Public Garden Management

Public Garden Management

Donald A. Rakow

Sharon A. Lee

WILEY

John Wiley & Sons, Inc.

Published by John Wiley & Sons, Inc., Hoboken, New Jersey

Published simultaneously in Canada

For general information about our other products and services, please contact our Customer Care Department within the United States at (800) 762-2974, outside the United States at (317) 572-3993 or fax (317) 572-4002.

Wiley also publishes its books in a variety of electronic formats. Some content that appears in print may not be available in electronic books. For more information about Wiley products, visit our web site at www.wiley.com.

Library of Congress Cataloging-in-Publication Data:

Public garden management /[compiled by] Donald A. Rakow, Sharon A. Lee.
      p.   cm.
    Includes bibliographical references and index.
  ISBN 978-0-470-53213-3 (cloth); ISBN 978-0-470-90457-2 (ebk); ISBN 978-0-470-90458-9 (ebk); ISBN 978-0-470-90459-6 (ebk); ISBN 978-0-470-95069-2 (ebk); ISBN 978-0-470-95082-1 (ebk)
    1. Gardens—Management.   2. Public spaces.   3. Gardening.   I. Rakow, Donald Andrew, 1951- II. Lee, Sharon A., 1944-
  SB467.8.P83 2011
  712'.5068—dc22

                                                                2010016949

Printed in the United States of America

10 9 8 7 6 5 4 3 2 1

The authors wish to dedicate this book to their spouses, Sue Rakow and Philip Lebowitz, whose patience, support, and encouragement were absolutely essential throughout the long process of developing this book.

They would further like to dedicate it to all current and future students and practitioners of public horticulture, who have chosen a field that truly does make a difference in the lives of people and the planet on which we live.

Contents

PART III
Administrative Functions 81

PART IV
Programmatic Functions 173

Acknowledgments

The authors wish to express their deep appreciation to Longwood Gardens for its generous and unwavering support throughout the process of developing this text. That support is in keeping with Longwood's well-established leadership in the promotion of professional educational programs. In the 1960s, Longwood recognized the need to have a formalized education program in public garden management and administration and established the Longwood Graduate Program in Public Horticulture in partnership with the University of Delaware. Longwood has continued that leadership by endorsing *Public Garden Management*, the first textbook on the operations of a public garden, and recognizing the significant impact that such a textbook will have on the continued development of professional courses on the subject.

To the following individuals, we offer our sincere appreciation for their conscientious efforts in reviewing specific chapters:

James M. Affolter, Professor and Director of Research, State Botanical Garden of Georgia

Eleanor Altman, Executive Director, Adkins Arboretum

David P. Barnett, President and CEO, Mount Auburn Cemetery

Jessica Blohm, Interpretive Specialist, New York Botanical Garden

Donald R. Buma, Executive Director, Norfolk Botanical Garden

Marnie Conley, Marketing Department Head, Longwood Gardens Inc.

Richard A. Colbert, Executive Director, Tyler Arboretum

N. Barbara Conolly, Public Garden Leadership Fellow, Department of Horticulture, Cornell University

Michael Dosmann, Curator of Living Collections, Arnold Arboretum of Harvard University

Holly Forbes, Curator, University of California Botanical Garden at Berkely

Charlotte A. Jones-Roe, Associate Director, North Carolina Botanical Garden

Jeremy Jungels, Public Garden Leadership Fellow, Department of Horticulture, Cornell University

Patrick S. Larkin, Executive Director, Rancho Santa Ana Botanic Garden

Carol Line, Executive Director, Fernwood Botanical Garden and Nature Preserve

Erin Marteal, Public Garden Leadership Fellow, Department of Horticulture, Cornell University

Scot Medbury, President, Brooklyn Botanic Garden

Scott Mehaffey, Landscape Architect

Bill Noble, Director of Preservation, The Garden Conservancy

Ken Schutz, Executive Director, Desert Botanical Garden

Adam Schwerner, Director, Department of Natural Resources, Chicago Park District

Holly H. Shimizu, Executive Director, U.S. Botanic Garden

Sonja M. Skelly, Director of Education, Cornell Plantations

Shane Smith, Director, Cheyenne Botanic Gardens

Frederick R. Spicer Jr., Executive Director, Birmingham Botanical Gardens

R. William Thomas, Executive Director, Chanticleer Foundation

Lisa K. Wagner, Education Director, South Carolina Botanical Garden

Ellen Weatherholt, Public Garden Leadership Fellow, Department of Horticulture, Cornell University

Peter White, Director, North Carolina Botanical Garden

To Dorothea J. Coleman, our thanks for her invaluable help in researching and preparing the references.

We are most grateful to the Portico Group, Architects, Landscape Architects, Interpretive Planners, and Exhibit Designers, in Seattle, Washington, for permission to use images of some of their public garden plans, and to the gardens illustrated: Buffalo and Erie County Botanical Gardens; Descanso Gardens; Hughson Botanical Garden; The Burden Center, Louisiana State University AgCenter; Portland Japanese Garden; San Francisco Botanical Garden; and Washington State University Arboretum and Wildlife Conservation Center.

Finally, we would like to acknowledge the assistance of the following in providing information for Appendix A, "Factors in the Development and Management of Canadian Public Gardens": Chris Graham, former Director of Horticulture at Royal Botanical Gardens; Doug Hevenor, Director of the International Peace Garden; Sharilyn J. Ingram, Assistant Professor, Brock University; Harry Jongerden, Garden Director, VanDusen Botanical Garden; Michel Labrecque, Conservateur, Jardin botanique de Montréal; Alexander Reford, Director, Reford Gardens/Jardins de Métis; and Freek Vrugtman, Curator Emeritus at Royal Botanical Gardens.

Foreword

In our tumultuous modern world, public gardens, with their orderly and diverse collections of plants and extensive educational programs, are ideally positioned to make major contributions not only to the amenity of our lives but also to the ways in which we envision the future. Throughout the United States, there is great interest in establishing new public gardens and building the capacity of existing ones to provide accessible, documented, and educational facilities that serve to attract visitors, but perhaps more importantly, serve as guides to the kind of sustainable, rich, and beautiful world that we would like to build together for the future. Many of us have found that there is no more rewarding profession than that of public horticulture as a way in which individuals can contribute to the enrichment of life and the preservation of the diversity and beauty that it represents. We hope that many who are considering a profession in this area find this book a source of guidance and inspiration.

All life depends on plants. They provide all of our food, directly or indirectly, with just over one hundred kinds of plants responsible for more than 90 percent of the calories we consume. Plants provide most of the medicine used throughout the world, as well as building and other raw materials, and they will be the sources of many more kinds of products that we have yet to discover or recognize. Plants beautify and enrich our lives and give peace to our souls. All of these are reasons why public gardens as showcases for enjoying and learning about plants have become so very important with the passage of years and with the challenges that we face in the modern world.

The global population has tripled within my lifetime to its present level of more than 7 billion people. More than 2 billion more people are expected to be added during the next four decades, an unprecedented number that will pressure a world already drawing some 150 percent of its sustainable capacity, according to GlobalFootprint.org. Consumption levels per person are increasing even more rapidly than population numbers, and so is the proportion of people living in urban centers, which makes the need for public gardens, with their extraordinary ability to connect city dwellers with nature, all the more important. The United States, with the highest consumption rates in the world, is growing much more rapidly than the world as a whole; the 310 million of us

now will increase to an estimated 440 million people by midcentury, with almost incalculable pressures on the environment resulting from this growth. We need public gardens and environmental awareness if we are to increase our ability to live as members of a world that can sustain us and everyone else on earth in a stable system.

In addition to direct pressures on habitats, the overharvesting of individual kinds of plants for particular purposes and the rampant spread of invasive alien plants and animals (such as garlic mustard, the emerald ash borer, and sudden oak death) in natural communities threatens their future. Global climate change, which has shifted the USDA established hardiness zones more than 150 miles northward over the past twenty years, is accelerating, and we seem to have limited ability to deal with it. Up to 40 percent of the endemic plants of California are projected to become extinct over the next several decades because of the elimination of their habitats. The Intergovernmental Panel on Climate Change has estimated that 20 to 40 percent of the world's plants could disappear from nature during the course of this century because of global warming, with its attendant changes in precipitation levels and distribution. This makes the role of public gardens in direct conservation efforts, as well as in education, all the more important.

The many and diverse functions played by public gardens in different settings are laid out especially well in Chapter 1 of this volume, but conservation has sprung to the forefront because of the challenges that our native plants and native communities face in the twenty-first century. The Center for Plant Conservation, a network of botanical gardens and arboreta throughout the United States, works collaboratively for the conservation of our plant species in their native habitats, in public gardens, and in seed banks. Its efforts have never been more important for the future. Beyond the importance of preserving our native plants, we also have a responsibility to contribute to the conservation of all plants. It is estimated that the world's public gardens hold more than 100,000 of the estimated 350,000 species of plants known worldwide—a rich endowment indeed, even if many of these species are represented by a single individual or too few individuals to constitute a genetically adequate sample. Public gardens, on their own or in cooperation with university departments of horticulture, are also prime sites for the maintenance of traditional cultivars of plants and the development and dissemination of new ones, all topics that are treated well in the pages of this text. The North American Plant Collections Consortium, supported by the American Public Gardens Association, represents a strong effort to coordinate and foster this aspect of our activities.

In view of the many and diverse ways that public gardens enrich our lives and facilitate our ability to envision a more complete and richer future than would be possible without them, it is a special pleasure to introduce this useful and accessible volume to its readers. I do so in the first instance by congratulating its authors, Don Rakow and Sharon Lee, for the fine work they have done drawing together a collection of useful and interesting chapters. With its examination of the functions that different gardens are playing and can play in their individual communities, this book will be of great use to the community of professionals and volunteers who are concerned with the presentation and management of public gardens and with the establishment of new ones. The book offers those of us who are responsible for the management of individual institutions much practical advice and guidance in the many aspects that add up to success in the very important field of endeavor that our public gardens represent.

The gardens in our care have the ability to heal our spirits in a troubled world and to lead us to envision a greater and nobler future for which we otherwise might not find time in the midst of our busy lives and the confused demands of the modern world.

PETER H. RAVEN
President, Missouri Botanical Garden
St. Louis, Missouri

PART I

Public Gardens and Their Significance

CHAPTER 1

What Is a Public Garden?

DONALD A. RAKOW

Introduction

If a public garden is any space that has been laid out for public enjoyment, then the history of public gardens can be traced back across both continents and centuries to such luminary garden creators as the Chinese emperor Shen Nung (ca. 2800 BCE), Queen Hatshepsut of the Eighteenth Dynasty of Egypt (ca. 1470 BCE), and the Greek philosopher Aristotle (384–322 BCE).

But in its modern context, a public garden is more than a property that holds a gathering of plants, even when those plants are laid out in an aesthetically pleasing manner. A public garden is both a *physical presence* that includes plant collections, buildings, and infrastructure and an *organization* that manages those elements and uses them to further its mission.

To answer the question posed by its title, this chapter will examine the essential criteria for a public garden, offer examples of the different kinds of institutions that meet those criteria, and identify the individuals and organizations that create public gardens and what motivates their efforts.

Essential Criteria

In its essence, a public garden is a mission-based institution that maintains collections of plants for the purposes of education, research, conservation, and/or public display. It must have a system for maintaining plant records and professional staff. Further, it must be open to the public and provide accommodations for access to all people.

This definition is also useful in identifying what is *not* a public garden. A park may have beautiful ornamental plants and they may be well cared for by the maintenance staff. Likewise,

KEY TERMS

Curation: selecting, organizing, and looking after the objects in a collection.

Systematics: the branch of biology concerned with classification and nomenclature; taxonomy.

Accession: a new item added to a collection in a museum or library.

Accessioning: the act of adding a new item to a collection.

Herbaceous perennial: a plant whose growth dies down annually, but whose roots or other underground parts survive.

Woody plant: any plants with stems and limbs containing lignin; as trees, shrubs, vines.

Ethnobotany: the scientific study of traditional knowledge concerning the medical, religious, and agricultural uses of plants.

Dendrology: the scientific study of trees.

Basic research: research that is driven by a scientist's curiosity or interest in a scientific question. The main motivation is to expand human knowledge, not to create or invent something.

Applied research: research that is designed to solve practical problems of the modern world, rather than to acquire knowledge for knowledge's sake.

Mission statement: a concise statement that defines why an organization exists, what are its primary activities, and whom it serves.

amusement parks, shopping malls, and even hotels can have lovely and diverse plantings, and community gardens devoted to food production may be public. But such sites do not meet the essential criteria of being public gardens unless there is a mission statement driving their efforts and their plants are actively curated, that is, cared for as objects that are part of the collection of a living museum. Chapter 20 deals in depth with all that is involved with the curation of collections at a public garden.

Mission Statement

Whether it is being applied to a public garden or to a private corporation, a mission statement defines why an organization exists, what its primary activities are, and whom it serves. A public garden's mission statement might focus on the types of collections it holds, how its collections are to be used, the focus of its programs and/or research, and who its primary audiences are. The mission statement should be the basis for all decisions and planning by the garden.

Plant Collections

Plant collections are fundamentally distinct from purely ornamental displays. Collections can be grouped either taxonomically (i.e., by family association), geographically (plants from one region of the world), functionally (groundcovers), or by plant needs (shade plants or plants for dry soil). One of the greatest challenges for public garden managers is how to merge the method by which collections are organized with the aesthetic goals of the garden.

Education/Research/Display

The degree to which a particular public garden is involved with education, research, or ornamental display will vary depending on the garden's mission. Whether for primary, secondary, collegiate, or adult audiences, educational programs at public gardens focus on increasing an appreciation of plants and their value to society. Programs generally include classes, workshops, tours, outreach, exhibits, visitor information, and special events.

Research at public gardens has traditionally focused on nomenclatural or plant systematics and plant breeding issues. But increasingly, many gardens today emphasize plant conservation and biodiversity research.

Plant Records

An essential component of plant curation for all public gardens is the accessioning and deaccessioning of individual plants. Each plant added to the collection is given a unique identifying number, and records are kept of each plant that is removed from the collections, along with the reasons for its removal. Start-up gardens may not be able to afford a plant records specialist and may assign this task to the gardeners or even to the director. Whoever has the responsibility for managing plant records and whether records are kept electronically or in a notebook, it is essential that every public garden maintain a record of all plants that have the potential to be long-term additions to the collections.

Professional Staff

Individuals who are attracted to work in public gardens typically possess a different set of qualities than people who go into parks management. While public garden staff members recognize the aesthetics of how plants are combined in collections, they also value how those plants are managed and are used to further the garden's educational or research mission.

The active management of plant collections therefore requires staff with specialized curatorial training, including a thorough knowledge of plant taxonomy and plant nomenclature. Typically, such individuals have backgrounds in horticulture, botany, or plant taxonomy, and are adept with the computer programs that many public gardens now use in curating their collections.

Open and Accessible to the Public

To be a public garden, a garden must maintain regular, posted hours and make reasonable efforts to accommodate those with disabilities or limited mobility. This does not mean that every section of every garden need be wheelchair accessible, but it does mean ensuring that every visitor is able to experience the garden in a meaningful way.

Types of Public Gardens

The origin of the public garden in the Western world dates to the sixteenth century in Europe. There—in cities such as Padua, Pisa, and Montpellier—medical universities created symmetrical, foursquare gardens filled with plants that were believed to be medicinally active. These *hortus medicus* gardens were then used as teaching sites for the medical and pharmaceutical students at these schools.

While public gardens have branched off in several directions since that time, all are living museums of curated plants, with programs in education, conservation, research, and/or display. In the following section on the types of public gardens, it is important to recognize that the distinctions between these types are becoming blurred. Increasingly, arboreta contain some herbaceous collections, botanical gardens usually have areas devoted to trees and shrubs, and display is certainly important to all institutions. In North America, approximately seven hundred institutions are currently considered public gardens.

Botanical Gardens

Botanical gardens contain a wide array of both herbaceous and woody plant collections, varied educational offerings for all ages, and research programs focused on plant improvement, conservation, ecology, or basic science. As the examples that follow demonstrate, if there is one characteristic that unites all botanical gardens, it is that they have botanically diverse, rather than simply aesthetic, collections of plants.

Brooklyn Botanic Garden, Brooklyn, New York

Established in 1910 on the site of a former city dump, today the Brooklyn Botanic Garden (BBG) occupies 52 acres in the heart of Brooklyn and contains world-class collections, including the Cherry Esplanade, the Cranford Rose Garden, the Japanese Garden, and the Steinhart Conservatory. But the breadth of BBG's programs and influence is exemplified by its educational and outreach work. The garden is home to the first and oldest children's garden in North America, and its education programs reach constituents in all age groups. One of its most innovative projects is the Brooklyn Academy of Science and the Environment, which the garden comanages along with Prospect Park and the New York City Department of Education. This mini–high school uses the resources of the garden and the park to educate young people on subjects related to the natural sciences and the global environment. BBG also offers an intensive Certificate in Horticulture program to individuals interested in professional careers in the green industry. Outreach efforts include locally based greening programs such as Greenest Block in Brooklyn and Brooklyn GreenBridge, family events, and research on the flora of the New York metropolitan area.

Chicago Botanic Garden, Chicago, Illinois

With 385 acres of natural beauty and twenty-three specialty gardens set on nine islands, the Chicago Botanic Garden (CBG) offers an incredible array of adult and children's educational programs nested within the School of the Chicago Botanic Garden. Beyond its collections and public programs, the CBG has developed a depth of intellectual activities that are seldom fully seen or appreciated by the casual visitor. With highly regarded scientists and facilities on-site, it is a recognized leader in conservation science and horticultural research. In addition to workshops and symposia directed at professionals in public horticulture, CBG has formed academic partnerships with Northwestern University in offering a master's program in plant biology and conservation, and with the University of Illinois at Urbana-Champaign in offering a bachelor's degree in horticulture. Through its outreach division, the Garden disseminates plant-based information and answers inquiries on subjects of interest to home gardeners.

Missouri Botanical Garden, St. Louis, Missouri

Located in St. Louis, Missouri, but with conservation and research programs that circle the globe, the scope and complexity of the Missouri Botanical Garden (MOBOT) and its work is truly inspirational. MOBOT was started by a young hardware merchant who desired to emulate the great gardens of his native England. In 1840, when Henry Shaw was only forty, he retired from his hardware business in St. Louis and spent the next decade traveling, learning botany, and laying the groundwork for what would for many years be called "Mr. Shaw's garden." MOBOT houses some truly fabulous horticultural collections, including those in the geodesic-dome-shaped Climatron, the 14-acre Japanese garden, and the Kemper Home Demonstration Gardens. But in other ways, the institution more closely resembles a plant-based university than a traditional botanical garden. It is a leading center of conservation and taxonomic research and houses a world-class library, herbarium, and laboratories. It supports many major endeavors in horticulture, including the Flora of North America and the Center for Plant Conservation. It also offers accredited courses on the university level and educational programs for every age group. A great deal of credit for all that it has become is due to Dr. Peter Raven, its longtime director and an acclaimed botanist and environmentalist.

The New York Botanical Garden, Bronx, New York

Much as Henry Shaw was stimulated by his European tour to create a botanical garden that would emulate the grand landscapes to which he had been exposed, the eminent Columbia University botanists Nathaniel Lord Britton and his wife, Elizabeth, were so inspired by their visit to England's Royal Botanic Gardens at Kew that they determined that New York should also possess a great botanical garden. A magnificent site of outstanding natural features was selected in the northern section of the Bronx. It includes dramatic rock outcroppings, a river and waterfall, rolling hills, ponds, and a 50-acre remnant of the forest that once covered the region. The land was set aside by the New York State Legislature for the creation of "a public botanic garden of the highest class" for the City of New

York. Prominent civic leaders and financiers, including Andrew Carnegie, Cornelius Vanderbilt, and J. Pierpont Morgan, agreed to match the city's commitment to finance the buildings and garden developments, initiating a public-private partnership that continues today. In 1896, the New York Botanical Garden (NYBG) appointed Nathaniel Lord Britton as its first director.

Today the Garden ranks as one of New York's premier cultural resources, with its fifty horticultural collections and its fabulous special exhibits. But the NYBG is also a world-class scientific institution, with researchers in its International Plant Science Center focused on exploring, documenting, and preserving the earth's vast biodiversity.

Fairchild Tropical Botanic Garden, Miami, Florida

While the previously described botanical gardens all house plant collections reflective of diverse geographic and environmental origins, the Fairchild Tropical Botanic Garden (FTBG) focuses its collections on species from tropical and semitropical regions of the world. Its palm and cycad collections are among the greatest in any public garden, and its collection of tropical fruits is internationally significant. In addition, the Garden has developed an internationally known and replicated education program, the Fairchild Challenge, which focuses on youth and plant science. Another of the efforts that distinguish the FTBG is its use of exhibits to attract greater and more diverse visitation. Some of these exhibits fit within the traditional purview of a public garden, such as "Windows to the Tropics," its permanent 16,428-square-foot conservatory of plants from the humid tropics. Other, more temporary exhibits—such as those featuring works in glass by Dale Chihuly or monumental sculptures by Roy Lichtenstein—stretch the definition of what is customary at a public garden.

The Desert Botanical Garden, Phoenix, Arizona

The Desert Botanical Garden (DBG) emphasizes the flora of one habitat type—the desert—rather than a pan-geographic sampling. Its collection of more than 20,000 plants features a particular focus on the American Southwest. The desert also serves as the unifying factor in the DBG's educational programs, which offer classes in desert landscaping, gardening, botanical art, photography, science, and healthy desert living. The survival of plants in the harsh desert environment is also the focus of the DBG's research programs in floristics, conservation, ecology, and ethnobotany.

Conservatories

A conservatory is typically a steel and glass structure for the display and study of tropical and other nonhardy plants. The earli- est known conservatories date from the seventeenth century when they were merely stone structures with extra glazing to allow in light. They were used by the British scientific community, nobility, and landed gentry to protect plants, especially those that had been collected on European tours and which they wished to grow in England's colder climate.

The heyday of British conservatories came in the nineteenth century after the tax on the weight of glass had been eliminated and the technology for steel production improved. It was then that Joseph Paxton designed the Great Conservatory at Chatsworth and London's famous Crystal Palace.

The Crystal Palace served as a design motif for the great conservatories constructed in the United States in the late nineteenth century. The earliest of these was the Conservatory of Flowers in San Francisco's Golden Gate Park. This majestic three-dome structure sits behind carpeted beds of annuals, adding to the Victorian appearance of the site.

Less well known, but no less impressive, is the conservatory of the Buffalo and Erie County Botanical Gardens. Also a three-dome structure, this conservatory was part of the grand plan for Buffalo parks laid out by the father of landscape architecture, Frederick Law Olmsted. The structure itself was constructed by the Lord and Burnham Co., noted for building many of the majestic conservatories of this era. The Enid Haupt Conservatory of the New York Botanical Garden also was designed by Lord and Burnham and was completed in 1902. It is considered one of the crown jewels of New York.

All of these historic structures have required extensive renovations, given their outmoded heating systems, the deleterious effect of internal humidity on wood and steel structural elements, and deteriorating beds and walkways.

While monumental efforts were undertaken to update and restore each of the aforementioned historic conservatories, a decision was reached in 1955 that the 1898 Conservatory in Mitchell Park, Milwaukee, Wisconsin, could not be saved. A design competition was held, and the winning architect, Donald Grieb, designed a three-dome conservatory, in which each beehive-shaped dome houses plants of a distinct climate.

The Mitchell Park Domes presaged the design of the Climatron conservatory, which opened in 1960 and has become a symbol of the Missouri Botanical Garden. The geodesic dome was inspired by the design of R. Buckminster Fuller. Covering more than a half acre, the Climatron houses some 1,400 species of plants in a natural tropical setting.

One of the most progressive conservatories in North America today is at the Phipps Conservatory and Botanical Gardens. A series of innovative design and engineering approaches—including passive cooling, earth tubes, a double-pane insulated roof, and a solid oxide fuel cell heating source—have been combined to make its Tropical Forest Conservatory the most fuel efficient in the world.

Arboreta

Arboreta, as contrasted with botanical gardens, focus on the study and display of woody plants, primarily trees and shrubs. They, too, typically offer educational programs for children, students, and adults. Their collections may be organized systematically, with each plant family assigned to its own area, or functionally, with plants located where their needs can best be met.

Arnold Arboretum of Harvard University, Cambridge, Massachusetts

Established in 1872, the Arnold is the oldest arboretum in the United States. Its first director, Charles Sprague Sargent, was one of the preeminent dendrologists and botanists of the nineteenth century. Sargent spent fifty-four years as director, shaping the policies and collections of the arboretum, and often collaborating with the illustrious landscape architect Frederick Law Olmsted. From the time of its founding, the Arboretum has maintained a complete record system, with a standardized accession number assigned to every plant on the grounds for use in tracking its name and origin. It is this detailed record system, along with the systematic organization of the collection on the grounds, that facilitates research by staff and other scientists. Currently, the living collections are used for research on a diverse range of subjects that include molecular systematics, plant physiology and morphology, vegetative propagation of woody plants, and evaluation and selection of new cultivars of woody plants with ornamental merit.

The Morris Arboretum of the University of Pennsylvania, Philadelphia, Pennsylvania

Many of the qualities that distinguish the Morris Arboretum today were established by brother and sister John and Lydia Morris when they first moved to the site: stewardship of the land, a dedication to horticultural excellence and collections diversity, a love of art and sculpture, and a focus on education.

Today, science, art, and the humanities are pursued through a variety of research, teaching, and outreach programs that link the Arboretum to a worldwide effort to nurture the earth's forests, fields and landscapes. Although formally affiliated with Penn, the Morris is also the official arboretum of the Commonwealth of Pennsylvania.

The Morton Arboretum, Lisle, Illinois

By including the phrase "and other plants from around the world" in its mission statement, Morton intentionally stretches the definition of what is considered an arboretum. The Arboretum has extensive herbaceous borders throughout its grounds. Among these are its Four Seasons Garden, Herb Garden, and Fragrance Garden. More recently, the Arboretum has added a 4-acre Children's Garden, one of the largest and most diverse such gardens in the country. The 1,700 acres of the Arboretum do hold collections of more than 4,000 kinds of trees and shrubs

So is the Morton Arboretum still an arboretum? Yes, in the mind of longtime president and CEO Dr. Gerard T. Donnelly, who sees an arboretum as a botanical institution that emphasizes the planting, display, and study of woody plants. Based on this definition, herbaceous plantings are not excluded, but trees are the central focus.

The North Carolina Arboretum, Asheville, North Carolina

The North Carolina Arboretum is a unique institution, as is clear from the first phrase of its mission statement: "The North Carolina Arboretum cultivates connections between people and plants through creative expressions." By immediately citing its location in the southern Appalachians, the Arboretum reveals the strong emphasis it places on its locale in carrying out its mission. Thus, its collections include a heritage garden, and annual events include a quilt show and a heritage crafts weekend to showcase the artistry of the region.

An arboretum for this area was first envisioned by the great landscape architect Frederick Law Olmsted, who was working at the nearby Biltmore estate. The Arboretum was founded in 1986 by the North Carolina State Legislature as a unit of the state university. It is therefore distinguished from other college or university arboreta that are associated with and governed by a single institution of higher learning.

Display Gardens

Display gardens expend more of their efforts on developing aesthetically pleasing exhibits of plants throughout the year. Often they offer both outdoor displays and extensive plantings in conservatories. Such gardens will frequently feature the newest cultivars of ornamentals or unusual tropical plants as ways of fulfilling their display mission. But to be considered *public* gardens, these institutions must still comply with the requirements of curated collections, as described earlier. While their focus may be on display, many of these gardens maintain lively educational programs and have highly skilled staffs managing well-documented plant collections, activities that enable them to qualify as public gardens.

Longwood Gardens, Kennett Square, Pennsylvania

Longwood refers to itself as the world's premier horticultural showplace, and it is hard to dispute this title. Longwood artfully combines plantings—both outdoors and in its extensive conservatories—with fountains, pathways, displays, and sculptures to create a true feast for the eyes. But Longwood is also a public garden that offers classes, tours, lectures, workshops, and internships to educate audiences on the beauty and importance of plants. In conjunction with the University of Delaware, the garden also offers the renowned Longwood Graduate Program in Public Garden Administration, which prepares candidates for leadership careers in public horticulture.

Chanticleer, Wayne, Pennsylvania

Like Longwood Gardens and Butchart Gardens, Chanticleer is a former estate, specifically of the wealthy industrialist Adolph Rosengarten. Rosengarten left his 31-acre estate to a private foundation, which opened the property to the public in 1993. Chanticleer is a shining example of the art of horticulture and rightly refers to itself as a "pleasure garden." Rather than concentrating on botanical collections, its focus is on plant combinations, which it executes through its exquisite container plantings, unusual textural and color combinations, and extensive reliance on foliage. Its educational mandate is carried out largely through collaborations with neighboring organizations.

Wave Hill, Bronx, New York

As an institution, Wave Hill falls somewhere between a display garden and a historic property. First settled in the early nineteenth century, Wave Hill has housed, at various points in its history, Teddy Roosevelt, Mark Twain, and Arturo Toscanini. In 1960, the Perkins-Freeman family deeded Wave Hill to the City of New York. Wave Hill Inc. was formed in 1965 as a not-for-profit corporation. Today, as one of thirty-three city-owned cultural institutions, Wave Hill provides an oasis of serenity and offers programs in horticulture, environmental education, woodland management, and the visual and performing arts. For many years, its director of horticulture was the esteemed Marco Polo Stufano, who was at the vanguard of a new and more expressive approach to ornamental display.

Historic Landscapes

All gardens are historic, and all landscapes are ever changing. Most sites that define themselves as historic and are open to

the public have also attempted to restore or re-create their landscape to a particular period or style. The authenticity of such landscapes is dependent on the level of documentation available to guide the plant selection and design process. As with display gardens, historic landscapes can be considered public gardens if they are driven by an articulated mission and have plant collections that are curated and used to support education and/or research.

The Fells, Lake Sunapee, New Hampshire

The former summer estate of John Milton Hay, a private secretary to Abraham Lincoln during the Civil War, the Fells is a historic, designed garden and cultural landscape with a large Colonial Revival house and 15 acres of gardens. Its organizational structure exemplifies how complex the management of a historic estate can be. The historic gardens are part of the larger 164-acre John Hay National Wildlife Refuge, shaped by three generations of Hay family agricultural activities and forest conservation practices. Sixty-four acres of the refuge, commonly referred to as the Fells, are now managed by the not-for-profit Friends of the John Hay National Wildlife Refuge, in cooperation with the federal property owner, the United States Fish and Wildlife Service. The Friends work in collaboration with the Lake Sunapee Protective Association, the Society for the Protection of New Hampshire Forest, and the Garden Conservancy to provide educational programs, to conserve natural resources, and to preserve the cultural landscape.

Stan Hywet Hall and Gardens, Akron, Ohio

The estate was built between 1912 and 1915 for F. A. Seiberling, founder of the Goodyear Tire and Rubber Company, who gave it the name Stan Hywet, Old English for "stone quarry," to reflect the site's earlier use. Stan Hywet reveals the high level of sophistication that the art of landscape design had reached in the early twentieth century. Originally more than 1,000 acres, the estate grounds were designed between 1911 and 1915 by renowned Boston landscape architect Warren H. Manning and, though reduced to just 70 acres today, remain one of the finest examples of his work. The English Garden was designed by noted landscape architect Ellen Biddle Shipman. It was completely restored in the late 1980s, using the original plant palette specified by Shipman. In 1957 the Seiberling family donated Stan Hywet to a not-for-profit organization for its preservation.

What qualifies Stan Hywet as both a historic estate and a public garden is that every effort is made in the gardens to use the plant types specified in the original landscape designs and careful plant records are kept of the trees, shrubs, roses, and perennials.

Sonnenberg Gardens, Canandaigua, New York

Sonnenberg has had an unfortunately turbulent history. The property was sold by the original owners' nephew to the federal government in the 1930s. The government then converted the property into the grounds of a new veterans' hospital. In 1970, a group of local citizens formed the Friends of Sonnenberg with the intention of restoring the grand estate to its former splendor. Despite their many successes, in the late 1990s Sonnenberg Gardens endured financial hardship, which climaxed with the arrest and conviction of its CEO for embezzlement. Just as the estate faced foreclosure, in 2004 New York State came to the rescue, purchasing the land and buildings and turning over the operations to a separate 501(c)(3) organization.

Throughout this rocky chronology, Sonnenberg has managed to hold on to many of its notable gardens. Chief among these is the Italian Garden, for which gardening staff lay out 15,000 bedding plants each spring. Other collections include the Rose Garden, Rock Garden, Moonlight Garden, and Japanese Garden.

Bartram's Garden, Philadelphia, Pennsylvania

No extant garden in America can claim to be more historic than the one founded by John Bartram in 1728. Recognized today as America's first great botanist, John and his son William roamed far and wide in their investigations of New World flora. John was eventually appointed royal botanist to King George III, and William's heavily illustrated journals became a seminal early text of American natural history.

Today the John Bartram Association is actively restoring a number of garden areas on the original farm site. As with other historic public gardens, the staff at Bartram's keeps records of each accessioned plant and has policies in place for guiding the acquisition of additional plants.

Zoos

As the zoological world has transformed itself from a focus on individual animals in cages to fauna displayed in native habitats, horticulture has taken on an increasingly important role. Some zoos have developed accessioned collections of plants curated by trained horticulturists, which serve the dual purpose of increasing the sense of verisimilitude of the simulated habitats and providing an additional visitor attraction in their own right. There is even an organization—the Association of Zoo Horticulturists—to address the professional development of individuals in this field.

Arizona-Sonora Desert Museum, Tucson, Arizona

The Arizona-Sonora Desert Museum is a world-renowned zoo, natural history museum, and botanical garden, all at one site. Its educational offerings span the range from ecological to horticultural and zoological, and it also conducts research on the ecology and preservation of the Sonoran Desert.

San Diego Zoo, San Diego, California

One of the most highly regarded zoos in the world, San Diego is a leader in progressive animal displays, animal breeding and conservation, and the integration of an arboretum into a zoo setting. Trees, shrubs, and herbaceous plants are used to simulate particular habitats, to add to the aesthetic ambiance of the zoo grounds, and to provide feed for rare animals. For example, the Zoo raises forty varieties of bamboo for the pandas on long-term loan from China, and it maintains eighteen varieties of eucalyptus trees to feed its koalas. Plants that are part of the permanent display are all accessioned and properly labeled, just as in an arboretum without zoo animals.

Brookgreen Gardens, Murrells Inlet, South Carolina

Brookgreen is an excellent example of a multifaceted cultural organization. It is a zoo, with exhibits of both the native fauna of the South Carolina low country as well as animals that have been domesticated in the South. But it is also a sculpture park, housing the Center for American Sculpture and more than 1,200 sculptural pieces displayed on the grounds. Finally, it must also be considered a public garden, with accessioned collections that range from live oaks to dogwoods, palmettos, and flowering perennials. An institution such as Brookgreen reveals the limitations associated with pigeonholing an organization.

For-Profit Attractions

Even some sites that are not generally perceived as public gardens can qualify based on our operational definition. For-profit sites fall into two general categories: tourist businesses and for-profit corporations supporting nonprofit activities.

Tourist Businesses

Tourist or vacation businesses that qualify as public gardens include extensive, curated plantings on their grounds. For-profit public gardens have as their primary motivation the realization of business profits. Therefore, while not-for-profits may focus on the education of their audiences or research in plant biology, plant managers at profit-driven organizations must justify their horticulture as benefiting the bottom line.

Walt Disney World

Beautiful, well-cared-for plantings can serve to increase attendance or justify higher admission prices. Plantings have always been a central component of Disney theme parks, and Walt

Disney himself felt that landscapes should provide shelter and shade for visitors, conceal visual intrusions, and support the storytelling by creating the right look for the setting. The Disney approach to theme park horticulture, including the extensive use of topiaries, has become so well recognized that the Disney organization now offers how-to seminars on this subject for other professionals in the field.

Mohonk Mountain House
The Smiley family has owned Mohonk Mountain House, in New Paltz, New York, since it was first built in 1869. The gardens are one of the prime attractions, along with the nature trails, lake, spa, and cuisine. The design approach is intended to capture the picturesque or romantic style of landscaping so popular in the Victorian era: irregular of form, featuring variety and boldness of composition, and fitting into the rugged nature of the site. But while the thousands of annuals are never formally recorded, the perennials, shrubs, and trees are all accessioned and cared for by a team of professional horticulturists. Mohonk also sponsors special garden-themed weekends each year, at which notable speakers present lectures or provide demonstrations.

Bellagio
A Las Vegas gaming hotel as a public garden? While this may seem incongruous, actually Bellagio takes great pride in the diversity, display, and quality of its botanical collections. With more than 140 horticulturists on staff, the Bellagio is able to change its display several times each year and to effectively accommodate the 14,000 visitors the garden receives each day. This is a much higher level of visitation than at any not-for-profit public garden in North America.

For-Profit Supporting Nonprofit
The second category is for-profit businesses that direct funds to not-for-profit entities that manage their public gardens. A prime example of this type of arrangement is Callaway Gardens. The Gardens are owned and operated by the nonprofit Ida Cason Callaway Foundation. But its wholly owned subsidiary, Callaway Gardens Resort Inc., is a corporation that operates the recreational, lodging, and retail facilities at Callaway Gardens. After-tax proceeds go to the Foundation to support its efforts. This issue is further muddied by the fact that, as a type of public garden, Callaway should be considered a historic landscape, in that it is located on the former estate of Cason J. Callaway and his wife, Virginia Hand Callaway.

Another example of a public garden supported by a for-profit corporation is Hershey Gardens, which is operated by the M. S. Hershey Foundation and receives enterprise income from admissions, weddings, and other rentals. But it also receives extensive support from the Hershey Corporation, the founder of which also created the Gardens.

Who Creates Public Gardens and Why
Public gardens are strongly influenced by their initial creators. Whether an individual, a group of individuals, an organization, or a government body, each entity that creates a public garden leaves its mark. Although most public gardens are started and owned by not-for-profit educational corporations, there are private public gardens and for-profit ones as well. The groups and organizations that start public gardens are incredibly diverse, so it is not surprising that the gardens they create are equally diverse, as the following examination will demonstrate.

Not-for-Profit Organizations
As their name implies, these are legally incorporated organizations formed by altruistic individuals. Not-for-profit gardens engage in their activities without any commercial or profit motives. Such organizations never offer stock, nor do board members directly benefit from the garden's revenues. The following examples demonstrate the multiplicity of motivations behind the creation of not-for-profit public gardens.

As a Grassroots Effort
The Cheyenne Botanic Gardens was started in 1977 as the Cheyenne, Wyoming, Community Solar Greenhouse Project. Since its inception, it has been dedicated to the twin goals of landscape sustainability and volunteer engagement. Its current facility was constructed in 1986, when the organization was incorporated into the Cheyenne Department of Parks and Recreation.

With a paid staff of only four, more than 90 percent of the labor at the Cheyenne Botanic Gardens is provided by volunteers. A high percentage of these unpaid laborers are seniors, disabled individuals, or at-risk youth. Thus the Gardens is simultaneously receiving help with the planting and care of its collections and serving as a site for horticultural therapy. The latter is reinforced in many of the Gardens' educational programs, as is information on ways to garden sustainably using plants of the high plains. The Gardens has received many awards for its grassroots efforts, including two presidential citations.

To Achieve Organizational Objectives
Some not-for-profit organizations create public gardens to help fulfill their mission or to provide a central venue at

which to present their programs. An example is the Chicago Horticultural Society, which has existed since 1890, hosting flower shows and horticultural competitions. But it was only in 1963 that the City of Chicago granted the society 300 acres of land on the outskirts of Chicago, a site that was then transformed into the Chicago Botanic Garden (opening in 1972). Today the society has an enormous capacity to carry out its tripartite mission of education, research, and conservation because of the Garden's popularity and its urban location.

To Complete an Individual's Inspiration

Alternatively, a particular individual may be the driving force in creating a not-for-profit garden. In 1906, industrialist Pierre S. du Pont purchased 202 acres of wooded farmland originally owned by the Peirce family to preserve the majestic trees on the property. But du Pont was so inspired by the magnificence of the site that he soon began the process of developing Longwood Gardens. He then used his considerable fortune to create Longwood's most notable features, including the conservatories, fountains, outdoor theater, and plant collections.

To Pursue a Research or Education Agenda

A fourth motivator behind the creation of a public garden by a not-for-profit is the pursuit of particular research or education goals. For example, the Rancho Santa Ana Botanic Garden was created in 1927 by Susanna Bixby Bryant with the specific goals of displaying as complete a collection of California natives as possible and working on the preservation of the state's native flora. The garden was eventually moved from Orange County to Claremont, and currently provides graduate training in plant systematics and evolution through the Claremont Colleges.

Another garden that combines many of these elements is the Fairchild Tropical Botanical Garden (FTBG). It was created in 1935 by Robert H. Montgomery, who named the garden to honor the botanist David Fairchild, his friend and colleague. Fairchild had collected plants from around the tropical zones of the world, and many of them are still on display at the Botanical Garden. Although Montgomery donated the land on which the garden sits to Miami-Dade County, the FTBG today is run by a private 501(c)(3) nonprofit organization.

To Preserve a Historic Property

Because the cost of restoring historic landscapes to their former grandeur can be prohibitively expensive, many such properties are donated to municipalities, friends organizations, or historical societies. But these municipal or private groups must have compelling reasons to accept such donations and the heavy challenges that go along with them. Motives can include an altruistic desire to preserve important cultural resources, an expectation of revenue resulting from an enhanced tourist attraction, and a hope that the restoration will positively affect a declining neighborhood or city.

Many critical issues must be addressed by groups entrusted with the oversight of historic properties. Chief among these is the historic period to be depicted in the restored landscape: the period in which the landscape was first created or had its greatest prominence, or the one for which the most complete records exist. Related to this issue is the difficulty of locating particular plant cultivars appropriate for the period of restoration.

The Garden Conservancy is an organization that is devoted to the preservation of significant American landscapes and has assisted many such sites in making the transition from private to public status and in establishing their not-for-profit position.

TREATMENT OF HISTORIC PROPERTIES

Depending on its current condition, the landscape's significance and character is typically recaptured by one of the four approaches established by the secretary of the interior's *Standards for the Treatment of Historic Properties:* preservation, rehabilitation, restoration, or reconstruction.

- *Preservation* is the act or process of applying measures necessary to sustain the existing form, integrity, and materials of a historic property. It is therefore the most conservative of the four approaches and is applicable when the property's buildings and landscape elements are already in good shape.

- *Rehabilitation* preserves those portions or features of the landscape that convey its historical, cultural, or architectural values and conducts repairs, alterations, and additions on nonauthentic elements.

- *Restoration* is the process of accurately restoring the form, features, and character of a property as it appeared at a particular period of time by means of the removal of features from other periods in its history and reconstruction of missing features.

- *Reconstruction* is the process of depicting, by means of new construction, the form, features, and detailing of a nonsurviving landscape for the purpose of replicating its appearance at a specific period of time and in its historic location.

Government Organizations

Cities, counties, states, and nations create public gardens for a number of reasons: as engines to drive urban renewal of run-down neighborhoods, to spur tourism, to raise cultural standards in a locale, or to elevate the ambience and aesthetic appearance of a municipality. Many of these motivating factors are illustrated in the following examples of gardens created by governmental organizations.

Municipalities

Most municipalities involved in the creation of public gardens have done so by partnering with independent friends groups. The roles and responsibilities of municipalities and 501(c)(3) groups vary with the institution. The site of the San Francisco Botanical Garden is owned and the director is hired by the City Department of Parks and Recreation. But the San Francisco Botanical Garden Society is responsible for the educational programs and collections curation. Similarly, the Los Angeles County Arboretum and Botanic Garden is jointly operated by the Los Angeles Arboretum Foundation and the Los Angeles County Department of Parks and Recreation. Still other relationships are even more complex: the University of Washington Botanical Gardens is jointly administered by the university, the City of Seattle, and the Arboretum Foundation.

While such administrative arrangements offer the public gardens the benefit of tapping into the resources of each of the partners, they can also create significant challenges. Problems that have surfaced at such gardens include having two directors, each responsible for administering part of the staff; a staff divided by differing wage rates, benefits contracts, or working conditions; and municipal managers or workers who do not follow expected levels of horticultural expertise at the garden.

To Improve Neighborhoods

The Garfield Park Conservatory (GPC) in Chicago, which first opened in 1908, became increasingly neglected and run-down during the 1980s and early 1990s. But as the West Side of the city became a focus for urban revitalization in the 1990s, the Garfield Park Conservatory was viewed as the centerpiece of this renewal. A support group, the GPC Alliance, was formed in 1998, and the conservatory was extensively renovated and restored to its former glory.

The result is that the conservatory is now the pride of this up-and-coming neighborhood, and attendance has grown from less than 10,000 annually to 200,000 in 2006.

To Counteract Economic Hard Times

The Montreal Botanical Garden was founded in 1931 by then mayor Camillien Houde at the height of the Great Depression to provide an economic stimulus. But the real credit for the garden's creation goes to the great botanist Brother Marie-Victorin, who campaigned for it for years. Today this garden is a major cultural attraction for Montreal and boasts one of the largest plant collections in North America, with more than 21,000 taxa under cultivation. It serves to educate the public in general and students of horticulture in particular and is deeply involved with the conservation of endangered plant species, and with botanical research (for more information, see Appendix A).

To Maintain Open Space

By the 1950s, it was clear to the civic leaders of Denver that growth was squeezing out available open space and that bold efforts needed to be taken to maintain the desired quality of life in the city. The first attempt at establishing the Denver Botanical (later Botanic) Gardens, on the site of a 100-acre park, ended in failure when too many of the young plants were stolen by poachers. But the city, county, and private citizens persisted in their dream, and in 1958 an old cemetery was identified as the future garden's permanent home. The Denver Botanic Gardens is now a heavily visited green space in a densely populated and vibrant city.

To Rescue a Facility from Imminent Collapse

Other municipalities become involved with a botanical institution in order to save them from the bulldozer. Such was the case for the City of St. Petersburg, Florida, which purchased Sunken Gardens in 1999 from the Turner family, which had owned it for nearly a hundred years. So highly regarded was this site by the residents of St. Petersburg that they approved a special tax levy to fund the purchase.

To Create a Larger Municipal Museum Complex

By clustering together several cultural centers, a municipality can make the complex a more attractive venue for tourists and other visitors. The Rio Grande Botanical Garden is a unit of the Albuquerque Botanical Park, which also includes the Albuquerque Aquarium and the Rio Grande Zoo. Visitors can purchase a combination pass that provides admission to all three sites. The arrangement also allows for economies of scale, with the three facilities able to share staffing, equipment, and promotional costs.

U.S. Federal Government

The proposal of a botanical garden for the citizens of the United States in 1816 eventually led to its establishment in 1820 by the U.S. Congress. While the site of the garden has moved several times, the U.S. Botanic Garden currently includes a renovated and greatly beloved conservatory, the National Garden, and Bartholdi Park. It receives the bulk of its funding from Congress and is administered by the Architect of the Capitol.

Also created by an act of Congress, the U.S. National Arboretum is administered by the U.S. Department of Agriculture (USDA), not Congress. It fulfills its mission of "serving the public need for scientific research, education, and gardens that conserve and showcase plants to enhance the environment" through extensive arboricultural and herbaceous collections and its education programs, publications, and research efforts. Its annual allocation from USDA is supplemented with support from the Friends of the National Arboretum, Herb Society of America, National Bonsai Foundation, and both the national and several capital-district garden clubs.

U.S. State Governments

The State of Nebraska has taken a unique approach to the administration of public gardens. Rather than designating a single site as the state garden, it has created the Nebraska Statewide Arboretum (NSA). Under the auspices of Nebraska State University, the NSA is a network of arboretum sites, parks, historic properties, and other public landscapes located in dozens of communities across the state. The NSA provides technical support to each of the sites and helps nascent operations with their development process.

Colleges and Other Academic Institutions

In recent decades, one of the fastest-growing segments in public horticulture is that of the college- or university-affiliated garden. The many reasons why institutes of higher learning create public gardens are outlined in the following examples.

Unifying the Campus

A campus garden or arboretum can serve to unify the campus by providing a central design element in the overall layout of the landscape. It can also intellectually unite the campus. At the University of California, Davis, for example, the GATEways (Gardens, Art, and the Environment) Project will use the UC Davis Arboretum as the front door for the entire campus. Such innovative efforts can support synergies between faculty members from disparate disciplines and bring the campus community together around themes such as environmental sustainability or physical beautification.

Thresholds to the Larger Community

Because colleges and universities are often viewed as lofty or even intimidating institutions, a botanical garden can serve as a threshold to the larger community. A family may tour the university's gardens but would never consider exploring a molecular genetics lab (and probably would not be invited to do so). In this way, the garden can play a vital role in ameliorating town-gown conflicts and generate goodwill that can benefit the university when the next controversy flares.

Supporting University Research

The University of California Botanical Garden was established in Berkeley in 1890 by E. L. Greene, the first chairman of the Department of Botany. His intention to create as complete a collection of the native flora of California as possible has formed the nucleus of both collections development and use. Until the 1960s, the garden was used almost exclusively to support university research and teaching. Although a strong public outreach component has been in place since that time, worldwide research in plant biology continues to be an integral portion of its mission.

Not all research at university-based public gardens is basic in nature. The evaluation of plant breeding efforts has traditionally been a popular form of applied research at college- or university-based public gardens, especially those affiliated with land grant institutions. Sometimes the plants displayed are the products of breeding efforts within the institution or offerings from a national or international trade organization, such as the All America Selections for bedding plants.

An excellent example of a university garden with this type of mission is the JC Raulston Arboretum of North Carolina State University. The Arboretum is primarily a working research and teaching garden that focuses on the evaluation, selection, and display of plant material gathered from around the world. Plants especially adapted to Piedmont North Carolina conditions are identified in an effort to find better plants for southern landscapes.

Gardens as Living Classrooms

College and university gardens have also traditionally functioned as living classrooms to enhance undergraduate or graduate instruction. Institutions with colleges of agriculture or natural resources typically offer courses in many disciplines— from horticulture to plant pathology, entomology, landscape architecture, international agriculture, plant breeding, and forestry—whose students benefit from study inside the garden. Cornell Plantations, the arboretum, botanical garden, and natural areas of Cornell University, uses its 4,300 acres of extremely diverse holdings to serve faculty and students in more than a hundred courses.

Gardens may have special areas devoted to meeting the needs of particular instructors or courses and may feature certain plants or collections for use in classes. By making inquiries to the departments that would most typically utilize the collections, curators can ascertain how the garden might support the academic program.

Gardens to Fulfill an Outreach Mission

Many colleges and universities, especially land grant institutions, also carry an outreach mandate as part of their institutional mission. Gardens can help to fulfill that outreach role by providing tours, classes, workshops, or other continuing educational activities to the audience beyond the campus. Alternatively, staff from the garden can reach out to school groups or community organizations as part of their extension efforts.

One public garden that is extraordinarily effective in its outreach activities is the Minnesota Landscape Arboretum. Creating engaging plant- and nature-based educational experiences for audiences of all ages is at the heart of the Arboretum's mission. It touches the lives of more than 53,000 schoolchildren each year through field trips, urban gardening programs, and a roving Plantmobile. It also programs effectively for adults and families and has an extensive program in therapeutic horticulture.

Providing a Competitive Edge

Institutes of higher learning compete to attract the most competitive students. While the academic standing of the school is the strongest drawing card for top-ranked students, the campus appearance or ambiance is also an important determining factor. The presence of a botanical garden or arboretum adds to campus beauty and allure. In some cases, the campus *is* the botanical garden, as is the case at the Scott Arboretum of Swarthmore College. Although the college offers no program in horticulture, the Scott manages impressive collections of conifers, witch hazels, crabapples, flowering cherries, hollies, hydrangeas, magnolias, roses, and tree peonies.

Serving as Living Museums

Because botanical gardens and arboreta are living museums, they contribute to the college or university's network of museums, which might also include art, history, anthropology, or local culture. Beyond whatever research or pedagogical roles they play, these museums are also prestigious centers for the institution and play a role in attracting not only great students but also top faculty, major grant funding, and local, state, or alumni support. Returning to the example of Harvard University, the Arnold Arboretum takes its place as one of the great museums of the university, along with the Fogg Art Museum and the Museum of Natural History.

Summary

In this chapter, we examined the basic criteria that are universal to all public gardens: having a mission statement; having professionally managed, accessioned collections; conducting some form of research and/or education programs; and being open and accessible to the public. We then explored the various types of public gardens and provided examples of each. Finally, the reasons why individuals or groups develop public gardens were presented, along with prototypical examples of each.

Students should now have a through understanding of how a public garden is distinguished from other sites in which plants are on display, and what the essential requirements are to create a public garden.

Annotated Resources

Berrall, J. A. 1966. *The garden: An illustrated history.* New York: Viking Press. Provides a broad overview of gardens and garden design over many centuries.

Birnbaum, C. A., and C. C. Peters, eds. 1996. The secretary of the interior's standards for the treatment of historic properties with guidelines for the treatment of cultural landscapes. Washington, D.C.: U.S. Department of the Interior, National Parks Service, Historic Landscape Initiative. Source of definitions for differing levels of historic preservation of landscapes.

A Brief history of the Brooklyn Botanic Garden. 2008. bbg .org/abo/history.html. Website traces the evolution of one of the nation's oldest botanical gardens.

Byers, B., G. Dreyer, R. C. Bumstead, G. Lee, R. E. Lyons, N. Doubrava, P. W. Meyer, and M. Zadik. 2003. College and university gardens: Profiles of seven diverse institutions. *The Public Garden* 18(4): 26–35. Profiles illustrate the breadth of public gardens affiliated with institutions of higher learning.

Hobhouse, P. 1992. *Gardening through the ages.* New York: Simon and Schuster. Essential text on how gardens have changed from ancient Egypt through the twentieth century.

Hubbuch, C. E. 1998. What is a botanical garden? *The Public Garden* 13(1): 34–35. Provides a concise definition for botanical gardens, distinguishing them from parks and other types of museums.

McNulty, E. 2009. *Missouri Botanical Garden: Green for 150 years.* St. Louis: Missouri Botanical Garden. In addition to providing a detailed history of America's first botanical garden, an introductory chapter also gives a short history of botanical gardens.

CHAPTER 2

The History and Significance of Public Gardens

CHRISTINE FLANAGAN

Introduction

Gardens do not exist without people, and nature untouched by humans is not a garden. This fact acknowledges that gardens come from willful acts requiring forethought and commitment on the part of individuals and societies alike. Gardens whose functions transcend food production—for example, for ceremony, pleasure, or religious use—are the subject of this chapter. They have been a persistent feature of complex human societies throughout history, implying that they result from a fundamental motivation originating in the human psyche.

The making of a "public" garden implies a social need or purpose in sharing the garden with others. In early human history, gardens were constructed by the ruling or religious elite for their pleasure and/or for political and social functions, such as performing a ritual or ceremony that demonstrates the wealth and importance of the rulers or cements their connection to the gods, thus reinforcing their claim to power. Only a few public gardens have this genesis. From an American post-Renaissance perspective, public gardens have often been formed when large private gardens or estates eclipse the longevity, interest, or wealth of the family that created them, and the estates are bequeathed to a public or private entity for use and appreciation by the public. In this chapter, we shall explore the variety and meaning of public gardens in order to understand why they are created and supported by human societies, and discuss the enlightened roles that public gardens play in the twenty-first century.

> ### KEY TERMS
>
> **Systematics:** the branch of biology concerned with classification and nomenclature; taxonomy.
>
> **Ethnobotany:** the plant lore and agricultural customs of a people; the systematic study of such lore.

Humans Are Place Makers

Why and for whom do we garden? Following the construction of shelter, garden making is one of the earliest forms of enduring manipulation of the environment and is associated with food production, spiritual place making, social discourse, and territoriality (Turner 2005). The history of garden making is as old as horticulture, or the growing of plants individually. Horticulture likely predates the clearing and formation of arable land for the collective planting and growing of plants, or what we usually think of as agriculture (Tudge 1998). The eighteenth-century garden designer Humphry Repton defined a garden as "a piece of ground fenced off from cattle, and appropriate to the use and pleasure of man; it is, or ought to be, cultivated" (Hunt 2000). The fence or boundary is key, for it defines the limits of stewardship and place: the garden is within, not beyond, and access to it may be controlled. The words *garden* and *yard* are derived from the Old English word *geard*, meaning "fence."

The concept of "garden" has been freighted with symbolism from the beginning of history. *Locus amoenus*, Latin for "pleasant place," is a literary term introduced by Aristotle in 384 BCE. It generally refers to an idealized place of safety or comfort, paradise, or Eden. A *locus amoenus* has three basic elements—trees, grass, and water—and is considered a place of refuge from the processes of time and mortality, a description ascribed to public gardens by many visitors and certainly evocative of the emotion motivating the creation of private gardens. Gardens are constructed to be shared, either literally with family or a segment of the public, or figuratively with the society as a whole when they serve as a venue for important symbolic ritual.

Ancient gardens were not public in the modern sense, but they were part of the public consciousness as an accepted, even necessary part of place making and community. Archeological evidence of gardens, and even the oldest surviving gardens from ancient Egypt, Greece, Rome, and throughout Christendom (Turner 2005), are associated with religion and powerful symbolism and thus served the innate psychological need for the understanding, control, or influence of fate and the quest for spiritual, if not corporeal, well-being. The forms of these gardens communicated the nature of the world and social order and represented the oldest manifestation of the design of outdoor space (Figure 2-1). These gardens were used by priests, pharaohs, and others in power but may have been accessible to some members of the public on festival days. They represented the achievement of beauty, organization, and control far beyond the scope of individual effort, satisfying the need of individuals to be a part of something significant and greater than their own lives. To a great extent, public gardens continue to fulfill that role.

Gardens Are an Expression of Culture, Social Norms, and Power

Archeological evidence of gardens and reference to them in art and recorded history are contemporaneous with the rise of culture and complex human societies. Establishment of human settlements coincident with the development of horticulture and agriculture enabled the production of excess food, the division of labor, and, over a period of more than 10,000 years, the evolution of socially stratified states with complex and rich cultures. The oldest human civilizations arose in six key regions (Table 2-1).

Nation-states, both ancient and modern, are characterized by large populations, complex economies, taxation, recording of information, organized religions, social classes, art, and monumental architecture, including monumental gardens. It has been argued that monumental gardens only emerge in and are diagnostic of complex cultures, and are an expression

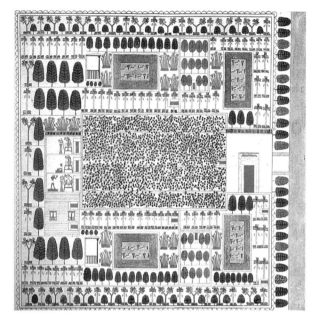

Figure 2-1: Painting of an Egyptian garden (1400 BCE) found in the funerary chapel above the tomb of Sennufer, overseer of the Gardens of Amun. The original wall painting has been destroyed, but Rosselini, an Italian Egyptologist, copied it in the nineteenth century. The garden is thought to be a palace garden and likely belonged to a pharaoh.

Tom Turner/Gardenvisit.com

of a mature and distinctive artistic tradition signifying intellectual development (Evans 2007). Some ancient gardens, such as the Hanging Gardens of Babylon and the Shalimar Gardens at Lahore and Kashmir, are still counted among humanity's greatest achievements, requiring sophisticated engineering and great expenditure of labor in their creation and maintenance. The Inca civilization is an exception. The Incas produced monumental architecture but left no monumental gardens, despite the significance of their agricultural constructions in the form of terracing of the steep Andean slopes.

Gardens have long been an expression of political power and a means of reinforcing cultural identity. Monumental garden construction and maintenance, requiring mobilization of resources, forced labor, and long-term commitment, is made possible because of the power inherent in the class structure. The gardens of Cyrus the Great (begun ca. 546 BCE) at Pasargadae in Iran (Figure 2-2), the monumental gardens of the Aztecs in Mesoamerica (1100–1500 CE), the Mughul gardens of India and Pakistan, and the gardens at Versailles near Paris (Figure 2-3) are all examples of palace pleasure gardens that demonstrated power, social control, and wealth (Turner 2005; Evans 2007).

Table 2-1: Gardens in Earliest Centers of Civilization

I. Old World

a. **Mesopotamia (southwest Asia):** Assyrian hunting parks (1100 BCE); palace gardens–Hanging Gardens of Babylon (Ninevah?, ca. 700 BCE); Iran-Pasargardae (Cyrus the Great, 550 BCE)

b. **Mediterranean region:** Nile River Valley (northeast Africa), ancient Egypt, Sennufer's Garden (palace garden, 1400 BCE) and Temple gardens (2065–1100 BCE); ancient Greece and Rome, religious, sport, and teaching gardens (430 BCE–130 CE)

c. **Indus River Valley (Indian subcontinent):** surviving examples are from the Islamic Mughal Empire (1500–1654 CE), including Shalamar Bagh (in Lahore, 1633 CE, and Kashmir, 1620 CE) and Taj Mahal (1632 CE)

d. **Valleys of the Yangtze and Yellow rivers in north-central China:** palace gardens developed during the Shang Dynasty (1600–1046 BCE) and developed further by successive dynasties into imperial hunting parks; by the time of the Han Dynasty (206 BCE–220 CE) , Chinese gardens could be classified as royal, religious, or scholarly

II. New World

a. **Middle America:** Aztec Empire and Mexica Dynasties, 1375–1519 CE; Chapultepec (ca. 1400 CE); Texcotzingo (1430–1450 CE); Huaxtépec, a pleasure park and horticultural garden (1450–1470 CE)

b. **Northwestern South America:** Inca civilization, 1200–ca. 1550 CE (when conquered by the Spanish), capital at Cuzco (10,800 ft [3,300 m]); legacy of significant terraforming and cultivation activities in the form of terraced agriculture

(Compiled from Turner 2005; Evans 2007; Lawler 2009)

Figure 2-2: At Pasargadae, the remains of the palace and garden of Cyrus the Great (ca. 546 BCE) are the oldest surviving stone watercourses and thought to represent an early form of the classical Persian garden plan.

Tom Turner/Gardenvisit.com

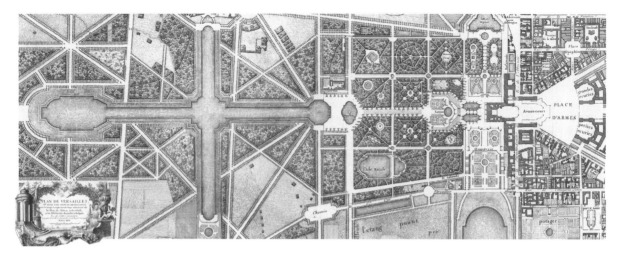

Figure 2-3: The gardens at Versailles, France (designed 1661–1700), center of government for King Louis XIV, are arguably the grandest of all gardens and provided inspiration for the national capital cities of Washington, D.C., Delhi, and Brasília.

Gardens Are Places of Pleasure, Spiritual Connection, and Expression of Social Value

Human intelligence applied to self-awareness has led to the distinction of body, mind, and spirit. Gardens, from the very beginning, reflected these distinctions. Vegetable and fruit gardens, as well as those devoted to exercise, served the body. Medicinal, zoological, and botanical gardens, arboreta, alpine gardens, rock gardens, and others were places for study and the growth of knowledge and intellect. Among the oldest surviving gardens are the sacred groves, temple gardens, ceremonial spaces, palace and sculpture gardens, and other spaces designed for beauty, contemplation, ritual, religion, celebrations, or expressions of doctrine (Figure 2-4). They were often located relative to significant geographical features or aided in the observation of significant astronomical events. These gardens helped people understand their relationship to the physical world, the role of society in providing social stability, and the place of humankind in the universe. Many gardens served more than one function.

Faced with the certainty of physical death, humans have long sought the means to immortality, or at least the exertion of influence beyond death. The creation of great gardens by the wealthy and powerful, with trees, stone, water, landforms, built structures, and other features that endure beyond a human lifetime, is among the most powerful means of achieving spiritual connection and asserting a personal viewpoint and statement of social dominance across generations (Figure 2-5). Many of the great public gardens around the world began as private estates.

Figure 2-4: This relief from ancient Greece (Hellenistic period) depicts a youth laying a wreath at a temple beside a sacred tree inside a shrine dedicated to the gods.

Tom Turner/Gardenvisit.com

Figure 2-5: George Vanderbilt completed Biltmore in 1895, and at that time it was the largest private residence in the United States. He commissioned architect Richard Morris Hunt, who modeled the house on three châteaux built in sixteenth-century France, and landscape architect Frederick Law Olmsted, who designed the grounds of the 125,000-acre estate. In addition to acres of developed gardens, Olmsted reflected Vanderbilt's environmental ethic and established America's first managed forest on the grounds. Still owned by the family, Biltmore is now a public garden and resort.

Photo used with permission from the Biltmore Company, Asheville, North Carolina.

Gardens As a Reflection of the Human Psyche

Both the private domestic garden of a residence and the public garden or park of a city are expressions of a basic human drive for connection to the living world, termed *biophilia* (Wilson 1984; Kellert and Wilson 1993). From this viewpoint, humans need nature and subconsciously seek it out as a result of our evolutionary history. The human penchant for collection, transport, and study of novelties, especially plants, is evident early in history. In what may be the earliest known garden boast, Assyrian king Tiglath-Pileser I (1115–1077 BCE) proclaimed: "I carried off from the countries I conquered, trees that none of the kings, my forefathers, have possessed, these trees have I taken, and planted them in mine own country, in the parks of Assyria have I planted them" (Gothein 1928). Thus, the

manipulation of landscapes and the importation of plants into gardens has long been part of the human behavioral repertoire. A contemporary expression of connection to the living world and intellectual understanding of the universe is the Garden of Cosmic Speculation (Figure 2-6), designed by Charles Jencks.

We owe the embedding of this instinct to the fact that the tendency to nurture living organisms has contributed to our own survival and, by inference, the survival of civilizations. In a sweeping study that applied the principles of ecology to a study of human history, Diamond (2005) has documented that societies that fail to steward the surrounding environment will outgrow their support systems and ultimately collapse. Evidently, at the level of the nation-state, this represents a failure of biophilia to compete in political discourse with the

Figure 2-6: Designed by Charles Jencks, the Garden of Cosmic Speculation at Portrack in southwest Scotland is a sensory exploration of recent scientific discoveries and the fundamental laws of nature arrayed in the design of landforms, water, rockwork, plantings, and artwork. The garden can be seen as an expression of biophilia in its most abstract form.

Image © Charles Jencks. Reproduced from *In Search of Paradise: Great Gardens of the World* by Penelope Hobhouse, published by Frances Lincoln, 2006.

motivation to provide for defense, war, justice, religion, education, and health, despite the certain and unfavorable outcome of degrading the environment. Lack of experience with nature during youth profoundly influences attitudes toward the environment, exacerbating the disconnection. According to the United Nations Population Fund, in 2008 more than half of the world's population lived in urban areas, with the greatest increase in urbanization occurring in Africa, Latin America, and China (UNFPA 2007). As more of the Earth's citizens are packed into cities, our public gardens, zoos, national parks, wildlife refuges, preserves, and similar sites will become the access points for people to appreciate and learn about nature, and therefore will play an increasingly important role in staving off societal collapse.

Public versus Private Gardens

Traditionally, owners of the garden, whether royal, familial, governmental, private, for-profit, or nonprofit, have determined who will have access. It is helpful to understand that the term *public* as it is now commonly understood may have applied (especially in ancient times) only to select social strata or religious groups. Private ownership of land under the domain of the common citizen is a relatively modern concept. The most ancient gardens and surrounding territory were under the control of the elite. Areas of commons on which gardens were developed may have served a public function but were private in the sense of who controlled access to them, blurring the distinction between public and private.

Thus, a private garden, reserved for the use of a family (regardless of the family's social station), is distinguished from a public garden, used for a broader function and broader section of society. In the twenty-first century, *public garden* implies the availability of the garden for the enjoyment of the public at large (as defined and determined by the surrounding society), irrespective of the garden's ownership. The point is not as simple as it seems; for example, consider how the decision to charge admission to a garden discriminates economically against a sector of society, a conclusion leading some public gardens to have free admission days. Other, more subtle forms of exclusion of certain subgroups of the public (e.g., whether the garden may be reached by public transportation) may be less obvious but still significant, apparent only after focused visitor study. Awareness that some groups are underrepresented in a public garden's audience has produced efforts to broaden programs in the hopes of attracting specific demographics. In the United States, *public* may also be used in the sense of "owned by the people," that is, the government. Only a small minority of public gardens are owned by local, state, or federal government entities.

The oldest gardens for public use can be traced to sacred groves where shrines were established for religious ceremony and later used for recreation and sporting events. The gardens at Olympia, dating from about 2000 BCE, contained the Temples of Zeus and Hera, the Altar of Zeus, and the Prytaneum, with its perpetual fire and great fountain. Olympia, the site of the oldest stadium in Greece, hosted the famed Olympic Games, held every four years from the eighth to the fourth century BCE. The modern Olympic Games began in 1896, and many Olympic venues strive to reflect the garden atmosphere present in the ancient sports parks, which symbolized the harmony of intellectual, artistic, and physical pursuits. Now, however, competitive sports in public green spaces are restricted to recreational parks that carefully segregate their pleasure gardens and walking spaces from ball fields and other sport venues.

Gardens Mirror the Surrounding Society

European gardens have had the greatest influence on the development of public gardens in the United States. Many of today's public gardens in Europe and the United States began as royal or grand private estates, and their design reflects the surrounding societal, religious, and historical context at the time of their creation. During the Middle Ages, the structure of private European gardens reflected Greek and Roman influence and often reflected Christian religious principles in their overall design. The plantings in monastic gardens in particular preserved the knowledge of plants and their uses from antiquity, bridging the intellectual desert of the medieval period. The Renaissance inaugurated a time of rapid social evolution that extended throughout all aspects of society, including the establishment of private and public gardens.

During the Age of Discovery (fifteenth through seventeenth centuries), the first botanical gardens in Europe were established in Italy, followed by rapid establishment of gardens in the major cities of the Continent by the mid-1600s. Evans (2007) suggests that the European botanical garden is a legacy

of the Aztec monumental parks, noted for their diverse collections of plants by Spaniards during the Conquest that began in 1519. However, the sixteenth century was a time of intellectual awakening in Europe, and the need to develop a better understanding of useful plants was inevitable. In Europe, knowledge of medicinal properties of plants had not progressed far beyond rote copying of *De materia medica*, first published by Pedanius Dioscorides, a Greek physician of the first century CE. The need to promote the study of medicinal plants was widely recognized in Italy, resulting in the establishment of medicinal study (physic) gardens at Pisa in 1544, Padua in 1545, Firenze in 1545, and Bologna in 1547. All were established at universities, thus highlighting the need for continuous study and access to the plants by scholars. The blossoming of world trade also led to importation and study of exotic plants and a broadening of interest beyond medicinal plants. Botanical gardens in Europe and in ports around the world were established to house and study plants discovered during explorations. The need to describe, categorize, and develop a means of identification of plants produced interest in taxonomy and classification, thus freeing the science of botany from its medicinal origins. In the eighteenth and nineteenth centuries, it became popular to display plants grouped by relationship, often in orders and families, producing the educational or teaching "botanical garden."

The Baroque period (1600–1750) marked a time of rapid social change. The advent of cannon warfare, the weakening of church authority, the exploration and navigation of the world oceans, and the development of science broke down barriers between the physical, social, political, and religious. Integration of disciplines, coalitions of city-states, and growth of knowledge were reflected in the design of gardens of the period. Mathematical harmony was manifest in progressively complicated axial designs, first within gardens and later in transverse and radial designs that transcended garden boundaries to include features of the surrounding town or landscape. Among the most influential and well known are the grounds of Versailles, built by King Louis XIV of France; the intricate complex of gardens in Isfahan; and the gardens along the National Mall, integrated with the radial thoroughfares of Washington, D.C.

In North America, colonization was rapidly followed by the discovery of new plants by botanist John Bartram and other prominent naturalists. Bartram's specimens became widely known to Linnaeus, Dillenius, Gronovius, and other European botanists as well as to hobbyist collectors, spurring transatlantic commerce in plants (Figure 2-7). Overall, the period was characterized by exploding interest in the study of plants and establishment

Figure 2-7: Bartram's Garden in Philadelphia preserves the legacy of America's first great botanist and plantsman. John Bartram's collections spurred interest in America's plants on both sides of the Atlantic.

© John Bartram Association, Bartram's Garden, Philadelphia

of botanical gardens featuring taxonomic collections. Bartram, with Benjamin Franklin, promoted the growth of science in the new nation with the founding of the American Philosophical Society in Philadelphia in 1743. Bartram's own garden, thought to have been established in 1728, is America's oldest surviving botanical garden and became public in 1891 when it was turned over to the City of Philadelphia.

Arguably one of the oldest public parks in the United States dates from about 1830, when cattle were banned from Boston Common, a space first dedicated for public use in 1634. By 1836, an ornamental perimeter fence enclosed the Common and its five perimeter recreational malls, continuing a trend

of improvements that had begun in 1726. This period marks a rapid growth in public parks and public gardens in the new democracy, with the formal founding of the Public Garden in Boston in 1837, the United States Botanic Garden in 1850, the Missouri Botanical Garden in 1859, and the acquisition of land for Central Park in New York City between 1853 and 1856. During this period botanical gardens were seen to have pragmatic value integral to the development of industry and science for the growing nation (Fallen 2007).

Public Garden Management and the Legacy of History

Many of the board discussions, budget justifications, and donor or foundation investments that drive the establishment, strategic planning, development, and everyday management of public gardens hinge on personal understanding of the purpose of the garden and its perceived relationships to the community and society at large. At financial or political junctures, the most passionate of garden management and governance discussions often surround questions raised by mission and priorities for funding and land use: Is the garden for beauty and contemplation or for education? Are its green spaces valued for plant conservation, wildlife habitat, and ecosystem services? What are the roles of art, science, and religion in its programs? Will the garden embrace evolution, genetically modified plants, or intellectual property rights of native peoples? What is the original vision of the garden, and can it (should it) evolve? Does the garden earn its keep from the perspective of the surrounding community? The stakeholders of a public garden—for example, garden staff, board members, academicians and researchers, volunteers, funders, donors, government, citizen advisers, schools, and garden visitors—are its strength. They represent a variety of educational, religious, and social backgrounds and often have differing priorities for the many roles that gardens may serve. It is helpful to remember that the diversity of public gardens in the United States is a direct reflection of the freedom of thought nurtured by a democratic society and historical events that led to their establishment. The continued relevance of a public garden to the local, regional, or national communities depends on the vision of the people who shepherd it into the future.

The Significance of Public Gardens in the Twenty-first Century

Public gardens show remarkable diversity in their relationship to society at large and to their local communities. Whether large or small, old or relatively new, most public gardens fulfill many roles simultaneously. To highlight the different ways that public gardens serve their local, regional, and national stakeholders, institutions have been selected that exemplify a particular purpose or activity.

Public Gardens Function as Reservoirs and Generators of Knowledge

Public gardens promote human relationship with and knowledge of the plant world by being places where botanical science, ethnobotany, horticulture, cultural traditions, and other plant-related activities are ongoing. Much like universities and museums, they preserve knowledge and perspectives that may not at times be sufficiently valued to be retained by the actions of wider society. However, unlike the boards of natural history museums and universities, public garden boards govern with priorities and perspectives driven by the needs of a plant-centered institution.

The New York Botanical Garden (NYBG) has a storied history of research in botany and in the taxonomy and systematics of plants. Since its founding in 1891, it has contributed significantly to the study and cataloging of the plants of the world by conducting expeditions, publishing original research, and serving as an international training center for plant systematists (Figure 2-8). As a result, its library and herbarium are internationally recognized as preeminent resources for the study of plant classification, taxonomy, and the new field of genomics.

NYBG also serves as a center for the study of economic plants and ethnobotany, with a focus on therapeutic plants. NYBG scientist Michael Balick specializes in the identification and documentation of the use of plants for healing in tropical indigenous cultures. These studies capture the putative nutritional, therapeutic, ceremonial, and other properties of plants heretofore largely unknown to Western science.

Similarly, in response to the threats of invasive exotic plants, habitat loss, and erosion of cultural knowledge, the National Tropical Botanical Garden based in Kalaheo, Hawaii, is working in the islands of the Pacific to document plant uses and survey plant populations. This work, which is also ongoing in many other public gardens, is important in a rapidly modernizing and globally connected world where ethnobotanical information and the plants themselves are often lost before their value is realized.

The Missouri Botanical Garden, one of the most famous and visited public gardens in all of North America, is known for its research on the world's flora as well as the taxonomy and systematics of plants. Perhaps less well known is the Garden's commitment to promoting public knowledge of and participation in horticulture. Its William T. Kemper Center for Home Gardening provides home gardeners with resources, instruction, expert advice, and 8 acres of teaching and demonstration gardens.

Figure 2-8: The New York Botanical Garden Library Building houses one of the world's largest and most important botanical and horticultural research libraries, with more than one million accessioned items (books, journals, original art and illustrations, seed and nursery catalogs, architectural plans of glasshouses, scientific reprints, and photographs) and more than 4,800 linear feet of archival materials.

Photo by Robert Benson, courtesy of the New York Botanical Garden

Figure 2-9: Named in honor of its late director and founder, J. C. Raulston, Ph.D., a passionate plantsman who founded it in 1976, the Arboretum is widely known for its dedication to horticultural education, ornamental plant introduction, and educational outreach to the green industry.

Photo courtesy of JC Raulston Arboretum at North Carolina State University

Public gardens, especially those based at colleges and universities, preserve not only horticultural skills and knowledge but also their outcomes in the forms of germplasm, individual plants, and gardens. The JC Raulston Arboretum in Raleigh, North Carolina, features the most diverse collection of cold-hardy temperate-zone plants in the southeastern United States. As a part of the Department of Horticultural Science at North Carolina State University, the Arboretum is primarily a research and teaching garden that focuses on the evaluation, selection, and display of plant material gathered from around the world.

Horticultural research may also be preserved at nonacademic institutions. The Luther Burbank Home and Gardens, in Santa

Rosa, California, includes more than an acre of gardens. The cacti, walnuts, and fruit trees displayed there are among many of Luther Burbank's unique horticultural contributions and serve as living reminders of the significance of Burbank's research. At the U.S. National Arboretum, part of the Agricultural Research Service of the U.S. Department of Agriculture, plant breeders develop new cultivars for introduction to the landscape industry. The Arboretum also displays specialty collections such as the Gotelli Collection of Dwarf and Slow-Growing Conifers, the U.S. National Herb Garden, and the National Bonsai Collection. The Rancho Santa Ana Botanic Garden and the Santa Barbara Botanic Garden invite use of their collections of California flora by offering graduate programs in plant studies.

Public Gardens Preserve Social Memory and Sense of Place

Humans, individually and in societies, tend to move forward, often leaving behind past perspectives. However, the ways that humans inhabit the landscape are often preserved, providing a societal perspective that connects past to future. Gardens especially tend to produce a lasting imprint on the land.

The house and gardens at Filoli, the estate of prominent San Franciscans Mr. and Mrs. William Bowers Bourn, were constructed between 1915 and 1929 on 1,800 acres south of San Francisco. Much of the lower, flatter area was used for pasture, but the steeper, upper portions were returned to their natural growth and today support the typical California native flora of mixed evergreen, oak-woodland, and redwood–Douglas fir forests. The estate, an outstanding showcase of early twentieth-century architecture and garden design, was purchased in 1937 by Mr. and Mrs. William P. Roth. In 1975, Mrs. Roth donated Filoli with 125 acres to the National Trust for Historic Preservation. Filoli provides an inspiring vision of an era of enlightened stewardship of bountiful land, plentiful resources, and an emphasis on self-sufficiency. The Filoli Center manages the remaining 654 acres of the estate and preserves it as open space, wildlife habitat, and pristine watershed for the city of San Francisco.

The State Arboretum of Virginia and Blandy Experimental Farm, a field research station of the University of Virginia, preserve a portion of the property of Graham Blandy, a stockbroker from New York, who bequeathed the land and a sizable endowment to support it to the university. A dominant feature of the Arboretum is the distinctive architecture of the former slave quarters (Figure 2-10), now part of the research laboratories and administrative headquarters. The miles of dry-stack limestone walls tell the story of the clearing of the forest and farming the land during establishment of the early nineteenth-century Tuley family estate. The Arboretum's vast

Figure 2-10: The historic slave quarters in Clarke County, Virginia, is believed to have been constructed between 1825 and 1830. It is located at the State Arboretum of Virginia at Blandy Experimental Farm and is now one wing of the University of Virginia field research station headquarters.

Photo by Tim Farmer, Blandy Experimental Farm

plant collections and central landscaped allée are the legacy of Orland E. White, the first director and mentor of more than thirty plant scientists who went on to establish significant plant research programs across the United States. The story written in the Arboretum's dramatic landscape tells of Hessian soldiers from the Revolutionary War, slaves and landed gentry, early scientific research, the establishment of research-based plant collections, and now an environmental research station training new scientists.

Tohono Chul Park in Tucson, Arizona, preserves 49 acres of upland Sonoran Desert. Surrounded by modern suburban development, the park tells the story of the desert and its continuous human occupation, including some seventeen indigenous cultures that have occupied the region, beginning with the Hohokam of 300 BCE–1150 CE. Today, Anglos, Latinos, Africans, Chinese, and other immigrants are also leaving their mark on the landscape.

Bartram's Garden in Philadelphia, Bok Tower Gardens in Florida, Tryon Palace in North Carolina, the Gardens at Colonial Williamsburg, and many others across the nation preserve the imprint of local history on the landscape and are a living legacy of place making, contrasting different times, social norms, and priorities in U.S. history.

Public Gardens Provide Local Ecosystem Services

Public gardens that preserve large tracts of land intact, with minimal disturbance, provide important services to the local environment. Examples include the 2,400-acre Shaw Nature Reserve, a part of the Missouri Botanical Garden located 35 miles southwest of St. Louis. Most of the property is managed as natural Ozark border landscape, with 1.5 miles of Meramec River frontage on both banks. It strives to inspire responsible stewardship of the environment through education, protection and restoration of natural habitats, and public enjoyment of the natural world. Its forests, prairies, and wetlands provide opportunities for ecological research while cleaning the air and water, recharging the aquifer, and providing significant natural habitat for native flora and fauna. Similarly, Mt. Cuba Center in Delaware preserves more than 600 acres of natural Piedmont forest, wetlands, and open fields, in addition to more than 50 acres of cultivated gardens that focus on the native Piedmont flora.

During the Great Depression, civic leaders in Madison, Wisconsin, purchased land in an effort to preserve open space for the city's residents. Most of the University of Wisconsin–Madison Arboretum's current 1,200 acres came from these purchases. In addition to inexpensive land, the Depression brought a ready supply of hands to work it. Between 1935 and 1941, crews from the Civilian Conservation Corps provided most of the labor needed to begin reestablishing ecological communities. Widely recognized as the site of historic research in ecological restoration, the Arboretum (Figure 2-11) includes one of the oldest and most varied collections of restored ecological communities in the world, including tallgrass prairies, savannas, several forest types, and wetlands. The Arboretum has sought to enhance the quality and ability of its land to provide ecosystem services while integrating this role with

Figure 2-11: Ahead of its time, the University of Wisconsin–Madison Arboretum, founded in 1934, is the result of the vision of civic leaders and Arboretum leadership who recognized the value of open space and ecosystem services to the future well being of the city and its environs.

© University of Wisconsin–Madison Arboretum

research and programs to teach citizens and schoolchildren environmental sciences.

Public Gardens Create Partnerships to Address Societal Problems

Through the creation of partnerships among universities, governments, nonprofit organizations, and private enterprise, public gardens are responding in innovative ways to the plant-related needs of society and citizens. More nimble than governments, more flexible than university programs, and more altruistic than private enterprise, public gardens have found ways to forge important academic, conservation, and therapeutic programs.

The Chicago Botanic Garden (CBG) has established the Regenstein School of Continuing Education, Horticulture Therapy Services, and the Buehler Enabling Garden, which all focus on adult education. It offers the nation's first Healthcare Garden Design Certificate of Merit and a Horticulture Therapy Certificate. While many graduate-level botany programs are threatened by declining enrollments, CBG's new Plant Sciences Center partners with Northwestern University to offer advanced degrees in plant science and conservation. Faculty and staff at CBG conduct research in plant sciences and conservation, including studies on the effects of global climate change on natural ecosystems. CBG has committed to tackling urban

hunger and job training through an urban agriculture program called Windy City Harvest. By working with a broad coalition of other groups, the Garden hopes to lessen hunger, increase availability of food, and foster vital connections between gardens, growing plants, food, livelihood, and human well-being. Similar programs have been established at the Cleveland Botanical Garden and other gardens.

Public gardens have been leaders in the promotion and establishment of children's gardens and school gardens. The Brooklyn Botanic Garden established the nation's longest-running children's gardening program in 1914. The University of Washington Botanic Gardens has established one of the nation's most effective programs to involve the public in the emerging battle against exotic invasive plants. The Lady Bird Johnson Wildflower Center at the University of Texas–Austin, a leader in espousing native landscaping and drought-resistant approaches to gardening, has partnered with the U.S. Botanic Garden and American Society of Landscape Architects to develop guidelines and benchmarks for sustainable landscape design and construction standards, called the Sustainable Sites Initiative (SITES). Similar to the LEED program for architecture, SITES has the potential to change the appearance, healthfulness, and sustainability of our nation's human-centered landscapes.

Figure 2-12: The Chicago Botanic Garden works closely with the community to offer College First, a dynamic paid internship program for eligible Chicago public high school students consisting of career mentorship, field ecology and conservation science, and college prep and assistance. Emphasis is placed on college as a pathway to careers.

Photo by Robin Carlson, courtesy of Chicago Botanic Garden

Public Gardens Serve as Plant Museums

Visitors and communities are beginning to view public gardens as living plant museums, that is, as institutions of accumulated knowledge about plants, endowed with privileges and responsibilities to the greater society. A plant museum is more than a plant display garden, just as a natural history museum is more than a collection of natural objects. Plant museums have at their core a living collection of scientifically ordered plants with provenance documentation governed by a set of management and development documents that clearly tie the collections to the mission of the institution. Being a plant museum means following best practices in education, collections curation, administration, governance, facilities management, exhibition, safety, security, visitor services, and other critical museum functions. Plant museums interpret the significance of plants to society, educate about plants and their interconnections to other life-forms, follow national laws and international agreements concerning obtaining and transporting plants, and work to protect plants and the Earth's environment.

Arizona-Sonora Desert Museum (ASDM), an institution dedicated to preserving and interpreting the life of the Sonoran Desert, has long acknowledged the international nature of its work. The protection of the desert and its populations require that conservation efforts, research, and educational programs transcend the U.S. border with Mexico. At ASDM visitors learn about the human, plant, and animal denizens of the desert, including wayfaring migratory species as well as those

in danger of extinction from climate change, habitat loss, and wild collection (Figure 2-13). They also learn about the critical role of water and how its uses by the public must become more sustainable.

Public Gardens Celebrate Our Connection to Nature and Our Ability to Create Human-Centered Space in Nature

The seeming contradiction of both appreciating nature and manipulating it is resolved in a garden. In cities where the noise, pollution, dirt, and coarse anonymity of the buildings render nature unrecognizable, public gardens provide an aesthetic respite that nourishes our sense of well-being and stimulates creativity. Public gardens democratize the experience, making the value of the garden environment available to citizens of all stations and circumstances. The social worth of the public garden is recognized by the populace when the gardens are funded (albeit partially) through tax districts or other public sources of revenue. Simply put, cement, asphalt, monumental buildings, and traffic wear us out; public gardens build us up and remind us that we have choices in the kind of environment we create.

Chanticleer in Wayne, Pennsylvania, unabashedly wears the mantle of pleasure garden, inviting the public to escape the modern reality of busy lives to simply enjoy beauty. The horticulture at Chanticleer is superb and focused on conveying the idea that gardens are artistic compositions, a kind of living

Figure 2-13: Blooming foothills palo verde trees (*Parkinsonia microphylla*) lure visitors to wander the Desert Loop Trail and leave behind forest and pastoral sensibilities about beauty in nature. Its trail system is one of many ways that the Arizona-Sonora Desert Museum encourages visitors to respect and appreciate this richly diverse biome.

© Arizona-Sonora Desert Museum. Photo by M. A. Dimmitt.

performance art writ in the landscape. At Chanticleer, fine art objects and crafts appear almost serendipitously, providing embellishments that complement the color, form, and texture of the garden spaces. Other public gardens that celebrate aesthetics in the garden include Cheekwood in Tennessee, the Frederik Meijer Gardens and Sculpture Park in Michigan, the Morris Arboretum in Pennsylvania, and the many estate gardens, including Longwood Gardens; Winterthur Museum and Country Estate; Hillwood Estate, Museum, and Gardens; Huntington Botanical Gardens; and Biltmore.

Public Gardens Are Places of Spirituality, Healing, and Solace

Just as public gardens can trace their genesis to places of religious and spiritual activity early in human history, gardens may still be places of interment and memorial. Mount Auburn Cemetery in Massachusetts is a national historic landmark and one of many public gardens whose landscape and burying grounds embrace the mortality of humans in unity with the immortality of nature. Although not cemeteries, other public gardens are places of solace and healing as well.

As places that celebrate the vitality, wonder, and splendor of plant life, gardens are incongruent with war and other forms of human violence. Their quiet beauty and slow, unfolding pace of change encourage contemplation and acceptance.

At Sawtooth Botanical Garden in Idaho, the Garden of Infinite Compassion invites people of all faiths to come, reflect, and find peace. Paleaku Gardens Peace Sanctuary in Hawaii is a 7-acre botanical garden that facilitates educational, spiritual, and cultural programs and offers a "sanctuary for the advancement of individuals toward peace and harmony." Gardens for Peace is an international network that recognizes the role of gardens in nurturing society and celebrating peace. It currently lists sixteen public gardens that include specific areas for spiritual healing.

Gardens and the Future of Civilization

The second decade of the twenty-first century presents exciting opportunities and challenges, even perils, for public gardens. The recession of 2009 was a preview of the future competitive environment for scarce resources, and in making the case for their support it is important to clearly understand how public gardens relate to society and the stakes at hand. Many suggest that the next forty years are crucial in tackling the Earth's monumental environmental problems, including our thirst for energy and the reformation of unsustainable lifestyles.

Public gardens are the keepers of plants and knowledge of human relationships to plants. Some fulfill this role explicitly, while others reinforce through their actions the innate human need to connect with a nurturing landscape. Of all the work of public gardens, the most fundamental and important role is to remind individuals and societies that plants (and gardens) are not optional for any civilized society. All of the food (the chemical energy that sustains our bodies and nearly all biodiversity) comes ultimately from plants, either directly or indirectly through the food chain; plants relieve mental and physical suffering by providing medicines, analgesics, and places of solace; plants provide shelter and other products to support our lives; and plants provide sources of pleasure and delight that make life worth living. Public gardens not only keep alive this knowledge; they also literally keep plant germplasm, and the skills to work with it, alive.

Humans may not need all of the estimated 400,000 plants found on the Earth to survive, but we certainly need more than any one institution or country can grow or appreciate. Even as the world's population continues to grow, we are only now beginning to understand the awesome power of humans to poison the planet and destroy its ability to support us and other complex life-forms. Plants anchor the ecosystems that clean our air and water and soil, sequester heavy metals, provide sustenance to all forms of consumers, and remind us of our innate need for beauty and creativity. By 2050, nearly one out of every three plant species in the United States, and more than 34,000 worldwide, may become extinct. While there is no doubt that humans will continue to exist with fewer plants, why would we choose to? In fact, the choice has already been made, for we cannot grow all the plants that we need in our fields and gardens.

Technology now can prove that there is no place on earth untouched by humans; in a sense, the entire planet has become our garden, and we must steward it. Who better to lead in making that case than public gardens? Our future will, of necessity, include plants. Public gardens are the institutions best positioned to demonstrate through actions that we can choose the kind of future we want.

Summary

This chapter examined the five-thousand-year history of public gardens—that is, gardens that have a use or function extending beyond a specific family and serve a societal function other than providing food. A common feature is that their construction and maintenance require significant labor or other resources, often drawn from the community at large. Across history, these gardens have served one or more purposes accorded by the populace—for example, recognition as places where religious, political, ceremonial, programmatic, or pleasure observances took place. The student will understand how the concept of "public" has changed over the millennia and how garden functions and design have evolved as a reflection of the philosophy and sociopolitical norms of the surrounding society. Finally, examples are presented of how present-day public gardens relate to their communities and the emerging roles of public gardens as places for plant advocacy, conservation, and environmental connection.

Annotated Resources

Evans, S. T. 2007. Precious beauty: The aesthetic and economic value of Aztec gardens. In *Botanical progress, horticultural innovations, and cultural changes*, ed. M. Conan and W. J. Kress, 81–101. Washington, D.C.: Dumbarton Oaks Research Library and Collection and Spacemaker Press. An eclectic collection of specialist papers exploring the impact of horticulture and plants upon specific cultures.

Turner, T. 2005. *Garden history: Philosophy and design 2000 BC–2000 AD*. New York: Spon Press. A detailed summary and analysis of gardens throughout the history of Western civilization. A definitive reference for history, design, and evolution of estate and public gardens.

PART II

The Emerging Garden

CHAPTER 3

Critical Issues in Starting a Public Garden

ROBERT LYONS

Introduction

A new or emerging garden is often more reflective of its founding individual or group than of a pressing need for a brand-new public garden. The garden is the vehicle or the instrument by which the individual or group can express a vision, new dreams, philosophies, strategies, and/or ideas that they believe are not expressed elsewhere. Even when other public gardens are relatively close, to the new founders those existing gardens lack particular qualities and learning opportunities in which they have more confidence.

Sooner or later, reality subdues initial naïveté and a steep learning curve is initiated, leading to the articulation of priorities and, often, to the development of a garden master plan. The most successful founders orchestrate an intricate and synergistic mix of calculated decision making with the original, unbridled passion that spurred them on in the first place.

Motivations

Carefully thinking through the founders' motivations for establishing a public garden may be one of the most important and most overlooked prerequisites for embarking on the creation of a new garden. Those initial motivations are critical because any one or all of them can help to shape a developing mission.

- *Personal motivations* provide the drive to persevere, no matter how hard the times ahead may be, and can be selfish, altruistic, or even therapeutic in nature.

- *Educational motivations* should be at or near the top of the list. Active or passive opportunities to seize a "teaching moment" are tailor-made within gardens and should not be

undervalued. The public, green industry professionals, and students of all ages are the most obvious recipients of the garden's educational message, but potential audiences also include master gardeners, garden clubs, and similar organizations.

- *Green motivations* may be based on a passion for the collection and display of plants in general, one or more functional purposes they possess, or particular families or genera of plants. Or they may be founded on a strong plant conservation ethic and an aspiration to use the public garden to further this agenda.

- *Recreational motivations,* when considered broadly and thoughtfully interpreted, serve to differentiate public gardens from simple parks and open green space. While the term *recreational* often infers a focus on physical activity, it can also include personal solace, reflection, relaxation, and decompression from job and personal stresses, all within a purposely planned collection of plants.

- *Financial motivations.* It would be unusual for the creation of a public garden to be considered solely to provide a revenue stream where none currently exists. While financial considerations are generally included in the initial planning process to support the new garden's survival and growth, they are often not the first steps in the founder's development strategy.

- As the economic, social, and educational environments become more globally focused, *international motivations* offer additional reasons for establishing public horticultural institutions. Gardens can serve as anchors for exchange programs, forums for cultural understanding, and expressions of diverse aesthetics.

Allies

Founders must make sure that their early priorities include developing a solid base of political, professional, and private sector allies. Their knowledge, connections, expertise, insights, access, and acumen will be invaluable as founders navigate their way through site development and organizational protocol. While garden creators may never need to call upon such allies, if they do they will really appreciate their friendship. The most logical groups from which to cultivate buy-in include key local administrators as well as local and statewide green industries. The latter's potential contributions can be immeasurable, and they are often just waiting to be asked.

In one particular instance at the JC Raulston Arboretum, a very complicated landscape situation remained after a new education center was constructed. The director recognized the physical complexity of the site and realized that any appropriate restorative and design action would require skills and equipment that extended well beyond the Arboretum's capabilities. Inviting representatives of the green industry to evaluate the site subsequently led to a new landscape design and a two-day construction and plant installation effort by industry professionals. The project was a perfect example of industry involvement and assistance and, most important,

getting something done that might have been nearly impossible without the collaboration.

Information Needs

While the founders' high energy and optimism about the planning process can't substitute for the wisdom, experience, and advice available from external resources, the best strategy for those trying to start a new garden is to avoid being paralyzed by the sheer volume of information they are likely to encounter, and to trust their instincts and adapt advice to their own situation.

- *Other public gardens and cultural institutions* can help founders avoid or conquer common obstacles, since it is highly unlikely that their problems will be unique—somebody somewhere has experienced similar obstacles and will be very willing to help.

- *The American Public Gardens Association (APGA),* the anchoring organization for public horticulture professionals in North America, is replete with resources to help those starting new gardens. APGA also has a Small Public Gardens Professional Section that encourages interaction among newly formed public gardens.

Figure 3-1: In the wake of building construction, the JC Raulston Arboretum's close relationship with the North Carolina landscape and nursery industries led to contributions of design expertise, hardscape and turf, equipment use, and labor to solve the site difficulties that the Arboretum staff could not handle alone.

JC Raulston Arboretum

Figure 3-2: Approximately a year after completion of the industry-assisted site in front of the Education Center, the Arboretum was able to showcase additional plants from its nursery inventory due to the slope management and drainage considerations included in the final site.

JC Raulston Arboretum

- *The American Society for Horticultural Science* sponsors a Public Horticulture Working Group that is composed primarily of academics who have some responsibility for campus-based gardens.

- *The networking possibilities across professional lines* can be extraordinary outlets for personal advice, counsel, and future consultation, which is why the American Association of Museums is another resource.

Beg and Borrow

Founders need to be savvy, creative, and imaginative individuals who have also learned to master the fine art of bartering. The backbone of many existing plant collections is often the result of the generosity of other gardens. Peer institutions are often quite willing to share their plants with start-up gardens. Alternately, plants can be "rescued" from sites that are scheduled for development.

Plant collections can define institutions and need to be started early, as does a network of sources. Some caution is also necessary, however. Plant acquisitions, even when offered gratis, should fit within the garden's collections priorities, usually spelled out in a collections policy (see Chapter 20). Also, certain taxa that may behave well in one climatic zone may be weedy and invasive in another.

While a bit more difficult, acquiring hardscape materials and construction assistance for a fraction of their market cost is possible. The Linnaeus Garden, in Tulsa, Oklahoma, for example, received donations of all of the bricks it needed for pathway development. Founders must keep in mind that safety, longevity, and aesthetics must always be key considerations and that the quality of materials and expertise should not be sacrificed for the sake of frugality. Excellent craftsmanship may be available within existing support groups, including volunteers, friends groups, and the green industry. Hardscape materials can be solicited directly from job surplus inventories or as targeted donations from sponsors. Benches, for example, are commonly offered to donors as potential sponsorship opportunities, and names or phrases can be directly engraved on one of the rails or on a plaque. When bricks are required for patios, walkways, and other purposes, they, too, can be engraved with donor names for a reasonable gift level over the cost of materials.

Even equipment and selected maintenance services have been creatively acquired by garden start-ups. Turf management firms may offer free use of their mowers with an understanding that they receive some form of publicity in return, in much the same way that irrigation companies may install a system at a discount in return for similar publicity.

Starting a garden is an experience filled with serendipitous moments, goodwill gestures included. Of course, anything the founders beg or borrow is really some form of in-kind support in the absence of any meaningful operational budget. It may not be the most comfortable strategy, but it is one that few new garden founders can ignore. When done astutely and respectfully, such cultivation of resources will also initiate, strengthen, and expand a broad base of support. This is neither tangible nor measured in currency, but it can lead to timely political clout and significant help in the future in ways that are yet to reveal themselves. It is also very important to publicize such gifts through the local media and on the garden's website; sharing news about in-kind gifts is often helpful in garnering additional gifts.

Recognize Your Limitations

The founders must realize that they cannot do this alone. Starting a public garden is much more complex than starting a home garden; weekends and evenings alone will not lead to the necessary progress. The sooner founders come to terms with their own individual limitations to make this dream tangible, the faster the dream may actually materialize, but only with the help of others.

Organize Volunteers

The value of volunteers is immeasurable and will only increase over time. They work because they want to be there, asking nothing more than to share in the new garden's progress, learn from the founders, and maybe get a free plant now and then. Many volunteers are retirees with flexible schedules, but it is also important to include gardening opportunities for individuals with 9-to-5 jobs in order to continue to build allegiances and local support. A savvy volunteer manager will recognize all possible blocks of volunteer time among interested but underutilized garden supporters. The integration of volunteers into garden maintenance opportunities to assist the paid staff can lead to improved plant collections and site conditions as well as the development of new groups of gardening volunteers who come, for example, during evenings and on weekends, times which more traditional daytime volunteers prefer to avoid. Teenagers are also potential volunteers. New gardens can take advantage of Eagle Scout candidates in need of projects. It might even be worthwhile to involve youth who have been assigned to work in the community for minor and/or nonviolent infractions (see Chapter 8).

Figure 3-3: The Japanese Garden at the JC Raulston Arboretum, many years after its installation with the help of staff, students, and volunteers, illustrates the impact of time in revealing the original intent of good designers.

JC Raulston Arboretum

Develop a Philosophical and Financial Support Base

An excellent source of support can come from the surrounding community. The neighbors of new gardens often view them as novel, nearby places of beauty, solace, learning, and pride, and can serve as the base for any fledging friends or membership groups. In fact, having a public garden nearby may increase the value of adjacent properties. Such groups are a natural connection for most gardens, and ones that typically provide annual support for general operations and maintenance, the greatest challenge for any director of a new garden.

Finally, the green industry represents one of the most important of all potential support groups and perhaps one of the most overlooked. New gardens promote the use and diversity of plants. Simply put, visitors see plants they like and request them from local retailers. In effect, public gardens are tasteful billboards for using plants.

One of the best examples of a garden working with the green industry is the JC Raulston Arboretum, whose expressed mission is to seek out, acquire, and evaluate new ornamental plants for landscape use. The Arboretum provides the green industry with propagation material for promising new plants, and the industry moves them to market. If asked, there is virtually nothing that the North Carolina green industry wouldn't do for the Arboretum because of the strength of this relationship.

The University of Delaware Botanic Gardens functions similarly, with "boundary-free" borders. Representatives of the industry generally alert the Gardens' director of their intention to collect propagation material and often return in the fall for a planned exposition, where guided tours and speakers apprise industry members of new plants and the performance of existing species and cultivars.

Become Relevant, Irreplaceable, and Memorable

It's easy to advise founders to make their gardens relevant, irreplaceable, and memorable, but this advice is often poorly implemented. Founders need to engage the local, regional, and statewide press in their efforts and make it easy for them to publicize the garden's efforts. Founders should never forget to invite local media to seasonal activities and special events. The new electronic media (websites, blogs, and social networking) is also quickly gaining importance as a way to get the word out about a garden's activities directly to its fans and potential new supporters (see Chapter 19).

The year was 1984; the scenario was perfect for opening discussions about the possibility of a new university-based public garden on campus. The department head was very new, several early-career faculty had been hired following an unusual number of retirements, and the campus site of interest (a 1-acre herbaceous plant trial garden) was losing its manager and open for a mission change. The department head had a personal interest in plant materials and recognized that the campus lacked a location to display and study plant collections within a purposefully designed setting.

Three faculty members who represented expertise in woody ornamentals, herbaceous plants, and landscape architecture were called into the department head's office to hear his vision for a new campus garden on the site of the existing trial gardens. He had no master plan, no start-up money, no ongoing budget base, and no promise of support staff or plant sources, yet somehow these three took the bait . . . enthusiastically!

What were they thinking? Well, like any new and energetic teachers, they saw this as an educational opportunity not to be missed. The thought of a convenient, multipurpose outdoor classroom for horticulture and landscape design was too good to be true. They may have questioned their sanity for a split second, but shrugged off their trepidations and immediately involved students by tailoring a special academic course around this opportunity to build a garden.

What is now the Hahn Horticulture Garden at Virginia Tech was first conceptualized by several upperclass landscape design students under the guidance of the three original faculty founders in a special-study course. The students traveled to see other regional gardens with similar missions, listened to the needs of the department, divided into teams, and embarked on the master planning process.

Shortly after the unofficial groundbreaking in 1984, credit-based courses in public garden maintenance and management were established to continue to engage students in overall operations and maintenance. Although elective in nature and never actually requiring students to help out, these courses were filled each semester, despite the often disingenuous complaints about "slave labor" from students during busy times.

Equally important to the Garden's initial growth and development were the creation of a volunteer corps (which still meets regularly) and early alumni support, which materialized as donated plants, funds from time-limited and inexpensive "bed sponsorships," donated benches, a memorial gazebo, and a pivotal internship endowment. The latter was a true turning point, coming as it did within five years of the Garden's establishment. A bequest from the family of one of the department's earliest alums provided a $50,000 endowment to support a summer intern, easing the demands on faculty time and leading to a much faster pace of accomplishment. After twenty years, the endowment remains in place and is often granted matching funds for a second intern through the generosity of a departmental student organization.

Potential Obstacles
Financial Needs

When considering difficulties related to cash flow and financial support, some of the worst headaches can be either avoided or mitigated by advance financial planning and plain common sense. The founders must know where the money will come from. While there is something to be said for embarking on some garden development on a shoestring budget, these efforts should have the clear purpose of enticing future donors to support growth of plant collections, required structures, and/or new staff positions. Starting garden development in the absence of sufficient support often backfires, resulting in unappealing aesthetics, overworked and demoralized staff, woefully scarce and poorly interpreted plant collections, suboptimal plant health and condition, presentation of an unclear message or mission, and a visitor experience that lacks educational and/or recreational value.

The Naysayers

Not everyone will share the founders' vision. Naysayers will look for any reason to marginalize the founders' efforts and broadcast what they see as folly. Like a contagious virus, their

Figure 3-4: Construction costs of the Ruby C. McSwain Education Center at JC Raulston Arboretum were entirely covered by private donations. While its construction consumed several acres, temporarily diverted pedestrian flow, and compacted the surrounding soil, the final building provided an anchor for Arboretum activities and much-needed space.

JC Raulston Arboretum

criticisms can have a debilitating impact on potential supporters and the founders' confidence. Therefore, it is imperative that the garden founders take a preemptive approach, anticipating possible arguments against their effort and developing credible responses to these criticisms.

Bureaucratic Impediments

It would be rare not to encounter bureaucratic impediments. The best advice is to get to know the system in which one works and the individuals within its ranks. They can help as easily as they can impede a garden's progress. Keep them informed and study the pertinent legal and/or covenant issues of your site. Do research. What rules and regulations govern potential parking, alcohol use, land development and management, crowd limitations, noise, and selling anything, particularly plants? Plant sales seem to be one of the universal mainstays of any garden, so examine any restrictions to holding them at the garden.

Lotusland is one of many institutions encountering such challenges. Situated within Santa Barbara, California, Lotusland has worked carefully to generate a visitor-based revenue stream amid the covenant demands of a surrounding community that wishes to protect itself from the impact of an institution open to the public. This impact, whether perceived or real, has Lotusland operating under a conditional use permit from the city, which specifically and legally regulates many aspects of its day-to-day existence, including opening and closing hours, maximum number of vehicles per day and number of visitors per year, music levels, event planning, special programming, and parking restrictions on surrounding residential streets. The Lotusland staff understands that relationship building is the key to operating successfully within the confines of its conditional use permit and, ultimately, pursuing its mission as a public horticultural institution within a very restrictive environment.

Renegotiating conditional use permits to better suit the institution can be risky and complicated, especially since the effort to soften the existing terms may backfire, resulting in even more restrictive covenants. This is particularly important to know for any new director wishing to revisit the reasons for the permit in the first place.

One Acre Looks Like a Thousand

The irony of land acquisition for new garden development becomes apparent when the excitement of planning and implementation collides with the realization of what it will take to do the job. What looked like a welcome challenge on the master plan may suddenly seem daunting, scary, and even unachievable. The best advice is to ensure in advance that the master plan clearly describes a logical sequence of construction, installation, and maintenance, but reality has a way of defying logic, and circumstances may not always provide for the luxury of ideal master planning. The best strategy for founders is to step back and identify key areas within the entire plan and to concentrate on them, focusing less attention on secondary areas. The public wants to see some measure of completion even if it's not the entire site, and progress is often observed and measured by key constituents who will communicate the garden's incremental successes with excitement to possible donors, partners, and a wider audience (see Chapter 6).

Figure 3-5: Construction and site preparation in 2008 for the Perennial Border at the Paul J. Ciener Botanical Garden in Kernersville, North Carolina.

F. Todd Lasseigne

Figure 3-6: The Perennial Border at the Paul J. Ciener Botanical Garden in 2009 illustrates how quickly herbaceous plants can cover a new garden space and create the impression of completion among other incomplete sections of a new garden.

F. Todd Lasseigne

Managing the New Garden

Every public garden founder or founding group thinks of one and only one thing at the outset: the plants. Regardless of the affiliated organization (university, municipal, or private/nonprofit), spreading the "I love plants and so should you" message can be any new founder's raison d'être. Yet the real test over time will be to maintain the essence of this message amid the growing complexities of institutional management that can challenge founders and determine the long-term success of new gardens.

Examples of successful management styles and strategies abound, and new ones emerge with surprising regularity. While many have proven suitable for the established public gardens and their staffs, they are often less useful within the context of a start-up garden or one that is quite new in its own evolution. Identifying a management style and/or philosophy is a fluid process and may be unexpectedly complicated by the simple personnel structure of new gardens. That is not to say that small institutions present few management challenges; in fact, the opposite is often true. Most new gardens typically have a staff of one (excluding board members), and that one person (often the original founder) must direct his or her actions toward achieving the vision for the garden. The next level of staff growth generally consists of a small professional support staff, a limited corps of volunteers, and a change in the use of pronouns from "I" to "we." During these early stages, the personal instincts, intuition, and life experiences of the new garden's leadership will often form the basis of the institution's management style.

Management by One, of One

Few would argue that a commitment to seeing a dream to completion does not come without personal sacrifice, but the reality of those sacrifices is often underestimated and exhausting. Remarkable things can be accomplished with a staff of one, but not without an understanding that eventually the staff will grow in number and with it an acceptance that some important personal management strategies need to be implemented.

- Effective time management is the key to surviving new and frequently unexpected demands. Conversely, poor time management and the resultant lack of time (or perception thereof) impede progress and can sour the optimism and anticipation that launched the garden in the first place. The personal energy and enthusiasm to move forward is built on a foundation of accomplishments and successful problem solving. A list of unachieved goals can be disheartening for any new garden leader. Checking tasks off the proverbial to-do list builds and maintains the motivation to keep going.

- The early days of a garden's establishment are important to building a vital support base. New garden leaders need to cultivate that support through a welcoming and engaging response to all who show an interest in the emerging institution. It is important for new leaders to make themselves available to speak at meetings of service clubs and garden clubs and for local radio and TV interviews. These are opportunities to tout the project with enthusiasm, create a shared vision, and be open to suggestions and input from the public.

- The leaders of new gardens must be willing to learn every day, no matter what prior experience they bring to the position. Learning from one's own mistakes (and not repeating them) could be one of the most significant management lessons for any new leader.

Management of Additional Staff

One of the most important ingredients for garden prosperity involves assembling a staff of talented individuals who understand their role in the institution's mission and creating an atmosphere in which staff members feel like contributing members of a team with a common purpose.

This is the new garden director's task. It requires the ability to delegate authority and to teach staff the value of their contributions. Institutions in their early stages of development seldom have enough staff, and it is common for staff members to wear many hats to implement the institution's mission. The necessity of multitasking should be clearly articulated in the hiring process, along with the longer hours at no additional pay that often come with multiple responsibilities and work at a new garden. These expectations should never come as a surprise to any staff member. On the other hand, in managing a small staff with the limited resources of a typical new garden, directors must not only provide the staff with positive reinforcement but also demonstrate trust in their abilities and support for their work.

Conclusion

Starting a new garden carries with it the special thrill of balancing on a bicycle without falling for the first time and continuing to ride with ease and steadiness from that point on. Nothing compares with the euphoric sense of accomplishment associated with that first ride and the confidence that results from success. Moving a garden forward will no doubt present challenges, but overcoming them will reveal the founders' own unrealized potential strengths and lead to a beloved destination filled with countless educational opportunities and the appreciation of many unknown supporters. The founder may move on, but like that first ride, establishing that first garden in one's career is an indelible accomplishment like no other yet to come.

Annotated Resources

Gagliardi, J. 2009. An analysis of the initial planning process of new public horticulture institutions. MS thesis, University of Delaware. An in-depth analysis of the planning, initiation, and implementation of the Paul J. Ciener Botanical Garden in North Carolina in its earliest stages. Excellent resource for individuals wishing to embark on new garden establishment in a nonacademic, nonprofit setting; considers everything from creating a board to strategies for community engagement.

Lyons, R. E. 1999. Arboreta and gardens: Teaching laboratories in the undergraduate curriculum—introduction. *HortTechnology* 9: 548. This special issue focuses on academic settings and the rewards and challenges of operating within educational institution boundaries.

Rakow, D. 2006. Starting a botanical garden or arboretum at a college or public institution, part I. *The Public Garden* 21(1): 33–37.

Rakow, D. 2006. Starting a botanical garden or arboretum at a college or public institution, part II. Moving from planning to reality. *The Public Garden* 21(2): 32–35. Both parts of this series provide specific and thoughtful strategy considerations from a seasoned director who himself works within an academic environment.

Stephens, M., A. Steil, M. Gray, A. Hird, S. Lepper, E. Moydell, J. Paul, C. Prestowitz, C. Sharber, T. Sturman, and R. E. Lyons. 2006. Endowment strategies for the University of Delaware Botanic Gardens through case study analysis. *HortTechnology* 16: 570–578. Outlines valuable considerations for endowment development for an institution moving from its founding as a public garden with limited staff and volunteers to an organized entity with recognized achievements and reputation.

CHAPTER 4

The Process of Organizing a New Garden

MARY PAT MATHESON

Introduction

The process of creating a new public garden should progress through a prescribed series of steps that starts with the formation of a core group and identification of key stakeholders and continues with the creation of a formal organization, the establishment of a board, and the development of a mission and goals. Organizers can avoid the mistakes made by other start-up groups by carefully adhering to these steps and not allowing initial enthusiasm to overwhelm the process.

Identifying and Organizing a Core Group

As most garden directors can attest, the process of organizing a new garden usually begins with one or two people who have a vision for the garden, one founded in their passion for the field and their sense that every community needs a public garden. Many of America's finest public gardens began with the individual; for example, Longwood Gardens was created through the inspiration and financial capabilities of Pierre S. du Pont. But not all gardens start out with such fortune. Many are born out of inspiration and tenacity without the benefit of land or financial support. That is why the first step in developing a new garden begins with a core group, those founding members with the dedication and vision to convince others in the community of the "possibilities" of a public garden.

Why Is the Core Group Needed?

The core group is essential to the success of a new garden because its members develop the idea, convince others in the community that it is viable, organize the structure of the

garden, and launch the new garden's first mission and vision for the future. While it may be one or two individuals with the original vision, an expanded group is important to provide stability, diverse ideas, and credibility to the concept. Initial steps in developing a new garden, including identifying available and appropriate land, funding or leasing the land, and establishing a nonprofit entity, require resources and specific knowledge of public gardens. As such, it is important to build a core group that will aid in the garden's development, a group with skills and abilities in such areas as the law, financial planning, horticulture, and garden management. Beyond this expertise, members of the core group may have personal connections and networks in the community that will help broaden the base as the project moves forward.

Powell Gardens is an adolescent in terms of its existence as a public garden. As with many new gardens, its story began with one person, George Powell Sr., a man with a deep appreciation of the land, a love that remained with him for life. In 1949, he acquired a large tract of land to develop a gentleman's working farm. His close ties to the land and commitment to maintaining the property were shared by other family members, including his son, George Powell Jr. Eventually the desire to farm waned, and the Powell family sought a way to preserve the land for use as a natural resource and horticultural center. While the original core group consisted of family members, it became clear that the protection of the land and vision to put it to public use required additional expertise. As a result, a member of the University of Missouri's School of Agriculture was asked to become involved in the enterprise, eventually leading to the university's agreement to manage the property.

After some time, the Powell family and the university mutually agreed to dissolve the relationship. The university management of the property had slowed down the project and become cumbersome to the effort to develop a horticulture center. With the property back under the control of the family members, the core group decided to establish a private, not-for-profit organization to manage the project, and formally established Powell Gardens Inc. in 1986. Again the core group recognized the need to add more diversity and expertise to the effort, so the four family members who made up the board invited two individuals with specific expertise and knowledge to join the effort. One was a professor from the University of Missouri who added the horticultural knowledge, education expertise, and connection to the university that remains today. The second outsider was well connected to the broader community, someone capable and willing to lead the development of a friends group, which is now four thousand strong.

Powell Gardens has become a thriving public garden serving the region and inspiring visitors with spectacular displays of horticulture and natural ecosystems. The vision and mission have expanded over time, as has the board of directors. What started as a core group of family members has expanded to twenty trustees with only two family members on the board. Their vision for Powell Gardens as a place of inspiration focused on plants and regionality has become a reality. The Gardens recently opened the largest edible garden in the United States, the Heartland Harvest Garden.

Figure 4-1: The blending of a horticultural landscape into a native woodland backdrop at Powell Gardens.

Courtesy of Powell Gardens

Finding the Core Group

Core groups often evolve from the inception of the idea. Individuals with land or money and a vision for a public garden are typically the initiators who find colleagues and friends to join in and assist with the development of the new garden. Powell Gardens outside Kansas City, Missouri, is an interesting example of how a garden was developed through the vision of a single family.

Figure 4-2: Garden paths are designed to follow the lay of the land through a wooded grove leading to a prairie landscape.

Photo by Alan Branhagen, courtesy of Powell Gardens

Finding the core group members is one of the key ingredients for a successful initiative to build a new public garden. Not all efforts begin with wealthy landowners. Some are driven by a vision and a group of volunteers who are willing to work toward that vision and are savvy enough to make the right connections in the community. Among the attributes to look for in forming a core group are personal wealth, community connections, leadership, legal expertise, and persistence (or "insistence with a smile"). It's unwise to underestimate this last one—many successful gardens can claim in their history one person who had the vision, passion, and tenacity to get the job done.

Who Are the Right People?

Finding the right people starts with the concept and land opportunities. There are several models for public gardens, including private nonprofit gardens governed by a board of trustees, municipal gardens managed or funded in part by a city or county, and gardens affiliated with a parent organization such as a college or university. Those initiating the concept of a garden will likely identify with one of the above models. The selection of land may also dictate whether the garden is to be an independent nonprofit or connected to a municipality or university. Identifying the right group of people to serve as

the founding members will depend upon which organizational model best suits the emerging garden.

Public gardens associated with colleges and universities are often initiated by a few professors or key personnel with the vision to either preserve the campus landscape through official designation as a public garden or establish a campus garden that will help the university accomplish specific goals. In the university model, key members of the core group are those donors influential with the university administration as well as those in positions of authority. Deans, department heads, faculty members, campus planning executives, and university donors are all important to the successful launch of a new university public garden.

In a private initiative, where a new nonprofit public garden is the desired outcome, the core group needs to include community leaders as well as people of wealth to ensure the acquisition of private land or the lease of public land in the case of a public/private partnership. Members of garden clubs and horticultural societies are often a part of the mix of the core group. The Coastal Maine Botanical Gardens is a very good example of a garden started entirely with the vision of a few people with the dedication and connections needed to develop a new garden.

The Coastal Maine Botanical Gardens began with a kernel of an idea generated by one resident of Boothbay Harbor. He and other midcoast Maine residents shared the belief that northern New England in general, and Maine in particular, needed a botanical garden; they founded the grassroots organization in 1991. Early members of the board of directors envisioned ornamental gardens, enhanced natural woodlands, and quintessential Maine landscapes meeting the nature education, research, and horticultural needs of the region and state (Coastal Maine Botanical Gardens 2009).

After a prolonged and thorough search for an appropriate site, in 1996 members of the board of directors purchased 128 acres of pristine land with 3,600 feet of tidal shore frontage in Boothbay. This was possible due to the unhesitating willingness of some directors to use their own homes as collateral. To accomplish their prodigious feat of purchasing the land and starting up the organization, they also undertook a charter membership drive, applied for grants, and solicited individual gifts. Those first directors and others who came to share the vision worked tirelessly to fulfill the organization's mission: the protection, preservation, and enhancement of the botanical heritage of coastal Maine for people of all ages through horticulture, education, and research. With steadfast commitment to the organization's vision, these members and hundreds of volunteers established a foundation, whose insightful planning helped to make Coastal Maine Botanical Gardens a jewel of rare quality among North American gardens

By early 2007, members of the board and staff had raised $8.25 million from individuals, foundations, and the State of Maine, providing an auspicious start. After sixteen years of planning, planting, and building, the grand opening of Coastal Maine Botanical Gardens was celebrated on June 13, 2007 (Coastal Maine Botanical Gardens 2009).

Figure 4-3: Exuberant blooms delight visitors from spring through fall at Coastal Maine Botanical Gardens in Boothbay.

Photo by Barbara Freeman, Coastal Maine Botanical Gardens

Figure 4-4: The Lerner Garden of the Five Senses at the Coastal Maine Botanical Gardens.

Photo by Barbara Freeman, Coastal Maine Botanical Gardens

Figure 4-5: Rhododendrons line stone-edged walkways in the Giles Rhododendron and Perennial Garden at Coastal Maine Botanical Gardens.

Photo by Barbara Freeman, Coastal Maine Botanical Gardens

Structure of the Core Group

Once a core group is identified, the next step is to get organized by assigning roles and responsibilities and identifying goals that will help to focus the team. First, the core group needs to identify a leader, someone who is respected by the members of the group and has the ability to both lead and listen. Other major areas of responsibility for core group members are organization, communication, documentation, facilitation, and research. Identifying who in the group has the needed skill sets to address these responsibilities will make it easier to move the project forward in a purposeful way.

The leader assigns duties to the group, including those of note taker (prelude to secretary), financial management, advocacy, management of legal issues, program development, planning, communication, fund-raising, and community initiatives. Often, key donors will take on leadership roles in the acquisition of property and development of the garden concept. Whoever takes the lead here, it is important to note that all core group members should participate in property and concept discussions and have their ideas valued and incorporated into the ultimate vision for the garden. A key mistake in the early days is to have one individual (often a major donor, but not always) drive the entire vision for the garden. This approach leads to the exclusion of other valuable ideas, disenfranchisement of core group members, and the possible loss of participants.

Moving the Garden Concept Forward

The critical next step is to identify the essential concept for the garden. This step requires research to find the models and information that will help facilitate decision making and setting up the project for success.

Reviewing the mission, vision, structure, and long-term plans of existing public gardens is a useful next step as planning for the new garden begins. Members of the core group should consider dividing responsibilities for the research phase, which should include talking to other garden leaders and even visiting public gardens that have attributes like those of the developing garden.

Discussions among the core group members and with community leaders will ensure that the vision for the new garden is appropriate to its community and substantial enough for long-term success. Learning from other gardens will enable the core group to develop an exciting vision and mission for the new garden that is unique nationally, locally relevant, and viable in the long term.

Some of this analysis will be obvious, particularly if a garden site has already been offered, a donor has already agreed to purchase land, or a community has designated a site for the garden. The structure of the garden and its purpose may emerge clearly from those decisions. If not, the next step is to identify a site that would be appropriate for the garden's mission, concept, and goals. Keep in mind that the site should have natural beauty, enjoy easy access to major thoroughfares, and be in an area where commercial development is acceptable. Further, a sizable population base will help with capital fund-raising, and later the operating budget, by providing an audience for visitation, membership, fund-raising,

and programs. Establishing a garden in some neighborhoods can be very problematic, as neighbors may be opposed to the kind of traffic and congestion a public garden can impose.

The idea of a garden is often driven by the opportunity to acquire a piece of property that has been offered or has some history with the core group. If so, the group should still do an analysis of the land to ensure that it is viable for a public garden and is worth the long-term effort of building the garden (see Chapter 5). While a new public garden can help to lift up a struggling neighborhood, property in blighted areas can be very difficult to protect from vandalism and may have limited visitation. It's always worth making sure a gift of land will live up to the potential of the garden concept. Selecting a piece of land must be done thoughtfully and with a long view, for the garden may be in the community for many years to come.

Later chapters discuss the attributes of land for a public garden and make suggestions about how to approach the land from a master planning perspective. Assuming that the group has identified land and has concluded the necessary legal steps to take ownership, it's clearly time to develop a master plan. This is one of those moments in a public garden's history that determines whether it will become great or mediocre. The temptation of some core groups to build the garden themselves can lead to

Lauritzen Gardens is an example of a garden that was started as a concept by a group of volunteers with a vision, a passion for gardens, and a will to develop a public garden. Their goal was to build a garden for Omaha that would be as impressive as the then new Des Moines Botanical Center. The core group had the passion but limited access to the affluence or influence necessary to actualize the idea. As with many emerging nonprofits, the original visionaries were not able to develop the plan and raise the funds necessary to implement the concept on their own. Influential civic leaders were asked to join the original group to take their vision of a public garden for Omaha to the implementation stage, which resulted in the creation of a garden that has demonstrated robust growth over the last twenty years.

This case study exemplifies several interesting and important factors in the development of a successful new public garden. One is that the core group may change over time and that a new group of individuals with specific expertise or connections may be needed to replace or supplement the skills of the original group. The concept of affluence and influence is important when initiating a long-term, costly project such as a public garden; the ability to give significant funds to the project correlates directly to its success. In addition, individuals with influence in the philanthropic community are able to drive the project to success by attracting donors and establishing credibility for the project and its core group of passionate advocates.

In the case of Lauritzen Gardens, the second core group included two influential women, one the wife of the retired CEO of a Fortune 500 corporation and the other the wife of the retired president of a major university. Their spheres of influence were key to the success of this garden. Together, they were able to raise funds, make important long-term partnerships, and convince the core group to hire a professional executive director to lead the development of the Gardens. Their involvement helped to create a ripple effect of support, drawing new resources to the project.

The early hiring of a professional executive director proved to be one of the core group's most significant actions, one that enabled Lauritzen Gardens to grow rapidly and develop an impressive donor base. This key hire enabled the board to "stay out of the weeds" and focus on long-range planning, master plan development, a capital campaign, and the expansion of the Gardens as one of the community's most important cultural assets. Young boards often make the mistake of taking on the role of staff and directing the horticultural practices instead of the future of the Garden.

The core group that established Lauritzen Gardens changed over time, respecting those who initiated the garden but including new members to help with implementation strategies. As a result, they were able to attract a very important donor, the Lauritzen family, for whom the Gardens is named. This lovely garden lives up to the early, lofty mission that remains today as it was written in the early 1980s: "Lauritzen Gardens will create a living museum of unique four-season plant displays, maintained to the highest standards consistent with environmental stewardship. It will provide memorable educational and aesthetic experiences for all."

Figure 4-6: Lauritzen Gardens' humble beginnings are seen here in one of the early projects that relied on volunteer labor and contributed material.

Courtesy of Lauritzen Gardens, Omaha's Botanical Gardens

Figure 4-7: The generosity of the Omaha philanthropic community and the passion of the founders of Lauritzen Gardens contributed to its transformation from a small volunteer-based organization to a multifaceted revenue-generating facility.

Courtesy of Lauritzen Gardens, Omaha's Botanical Gardens

Figure 4-8: A strong sense of regionalism is evident in the designs for all the projects at Lauritzen Gardens. In this case, the Garden in the Glen was created in a natural drainageway under a canopy of existing trees. A form of the native limestone was used for the construction of the stream corridor.

Courtesy of Lauritzen Gardens, Omaha's Botanical Gardens

Figure 4-9: Private investment was critical to the successful building of Lauritzen Gardens. The construction of the Victorian Garden was made possible by a foundation gift from one of its earliest and most ardent supporters.

Courtesy of Lauritzen Gardens, Omaha's Botanical Gardens

the downfall of the new garden. The job of the board, which the core group will likely become, is to guide the planning, not to undertake the physical work of building the garden. While it may be difficult to resist this temptation, it is important that core groups take the time to raise funds to create a proper, thorough, and well-analyzed master plan. In so doing, the core group will set the stage for a successful public garden long into the future.

One final but important tip: core groups should not think small. Rather, they should remember that the garden they envision today will likely be around for a long time and might be one of the community's remaining intact green spaces where people can interact with nature and connect with plants on a large scale. The message to core groups is to think big, plan big, but be modest and thoughtful in developing short-term goals. It's important to have those big hairy audacious goals for the future, but to be realistic about the next ten years.

Identifying Key Stakeholders

In many cases the core group will not have all of the expertise, influence, and affluence necessary to create a new public garden, so the next important step is to identify the stakeholders and to develop strategies for engaging those stakeholders in the project.

Given that most American public gardens are operated and developed with contributions from donors, the most important stakeholder group to consider is the philanthropic community. Finding individuals with wealth and a giving history is essential to success. They will also open doors to others with the ability to support a new project, so equally important are the personal relationships of prospective donors.

Community leaders are also critical stakeholders. They are in positions of influence and may assist in advocating for the vision of the garden and its potential impact on the community at large. While a garden may be conceived out of a love of gardening, the contemporary public garden is also an investment in the community, supporting educational needs, enhancing green space, and providing cultural vitality to its city. Members of the local chamber of commerce may have a particular interest in the economic benefit that a public garden provides through tourism, public programs, traveling exhibitions, and conferences.

As the plans for the garden develop, approaches to a diverse set of stakeholders should emerge. Individuals are motivated by different things, so it's important to find each stakeholder's primary area of interest and work to connect the garden initiative to that.

Public gardens are diverse, and their governance and operating structure as well as their primary mission will help to direct the core group to key constituencies. The university garden will have a completely different set of stakeholders than a historic estate garden. Understanding who those important groups are will lead to better success in developing the garden and establishing a base of support for its future operations. Early stakeholders are also future donors, members, and community advocates who will become the base of the garden's friends group.

Key Stakeholders for College or University Gardens
- University administration
- Faculty
- Students
- Donors
- Legislators
- Key alumni
- Public

Key Stakeholders for Government-Related Gardens
- Government leaders
- Legislative branch
- Donors
- Foundations: corporate and/or family
- Public
- Chambers of commerce, convention and visitors bureaus, park districts, historical societies
- Neighborhood groups and nonprofit alliances

Key Stakeholders for Nonprofit Gardens
- Neighbors
- Donors
- Community leaders
- Gardeners, garden clubs, plant societies
- Public
- Corporations
- Chambers of commerce
- University partners

Key Stakeholders for Historic Properties and Existing Gardens
- Family
- Donors
- Historical and preservation societies
- State and federal government
- Public
- Neighbors

Formalizing the Organization

While some new gardens may be able to function under the auspices of an existing nonprofit in their early years, eventually the time will come to formalize the garden, giving it a name and official status as an organization, whether that be as part of another institution (e.g., a college, university, or art museum), as a stand-alone nonprofit, or as a governmental unit.

Several factors determine the timing of this important step, but it is one that changes the core group from an informal group to an official body bearing the title of board or advisory board and the consequent management responsibilities. If the project is to be a college or university garden, the initiative may require an official designation from the college or university board of trustees and an official reporting structure.

This step should be taken with forethought and an understanding that the official designation changes the project forever.

An official designation, be it as not-for-profit or a university arboretum, brings automatic credibility to the project and establishes rules, regulations, and a legal designation that require a much higher level of formality and process. This step changes the project from a dream to a reality and will enable the group to begin important initiatives such as acquiring land and raising funds.

The dedication, purchase, or donation of land for the planned public garden requires that a nonprofit organization be established in order to receive or purchase such land. The legal issues related to owning and managing land for a public purpose will require more formal procedures and operations as well as necessary insurance and risk management policies to address liability issues.

Any newly formed garden will need its organization formalized in order to provide donors the benefits of tax deductions for their donations. The establishment of the organization as a 501(c)(3) charity enables the board and staff of the garden to solicit funds from individuals and corporations and to apply for foundation and public grants.

Types of Governance and Board Structures
Nonprofit Governing Body

A nonprofit public garden is overseen by a board of trustees responsible for governance, finances, and the legal operation of the garden. This type of governing body carries the fiduciary and legal responsibilities of the organization and can involve financial obligations should things go awry. Therefore, it's very important that the board obtain legal counsel for such things as the establishment of bylaws, operating policies, human resource policies, and financial accountability. Starting out right will ultimately protect members of the governing body from liability and ensure that the operation of the garden is accountable and managed ethically. At this stage, directors' and officers' insurance should be purchased to protect board members and executive staff from personal liability with regard to managing the nonprofit.

The key roles for the board of trustees, include long-range planning, fiduciary oversight, recruitment and management of the executive director, and fund-raising. Each role is critical to the success of the garden, but in many cases, the board of a young public garden migrates to those things that come more easily, such as planning and horticulture, and ignores the fund-raising responsibility. Finding board members willing to ask for money will enable the garden to succeed in its dreams. When fund-raising is ignored, the board will talk about building a garden long into the future, but the dream may stall.

The fiduciary responsibilities of a board are important to the sustainability of an emerging garden. The commitment of a few people with financial expertise can position the garden for success into the future. Establishing financial policies and developing a business plan are two critical steps that the board finance committee should initiate early in the garden's development. The business plan will inform and help direct the master planning of the garden by identifying the importance of earned revenue to the garden's financial health. If earned revenue is a part of the business plan, the garden will likely need facilities for private events such as weddings, corporate retreats, and other social gatherings. The business plan will also identify the garden's potential audience, which will inform the planning for parking, restrooms, and other visitor amenities. The long-range planning and business plan go hand in hand and require savvy and dedicated board members to guide the process with thought and a strategic approach.

Advisory Board for Gardens that Are Part of a Larger Governing Unit

Public gardens at universities usually have advisory boards whose role is similar to that of a governing board, without the legal and fiduciary responsibilities. Advisory board members are important advocates for the garden within the larger institution and should have a strong role in the long-range planning for the garden. Again, there is an important fund-raising responsibility for advisory board members, though they will have to be guided by the university process when approaching donors. Some universities engage in "gatekeeping," restricting access to certain donors. While the public garden staff must adhere to the approval process for university donors, advisory board members still can attract such donors with information about the garden's activities and progress. This approach often leads to a donor requesting an opportunity to learn more and potentially making a gift with the university's approval.

Governance of Gardens Owned by Governmental Units

Gardens that are owned and operated by a city, county, state, provincial, or national government often have multiple governing authorities: the governmental unit and the nonprofit foundation's board. Sometimes cynically dubbed the "double-headed monster," this challenging governing structure creates a dual reporting system, dual human resource system, and confusion about who has ultimate authority over the garden. Some institutions have learned to live with these challenges, and others have been able to convince the governmental unit to privatize the garden by turning its development and operation over to the nonprofit foundation and board. The governmental unit benefits because its financial commitment can be limited to current levels, thereby saving the community tax dollars into the future, and the garden benefits because the foundation is able to raise more private funds and has fewer bureaucratic restrictions. In starting such a new garden, advocates should look closely at public/private partnership models that create one system of governance, whether through privatization or having the same executive director for both the public side of the garden and the private foundation.

Legal Process of Creating an Organization

To become a legal nonprofit, a public garden must be recognized as a tax-exempt charity under section 501(c)(3) of the U.S. tax code and receive a determination letter from the Internal Revenue Service (IRS). To qualify as a charity under section 501(c)(3), none of the organization's profits may inure to any private shareholder or individual. The section also excludes action organizations whose purpose is to influence legislation or support political candidates. The creation of a charitable organization under section 501(c)(3) of the tax codes allows for tax-deductible charitable contributions to be made to the public garden. The process is not difficult, and information about it is easily found on the IRS website. Before filing, the garden needs to have a mission statement, board of directors, and established financial accounting procedures and policies. Bylaws and articles of incorporation are also important steps to becoming a charitable organization, though these may require the services of an attorney. Once complete, the garden is a nonprofit enterprise that will need to be managed with strategic and thoughtful approaches and an eye to the steps necessary to put good planning into action.

The Contemporary Board: Get Started Right

A crucial step in the garden's transformation from idea to enterprise is the establishment of a board of directors. Several resources available on the Web and in libraries provide details about the role of the board. One of those is Boardsource, an excellent resource that provides information and programs on developing and managing effective boards.

The Minnesota Council of Nonprofits has a clear and succinct description of the board's role:

> Board directors are trustees who act on behalf of an organization's constituents, including service recipients, funders, members, the government, and taxpayers. The board of directors has the principal responsibility for fulfillment of the organization's mission and the legal accountability for its operations. This means that as a group they are in charge of establishing a clear organizational mission, forming the strategic plan to accomplish the mission, overseeing and evaluating the plan's success, hiring a competent executive director and providing adequate supervision and support to that individual, ensuring financial solvency of the organization, interpreting and representing the community to the organization, and instituting a fair system of policies and procedures for human resource management.

For the young garden, a small board is recommended, with defined committees whose assignments focus on the steps for the garden's growth. While there is no established perfect board size, a typical board is between ten and thirty people, with each member serving on at least one committee. The emerging board may be smaller than ten, which makes it flexible and manageable. A large board in the early years can be unmanageable, and board member experiences may fall short of expectations.

Committees are the active part of the board and are essential for progress to be made. Although there may be others depending on the nature of the garden and its current focus, the following are key committees for public gardens.

- **Executive committee:** comprises board leadership (chair, vice-chair, finance chair or treasurer, and committee chairs)

- **Finance committee:** implements financial oversight, business planning, financial policies

- **Strategic planning committee:** oversees the planning process, assists with the business plan

- **Master planning, design, and construction:** may focus on any of those three areas of responsibility, depending on phases of garden growth; assists with hiring designers; oversees physical development of the garden

- **Education:** focuses on programs, exhibits, educational goals

- **Collections:** helps to establish direction and focus for the horticultural collections

- **Development:** is essential to the organization's financial success and capital growth; responsible for membership development and fund-raising for annual campaign, major gifts, and capital projects

- **Human resources:** establishes human resource policies; may assist with recruitment and selection of executive director; establishes pay scale and oversees human resource management

Board members have a responsibility to make donations to the organization. By making a personal gift to the garden, a board member demonstrates his or her commitment to the mission and is positioned to ask others to do the same. On a contemporary board, 100 percent of the members should contribute financially to the organization. It is not uncommon to have a mandatory minimum level of giving as a part of a board member's responsibility. One of the mistakes young boards make is to ignore giving requirements. Avoiding the uncomfortable conversation about a board member's financial responsibility will result in little or sporadic giving.

Building a generous and giving board starts with clear expectations that are communicated to prospective board members in one-on-one meetings and written job descriptions. It is wise to be clear in defining giving expectations and encourage multiple gifts throughout the year to support membership, annual fund drives, and special projects. Some board members will be in a better position to influence others than to give personally, but they still need to make the minimum contribution in order to achieve 100 percent board giving.

Establishing a working board with defined responsibilities and a job description with agreed-upon expectations will ensure that board members focus on the important aspects of their job and propel the garden toward its future.

Development of Vision, Mission, and Goals

Corporations are measured by their profitability; nonprofits are measured by the fulfillment of their mission. The development of a succinct mission, one that identifies the broad purpose of the garden, is critical in the development of a young garden. Missions reflect the garden's public role in serving the community and its focus with respect to plants. With mission statements, it is very easy to get bogged down in wordsmithing. While it is important to have a meaningful and focused mission statement, the most important part of the process of developing the mission is to create a framework that will drive the garden's strategic plan, programming, collection focus, and master plan. The mission statement is about what the garden is, what it does, and why it is involved in its major efforts.

It is very common to have a vision statement that supports the mission statement, but on a much grander scale. The vision is an emotional and high-reaching statement that sets the tone for a certain phase of the garden, a statement that reaches for the stars. While the vision may not be achieved in the course of a decade, it will set a lofty ideal that board members, staff, and donors can work toward for the greater good.

It sounds simple to write mission and vision statements, but the process of doing so is an important journey, a means to an end for the organization. Often a facilitator can assist the core group with the development of the mission, vision, and objectives. A good facilitator will ensure that everyone has a voice and that all ideas are heard and respected, and will lead the team through the paring down of ideas to the more critical concepts. The journey helps to build a team that shares a single vision for the garden. Such a team is more likely to succeed than one that lacks focus or disagrees about objectives and larger goals. Developing objectives at this stage establishes key priorities for the garden, enabling the board to proceed with the garden's development.

With mission, vision, and key objectives determined and clearly understood, the board is ready to begin the next phase

PUBLIC GARDEN MISSION STATEMENTS

Garvan Woodland Gardens
Garvan Woodland Gardens is a viable and sustainable entity within the University of Arkansas. The organization preserves and enhances a unique part of the Ouachita Mountain Environment while providing people with a place of learning, research, cultural enrichment, and serenity. Developing and sustaining gardens, landscapes, and structures of exceptional aesthetics, design, and construction is a core purpose. Garvan partners with and serves the communities of which it is a part.

Missouri Botanical Garden
To discover and share knowledge about plants and their environment, in order to preserve and enrich life.

Cornell Plantations
Our mission is to preserve and enhance diverse horticultural collections and natural areas for the enrichment and education of academic and public audiences, and in support of scientific research.

Cheekwood
Cheekwood is a 55-acre botanical garden and art museum located on the historic Cheek estate. Cheekwood exists to celebrate and preserve its landscape, buildings, art, and botanical collections and, through these unique means, provide an inspiring place for visitors to explore their connections with art, nature, and the environment.

Franklin Park Conservatory
Franklin Park Conservatory nurtures plants and people. We promote environmental appreciation and ecological awareness for everyone. Our unique botanical collections provide lifelong learning opportunities in a friendly and accessible setting, which preserves tradition and provides a refuge for the soul.

San Diego Botanic Garden
The mission of the Garden is to inspire people of all ages to connect with plants and nature

Brooklyn Botanic Garden
The mission of Brooklyn Botanic Garden is to serve all the people in its community and throughout the world by:

Displaying plants and practicing the high art of horticulture to provide a beautiful and hospitable setting for the delight and inspiration of the public.

Engaging in research in plant sciences to expand human knowledge of plants, and disseminating the results to science professionals and the general public.

Teaching children and adults about plants at a popular level, as well as making available instruction in the exacting skills required to grow plants and make beautiful gardens.

Reaching out to help the people of all our diverse urban neighborhoods to enhance the quality of their surroundings and their daily lives through the cultivation and enjoyment of plants.

Seeking actively to arouse public awareness of the fragility of our natural environment, both local and global, and *providing information* about ways to conserve and protect it.

of development, whether that is the hiring of an executive director or a master planning firm. From a dream to a reality, the board has taken the idea of a public garden, formalized it, and identified its core purpose, all steps that lead to the physical development of the garden itself.

As young gardens evolve, their missions may be evaluated and rewritten to better reflect the times and age of the institution. The Coastal Maine Botanical Gardens rewrote its original mission statement in 2009.

Former Mission Statement

Coastal Maine Botanical Gardens is committed to the protection, preservation, and enhancement of the botanical heritage of coastal Maine for people of all ages through horticulture, education, and research.

New Mission Statement

To grow a living legacy of gardens that will inspire young and old alike to study, conserve, and treasure Maine's coastal landscape.

Summary

The process of organizing a new garden is one born of passion and a strong belief in the important role a public garden plays within its community. With a thoughtful and strategic approach, the core group can successfully launch a new garden. The key is to establish a core group with diverse skills, attract people with influence and affluence to the core group, listen to ideas and respect group members, and organize the group with defined responsibilities. As the concept develops, the group will eventually need to formalize the organization by establishing a nonprofit entity or having the garden concept officially designated by a parent institution. This important step leads to formal procedures, legal and financial accountability, and the formal establishment of a board of directors or advisory board. A mission and vision statement for the garden are important steps in preparing for the formalization of the garden. The development of a mission is crucial, as it identifies the primary purpose for the garden, the means by which the purpose is served and the core values. The development of such a mission is a step that leads to a single focus by the board and identifies objectives that will lead to future steps such as a master plan and a programmatic plan.

With a strong focus, a single vision, and a commitment to the project, the board will lead the garden to its future.

Annotated Resources

Boardsource (www.boardsource.org). Provides information about governance, roles and responsibilities of the board, job descriptions, and other pertinent information.

Internal Revenue Service (www.irs.gov/charities). Provides information about setting up a 501(c)(3) nonprofit organization.

Minnesota Council for Nonprofits (www.mncn.org/info_govern.htm). Provides information about establishing governance, board roles, and responsibilities.

CHAPTER 5

Land Acquisition

MAUREEN HEFFERNAN

Introduction

Many public gardens originally started with an idea and then land was identified; in other cases, the availability of land served as the impetus for creating the public garden.

Acquiring land for a new garden can vary from easy (e.g., when the land is gifted or donated to a group or community to develop) to arduous (e.g., when a group planning to create a public garden undertakes an often lengthy, comprehensive search for land suitable and sizable enough to fit its mission, vision, and logistical needs). The size of the garden plans and land necessary to achieve those plans often correlates to the size of a nearby population center, the founding group's ambition, and the amount of money it will be able to raise.

This chapter will discuss the major ways most public gardens acquire land, factors to research before settling on a piece of land, and case studies of how four newer public gardens acquired the land they used to build their gardens and facilities.

Gifted Land

When land becomes available to a community or nonprofit organization, that organization may decide that a public garden would be the best use of the land because of perceived economic, educational, and environmental benefits for the community and wider region.

A military base may be decommissioned, leaving a large tract of land available for development. An individual or family may donate undeveloped land, an estate, a nursery, or a farm to a community or organization. Undeveloped or developed land may become available at a college or university to be transformed into a public garden for both educational and recreational purposes, or a large financial gift may be given to a college to develop a garden on an unused area of its grounds. To improve the quality of life and economic vibrancy of its community, a city may create a public garden on vacant land or give that land to a nonprofit group (not as outright owner but with a long-term lease at no expense) to develop as a public or community asset.

These types of land gifts can be a surprise, or they can be a planned gift, one that a group or community knows will become available upon the death of an individual. The latter type of gift might come with an endowment to create and maintain a garden; if not, funds must be raised to develop and sustain the site and facilities.

Groups need to carefully assess these gifts and not underestimate what it takes to create and maintain a quality public garden. Horticultural associations may find themselves with a gorgeous but expensive-to-manage mansion, garden, and grounds that, while beautiful and with much potential as a garden attraction, can drain them of money and time that otherwise could be directed toward their primary educational and information service mission.

The organizing group needs to analyze the site to determine if that land will be suitable for development as a public garden. Even though the land and facilities are free, the site may be too constrained by its built features or need too much overhaul or cleanup to be developed. For example, an estate may have an older mansion or old greenhouses and barns that would be very expensive to repair or maintain. In such cases, undeveloped land may end up being a better option and as a blank slate provide more master planning options.

Purchased Land

When an individual or group wants to start a public garden without a particular tract of land in mind, then the organizing group needs to begin a search for land with the desired features and location that make it feasible to develop and sustain as a public garden. They most often work with local residential and/or commercial realty companies to find available land and extensively network with area residents, businesses, local or state government officials, and others to acquire the land.

Whether land was gifted to an organization or purchased by it, a deed of transference or sale must be filed in the local municipality to officially record that the group is now the legal owner of this property.

Leased Land

A number of gardens acquire use of land by leasing it, often from the municipal entity that owns the land. Leases are basically rental agreements where the lessee rents or leases the land only. These arrangements are most often undertaken when a city or other government entity extends a long-term lease to a public garden for a nominal amount of money per year so that the public garden may develop.

Financing the Land: Owning vs. Leasing or Renting

Owning the land outright is probably the most desirable situation because ownership means that there will be no change in leasing terms or leasing costs. When the organization owns the land, there are fewer restrictions on how the land is developed (within environmental guidelines and local covenants), and insurance and other liability issues are clearer.

However, leasing can be a more affordable option with lower monthly costs than a mortgage. Careful and precise legal agreements must be crafted so that both parties' rights, investments, and long-term interests are safeguarded. For example, the entities should agree in advance as to who is responsible for maintaining utility and water lines, who pays for insurance on the property and the cleanup of any toxins identified on the site, and what rights the lessee has in retaining the value of its investments after the lease is up.

When purchasing property, it is critical to engage experienced legal counsel, to conduct a professional appraisal, and to assemble an experienced team consisting of a realtor and bank loan officer to advise and help lay out options for financing the land purchase through a variety of mortgage or loan packages. The organizing group should already have initial short- and long-term plans for fund-raising, cash flow, and longer-term financial health.

Commercial or individual landowners selling their land may be amenable to donating or greatly discounting part or all of the land for tax purposes. Again, groups should retain good legal counsel to work out possible options to propose to prospective sellers of land that they would like to acquire.

Once the land is secured, insurance is a necessity. It protects against liability for anyone injured while on the site and becomes even more important as more organizers, contractors, planners, and ultimately visitors work on and use the property.

In addition, the group will need to select a master planner/landscape architect to begin the process of designing the garden and developing a full master plan for the site, including utility and communications infrastructure, septic facilities, parking, gardens, trails, support buildings, and more (see Chapter 6).

Mission, Resources, and Land Size

The appropriate size of the property is determined primarily by the core mission of the planned garden as well as the organizing group's financial resources and fund-raising ability. It also correlates to what the group hopes to accomplish in terms of the type of plant collections it would like to create, natural areas it wants to conserve or showcase, the number of visitors it needs or would like to attract, and the amount of land available in the target region, especially in urban and suburban areas, where available or appropriate land is limited.

If the mission of a new public garden is primarily to collect and showcase trees, it needs a large tract of land because trees need more space to grow and mature than do perennials or annuals. Sometimes, however, organizing groups may have to scale back or change collection plans in order to work with the amount of land that is ultimately available to them.

Many new public gardens aim to showcase their region's indigenous landscape and flora, including topography and other natural land features, as a way to resist the homogenization of landscapes. In such cases, the garden's organizing group will want to find an undeveloped tract that contains the native plants and ecological habitats of its region.

Finding property that is near other cultural or recreational facilities greatly helps attract more visitors to each entity. A gorgeous tract of land that is located far from any other destination may struggle to attract visitors, especially after the initial excitement of the first year has waned.

A useful planning tool for new groups is to undertake benchmarking studies. Contacting existing public gardens that have successfully operated for a number of years with similar missions, resources, location, and climate can lead to helpful advice and information about land that is appropriate for the group's planned garden, visitors, members, visitor amenities, education facilities, and parking.

Land for Parking

Another consideration in determining the amount of total land needed is parking. If benchmarking research suggests 50,000 visitors annually, with most visitors coming in the summer months, then at least 150–200 parking spots would be required, with a minimum of six for the disabled and special room for at least three large tour or school buses. Additional questions related to visitor transportation include: Is there room for parking expansion as visitor numbers grow? Is the site adjacent to public transportation, which is an important consideration in a more developed or urban area? Are there any nearby sites that could handle overflow parking and/or shuttle services for special events?

Working with an experienced landscape architect or master planner will help a group understand and plan for enough parking from the opening day onward.

Buffer Land

While a discrete area of land is necessary for initial development, a group may try to acquire new parcels as they become available to allow room for future expansion and especially to create a buffer zone around the collections. The latter will enable the garden to maintain a sense of being an oasis screened from commercial, residential, or roadway development. The buffer can also shield neighbors from noise or distraction coming from the garden—anything from construction to festivals. The group may also want to help conserve undeveloped land adjacent to the garden by purchasing as much as possible initially and then acquiring adjacent lands as resources allow.

Additional Capacity

Adequate land should be planned for adding support buildings, storage areas for maintenance and horticultural operations, enough room for machinery and other equipment, space for staff, and possibly propagation or greenhouse operations (see Chapter 25).

Other Site Considerations
Topography

The topography of the site determines if it is suitable. A variety of topographical changes may be desirable for aesthetic and design options. In most cases, however, these changes should be gentle; if the land slopes too steeply in key areas, it could cause safety, building, and erosion hazards. It could also increase development costs and the expense of complying with Americans with Disabilities Act guidelines for walkway grades. In addition to elevation changes, other topographical features to consider are bodies of water, ledges, rock outcrops, and built features, which may include buildings, roads, landfills, and utility poles.

Soils

In urban, suburban, or reclaimed industrial sites, thorough testing for water and soil contamination or toxic wastes of any kind is critical. Past site use and history should be explored, not only for possible toxic substances but also for historical purposes and permitting. If certain types of objects, such as Native American artifacts, are found on the site, considerable archeological exploration and documentation will be necessary before the site may be developed.

Tests for pH and nutrient and organic content will determine how much amendment the soils will require, and simple perk tests will reveal the drainage characteristics of varying sites. If a master plan is in place, the plantings specified in the plan should be evaluated to determine whether the site will need more soil depth, higher or lower soil pH, or amendments for desired plants to thrive, and what it will cost to undertake and maintain any changes.

Drainage and Watersheds

How the site drains or retains water is important. Wetlands that must be preserved or avoided during development may make the site challenging or even untenable for a public garden. Environmental permitting will require that any large watershed areas be identified, so that development can insure that water draining into watersheds is not polluted and will not cause erosion on the land or washouts on any adjacent roadways.

Microclimates

A variety of microclimates is desirable as a way to extend the range of the plant collections. Higher elevations, depressions, south-facing hillsides, and protected areas can all feature different plantings that are hardy to that condition. Showcasing a variety of microclimate sites is also an excellent educational tool to teach visitors how to select plants, group plants, or create garden themes for specific areas.

Conducting A Biotic Inventory

Whether or not the site attracts and supports a variety of plants and wildlife is an important consideration, especially if plans call for the garden to showcase native or regional ecology and plant and animal interactions.

A site inventory with a trained botanist or wildlife ecologist is a useful way to identify both native and invasive plants and animals on the site. The wildlife analysis should also consider such issues as whether the land contains wildlife corridors that are important to keep undeveloped and whether there are endangered habitats that would be destroyed or compromised. If deer or other highly destructive herbivores are present, the costs of building perimeter fencing should be considered.

The botanical inventory entails compiling a comprehensive list of the entire flora growing on the property, including groundcovers, trees, and herbaceous and woody plants. The inventory is often done over at least a twelve-month period so that all plants, including spring ephemerals, can be documented.

An inventory is also helpful in determining whether the land contains the plants and ecosystems that are important to the mission of the new garden and provides useful information for the master planning process and state environmental permitting process. For example, if the inventory identifies locations that include rare or endangered species, those areas may need to be off-limits for development or carefully developed so that visitors can view the plants but not endanger their habitats. The inventory might also show a rich and extensive woodland area filled with native wildflowers that could be developed as a naturalized garden, or showcase an area rich in

a variety of mosses and ferns. In the process of collecting live botanical samples, the botanist or horticulturist undertaking it can create a herbarium record for the organization.

Noise Levels

What is the noise level at the site? Is the land near a major highway, airport, hospital, or train track, where traffic, sirens, or horns will disturb the peaceful experience of being in a garden? Most sites vary in the degree of ambient noise. It may be advantageous to select the quietest area for the entrance or visitor's center.

Surrounding Views

What are the views from the perimeter of the site into the adjacent landscape or built areas? Are there pleasing "borrowed" views that won't get developed, or are there views into unsightly areas that cannot be screened? The Cleveland Botanical Garden has lovely borrowed views of a city park that abuts its property, making the Garden seem much larger than its nine acres. Part of the dramatic appeal of Wave Hill, in the Bronx, New York, is that the garden's perimeter seems to extend to the forested shore on the other side of the Hudson River.

Another critical consideration is possible future development near the proposed site that could have an adverse impact on the public garden's views. Whether through a donation or purchase, gardens that have the resources often try to acquire buffer lands to protect their "viewsheds." Organizations should check with municipal or regional planning entities to determine what development projects may be planned in the short or long term that are within the garden's visual zones.

Zoning Laws

Understanding possible restrictions or the lack of restrictions on development, both on the site and on nearby land, requires a careful reading of applicable zoning laws. Garden property or neighboring acreage that is zoned for fast-food franchises, malls, or housing subdivisions may not be a good long-term location for a public garden. Likewise, zoning laws that severely restrict development may limit the garden's ability to erect new buildings.

Traffic Impact

Traffic studies may be needed to determine the impact of visitors on existing roads. If roads connecting to a site under consideration are currently congested, that site may not be appropriate for a new garden or may require working with a local traffic or planning entity to install traffic lights, traffic-calming devices, or stop signs. However, a site near bike trails, greenways, or sidewalks would be attractive as a destination for bikers and walkers.

Potential Natural Hazards

Another consideration is a site's potential for natural disasters such as earthquakes, tsunamis, wildfires, hurricanes, landslides, or floods. Such potential may not disqualify the land, but an evaluation of possible natural disasters allows the planning group to take measures to prevent, mitigate, or deal with these disasters if they occur.

Environmental Permitting Process

Once the master plan is developed, the process of obtaining environmental and building approvals from local, state, and possibly federal levels (if federal grants or earmarks are involved) must be undertaken. The land itself, as well as the intensity of the master plan's impact on the land, will determine the overall length and complexity of the permitting process. At least six months to one year, or even more, may be necessary to complete the required environmental approvals.

To summarize, the major steps in the process of obtaining the necessary permits will involve hiring consultants and experts to do the following:

- Survey the land

- Identify wetlands, floodplains, and riparian corridor areas that may need special protections from development

- Identify areas that have eroded or may be prone to erosion

- Identify aquifers and watersheds

- Identify rare or delicate habitats such as vernal pools or endangered flora or fauna species

- Determine if land has any historical or archeological significance

- Test the site for any contamination in soils or ground or surface water or any uncapped wells, particularly oil wells

- Analyze the impact of development on surrounding roads and properties

This process demands patience and an ability to carefully complete the necessary and extensive site research and paperwork to obtain environmental approval for a project. The permitting process should be undertaken at least a year or more before any development is planned for the site.

After the site has been thoroughly inspected and tested, the founding group may need to consider the costs of restoring or improving the site before constructing new buildings or gardens to see if it is feasible to undertake not only the costs of new construction but also the costs of reclamation and cleanup of hazardous wastes.

Research and Networking: Critical for Land Planning

The participation of a landscape architect in the investigation of possible sites can be invaluable. Landscape architects can offer vital insights about potential sites and provide information on the amount of land needed for proposed programs and uses as well as desirable land traits.

Commercial realtors and various city and county officials are good sources of information about available land. Cities and counties are sometimes willing to donate or lease land, including neglected or unused city parks and vacant or abused sites, to groups willing to responsibly develop it as a quality attraction.

Environmental organizations, such as the Nature Conservancy or local land trusts, that are experienced in purchasing land, gaining conservation easements, and accepting donations of land may also provide helpful information and tips on acquiring land through donation or purchase.

CASE STUDY: COASTAL MAINE BOTANICAL GARDENS

Acquisition of the site for what became the Coastal Maine Botanical Gardens (CMBG) involved both a long, careful search for land to purchase and the unexpected receipt of a large donated tract.

The founding group researched and visited other public gardens throughout the country to determine the type of land that would be suitable and necessary for the new garden's mission and vision. The result was a wish list of desirable natural features as well as a list of logistical characteristics. The natural

features wish list included characteristics that would make the site more educational and compelling as a quintessential Maine attraction. These included waterfront property with dramatic stone ledges; vernal pools; stands of older-growth pine, spruce, and birch trees; old stone walls typical of Maine; salt marshes; wildflower meadows; and intertidal zones where visitors could walk out along the water's edge and rocky coves at low tide.

The logistical parameters included proximity to a major interstate or tourist route; proximity to other commercial and cultural attractions; a site within a two-hour drive of the majority of Maine's year-round and summer populations; a varied topography, but one with enough relatively level space for buildings and infrastructure; and a site near town water and electrical lines to reduce utility and communications hookup costs.

Assisted by students in the graduate landscape design program at Radcliffe College, the founding group determined that 75 to 100 acres was necessary to build a public garden with conserved waterfront land. Working with realtors and networking with friends, family, local businesses, and nonprofit organizations, the group initiated a search for coastal property within 60 miles north and south of Boothbay.

In 1996, the group found and purchased a failed subdivision—128 acres of pristine land in Boothbay with all of the desired features, including half a mile of frontage on a tidal river. The Boothbay location not only was easily accessible from Route 1, the state's primary coastal highway, but also provided the critical advantage of being in a picturesque village that is a popular seasonal tourist destination. The property was bounded by light residential development that would not constitute a problem if the Gardens wanted to develop more collections and trails outside of the initial 10 acres planned for the collections and support structures. The site had a gentle but steady rise to the property's highest point, which would lend itself to a dramatic entry drive experience for visitors. At its crest, the site had a sizable flat area with southern exposure that would work well for a visitor center and surrounding gardens that could have accessible paths.

In 2005, CMBG received an unexpected gift of an additional 120 acres of contiguous waterfront land from a local family that wanted to conserve the land and felt CMBG would be a good steward. The land was undeveloped and had no red flags—no maintenance-intensive structures and no environmental violations or other possible liabilities. The gift gave the Garden the benefits of increasing its natural land holdings, room to create more waterfront trails, added educational opportunities, and a greater buffer zone around the developed main campus.

Figure 5-1: The founders of Coastal Maine Botanical Gardens searched for land that included such natural features as changes in elevation, coastal frontage, ledges, native pines, ferns, and wildflowers.

Barbara Freeman

Figure 5-2: The cleared land area selected to serve as the main campus of the Coastal Maine Botanical Gardens.

Barbara Freeman

Figure 5-3: The same site several years later, with ornamental gardens, a great lawn, and visitor center.

Barbara Freeman

Figure 5-4: Aerial view of the Coastal Maine Botanical Gardens' 248-acre waterfront land, of which 128 acres were first purchased through a mortgage and 120 acres were later donated.

Barbara Freeman

Figure 5-5: A waterfront trail on the 120-acre property donated to the Coastal Maine Botanical Gardens.

Barbara Freeman

CASE STUDY: BOTANIC GARDEN OF WESTERN PENNSYLVANIA

Pittsburgh is home to the well-known Phipps Conservatory and Botanical Gardens, but a group of individuals felt strongly that Pittsburgh should have a major outdoor public garden that could also serve as an educational and economic development resource for western Pennsylvania.

The founding group, the Horticultural Society of Western Pennsylvania (HSWP), consulted other public gardens and hired Marshall Tyler Rausch to help plan the new public garden. After initial discussion, the group decided it needed a site with substantial acreage to accommodate the new garden's mission to develop ornamental gardens and to educate audiences on the natural ecosystems of western Pennsylvania. The site needed to be accessible and not more than forty-five minutes from Pittsburgh, have the region's characteristic ecological networks and natural features including natural forests with natural watersheds for irrigation, and offer enough land to provide a buffer against possible new development.

In 1998, after a four-year search, HSWP acquired a ninety-nine-year lease for $1 a year from the Alleghany County Board of Commissioners for 400 acres of land in Settler's Cabin Park, twenty minutes west of downtown Pittsburgh. It is a site rich in city history and natural beauty and exemplifies western Pennsylvania's natural landscape of rolling hills, hollows, and native forest flora of red pine, elm, oak, locust, and cherry trees.

In 2000, Pennsylvania's Department of Conservation and Natural Resources awarded HSWP a $100,000 matching grant to begin the master planning process. After the master planning process was completed, the group leased an additional 52 acres of county land to accommodate parking, a visitor center complex, and new garden areas, bringing the total land acquired to 452 acres.

While the property had many desirable features, it also had some significant problems, including contamination from coal, oil, and mineral extraction and significant invasive plant species populations in some areas. Working closely with the Pennsylvania Department of Environmental Protection and with the help of an army of volunteers, the group is responsibly repairing and cleaning the site to serve as a public garden and environmental education center.

Located in Fayetteville, North Carolina, which has a population of 342,000 in the greater metropolitan area (including a large military presence), Cape Fear Botanical Garden was started by a small but committed group of residents who believed their community could benefit from a public garden that would improve the quality of life and attract more tourists and economic diversity to the region. In 1989, the Friends of the Botanical Garden was formed, which was the catalyst for raising funds and starting the planning process.

In its search for land that was accessible to the city and appropriate for a garden site, the Friends toured a neglected city park that had the ideal characteristics: it was easily accessible (just two miles from downtown Fayetteville); it was located at a historically significant site (at the confluence of the Cross River and Cape Fear River, where Fayetteville was originally founded); it had scenic water views and level land that could be developed

as ornamental gardens; and it was a relatively undeveloped site that was still rich in native pine and hardwood forests that are characteristic of the region.

The Friends group approached the City, which agreed to lease the 72-acre property indefinitely for $1 a year. Several years later, a donor was found to provide funds for the Garden to purchase an additional contiguous 5 acres as a buffer zone to protect key perimeter areas. After leasing the land for thirteen years, the City deeded the entire 72-acre site to the Garden.

Since acquiring the land, the Garden has completed a number of major themed garden areas, including a Water Wise Garden, focused on water conservation strategies, and has built up a nationally respected collection of daylilies, camellias, and hostas. The Garden also has conserved more than half of its acreage as natural areas to showcase the region's native plants, trees, and wildlife.

Figure 5-6: Shown is part of the 72-acre city parkland initially leased and then given to Cape Fear Botanical Garden.

Jim Higgins

Figure 5-7: The developed gardens and visitor center at Cape Fear Botanical Garden.

Jim Higgins

CASE STUDY: LAURITZEN GARDENS

Lauritzen Gardens started in earnest in 1982 when five individuals met to begin planning the first botanical garden in Omaha, Nebraska. Even with a greater metropolitan area population of 838,000 and with 1.2 million people living within 50 miles of the city, Omaha did not have a public garden. The group's mission was to create a garden that would be a living museum of unique four-season plant displays maintained to the highest standards consistent with environmental stewardship and to provide memorable educational and aesthetic experiences for all visitors.

The group searched for suitable land to purchase or lease. Finally, in 1994, the group negotiated a public/private partnership with the City of Omaha, through which the group received an easily accessible 70-acre parcel of land free of charge under a long-term management agreement. The land boasted natural woods and rolling terraces on a bluff just west of the Missouri River but also presented some development challenges: it had been used

as a landfill, and both soils and water needed to undergo extensive testing for contaminants. In addition, potential soil settling issues had to be accommodated in the master planning process.

Construction of the first trails and gardens began in 1995. In 1998, the Garden was able to purchase an additional 30 acres of contiguous land thanks to a donor who provided the funds for the acquisition. The new land was desirable because it afforded the garden visibility and vehicular access from Interstate 80 and provided a buffer zone, all critical elements in attracting more visitors. Like the first parcel of land, this new site had some drawbacks as well. The land had been used as a soil-mining site, which resulted in extreme elevation changes and required a significant financial investment to regrade to make it suitable for building and garden development.

Lauritzen Gardens now has a total of 100 acres, of which it manages 70 acres and owns an additional 30 acres.

Figure 5-8: The 70-acre landfill site that became Lauritzen Gardens. Extensive site grading requiring the movement of hundreds of thousands of cubic yards of soil was necessary due to previous soil-mining facilities that occurred on a portion of the site.

Lauritzen Gardens

Figure 5-9: Shown are the gardens and visitor center at Lauritzen Gardens on a site once used for soil mining. A commitment to using native plant material in the parking facility helped restore the original character of the site, with retention ponds used throughout the parking facility to capture storm runoff.

Lauritzen Gardens

Summary

How land is acquired to start a public garden varies greatly. In some cases land is made available to newly formed public garden groups through a long-term leasing or management agreement with a governmental unit. In others, the land, while not ideal, comes at a nominal cost or is free of charge to a founding group that can afford the reclamation or remediation costs and agrees to follow environmental restrictions and municipal building and maintenance codes. Other gardens have been able to privately purchase land through long-term financing arrangements and/or through the generosity of a major donor who donates the initial plot of land to gain momentum for a project. Finally, there are also hybrid examples where public gardens have both leased or loaned land from a city or county as well as owned land.

Annotated Resources

American Planning Association (planning.org) has excellent information and training resources for learning more about community planning, urban planning, and planning more livable and sustainable cities and towns.

American Society for Landscape Architects (asla.org) provides information on land assessment, master planning, and environmental permitting.

Butler, K., and F. R. Steiner, eds. 2007. *Planning and urban design standards,* student ed. Ramsey/Sleeper Architectural Graphic Standards series. Hoboken, N.J.: John Wiley and Sons. A useful introductory student guide to land planning.

Clark, S. 2007. *Field guide to conservation financing.* Washington, D.C.: Island Press. A practical book for groups to determine their organizational and financial readiness to acquire land, how to make a deal on land, and legal considerations to be aware of throughout the purchasing process.

Endicott, E., ed. 1993. *Land conservation through public and private partnerships.* Washington, D.C.: Island Press. Features information on a variety of different kinds of public and private partnerships that seek to conserve land or acquire land for parks, greenbelts, and sustainable development.

Environmental Protection Agency (epa.gov) has extensive online information regarding guidelines for new developments and permit processes.

Institute of Civil Engineers (ice.org.uk) has information resources on site assessments, risk analysis of sites, and risk assessment of developments on damaged or contaminated land.

LaGro, J. 2008. *Site analysis: A contextual approach to sustainable land planning and site design.* Hoboken, N.J.: John Wiley and Sons. Excellent information about how to incorporate sustainable thinking into site and project planning.

LaGro, J. 2001. *Site analysis: Linking program and concept in land planning and design.* New York: John Wiley and Sons. This is a uniquely helpful book to assess a land site for a program or mission purpose.

McMahan, E., and M. McQueen. 2003. *Land conservation financing.* Washington, D.C.: Island Press. Good ideas and information on a variety of ways to finance land purchases.

Platt, R. H. 2004. *Land use and society: Geography, law, and public policy.* Washington, D.C.: Island Press. More scholarly discussion of how land use is affected by changing laws, public and environmental needs, and public policy.

Designing for Plants and People

IAIN M. ROBERTSON

Introduction

Public garden design is the process of fitting garden facilities, collections, and uses or programs to the specific site conditions for which the garden is to be designed and in which it will grow. Stated this way, the process sounds simple and straightforward, but in practice it is complex and frequently convoluted. In a well-designed garden, the fit between garden features, collections, and uses and the site seems comfortable and sensible: everything is appropriately placed and physically convenient, the garden layout is comprehensible, and the experience delights the spirit. In a brilliantly designed garden the fit appears inevitable. By contrast, walking into a poorly designed garden feels physically awkward and perceptually confusing, and the experience is disturbing. This chapter describes the design process and how garden staff should participate in the process to create well-fitting rather than ill-fitting garden designs.

The Garden's Origins and Its Design

New public gardens don't arise out of nothing; they have origins that influence all aspects of their development and operation. The history of the site and genesis of the garden are components that are equal in importance to the garden's physical design. Those entrusted with the garden's design must understand its origins because they are the nucleus of the garden's purpose, suggest the focus or direction that the garden should take, affect the scope of design services it requires, and influence the resulting garden facilities. The following examples illustrate this point:

- If a new public garden is developed from an estate donated by an individual or family to a nonprofit group, its designers will be faced with the problem of how to adapt what was a private facility to function as a public garden. In such situations, issues of whether the owner's personal idiosyncrasies are integral to the garden or can be modified or removed for functional reasons become crucial design questions. Developing designs for such gardens can include working closely with family members to ensure that the mission and facilities fit the donor's wishes and balancing these concerns with legal requirements and functional needs of public gardens.

- If a new public garden results from efforts by a community group or a nonprofit environmental organization to preserve an undeveloped piece of land, then a different dynamic prevails, and the garden's designers develop conceptual ideas for the garden while a loose-knit group coalesces into a functioning organization, volunteers give way to paid staff, and the garden's mission crystallizes.

- Public gardens founded by government agencies or public institutions often have a staff in place and a mission derived from their institutional mandate, such as providing demonstration gardens, offering research opportunities, or promoting specific kinds of plant collections. In such situations, the garden's designers must ensure that facilities reflect the institution's larger mandate so that the garden is seen as integral to its mission.

- Designers are frequently called upon to redesign established gardens. In these situations, the design process should begin

Client: the individual, or more commonly the staff team, that works with the design team on a design project. The client should represent all components of the garden staff and must possess the legal authority to approve and accept work on behalf of the garden.

Contract documents: the legal documents between a garden and a contractor to build or install a specific exhibit, garden feature, or plant collection. Contract documents include construction drawings and written specifications.

Contractor: an individual business, or more commonly a general contractor and subcontractors, hired by a garden to install a specific exhibit, garden feature, or plant collection. Subcontractors may include civil, structural, mechanical, and electrical engineers and landscape and irrigation contractors.

Design teams/consultants: the design firm, or more commonly team of firms, hired by a garden to plan and design gardens from conceptual design to installation of gardens. Firms commonly include landscape architects, architects, planners, and different types of engineers, such as civil and environmental, geotechnical, structural, mechanical, and electrical. Individuals from a wide range of specialist services may be required on some teams, including exhibit designers, financial and fund-raising consultants, anthropologists, archeologists, ecologists, botanists, wildlife experts, and artists.

Design services: the scope of work that a design team is contracted to provide a garden. Contracts for design services should not be confused with construction contracts.

Physiography: the shape and character of the land's surface. When unaltered by human activity, physiography provides information on underlying geology, soils, and hydrologic processes. It also has important spatial qualities that affect the experience of the site, such as exposed vantage points and enclosed valleys.

Programs: the facilities, activities, and experiences that the client wishes to accommodate in the proposed garden. Programs may be described in terms of activities such as educational and recreational programs or in terms of physical features, plant collections, building room spaces, etc.

Design process: the iterative or step-by-step process of turning a garden's aspirations and goals into physical gardens. The design process proceeds through overlapping steps, from conceptual or sketch designs to progressively more detailed design drawings, followed by construction drawings for installing the design. The design process includes the construction stage and eventual garden maintenance, when decisions must be made about how to manage the plants.

RFPs and RFQs: requests for proposals and requests for qualifications are published or privately solicited announcements for design services needed by gardens. RFQs are more general and confine themselves to information on a design firm or team's qualifications, while RFPs solicit proposals for how a design team would address a specific project.

Site analysis: the process of collecting or inventorying the natural, social/cultural, and experiential qualities of a site; analyzing them to determine the site's conditions that might affect garden development; and synthesizing this understanding into a map of opportunities and constraints that can guide subsequent design explorations.

with determining why a new design is necessary. At one end of the spectrum of reasons may be the fact that visitor numbers have grown dramatically and the garden must change to keep pace with new needs, programs, facilities, or research. Gardens at the other end of the spectrum may have fallen into decline due to neglect or abandonment and now must be restored.

Understanding why a garden developed as it did is crucial to determining future options.

Design Services

Public gardens use design consultants for a range of planning and design functions, but typically when a new garden is being planned or an existing garden being completely redesigned, designers are hired to develop comprehensive master plans for the entire garden.

Before the design process can begin, those who are charged with organizing the creation of a new public garden must decide what design services they need. A necessary prelude to that decision is clarification of the new garden's purpose and mission and the kinds of programs and facilities the garden will need to achieve that mission. Thinking through the physical implications of the planned garden's mission and programs in advance results in a more successful design.

In the context of the design process, scope of services means the work that a garden hires a design team to produce. To avoid problems, gardens should develop detailed descriptions of the products and services they expect design consultants to provide. The garden needs to identify not only the scope of services but also how it plans to use each of those products, because different uses will subtly change the focus of the work.

The scope of services should be tailored to meet the garden's specific needs, aspirations, and resources. A master plan for a small garden with limited resources may consist of a simple analysis of site conditions, a brief description of program features and collections, and an illustrative plan of the completed garden. At the other end of the spectrum, a master plan for an elaborate garden on a large site may include a report describing site conditions in great detail; a beautifully rendered illustrative plan; plans of the conceptual organization of garden features, collections, and circulation systems; and cost estimates for construction and operation.

Services Provided by Design Consultants

Consultants may develop detailed designs for specific portions of a new public garden, such as a plant collection, exhibit, or display garden. Although based on the master plan, these designs and cost estimates for specific areas are developed in greater detail; they may closely follow the plan or depart from it in response to new information or a deeper understanding of the need for the facilities. When construction funds have been secured, the design team will prepare construction documents for installing projects. Design consultants may be retained to oversee construction work, though not to do the work itself, unless the contract is for design/build services.

Design consultants may prepare phasing plans if a garden is to be developed over several years, as well as and illustrative drawings, reports, brochures, and video presentations suitable for fund-raising for both master plans and individual projects. Design consultants may work with garden staff to develop interpretive and educational materials for specific exhibits. In addition to preparing capital cost estimates for master plans and specific exhibits, design consultants may also provide estimates of operating costs and staff needs for the projects they design.

Through discussions and workshops, design consultants play a less tangible but no less important role of revealing the varied hopes and aspirations of garden staff, boards, and visitors; weighing their significance; resolving conflicts; and reaching consensus.

Making Good Use of Design Services

All successful public gardens are the result of close and mutually supportive collaborations between design teams and garden staff, including directors, governing boards, volunteers, and users.

Being an effective client is the best way for a garden to ensure that the design team does not waste time and the garden's money performing unnecessary work. Effective clients, for example, collect and provide the design team with as much accurate and current supporting information as possible, particularly with respect to site conditions. They also make timely decisions to

allow work to proceed, which include reviews and comments on the work submitted by the design team.

Designs develop over time through discussions between clients and design teams, and it is not unusual for the scope of design services to expand as new activities or products are discussed. To avoid unanticipated cost escalations due to "scope creep," clients and design teams should agree in writing on changes and additions to design services when these are made.

Steps in the Design Process

The design process is not a linear one that is gone through once and once only to create a design. Rather, it is an iterative process, resulting in design products that are progressively more focused, detailed, and appropriate for the specific needs of the garden being designed. Think of the process as reaching a progressively closer fit between the garden's program needs and aspirations, its available or potential resources, and the site's specific potentials. This is important for garden staff to understand because their input as clients is essential throughout the process.

Essentially, the same design process steps occur in the development of the master plan and in the development of specific parts of the master plan for implementation. The difference is that in the latter, each stage is carried out in far greater detail and specificity. While the products of the master planning stage are thoroughly developed ideas presented in compelling illustrative drawings and reports that may be used to gain community support for the garden, agency approval, and financial support, project development products are construction drawings and specifications that are used by contractors to estimate the work and material costs to build the project and to prepare bids to perform the work. Construction documents are detailed, specific, and technical and frequently take longer to develop than master plan documents.

The design process commonly includes the following steps:

- Site and program analyses

- Development of alternative sketch, or concept, designs

- Assessment and selection of preferred alternatives

- Development of the preferred alternatives through design development into a final design.

- Construction drawings

- Implementation of the design

Site analysis consists of assessing the potential of the site to accommodate a desired program. Program analysis consists of tailoring the garden's desired facilities to the realities of site conditions and financial resources. To ensure an effective integration, site and program analyses should be done simultaneously. Sketch designs are loose drawings exploring a range of possible programs and ways of fitting programs to the site. They allow the design team and client to assess which approach they prefer, and this becomes the direction that subsequent design development drawings explore. When a final design is accepted and approved by the client, the design team prepares construction drawings and a contractor is hired to implement or construct the project. The construction drawings and specifications then become part of a legal contract between the garden "owner" and the contractor selected.

Gardens are not built directly from master plans. The functions of a master plan are to provide a robust but flexible structure for a garden; give spatial definition and form to a garden's mission; provide a long-term, phased road map for the garden's future; and provide materials for fund-raising to implement the plan. Master plans serve larger functions beyond these practical considerations, articulating and expressing each garden's vision for what it wishes to become. To be successful, master plans must be cogent, eloquent, and inspiring.

Master planning is a visioning and feasibility process that concludes with drawings, reports, models, and possibly computer-simulated walk-throughs of the proposed garden. These are presented in a form that describes the garden or exhibit's vision in engaging and exciting ways. Master plans may also contain business plans for how the garden will support itself.

The design process continues with the implementation of the design, and here, too, design decisions must be made, for no matter how carefully developed the construction documents, circumstances arise that make interpretations or changes necessary. For example, unusually adverse weather conditions may prevent completion of work according to the contract schedule. Since the designers are not parties to the construction contract but understand the work involved, they may act as unbiased arbiters, determining how much additional time the contractor should be allowed in order to complete the work. Physical changes may also have to be made to the design during the construction phase—for example, when a plant species or material is not available and substitutes must be selected, or when a path must be rerouted to avoid a utility vault. In other words, design decisions continue to be made throughout construction and in the process of approving the contractor's work; these decisions are also part of the process of successfully fitting design goals to site conditions.

Site Analysis

The purpose of a site analysis is to get to know all aspects of the site, including natural conditions, features and processes,

and cultural and historical features. Site analyses must consider not just the site itself but also its local or neighborhood context as well as its regional context. A site analysis checklist is a useful tool to ensure that all site factors are considered. Checklists should include information on natural factors and human factors as well as intangible perceptual considerations. The latter may provide insights into possible garden experiences, answering questions such as "Where is the heart of the site?" "What moods or feelings does this place evoke?" and "How is this place representative and expressive of regional character?" While these considerations are subjective and not amenable to precise mapping in the way that we map factual data such as soil or microclimate conditions, they are important site considerations. The people best able to answer these questions may be those with long and intimate ties to the site and region, including garden staff or local residents. Garden staff should also explain to the design team what it is about the site that they value, whether it is specific features and physical attributes or things that give it its unique character and delightful experiences.

Municipal, county, state, or federal geographic information system (GIS) databases provide enormous quantities of factual information that may offer valuable insights into the regional or local context but that often is not sufficiently detailed to be useful for master planning or project design. Garden staff can help the design team determine which data will be useful and which will not.

Collecting published information on natural and man-made factors is important but is no substitute for careful, observant, thoughtful on-site explorations. Since plant collections and displays are likely to be a large part of garden facilities and experiences, on-site explorations should ideally occur in all four seasons to understand their varying effects. Design consultants typically observe site conditions in one or two seasons and must rely on the expertise of garden staff to provide an understanding of year-round site conditions and likely garden use patterns.

While the purpose of the site analysis is to get to know site conditions intimately, this is not an end in itself; rather, it enables planners to draw conclusions about the site's unique potentials and liabilities as a garden location. The site analysis stage concludes with a synthesis of this understanding in a site constraints and opportunities map, an important tool for subsequent design decisions.

By highlighting what can and cannot be done on the site, the map provides boundaries for design explorations. Although the word *constraints* sounds negative, constraints are extremely helpful in design because they provide boundaries as to what is and what is not possible on the site, thereby directing and focusing design explorations in viable directions. By contrast, site opportunities may give the garden its unique and distinctive physical character or may inspire specific garden programs and uses.

A checklist is a comprehensive catalog of topics that should be considered in a site analysis. Not all topics listed below are relevant for every site.

Natural Factors

Site location: regional context, physiographic province; relationship to off-site physiographic features; north point/orientation

Physiography and orientation: elevations and variations; topographic or physiographic features; slopes: steepness, length, stability, aspect, and exposure

Geology: geologic formations; rock types; depth to bedrock, rock outcrop

Hydrology: surface water (streams, lakes, marshes, bogs); flow characteristics; water quality; subsurface water (aquifers, groundwater); flooding; legal flood plains

Soils: types, fertility; percolation rates; texture, hardpan, stability; characteristics; adaptability to land uses (forestry, agriculture, development/construction, bearing capacity); surface and subsurface soil pollution and contamination

Climate and microclimate characteristics: rain/snowfall, hours of sunlight, wind patterns, seasonal temperatures, storms; microclimate considerations as a result of topography, vegetation, buildings (sheltered/exposed areas, frost pockets, warm/cool slopes)

Vegetation: regional vegetation patterns; plant communities on-site; trees, shrubs, herbaceous plants: size/age, canopy, condition; extent of major species; rare or endangered plants, indicator species, and weeds; native and exotic species; signs and types of natural and man-made disturbance/maintenance

Wildlife: extent and species composition; indicator species

Human Factors

Access and circulation: vehicular road capacities and conditions, volume, parking; pedestrian, bicycle, public transportation circulation and access

Structures: character, uses, historic/visual qualities, size, and condition of structures and fencing; plans for new or changes to existing structures; relationship of existing building uses to proposed uses

Utilities: overhead and underground water, gas, electricity, storm, and sanitary; sewers and emergency services; capacity, connection points, future service plans; implications of overhead wires and underground lines; easements; location/condition of gutters, drains, curbs, steps, walks, paving, utility poles

Land use, ownership, zoning: on-site and adjacent areas and setbacks, building lines/heights to be maintained

Perceptual Factors

Tangible visual and aesthetic factors: important views and visual features on-and off-site; preservation, screening, or creation of views to and from adjacent areas; site's visual/aesthetic character; spatial character of site, surroundings, and region; edges; predominant colors, light quality, textures, lines, and scale of site; unifying/dividing characteristics

Intangible perceptual factors: emotional, intellectual, and cultural responses that assist in understanding the relative importance of the above factors, including the meaning of place, the feeling it invokes, its symbolic significance, the design responses suggested by the site, and the relationship between site, community, and region

Garden staff should study the site analysis constraints and opportunities map closely to ensure that they agree with its conclusions and design implications and assess whether the design team has correctly interpreted which site conditions are fixed and immutable and which can be modified, whether easily or with effort.

Program Needs and Uses

The word *program* is used here to mean all of the activities and facilities the garden is intended to accommodate. Program development is discussed in other chapters, but in summary, garden programs include elements of education, research, conservation, recreation, and aesthetic pleasure. Just as the site is a garden's physical foundation, programs are the heart of its purpose.

Making decisions about a garden's programs is a crucial activity of garden boards and staff. In a very real sense a garden's program illustrates its mission, what it aspires to be as an institution,

and what forms it will take. Ideally, gardens retain design teams after they have formulated a clear understanding of their mission and programs but before they have locked in their programs. At this stage, when the design program is being refined, design teams provide a series of conceptual designs that demonstrate to garden staff the implications of different program emphases, elements, and arrangements on the site. Thus, one of the roles of the design team is to present alternative development scenarios to test the viability of different design programs and to assist staff in making decisions about how to fit programs to sites.

Because the team may press garden staff to define the meaning of different aspects of the program more precisely or decide which elements are more or less important to the garden, this stage can be misunderstood as the design team making program decisions for the garden—which should not occur. Program decisions are the responsibility of the garden staff, not the design team. However, a good working relationship between garden staff and designers is one in which designers offer suggestions for possible program elements, question program decisions, and demonstrate the physical planning implications of different program choices.

This stage in the design process is more complex for public gardens than it is for most institutions because their programs are typically more fluid and multifaceted, and as a result, gardens may be used by visitors in a wide variety of ways. For example, plant collections and exhibits that some visitors use for educational purposes may also be excellent settings for aesthetic delight and therapeutic enjoyment. There is no reason why garden features cannot be designed to serve multiple uses: research, education, recreation and relaxation, experiencing nature, social gatherings, community building, and neighborhood events. Deciding on the relative importance of these uses is the responsibility of the garden staff or board. There should be a clear connection between decisions about the programs, the garden's features and collections, and its mission statement. Ultimately, all garden programs derive their legitimacy from being firmly rooted in a garden's mission.

Another invaluable result of testing programs through alternative designs is that unstated and implicit program assumptions are made explicit. Skillful designers ensure that a wide range of options and possibilities are considered by all segments of the garden community, but in the end, final decisions by administrators, staff, and board are rooted in the garden's mission.

The difference between promoting and orchestrating broad discussions of programs and explaining the physical design implications of program decisions and making program decisions for the garden is subtle, but when a design is perceived to belong to the design team rather than the garden staff and users, trouble inevitably follows.

Design Alternatives: Fitting Programs to Site

The design team's earliest drawings typically show design ideas in sketchy, diagrammatic, or abstract fashion. Hence, these drawings are often described as sketch or conceptual designs. As noted, these can be used to test program decisions and understandings of site conditions and offer a first idea of how programs might be fitted to sites. Such drawings are exploratory rather than definitive; they suggest ideas rather than describe firm decisions. This point is important because to keep the design process moving forward garden staff must respond to drawings at the appropriate level. Design alternatives illustrate big-picture ideas—dramatically different ways in which gardens might develop—and should be assessed conceptually rather than in detail. Which alternative, or combination

of alternatives, best captures the future the staff and board envision for the garden? The process of assessing different conceptual alternatives against a garden's mission, program, resources, and site conditions results in a preferred alternative that will be further refined through subsequent design stages. Restraint in the subsequent development of concepts is important; they are essential guides in the development of design ideas but should be subtly present in the final design, not overtly obtrusive. Effective concepts should pervade completed gardens like excellent butlers: omnipresent but invisible.

The conceptual design stage is often the most difficult for nondesigners to understand because it makes the leap from abstract or nonspatial ideas, such as "a collection of hardy *Sorbus* species," to a plan that locates, sizes, and shapes spaces for each program element. Concepts are ideas that designers use to transition from nonspatial ideas to spatial forms. Thus, the concept for arranging a *Sorbus* collection could be "a formal allee" or "an informal grove," or *Sorbus* species could be included in an ecogeographic collection. This example is straightforward, but garden staff should be prepared to consider more playful or fanciful concepts. All conceptual explorations are acceptable so long as they prove to be relevant to the design context and are effective at translating programs into plans. A more poetic conceptualization of a program need for "a meeting place in a shade garden" could, for example, use a baseball mitt as a concept to transform the idea of a meeting place into a shallow amphitheater surrounded by enclosing shrubs. Further, it could add a fringe of trees—a baseball cap!—to shelter amphitheater users from the sun.

To generate appropriate conceptual ideas, designers listen carefully to garden boards, staff, volunteers, and visitors to develop an appreciation for their values and aspirations. It is crucial throughout the development of designs that garden staff members provide the design team with clear explanations of what they wish to accomplish and with thoughtful and detailed feedback as ideas develop. Effective clients are fully and continuously engaged with their design team. In fact, as the work progresses, they become essential and integral parts of the design team.

The Descanso Gardens conceptual organization depicted in Figure 6-1 is an example of a conceptual diagram for a large public garden. It divides the garden site into six areas, each with an evocative name that relates to the Garden's mission and references existing site features. Note, for example, that the parking lots, which are usually assumed to be negative features in public gardens, are labeled "orchard," thus conceiving of this functional need in a manner that relates positively to the garden's mission. The six "bubbles" are not randomly located or sized but respond to the site's topography, vegetation, and historic features, as well as to each other. The bubbles are connected in three ways: by four axes that provide the garden with a strong visual structure to orient visitors to its main features; by loosely suggested trails that set up an organization and structure for the garden experience; and by lines showing water features that are a central part of this Southern California garden's educational program. Thus, a simple diagram contains a wealth of understanding of site conditions and program possibilities and suggests a structure for the garden that has spatial, perceptual, cultural, and environmental dimensions. Accepting the conclusions of this conceptual diagram narrows and focuses subsequent design explorations.

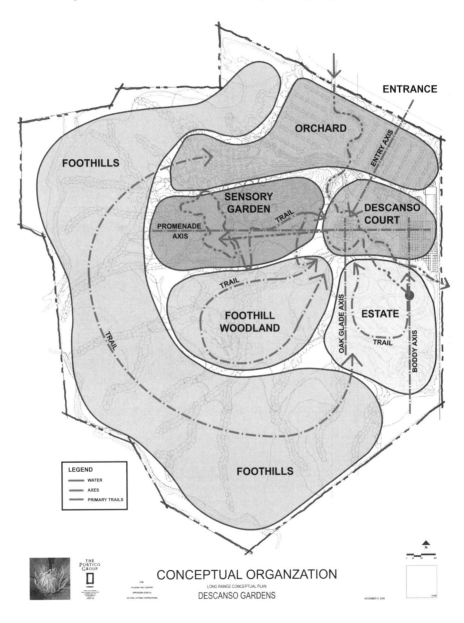

Figure 6-1: Plan showing conceptual organization of garden elements, Descanso Gardens, La Canada Flintridge, California.

The Portico Group

Figure 6-2 is a conceptual master plan for an arboretum and wildlife conservation center at Washington State University (WSU). As a result of continual refinement of ideas in discussion with the client, this conceptual plan is much more elaborate than the Descanso Gardens diagram, but it, too, illustrates how program elements, spaces, and circulation are organized and located to fit site conditions. It also begins to suggest the qualities of the experiences of different arboretum elements.

The Palm Dome, shown in Figure 6-3, is another conceptual plan, but at a much smaller scale than the WSU plan. It illustrates ideas for redeveloping the central dome of a greenhouse. The annotations assist our understanding of the intent of the conceptual plan. They describe how the overarching conceptual idea for a palm dome can be elaborated on and fleshed out with more detailed depiction of plants, paving, and water

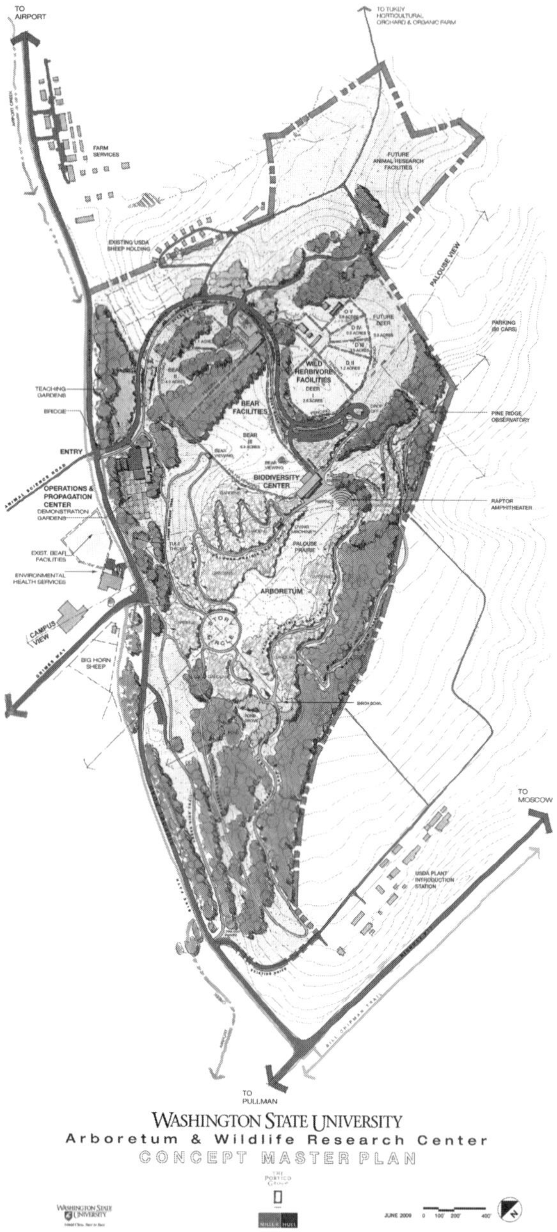

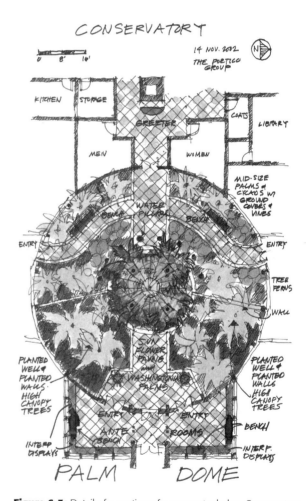

Figure 6-2: Conceptual master plan for the Washington State University Arboretum and Wildlife Conservation Center, Pullman, Washington.

The Portico Group

Figure 6-3: Detail of a portion of a conceptual plan. Conservatory Palm Dome, Buffalo and Erie County Botanical Gardens, Buffalo, New York.

The Portico Group

features. Evocative labels add an important element. Although the circulation is relatively simple and straightforward, the spatial experience is nevertheless rich and complex, consisting of a transition through an anteroom from outdoors to indoors with resting places and interpretive panels, followed by a narrowing down of the path before it opens into a central palm-and-water crescendo. Integrated with this spatial sequence is a series of plant sequences that the conceptual design describes in terms of height, character, and types of plants—tree ferns, palms, cycads, groundcovers, and vines.

Each of these plans illustrates the essential point that effective design concepts are not imposed blindly on a mute site but evolve in an organic manner from a thorough appreciation of site potentials and distinctive program needs. Effective clients respond positively when their design teams challenge their preconceptions by developing conceptual drawings showing a diverse range of possible futures.

Master Plans and Reports

The defining element of a master plan is the plan itself, typically drawn in an illustrative style, that is, one that easily communicates to the public what the garden wishes to become.

Master plans are often used to build community and political support for a garden and as fund-raising tools. However, if organizations leave consideration of capital and operations costs until the design is completed, they are likely to discover that the design they have set their hearts upon is too costly and too difficult to maintain.

To be successful, a master plan should differentiate its garden from others by describing its specific purpose and identity and how it is uniquely appropriate for its location and community. Master plans should be both visionary and achievable, a balance that might be described as "practical sustainability." Thus, beautiful illustrative plans are accompanied by detailed analyses of specific garden exhibits, collections, and facilities as well as capital cost estimates and garden operations costs. Master plan reports describe the purposes of the garden and its collections, displays and exhibits, as well as their value and benefits to different audiences or users, and they include cost estimates for developing, operating, and maintaining each portion of the garden.

Master plans frequently include aerial perspectives and character sketches—crucial tools to convey the experience and character of a garden to the public in ways that plans

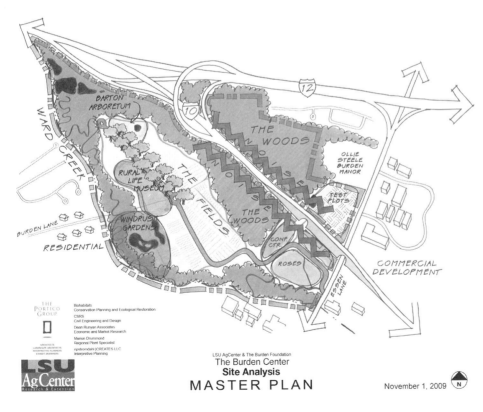

Figure 6-4: Site analysis conclusions locating and naming the principal site features. The Burden Center, Louisiana State University AgCenter, Baton Rouge, Louisiana.

The Portico Group

Figure 6-5: Plan naming the principal master plan components, including a botanical garden, a rural life museum, research areas for food and fiber, forestry, and ornamental plants and turf research station, at the Burden Center, Louisiana State University AgCenter, in Baton Rouge.

The Portico Group

Figure 6-6: Plan showing site surface water and drainage patterns at the Burden Center, Louisiana State University AgCenter, in Baton Rouge.

The Portico Group

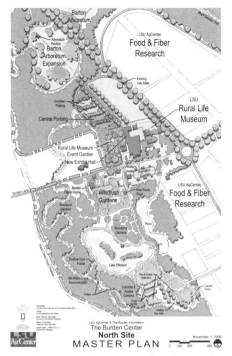

Figure 6-7: Master plan of the northern botanical garden naming principal features. The Burden Center, Louisiana State University AgCenter, in Baton Rouge.

The Portico Group

cannot do. These are often described as artist's conceptions for the garden. Figures 6-8 and 6-9 show aerial perspectives of the proposed Hughson Botanical Garden in California and an expansion of the Japanese Garden in Portland, Oregon. Viewers can imagine themselves in the scene engaging in and enjoying the garden's features and attractions. Lively, evocative, and appealing drawings such as these explain each garden's goals and can be very helpful for soliciting support for the plan. Figure 6-10 is a perspective of the lawn at the entrance to the San Francisco Botanical Garden from a viewpoint at ground level rather than an aerial perspective. Aerial perspectives provide garden overviews, while ground-level perspectives place us within the proposed garden.

Detailed Design and Project Design

Presentations to the public, support groups, and organizations along with grant proposal writing and fund-raising typically follow completion and adoption of a master plan. These tasks are the responsibility of garden directors, boards, and staff and may extend over long periods of time. Unless they are very small, gardens are rarely constructed in their entirety at one time. More typical is phased construction on a project-by-project basis. When support for development of a portion of the master plan has been obtained, the design team begins work on developing that portion of the master plan in greater detail.

Figure 6-8: Aerial perspective of the Hughson Botanical Garden, Hughson, California.

The Portico Group

Figure 6-9: Aerial perspective of the Portland Japanese Garden, Portland, Oregon.

The Portico Group

During the project development stage, design ideas become more real, more specific, and more practical. Throughout this stage, staff should ensure that the developing designs are indeed what they want and can be built and maintained with available resources. However, they should also ensure that the larger master plan vision is not lost. Successful completion of the first phases of a master plan is of utmost importance, as they will become benchmarks by which the public and potential donors judge the efficacy of the master plan and the long-term success of the garden.

Figure 6-10: Ground-level perspective view of San Francisco Botanical Garden entrance, San Francisco, California.

The Portico Group

As designs are refined, they will increasingly be generated as CAD (computer-aided design) documents and as complex written specifications. Almost without exception, all construction documents are produced electronically because reviewing and approving agencies require them in this form and contractors bidding on work expect them in this form. The firms that constitute the design team communicate efficiently with each other using these standard computer programs. Specifications and CAD drawings are a "language" that facilitates communication between agencies and professionals but makes drawings and specifications less accessible to the public. Garden staff must be able to read such documents so that they can assess whether the work described meets their needs. To ensure broad agreement and participation, this skill should not be confined exclusively to a few staff members.

Construction Drawings, Bidding, and Implementation

The purpose of the project design stage is to develop portions of the master plan in greater detail, obtain acceptance of these projects by all parties including regulatory agencies, produce cost estimates to ensure that projects remain within the garden's budget, and prepare drawings and specifications for contractors to bid on and install the work.

Construction drawings and specifications are commonly referred to as "contract documents" because they are part of a legal contract between the garden (the "owner") and a contractor to build the work. Construction contracts are not the same as contracts between gardens and design teams to produce the construction documents.

As construction documents are refined, they typically go through several review stages, such as at 30, 60, and 90 percent completion, before the final set is produced. Interim reviews ensure that the work remains on track and that the contributions of each subconsultant are completely integrated with all others in the final document package. The complete document set is used to solicit bids from contractors to perform the work. How the bidding process is conducted will depend on whether the garden is a public or private organization and the size and complexity of the contract. Public and nonprofit gardens may be required to go through a public solicitation and bidding process and select the lowest qualified bidder. Private gardens typically have more flexibility in how they enter into construction contracts.

Once a construction contract has been signed, the job of the design team may be over or may change if the garden wishes to retain the design firm to assist with reviewing and accepting construction work as it proceeds. On large and complex jobs the owner's representative should be familiar with all aspects of construction in the contract, fully conversant with the scope of work in the contract, and knowledgeable about contracting practice and law. Wherever possible, gardens should avoid making design changes after a contract is signed because such changes are likely to result in significant increases in the contract costs or a delay in the completion of work. During construction, access to the site by garden staff may be controlled by the contractor for safety and liability reasons. Following completion of the construction, an elaborate process of reviewing and accepting the work, remedying "defects and omissions," fulfilling warranty maintenance on landscape work, and making final payments takes place.

Hiring a Design Team

Gardens solicit design services by contacting local or national design firms or by advertising in trade newspapers, professional publications, or online for requests for qualifications (RFQs) or requests for proposals (RFPs). RFQs ask firms to provide brochures describing their qualifications for this type of work, while RFPs are more specific and ask for proposals for a scope of work described in some detail. Senior garden staff and board members (and possibly representatives of support groups) should participate in developing assessment criteria, reviewing firm credentials, deciding which firms to interview, the interview process itself, and the selection of a design team. Interviews should be structured to provide the design team with as much information about the garden as possible and to allow garden staff to observe the team in a variety of contexts, professional and social.

The process of responding to RFPs and participating in interviews is time-consuming for garden staff and costly for firms. Gardens should therefore interview only good candidates and minimize the number of interviews. When interviews have been completed, gardens should conduct contract negotiations with the selected team as quickly as possible and inform teams that were not selected as soon as negotiations have been completed and a contract signed.

Negotiations will include defining a scope of services and determining the "deliverables," or products to be provided. To allow the design team to accurately assess its time and work commitments and to avoid confusion at later dates, the scope and deliverables should be spelled out in as much detail as possible. Design teams are likely to possess more experience in the design process than garden staff. Thus, although gardens should have a clear idea of what they want the outcome of the work to be, they need to be open to suggestions from the design team.

To avoid confusion and ensure efficiency of communication between the garden and design team, garden administrators, staff, and board members must be clear about their respective roles and responsibilities. Typically, the garden director acts as the client's voice and has the last word in discussions with the design team and in making decisions for the garden. An effective garden quickly establishes clear channels of communication for its staff and supporters and makes everyone aware of decision-making authority. Similarly, the design team must establish leadership and decision-making responsibilities among consultant staff and subconsultants.

A design team that arrives on the job with preconceived notions of "what you need" and a prescribed process for developing a design is unlikely to be responsive to the garden's unique situation and potentials. Conversely, a design team that offers no ideas of its own or cannot compellingly articulate alternative points of view is unlikely to bring to light ideas latent in the group. Establishing good communication, mutual respect, efficient working relations, and trust at the outset are essential to successfully navigate the ups and downs that inevitably occur during the design process.

The size and composition of design teams will depend on the scope and complexity of the work. In small gardens the process may consist of hiring a local landscape architect, while start-up gardens may seek design help to prepare a pro bono design. Design students from local colleges might prepare plans as part of a class or a garden internship. Design teams for large projects typically include a landscape architecture firm; architects may be included if significant building work and a range of subconsultants are contemplated. If the project is large and prestigious, a garden may seek a nationally known design firm. To ensure that the design team includes the necessary expertise, garden administrators must anticipate the program so that design consultants can assemble appropriate teams.

Changing the design team during the design process can be costly and result in lost time, but if the client and team are incompatible, this may be a necessary course of action. However, unless there are good reasons for not doing so, gardens typically retain the same firm to prepare their master plan and the design of specific projects, which tends to ensure efficiency and continuity. Similarly, it is advisable to retain the design firm that prepared the contract documents to provide advice as necessary during the installation of the work. On very complex contracts, particularly architectural and civil engineering ones, a project management consulting firm may be hired to manage the construction contract, but even in this situation it is advisable to retain the design firm to advise on situations where the intent of the design is in question.

Deciding which design team to hire is critical. Information gleaned from interviews and from careful review of materials submitted by design firms through the RFP and RFQ process must be supplemented by discussions with former clients and, if possible, visits to gardens designed by the firms. Among the factors to consider in the selection process are:

Expertise. Does the team possess the expertise necessary to provide the design services needed by the garden?

Compatibility. Are team members people with whom garden staff feel they can work cooperatively and empathetically? Are the team's values compatible with those of the garden's mission and staff?

Familiarity with locale. Are members of the firm familiar with local soil conditions, weather patterns, plant hardiness lists, and social and cultural norms?

Experience with public gardens. Has the firm developed physical master plans and implemented designs for other public gardens? Do these plans and designs demonstrate a sensitivity to the unique circumstances of each garden?

Commitment to collaborative process. How committed is the firm to responding to client wishes and needs? How do team members describe their skills and past successes? Are team members good listeners as well as good communicators?

Affordability. This factor should be considered after other factors, not first. The old adage "You get what you pay for" always applies.

Summary

The most visible products of the design process are, of course, completed public gardens, but successful outcomes are not measured solely by physical products. The time-consuming, often arduous and contentious process of conceiving, developing, and building a garden must also unify and reinvigorate the entire garden community: staff, board members, volunteers, support groups, and visitors. The communities that created and must now manage these gardens must be strongly committed and unified to ensure the garden's long-term success. Successful design processes consider all perspectives and interests and integrate these into coherent missions and goals, producing garden communities that are firmly united rather than divided into factions.

Successful public gardens are memorable and distinctive; they fit their place and time uniquely and appropriately, doing so with quiet but firm self-confidence. Successful gardens are not imposed on their sites and communities but grow out of them. Reaching a happy fit is never easy, nor is the fit ever finished: gardens and communities are dynamic, constantly growing, changing, and evolving. Successful designs recognize this dynamism and accommodate constant adjustments to maintain that happy fit throughout their lives.

Successful design processes simultaneously create meaningful gardens *and* organizations dedicated to their development, care, and stewardship.

These are essential characteristics of sustainable gardens and organizations. Ultimately, sustainability and fit are the products of successful design processes.

Annotated Resources

Master plan reports and drawings, obtained from other public gardens, may be valuable examples that can help a garden make decisions about how it wishes to tailor its own design process, but, of course, these cannot be applied verbatim.

In addition, most landscape architecture firms include information about their work on their websites. Check, for example, the websites of the following landscape architecture firms known for their work with public gardens:
Deneen Powell Atelier, Inc. (www.dpadesign.com)
Mesa Design Group (www.mesadesigngroup.com)
M-T-R Landscape Architects (www.mtrla.com)
Oasis Design Group (www.oasisdesigngroup.com)
The Portico Group (www.porticogroup.com)
Rodney Robinson Landscape Architects (www.rrla.com)
Rundell Ernstberger Associates (www.reasite.com)
Terra Design Studios (www.terradesignstudios.us)
The American Society of Landscape Architects website (www.asla.org) provides professional information about landscape architecture.

PART III

Administrative Functions

CHAPTER 7

Staffing and Personnel Management

GERARD T. DONNELLY AND NANCY L. PESKE

Public gardens originate in many different ways. Some are conceived and planned as entirely new gardens to be created; others may involve the organization, professionalization, and development of existing gardens or landscapes. Certain gardens originate as independent organizations, while others may emerge within existing institutions, such as within a park system, municipality, university, or government agency.

One or more individuals may plan the concept and purpose of the garden and organize its establishment. These organizers often have the passion to work as volunteers to start the garden, and may serve as unpaid staff.

Organizational work, planning, and fund-raising are usually among the greatest needs of a new or developing garden. These efforts are normally led by a garden director, who may be a volunteer or a paid employee.

KEY TERMS

Benefits: nonwage compensation, such as medical insurance, retirement plans, and vacation and sick leave.

Collective bargaining agreement: a contract negotiated between management (for the employer) and union representatives regarding issues that affect employment conditions, such as wages, benefits, hours, and working conditions.

Compensation: the wages, salaries, and fringe benefits provided to an employee in exchange for work.

Exempt employees: employees who are exempt from certain Fair Labor Standards Act requirements, such as overtime compensation; generally, salaried employees. The position must meet specified criteria for one of the exemptions—administrative, professional, or creative—that relate to duties, supervision, or salary.

Fair Labor Standards Act (FLSA): federal law that establishes a national minimum wage, requires overtime compensation for certain jobs (nonexempt employees), and prohibits the employment of minors, among other provisions.

Human resources: a term that describes all management aspects related to the employer-employee relationship; also known as personnel management. Also refers collectively to the paid and volunteer staff of an organization.

Nonexempt employees: employees who are covered by FLSA regulations; generally employees paid by the hour. Positions are generally classified as non-exempt unless they meet one of the exemptions defined above for exempt employees.

Organizational chart: a diagram depicting the titles, levels, and reporting relationships of positions or departments of an organization; may include employee names.

Staff: the paid employees or volunteers that are engaged to do the work of an organization. The development, accomplishments, and quality of a public garden are directly related to the size and quality of its staff. The mission and purpose of the garden help define the kind of staff positions required and priorities for hiring. Staffing and personnel practices naturally evolve as gardens are established and develop over time. Garden size and strategic plans will determine how employees, supervisors, departments, and organizational structure are configured. To attract, retain, and motivate quality employees, a garden's personnel practices should be based on best practices in hiring, compensation, performance management, and training and professional development.

Staffing the Start-Up Garden

Regardless of the circumstances of garden establishment, at some point the decision may be made to hire one or more paid employees. The mission and purpose of the garden will likely dictate priorities for early staffing, and will certainly guide later staff development. In addition to a garden director, horticultural plant establishment and care may be among the early priorities, in which case a gardener or horticulturist will be needed.

Priorities for additional staffing can be addressed as funding becomes available for the start-up garden. In addition to a director or other garden leader and one or more gardeners/horticulturists, other priority positions may include ones in horticulture, curation, education, and fund-raising and promotion for the garden.

Commonly Prioritized Positions

Director

As the lead staff member of a garden, the director is responsible for working with the governing board or other authority to create the vision, direction, and plans for the garden through time, and to lead the organization and staff operationally to achieve the garden's mission and goals. The director is also responsible for the advancement of the garden through fund-raising, promotion, government relations, and positioning within the public garden profession and the community. A principal role of the director is to be the champion for the garden's horticultural, conservation, or scientific mission, which requires an appropriate level of passion, experience, and academic training. In start-up or small gardens, the director may bear myriad responsibilities, including horticultural supervision, budgeting, accounting, staffing, management of compensation and benefits, legal matters, and more. The search for a director with competency in all of the areas of responsibility typically expected can be challenging.

Gardener or Horticulturist

The plants in a garden need the care and attention of a gardener or horticulturist. This professional plants, weeds, waters, prunes, and otherwise cultivates plants in the collections, garden areas, or greenhouses. A working knowledge of plants and horticulture, developed through experience and academic study, is required. In a public garden, gardeners or horticulturists often interact with visitors interested in their work and may teach or share their knowledge informally or in the garden's educational programs. There is no technical difference between the titles of gardener and horticulturist, but the latter is sometimes used to suggest a higher level of professional or academic training. As the number of gardeners/horticulturists grows, a need will develop for a horticulture supervisor or manager who can coordinate the work of the horticultural staff.

Figure 7-1: Public gardens need to be tended, and gardeners or horticulturists are among the first employees to be hired at a new garden.

The Morton Arboretum

Curator

If the mission of the garden includes the creation and management of plant collections for botanical, horticultural, or conservation purposes, the hiring of a curator is a significant priority. A curator is the steward of the collection, responsible for development and care of the collections through time. Curators develop plant collections policy, acquire plants for the collections, arrange appropriate record keeping and labeling, ensure proper horticultural care and protection, conduct evaluations of plant performance, and arrange access to the collections for study or use by others. A substantial knowledge of and passion for plants, plant systematics, and horticulture are needed for the effective curation of plant collections.

Education Coordinator

Public gardens traditionally offer organized educational programs to the public, and an education coordinator plans these programs to support the mission themes of the garden and the needs and interests of the audience and community. The education coordinator hires and schedules instructors or docents to conduct classes, tours, and activities, and may serve directly in such educational roles. Educators and plant specialists alike may be appropriate candidates for the position of education coordinator, as long as the individual has a special interest in the subject matter and a familiarity with and skill in engaging students of all ages in the informal educational setting of a public garden.

CASE STUDY: KEY WEST TROPICAL FOREST AND BOTANICAL GARDEN

Although the Key West Botanical Garden was first established in the 1930s, it endured periods of neglect and resurgence, and was ultimately reinvented as the Key West Tropical Forest and Botanical Garden in 2001. A group of concerned individuals in the community rehabilitated the 7.5-acre site and raised funds to build a new visitor center. Volunteers supported the rehabilitation and continue to contribute services that might otherwise require paid staff.

The first paid employee hired in 2004 was a part-time executive administrator, who was among the founding board members of the reinvented botanical garden. In addition to volunteers, the Garden uses contracted services to support operations. Contractors supplied accounting services, landscape maintenance, and tree care early on and continue to do so. In 2005, a full-time grounds maintenance/custodian employee was hired, and 7.5 more acres were added to the property.

A full-time executive director was hired in 2006, the garden administrator was increased to full-time, and a contracted grant writer was hired. The administrator then focused on membership and visitor programs, events, and visitor center operations. In the following year, a grant was secured to establish educational programs. A part-time director of education was hired, together with a full-time education coordinator and two full-time environmental educators. A part-time botanist was also hired in 2007.

In 2008 the executive director retired, and the board of directors decided to focus staffing on midlevel positions; a board member became the executive director on a volunteer basis. A resource manager was hired in 2009 to help coordinate volunteers and personnel management, inventories, equipment, and other resources. In 2010 a part-time director of conservation was hired under contract. The future staffing plan includes a paid executive director and, with the planned development of horticultural landscapes and conservatories, full-time horticulturists.

Although each public garden is unique in its development path and the evolution of its staff, the Key West Tropical Forest and Botanical Garden provides an interesting example of staffing at an establishing garden. The ongoing use of contracted services suits this garden well because of its small but evolving size, its seasonal audience and programs, and its remote location, far removed from population and employment centers. Establishing gardens in other areas might consider using contractors for certain services to allow flexibility instead of committing to paid positions.

The Key West Botanical Garden Society is maintaining and developing the historic Key West Tropical Forest and Botanical Garden as an arboretum, botanical garden, wildlife refuge, and education center (www.keywestbotanicalgarden.org). The garden is dedicated to growing and interpreting the plants and ecosystems of the Florida Keys and the Caribbean, and has active plans for a vibrant future.

Figure 7-2: Volunteers and paid staff work hand in hand at the Key West Tropical Forest and Botanical Garden and at most public gardens.

Key West Botanical Garden Society/Peter Arnow

Fund-raising and Marketing Coordinator

With a small garden staff, one person is typically designated to help raise financial support and build awareness for the garden in the community. Both roles are of significant importance to the well-being and development of a public garden. Donors will not surface or contribute significantly to organizations that they do not know or that do not have a significant profile of service and value in the community. And community needs cannot be met without adequate funding to develop the garden and create meaningful programs and services. Key qualifications include a dedication to the mission and purposes of the garden and an ability to interact effectively with the public, donors, community leaders, and the media.

Staffing the Developing Garden

Staffing patterns evolve as a garden develops and grows, and vary depending on the garden's ultimate size. Job functions, responsibilities, and titles shift with garden size or growth, trending from generalist employees with multiple responsibilities for newer and small gardens to more specialization as the garden evolves or increases in size.

An organizational structure will also emerge as the scale of the garden and number of employees increase. A larger staff will require increased supervisory roles. Changes in the number and naming of job titles will sometimes reflect the developmental stages of a growing garden. As an example, multiple gardeners will require coordination and supervision, perhaps by a horticulture supervisor or crew leader. Later, one or more horticulture supervisors may be led by a horticulture manager. In a more mature or large garden, managers may be led by a director of horticulture or vice president of horticulture and operations.

For most public gardens, personnel costs for compensation and benefits represent the single greatest expense in the budget. Staff expansion is contingent on the financial resources available to the garden and requires careful financial planning. Staffing additions must relate to the garden's core mission and should be considered only if sustainable funding is ensured.

Public Garden Jobs

The number and diversity of jobs in public gardens increase with the size and complexity of the garden. Public gardens, like other types of museums, often have a greater diversity of staff positions than similarly sized for-profit companies, which usually have a more targeted business model. A sampling of public garden positions and job groupings follows.

Administrative Positions

Leadership, management, and operations positions are part of a garden's administration, and are distinguished here from horticulture, education, and research positions, described later.

Director/Executive Director/President/CEO

As a garden grows in scale and complexity, the responsibilities of the director or lead staff member shift to focus more on leadership-level functions, community and board relationships, and fund-raising. Although the director bears ultimate responsibility for all aspects of the garden, larger public gardens hire staff and staff leaders to cover horticultural, scientific, educational, visitor, and business functions. Resources and public support must be used wisely, for mission purposes, and with business-like efficiency to deliver the public benefits that are defined for nonprofit organizations. The series of titles used for the lead position typically reflects the size and complexity of the organization, with the title changing from director to executive director, then president, and perhaps president and chief executive officer (CEO) as the garden matures.

Business Manager/Chief Financial Officer (CFO)

The business functions of budgeting, accounting, financing and investments, payroll, and other financial responsibilities are best managed by professionals with training in business, accounting, and finance. Independent audits are required of larger public gardens and include reviews of proper accounting and internal control procedures and regulatory compliance. In larger gardens, the business manager or CFO is supported by accounting and bookkeeping staff.

Personnel Manager

Responsibilities for personnel or human resources management grow with the size of the staff. Employment law and regulations continue to evolve, adding complexity to the role of managing the hiring, training, compensation, evaluation, safety, and termination of garden employees. Human resources professionals are experts in this area; in larger gardens they may be supported by specialist positions in benefits administration, labor and union relations, and staff training.

Marketing Manager/Communications Director

Building awareness and audiences are essential objectives for public gardens, and marketing, public relations, and communications specialists position the garden for successful public engagement. A public relations coordinator may be needed to develop and maintain effective relationships with the media.

Other related positions include writer, editor, graphic designer, webmaster, and social media specialist.

Development/Membership Director
Cultivating relationships with visitors, members, and donors is an important way of ensuring public support through contributions. Coordinators, directors, or vice presidents of development lead these efforts and often hire additional staff to support the philanthropic program. Fund-raising staff may specialize in annual giving, major gifts, capital campaigns, or planned giving. Grant writers pursue support from corporations, foundations, and government sources. Membership programs, led by a membership manager and other staff, are often successful in establishing ongoing relationships with members that can lead to more significant contributed income in support of garden operations.

Visitor Services Manager
Visitor services positions must have a high priority in public garden staffing. Such individuals are responsible for anticipating visitors' needs and ensuring that those needs are adequately addressed. In addition to the leadership role of manager or director, some gardens employ coordinators for group tours and special events, facility rental managers, and gate attendants/ticket takers.

Facilities Manager/Chief Operations Officer
The number of employees necessary to manage and operate a garden's facilities and business operations depends on its size. A chief operations officer (COO) may provide leadership for operations in a large garden, but other possible positions include facilities manager, security coordinator, director or specialist in information technology, and managers of gift shops and food services. A new and emerging role at public gardens is for leadership of sustainable practices related to resource use and carbon impact.

Horticulture Positions
The horticultural staff typically is the largest employee group at a public garden. In addition to gardeners/horticulturists and the leadership roles of manager, director, or vice president of horticulture, many other public garden jobs fall into the horticultural category.

A grounds manager may be responsible for general landscape care, mowing, and site construction. Conservatory managers coordinate horticultural display efforts under glass. Greenhouse/nursery production managers propagate and grow plants for collections, display, and study. Plant records managers

Figure 7-3: Welcoming and assisting visitors is an essential role of a public garden's employees.

Gene Almendinger/Desert Botanical Garden

keep the essential records on plants in the collections and ensure the accuracy of plant labels. Landscape architects or design consultants are employed at some larger gardens to guide master planning and landscape design. Gardens with significant natural areas may need a manager and staff for their stewardship and management. In addition to the regular staff, most public gardens employ seasonal horticultural employees who support the larger demands of the growing season.

Education Positions
Public gardens are institutions of learning and inspiration. Leading these efforts is a manager, director, or vice president of education. Depending on the scale of educational offerings, specialist coordinators may be focused on formal youth education, school programs, and continuing education. Some gardens have partnerships with colleges and universities that also require staff participation.

Critical to a garden's informal education program is a staff member responsible for interpretive programs that support the garden's mission. Interpretation and exhibition managers or specialists create exhibits and interpret the plants, gardens, and programs of the public garden. Paid or volunteer docents often provide personal interpretation and tours for garden visitors.

Research Positions

Botanical gardens and arboreta are traditionally based in science, and many public gardens today include scientific research in their mission and staffing plans. Conservation and environmental science programs have grown in recent years in response to environmental concerns. A head, director, or vice president of research leads the scientific program. At some gardens, research scientists with specialized academic degrees focus on taxonomy and systematics, conservation, genetics/genomics/plant breeding, or other botanical and horticultural research; postdoctoral scientists, graduate students, research associates, and laboratory and field assistants support their research.

Organizational Structure

In a start-up garden, the organization may be quite simple, with all employees reporting to the garden manager/director. As the garden develops, employees will be added, more specialized job roles and supervisory relationships will emerge, and employee work groups or departments will be defined. Layers of reporting and management become necessary, resulting in a hierarchy of responsibilities and groupings of functions or departments. The director or human resources staff may develop an organizational chart that shows the relationships between positions, functions, departments, or work groups.

The case study that follows illustrates the organizational structure and staffing of a large, established public garden. The merits of multiple layers versus a flatter organizational structure and reporting are often debated, but no one approach is appropriate for all organizations.

Although larger gardens can appear compartmentalized, garden management must ensure cohesion, communication, and interdepartmental cooperation. Leadership teams of senior managers and cross-departmental project teams are effective tools for maintaining organizational integrity.

Personnel Management

Because a public garden's mission and goals depend primarily on the efforts of its employees for their achievement, it is essential to recruit and hire the best employees the garden can afford and find, compensate them well enough to retain them, train them, evaluate and encourage their work, and manage these human resources effectively. Human resource management is focused on these needs as well as the need to maintain the garden's compliance with the growing body of laws and regulations governing personnel and labor practices.

Recruitment and Hiring

Each employee is hired to make positive and significant contributions to the organization. An organized and consistent process for recruitment and selection that uses best practices and conforms to all legal requirements provides a solid foundation for hiring the most qualified candidates. (See "Recruitment and Hiring Steps.")

It is essential that the cultural diversity of the staff of a public garden reflects the diversity of the audience the garden serves or hopes to serve. But the plant sciences and the field of public horticulture have yet to attract a broad enough diversity of students or job candidates to satisfy that obligation. Focused efforts are needed to encourage career awareness, provide professional development opportunities, and recruit and hire individuals of color and cultural diversity to make gardens more effective in serving the entire public.

CASE STUDY: STAFFING AT A LARGE, DEVELOPED GARDEN— THE MORTON ARBORETUM

The Morton Arboretum provides a good example of staffing and organizational structure at a large, fully developed garden. The Arboretum was established in 1922 as a private, nonprofit organization dedicated to the planting and conservation of trees. It is a scientific, educational, and public service organization located in the western suburbs of Chicago, Illinois (www.mortonarb.org).

The Arboretum consists of 1,700 acres of land, on which are located plant collections, gardens and horticultural landscapes, research facilities, natural areas, buildings, and support facilities. Attendance in 2009 amounted to 831,000 visitors, and 34,000 members helped to support an operating budget of $24 million in that year.

In 2009, the Arboretum employed 143 full-time employees, 103 part-time staff, and 100 seasonal workers. This staffing level equates to a full-time equivalent of 206 employees. Together with more than 940 active volunteers, the Morton Arboretum is supported by a substantial human effort that is managed and organized for optimal achievement of its mission.

Figure 7-4 illustrates the organizational structure and senior staff of the Morton Arboretum. Six vice presidents report to the president and CEO, who is accountable to a board of twenty-five trustees. Plant collections, science, and education functions are each supported by a vice president, as are the fund-raising, marketing, and financial enterprises. Vice presidents partner with

the president to provide strategic leadership for their area of responsibility, and they are active in external relationships and resource development for their programs.

Directors and heads of program areas work with the vice presidents to lead specific operations, and a series of managers, coordinators, specialists, and other employees carry out the objectives of the organization. Given the importance of an effective and well-supported staff, the director of human resources at the Morton Arboretum reports directly to the president and CEO.

To ensure effective leadership and integration in this large public garden, the president and CEO, vice presidents, and directors of the Morton Arboretum work together as a leadership team, addressing matters of strategy, planning, administration, and operations. Working teams of employees from different departments are organized to advance institutional strategic themes (e.g., climate change, community greening, tree health) and are also used to gather multiple perspectives for special initiatives (e.g., art exhibition planning).

Effective staff communication is essential, especially in a large organization. The Morton Arboretum uses a variety of means for information exchange, including regular staff meetings, an intranet for staff, email communications, personal interaction, social media, and quarterly employee forums with the president and CEO.

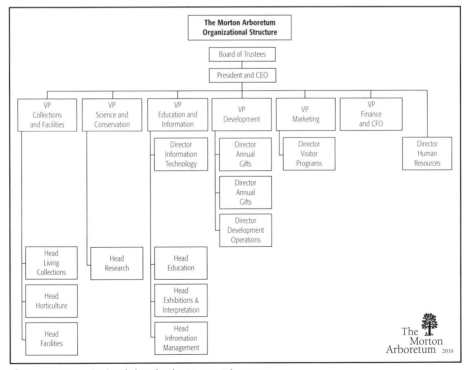

Figure 7-4: Organizational chart for the Morton Arboretum.

Job Descriptions

A job description defines the garden's expectations for each position in the organization and provides clarity in hiring and performance evaluation. A well-developed job description includes a high-level overview of the position; essential job-related duties; the knowledge, skills, and abilities required to perform the job; and the general working conditions for the position. (See "Elements of a Job Description.")

Compensation and Benefits

Given the importance of the staff in achieving a garden's mission and goals, it is essential that the organization provides fair and competitive pay and benefits that can attract and retain high-quality employees. A systematic approach to compensation is necessary and should be based on objective data, available institutional resources, and the organization's overall philosophy toward pay and benefits.

An assessment of the current market value of a position is based on the skills, knowledge, and abilities of competent individuals in similar positions in the marketplace; published salary data are available from local, national, and industry-specific surveys. When the market average for a position is established, the institution's pay philosophy can be applied to this information, which might be to pay at the market rate, lead the market with attractive premium compensation, or pay less than the market rate. The compensation system must be flexible enough to ensure that the garden is able to recruit and retain a highly qualified workforce, yet provide the structure necessary to effectively manage the overall compensation program. Once in place, a continued systematic approach will keep pace with compensation information over time.

This same benchmarking approach should be utilized when determining the types of benefits offered to employees, including medical, dental, and retirement benefits, and the cost sharing of any premiums. The organizational philosophies for salaries and benefits need not match—a garden that lags the market in pay may choose to lead the market in benefits.

Outsourcing and Independent Contractors

In addition to hiring employees, a garden may outsource one or more of the garden's functions or use independent contractors to accomplish the necessary work of the garden. Outsourcing is the utilization of an independent company to assume responsibility for a specific function of a garden. Almost any function can be outsourced; two examples are custodial services and human resources management. Advantages are savings in hiring, wages, benefits, and overtime cost, and access to expertise that cannot be readily hired. Conversely, such an arrangement may include paying a premium price to the provider. Outsourcing is a partnership that involves shared control and requires stronger, focused efforts in communication between the garden and the hired company.

Independent contractors are individuals hired to provide services or outcomes defined in an agreement or contract. Specific Fair Labor Standards Act (FLSA) rules apply that distinguish between employees and independent contractors. Independent contractors are not subject to direct supervision; they determine the methods, details, and means of providing the specified services, and should not use garden resources to fulfill their agreement. Contractors are typically paid at completion of the job, not by the hour or week. This type of flexible staffing arrangement is well suited for short-term needs or specific projects.

Legal Compliance

The human resources function, including compensation, benefits, recruitment and hiring, and performance management, is likely the most regulated area of a garden. Numerous federal, state, and local laws and regulations protect employee rights and prevent unlawful discrimination in all aspects of personnel management. Some of the more significant federal labor laws include:

- Age Discrimination in Employment Act (ADEA): prohibits discrimination in employment for people age forty and over

- Americans with Disabilities Act (ADA): prohibits discrimination in employment on the basis of a disability

- Civil Rights Act of 1964, Title VII: prohibits discrimination or segregation in employment based on race, color, national origin, religion, and gender; created the Equal Opportunity Employment Commission (EEOC)

- Consolidated Omnibus Budget Reconciliation Act (COBRA): provides for continuation of health care benefits for former employees and their families

- Employee Retirement Income Security Act (ERISA): established basic standards for retirement and health benefit programs to maintain their tax-favored status

- Fair Labor Standards Act (FLSA): regulates employee overtime status, child labor, minimum wage, overtime pay, record keeping, and employment matters

- Family and Medical Leave Act (FMLA): provides employees with the opportunity to take up to twelve weeks of unpaid leave for the birth or placement of a child, for the serious health condition of a family member, or for the employee's own serious health condition

- Pregnancy Discrimination Act (PDA): prohibits discrimination related to pregnancy, childbirth, and related conditions

Many of these regulations apply to all organizations, without regard to the number of employees. Others apply only when an organization has a certain minimum number of employees. Understanding and complying with these regulations is important because they help organizations and managers act in a responsible and appropriate manner and minimize potential liability to the organization or an individual.

Labor Relations

Employees at some public gardens may be organized into a labor union. Unionized labor is often associated with government-affiliated gardens and with many college and university gardens. Union employees are covered by a collective bargaining agreement, or union contract, that mandates specific provisions regarding pay, benefits, performance management (disciplinary action), work hours, and other working conditions. Gardens may have both union and nonunion employees, requiring different systems of personnel practices, policies, and benefits.

Collective bargaining agreements are negotiated between management and union representatives on a periodic basis, as determined by the length of the agreements. Specific labor laws related to union employment contained in the National Labor Relations Act provide guidance to both employers and employees.

Personnel Policies

In addition to the compliance issues necessary to operate a successful organization, the garden needs to develop personnel policies and guidelines to establish a strong foundation for legal, ethical, and appropriate behavior by employees. (See "A Sampling of Personnel Policies.") The Sarbanes-Oxley Act of

- **Alcohol- and drug-free workplace:** addresses the possession, use, and/or consumption of any substance that may impair an employee's ability to safely perform his or her job

- **Antiharassment:** asserts the garden's commitment to maintaining a workplace free from unlawful harassment, discrimination, and intimidation, and outlines the process for making and investigating a complaint

- **Attendance:** establishes standards and expectations for attendance and punctuality, and outlines procedures related to illness, notice, and absences

- **Cell phone use:** provides guidelines for the use of cell phones during work time, including the use of cell phones to conduct business while driving

- **Conflict of interest**: requires reporting and disclosure of situations, activities, and relationships that might be considered a conflict or potential conflict of interest

- **Discipline:** outlines unacceptable conduct and behavior that would lead to disciplinary action, and disciplinary measures used by the garden

- **Document retention:** addresses the systematic review, retention, and destruction of records and documents received or created in the course of garden business

- **Ethics:** communicates expectations for ethical conduct, in accordance with legal and professional standards by employees and representatives of the garden

- **Gifts and gratuities:** addresses the acceptance of gifts by employees from outside business sources

- **Intellectual property:** defines the conditions under which work products developed by employees are considered the intellectual property of the garden

- **Outside employment:** states the garden's view on outside employment that may compete or pose a conflict of interest with an employee's ability to perform his or her duties

- **Overtime compensation:** defines overtime pay for work in excess of forty hours in a week, as provided for in the FLSA

- **Safety:** conveys the safety philosophy of the garden and applicable accident or safety hazard reporting procedures

- **Travel and business expense:** sets the standards and reimbursement practices for expenses incurred in connection with approved garden travel or business

- **Violence in the workplace:** addresses violent behavior and the possession of weapons on garden property

- **Whistle-blower protection:** ensures opportunities for employees to report suspected or actual violations of applicable policies, laws, or regulations; includes investigation procedures, confidentiality, and antiretaliation provisions

2002 mandates nonprofits to adopt certain policies, including ethics, whistleblower protection, and document retention.

An employee handbook is a valuable resource and communication tool for employees to understand job-related policies and guidelines, information about employment and benefits, and organizational expectations. A handbook should be a living document that is made available to employees and updated as policies change and evolve.

Performance Management

A key component of supervisors' leadership role is managing the performance and development of their staff, including hiring/promoting appropriate employees, coaching and guiding staff to the accomplishment of goals, providing timely recognition of achievements, and setting clear and realistic goals for employees. When warranted, supervisors must provide feedback about negative performance and possibly take disciplinary action, such as oral and written warnings, a performance improvement plan, suspension, or termination.

Ongoing and systematic performance feedback is essential to the employee-employer relationship. It is the supervisor's responsibility to provide recognition for an employee's efforts and successes and to identify areas where further job related training or development may be warranted. At a minimum, an annual performance evaluation meeting should take place as one method of performance management and feedback. Frequent and regular feedback and dialogue between supervisor and employee is recommended to establish an ongoing, mutual understanding of performance expectations and results.

Performance appraisals are used for formal evaluation of employee performance and accomplishment of goals, to provide feedback and counseling, and to address areas of improvement or where additional training is needed. Appraisals can improve productivity, clarify expectations, and establish work-related goals for the upcoming appraisal period. Performance appraisal methods include category rating, with a predetermined form or checklist; narrative, with written commentary on performance; and comparative, with rankings of all the employees in the working group.

Training and Professional Development

Employee training and development should commence the first day of employment and continue throughout the employee's time in the job. Effective orientation to the organization and job training and instruction are essential. Some employers use

Figure 7-5: Supervisors provide ongoing training and feedback to employees to help them do their job.

The Morton Arboretum

the initial employment period to measure an employee's early progress and performance and assess expectations and needs for additional training or support.

In addition to initial orientation and training of new employees, supervisors need to play a direct role in the ongoing training and professional development of garden employees, ensuring that resources and systems are in place to support continuing education. As part of the annual goal-setting process, it is valuable to consider an employee's interest in and perspective on ongoing professional development in addition to the training identified by the supervisor. Benefits include improved performance, increased retention, internal transfer and promotion opportunities where appropriate, and professional networking. To ensure that continuing education programs are a good fit, it is important to consider how employees' professional development and career goals align with the goals of the garden. Additional academic training, participation in professional associations and conferences, new skill development, workshops, job shadowing or exchange, mentoring relationships, and special projects are some of the many forms of professional development opportunities possible.

Summary

Many fascinating opportunities for employment exist in public gardens, in a wide range of disciplines. Academic and professional development programs now in place are fostering a larger pool of well-educated professionals within the field of public horticulture. Public gardens as organizations also continue on a path of greater professionalization. This occurs as

individual gardens grow and mature, but is also occurring for public gardens as a group.

The American Public Gardens Association (www.public gardens.org) and the Center for Public Horticulture (www .publichorticulture.udel.edu) are dedicated to making public gardens and the individuals who work at them more effective and professional.

This chapter on staffing and personnel management addressed the evolution of staffing as a garden becomes established, develops, and matures. The number, specialization, and level of jobs change as the garden develops, as does the organizational structure of the garden staff over time.

The employer-employee relationship is critically important to the success of a public garden, and managing employment is a complex process. Effective management of the human resources of a public garden leads to an employment environment that is attractive to potential employees and encourages employee retention, motivation, and productivity.

Employment at a public garden is one of the most satisfying pursuits in the world of work, and it is gratifying to see what public horticulture professionals can accomplish by engaging people with plants in a garden setting.

Annotated Resources

American Association of Museums Career Center (www.aam -us.org/aviso/index.cfm). Job postings in museums, including public gardens.

American Public Gardens Association. 2008. *2008 compensation and benefits study.* Kennett Square, Penn.: American Public Gardens Association. Benchmark salaries and benefits for public garden jobs.

American Public Gardens Association Career Center (www .publicgardens.org). Job postings in public gardens; click on Member Resources, then Career Center.

American Public Gardens Association Resource Center (www .publicgardens.org). Model job descriptions, personnel policies, and organizational charts from different public gardens; click on Member Resources, Resource Center, Human Resources.

Barbeito, C. L. 2006. *Human resource policies and procedures for nonprofit organizations.* Hoboken, N.J.: John Wiley and Sons. A useful reference for personnel practices at nonprofit organizations, with model policies and procedures.

Botanic Gardens Conservation International (www.bgci.org/
resources/jobs). Job postings in public gardens.
Center for Public Horticulture (www.publichorticulture
.udel.edu/careers). Video career profiles by public garden
professionals.
MuseumProfessionals (www.museumprofessionals.org). Job
postings in museums, including public gardens.
Pynes, J. E. 2004. *Human resources management for public and nonprofit organizations: A strategic approach.*

Hoboken, N.J.: John Wiley and Sons. A comprehensive
reference on human resources management in nonprofit
organizations and public agencies.
Society for Human Resource Management (www.shrm.org).
Comprehensive HR site and resources, including tool kits,
sample forms, glossary, and regulatory matters.
United States Department of Labor (www.dol.gov). Source
of information on federal labor laws and employment
practices.

CHAPTER 8

Volunteer Recruitment and Management

ARLENE FERRIS

Introduction

Many of North America's public gardens were originally founded by volunteers, and today volunteers contribute to the programs and activities at most, if not all, public gardens. Volunteers help a garden grow and thrive in countless ways, but their involvement must be planned for and managed. Although a garden will grow and increase its staff, programs, and financial support, it will never outgrow its need for volunteers, who are invaluable assets both within and beyond the garden gates.

The Value of Volunteers

A garden may try to determine the value of volunteers by counting hours donated and multiplying that figure by an average hourly rate to show how much was saved in labor costs. But measuring their contributions only in monetary terms understates their value. Volunteers bring energy, talents, skills, and knowledge to enrich a garden in obvious as well as unexpected ways. Their contribution of time is a testimony to the importance of the garden's mission. A volunteer program allows members of the community to become partners in achieving the garden's goals. In turn, volunteers take the garden's message out into the community, where they share their knowledge and passion with others.

Planning a Volunteer Program

A volunteer program requires an investment of time and money. The goal of planning is to make sure that the garden's investment in volunteers has a satisfactory rate of return by creating a program that meets the needs of both staff

and volunteers and effectively integrates volunteers into the organization.

Assessing When, Where, and How Volunteers Can Help

Although most public gardens utilize the assistance of volunteers, the extent of their involvement depends on the size of the garden and its staff, its stage of development, and the numbers and types of programs offered. Asking "Where are we now? Where do we want to go? How can volunteers help us get there?" will guide a garden's broad vision for its volunteer program. In order to assess its immediate needs, a garden should determine the following: What positions must be filled? Is there funding to hire staff for the positions? Can volunteers assist in carrying out the duties of the position? In what ways can volunteers help deliver programs and services? Who will be responsible for recruiting and training those volunteers? Although a garden's need for volunteers will continually evolve, answers to these questions can serve as a starting point.

In new gardens, volunteers may do everything from planting to planning, from writing to fund-raising. As the garden grows, staff will assume duties that require more time, specific skills, and greater accountability. Volunteers may be skilled and dedicated, but rarely will they want to volunteer for twenty to forty hours each week on the fixed schedule most jobs require. Eventually a balance is found between duties best allocated to paid staff and those most suited to volunteers.

Established gardens typically have volunteers providing substantial levels of support in horticulture, education programs, visitor services, administrative offices, conservation projects,

Figure 8-1: Horticulture volunteers play an important role in caring for the plant collections at most public gardens.

Courtesy of Fairchild Tropical Botanic Garden

plant sales, the herbarium, and the gift shop, as well as at special events. Gardens will continually seek new or expanded opportunities for volunteer involvement, building on the success already achieved with their help. Volunteers will be an invaluable source for ideas about additional ways they can help the garden and the staff.

Understanding What Motivates Garden Volunteers

When prospective volunteers are asked why they want to volunteer, many say it is because they want to support a garden that is important to them and to their community, but volunteers also have tangible needs that must be met to keep them motivated.

- **Volunteers want personal enrichment.** People volunteer to engage in interesting, stimulating pursuits, and for lifelong learning opportunities.

- **Volunteers want to meet others.** Volunteers want to meet and socialize with people who have similar values and interests.

- **Volunteers want to participate in meaningful programs.** Volunteers want to help educate children, preserve important plant collections, guide visitors, and be involved firsthand with conservation and research projects.

- **Volunteers want to learn new skills.** People pursuing careers in horticulture and related fields can increase their

knowledge, gain experience, and network with others in the field.

- **Volunteers want to work in a garden setting.** People interested in plants value the opportunity to learn firsthand about horticulture and to help create beautiful public gardens.

Gaining Staff Support

Support from the top is a key element of a successful volunteer program. According to Susan Ellis, a leader in nonprofit management, top administrators have a vested interest in the development of a successful volunteer program because of the great potential of volunteers to advance the organization's mission.

Equally important is gaining staff buy-in early in the process of establishing a volunteer program. Volunteers work best in a friendly, nurturing environment, and staff reluctance to work with volunteers will hinder their integration into the organization. Involving staff in the planning process will help to address possible concerns and give staff a vested interest in a successful outcome.

Volunteers and Paid Staff

All garden employees, union and nonunion, must be assured that volunteers are not substitutes for paid staff. Collective bargaining agreements with union employees may impact a garden's ability to utilize volunteers in certain jobs. Staff members at gardens that have successfully negotiated with collective bargaining units are useful sources of information on this issue.

What distinguishes volunteers from paid staff?

- Volunteers are not paid.

- Volunteers control their own schedules.

- Volunteers don't have to do something they don't want to do.

- Volunteers, in general, do not perform sustained heavy labor or operate machinery.

Managing the Volunteer Program

Though small or emerging gardens may not need a volunteer program manager, a volunteer program may grow to a size where a designated person is needed to recruit, orient, coordinate, and track volunteers. A volunteer manager's primary responsibilities are to facilitate volunteer support of the mission, goals, and work of the garden and its staff, interface with the volunteers, and coordinate all of the elements of the program. The volunteer manager can be part-time or full-time, a staff member with multiple duties, or a qualified volunteer. An alternative model is to have each department recruit, interview, train, and manage its own volunteers.

Designing Volunteer Jobs

Staff requests for volunteers should always be designed using a job description form as a template. To complete the form, staff members must identify the significant elements of the job, which will help in selecting the right volunteer for the position. Because job description forms state expectations up front, applicants without the required skills or abilities are more likely to understand why they have not been selected for a position for which they are not qualified.

Volunteer Policies and Procedures

In tandem with the creation of volunteer jobs is the creation of policies and procedures that will guide volunteer involvement and will facilitate the integration of volunteers into the organization. It is important to have garden-wide policies as well as those issued at the departmental level.

Garden-wide policies and procedures should be listed in the volunteer handbook, and volunteers should sign off on receiving and agreeing to the policies. Departmental policies are issued to volunteers by their staff supervisors. Other versions may be created for volunteers helping at one-time-only events. New gardens can look to established gardens for examples of policies and procedures, and gardens can also look to their own employee handbooks for additional ideas about what to include.

ELEMENTS OF A VOLUNTEER JOB DESCRIPTION

Position title and description

Supervisor

Location of work

Duties and responsibilities

Required skills, knowledge, abilities, attitudes

Days and times required

Minimum/maximum length of assignment

Training and evaluation procedures

How this work helps fulfill the garden's mission

Benefits to the volunteer

SUGGESTED VOLUNTEER POLICIES AND PROCEDURES

Absences, scheduling, recording volunteer time

Assumption of risk and release of liability forms

Background checks

Computer use

Customer service standards

Dress code

Emergency procedures

Evaluation procedures

Grievance procedures

Membership, admissions, and guest policies

Operation of garden vehicles

Parking

Plant collecting

Prohibitions (drinking, drugs, smoking)

Safety

Sexual harassment

Training requirements

Risk Management Issues

Staff should assess the potential risks in volunteer jobs and work sites and provide training, tools, equipment, and supervision to minimize or eliminate those risks. Some volunteer jobs are inherently risky: horticulture volunteers may come in contact with stinging insects, spiny plants, or severe skin irritants, for example, or injure themselves using sharp tools. All volunteers who work outdoors can be affected by varying weather conditions, and procedures should be established to help them deal with those occurrences.

Volunteers working with children or other vulnerable populations, including the elderly or those who are disabled, must be properly screened, trained, and supervised to meet the higher standard of care required.

Other high-risk volunteer jobs are those that involve driving garden vehicles or using potentially dangerous equipment or chemicals (Figure 8-2). If the risks associated with certain tasks cannot be tolerated, those tasks should be modified or assigned to paid staff.

Figure 8-2: Volunteers at Fairchild provide shuttle service for disabled visitors and others who need assistance. Shuttle drivers receive training on equipment and procedures to protect the safety of passengers.

Courtesy of Fairchild Tropical Botanic Garden

Volunteer Recruitment and Placement

The challenge in recruitment is not just to find people who love the garden and are willing to help but to find people with the time available and the ability to do the jobs at hand. Not all volunteers need to have the same capabilities. Accommodations such as handicapped-accessible potting tables and wheelchair-accessible workstations can provide access to greater numbers of potential volunteers. Older or less physically able volunteers can perform a variety of tasks, from writing gift acknowledgment cards to serving as greeters.

Create a Message

Recruitment messages should convey that volunteers are needed, that the work is rewarding, and that volunteering

Figure 8-3: A recruitment brochure should contain attractive images, the garden's mission, requirements for volunteering, and contact information for prospective volunteers.

Courtesy of Fairchild Tropical Botanic Garden.

requires a commitment. The volunteer website, brochure (Figure 8-3), and other recruitment materials can elaborate on the details of jobs, introduce some of the current volunteers, and inspire people with positive messages. It is best to avoid the temptation to claim that "there is something for everyone to do at the garden," because it may be a promise that the garden can't keep.

POTENTIAL GROUPS OF VOLUNTEERS

Garden members and visitors

Neighborhood residents

Members of civic groups

Members of garden clubs, master gardener groups, plant societies, environmental organizations

Public and private school students, home-schooling organizations

Recruits from college and university volunteer centers, fraternities, sororities

Residents at retirement communities and organizations of retired professionals

Employees of corporations

Court-ordered community service participants

Figure 8-4: The Atlanta Botanical Garden hosts Thursday evening social events to attract new audiences and prospective volunteers. Courtesy of Atlanta Botanical Garden.

Recruitment Events and Tools

Some gardens have a steady stream of applicants because the garden is popular among plant- and nature-lovers in the community. But for most gardens, active recruitment campaigns are necessary to get the numbers and types of volunteers needed. Recruitment campaigns require a multiplicity of announcements: notices in garden publications and on the website; emails and direct mailings to members and community groups; recruitment literature and displays at the garden; coverage in the local media; and postings on community volunteer sites, social networking sites, and bulletin boards. People also respond to being personally asked to volunteer by staff or other volunteers.

Many gardens have regular recruitment or special events that allow the public to visit the garden and learn about the volunteer program (Figure 8-4).

Whether or not there is an immediate need for volunteers, gardens should always showcase their volunteer programs to recognize the contributions of those already serving and as a reminder of the program's existence.

CASE STUDY: CHEYENNE BOTANIC GARDENS

The unique history and success of the Cheyenne Botanic Gardens demonstrate how volunteers and community groups can sustain a garden at every stage of its development.

The Cheyenne Botanic Gardens' earliest incarnation was a solar-powered greenhouse, funded through low-income assistance programs, where senior, disabled, and at-risk youth volunteers grew ornamental and edible plants. The greenhouse eventually evolved into a 9-acre public garden and a 62-acre arboretum operated by Cheyenne's Parks and Recreation Department, and seniors, disabled individuals, and at-risk youth still constitute the majority of volunteers in this award-winning volunteer program. The Gardens has one of the highest volunteer-to-staff ratios of any public garden, with volunteers providing an estimated 90 percent of the physical labor needed to maintain the garden and its collections.

Community support for the garden is cultivated by the staff, led by garden director Shane Smith, who actively encourages involvement by civic groups and invites community participation. The Gardens' nonprofit arm, the Friends of the Cheyenne Botanic Gardens, raises funds for the design and construction of new landscapes as well as for the volunteer program and staff training, and advocates for the Gardens at municipal budget hearings.

The Application

All prospective volunteers should complete an application form in advance of an interview so that garden staff can determine if the applicant is a good prospect. Equal employment opportunity statutes provide guidance on what may and may not be asked on the application and during the interview, but generally applicants can be asked about medical conditions or physical limitations that need to be considered for certain jobs.

Many garden websites include a link to a volunteer application. Some gardens use volunteer management software with electronic application forms that feed directly into the database for ease in sorting, tracking, and reporting.

The Interview

When a garden has a viable applicant, a personal interview is needed to get to know the person better and determine whether, when, where, and how to proceed with a volunteer placement. A list of questions and information to cover is a useful way to keep an interview on track. Initial phone or drop-in inquiries are an opportunity to prequalify candidates to determine if they have the time or interest for the positions available and, if so, to schedule an interview for a later date.

An interview can end with a placement, a conditional placement, or a decision that a placement is not possible at the time. In some gardens, a second interview with the staff supervisor of the position is necessary before the placement is finalized.

If there is no match and none anticipated, it is permissible for an organization to turn away a volunteer. Sometimes the reasons will be apparent: for example, the volunteer cannot commit to the required schedule or is not able to perform the necessary tasks specified on the job description form. Tact and diplomacy are critical. In some situations it is appropriate to refer the volunteer to other organizations in the community that are seeking volunteer assistance.

Screening, References, and Background Checks

Some states and municipalities require screening of all volunteers or only those in certain jobs, such as youth education program assistants. Potentially, volunteers could be subject to criminal record checks, sexual offender searches, and credit or driver's license history checks. The volunteer application form should include screening requirements, and the garden should budget for the costs of this increasingly common requirement

Placement

A new volunteer needs a temporary name badge and a handbook, the garden map and brochures, and schedules of upcoming trainings, orientation dates, and garden events. The volunteer should receive written confirmation of the assignment with the staff supervisor's name, when and where to report for work, and recommendations for equipment to bring or to wear. The staff supervisor should receive a copy of the confirmation and the applicant's contact information. The volunteer program manager should check with the staff member and the volunteer within a month to assess the suitability of the assignment and help iron out difficulties.

The Volunteer Handbook

A volunteer handbook contains all of the information needed by a new volunteer. Though much of the information may have been provided verbally during the process of recruitment, interview, and placement, the handbook gathers it all in one document. In addition to garden-wide policies and procedures, a handbook should contain a welcome from the garden director, an introduction to the volunteer program, the garden's mission statement and history, up-to-date facts and figures, and an overview of program areas and activities. At some gardens volunteers receive a staff directory when they receive a handbook.

Volunteer Training

Training volunteers can involve several steps, including orientation, garden-wide training, and departmental training, depending on the circumstances of any particular garden. If volunteers are recruited and placed continually throughout the year, the training steps may not occur in sequence.

Orientation

Orientation possibilities include a tour with specified content for newly placed volunteers or a program for prospective volunteers to help them decide if and where they fit into the organization. Whatever form it takes, it must provide volunteers with a higher level of information about the garden than they would get as a member or visitor, along with an explanation of why this information will be important to them as volunteers.

Training

A series of formal classes, presentations, and/or Web-based trainings for all volunteers provides the foundation of institutional information that volunteers need in order to be effective spokespeople for the garden. The department-level training may be done formally or informally and in many gardens is accomplished by on-the-job training. Because most volunteers will only be at the garden three or four hours a week, it will take them many weeks or even months to acquire the knowledge necessary to be an integral part of the institution.

Nancy White, Desert Botanical Garden, Phoenix, Arizona

The goal of Volunteer U is to appropriately train new volunteers and to keep volunteers learning and growing throughout their involvement with the Desert Botanical Garden. Volunteer U is offered in sixteen-week cycles twice a year. A printed schedule of classes with dates, times, and locations is developed each fall and spring.

The Garden defines training as classes required to perform a specific role in a volunteer program. There are twenty-two different volunteer opportunities, such as docents, horticulture aides, garden shop, and special events. Classes are developed by the staff to meet Garden needs and are taught by staff or experienced volunteers. Every department in the Garden uses trained volunteers.

The first required class for all new volunteers is How to Be a DBG Volunteer. This class, which includes fundamental

Garden information, volunteer policies, commitment and training requirements for volunteer programs, and customer service training, ensures that volunteers have the basic information needed to be successful. Volunteers then choose the program they would like to work in and begin taking the required training classes. For example, requirements for horticulture aide and docent include the foundation science courses Ecology and Plant Biology as prerequisites before specific horticulture and docent training. Other areas, such as special events or special exhibits, require less training.

Though some volunteers come to the Garden with a great deal of relevant education and life experience, they must still take all required classes. It is important that they are up-to-date on the most current information in each field to do their job well and provide accurate information to visitors.

Figure 8-5: As part of the Fairchild's Core Training Program, University of Miami professor Joanna Lombard teaches volunteers about the garden's historic landscape design.

Courtesy of Fairchild Tropical Botanic Garden

Continuing Education

Public gardens are like nature universities—they never run out of subjects for the continuing education of volunteers. Staff can use continuing education programs to keep volunteers informed about research and conservation projects, collecting trips, and other staff

achievements that have special meaning to the volunteers. Good training and quality continuing education classes keep volunteers informed, productive, and happy. Today's volunteers are lifelong learners. It is quite common to hear volunteers say, "No matter how long I've been here, I am still learning new things."

Figure 8-6: Basic horticulture classes are offered annually to all Fairchild volunteers. In addition to learning good gardening practices, the classes allow the volunteers to meet and interact with the horticulture staff.

Courtesy of Fairchild Tropical Botanic Garden

Figure 8-7: Marty Petillo, volunteer services manager at Olbrich Botanical Gardens, instructs new interns about working with volunteers. Classes cover everything from the basics of supervision to correcting performance problems.

Photo by Katy Plantenberg, courtesy of Olbrich Botanical Gardens

Training Staff to Work with Volunteers

Neither the volunteer program manager nor the garden's director should assume that all staff members will be good volunteer supervisors. While new staff will need mentoring and coaching, all staff members can benefit from formal training to improve their supervisory skills. At Olbrich Botanical Gardens, the volunteer services manager developed a series of classes for training staff supervisors; these are offered to staff and interns on a regular basis. The volunteer and internship coordinator at the Morton Arboretum conducts yearly staff training during which staff members are invited to share best practices with colleagues.

If formal training is not possible, the basics can be acquired by staff by researching the literature, attending conferences and workshops, viewing training modules, and speaking with staff at other gardens. Information can be shared at staff meetings, and articles can be circulated. Handouts can be prepared with helpful hints, such as never waste a volunteer's time; make sure volunteers have the tools, equipment, and information needed to do the job; treat volunteers with consideration and respect; never ask volunteers to perform tasks that staff members wouldn't do themselves.

Overseeing and Evaluating the Volunteer Program

Overseeing the program involves communicating with volunteers to update them about garden activities and volunteer-related news, spending time interacting with volunteers (also known as "management by walking around"), and keeping track of their contributions and hours. In small or emerging gardens with limited numbers of volunteers, tracking can be simple, but at the country's largest gardens, with between 1,000 and 2,000 volunteers, keeping track of them is a monumental task.

Record Keeping and Reporting

Maintaining a volunteer roster, volunteer records, and reports of hours worked are essential duties of the volunteer manager; the numbers of hours worked is the gold standard for measuring volunteer involvement. In 2008, volunteers at the New York Botanical Garden gave 84,000 hours; volunteers at the Missouri Botanical Garden gave 135,000 hours. These numbers indicate the extent of a garden's community support and show volunteers the size of their collective contribution. Numbers of volunteers and hours worked are benchmarks that are used in grant applications, annual reports, and presentations to members, donors, and the media. There are software

SUMMARY OF FAIRCHILD TROPICAL BOTANIC GARDEN VOLUNTEER HOURS FOR 2009

Education : Challenge, Discovery, Explorer – **4,715**

Horticulture: Aquatics, Arid, Butterfly, Cycads, Conservatory, Early-Birds, Flower Garden, Groomers, Heliconia, Nursery, Palms, Plant Records, Propagation, Plant Sales, Rainforest, Special Projects, Victoria Pool, Vine Pergola – **8,657**

Center for Tropical Plant Conservation: Archives, Conservation, Herbarium, Library – **8,139**

Visitor Services: Admissions, Information Desk – **5,024** Membership and Shop –**3,755** Tram and Walking Tour Guides, Shuttle, Host –**12,47**1

Festival and Events: Butterfly, Chocolate, Mango, Orchid, Ramble – **16,183**

All Other Areas: Development, Friends of Fairchild, Office, Special Projects, Training, Tropical Fruit, Trustees – **8,956**

Figure 8-8: The contributions of garden volunteers are recognized when the garden publicizes the number of hours donated and the scope of work performed.

Courtesy of Fairchild Tropical Botanic Garden

packages available for volunteer data management, but small or emerging gardens can begin with a spreadsheet that most software manufacturers will transfer into a package when their product is purchased.

Evaluating the Volunteer Program

Soliciting regular feedback from staff informally and via survey forms will indicate how well volunteers are meeting the garden's needs. Are staff members getting the quantity and quality of volunteers needed? Do volunteers need more training or better orientation? Do staff supervisors want training in managing volunteers? The answers will help program managers meet the needs of the garden and the staff.

Volunteers should be surveyed about the quality of their experience. Are volunteers getting adequate training, supervision, and feedback in their jobs? Are the necessary tools and information provided? What do volunteers like most and least about volunteering at the garden? Do volunteers feel recognized for their contributions? The answers can provide guidelines for program modifications that will lead to higher levels of job satisfaction and higher retention rates for volunteers.

Evaluating Volunteer Performance

At most gardens volunteers are evaluated informally by staff who oversee their work and recommend changes and improvements as needed, always with tact and sensitivity to the volunteer's feelings. When staff set standards and expectations in advance and provide training and adequate supervision, the need for formal evaluations is minimized. However, gardens should formally evaluate their guides, testing them on the accuracy of the information and the effectiveness of their presentation. New guides can be tested on both points during checkout tours given to staff or trained volunteers. Guides can also be required to take written exams on the material covered, and should be informed that they will be periodically evaluated to ensure continued accuracy and effective delivery. Volunteers who teach classes have to meet established criteria before the start of their teaching assignment and have their performance reviewed periodically by staff and by class members.

Recognizing, Rewarding, and Retaining Volunteers

Volunteers will remain loyal to and involved at a garden if they enjoy what they are doing, understand how their work contributes to the achievement of the garden's mission, and are supported in, recognized, and thanked for their role in the garden's success.

Staff can recognize and reward volunteer efforts on a daily basis with simple courtesies. Recognition takes place each time volunteers are greeted with a smile, when staff members show respect for their time by preparing for their work in advance, when they are sincerely thanked, and when they are treated with friendliness and consideration. It is important that staff members offer volunteers assistance when needed, inquire about a recent absence or a special event in their lives, and notice and compliment them when a job is done well.

Possible tangible ways to thank volunteers include:

- A newsletter to keep volunteer informed, recognized, and thanked

- Articles and pictures in the garden's magazine and on its website

- An annual appreciation and recognition event

- Celebrations of milestones in their service with pins, plaques, or certificates

- Opportunities for volunteers to serve as mentors

- Increased responsibilities or the opportunity to work on special projects

- Seeking their advice when planning activities, programs, and new volunteer jobs

Figure 8-9: An annual gift for the volunteers is a tangible sign of appreciation for their important contributions.

Courtesy of Fairchild Tropical Botanic Garden

- An annual gift such as a water bottle, tote bag, or T-shirt

- Regular or occasional snacks, beverages, or refreshments

- Birthday cards, personal thank-you notes

- Staff spending time with volunteers on breaks

Recognizing and rewarding volunteers benefit both the volunteer and the garden. The volunteers benefit from knowing their contributions have been recognized as worthwhile, and the garden benefits because recognition leads to retention of volunteers.

Summary

Volunteers can help public gardens increase the breadth and depth of almost every program area, but their involvement must be planned for and managed to be effective. The value of volunteers comes from the work they do, from their validation of the value of the garden's work and mission, and from their role as ambassadors for the garden, both within and outside the garden gates. How much value a garden gains from a volunteer program is directly related to the time it devotes to recruiting, training, managing, and retaining dependable, qualified volunteers.

Figure 8-10: Volunteers are a garden's best ambassadors. By greeting visitors and giving tours, volunteers make a personal connection with almost everyone who comes to the garden.

Courtesy of Fairchild Tropical Botanic Garden

Annotated Resources

American Public Gardens Association (www.publicgardens.org). Information on volunteer programs is available from the Resource Center and the Professional Section for Volunteer Managers.

Campbell, K., and S. Ellis. 1995. *The (Help!) I-don't-have-enough-time guide to volunteer management.* Philadelphia: Energize. Practical suggestions for team building.

Ellis, S. 1996. *From the top down: The executive role in volunteer program success.* Philadelphia: Energize. A comprehensive reference for organizational leaders.

Energize. www.energizeinc.com. Lists resources and provides links to information on recruiting, training, and managing volunteers.

Graff, L. 2003. *Better safe . . . Risk management in volunteer programs and community service.* Ontario, Canada: Graff and Associates. Detailed explanation of risk management issues.

Hands on Network. www.handsonnetwork.org. Posts volunteer opportunities online.

Independent Sector. www.independentsector.org. Provides statistics on volunteers nationwide.

McCurley, S., and R. Lynch. 1996. *Volunteer management: Mobilizing all the resources of the community.* Downers Grove, Ill.: Heritage Arts. A complete survey of volunteer management issues, including terminating a volunteer.

Nonprofit Risk Management Center. www.nonprofitrisk.org. Addresses current risk management issues.

Points of Light Foundation. www.pointsoflight.org. Links to hundreds of resources for volunteer managers.

Stallings, B. www.bettystallings.com. Links to numerous resources, including the twelve-part series *Training Staff to Succeed with Volunteers,* available electronically.

University of Delaware Center for Public Horticulture. www.publichorticulture.udel.edu/resource-center. Links to theses on volunteer management.

Volunteer Match. www.volunteermatch.org. Lists volunteer opportunities.

Volunteer Today. www.volunteertoday.com. Users may submit questions on volunteer management issues.

CHAPTER 9

Budgeting and Financial Planning

RICHARD PIACENTINI AND LISA MACIOCE

Introduction

Successful organizations focus on the bottom line—at least that was the mind-set and the way many businesses operated in the past. Recently, attention has shifted to the triple bottom line, such that organizations consider their ecological and social performance when accounting for their overall performance. While the purpose of this chapter is to focus on key traditional accounting methods and procedures, it is important for gardens to recognize and lead in the other two key areas of measuring overall performance. A focus on profits should not be taken at the expense of important social and environmental issues.

Being nonprofit is not a license to lose money. No organization, whether for-profit or nonprofit, can survive in the long run if it does not carefully monitor and control its income and expenses. It is also important to recognize that donors like to support winners. Gardens are more likely to be successful in fund-raising if they have a track record of carefully managing their operations. Careful attention to operating, restricted, and capital budgets is critical to success.

In this chapter we explain key terms and principles for accounting, budgeting, and monitoring the finances of an organization. A carefully crafted budget is the single most important financial document an organization can produce. The best budgets focus on institutional priorities, help set direction, and identify key areas of revenues and expenses. Success, however, does not end with producing the budget. Careful monitoring, reacting, and adjusting are the critical steps to success.

Why Budget?

Budgeting provides any organization, whether for-profit or not-for-profit, with a plan for the fiscal year or years ahead. The budget process should be an important part of the strategic initiatives and planning of the organization. Peter Drucker notes that "performance in the nonprofit institution must be planned. And this starts out with the mission. Nonprofits fail to perform unless they start out with their mission" (Drucker 1990). That being said, limited resources require the not-for-profit to set goals and forecast resources based on internal and external pressures, including the organization's mission, staff, board of directors, and donors, as well as changes in the economy, demographics, or politics (Oster 1995). Not-for-profit organizations also benefit from budgeting, as most entities are dealing with directives from a variety of constituencies, including users of their services, the organization's board of directors, governmental authorities, donors, granting agencies, and even the community.

Perhaps most important, budgets ensure accountability, not only at the organizational level, but at department levels as well. "Budgeting is an on-going process" (Dropkin and LaTouche 1998). It is important that a budget be evaluated on a consistent basis throughout the year. Variance analyses comparing budgeted amounts to actual results should be prepared and reviewed on a monthly basis at an organization-wide level to not only identify potential problem areas but also indicate where there may be successes. Based on these analyses, managers should be held to the initial departmental

Accrual method of accounting: transactions are recorded when the order is made, the item is delivered, or the services occur, regardless of when the money for them (receivables) is actually received or paid.

Budget target: level of expenses set at organization and department levels prior to the start of the budget process.

Capital budget: a plan to finance long-term outlays, such as for fixed assets like facilities and equipment.

Capitalization policy: the policy that defines the fixed assets and projects that will be capitalized by the organization. The policy includes information on the minimum dollar amount that can be capitalized, identification of useful lives of certain categories of assets and projects, and an outline of the method used to calculation depreciation.

Cash method of accounting: the more commonly used method of accounting in small business. Under the cash method, income is not recorded until cash (or a check) is actually received, and expenses are not counted until they are actually paid.

Fixed asset: item of value that will be used for an extended period of time and is not expensed in the year purchased. These items are capitalized in the current year, that is, recorded as an asset. The expense for a fixed asset is recorded over its useful life and is referred to as depreciation. Fixed assets are also referred to as property, plant, and equipment (PP&E) and normally include items such as land and buildings, motor vehicles, furniture and fixtures, equipment, and machinery.

Fixed expense: expense that remains the same regardless of the level of activity occurring in an organization.

Form 990: the Internal Revenue Service form that nonprofits use on a yearly basis to disclose financial information, including revenue, expenses, and assets.

Functional expense: expenses grouped into one of three categories: administrative, program, and fund-raising. Program services are mainly those activities that further the organization's mission; fund-raising expenses are the expenses incurred in soliciting contributions, gifts, and grants; and administrative expenses relate to the organization's overall operations and management.

Markup percentage: the percentage added to the cost of an inventory item to determine sales price. Marking up an item 100 percent doubles the cost.

Materiality: the significance of an item compared to the entire budget.

Open to buy: a financial model used by retailers to determine the proper levels of inventory to be kept on hand for the amount of sales expected to be generated.

Operating budget: a budget that identifies expected revenue and expenses over a period of time, typically a fiscal year.

Program supplies: items purchased for furthering the organization's mission.

Triple bottom line: also known as "people, planet, profit," it provides criteria for measuring an organization in three areas of success: economic, ecological, and social.

Variable expense: expense that fluctuates based on the level of activity incurred in an organization.

budgets and be asked to provide reasonable explanations for any variances. In short, budgets allow management "to measure and guide the nonprofit's immediate and long-term financial health and operational effectiveness" (Dropkin and LaTouche 1998).

Types of Budgets

Organizations may prepare operating and capital budgets on an annual basis. In conjunction with these budgets, the garden will need to evaluate the effect of restricted or endowment funds on its operations and programs.

The Operating Budget

The operating budget is the main focus of this chapter, as it summarizes an organization's day-to-day activities. This represents the total revenue and expenses over some period of time, typically a fiscal year, and could include revenues such as admissions, memberships, donations, interest income, and gift shop sales, as well as expenses such as salaries and benefits, plants, soil, maintenance contracts, program supplies, depreciation, and cost of goods sold.

The Capital Budget

For many organizations, the capital budget is as important as the operating budget. It identifies equipment and projects that the organization can record as assets rather than expenses in the initial year of purchase or completion. That is, the organization can capitalize the item or project and recognize the expense of that piece of equipment or project over its useful life through depreciation. The dollar value of items that should be capitalized may vary from organization to organization and depends upon the capitalization policy as well as the materiality of the projects to the garden as a whole. The capital budget for the fiscal year should list the items that the garden intends to buy or construct, the estimated cost of these items, and the source of the funds that will be used to pay for them.

When major changes to the operations and facilities of an institution are contemplated, a business plan should be developed to ensure that adequate revenues can be secured to offset increased operating expenses. Both operating and capital budgets can be affected by a variety of other funding sources. Monies received for restricted purposes or allocations from endowment funds should be considered as part of the budget process.

The Relationship Between Budgeting and Cash Flow

Although an in-depth discussion of cash flow is beyond the scope of this chapter, it is important to understand that the cash flow of an organization is affected by the budget. While one may immediately think that operating revenues and expenses that are projected in the budget automatically equate to cash inflows and outflows, this is not always true. For example, revenues that are recorded with related receivables do not have cash flow effect until the balance owed is received. Similarly, expenses that are accrued for a future purpose do not affect cash flow until payment of the invoice is complete. Therefore, items such as these have to be considered in the spread of the budget across the year, as they may affect cash flow in one month over another.

The capital budget also has an effect on cash flow. While capitalized items are not recorded in the income statement on which the operating budget has been based, there is a cash outflow at the time payment is made for the project or item.

In addition, the purchase of inventory for gift shops or cafés must be considered. While the cash outflow for these items occurs at the time of purchase, the budgeted expense for these items is the cost of goods sold. That is, the expense related to gift shop revenue is recorded at the time of sale, while the cash outflow for the inventory may have occurred months earlier when the item was purchased. Inventory levels and purchases should be monitored carefully and can be estimated using an inventory model such as open to buy.

Lastly, cash flow related to the operating budget can be positively affected by utilizing existing restricted grants or endowment funds.

Without the complete picture of the cash inflows and outflows of an organization, liquidity can suffer. While cash flow directly relates to the budget in many respects, other items out-side the normal budgeting process can negatively or positively affect it. As such, the operating and capital budgets must be reviewed in tandem. In addition, other items that affect cash flow, such as inventory purchases or the use of other funding pools, must be considered.

Tools for Budgeting

There are several tools that can be used to prepare the budget, including spreadsheet programs such as Microsoft Excel, software packages such as Blackbaud Financial Edge, Sage MIP, or Intuit QuickBooks, and outside professional assistance. Also, there are many options for both live and Web-based instructional courses on budgeting. These courses are often offered in conjunction with the software packages, provided for clients by the local certified public accounting (CPA) firm that prepares their audit, or given by independent entities. All of the tools described here can be used alone as well as in combination with each other.

Spreadsheets

Depending upon the size and complexity of the budget, a simple spreadsheet or series of spreadsheets may be all that is needed to document and monitor the budget. Detailed categories can be documented and linked to a final summarized spreadsheet, and advanced features in Excel such as macros and look-up tables may assist in performing actual-to-budget comparisons. Many times departmental budgets can be accumulated in an Excel spreadsheet and later exported to another software package. Because most packages do not offer Web-based budget entry for more than a few people, spreadsheets are an easy method of obtaining detailed budget information at another department level. It is important to note that spreadsheets may have to be in a certain format in order to be exported.

Software Packages

Although spreadsheets are useful, software packages offer more flexibility and reporting features. In many cases, budgeting is a module of a larger suite of accounting software that includes a general ledger. With these types of packages, the budget can be easily compared with actual results on a monthly, quarterly, and yearly basis. Budgeting software allows for budget information to be entered in detail by department, expense or revenue category, program, or other more detailed segment. As noted above, a spreadsheet may be used at a department level to gather budget information and import it into the software package. In addition, these packages often include a forecasting feature that will assist throughout the year in performing projections of final results based on certain scenarios.

Professional Assistance

Outside professional assistance is also an option for organizations that may not have an accounting professional on staff. Independent CPAs can offer their services for a fee to prepare the organization's budget and even set up a process whereby the garden can obtain the information and prepare the budget on its own. Another option is locating a professional who will assist in preparing the budget on a pro bono basis. The RSVP Senior Corps, a program of the Corporation for National and Community Services, is composed of retired individuals with a variety of skill sets who volunteer their time in organizations to perform tasks such as budget preparation. Lastly, state and local CPA professional organizations often have volunteer corps as well and can offer similar services.

The Budget Formulation Process

The overall budget process begins with setting priorities and goals for the upcoming year, identifying fixed and significant expenses, and formulating budget targets for the organization and for each department and program. A budget calendar should be prepared to identify a specific timeline with milestones for tasks to be completed by the parties involved in the process. Once priorities are set and the calendar is finalized, a budget kickoff meeting should be held for all parties that will have a role in the preparation of the budget to review the priorities, time lines, process, and expectations. After the initial departmental budgets are completed, a consolidated budget will be prepared and analyzed prior to being presented to the board of directors or other supervisory authorities for final approval. This process can take a few weeks to a few months depending on the complexity of the organization.

Planning, Priorities, and Goals

The budget process begins with planning and collaboration between the executive director or president of the organization and the department directors as to the priorities for the upcoming fiscal year. In smaller organizations, where a set hierarchy of personnel may not be in place, individuals at the staff level may also be involved in this process. In some organizations, the initial planning at this stage can also include the board of directors. It is important to establish priorities and goals before the budget process begins so that everyone is aware of the direction for the upcoming year and can plan accordingly. In addition, involvement of departments at this level creates buy-in and participation in the budget itself, leading directly to accountability by the departmental directors and staff. The priorities set at the beginning of the budgeting process can be as simple as what programs will be instituted, continued, or discontinued

in the upcoming year or as complex as planning to open a new gift shop or restructuring the staffing of the organization. All of the priorities have a variety of effects on the budget and need to be evaluated carefully.

Setting Revenue Targets

The second stage in the budget process is to set the overall revenue targets for the organization. There are three types of revenue streams for gardens: earned income, including admissions, café, gift shop sales, space rentals, and education programs; contributed income such as donations and sponsorships; and endowment or parent organization support. Many gardens are stand-alone nonprofit entities, while others are government-run or associated with a parent institution. For these gardens, the financial goal is to maintain a break-even budget. As such, until the most likely revenue sources are quantified, the expense portion of the budget cannot be calculated. In this part of the process, the garden needs to be realistic but conservative as to what types and amounts of revenue to expect in the upcoming fiscal year. Gardens that are heavily reliant on endowments typically will use a rolling three-year average to smooth out peaks and valleys in the investment results and add more consistency to the budget. Gardens that rely on government or institutional support need to obtain commitments as soon as possible to help set realistic budgets. It is also important to include "stretch goals" where appropriate. Stretch goals are important especially in terms of garnering operating contributions, grants, memberships, and even gift shop sales. The people overseeing these areas should be given goals that motivate them to attain additional revenue.

Earned income, such as that from admissions, gift shops, food concessions, facility rentals, and education programs, can be budgeted in a variety of ways. Start-up gardens may have to obtain supporting information from similar gardens, data from similar local venues such as zoos or museums, or statistics from local visitor bureaus to estimate the first year of operations in these areas. More established gardens that have a few years' attendance data can calculate the projection of revenue from admissions, gift shops, and food concessions much more easily. In addition, knowing the extent to which classes are attended or spaces are rented will assist in projecting the earned revenue of the following year.

Admissions Revenue

Admissions revenue is most easily projected based on an expectation of yearly paid and unpaid attendance. First, one must set the expectation of the full year attendance. The questions to determine this are: How much do we intend to grow or shrink? What events or exhibits will draw more or fewer guests in the upcoming year? Should we raise admission rates? How many times on average do our members visit, and how does that affect the calculation? The determination of full-year estimated attendance may be unscientific or very detailed. The calculation may simply be the prior-year figures plus a growth or shrinkage percentage, or it can be based on a trend over the past five years in every category of guests. Once the full-year attendance is set, it can be broken down into monthly and even daily projections based on prior statistical trends. The prior-year percentage of guests visiting by month or day as well as by category (adult, child, senior, or member) should be calculated, as well as the average price paid per guest. The average price, or price per capita, can be calculated by taking the prior-year admission revenue and dividing it by the number of visitors. Once these statistics are obtained, the following formula should be used to calculate the full revenue budget for admissions:

$$\text{Attendance} \times \text{Average Price} = \text{Admissions Revenue}$$

Gift Shop and Food Concessions Revenue

In the area of the gift shop or food concessions, the revenue projection is most easily done on a per capita attendance basis, which can be calculated as follows:

$$\text{Sales} \div \text{Total Attendance} = \text{Per Capita Sales}$$

If the garden attendance tends to be cyclical in nature, with different seasons and events that cause attendance to increase or decrease, this calculation is best done on a monthly basis, as there can be large fluctuations in per capita calculations throughout the year. Note that the total attendance number used here should be adjusted by those groups of guests that may be counted in attendance but would not frequent either of the locations. For example, school groups, facility rental clients, and education program attendees would probably visit the garden but not the gift shop or food concessions, and thus they should be excluded from the calculation.

Facility Rental Revenue

Facility rental revenue can be based on prior-year usage statistics or, if a garden books space a year or more in advance, on a combination of the expected revenue from booked events and prior-year expectations of the remaining open space. This is an area where stretch goals may be appropriate. Is there an opportunity for the manager or staff in the area to go out to "sell" the space? Do they attempt to sell additional services with current clientele? Are there creative ways to make more revenue by offering more services?

Education Program Revenue

In the case of education program revenue, the prior year may be the best indicator of class attendance. The rates charged for each class and the different pricing categories (members and nonmembers) should be reviewed at the time of the budget calculation. If the offering of classes and rates is basically the same for each class semester, the estimate may be calculated as follows:

$$\text{Rate Per Class} \times \text{Number of Attendees} \times \text{Number of Classes}$$
$$= \text{Education Program Revenue}$$

However, if the offering is significantly different, the types of classes and rate structures may need to be evaluated in more detail.

Membership and Contribution Revenue

Annual giving comes to the garden generally in two forms: memberships and unrestricted contributions. Generally, public gardens include memberships under the earned income category. The explanation for this is included in Chapter 11. For a start-up garden, these two categories will be difficult to estimate; relationships with members and donors have to be cultivated, and it may take a number of years before a solid base of these supporters is attained. With experience and a solid membership base, however, the estimate of revenue related to member dues or fees can be calculated. The tracking of people in each category of membership is very important. In addition, the membership levels offered and pricing in each level need to be reviewed to determine if any changes should be made. Unrestricted contributions are more difficult to ascertain in any organization due to a variety of factors, including economic conditions, donor sentiment, and local demographics.

Underwriting Revenue

Foundations, corporations and government entities can also supply a revenue stream, which may be in the form of underwriting and sponsorship of seasonal shows, special events, or specific programs. Many government entities also provide operating support for a variety of education-related programs or simply for the garden's day-to-day operations.

Cultural Tax Districts

Cultural tax districts are another source of revenue for gardens. These districts exist in cities throughout the United States, such as Pittsburgh (Allegheny Regional Asset District), Denver (Scientific and Cultural Facilities District), St. Louis

(Zoo-Museum District), Salt Lake City (Zoo, Arts, and Parks District), Cleveland (Cuyahoga County cigarette tax), and St. Paul (Sales Tax Revitalization). In these areas, a portion of specific tax revenue collected is allocated to cultural institutions, parks, and other related organizations to supplement their budgets. These districts were born of a variety of situations, including entities that cities could no longer afford to wholly support, financial crises of certain nonprofit cultural institutions in the city, loss of funding sources by nonprofits, and the fear that population decline in an area would cause cultural institutions to struggle. Each district has different and sometimes complex rules regarding the funding of the organizations in its district. In simple terms, the organizations are provided support through revolving loans or grants.

Supporting Entities

Oftentimes the garden may be affiliated with a university, museum, governmental unit, or separate nonprofit organization. As a result, the garden may be granted an allocation each year to support its budget or receive some type of free or reduced services. For example, in the case of the San Francisco Botanical Garden and the nearby Conservatory of Flowers in Golden Gate Park, two nonprofit entities, the San Francisco Botanical Garden Society and the San Francisco Parks Trust, assist in supporting each operational budget. The San Francisco Botanical Garden Society is very active in fund-raising and its support includes funding for positions as well as managing the volunteer and educational programs. In addition, the City of San Francisco provides a portion of the budget for the botanical garden as well as park patrol and utilities. In the case of the Conservatory of Flowers, the Parks Trust has provided assistance in certain projects and comanages the facility. There are many different types of supporting entities that may assist in funding the garden's budget. It is important that all sources of revenue and coverage of expenses are considered during budget preparation as well as evaluation throughout the year.

The Effect of Restricted and Endowment Funding

The operating revenue budget can be affected by outside funding for restricted purposes or funding allocations from endowment funds. Project support is often restricted by purpose and time frame. Purposes can range from coverage of salaries and benefits of staff in specific programs, interns, and capital projects to funds for certain areas of the gardens. However, this restricted funding can have an effect on the operating budget. For example, a local garden club may agree to give the organization $1,000 per year to fund the salary of a summer intern to care for a particular garden. Funds such as these are for a restricted purpose and must be accounted for separately from the operating budget so that the funds expended for the restricted purpose can be tracked. Would the intern have been hired regardless and paid as part of the operating budget? In that case, there may be savings in the budget that year. Or if it is known that these funds are recurring each year based on a written agreement, there is no need to budget for the expense in the operating budget, thereby making funds available for other purposes.

Endowment funds are another potential source of income, although likelihood of this funding source there is less for start-up gardens. Like restricted funds, endowment funds are often given to the organization for a specific purpose. However, the stipulation related to endowment funds is that the principal or original donation must remain intact while a portion of the appreciation on the funds can be allocated for use by the organization each year. The allocation is typically approved by the organization's board of directors and often follows state law as well. Although it can be more challenging to raise endowment funds, there are advantages to increasing the proportion of the budget that is underwritten by an endowment that provides support in perpetuity.

Identification of Fixed and Significant Expenses

After the revenue target has been set for the operating budget, the next step is to identify fixed expenses as well as other significant recurring expenses. Fixed and significant expenses include some categories of salaries and benefits, insurances, utilities, depreciation, cost of goods sold, and certain contracted services. Specific gardens may identify other expenses that are considered significant and should be evaluated at this point in the budget process.

Salary and Benefits

Salary and benefits are typically the single largest expense budget line item in most gardens and, as such, are significant enough to warrant specific analysis before any other expenses are budgeted. The first step in the calculation of the salary budget is the identification of all staff and their current rates. At this point, salaries that are variable based on level of activity should be quantified. For example, the garden may be able to staff the admissions desk and gift shop with fewer personnel on days when activity is low. Likewise, salaries of rental and education assistants may vary depending on the number of events or programs offered. The department directors in these areas should map out the full year of expected hours based on the priorities set earlier in the budget process. Once the variable hours are determined, the salaried and hourly staff that have consistent work schedules should be quantified. At this point, total wages per person and average expected merit and cost-of-living increases should be calculated. In instances where there are open positions that are expected to be filled in the coming fiscal year, a vacancy factor can be used to reduce the amount of salary budgeted for the garden. That is, if a certain position will not be filled until April and the fiscal year begins in January, the garden may decide to budget for only nine months of salary for that position rather than the full twelve months. Vacancy factors should be used only if there is relative certainty as to when the position will be filled.

Part-time and seasonal employees are a mainstay of many organizations. As such, a meaningful statistic for the budget is full-time equivalents (FTEs). Based on the total number of hours of all employees, this statistic is often more telling than the number of employees. The number of FTEs can be calculated as follows, assuming a typical workweek is forty hours:

Number of hours worked by all employees per year ÷ 2,080 hours per year = FTEs

Overtime can also be quantified and budgeted. While some organizations budget for overtime, others do not. Some overtime may be unavoidable, such as in gardens with short time frames for installing special exhibitions. In this case, the garden may want to quantify this amount and budget for it ahead of time for better control of the budget. In cases where only small amounts of overtime are expected, the organization may decide to budget it at a zero level as a means of tightly controlling staffing costs.

The benefit budget can be much more detailed than the salary budget. While all personnel typically receive a salary, not all staff may be eligible for benefits. Moreover, federal and state taxes that need to be paid by the employer should be quantified and budgeted at this step. Each staff member should be evaluated for all benefits offered and paid for by the employer. These could include health, dental, and life insurance, long-term disability, and pension contributions. For positions that are not filled at the time the budget is completed, it is best to be conservative and estimate that the position will carry the majority of the benefits at midrange levels. Another important item to consider is that human resource benefit eligibility policies often make staff ineligible for benefits until they have reached a certain number of days of employment. Lastly, the rising cost of health care and other benefits is a factor as well. The garden's health care provider or insurance broker should be able to estimate the expected increase in certain benefit costs for the coming year. Once these calculations are made on an employee-by-employee basis, the complete benefit budget can be quantified.

Insurance

Insurance costs are a significant expense that should be quantified early in the budget process. The garden's broker or insurance agent should be able to assist in estimating the inflationary factor that should be used to account for a possible future premium increase. At this time, consideration should also be given to the amount of coverage in force: Are there any special needs in the upcoming year that need to be added into the policy? Are there any items that can be removed? This review should be performed at least once per year.

Utilities

While utility expense may not be a fixed cost, it is typically significant. Utilities vary based on usage of the facility, the number of days or hours that the facility is open, the number of rental events, the weather, and other factors. Local utilities may be willing to negotiate new rates every few years, and this should be considered as the budget is prepared. The garden may also want to look at ways that these costs can be lowered through usage reduction. Utility usage trends by month along with a review of current rates should be evaluated for the past few years to determine the projected utility cost for the upcoming budget.

Depreciation

The projection of depreciation expense should be performed in conjunction with preparation of the capital budget. The depreciation expense on existing items can be calculated from a spreadsheet or database of the currently held fixed assets. Once the capital budget is completed, the items' estimated cost and useful life must be found. Depending on the depreciation policy of the garden, depreciation on items in the first year of life could be prorated based on purchase date, or a full year or six months of depreciation could be taken. After these items are quantified, the calculation should be completed and added to the depreciation expense of existing items. Accounting for depreciation in nonprofits can present a challenge, especially in organizations with a significant amount of capital improvements. In these cases, presenting depreciation in the operating budget can lead to large operating losses.

Cost of Goods Sold

Gardens with a gift shop or food concessions need to determine the cost of goods sold and cost of food and beverage using the estimated revenue and average markup percentage used to determine profit. For example, if gift shop products are marked up 100 percent and the gift shop revenue is estimated at $80,000, cost of goods sold expense would be estimated at $40,000.

Contracted Services

The garden must identify any contract services that will be paid regardless of the activity level. These contracts could include legal, accounting, security, software licensing and maintenance, and equipment leases and maintenance. Also, the garden should consider any new contracts that may be executed during the upcoming year for equipment or systems that will no longer be covered by warranty as well as for new services that will be outsourced.

Identification of Variable Expenses

After calculating the revenue budget and identifying fixed and significant expenses, the remaining expense budget to be allocated to departments should be calculated. Simply put:

Revenues − Fixed and Significant Expenses = Remaining Department Expense Allocations

The method used to allocate the remainder to each department to perform its detailed budget calculation is a matter of preference. It may be the percentage of each department's actual activity to total activity in a prior year, or it may be an allocation based on the known priorities for the coming year. The final amount that the department receives for the allocation of its remaining expenses can be termed its budget target.

The remaining variable expenses can be budgeted by department directors or staff based on the budget target and priorities that have been set. These expenses can include items such as plant and dry materials, maintenance supplies, tools, program supplies, marketing and promotion costs, travel and professional development, printing and publications, computer hardware and software, minor equipment, fuel, merchant and investment fees, postage and mailing costs, dues and subscriptions, and office supplies. Some consideration should be given to applying an inflationary factor to certain expenses. Depending on the expense category, the local economy, or other factors, the garden may want to increase certain expenses by 1 to 5 percent. Lastly, departments should be instructed to provide supporting documentation or explanatory information for each budget category.

This step can eliminate the need to ask questions later regarding differences discovered during monthly variance analyses. It also provides important information to the departments during the budget year as to why they may have increased or decreased spending in one category over another.

Often the department director may not have sufficient information related to certain expense categories at the time the budget is prepared. As a rule of thumb, as long as any department does not exceed its total yearly budget target, it is not necessary to budget every category exactly. The most important item to remember is that a budget is an overall guideline; operations change and emergencies arise.

Budget Evaluation Analyses and Meetings

Once the departments have completed their budgets, as shown in Table 9-1, several analyses should be performed. The first analysis is an overall review of the budget to determine if it breaks even. If the budget must be cut in order to meet the overall target, executive management should discuss the situation with department managers and staff and revise the budgets before any further analysis.

As presented in Tables 9-2a and 9-2b, the first analysis to be prepared should illustrate total expenses both by department and by expense category compared to prior-year actual results. This is a valuable tool because it allows for significant variances to be evaluated before the budget is approved. Often the comparison of departmental expenses in total will appear consistent year to year. However, when specific expense categories are compared to the prior year, there may be situations for which there are significant differences. For example, the category of mailing costs has a large variance when compared year to year. There may be a logical explanation related to the increase or decrease; however, the category should be analyzed to determine if a department overcalculated the expense based on expected mailings or if a department omitted an important brochure mailing by mistake.

After these analyses are performed, meetings with each of the departmental directors or staff should take place to review their budgets. At this point, executive management should review the budget and the supporting documentation and make any further changes to finalize the departmental budget. The departmental directors should then allocate the budget by month based on when they believe the expenses will be incurred.

In most gardens, a financial committee of the board of directors will review the budget in detail before it is presented to the full board of directors for final approval.

Table 9-1 Sample Departmental Budget

Daisy Public Garden
Departmental Budget 20XX

EXPENSE CODE ▽	0060-Horticulture	ACTIVITY CODE ▷ 003 Seasonal Show	044 Outdoor Gardens	047 Welcome Center	048 Children's Garden	051 Butterflies	052 Front Lawn/beds	099 Daily operations	Total
0119	Soil/mulch							$15,000	$15,000
0129	Chemicals		50					4,000	4,050
0139	Containers							7,500	7,500
0159	Tools & equipment		200					1,000	1,200
0169	Butterflies					28,000			28,000
0179	Safety							3,500	3,500
0189	Beneficial insects							10,000	10,000
0199	Other ground supplies		1,000					5,000	6,000
0221	Seeds						15,000		15,000
0230	Prefinished plants	25,000	3,500	2,500	5,000		12,529	6,000	54,529
0301	Telephone							240	240
0414	General office supplies							2,200	2,200
0438	Program supplies							2,000	2,000
0578	Printing							800	800
0599	Regular mail							50	50
0629	Uniforms							3,682	3,682
0652	Copier							50	50
0717	Training							3,600	3,600
0725	Auto							200	200
0829	Other professional fees							18,900	18,900
0838	Design	15,000							15,000
0841	Dues/memberships							348	348
0860	Subscriptions							221	221
0862	Permits/licenses							500	500
	Total	$40,000	$4,750	$2,500	$5,000	$28,000	$27,529	$84,791	$192,570

Budget Oversight and Financial Planning

The budget process does not end with the compilation of the budget itself. It is important to review budget-to-actual variances, forecast results, and evaluate certain programs, departments, and special events in terms of financial viability throughout the fiscal year.

Frequent Budget Evaluation

As variances are discovered throughout the year, it is not good practice to alter the original budget to accommodate new information. The budget should remain static, and the explanation of variances should serve as the support for why certain categories have experienced differences from initial projections. This does not mean that one should ignore variances in the budget.

Table 9-2a: Sample Operating Budget, by Department

Daisy Public Garden
20XX Operating Budget with Comparative Information

	Prior Year Budget	Prior Year Actual	20XX Projected Budget
REVENUES			
Earned Income			
Admissions	$1,458,657	$1,389,010	$1,242,617
Gift shop sales	795,630	679,852	651,746
Interest income	148,875	135,000	124,698
Special events	218,650	150,415	121,544
Rental income	505,222	556,788	684,521
Memberships	615,000	618,000	599,029
Education	172,255	175,622	178,950
Subtotal	$3,914,289	$3,704,687	$3,603,105
Contributed Support			
Grants: general operating	$56,000	$45,000	$50,000
Contributions	295,000	325,000	376,000
Other (special events)	-		-
Sponsorship/underwriting	300,000	542,000	295,000
Subtotal	$651,000	$912,000	$721,000
Miscellaneous			
Miscellaneous	$1,100	$950	$804
Subtotal	$1,100	$950	$804
Cultural Tax District Allocation	$2,000,000	$2,000,000	$2,000,000
TOTAL REVENUES	$6,566,389	$6,617,637	$6,324,909
EXPENSES BY DEPARTMENT			
Admissions	$328,985	$257,453	$265,177
Administration	1,405,195	1,395,687	1,585,021
Facilities	1,299,919	1,301,645	1,349,002
Food concession contract	1,000	25,487	51,634
Development	233,787	221,357	225,604
Education	474,118	395,687	381,752
Gift shops	604,213	579,845	508,780
Horticulture	1,116,835	998,621	972,596
Marketing	628,492	650,485	503,783
Membership	80,610	75,415	70,638
Rental	157,459	287,632	318,619
Special events	145,984	111,898	79,732
Interest	89,792	25,654	12,571
TOTAL EXPENSES BY DEPARTMENT	$6,566,389	$6,326,866	$6,324,909
Net Surplus/(Deficit) before depreciation and capital gains	-	290,771	-
Depreciation	$1,041,966	$899,635	$908,721
Capital gains	$0	$24,187	$0
Net Surplus/(Deficit) after depreciation and capital gains	($1,041,966)	($584,677)	($908,721)

Table 9-2b: (Continued)

Daisy Public Garden
20XX Operating Budget with Comparative Information

	Prior Year Budget	Prior Year Actual	20XX Projected Budget
REVENUES			
Earned Income			
Admissions	$1,458,657	$1,389,010	$1,242,617
Gift shop sales	795,630	679,852	651,746
Interest Income	148,875	135,000	124,698
Special events	218,650	150,415	121,544
Rental income	505,222	556,788	684,521
Memberships	615,000	618,000	599,029
Education	172,255	175,622	178,950
Subtotal	$3,914,289	$3,704,687	$3,603,105
Contributed Support			
Grants: general operating	$56,000	$45,000	$50,000
Contributions	295,000	325,000	376,000
Other (special events)	-		-
Sponsorship/underwriting	300,000	542,000	295,000
Subtotal	$651,000	$912,000	$721,000
Miscellaneous			
Miscellaneous	$1,100	$950	$804
Subtotal	$1,100	$950	$804
Cultural Tax District Allocation	$2,000,000	$2,000,000	$2,000,000
TOTAL REVENUES	$6,566,389	$6,617,637	$6,324,909
EXPENSES BY DEPARTMENT			
Salaries and benefits	$3,462,322	$3,010,251	$3,100,559
Facilities maintenance	88,600	119,675	115,300
Horticulture/plants	364,075	357,684	328,437
Utilities	294,523	452,675	471,955
Advertising and promotion	143,200	168,533	160,000
Insurance	129,000	148,600	150,200
Office supplies	25,350	24,222	23,425
Program supplies	216,622	198,666	187,530
Cost of goods sold	397,815	355,233	325,873
Printing	167,430	159,864	142,983
Postage/freight	74,257	66,999	54,885
Rental/leases/equipment	163,737	233,458	285,327
Travel /training/meetings	125,310	120,456	115,000
Contracted services	643,664	635,000	594,333

Table 9-2b: Sample Operating Budget, by Category

	Prior Year Budget	Prior Year Actual	20XX Projected Budget
EXPENSES BY DEPARTMENT			
Design	94,401	100,256	113,720
Bank fees	62,962	84,354	95,837
Dues/periodicals	16,530	19,497	22,513
Interest	89,791	65,888	32,732
Miscellaneous	6,800	5,555	4,300
TOTAL EXPENSES BY DEPARTMENT	$6,566,389	$6,326,866	$6,324,909
Net Surplus/(Deficit) before depreciation and capital gains	-	290,771	-
Depreciation	$1,041,966	$899,635	$908,721
Capital gains	$0	$24,187	$0
Net Surplus/(Deficit) after depreciation and capital gains	($1,041,966)	($584,677)	($908,721)

It is very important that the organization react to changes in the operating environment and make and document changes accordingly. Many times the results are controllable, especially in terms of variable expenses. Departmental directors must reevaluate the budget each month as actual results are received and identify problem areas where there are or will be significant variances (see Table 9-3). In these cases, the departmental budget must be reviewed to determine where there may be budget dollars available to cover potential problems. It is also important that the actual results are recorded correctly by category throughout the year, as they may be used the following year for evaluation of the targets for the budget process. In other words, even though the budget resides in category X and the actual expense is occurring in category Y, the item should be recorded in category Y so that actual results are accurate for current and future years' reference.

Variance Analysis

On a monthly or quarterly basis, each income and expense line item should be evaluated relative to the monthly and year-to-date budget along with prior-year results for the same period, if available. Significant variances should be evaluated, explained, and documented. The level of significance is a decision that must be made internally by professional accounting staff and executive management. The materiality of the category to the budget as a whole should be considered when evaluating variances. There is not a hard-and-fast rule, but level of significance is typically as simple as a percentage, say a 10 percent difference from the year-to-date budget.

Both positive and negative budget-to-actual variances should be investigated. Often variances are due to timing of the incurrence of expenses. For example, perhaps expenses related to plant materials were expected to be incurred in May but were actually incurred in June due to the placement of a late order. In this case, while there may be a positive budget variance in plant materials in May, it will not continue to be positive past that month. In another example, it may be that the plant materials were expected to be incurred in May, but the exhibit that they were to be used for was cancelled and will not be rescheduled. In this case, there is also a positive budget variance, but it will continue to remain positive in that line unless other plant materials are purchased in their place. In the case of negative variances, it is important to determine if the variance will continue to grow throughout the remainder of the year or if the amount of the variance will stay at a consistent level. For instance, a monthly expense on a maintenance contract was expected to be $500. However, because of the addition of another piece of equipment, the monthly contract amount was increased to $600. In this case, the variance will continue to build throughout the year at the rate of $100 per month. The department director should evaluate the remainder of the budget to ascertain if another budget line will not be used in its entirety so that the increased maintenance contract expense can be covered. In another example, a tool may

Table 9-3: Sample Education Department Budget

Daisy Public Garden Education Department
Income Statement & Variance Analysis
June 20XX/YTD vs. Budget

	Current Month Actual	Current Month Budget	Favorable (Unfavorable) Variance	YTD Actual	YTD Budget	Favorable (Unfavorable) Variance
Revenues						
School classes	$3,230	$3,500	($270)	$19,141	$18,506	$635
Summer camps	1,595	3,000	(1,405)	5,214	4,500	714
Adult class registration	7,807	8,083	(277)	51,201	51,167	34
Supplies fees	1,727	583	1,144	6,874	3,500	3,374
Symposium registration	-	-	-	12,105	10,000	2,105
Trip fundraisers	-	-	-	12,000	9,700	2,300
Total Revenues	$14,359	$15,166	($808)	$106,535	$97,373	$9,162
Expenses						
Salaries	$8,780	$8,605	($175)	$51,863	$52,302	$439
Payroll taxes	629	771	142	8,170	7,492	(678)
Benefits	1,424	1,424	-	8,544	8,544	-
Telephone	-	-	-	32	-	(32)
Office supplies	93	167	74	672	1,000	328
Program supplies	1,200	1,207	7	7,200	7,200	-
Brochures	-	-	-	1,950	1,250	(700)
Bulk mail	-	-	-	2,955	2,000	(955)
Regular mail	132	133	1	857	800	(57)
Meetings	-	33	33	119	200	81
Travel	500	250	(250)	500	750	250
Training	-	167	167	150	200	50
Auto	146	188	42	245	1,125	880
Instructor fees	480	800	320	6,707	8,805	2,098
Outside services	100	300	200	507	1,800	1,293
Bulk mail service	560	200	(360)	560	550	(10)
Dues/memberships	35	-	(35)	370	100	(270)
Bank fees	46	438	392	899	1,400	501
Total Expenses	$14,125	$14,683	$558	$92,300	$95,518	$3,218
Net Surplus/(Deficit)	$234	$483	($250)	$14,235	$1,855	$12,380

have to be purchased for a project earlier than expected, say in February rather than in March. While there would be a negative variance in the current month and year-to-date in February, at the end of March the actual results and budget would be accurate. However, if the tool was needed but not budgeted for at all, the negative variance would continue for the year, and again the department director would have to determine how to cover the unexpected additional expense.

Comparing current-year results to the prior year is another way to perform variance analysis. This analysis can provide insight into current-year operations and whether budget priorities are being met. This assessment allows for open dialogue concerning items such as why certain donations have not recurred, why attendance has increased or decreased in certain periods, or why salaries and benefits have increased more than was anticipated.

Evaluation of Programs, Special Events, and Departments

Another important set of analyses are profit-and-loss statements by program, special event, or department (see Table 9-4). Because expenses for programs and special events may cross over several different departments, it is important to accumulate all of the financial information to assess the true financial results. For example, a large plant sale may incur expenses in the departments of horticulture, education, marketing, gift shop, and administration—horticulture is purchasing the plants, education is producing the associated plant identification materials, marketing is promoting the event by obtaining advertising, the gift shop is recording the sales revenue, and administration is providing the mailing costs and incurring the credit card processing fees. If the garden is using software to process its revenues and expenses, expenses for an event such

as this can be tracked by assigning a code to the expense as it is processed through the system. Reporting can then be done based on that code to determine the financial results. If the garden is not using software, accumulating information in a spreadsheet is just as effective.

Expenses that tend to be overlooked in this process are the effort that staff put forth before, during, and after the event as well as overhead costs related to administration of the event. While the real expenses can be identified by invoices, staff time is an area where, without proper time tracking, there is no easy way to identify time spent on a particular event. Once the hours of the participants have been identified, the rate by person should be applied to the hours to determine the amount of wages that should be allocated to the event. In addition, a benefit percentage may be added based on an estimate from the prior year. For instance, if in the prior year 25 percent of

Table 9-4: Sample Profit-and-Loss Statement

Daisy Public Garden
Special Event Income Statement
June 30, 20XX

	Actual	Budget	Favorable (Unfavorable) Variance
Revenues			
Ticket sales	$57,875	$42,00	$15,875
Sponsorship	23,175	25,000	(1,825)
Total Revenues	$81,050	$67,000	$14,050
Expenses			
Salaries/benefits allocation	$2,986	$2,500	($486)
General office supplies	28	-	(28)
Program supplies	3,488	3,800	312
Print brochure	50	-	(50)
Stationery/invitations	3,400	3,000	(400)
Printing	147	250	103
Bulk mail	58	450	392
Regular mail	837	750	(87)
Equipment rental	7,150	7,000	(150)
Security	143	200	57
Professional services/catering	21,794	22,000	206
Performers	850	-	(850)
Bank fees	1,431	-	(1,431)
Total Expenses	$45,742	$42,950	($2,792)
Net Surplus/(Deficit)	**$35,308**	**$24,050**	**$11,258**

total salary and benefit expenses for the garden were benefit-related, this percentage should be applied to the calculated wages. Once this calculation is complete, the amount of salary and benefits associated with the event can be allocated as part of the financial results noted above.

Lastly, overhead must be allocated to a program, special event, or department. Overhead can include such expenses as insurance, utilities, and various administrative processes. Often the easiest way to find an overhead percentage is to determine the amount of organization-wide expenses that are administrative in nature. If the organization prepares a Form 990 or functional expense statement as part of its year-end financial statement process, the allocation of administrative costs will already be complete (see Table 9-5). However, if this needs to be calculated separately, expenses incurred throughout the organization must be reviewed and placed into the groupings of program costs, fund-raising costs, and administrative costs. Note that some expenses may span multiple categories. For example, mailing expenses may be related to program (class offering brochures), fund-raising (annual appeal requests), or administration (contract mailings). And in the case of salaries and benefits, it is likely that certain individuals' time should be allocated among the three categories. For example, the executive director is probably involved in all three activities, including planning exhibits (program), meeting with donors (fund-raising), and evaluating the organization's finances (administration). An estimate of this time needs to be made on a yearly basis. On the other hand, some expenses such as program supplies can be completely allocated to the program category, and the salary of the director of development will most likely be fully categorized as fund-raising expenses.

If the program or event is not breaking even or making a profit, serious consideration should be given to its elimination in the future. However, while a garden does not want departments to subsidize unprofitable programs and events, there

Table 9-5: Sample Functional Expense Statement

Daisy Public Garden
Statement & Functional Expenses
As of June 30, 20XX

	Program	Administration	Fundraising	Total
Salaries and related costs	$122,668	$17,423	$12,613	$152,704
Depreciation	13,670	23,606	722	37,998
Professional fees	540,378	28,333	12,016	580,727
Building and ground maintenance	1,062,012	150,841	109,195	1,322,048
Utilities	218,001	-	-	218,001
Advertising and promotion	186,183	7,347	1,282	194,812
Other program costs	5,698	5,367	464	11,529
Design	9,402	1,997	252	11,651
Equipment rental	4,854	1,869	-	6,723
Insurance	149,728	-	-	149,728
Printing and postage	176,414	1,153	5,469	183,036
Accounting and legal	13,172	869	86	14,127
Investment fees	85,899	-	-	85,899
Travel	60,055	7,662	9,133	76,850
Dues	243,226	34,757	70,961	348,944
Office supplies	66,248	2,098	403	68,749
Equipment	17,779	1,009	4,062	22,850
Interest	16	-	-	16
Total Expenses	$2,975,403	$284,331	$226,658	$3,486,392
Percentage of Total Expenses	85%	8%	7%	100%

may be specific reasons for continuing activities that are mission-driven or tied to community involvement initiatives.

Short-term Forecasting

The final piece of budget oversight and financial planning involves forecasting short-term and long-term results. A projection for the remainder of the year is typically more meaningful following completion of the first quarter of financial activity. Depending on the activity during those periods, it may make more sense to wait an additional quarter to complete the initial projection. For instance, the most significant exhibit that the garden hosts may occur at the end of the second quarter, and prior to that time business is typically slow. Waiting to project the remainder of the activity for the year is best left until after the second quarter so that the most significant activity can be included in the projection.

The importance of regular variance analysis and short-term forecasting should not be underestimated. If deficits are predicted, the sooner an organization takes action, the easier it will be to make adjustments in future months. For gardens on a calendar-year budget cycle, it is far better to implement minor budget reductions across the board in April rather than waiting until November to act, when drastic actions, such as layoffs, may be necessary to generate enough cuts to break even.

There are several methods of forecasting short-term or year-end results. Two specific methods include projecting the remainder of the year at levels initially budgeted and adjusting the remaining budget for known changes in operations. A pro forma example of the latter analysis is presented in Table 9-6. The first method involves taking year-to-date activity and projecting the remainder of the year at the level already budgeted. If the organization has been nearly on target for the year thus far, this may be all that is needed to determine the remainder of the year. The second method can be a hybrid of this, using the budget to project the remainder of the year but also adjusting for any known changes that will occur in operations in the ensuing months. For example, positions that will not be filled, programs that have been cancelled or reduced, and supplies that will not be purchased all provide opportunities to reduce the projection of expenses for the remainder of the year. On the other hand, there may be changes in priorities throughout the year, and perhaps it will be necessary to add a position or an additional maintenance contract. In such cases, the expense projection may have to be increased.

Revenue for the remaining months can be projected in a variety of ways. Current trends in attendance, either positive or negative, can be used to project admissions, gift shop, and food concession revenue. On the other hand, donations may be more unpredictable than other sources of revenue, and prior-year trends, if available, may not be a strong indicator for the remainder of the current year. It may be beneficial to have the person handling development efforts assist in the forecasting of such revenues. Overall, if prior-year information is available and the current-year trends appear to be consistent with prior years, a reduction or increase in the remaining months may not be needed. In general, the forecast must be reviewed and revised each month as the landscape changes. If it appears that the budget may not be met by the end of the year, open discussions between executive management and the departmental directors should occur to determine whether to cut expenses, use creative ways to increase revenue, or both.

Cash flow evaluation is an important part of the short-term forecast. While variance analysis and projection of financial results are important tools to ascertain the effectiveness of the budget, without a healthy cash flow the organization will not survive. As noted previously, not all revenues and expenses represent immediate cash inflows and outflows to the organization. For example, revenues with related receivables, cost of goods sold, and large accrued expenses will affect cash flow in periods other than when the revenue or expense is recognized. The garden should evaluate the amount of cash inflows and outflows each month and use the budget for the remainder of the year to determine the expected cash results for the upcoming time frame.

Long-term Forecasting

Long-term forecasts are most effective as an integral part of the organization's overall strategic plan. The strategic plan should address the mission statement, what makes the garden unique, and future plans for expansion or changes in programs. Organizations may elect to complete a high-level forecast for an additional two years as part of this process to ensure that future institutional priorities receive adequate funding. Forecasting beyond three years is not considered useful due to uncertainties and constant changes in the economic environment. Not as detailed as the budget process, this projection can be done using current-year results adjusted for inflation, attrition, or new positions as well as additions or eliminations of significant programs, increases in depreciation related to expansion, and expected attendance increases or reductions. This type of calculation provides a road map for future years and will assist in setting priorities for future budget processes.

Table 9-6 Sample Projection of Financial Results

Daisy Public Garden
Projected Financial Results – Year Ending June 30, 20XX

Revenues	YTD Actual	April Budget	May Budget	June Budget	Projected Year-End Results	Known Adjustments Through Year End	Revised Projected Year-End Results
Business office	$1,563,916	$208,242	$208,242	$208,345	$2,188,745	$0	$2,188,745
Gift shop	332.594	48,641	44,622	108,879	534,736	141,000	675,736
Admissions	761,719	83,023	72,450	217,052	1,134,244	-	1,134,244
Rentals	354,034	49,720	40,043	44,239	488,036	225,000	713,036
Membership	416,487	53,927	56,522	100,093	627,029	-	627,029
Development	228,070	39,963	159,463	321,463	748,959	(25,000)	723,959
Special events	72,375	30,423	6,113	11,313	120,224	12,550	132,774
Education	137,141	16,609	16,296	14,321	184,367	15,700	200,067
Volunteers	15,159	5,138	4,963	4,963	30,223	-	30,223
Projected total revenue	**$3,881,495**	**$535,686**	**$608,714**	**$1,030,668**	**$6,056,563**	**$369,250**	**$6,425,813**
Expenses							
Business office	$506,853	$43,680	$44,180	$58,744	$653,457	$250,000	$903,457
Human resources	99,651	15,311	15,536	29,318	159,816	-	159,816
Information technology	130,306	21,298	14,305	16,204	182,113	-	182,113
Director's office	306,610	29,037	31,007	136,145	502,799	(46,450)	456,349
Facilities	864,238	96,749	106,543	133,309	1,200,839	-	1,200,839
Gift shop	283,493	36,257	34,229	74,625	428,604	-	428,604
Admissions	148,711	17,550	18,180	27,096	211,537	-	211,537
Food concession contract	70,876	7,689	10,689	11,689	100,943	-	100,943
Rentals	176,897	21,185	22,802	28,945	249,829	101,564	351,393
Membership	59,133	7,775	9,521	10,921	87,350	-	87,350
Horticulture	697,522	93,339	99,196	74,766	964,823	-	964,823
Development	130,427	26,863	20,603	26,625	204,518	(32,000)	172,518
Marketing	476,962	26,131	62,043	64,708	629,844	-	629,844
Special events	74,176	13,983	21,839	7,930	117,928	-	117,928
Education	232,688	24,946	26,111	38,998	322,743	-	322,743
Volunteers	37,388	6,681	5,651	7,402	57,122	-	57,122
Projected total expenses	**$4,295,931**	**$488,474**	**$542,435**	**$747,425**	**$6,074,265**	**$273,114**	**$6,347,379**
Projected surplus/(deficit) before capital gains and depreciation	(414,436)	47,212	66,279	283,243	(17,702)	96,136	78,434
Capital gain/(loss)	80,093	-	-	-	80,093		80,093
Depreciation	820,930	106,426	106,426	106,423	1,140,205	(46,430)	1,093,775
After capital gains	**($1,155,273)**	**($59,214)**	**(40,147)**	**$176,820**	**($1,077,814)**	**$142,566**	**($935,248)**

Summary

Budgeting is a significant part of any organization's overall strategic initiatives and provides financial direction in the form of a plan for the current as well as future years. During the budget process, it is important to set overall priorities for the budget year, outline appropriate time lines, and calculate revenue and expense targets both at a department level and for the organization as a whole. Various analyses comparing expense categories and departments to prior years should be evaluated before meeting with each department for a final review and providing the budget for approval by the board of directors. However, the budget process does not end with final board approval. It is important to continue to perform variance analyses throughout the year to compare actual results to the budget as well as to forecast the expected financial results for the remainder of the year.

While there are many different tools for and methods of budgeting, forecasting, and planning, the most important point is this: a financially sound, thoughtfully prepared budget ensures accountability both organization-wide and at department levels. It also serves as an important tool for management and the board of directors to measure not only the financial results of the organization, but also its operational efficiency and effectiveness. While this chapter focused on traditional accounting measures, it is important to include the other key measures of the triple bottom line, the social and ecological, in planning and operating the organization.

Annotated Resources

Drucker, Peter F. 1990. *Managing the non-profit organization: Practices and principles.* New York: Harper Collins.

Dropkin, Murray, and Bill LaTouche. 1998. *The budget-building book for nonprofits: A step-by-step guide for managers and boards.* San Francisco: Jossey-Bass.

Epstein, Marc J. 2008. *Making sustainability work: Best practices in managing and measuring corporate social, environmental and economic impacts.* San Francisco: Berrett-Koehler.

Oster, Sharon M. 1995. *Strategic management for nonprofit organizations: Theory and cases.* New York: Oxford University Press.

Savitz, Andrew W., and Karl Weber. 2006. *The triple bottom line: How today's best-run companies are achieving economic, social and environmental success—and how you can too.* San Francisco: Jossey-Bass.

Western States Arts Federation and the Washington State Arts Commission. 2008. *Perspectives on cultural tax districts.* Proceedings from a seminar, February 11 and 12, Seattle, Washington.

CHAPTER 10

Fund-raising and Membership Development

PATRICIA RICH

Introduction

Would that money really grew on trees—then public gardens would not have to worry about fund-raising. No matter the sources of a garden's income, at some time virtually all gardens look for private dollars to enhance their funding mix along with endowment income, public funding, and earned revenue. Private philanthropy can be essential to fund basic operations or to provide the margin of excellence for programs and projects. As public gardens develop and grow, almost all add a development office. In larger gardens, the development office may have staff members who work on membership, proposals to foundations and corporations, fund-raising events, major gifts, capital campaigns, and other fund-raising programs. All fund-raising is a matter of working with people. This chapter will discuss where the funds come from and how gardens can access them.

Sources of Funding

Public gardens need multiple funding sources. Some have an endowment that provides a significant part of the revenue (e.g., Longwood Gardens). Some receive essential funding through the university they serve (e.g., Red Butte Garden and Arboretum, University of Utah). Others are public entities, part of a governmental unit from which they receive funding (e.g., Harry P. Leu Gardens, Orlando, Florida). And some exist totally on private funds (e.g., Bloedel Reserve, Washington). Most gardens have a combination of some or all of these funding sources. A mix provides a solid funding base in case one of the income streams is not consistent, gives a garden the possibility of increasing its programs and services over time, and provides opportunities to develop the garden's constituencies.

No matter the source, it is the relationship between the garden and the funders that is paramount.

Unrestricted Funds

Gardens raise two types of money, unrestricted and restricted. Unrestricted funds can be used for any needs. They often provide the basic operating revenue. It is this funding that pays salaries and keeps the lights burning. Unrestricted funds usually come from parent institutions (e.g., universities), government or taxing districts, annual giving from private donors, special events, earned income, and bequests.

Restricted Funds

Restricted money is for specific projects and programs. It may come from any source but is raised for a purpose. It can be the result of a request to an individual, foundation, corporation, or government entity. It is also the focus of capital campaigns. Ethically, and sometimes legally, these funds are restricted by donor intent. One question often asked of development officers is why they would want to raise restricted funds. The answer is that donors often give far more to restricted funds, such as those for a particular collection or project, than they will give as unrestricted gifts.

The garden's governing board has the power to establish board-restricted funds, which are monies that have not been restricted by donors. For example, board policy may be that all unrestricted bequests are put into the fund to support horticultural development, even if the donor did not specify this action. At a later date the board may vote to use the money another way, which is why auditors do not treat such board-restricted funds as restricted funds.

Public Funding

Public funding comes in many ways and from multiple sources. Creating and increasing public funding can be a significant revenue strategy for a garden. Most of the gardens in New York City (New York Botanical Garden, Brooklyn Botanic Garden, Queens Botanical Garden) receive some funding from the City of New York Department of Cultural Affairs. In some cities, the public garden is actually a unit of the city government, often in the parks and recreation department (e.g., Leu Gardens). In a few cases a special taxing authority supports the garden (see Chapter 9). Creating and increasing public funding can be a significant revenue enhancement strategy for a garden.

Indirect public funding is through an intermediary, a local, state, or federal agency that contracts with the garden for services. It can be unrestricted or restricted. Examples include federal sources such as the Institute of Museum and Library Services or the National Science Foundation. For gardens, the most likely projects that would be funded through a government grant are those related to education, science, art, environmental programs, and historic preservation. In the United States, a federal government website (www.grants.gov)

lists all of the federal agencies with granting programs. Many states and large municipalities have similar websites.

Private Funding

Private funding from individuals, corporations, foundations, and civic groups can be the foundation of a garden's finances or the extra funds that move the garden toward excellence. Each donor is unique; the challenge for the development staff is to find the right way to approach a donor at the right time and with the right proposal to gain the greatest resources for the garden.

Individuals

Individuals are the backbone of private dollars raised for a garden. They may begin their financial support as a member and move on to become a volunteer, then a major contributor, and then leave the garden a bequest. Individuals tend to be the most consistent donors and the garden's advocates in the community. For college and university gardens, the majority of individual donors tend to be alumni.

Corporations

Corporations are interested in public gardens as community resources. Some want access to the garden and its information for their employees. For some, a garden fits into their business strategy, such as supporting cultural resources where the company is headquartered. Others see public gardens as a way to enhance their "green" image.

Much corporate funding comes in the form of sponsorships for public events that bring visitors to the garden and special events designed to raise funds. The exhibition of artworks in glass by Dale Chihuly at a number of gardens raised major event sponsorships. The corporate name on an event, a program, or a building can be a good fund-raising opportunity for a garden and a strategic marketing decision for a company; for example, the Monsanto Center at the Missouri Botanical Garden is that garden's major research facility. Many corporations also have matching gift programs, through which an employee's gift is matched by the company.

Foundations

Philanthropic foundations provide funding for institutions and programs in which they have an interest. Family foundations are often created by people to ensure that some of their wealth is used to benefit society. Family foundations that are still managed by the family should be viewed as individual donors. Corporate foundations are usually viewed as corporate donors. Typically, most foundation support for public gardens is directed to outreach efforts, educational programs, conservation programs, or scientific research.

To identify potential funders and their specific requirements for grants, organizations conduct prospect research using the Internet and tools created by the Foundation Center, a national organization that provides a directory of private philanthropic and grant-making foundations (www.foundationcenter.org). Some public and university libraries provide Foundation Center materials and offer resources for nonprofits, including Internet access to a variety of databases helpful in locating potential funders and training in how to use the materials.

Civic Groups

Many civic groups, including garden clubs and Rotary clubs, raise funds from members and events and make grants to organizations that provide the services they support.

Fund-raising in a Garden

Fund-raising is both the effort to make certain the garden will have the financial resources it needs and the way to build an identifiable constituency. At its core, the purpose of fund-raising is to help the garden fulfill its mission. Having supporters gives the garden significance in the life of the community.

Fund-raising is about relationships ("people give to people"), which take time to develop. It is incumbent upon the executive director and the board chair to build a culture in which all staff and board members nurture relationships with existing and potential donors—in fact, with everyone who comes into contact with the garden.

The Board

The board's fiscal responsibility includes fund-raising, and each member of the board has a responsibility to make donations to the garden. Some boards set a minimum gift per member or an expected total giving level for the board as a whole.

Many public garden boards have a development committee that helps to identify and open doors to potential donors, works to cultivate donors by connecting them to the garden, and along with the staff solicits gifts. Many boards urge their members to give gift memberships to family and friends. This is an excellent strategy for identifying individuals with higher-level giving capabilities. The board also adopts fund-raising policies, one of which should be a gift acceptance policy that defines acceptable gifts, including cash, securities, land, types of planned gifts, and types of in-kind gifts. There should also be a gift recognition policy about how gifts at different levels will be acknowledged.

The Staff

The garden's executive director plays an active role in development by soliciting gifts, interacting with donors, and in general serving as the garden's public face. He or she also needs to develop close relations with each member of the board. It is the job of the development staff to implement and evaluate fund-raising programs, work with the director and donors, and engage the board and volunteers in meaningful and appropriate ways. This staff must also work closely with the executive director and other program directors to fully understand the priorities of the organization.

For a serious commitment to fund-raising, a garden should have, at a minimum, a development director and an administrative assistant. The membership program and the development program should be in the same office. The development director writes the development plan, implements all of the elements of the plan, and establishes relationships with members and donors. As the program grows, a membership manager becomes essential, as does a special events manager. Sometimes communications and marketing functions are also included in the development office. The size of the staff depends on the size of the program. At colleges or universities, the garden's fund-raising staff typically works closely with central alumni affairs and development staff.

Development Plan

The first step in fund-raising is to create a development plan. With a plan in place, development efforts are focused, efficient, and effective. The plan includes goals and measurable objectives, which become management measures for development, and a calendar. The basic steps in the creation of a plan are outlined below.

1. Create a membership and development planning committee. The committee should include development staff and board development committee members. It is important to include the board members who will help implement the plan.

2. Review the garden's funding history: the prior three years of annual giving, parent institutional support, public funding, corporate/foundation support, enterprise income.

3. Develop a SWOT (strengths, weaknesses, opportunities, threats) analysis:

   a. Strengths (internal): What does the development department do very well (e.g., implement events)?

   b. Weaknesses (internal): What might the department do better (e.g., record keeping)?

c. Opportunities (external): What could the department take advantage of (e.g., the public's interest in all things green)?

d. Threats (external): What might have a negative impact (e.g., the economy)?

4. Establish goals (major accomplishments) that flow from the SWOT analysis and recommendations (e.g., increase membership by a certain percentage).

5. Develop SMART (specific, measurable, achievable, results-oriented, time-determinate) objectives for each goal—for example, gaining 500 new members through on-site sales by December 31 is the responsibility of the membership manager (Seiler 2003).

6. Create action plans for each objective: how will this be accomplished?

7. Write the plan, including all of the above.

8. Prepare the budget, including both revenue and expenses.

9. Construct a calendar, making certain that the workflow is achievable.

10. Gain approval from the director and the development committee.

11. Work the plan, implementing all of the activities.

12. Evaluate.

Role of Technology

A garden must keep records to be successful at fund-raising. Database software is the fundamental tool for the department. To reconnect with previous donors, it is necessary to have contact information, know how much they gave, when they gave, and why. All of this can be maintained in a database. Software systems can indicate when membership renewals are due, generate thank-you letters, report and track grants, and record major donor cultivation efforts, special events, and more. Fund-raising software systems are available for purchase or lease and fit any size garden.

The Giving Cycle

The development process is known as the "giving cycle" and has five components: the case statement, donor identification, cultivation, solicitation, and recognition.

Case Statement

The case statement conveys to potential donors the impact of their gift. It includes the rationale for the project or program, its

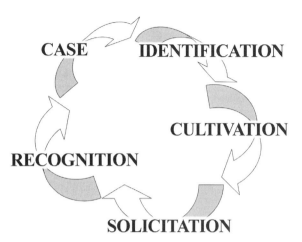

THE GIVING CYCLE

Figure 10-1: The giving cycle.

importance to the community, and how it will be implemented and evaluated. Successful case statements connect with the values of potential donors and get them excited about supporting the garden or a particular initiative. They are used in proposals to foundations and corporations and as the basis for printed pieces to hand to donors. There is often a case statement for the garden as a whole and separate ones for individual projects and programs.

CASE STATEMENT CHECKLIST

Is your case statement effective? Does it . . .

- Describe a worthy cause?
- Show a genuine need?
- Provide a solution for meeting the need?
- Contain facts that make the case?
- Demonstrate that the organization has a proven record?
- Show the impact of the donor's gift?
- Have a positive feel?
- Appeal to both the head and the heart?
- Have a sense of urgency?
- Do all of this briefly?
- Portray the situation in a way that is easily remembered?

Donor Identification

Anyone who has a connection to the garden is a potential donor. In the case of college and university gardens, all alumni should be considered potential supporters. Besides their time and expertise, board members should also donate to the garden. If board members, those closest to the organization, are not willing to give, why should anyone else? Some funders now ask how many board members donate. Public and private funders look to the percent of board participation as a sign of commitment to the organization. The senior staff at the organization should also consider contributing. The development director and executive director can provide examples by making the first gifts. Requests should be made without any pressure, and without identifying any specific amount.

High on the list of those who should be solicited for gifts are the garden's volunteers. Fund-raising research (Havens, O'Herlihy, and Schervish 2006) shows that volunteers are one of the groups most likely to support the organization. In addition, casual visitors are sometimes willing to support the garden. To solicit those gifts, gardens provide donation boxes at the entrance and other locations. Those who come to educational programs or attend special events should be encouraged to become members and included on lists of potential donors. Finally, new donors can be solicited through direct mail, usually in appeals for membership.

Cultivation

Cultivation is a garden term with an analogous meaning in fund-raising. It includes all activities and contacts with potential donors that lead to their involvement in the garden and interest in supporting its work. Existing donors are also cultivated in hopes that they will increase their level of giving. Examples of cultivation methods include personal letters (or emails); personal phone calls from the development officer, director, or board members; personal visits to the potential donor; invitations to events; plant information services and plant giveaways; and garden tours.

The level of cultivation is often proportional to the giving potential of the individual or family being cultivated. For major donors, the executive director and development director may have multiple contacts over several years before a gift is requested.

Solicitation

The main reason people give is because they are asked. People give to public gardens because gardens are a community resource,

WHY PEOPLE GIVE

They . . .

- Were asked
- Believe in and understand the cause or mission of the organization
- Have had a personal experience with the organization
- Want to support an organization that friends support
- Believe the organization is well managed
- Feel satisfied and find self-fulfillment through giving
- See the results of the organization's work
- Appreciate the way in which they were thanked—they feel cared for
- Receive a tax deduction

they love plants, they support environmental and conservation programs, they take education courses, and because gardens are beautiful places where they enjoy quiet walks and the interesting events that bring them back year after year.

Solicitation is the request for a gift, but involved in that request is what the Fund Raising School (2002) calls a "ladder of effectiveness" (see Figure 10-2). How a gift is solicited depends on the size of the gift, the relationship of the donor to the garden, and the program for which the gift is being solicited. For acquiring new or renewing current members, direct mail is often used. For donor renewals and thank-yous, the telephone is often effective. For foundations and corporations, the ask usually comes in the form of a written proposal. For significant gifts, personal solicitation is the most effective, but each garden has to decide what it will consider a major gift, as the scope and needs of the organization grow.

Technology also has a role to play in solicitations. Every website should be able to take memberships and donations. While email appeals seldom bring in large gifts, electronic media may be a cost-effective way to recruit first-time members and contributors, especially those in younger age groups. It is now also possible to cultivate and solicit donors with social media. Methods such as Twitter have proved helpful in generating attendance at events.

Acknowledgment

For each gift, acknowledgment is essential. Basic acknowledgment is a thank-you letter, but donors of major gifts should receive an immediate phone call. The garden will need to

- Personal: face to face
  - Team of two
  - One person

- Personal letter (on personal stationery)
  - With telephone follow-up
  - Without telephone follow-up

- Personal telephone
  - With letter follow-up
  - Without letter follow-up

- Personalized letter/Internet
- Telephone solicitation/phonathon
- Impersonal letter/direct mail/Internet
- Impersonal telephone/telemarketing
- Fundraising benefit/special event
- Door-to-door
- Media/advertising/internet

Figure 10-2: The ladder of effectiveness.

Fund Raising School 2002

furnish a tax receipt listing the precise size of the gift for tax deduction purposes. For gardens associated with colleges or universities, the parent organization will issue this receipt, and the garden should then send an acknowledgment with no mention of gift value.

Recognition

Recognition differs from acknowledgment in that it recognizes the name(s) of the donors or their designees. Common recognition tools include listing donors in the newsletter, annual report, or on the website. For large gifts, especially capital campaigns, rooms, buildings, or gardens are named for the donor. Endowment donors are often recognized in the naming of programs or positions. Many gardens also have programs through which donors may memorialize or pay tribute to a loved one by naming a tree, bench, or other object.

Fund-raising Programs

Fund-raising programs are the constructs around which the development program is created. The garden decides which programs to initiate and implement. A mature fund-raising department will have multiple programs. A new garden will start with a few and add new ones as programs build. While

new gardens often begin with a capital campaign to build the site, it is critical to start a membership program at the same time so that operating funds are available to implement programs and so that the organization will have contact information allowing future communication with this valuable pool of potential donors, volunteers, or advocates.

Membership

Membership is the entry level for identifying the garden's constituencies and building a base for support, education, and advocacy. When a garden needs community support, a membership base can be very useful. The members become the donor base for fund-raising activities, classes, and other programs. A well-run membership program brings net revenue to the garden. That revenue is unrestricted, making it particularly helpful (Rich and Hines 2002).

Because membership is the entry point, it is viewed as the base of the pyramid of giving, which shows the natural progression for many donors (Greenfield 1991). An entry-level member will often be asked to upgrade after two or three years. Entry-level members are more likely to be value members who say, "What do I get for my dues?" rather than, "I just want to help the garden in its mission." As described in Chapter 11, memberships are usually considered a form of earned income. A percentage of members will become part of a donor club with higher levels of membership. In this way, gardens are able to identify potential donors for major projects, such as a capital campaign. Having membership as an integral part of development facilitates internal communication and prevents competition between membership and fund-raising departments over individuals who support the organization.

Gardens sometimes have separate friends groups with their own nonprofit legal designation. Friends or member groups often do fund-raising for the garden. But issues arise when the garden's needs and what the friends want to fund are not the same. If the friends group is separate, then the garden must work diligently to develop a strong relationship with good communications. To ensure close coordination and mutual respect, it is often advisable to have the garden's executive director as a member of the friends group's board.

How to Develop a Membership Program

Membership is an exchange between the supporter and the garden. What will the garden offer? Free admission? Discounts? The American Horticultural Society offers a reciprocity program that allows members of one garden to gain free or reduced admission and/or reduced prices in gift shops at other

DONOR PYRAMID OF GIVING

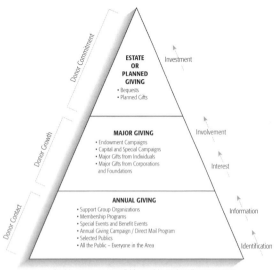

Fund-Raising, James M. Greenfield, copyright ©John Wiley & Sons 1991.
Reprinted by permission of John Wiley & Sons, Inc.

Figure 10-3: The pyramid of giving.

participating gardens. Membership programs are typically structured with levels of giving and more benefits at higher levels. Benefits should not negate net revenue. It is useful to look at other local museums as well as other regional and national gardens before deciding on a benefit structure. Table 10-1 shows a sample membership structure.

Membership Acquisition

The major ways to solicit memberships are through on-site sales, direct mail, garden publications, and the website. Gardens associated with a college or university may also acquire gifts and members through the campus phone-a-thon or phone bank. Listing the garden as a campus giving designation and volunteering to help with training of callers can be cost-effective ways to recruit students, faculty, staff, and alumni to give and become members.

Direct mail has long been a major method of membership and acquisition, and many gardens continue to use it. It can be a small endeavor, with letters sent to the friends and colleagues of board members, or very large, using purchased or exchanged lists (from magazines or other cultural institutions, depending on resources and the community). Before embarking on a major direct mail campaign, gardens should consult professionals in the direct mail field.

Offering memberships on-site is an opportunity for all gardens, no matter the size. On-site sales are becoming major acquisition points. This includes having membership brochures/applications at the reception desk, in the garden shop and café, and at events. The strongest selling location is usually the entrance to the garden. At Garvan Woodland Gardens of the University of Arkansas, which opened in 2001, volunteers staff the membership desk during the busiest times. The Gardens now has 3,300 members, with on-site acquisition and renewal. With a very small budget, one staff person, and a lot of volunteers, it is able to promote its program with great success. The Chicago Botanic Garden (CBG)

Table 10-1: **Sample Membership Structure**

	Member	**Friend**	**Contributor**	**Sponsor**	**Silver**	**Gold**	**Platinum**
Dues	$50	$100	$250	$500	$1,000	$2,500	$5,000
Newsletter and special email announcements	Yes	Yes	Yes	Yes	Yes	Yes	Yes
Admissions per visit	4	8	8	8	Unlimited	Unlimited	Unlimited
Discount in shop	10%	10%	10%	10%	10%	15%	15%
Discount for classes	10%	10%	10%	10%	10%	15%	15%
Discount for events		10%	10%	10%	10%	10%	10%
Early registration for classes			Yes	Yes	Yes	Yes	Yes
One garden publication				Yes	Yes	Yes	Yes
Invitations to special events					Yes	Yes	Yes
Tour and dinner with the director						Yes	Yes

acquires more than 60 percent of its members at a membership booth at the main public entrance. With a membership of 50,000, CBG has the resources to staff the booth during all open hours. The booth serves as a focal point for answering questions as well as acquiring new members and renewing current ones.

Membership Activities

Membership activities are opportunities for member cultivation. Regular communication keeps members informed, interested, and involved. Gardens post news on their websites and send out periodic printed and electronic information, including newsletters, listings of educational offerings, program materials, and invitations to events, some limited to members only. In addition to member participation in the garden's normal activities, some gardens have special horticulture education classes for members only. Others allow members to register early for popular classes. Still others have events that encourage use of the grounds. The Missouri Botanical Garden has a Rose Evening for members only when the roses are in bloom.

Members also need recognition, which can be through a "thank you for joining" packet complete with a membership card, a list of upcoming events, and an opportunity to volunteer. Members can be listed in the newsletter, in the annual report, and on the website. As the program grows, print recognition often becomes limited to donor club members. While a few people really do want to remain anonymous in their giving, and this should be scrupulously respected, most can't be thanked enough. Even those who don't want their names listed may enjoy being thanked. Stewardship through calls, visits, and letters is very important.

Donor Clubs

Because a membership program brings in a relatively small percentage (10–20 percent) of the funds needed by the garden to operate and move toward excellence, it is very important for the organization, especially the development director, to focus cultivation efforts on those individuals who have the greatest potential to make major gifts. Typically, 10 percent of the members give 90 percent of the money.

Donors who make large contributions should be recognized with membership in the appropriate major donor club. While these members receive benefits, their gifts far exceed the value of the benefits. Benefits such as personal tours, dinners, and special lectures are important means to both recognize members of these groups and bring them closer to the garden.

Corporate Memberships

Some larger gardens have a corporate membership program. The levels for these gifts tend to be higher than for basic membership and sometimes have only one or two levels with very high-level giving. Benefits can include admission for employees, special receptions for employees, or educational programming at the work site. At higher levels, opportunities such as free or discounted rental of facilities can also be a benefit. For the corporation, simply being associated with a green organization is often an added benefit.

Annual Giving

Annual giving consists of those fund-raising programs that bring in donations each year and provide basic funding, often unrestricted. Annual giving can be in response to direct mail (especially at year end), donation envelopes inserted in newsletters, email appeals, tribute and memorial appeals, and annual special events. Some donors give once a year; some give to multiple fund-raising appeals. Many gardens will target annual giving appeals at individuals who provided gifts in the previous year but not in the current year.

Second Gift from Members

At gardens, the first gift in the year is usually for membership, but members can and should be asked for other gifts during the year in response to a special solicitation, often a year-end appeal. Members may also give to a special project appeal, a fund-raising campaign for an identified project, such as the renovation of a garden area.

Tributes and Memorials

Every garden should have a tribute and memorial program through which individuals can make a gift in honor or in memory of someone. With its sense of renewal and beauty, a garden is ideal for this type of gift. Typically, these gifts are solicited by the family rather than by the garden itself (e.g., "In lieu of flowers contributions may be made to Lovely Garden"), or the family provides the entire expected gift. The garden should send note cards to the honoree or the family of the individual being remembered. Tributes need timely acknowledgment through the newsletter, website, and other means.

Many gardens recognize larger gifts in this category with plaques on benches or walls, bricks in sidewalks, or tagged trees or other plant material. The use of plants as memorials needs to be carefully handled so that staff can quickly find the plant on the grounds and donors can be informed when the plant material is no longer there (e.g., the tree dies) or the memorial tag is moved to another plant. The expected giving levels for memorial and tribute programs vary greatly from garden to garden, as does the length of time for which the recognition is maintained. Typically, gardens that offer perpetual name recognition and a commitment to replace the tree or object as necessary require the highest-level gifts.

Benefit Events

Virtually all nonprofits hold special events, which can be good ways to garner publicity, new participants, and some funding, but they are enormously time-consuming, and if time is considered, they often have a low return on investment. In addition, many special events can take a garden away from its mission and exhaust already overworked staff. Gardens should set realistic limits on the number and scale of special events staff can handle each year. Board members frequently think they are helping by proposing additional events, but staff hours required are usually many times more than board members recognize. Finally, special events should be considered "friend raisers" rather than fund-raisers, at least in the short term.

Many gardens hold gala dinners that become major social events in the community. The cost to attend is often significant.

The evening sometimes includes entertainment, awards, or an auction. Much depends on the garden, the availability of volunteers, and the philanthropic nature of the community. The most successful benefits are those with significant volunteer involvement, because volunteers can spend the time necessary to make the event successful and they will encourage their friends and colleagues to attend.

Events usually have multiple streams of income—ticket sales, table sales, sponsorships, purchases (i.e., auctions or sales), and donations. Sponsorships tend to be the greatest income generator. These can come from corporations, advertising, or individuals.

The event should include information about the garden. Whether it is a short talk, a video, signs, or a take-home favor with a brochure, there needs to be a way to instill the garden's mission into the event. The development department should follow up with participants through phone calls to large contributors, thank-you letters to everyone, and the addition of all participants to the next mailing for membership. On-site sales of membership during a large event (if appropriate) are effective.

CASE STUDY: SPECIAL EVENT—BEST OF MISSOURI MARKET

In 1991, volunteers from the Members Board of the Missouri Botanical Garden created the Best of Missouri Market, a yearly event held in October to raise funds and to increase attendance. It has been an enviable success. About 130 vendors who offer food, plants, and garden-related products and fine crafts are invited to participate. Vendors pay a flat fee of $350 for a single booth and the opportunity to sell to 22,000–27,000 shoppers in two days. The vendors come from Missouri and the metro southern Illinois area. They are rotated so that there are at least thirty new ones each year, giving attendees a reason to return. A member benefit is the opportunity to come early the first morning to be among the first shoppers and to enjoy coffee and pastries donated by local companies.

Member Board volunteers serve in major positions for the market. The chairs find, invite, and contract with vendors from across the state. Other volunteers sell ads in the market's directory. Aided by staff, volunteers garner sponsorships. More volunteers help with all the necessary jobs for the two days of the event.

The event began with one large tent filled with vendors and has grown to four. There is a food court in another area of the Garden. Deep in the Garden are children's events, including milking a cow, decorating pumpkins, and planting a seedling. A local hospital staffs a tent with child-friendly crafts and a pediatrician to answer parents' questions. The master gardeners make

fresh apple cider and talk to visitors about their program. The Garden's plant doctor is also on call.

The market is a major opportunity for people to join and current members to renew. Member admission is discounted, while all others pay a higher fee. The Garden finds that a significant number upgrade their membership to bring extra guests to the market. The market processes more than 1,000 memberships during the two days. With membership, vendor fees, sponsorships, the directory, and other sales, the net revenue is in the range of $250,000. The presenting sponsor is a local grocery chain. The volunteers lead this event. Two staff members, the membership director and an administrative assistant, help with coordinating all of the logistics and other Garden-related work and process vendor contracts.

What are the outcomes? Funding, of course. Another has become great collaborations with other organizations. Missouri Agri, part of state government, has as one of its goals encouraging small business. It helps sponsor the market because a number of vendors who started at the market have gone on to become flourishing businesses. The Bee Keeper Association has a demonstration area. The Girl Scouts volunteer. And in the community, the Shaw Neighborhood Association (from the Garden's own neighborhood) started its art fair to coincide with the market to take advantage of the crowds.

Capital Campaigns

Capital campaigns are major fund-raising campaigns that usually begin with a large building or garden project and take three to five years to complete. Funds for programs as well as endowment donations can be included. Once the needs are set, a feasibility study (a fund-raising marketing study) is often conducted by an outside consultant. The case for support for the project is tested along with funding amounts, levels of interest, leadership, and basic campaign marketing messages.

The campaign must have strong financial and volunteer support from the board. The campaign plan and a campaign committee are created. A gift chart is developed with the number of gifts necessary at each level to achieve the goal. Table 10-2 shows the potential gift levels for a $3 million campaign.

The initial gifts, including one or more lead gifts, are solicited in a quiet phase of the campaign and secured before the campaign becomes a public fund-raising campaign. In most campaigns, the lead gift is 10 to 40 percent of the goal. Once the campaign goes public, the entire membership can be solicited.

Capital campaigns range from $1 million to hundreds of millions of dollars. Of the gifts, 80–90 percent of the funding will come from 10–20 percent of the donors. With capital campaigns, gardens are named and built, positions endowed, and buildings created. They raise large sums of money and position the garden as a force in the community. A campaign can increase annual giving, add new donors, and give the garden much-needed space, programs, and ongoing income through the endowment.

If the goal has not been reached by the declared end date of the campaign, the garden can either extend the time limit (which can have negative public relations consequences) or declare victory with the lower than hoped-for total. If choosing the latter, the garden would then have to adjust its goals in line with available funds.

Planned Giving

A planned gift usually refers to a deferred gift—one that comes to the garden after the donor is deceased. Most planned gifts are bequests; that is, a donor has provided for the garden in his or her will. Anecdotally, fund-raisers have found that most bequests are from people who are not major donors to the organization. For gardens, they are often members at the basic level or those who love the garden but have never joined. Gardens should note in their publications and websites that bequests are welcome. While there is seldom a direct response to notes welcoming bequests or other types of planned gifts, it is important to have the information in full view for the one in a thousand individuals who is thinking about his or her will and legacy. Those who have made a provision in their will (and tell the garden) should be recognized with a donor club specifically for this group (e.g., the Heirloom Circle at Powell Gardens in Kansas City, Missouri).

There are a number of other planned gifts, including gift annuities, pooled income funds, insurance, and trusts. When a garden has a history (at least ten years) and a donor base, then a staff person or consultant can be retained to implement a comprehensive planned giving program.

Table 10-2: Sample Capital Campaign Gift Chart

Campaign for Lovely Garden Goal: $3,000,000 Gift Chart					
Level	Gift Range	No. of Gifts	No. of Prospects Needed	Total Dollars per Range	Percent of Total
7	$750,000	1	4	$750,000	25%
6	$500,000	2	8	$100,000	33.3%
5	$250,000	2	8	$500,000	16.7%
4	$100,000	3	12	$300,000	10%
3	$50,000	4	16	$200,000	6.7%
2	$25,000	6	24	$150,000	5%
1	<$25,000	MANY	MANY	$100,000	3.3%

In-Kind Gifts

In-kind gifts are donated objects that range from plant materials to sculpture to land. The garden needs an acceptance policy for these gifts. What will be accepted? Will the garden be able to dispose of the gift? A wish list of items the garden desires, published in the newsletter or on the website, is an effective way to make members aware of the garden's needs and to discourage offers of what is not needed.

Don't be afraid to turn down an in-kind gift the garden doesn't need, one that is off-mission, or one that the garden can't afford to keep up. Don't hesitate to ask the donors of an in-kind gift for a cash gift to help maintain the item they have donated. Since many donors of in-kind gifts will want to take a tax deduction, staff should be familiar with current IRS requirements. Also, before accepting a gift of land or a large item such as a greenhouse, staff need to make sure environmental assessments or other inspections are done to avoid acquiring a liability for the garden.

Evaluating the Development Program

To decide how to proceed the next year, the development staff members need to evaluate the various fund-raising programs on an ongoing basis. With the plan as the guideline, the objectives become the measures. Overall, attention should be paid to the number of donors, new donors, renewal rate, and money raised from the development effort as a whole and by each fund-raising program and technique individually. Some development offices also project and follow cash flow on a monthly basis so that the garden knows when to expect funds.

Summary

This chapter has covered the basics of fund-raising and membership development. Fund-raising's major goal is to provide funding for fulfillment of the garden's mission. By creating a development plan, selecting the programs and techniques for the appropriate funding sources, and implementing the programs, the development effort ensures that the garden can continue its important work. In the process, fund-raising also brings to the garden a constituency that can be involved in its work, become advocates for its programs, and elevate its stature in the community.

Annotated Resources

Association of Fundraising Professionals (www.afpnet.org) is the largest membership organization of fund-raisers, with local chapters offering fund-raising education. The website has a bookstore and up-to-date information on fund-raising and the nonprofit sector.

CHAPTER 11

Earned Income Opportunities

RICHARD H. DALEY

Introduction

The entrepreneurial spirit is alive and well at public gardens and manifested in earned income activities. Gardens have found numerous ways to develop this stream of income, from admission fees and gift shop sales to hosting weddings.

Virtually all public gardens rely to some extent on earned income for their financial success; some derive 40–50 percent of their income from earned income sources. In recent years, earned income has been one of the most consistent growth areas for revenue in the public garden world.

Earned income is derived from transactions, which can be from a membership fee, an admission fee, or an item in a gift shop. The key is that the person receives something back, in contrast to philanthropic contributions.

Boards of directors have pushed institutions in recent years to raise the percentage of income provided by earned income. There are several reasons for this. Historically some institutions have not been as aggressive as they might be in building this part of their income. Probably more important, though, are two factors: first, board members usually derive their own income from business pursuits, so this part of the nonprofit business makes good sense to them, and second, if a larger percentage of income can come from earned income, there may be less personal and collective pressure on board members to raise funds.

Earned Income Opportunities

Admission Fees

Most public gardens charge for admission. The obvious reason to charge an admission fee is to bring in income, but there are

KEY TERMS

Earned Income: income derived from any source where a product or service is provided for a fee, including income from programs, gift shops, food service, facility rental, and similar operations.

Risk capital: equity capital of a firm or organization, against which all losses are charged and that takes the full brunt of the effects of failures, misjudgments, uncertainties, and adverse circumstances

Unrelated Business Income Tax (UBIT): the U.S. Internal Revenue Service requires nonprofit organizations to pay tax on income that is derived from business activities that do not relate to the mission of the organization.

other reasons as well. Most Americans appreciate what they pay for more than they appreciate what is free, and when they pay for something, visitors often take better care of it. The fee itself discourages people who have little interest in plants, and admission stations at entrances serve as control points that improve security. Control points also give the institution the ability to collect information about visitors, such as zip codes, that can be used in developing marketing programs.

One of the most important reasons to charge for admission is that it promotes membership sales, a key stabilizing component of public garden revenue. A very high percentage of respondents in most membership surveys say that free admission is the single most important reason they join the organization. Of course, it is not free; the person is, in fact, just paying for admission in advance through membership fees. Public gardens that do not charge an admission fee usually have membership levels that are far lower (just 10–20 percent in some cases) than at similar institutions that do charge for admission or parking (Daley 2008).

How Much Do Gardens Charge?

Pricing is always a challenge because institutions want to serve the greatest number of people possible while simultaneously maximizing admission income. The best strategy is often to optimize the fee and find a level at which large numbers of people are served and substantial income is raised. The amount of the charge depends on the size of the garden (which relates to the length of stay for visitors), the complexity of collections within the garden, the quality of the gardens, and special features (such as conservatories), as well as local market conditions. In areas that have generally low fees for cultural institutions, the fees at gardens are lower than in areas where competitors charge substantial admission fees.

Special Features and Events

Special features are distinguished from regular ones in that they typically are not continuously available and may have a special admission fee. The Chicago Botanic Garden has an exquisite garden railroad exhibition at holiday times for which it charges an extra admission fee. The Missouri Botanical Garden charges an extra fee for its children's garden, which is available year-round.

A common problem for public gardens is that for many people there is no compelling reason to visit their day-to-day exhibitions. This is frustrating for staff and volunteers, who work hard to have beautiful displays all the time. As a result, gardens increasingly rely on special public events to build their earned income. The strategy is to create a sense of urgency with a time-limited event (from one day to two weeks, or an entire season for huge exhibitions).

Special events can be responsible for as much as one-third or more of a garden's annual attendance, which means the economics justify their presentation. Those special events with no additional fee for admission achieve their aims by attracting much larger audiences. Others, especially those events that occur after normal hours, have a specific fee. Besides admission fees, special events are excellent ways to build other earned income streams: memberships, retail sales, and food service sales.

There are many variations on the theme of special events, ranging from large-scale events such as concerts that require

The Arboretum at Flagstaff has developed a regularly scheduled program, modeled after one at the Arizona-Sonora Desert Museum, of free-flying raptors under the care of trained raptor staff. Now the Arboretum's single most popular program, with the equivalent of approximately 50 percent of its visitors attending one or more raptor presentations each year, the raptor program is a major factor in the continued increase in attendance and membership. Because there is no extra fee for the raptor program, the income it generates does not show up directly as a fee for service, but it is reflected in membership, admission, and gift shop sales. The program also generates excellent press for the Arboretum and has helped with both corporate philanthropy and local foundation support.

Figure 11-1: Volunteer raptor trainer and visitors, Arboretum at Flagstaff.

Arboretum at Flagstaff

large resources and have the potential for large returns to small events such as quilt shows, plant society flower shows, and art exhibitions. Although large shows and small events are not mutually exclusive, only the larger institutions can handle many events or even a single huge event because they are so staff intensive.

A popular strategy is to have an annual signature event that becomes a major attendance builder. The Dallas Botanical Garden and Arboretum has Dallas Blooms, the Missouri Botanical Garden has its Japanese Festival, the Denver Botanic Gardens has a major plant sale, Longwood Gardens has its Holiday Show, and the New York Botanical Garden has its biennial orchid show. Signature events come with many advantages. They are often tied directly to the garden's mission and existing features; they retain and build their popularity over many years; they remain a mainstay of the institution and help brand the institution; the staff and volunteers become quite expert at executing them, so the events become efficient to run; and since they create a regular following, their success each year is predictable. At large venues, these events draw tens of thousands of visitors. Because they are popular, local businesses often become regular sponsors, adding more reliable income. Some, but not all, of these major events have fees above the normal admission fee.

Another variation is the one-time special event, often produced by others and brought in to a garden for several months. Recent examples of these mega-events include shows that have traveled to numerous gardens include "Big Bugs," a display of gigantic artificial bugs of great appeal to families, and the Dale Chihuly glass exhibition, which includes installations customized to the venue. These one-time events can be extremely expensive, often costing tens of thousands and sometimes hundreds of thousands of dollars. Akin to the blockbuster shows at art museums, these shows nearly always require underwriting by major corporations, but they are enormously popular with the public and generate large crowds.

Figure 11-2: Public gardens of all sizes have success with concerts, such as this one at Denver Botanic Gardens.

Richard Daley, Daley Images LLC

In analyzing the success of a major exhibition, it is important to look at the change it brought to the institution across several measures. The exhibition of artworks in glass by Dale Chihuly has appeared at several public gardens, and all report major increases in many categories.

Impact of Chihuly Exhibition at Atlanta Botanical Garden
(Figures are from 2004 and are approximate.)

Total attendance	210,000	+136%
Admission revenue	$2.6 million	+243%
Membership dues	$1.7 million	+84%
Museum shop sales	$1.2 million	+215%

It is important to note that the figures listed are the earned income portion of the financial equation and do not include corporate support or other private philanthropy. In addition to generating earned income, major exhibitions such as this provide excellent opportunities to build contributed income and cultivate future potential supporters.

In evaluating major exhibitions and events, it is important to look at the long-term as well as short-term benefits. The Atlanta Botanical Garden found that while there was a very large increase in the number of members (58 percent) and membership income (84 percent), these both dropped significantly after the first year. Most important, though, the base levels moved to a higher threshold, so the increase in support through membership provided a long-term boost.

Membership

Membership programs are closely related to both earned income and contributed income. Because they are managed together with development programs, and because of the movement of members to donor status, membership programs are discussed in more detail in Chapter 10.

The income from membership programs, though, is best reflected on income statements as one of the earned income categories. An alternative is to record membership income up to, say, $500 in the earned income category and income from memberships at $500 or more in the development category. Typically, a very high percentage of members of public gardens are in the lowest member categories because it is less expensive to be a member than to pay for admission. These are largely "value members," and this is a transaction through which they receive benefits for their membership. In other words, they are buying a service, not making a philanthropic donation. This categorization of membership income under earned income is recommended by the American Association of Museums and allows for comparisons with other public gardens and other institutions

Figure 11-3: Exhibitions of Dale Chihuly glass have been popular and profitable at many public gardens, including this one at Desert Botanical Garden.

Richard Daley, Daley Images LLC

in a consistent way. It is important to recognize that this categorization has significant IRS implications in the United States. On its website, the IRS states that memberships are considered quid pro quo contributions if the donor receives goods or services that can be valued in exchange for that membership: "[Quid pro quo] is a payment a donor makes to a charity partly as a contribution and partly for goods or services. For example, if a donor gives a charity $100 and receives a concert ticket valued at $40, the donor has made a quid pro quo contribution. In this example, the charitable contribution part of the payment is $60."

Retail Sales

With shopping a major leisure-time activity in the United States, most public gardens have joined the trend and operate retail shops. Just as the size and complexity of gardens vary, so does the scale of shops, which range in size from a few dozen square feet to more than 5,000 square feet. Retail shops are nearly all located adjacent to the main gate so that visitors see the shopping opportunity as they enter and can plan to leave time on their way out to shop. While a few shops are located inside the charging point, it is much more advantageous to locate the shop before the charging point to encourage shop visits by local residents who might not shop if there is an admission barrier.

Garden gift shops normally have a decided gardenesque theme in their merchandising, with floral- or garden-themed gift items, gardening books, a selection of small garden tools and gardening gloves, and garden logo items such as T-shirts, hats, coffee mugs, and garden aprons. The larger shops offer garden ornaments, bird feeders and baths, pots and jardinières, and occasionally high-end garden furniture. The shop itself helps brand the institution and reinforces the institution's

mission. All merchandise must be related to the garden's tax-exempt mission, in accordance with IRS Unrelated Business Income Tax (UBIT) code. Significantly, the test of whether an activity or sales item may be related or not is *not* the use of the funds. In other words, simply because the income from the activity is used to advance the tax-exempt mission, does not mean the activity or item may not be taxed. The activity or item itself must be related to the tax-exempt purpose and the activity must be "substantial."

The IRS does recognize many exemptions to the tax, some of which apply to public gardens. For example, food service available to the public and staff is exempt from tax because it relates to visitor comfort; activities that are carried out entirely or almost entirely by volunteers on behalf of the organization are not subject to taxation; and activities provided primarily to members or employees are not taxable under UBIT. The IRS provides guidance through Publication 598, "Tax on Unrelated Business Income of Exempt Organizations," which is available online.

State and local laws can also affect tax issues for public gardens separate from UBIT issues. Of course, laws and regulations change, and an attorney familiar with UBIT and state and local laws should be consulted before engaging in a substantial activity that could trigger tax issues.

Typically, volunteers manage and do the buying for the shops at newer gardens. As the institution matures, attendance becomes larger, and membership increases, the decision is usually made to professionalize the shop with a paid manager and buyer, a change that often dramatically improves the shop's financial performance. Although adding staff is a big step, the financial investment in professional staff is nearly always more than justified by the increase in net income.

CASE STUDY: DESERT BOTANICAL GARDEN GIFT SHOP

The Desert Botanical Garden's gift shop consistently ranks among the most profitable at any public garden. The top categories of sales are plants, gifts, books, and T-shirts. The shop is conveniently located by the entrance and exit. The keys to its success are excellent buying, diverse price points for goods, unique items related to the American Southwest, good understanding of its customers, professional management, and strong support from Garden management. In addition to the annual influx of winter tourists to the area, the Desert Botanical Garden also has a large, loyal membership that supports the shop. Shops at public gardens, such as this one, that are in popular tourist destination areas have a great advantage over those at gardens located where few tourists visit.

Desert Botanical Garden Gift Shop Sales
(Figures are from 2008 and are approximate.)

Gross sales	$1,640,000
Cost of goods sold	$835,000
Gross margin	$805,000
Salaries	$330,000
Supplies	$15,000
Other overhead	$5,000
Net to DBG	$455,000
Gross sales per visitor	$4.80
Net per visitor	$1.35

Figure 11-4: Gift shops such as this one at the Cleveland Botanical Garden are mainstays of earned income at public gardens.

Richard Daley, Daley Images LLC

Plant Sales

Some garden gift shops offer plants for sale. These usually range from small cacti aimed at the tourist market to houseplants. Because they require more care and space and a quicker turnaround time, fewer garden shops offer perennials, bulbs, annuals, and woody plants. There is also more sales competition for these plants from the local nursery trade.

Many gardens have an annual plant sale that features outdoor plants even if these are not sold routinely in their shops. These plant sales can range in size from modest to enormous, with significant sales volumes and net income exceeding $100,000.

A major issue for gardens with plant sales is whether to raise their own plants, buy them for resale, or buy them on consignment. While most gardens offer at least some excess plants for sale that otherwise would be turned into compost, the question remains: grow or buy the plants? It is almost impossible for a garden to grow plants for sale economically, given the cost of staff time and utility costs for greenhouses. If the growing is done entirely by volunteers and if utility costs are low (unlikely for gardens outside the South and Southwest), then it can make sense if greenhouse space is available. For the majority of gardens, the economics simply do not allow for growing plants in quantity specifically for sale. The solution for most gardens is to buy the plants outright or purchase them on consignment.

Food Service

Just as with zoos, art museums, and other attractions, people come to gardens as a leisure-time activity, and they often want to eat. The larger the garden, the more important food service is as an amenity, because visitors stay longer. Similarly, gardens with few or no restaurants nearby have an added reason to provide food service.

Because most public gardens also need to provide food for special events and donor events and as part of facility rental, catering is a major factor in providing, managing, and assessing food service. In fact, the catering component of food service is often much more lucrative than the day-to-day food service.

The issues for food service management include:

- Should the food service be provided by an outside vendor or be run by the garden?

- How should the garden balance offering the high-quality food and service that donors and members desire with the need to provide higher-profit food service (e.g., faster, less nutritious, less appealing) for most casual visitors?

- If the food service is run by an outside caterer, should rental events be required to use that caterer?

- If the food service is run by an outside caterer, is the garden obligated to use that caterer for all its events?

- What is a reasonable financial arrangement with a caterer that provides good income to the garden and is also financially rewarding to the caterer, so food service becomes an asset for visitors (and for those renting facilities) and enhances, not detracts from, the garden's reputation?

Most gardens use an outside catering firm to handle food service, which makes sense. This is an ancillary business, not a core business where gardens can expect to have or should aspire to develop a core competency. Unless a garden either has an annual attendance of several hundred thousand visitors or a very large facility rental business (for weddings, for example), income from food service is often disappointing, particularly when compared to the income brought in by gift shops, often with less space.

Facility Rental

Facility rentals have been the fastest-growing source of earned income for many public gardens over the past decade. In recent years, several gardens have built visitor centers that are largely designed as spaces for rent. The Brooklyn Botanic Garden built a separate conservatory-style space to host weddings and celebratory events; it immediately became a prime spot in Brooklyn for events and has generated a very large amount of income. This is not true just of the largest gardens. Harry P. Leu Gardens in Orlando, Florida, a publicly owned garden, built its visitor center largely to cater to private events. Cape Fear Botanical Garden in Fayetteville, North Carolina, is doing the same.

Powell Gardens, located about forty-five minutes from the center of Kansas City, Missouri, provides an excellent example of how beautiful gardens even outside central urban cores can produce strong revenue streams from facility rentals. Powell Gardens is so popular for weddings that it built a small wedding chapel on the grounds. Because of its long and successful track record as a location for weddings, the social network among local brides promotes the Gardens as a venue. The Gardens also has its own bridal show in February to introduce the venue to potential clients and advertises in local bridal magazines.

Powell Garden Facility Rentals
(Figures are approximate and are from 2008.)

Chapel rentals	130 rentals
Arbor/grounds	10 rentals
Reception packages	110 packages
Meetings	30
Total rental events	280
Gross income	$227,904
Net income	$161,928

Public Program Income

Providing an array of programs for the public is inherent in the mission of public gardens. Public programs excite and inform people about plants and nature, about landscapes and plant collections, about how we use plants for food and decoration, and about conservation and stewardship. These programs can also be a source of significant earned income.

Generally, programs for children need to be priced at a level where they still require subsidies from grants, private contributions, or the general operating budget. While there are exceptions, such as youth summer camps that can sometimes pay for themselves, the public programs that are self-sustaining or generate net income are those aimed at adults: classes, lectures, workshops, and tour programs.

Plant Royalties

A few public gardens, such as the University of British Columbia Botanical Garden, the Chicago Botanic Garden jointly with the Morton Arboretum (see case study below), and the Denver Botanic Gardens (whose program is called PlantSelect), have experimented with developing cultivars to be sold in the retail trade, with a percentage of income returning to the garden.

These programs take a great deal of time from the professional horticulture staff and willing partners in the local nursery trade, but their value is considerable: not only is potential income generated, but because plants are tagged and identified with the public garden in the nurseries where they are sold, the programs also reinforce the brand of the public garden as a regional leader in horticulture.

The Denver Botanic Gardens has one of the most diverse programs for adult education in the country, including dozens of classes, a long-standing sponsored lecture series, two certificate programs, and occasional symposia. This program also has consistently generated significant net income, even after including expenses beyond the out-of-pocket costs for each program. Expenses covered by the fees include the coordinator's salary, all out-of-pocket expenses, and many other expenses often not charged back to the programs.

The following table shows the approximate participation, revenue, and expenses of Denver's public programs. About 15 percent of the income is from sponsorships, but even if this income were not available, the total program would still generate significant net income.

Program	Number of Programs	Number of Participants	Income ($)[1]	Expenses ($)	Net ($)
General adult programs	100	1,820	42,000	31,000	11,000
Lectures	5	365	38,000	25,000	13,000
Gardening certificate	30	500	32,000	22,000	10,000
Botanical illustration	60	700	105,000	70,000	35,000
Symposia	2	330	40,000	20,000	20,000
	~200	**3,715**	**~260,000**	**~170,000**	**90,000**

[1] Includes approximately $40,000 in sponsorships; figures are for 2008–2009.

Miscellaneous

A few public gardens, such as the Los Angeles County Arboretum and Botanic Garden and the North Carolina Arboretum, have rented their grounds to film companies. While this can be lucrative, it can also be highly disruptive to the casual visitor, depending on the length of the shoot. In some cases, a film company may want weeks of access, limiting public use of entire areas. Even if economically attractive, such extended commitments (and film companies typically need more time than requested, not less) may not be justified when compared to the interruption of normal activities, possible damage to plant collections and grounds, and the cost of staff required to coordinate with the film company and protect the collection.

Although travel programs often are not very profitable, many gardens offer such programs. They can be excellent ways to build donor loyalty, find new supporters, and excite key donors about special projects.

Public gardens find many other ways to earn income, ranging from producing and selling books to renting property for farming and providing consulting services on botanical and horticultural issues.

Managing Earned Income

The Business of Earned Income

Applying standard business procedures to the handling of earned income has become more and more of an accepted practice at public gardens. Those areas, such as retail sales, that have a clear bottom line are usually organized with financial goals. For areas such as public programs that have both a mission-driven component and an earned income expectation, garden administrators must clarify which goal takes priority and establish benchmarks that reflect those defined priorities.

Evaluation of New Projects

The first issue in approaching possible projects in a business-like fashion is to ask key questions to clarify expectations; those questions can later be used as part of the program's evaluation. As obvious as it sounds, the first steps in evaluating an idea with earned income potential are to decide if it supports the institution's mission and strategic objectives, including financial ones, and to clearly define the primary and secondary purposes. Is it to generate net income? Is it to build loyalty among members and donors? Or is it to diversify the audience? Very frequently, a new program or activity is proposed for one purpose (say, net income) and evaluated by a different measure ("It lost money, but we made a lot of friends").

Some of the key questions that need to be asked include:

- Does the garden have the expertise, or can it be found at a reasonable cost?

- Is it possible to experiment with this potential source of revenue without making a major investment at the outset?

- Has a feasibility study been conducted of the potential costs and benefits?

- How can income be maximized by using this new project to build other earned income?

- Will this enhance or hurt (1) general visitor experience, (2) members' experiences and view of the garden, (3) donor perceptions and loyalties, (4) the garden's overall reputation and brand?

- Will this have unintended consequences, such as disturbance of neighbors?

- Is this the best use of capital funds?

- Is it possible to give this project time to meet income expectations, perhaps three years?

- What is the competition like today, and what will it likely be in a few years?

- Who will manage this enterprise?

- What are the opportunity costs? (In other words, by deciding to pursue this project, what other projects will the garden choose not to do?)

Staff Structure and Use of Volunteers

Developing and managing earned income is usually decentralized and involves many departments and functions. On its face, it may not seem like proper management to have it so dispersed, but in practice the skills are so divergent that it would be difficult to consolidate these functions into a single department.

- At larger institutions, some but not all of the activities are concentrated in a visitor (or guest) services department. These usually include admission income, retail sales, food service, and facility rentals. If such a department does not exist, the responsibility to generate admission income often becomes an orphan project, with no person really assigned its overall management.

- To create the most seamless coordination of benefits, communication, and fund-raising requests between the membership and development functions, the membership component of earned income is best managed by the development department.

- Special events can also fall under the purview of the visitor services department. In some public gardens, it is part of the marketing function, which sometimes falls to the development department.

- Program income derived from educational activities belongs in that department (also sometimes called the public programs department, a broader and usually better description).

The finance director can play an important advisory role in many earned income activities no matter which department has the responsibility. At smaller gardens, the finance director may directly manage some of the functions. The finance director can also make a significant contribution in building the financial skills of garden department managers, most of whom have specialized backgrounds but often lack financial skills such as forecasting revenue.

Volunteers play an extraordinarily important role in some areas of earned income, particularly in special events, gift shops, and plant sales. The number of available staff is often too small to meet the personnel needs of major special events, so volunteers frequently serve as front-line staff, providing directions and information to visitors at events. They staff membership sales booths, and in gift shops they often serve as the primary sales force and sometimes staff the entire operation, including the buying.

Contracting for Services

For any component of earned income that is not operated internally, garden management must be keenly aware of how the operation affects its reputation for quality and service. From uniforms to service training, the public must see the operation as having the same quality as if provided by garden staff.

Food service is the one earned income area that is nearly always provided by contractors. Few gardens can manage this business as effectively as an outside catering service can. The financial return on food service at gardens is often disappointing. At first glance, the reason might seem to be that the caterer makes most of the profit, leaving little income for the institution. But the fundamental problems with managing food service are the highly perishable nature of the product, the very high turnover of staff in food service, and the critical importance of having a highly experienced food service professional to manage this business.

Earned Income at Emerging and Established Gardens

Earned income endeavors at new and emerging public gardens differ from those of larger, established gardens in several ways. The first is scale: small gardens cannot provide the number and diversity of activities, nor can they expect to bring in the same scale of revenue for even the same events. Small gardens have less risk capital, and so they have less tolerance for failure. They have fewer staff with expertise or experience in building earned income, and less money to hire outside people to do the work. In developing new income streams, emerging institutions have to prioritize more carefully than well-established institutions that are more able to try several new activities at once.

Newer gardens should begin with the basics: establishing and managing admission fees, establishing and developing a membership program, and establishing a small retail operation. Modest public programs and a few events represent the next stage of development. As a strategy, newer gardens have to focus on those areas with the greatest potential for return and may turn over some areas to volunteers with little staff involvement. Although having volunteers manage such projects alone can result in problems with consistency and accountability, sometimes it is the only realistic option.

Other Earned Income Issues

Mission versus Income

Gardens, like all other nonprofit organizations, do not and should not judge their success purely on financial grounds. Ironically, this is one reason that the great business guru Peter Drucker commented that nonprofits are often run *better* than for-profit organizations!

Even though nonprofits are not businesses, in their overall activities and in their earned income activities in particular they must be run like a business, using appropriate planning and evaluation techniques. But a focus on financial matters also creates tension within institutions. Often staff members complain that the CEO is "only interested in the finances" and feel that the board of directors is to blame. It is almost certainly true that for most institutions a large amount of the top management's time ends up being devoted to finding funds to support the ever-increasing costs of mission-related activities: horticulture, education, science, and conservation.

The tension arises in part because (1) most of the mission-related managers have backgrounds in specialized fields with little training in financial management, (2) top management does a poor job of explaining the relationship between income and the ability to support mission activities, and (3) some institutions follow every avenue of support with little regard to the mission.

Competition with Local Businesses

Occasionally a garden enterprise is seen as a significant competitor to local businesses, especially if the enterprise is located off-site. Although gift shops, food service, and facility rentals all could be said to compete with off-site, for-profit enterprises, those activities seldom becomes issues because these enterprises have become accepted museum guest services.

Gardens must look at the unintended consequences of new businesses. Sometimes the question of unfair competition is raised. For example, one public garden created a horticulture service to provide and care for plants in businesses. Local businesses complained, and the garden decided to divest itself of this business even though it was willing to pay the UBIT tax for it. While a new enterprise may make good financial sense, its effects on the community, on stakeholders, and on the garden's reputation all have to be factors in the analysis.

Summary

Earning income is an essential component of the revenue mix for public gardens. Virtually all have membership programs, most have admission fees, most have fees for some programs, and gift shops abound. There can be tension created by the drive to be entrepreneurial versus the desire to be mission-driven, and most public gardens find a good balance that allows the mission to remain central while simultaneously being a responsive, businesslike organization building the financial resources to sustain the institution.

Annotated Resources

American Association of Museums (www.aam-us.org) is a resource for information about many aspects of museum management.

American Public Gardens Association (www.publicgardens.org) collects and distributes a wide range of materials on public gardens, including information on admissions, memberships, and programs.

Museum Store Association (www.museumdistrict.com) is the primary resource for all kinds of museum stores.

CHAPTER 12

Facilities and Infrastructure

ERIC TSCHANZ

Introduction

Facilities and infrastructure are the physical backbone of a public garden. Proper planning and design of utilities, drainage, buildings, and roads are critical to the development of a successful institution. But as important as these items may be, a public garden is primarily about plants, people, and programs. The mission of a garden in relation to these essential components should drive the development of facilities and infrastructure.

Unfortunately, it is all too easy to start planting gardens and building walks without planning for the present needs and future infrastructure of a garden. The garden's master plan (see Chapter 6) is the long-term document that will guide facility and infrastructure requirements. Mission and collection statements will also help drive these physical requirements in a specific direction. Many start-up operations find it challenging to wait through this planning period and want to immediately start planting and building. It is possible to move forward quickly, but this should not happen until professionals have completed some initial work.

Land

As described in Chapter 5, the founders of start-up gardens dream of an ideal piece of land but often must take what is given to them. It might be a donor's estate or farm, or possibly land owned by a governmental entity, but rarely do the founders have funds to select and purchase a perfect site. If options are available, careful consideration must be given to future infrastructure development.

Surplus or free land might not be easily developed due to flood plains, residential restrictions, easements, dumps, or old mining activity. A low-cost or free site may be more costly to develop in the long run. If there are any questions concerning a site's developmental use, it would be wise to consult with a landscape architect and/or engineer.

Costly Pitfalls

Given present environmental laws, it is absolutely necessary to complete a professional environmental assessment before accepting title to any land. Buried gas tanks, hazardous residues from manufacturing, and even illegal dumps are just a few of the problems that can doom a site. After title has changed hands, any and all environmental problems become the responsibility of the new owner. Cleanup of a contaminated site can easily run in the hundreds of thousands of dollars.

A title search at the local courthouse should show any easements on the land, which can range from simple utility easements placed on the land by local utility companies to large easements owned by regional or national companies. These large easements can be major distribution lines needed to transport electricity or petroleum products throughout a multistate region. Each easement will have specific requirements. Most companies will not allow structures on their easements, nor will they be responsible for damage to plants if a repair on their easement is necessary.

Site Inventory

Once the site is selected, it must be evaluated for existing structures, buildings, arbors, and infrastructure components such as on-site utilities, roads, and ponds. This inventory will need to be done prior to a site analysis and master planning, and items should be located on a topographic map of the site. Although topographic surveys are costly and not necessary at this stage

Figure 12-1: Cleared electrical easement at Powell Gardens, Kansas City, Missouri.

of planning, the work will be required before detailed planning and construction design can be started. U.S. Geological Survey topographic maps can be used for this initial work and can be procured at a very reasonable cost. Most areas of the United States have been mapped by this agency.

A site inventory could be started by a landscape architect, architect, or engineer, or even a garden staff member with the appropriate expertise. Even at this early stage, these experts can determine if the present sizing of utilities, on-site or adjacent to the site, will be sufficient. If two sites are under consideration, this type of survey can provide actual comparisons and support a factual decision-making process. After a review of the site and existing infrastructure and facilities, one decision may be to look for another site.

CASE STUDY: LAND EASEMENTS

On Powell Gardens' 950 acres there are three major easements: a high-power electrical transmission line, a high-pressure 8-inch natural gas line, and a fiber-optic line, all of which bisect the property. The staff and board were fully aware of these easements, which were included in the original site analysis and master plan.

Two of the leases are more than fifty years old and legally vague, but given that they involve utilities, state and federal requirements must be followed. The gas and electrical line easements are cleared of all brush and trees as needed, and herbicides can be used for this work.

The gas easement posed another challenge, as it cut through the core of the Garden. The easement was as much as 100 feet wide, and structures are not allowed along its path. The

Garden chose to relocate the line at its expense, and it is now located between garden sites and will only be traversed by a trolley road.

The fiber-optic lease was written after the Garden's creation. With proper legal help, this lease was drafted in favor of the Garden. The line remains under a newly constructed garden, but the owners of the line are legally obligated to return the property to the preexisting condition after any repair work.

Land use easements come in all sizes and types and need to be distinguished from conservation easements. It is best to understand the legal requirements of the lease before master planning and to realize the challenges and potential costs that they might bring to the project.

Utilities

The locations of all utilities on the site—water, electric, sewer and gas—should be determined, along with their line widths. In rural areas and sometimes on surplus government land, utilities might not be on the site. If they are not, their proximity to the site should be determined. If possible, the age and necessary upgrades of these installations need to be determined. Utility companies are a great source of information about the size of service available at the meter.

Generally speaking, most underground utilities on the site will ultimately need to be replaced because they are rarely in the correct place or of the correct size. It is best to determine ahead of time costs for bringing in commercial electricity (described as three-phase electric), installing water taps, drilling wells, or developing sanitary systems. An engineer can develop cost estimates to upgrade or bring in the necessary utilities at the appropriate size. The availability of energy sources such as natural gas or oil can drive decisions for heating systems. Lack of a specific utility may or may not be a deal breaker, but it can be expensive to remedy.

Bringing utilities to a site can involve large costs that must be weighed against green alternatives and other, more sustainable systems. Opportunities abound to heat without natural gas or oil, ranging from solar panels to groundwater-source (from wells or lakes) heat pumps—all very efficient and proven technologies. On-site green sanitary systems can use plants to treat gray water or as the final polishing system for treating effluent, which can have an added benefit as an educational exhibit to show a sustainable way to handle sanitary water.

Water, Water Everywhere

All public gardens require some type of irrigation system and a source for water. City or county water is expensive and not always the best choice. Even potable water from water utilities may require treatment for pH, hardness, and other chemicals before it can be used for plants, which is costly and time-consuming. A thorough study of the site can show the potential for irrigation wells, lakes, or ponds. Given the fluctuation in the water level, an irrigation lake typically should not be the main water source for a garden.

Runoff from parking lots and buildings can be diverted into bioswales and directed into large holding basins or cisterns. Permeable paving can be used to direct water into percolation beds. This water is kept from entering the stormwater system, allowing it to percolate back into the water table. Cistern and pond water started as rainwater and usually requires less treatment than most water from utility systems.

Water regulations vary from state to state, and it is best to check with local authorities or consult with a hydrologist.

Roads and Walks

Access to the site from public roadways needs to be resolved. Besides present ingress points, it is important to check with the local authorities to determine if others are permissible. A garden can easily draw thousands of visitors in one day. Some residential neighborhoods with smaller streets cannot handle this type of traffic. If the entrance is off a major highway, deceleration and stacking lanes may be required.

Interior roads improved with a firm base and drainage ditches are the standard for public and maintenance roads. Muddy trails through the site are a liability. All parking spaces, whether on gravel or another hard surface, and all interior established roads and access points should be part of an infrastructure map. Also, to the degree possible, accessibility in compliance with the Americans with Disabilities Act should be maximized.

If the site has any garden paths or walks from earlier work, the quality and materials of their construction need to be assessed. All of these details should be logged on the site inventory to determine how they might affect the master plan.

Structures

Next to be noted on the site plan are any existing structures, including basic construction type, square footage, floor plan, utilities, and condition. Other considerations are whether the structures are historic, their accessibility, and their original intended use. The site inventory must focus on the facts, leaving emotional reasons behind. For instance, if a structure was the founder's home but is completely dilapidated, the survey needs to accurately reflect its current condition.

The Next Step

Once the site inventory is complete, a site analysis can be started. This document, generally in bubble diagram form, defines the challenges and opportunities of the site. Assuming that professional help has been obtained and a master plan is in the works, a garden might move forward with temporary gardens and structures or forge ahead with the building of the master-planned garden. But this step depends on the site, speed of planning, funding, and a host of other issues.

Raw land without structures can be a blessing because there are no demands to fit a previously built structure into the garden scheme, whether temporarily or permanently. The challenges start when the site has quality structures but not necessarily in the correct locations. A site analysis and/or well-thought-out master plan will help with these decisions.

Figure 12-2: Site analysis phase of Duke University, prepared by Terra Design Studios.
Duke University/Terra Design Studios

Temporary Gardens and Structures

Master-planning a whole site will take some time, especially if a variety of stakeholders is involved. To garner interest from the public and ultimately obtain funding, most start-up gardens will develop some type of temporary front door, garden, and office. Landscape architects are often asked to do an initial site analysis to determine the best location for a temporary garden, which may involve adding new temporary structures or reusing present facilities. This could be a completely temporary site that will later be abandoned or adapted for reuse. A temporary garden can also be within the bounds of the future garden, with the intent to remove or renovate it when the permanent garden is built.

Renovating Structures

Generally, start-up gardens need visitor reception space and office space. It is sometimes economical and efficient to renovate existing smaller structures, homes, or office/commercial spaces for such use, especially if they are part of a temporary garden, to fill in until the master plan is complete and permanent facility construction has been undertaken. The main considerations are costs

and potential reuse. An architect can provide helpful information, but a world-class architect isn't necessary for these decisions, and a design/build firm can often be an economical way to begin.

Code requirements for public buildings and the specific needs driven by the building program can increase the costs of renovation and sometimes outweigh the practicality of reusing a structure. Many gardens use homes renovated for offices, but given the need for visitor reception spaces and the number of required restrooms, a major addition or stand-alone structure is often necessary. The building program will dictate the square footage for public space, office space, and classroom space, and the number of bathrooms. Design consultants working with the governing body can shape this program and drive the renovation and any additions or the decision to build new.

Green Renovation

Although more costly to implement in renovation than in new construction, sustainable practices can be included in a renovation process and should be kept in mind. Two main areas to consider are heating and cooling and water conservation.

Kris S. Jarantoski, Executive Vice President and Director, Chicago Botanic Garden

Now a major public garden, the Chicago Botanic Garden was opened to the public in 1972 on 300 acres that had been sculpted into nine islands surrounded by lakes and natural areas, resulting in a landscape of water and turf-covered islands without much interest to the public.

The Garden's first director, Dr. Francis de Vos, wanted a beautiful and educational demonstration garden that would generate popular excitement and support for the unprecedented garden development to come. A one-half-acre Home Landscape Center built near the Garden's first public building contained an herb garden, vegetable garden, and gardens featuring the best landscape plants for the Chicago area on a scale with which the average city dweller could identify. Simple wood fences created garden rooms, railroad ties created raised beds and planters, and gravel walks allowed the pubic to view the displays. Seasonal plantings of bulbs, annuals, herbs, and vegetables kept visitors returning to see the changes taking place.

With the completion of a new Education Building in 1976, the focus of the Garden and public access to it shifted from the south end and the Home Landscape Center to the main island and the new Education Building. A new Home Demonstration Garden, much larger than the old one, opened to the public in 1981 near the new Education Building.

The old Home Landscape Center had been built with the idea that it would be temporary, until the real, final gardens could be built, but by that time many people had become attached to the garden. Much discussion led to the conversion of the Home Landscape Center into a plant evaluation garden with new bed lines, soldier-course brick outlining the walks, and planting beds throughout in which to rotate plants in and out as they were evaluated. The largest trees and shrubs were retained to give the garden a framework, and the converted garden opened in 1982 as the Pullman Plant Evaluation Garden.

A master site plan created in 1997 and updated in 2009 includes plans for the Pullman Plant Evaluation Garden to make way for an expanded Production Greenhouse area in the future. People are now attached to the Pullman Plant Evaluation Garden, and so another evaluation garden will consequently be expanded.

A master site plan with an integrated vision that moves the institution's mission forward will rally people to change. Institutional respect for the people and traditions that built the organization will go a long way toward assuring people that the institution is not going astray.

Figure 12-3: The vegetable garden component, circa 1979, of the Home Demonstration Garden at the Chicago Botanic Garden.

Kris S. Jarantoski

Figure 12-4: The original ornamental garden, with best plants for the Chicago region, in the Home Demonstration Garden at the Chicago Botanic Garden.

Kris S. Jarantoski

Figure 12-5: The Pullman Plant Evaluation Garden, Chicago Botanic Garden, site of the former Home Demonstration Garden.

Kris S. Jarantoski

If additional square footage is being added or if the original heating/cooling units are old, this is a great opportunity to review efficient ways to condition renovated facilities. Public bathrooms are cost-efficient spaces for sustainable practices. Fixtures such as on-demand water heaters, waterless urinals, and low-water-use toilets and faucets are no more costly than standard fixtures and provide an immediate financial payback. The type of renovation project and the amount of funding will determine the possibilities for the inclusion of sustainable practices.

Other Options

Some gardens have successfully used mobile structures and prefabricated facilities. Although a bit more costly than renovation, mobile structures are economical and readily available. Prefabricated structures can be designed for a specific building program and quickly constructed and delivered to the site. While lacking the look of an architect-designed building, these structures do have a nice appearance, and because they are new construction they will meet necessary codes. They are moved onto the site with large trailers and lifted into place with cranes, and they can be moved to other garden areas for future adaptive reuse.

Whether renovating or building new temporary facilities, it is important that the project align with the site analysis and that the planners consider the future for these structures and specifically whether they can be reused later for other staff purposes or if they will be in the middle of future gardens. Answers to these questions will help determine the feasibility of the investment for renovations, additions, or prefabricated structures.

CASE STUDY: START-UP STRUCTURES

The Atlanta Botanical Garden (ABG), now a world-class facility, had a humble start-up in a double-wide trailer. The board realized the need to have a presence on the property that included gardens and a physical structure. The trailer was moved onto the site in 1977 and served as staff office space, also housing a small gift shop and a multipurpose space for educational programs and meetings. The double-wide was used until 1985, when the Gardenhouse was opened and became the new front door for the ABG, with ticketing, a much larger gift shop, staff offices, and meeting rooms. In 2009 the visitor services component was separated from the Gardenhouse with the opening of the new Hardin Visitor Center. The ABG's growth demonstrates the value of a well-thought-out evolution in the use of its facilities.

Daniel Stowe Botanical Gardens, near Charlotte, North Carolina, is situated on a 480-acre site of old farmland and woods. The board and founding director established the site with a temporary structure and gardens. A 2,400-square-foot, two-story modular home was moved onto the site in 1991. It was quickly apparent that additional space was necessary, and another single-story double-wide was added to serve as a meeting room and classroom space. The entire complex was then surrounded by decks and covered porches. A log structure was also moved and restored on this site and used as a gift shop. Display beds continued to grow and expand in size.

Once the new visitor center and master-planned gardens opened in 1999, these facilities were turned into staff offices. For the first two years of the "new" gardens, visitors demanded to see the old gardens. Because the temporary gardens had been free, some visitors questioned the new paid admission. Although the temporary site was very attractive, Mike Bush, the Garden's second director, now questions if too much money was spent developing and operating temporary gardens versus focusing energy and funds on the future permanent gardens and structures and making them a reality more quickly.

Figure 12-6: Atlanta Botanical Garden's humble beginning—the office/reception space that started it all.

Atlanta Botanical Garden

Figure 12-7: The Gardenhouse at the Atlanta Botanical Garden was dedicated in 1985 and serves a multitude of garden functions.

Atlanta Botanical Garden

Figure 12-8: In 2009 the visitor service component was separated with the opening of the new Hardin Visitor Center.

Atlanta Botanical Garden

Figure 12-9: Daniel Stowe Botanical Gardens Visitor Center. Massive porches and extensive landscaping created strong visual appeal for this prefabricated building.

Daniel Stowe Botanical Gardens

Sites Without Structures

Sites without structures (or with structures that through a planning process are deemed unusable) will require a different strategy. If new structures will be permanent and part of the future garden, it is necessary to have the master plan complete in order to locate them correctly on the site. The same applies for all utilities.

Besides locating future structures and future gardens, it is necessary to plan for the layout of utilities and roads. An engineer working with a landscape architect can develop a utility master plan, a critical document. Among the common pitfalls is the failure to install enough capacity or large enough sizes for phone lines, water lines, or garden paths.

Figure 12-10: This structure was moved onto the site and restored as a gift shop facility.

Daniel Stowe Botanical Gardens

Because thousands of dollars will be invested underground for future facilities, the master plan and utility plan need to be well thought out.

Utilities

The utility master plan provides guidance for present installations that will impact future development. For instance, the water source must be sized for the future needs of the gardens, whether it is a tap to commercial water or on-site wells or ponds. Main irrigation lines must also be sized appropriately, allowing for the additional irrigation requirements of future gardens. The same can be said for electricity, gas, potable water, and sanitary systems. The installation of empty conduits under walks and roads for future water and electrical lines is very inexpensive. The extra upsizing at this point outweighs tearing up mature gardens a few years later. Upsizing or upgrading beyond the minimum will generally pay back in a short time.

Even small gardens have miles of pipes and wires underground, all of which need to be documented as they are installed and located accurately on an as-built overall utility plan. Since memories fail and employees move on, all work, additions, and repairs need to be described with sizing, valves, and junction boxes. The development of a file of digital photos to document complex utility installations will prove invaluable.

Irrigation

Gardens basically have two water systems that shouldn't be intermingled. The potable system is for the public's use in buildings and drinking fountains throughout the gardens. The irrigation system can use potable or nonpotable water but should not be considered potable. All irrigation valves should be marked in that manner, and the irrigation system needs a backflow preventer to separate it from any potable system, as required by codes. Without a backflow preventer, there is a possibility of backflow contamination into the potable water system.

Garden Roads and Paths

Garden paths, trolley paths, and maintenance roads are the major transportation network within the garden. Garden trams can be used for tours through the garden or serve as transportation to garden hubs from which the visitors then walk through the garden. Trams can be driven on garden paths, which is inconvenient for the walking visitor, or two systems can be built, which is more expensive. Because all garden and maintenance vehicles need to move through the garden, garden paths should be a minimum of 8 to 10 feet wide.

Because local building codes require access to major structures by fire trucks and emergency vehicles, roads need to be constructed to handle heavy loads and laid out for specific routes.

Figure 12-11: Underground utilities: a maze of plumbing photographically documented for the future.

Powell Gardens

Building New Structures

Depending on the mission of the garden, the sequencing of structures will vary, but most public gardens start with a visitor reception space, staff offices, and some type of education space. One size does not fit all, and the design of new permanent structures will depend on the master plan, mission of the garden, funding, demand, and a host of other issues. One of the best investments before making these decisions is a field trip to similar institutions, with the architect, planners, and board members all participating. If visiting is not possible, staff members should call their peers at other gardens. An amazing amount of information can be learned from a staff that has lived with a facility.

Buildings can be constructed for an initial purpose with a plan for change in use when future structures are completed; this requires a complex long-term strategy with a well-thought-out master plan and a disciplined staff and board focused on following the plan.

Another strategy is to build structures in phases, driven by demand and available funds. One building or a campus of buildings might be designed with the plan for construction in phases. For instance, a visitor reception space with a few offices could be constructed in phase one. As the need grew, more offices, bathrooms, and a multipurpose space for education might be added. The next phase might have education in a separate facility and the original visitor reception space now totally focused on visitor amenities, visitor orientation, bathrooms, gift shops, and food service.

The Future of Garden Facilities

Green and sustainable building practices can be incorporated into the design of all garden facilities. Phipps Conservatory and Botanical Gardens has demonstrated how the greatest energy user, a conservatory, can be built as a sustainable structure. The level of commitment should be limited only by time and money. As gardens move forward, green buildings will be the standard, not the exception. It will be mandatory to be knowledgeable about green/sustainable initiatives, such as LEED, Green Globe, and the Sustainable Sites Initiative.

Common Botanical Garden Facilities

No two botanical gardens are alike; they vary by mission, by location, and by climate. Although there are similarities in facilities, not all gardens will have all of the same types of facilities, nor will they have the same components within these facilities. In a general way, the following captures the primary facilities found in many gardens and the major components of these facilities.

Visitor Center

The visitor center is the most important building from a siting standpoint; it is the garden's front door and provides space for visitor reception, ticketing, information, and such visitor amenities as restrooms, gift shops, and food service. It also often houses staff offices as well as exhibit space and multipurpose spaces.

Education Facility

Education facilities need good access for school buses and parking. Due to noise and commotion, the entrance needs to be separate from the general visitor entrance. Classrooms should be sized for school classes, but with dividers they can be part of a larger multipurpose room and outdoor terraces to increase flexibility.

Administrative Offices

If the administrative offices are to be located in a stand-alone facility, they don't need prime real estate, but they should offer convenient access for donors, board members, and so on. Beside the administrative staff, this building could accommodate offices for accounting, development, human resources, and marketing, as well as meeting spaces.

Maintenance Facility

A maintenance facility needs good access for deliveries, fuel storage, large trucks, and garbage. It needs to be out of public view and fenced from the public to prevent acts of vandalism and to reduce liability. This is the space for general storage, shops for the different trades such as plumbing and electrical, and a garage for general equipment maintenance.

Growing Complex

Whether the garden grows plants for display, collections, research, or sales determines the size of the growing complex. Plastic double poly greenhouses are the most economical; standard glass houses are more expensive but have better longevity and are more attractive in public areas. In a multiple-greenhouse operation, a head house connects to the greenhouses and works as a potting area and a space for the gathering and distribution of plants and includes office space and storage for pots, soil, and fertilizers. Outdoor plant storage in a shade or lath house is included in this area.

Horticulture/Nursery

When not combined with the growing complex, this area includes spaces for horticulture staff offices, gardening tools and equipment, and often storage for bulk mulch and composting facilities. See Chapter 13 for more information on compost production.

Conservatory

A conservatory is the most expensive garden structure to build, operate, and maintain, and it requires specialized staff for the physical plant maintenance and horticultural operations. Conservatories are generally for display and exhibits and are more highly designed than greenhouses. They require specialized heating and cooling equipment, along with engineered glazed roof structures. Technology now exists to design a conservatory that can be truly sustainable and use a minimum of fuel.

Research Facility

A research building can stand alone and might include a library, herbarium, micropropagation labs, general labs, and more technical research greenhouses.

Garden Features

Depending on the design, many hardscape features can be added to a public garden, including fountains, gazebos, arbors, waterfalls, pools, stairs, and statuary. As with other structures, codes, maintenance, and flexibility all need to be considered when designing and building these components. In addition, the design team should consider how the style of each feature will fit with the overall style of the garden.

Performance Space

Many gardens with performing arts programs have developed outdoor amphitheaters, which can range from sloping lawns to full-scale outdoor theaters with stages, lighting, sound systems, and greenrooms.

Summary

Great botanical gardens, whether they are twenty-five or a hundred years old, don't happen without planning. From day one the proper planning for site access, utilities, roads, and structures will impact the future of the garden. Great botanical gardens start with a strong mission and collections statement coupled with a master plan developed by experienced professionals.

Before major plantings bloom in a garden, significant investments will be made in infrastructure components, many of which are buried underground. Given the costs involved and the potential for future garden disruptions, it is imperative that the proper consideration be given to the design and installation of these items.

Sustainable and green facilities will be increasingly important. Start-up gardens can easily plan and design for sustainable new facilities and include sustainable practices in plans for renovations to existing facilities.

Annotated Resources

American with Disabilities Act (www.ada.gov/stdspdf.htm). ADA standards for accessible design are listed on this site.

Green Building Initiative (www.gbi.org). Not-for-profit organization promoting green building approaches and Green Globe certification.

U.S. Green Building Council (www.usbgc.org/LEED). Lists complete information on the LEED certification program.

Sustainable Sites Initiative (www.sustainablesites.org). Website describing the mission and activities of this group.

U.S. Department of the Interior, U.S. Geologic Survey (http://topomaps.usgs.gov). Information on U.S. topographic maps.

CHAPTER 13

Grounds Management and Security

VINCENT A. SIMEONE

Introduction

High-quality grounds management is a major factor in any public garden's success. The way in which the grounds are managed is one of the primary criteria that distinguish a public garden from a park or golf course, and it can turn a garden into a masterpiece. The emphasis of a public garden grounds management program is on plants, as opposed to grass on a golf course or perhaps trees and their canopy shade in a park. A quality grounds management program ensures that the care of all plants is of fundamental importance and that they are managed as parts of collections rather than simply as landscape elements. As a component of grounds management, a security program can ensure that all of the physical resources of the garden are adequately protected, and that staff and visitors are safe while on the grounds.

A public garden is much easier to maintain if there is a successful relationship between landscape site conditions, garden design, and appropriate plant selection. Consideration of each of these key elements in conjunction with the others when planting a garden will reduce the time spent later on garden maintenance. Selecting plants that are resistant to pest problems, noninvasive, and less maintenance intensive goes a long way in helping to reduce overall maintenance. Also helpful is a landscape design that considers the level of maintenance desired in determining plantings and hardscape components.

Grounds Maintenance Needs

Grounds managers must first view the entire landscape to determine the level of maintenance that each garden section requires. Through this analysis, the manager can identify which sections require intensive weekly weeding and tending, such as vegetable gardens, herb plots, and perennial and annual borders, and which require only seasonal maintenance, such as woody plant collections and meadows. While aesthetics, collections management needs, and education programs must all be included in design considerations, the best designed gardens will have plants grouped according to the level of maintenance required.

Analyze the Site

Every public garden needs a comprehensive grounds maintenance schedule, which is refined and updated with each passing season and year. Before specific decisions on the levels of maintenance can be set, the following aspects of every garden area must be reviewed and analyzed:

- **Viewing distance.** How close will the public come to this garden area?
- **Specific plants.** What level of maintenance is required to keep them healthy and showy?
- **Access.** How does the topography impact access to the area and what are the levels of access to the area for equipment?
- **Soil and water.** Do the soils and access to irrigation for the garden area present any challenges?

It is important to start with an inventory of all plants and their locations before developing a comprehensive grounds management program. Once a list of plants with their maintenance requirements is ready, the next step is to develop a program of grounds management actions according to the season or month. This program outlines all of the major horticultural tasks necessary to achieve optimal care of the gardens.

Compost: completely decayed organic matter used for conditioning soil. It is dark, odorless, and rich in nutrients.

Decurrent growth habit: tree growth habit displaying a spreading crown and multiple main branches.

Emergency management plan: a plan that anticipates all potential emergencies that might befall a municipality or institution and provides immediate and longer-term responses to each of those scenarios.

Ericaceous: any of the plants in the family *Ericaceae*, most requiring acidic soils high in organic matter.

Excurrent growth habit: tree growth habit displaying a central leader or trunk from which emerges a scaffold of branches.

Friable: having a crumbly texture that makes a soil ideal for the root growth of plants. Friable soils are usually classified as loam.

Growing degree days: a method of predicting biological events such as date of flowering or date of insect hatch based on accumulated seasonal temperatures. Usually calculated as:

$$\frac{\text{Max. temp.} + \text{min. temp.}}{2} - \begin{array}{c}\text{Base} \\ \text{temperature}\end{array} = \begin{array}{l}\text{Daily GDD, in which} \\ \text{the base temperature} \\ \text{is predetermined}\end{array}$$

Hardscape: all of the nonliving elements of a landscape, including roads, pathways, parking, plazas, fountains, sculptures, etc.

Integrated pest management: an approach to garden maintenance that has as its main goal the development of sustainable ways of managing pests that minimize environmental, health, and economic risks.

Invasive plant: a plant that has the ability to thrive and spread aggressively outside its natural range. A naturally aggressive plant may be especially invasive when it is introduced to a new habitat.

Herbaceous: annual and perennial plants that have leaves and stems that die down at the end of the growing season to the soil level. They have no persistent woody stem above ground.

Mulch: a protective cover placed over the soil, primarily to modify the soil environment and reduce weed growth.

Recycling: processing used materials into new products to prevent waste of potentially useful materials, reduce the consumption of fresh raw materials, reduce energy usage, and reduce air pollution.

Sustainable development: development that meets the needs of the present without compromising the ability of future generations to meet their own needs (Brundtland Commission Report 1983).

Xeriscaping: landscaping designed specifically for areas that are susceptible to drought or for properties where water conservation is practiced. Derived from the Greek *xeros*, meaning "dry," the term *xeriscape* means literally "dry landscape."

Group Plants According to Maintenance Levels

All plants require maintenance, but not all require equal levels of maintenance. Many trees only require pruning once every three to five years to remove deadwood or to perform structural maintenance, but fruit trees require annual pruning if they are to set quality fruit. The same can be said for annual flowering plants: some require constant deadheading to keep flowering, while others require little or no maintenance and keep blooming throughout the season.

Different parts of the United States will have different plant maintenance regimes. For example, regular irrigating is a necessity in much of the Southwest, while protecting plants from extremes of cold is a given in the upper Midwest. Professional grounds maintenance websites, magazines, and books can provide examples of programs specific to the garden's region.

Grounds Management Staff

Expertise in all areas of garden maintenance is required to perform a consistent quality grounds management program. Staff must be knowledgeable about the plants (woody, herbaceous, and turf) and hardscape maintenance (walkways, parking lots, edging, water features, topography, and erosion control). The following are core grounds maintenance job classifications:

Arborist: maintains all the woody plants; knowledgeable about basic pruning techniques and the latest in the science of arboriculture as well as the common diseases, insects, and abiotic problems of trees in the garden's collections. Either manages contractors who actually climb and prune the large trees or, if a certified arborist, performs the tree pruning.

Equipment operator: operates licensed heavy equipment: bucket trucks, tractors, front-end loaders, grinders, and dump trucks. Understanding how to carry heavy weights, use outriggers, and balance loads is required.

Gardener: performs basic gardening skills such as planting, weeding, mulching, dividing, and pruning. Has the ability to detect plant problems as they develop and either react personally or refer the problems to staff with particular specialties.

Table 13-1: Sample Grounds Management Schedule

Type of Activity	Jan	Feb	Mar	Apr	May	Jun	July	Aug	Sept	Oct	Nov	Dec
PLANTING												
Container grown			X	X	X	X	X	X	X	X	X	
Balled and burlapped			X	X	X	X			X	X	X	
FERTILIZATION												
Trees			X	X	X	X			X	X	X	
Shrubs			X	X	X	X			X	X	X	
Herbaceous plants			X	X	X	X			X	X	X	
PRUNING												
Spring-flowering trees and shrubs (after bloom)					X	X	X					
Summer-flowering trees and shrubs		X	X	X								
Conifers (candle pruning)					X	X						
Broadleaf evergreens			X	X	X	X	X	X				
MULCHING	X	X	X	X	X	X	X	X	X	X	X	X
WEED CONTROL												
Pre-emergence		X	X	X						X	X	
Post-emergence		X	X	X	X	X	X	X	X	X	X	
TURF												
Establishment			X	X	X	X			X	X		
Overseeding									X	X	X	
Aerating			X	X	X	X			X	X		
Thatching		X	X		X	X						

Grounds manager/supervisor: skilled in managing people, dispatching and organizing work, teaching, and multitasking.

Horticulturist: plans, designs and installs entire garden areas. Experienced and knowledgeable in all aspects of plants, with a background in horticultural science and the ability to troubleshoot problems in the landscape.

Irrigation specialist: maintains all irrigation systems, which can be advanced installed electronic systems or manual and portable. Requires background in electronics and pipefitting and an understanding of soil structure and basic plant requirements.

Integrated pest manager: manages all plant pest problems such as insect, disease, weed, and cultural problems. A degree in horticulture, entomology, pathology, or plant science and excellent problem-solving and record-keeping skills are useful.

Turf specialist: maintains all turf areas. Knowledgeable about all types of turf; able to advise staff on turf-related questions and to work closely with irrigation specialist on managing water, a critical component of quality turf care. Understands and manages the turf-cutting contractor or staff.

Scheduling Staff

Scheduling staff is an important part of grounds management and is determined by the needs of the facility. While the majority of the staff work regular business hours on weekdays to facilitate maintenance of grounds, greenhouses, and buildings, some specialized staff must work on weekends, on holidays, and after regular business hours to serve specific functions, such as staffing special events or caring for vulnerable greenhouse collections. Schedules need to be evaluated and modified regularly to reflect changing priorities with changing seasons.

In some situations, part or all of the staff in a public garden may be unionized and have certain rights as part of a collective bargaining agreement. When dealing with unionized staff, specific job duties, benefits, work schedules, and disciplinary procedures must be observed. Often supervisors do not have the same supervisory flexibility with the management of unionized staff as they do with nonunionized staff.

Outsourcing Grounds Maintenance

Some public gardens elect to contract out certain grounds maintenance services. The advantages and disadvantages of outsourcing depend on resources, specific restrictions, and makeup of the facility. In some instances, grounds maintenance tasks are outsourced when staff do not have the expertise to complete the task or when the garden does not have the proper equipment for the work. It may not make financial sense for a public garden to own a blacktop-paving machine if this task is only performed once every two to three years. Sometime outsourcing is more cost-effective because it enables in-house staff to focus on core duties and responsibilities. Tasks that are commonly outsourced include lawn care, infrastructure maintenance, pesticide applications, and some arboricultural work such as pruning or removal of large trees.

On the downside, garden managers typically have less control over contractors than over their own staff. Also, contractors may not always be available when the work needs to be performed, particularly after an emergency situation such as a snowstorm or windstorm.

Total Plant Health Care

A grounds management program must take into account all aspects of the garden, including soil, turf, herbaceous and woody plant material, mulch, weeds, irrigation, fertilizers, pesticides, and pruning. The maintenance schedule for each plant collection must reflect all aspects of plant health specific to the plants in that collection.

Soil Preparation

All gardeners know that a healthy garden requires healthy soil. Time spent on soil preparation is well worth the effort, particularly prior to planting. The ideal garden soil is friable and rich enough in nutrients to yield healthy plants. Local extension services or private soil labs can provide soil analyses. Each soil

Figure 13-1: A complete soil analysis will yield a profile of soil fertility, pH, and composition. Such an analysis should be undertaken before determining how best to modify the soil to meet plant needs.

Smithsonian Institution, Smithsonian Gardens

test will indicate the makeup of the soil by percentage (clay, sand, loam, and organic matter) as well as the status of critical elements such as nitrogen, potassium, and phosphorus, along with soil pH.

The results of the soil analysis help determine what plants can properly be grown in that area. For example, if the soil pH is in the alkaline range, it will not be appropriate for ericaceous species, such as *Rhododendron*. Soils that are heavily compacted or have poor drainage can be improved to a degree with the addition of large quantities of organic matter or, in extreme cases, through the laying of drainage tile. Alternatively, the horticulturist responsible for such areas can select from the palette of plants tolerant of such soils. Soil testing and modifications should occur routinely throughout the life of a garden.

Mulching

All public gardens utilize mulching techniques throughout the landscape. Mulches can be divided into natural forms (such as wood chips, shredded hardwood bark, leaf mold, straw, pine needles, and nut hulls) and inorganic forms (including black plastic and landscape fabric). No single source of mulch is ideal for all situations, but both function and aesthetic appearance must be considered in a public garden setting. The benefits of using mulch are numerous: it cuts down on water loss, insulates roots from excessive heat and frost, reduces weed problems, and often provides aesthetic improvements to the landscape. In addition, organic mulch types provide a

Figure 13-2: A well-mulched tree can reduce soil moisture loss and weed growth while adding to the aesthetic appeal of the garden.

Alexis Alvey

slow-release form of nutrients for plants as they decompose and are cultivated into the soil.

Mulch can be a problem in the landscape if applied with unrealistic expectations. Mulches are not an effective method of controlling perennial weeds. Although they can temporarily mask the problem (which may be justified if a particular garden area needs to be spruced up in a hurry), the problem will recur within several weeks to months. The depth of the mulch layer should be less than 3 inches, particularly around the base of trees. Studies have shown that overmulching around tree trunks can make them more susceptible to trunk cracks and entry of pathogens.

Weeding

A weedy landscape severely impacts the overall quality of the public garden landscape. Before developing a weed management plan, the manager must identify the weed species and determine whether they are perennial (bindweed, quackgrass), biennial (garlic mustard, wild carrot, henbit), or annual (crabgrass, chickweed). Annual and biennial weeds and all weed seedlings can normally be removed by hand or by cultivation with a long-handled hoe or cultivator.

The most difficult weeds to remove are tenacious perennial species. Ideally, weeding occurs before the weed plant has had a chance to set seed and spread. Perennial weeds or biennials with very heavy seed set can be difficult or impossible to eliminate by cultivation. Perennials such as bindweed contain rhizomes, and hand-cultivating typically results in breaking the rhizomes into multiple pieces, each of which will produce a new plant. Biennials such as garlic mustard can be equally difficult to remove completely, and cultivating may only mask the problem for a short period. When dealing with persistent weeds, one option is to remove the existing soil to a depth of 8 inches, then cover the subbase with a layer of black plastic mulch or landscape fabric, and finally import new, weed-free soil to cover this. Alternatively, black plastic could be put on the surface for two years to prevent light from reaching the weeds, thus weakening or eliminating them. This has worked effectively against Russian thistle.

Another, less labor-intensive approach is the use of nonselective herbicides, such as those containing glyphosate. In most states, herbicides can be applied only by licensed pesticide applicators. Also, nonselective herbicides cannot be used in established perennial or groundcover beds unless one uses a special application technique such as sponge-wiping directly on the foliage of the offending plants. Another effective method of reducing weeds is to have densely planted beds with little bare earth exposed to light.

Irrigating

When designing or deciding on the type of irrigation system required, a primary consideration is the nature of the plant collection being maintained. Public garden landscapes typically consist of turf, planting beds with herbaceous and woody plants, stand-alone trees, evergreens, and tropicals. Each of these categories will likely require its own level of irrigation. When designing and selecting an irrigation system, specific irrigation heads for turf, shrubs, and other select collections should be considered.

Irrigation systems range from low-tech, manual systems to very high-tech automated ones. There are advantages and disadvantages to both, depending on the landscape situation and budget. Manual systems tend to be lower-cost and easier to repair but require more labor to operate. More sophisticated systems are more expensive to install and maintain but are more automated. An example of a low-tech, manual system would be the use of hose bibs, hoses, and sprinkler attachments. Hoses and hose bibs typically are available in ½-inch and ¾-inch sizes. However, these systems require regular monitoring and can become inefficient and wasteful.

In the realm of more advanced irrigation systems, again, there are levels of complexity. The simpler systems consist of in-ground piping of some type. The two main types of piping available are rigid PVC and more flexible polyethylene tubing.

PVC is more expensive and harder to install, but it is more durable and longer-lasting than polyethylene tubing.

One type of in-ground system utilizes quick couplers. These durable couplers are typically made of brass and are available in ½-inch, ¾-inch, and 1-inch receptacle sizes. Brass sprinklers are available specifically to fit these receptacles, which are at ground level. Although the materials can be expensive at initial installation, because of their durability and longevity quick couplers are economical over time. While this type of irrigation system is considered somewhat outdated and inefficient, it does provide a reliable and generous volume of water for landscapes that require it. These systems usually run under higher water pressure but require minimal maintenance.

With new technological advances, in-ground sprinkler heads have become much more efficient and effective. The newer sprinklers have pop-up heads that automatically rotate to the desired width and length of spray. These are also known as rotor sprinklers and are designed to use lower volumes of water while providing a uniform application of water (Grounds Maintenance 2010). These sprinkler heads are primarily made of lightweight plastic and stainless steel or another durable metal. They can range in style from lawn sprinklers that recess into the ground when not in use to taller, extended heads for shrub borders where vegetation is higher. With water conservation and availability an important issue, this technology continues to become more efficient.

Another type of irrigation system worth considering that requires less water to operate is a drip or weeper system. Drip irrigation can be used in flower beds, shrub borders, containers, and greenhouses. Weeper or soaker hoses can be used in flowerbeds and around trees and shrubs. The advantages to both in-ground pop-up sprinklers and drip or weeper systems are that they are relatively easy to install, are easy to repair, and are reasonably priced. These systems can be controlled manually or with programmable clocks.

In addition to advances and efficiencies in piping and sprinklers, innovations have also been made in irrigation control systems. While much of this technology is typically applied to farms, golf courses, athletic fields, and other commercial sites, it can also be very effective in a public garden. These systems are computerized, highly automated, and very efficient, and offer the ability to control irrigation by phone, radio transmitter, and even wireless connection. Soil moisture sensor networks can be linked to irrigation systems and monitored and controlled from a remote site. These systems will control the amount and frequency of watering based on a host of variables in the field. This new technology can provide water more efficiently

to landscapes while minimizing environmental effects such as runoff and nutrient leaching (Bauerle 2010).

For the sake of efficiency, it may be tempting to place entire sections of the garden under a single automated irrigation regime. But for many public gardens, such an approach would not accurately reflect the particular watering needs of individual taxa. In an herb garden, for example, some herbs may be heavy water consumers, while others might survive best when kept fairly dry. Overhead irrigation sprinklers may be okay for the former but would drown the latter. Plants that are improperly watered or subject to severe fluctuations in the amount of moisture in the soil will usually exhibit unwanted stress, which can compromise growth rate, flowering capability, and overall plant health.

As a general rule, longer, infrequent watering is preferred over short, frequent watering. Specific watering amounts depend of soil types, size and types of plants, density of planting (especially densely planted perennial beds where the interlocking root masses take up a tremendous amount of water very quickly), and size of area to be irrigated. For example, in the heat of the summer when plants in planting beds are not receiving enough natural rainfall, watering plants for two to four hours, once or twice a week, will provide a deep watering. Deep watering will encourage the establishment of a healthy root system.

Container plantings are in a special category for watering techniques. Many require daily irrigating to prevent them from wilting, especially during the heat of summer and when grown in full sun. Thoroughly wetting the soil is essential, which generally is achieved when excess water runs out of the bottom of the pot.

Unlike established plants, newly planted shrubs and trees should be watered consistently for at least the first two years after planting to ensure that they are properly established. This supplemental watering will allow the plants to develop a well-formed root system. In most cases, after a couple of years these plants can be incorporated into an ongoing irrigation schedule along with other established plantings in the garden. However, certain species such as ericaceous plants (family *Ericaceae*) may need a longer period to become established due to their fibrous, shallow root system.

Fertilizing

There are many commercial formulations of fertilizer, some specifically for turf, others for trees and shrubs, herbaceous plants, or greenhouse crops. Table 13-2 describes the major and minor nutrients found in fertilizer formulations.

Table 13-2: Plant Nutrients

Primary Nutrients	Secondary Nutrients	Micronutrients
Nitrogen (N)	Calcium (Ca)	Iron (Fe)
Phosphorus (P)	Magnesium (Mg)	Manganese (Mn)
Potassium (K)	Sulfur (S)	Boron (B)
		Zinc (Zn)
		Copper (Cu)
		Molybdenum (Mo)
		Nickel (Ni)

Fertilizers are generally divided into organic or inorganic and fast or slow release. The speed of release reflects the relative rate at which nitrogen is available for root uptake. Nitrogen is a primary component of proteins and is usually more responsible for increasing plant growth than any other nutrient. An organic fertilizer is derived from a plant or animal source such as manure, cottonseed meal, or dried blood. Organic fertilizers tend to be slower-release because microorganisms generally have to break down the organic nitrogen to a more soluble, usable form.

Inorganic or chemical fertilizers are generally available at a lower cost per unit of nitrogen. These fertilizers can be either slow-release or fast-release depending on their chemical makeup. Slow-release fertilizers have a longer residual, lower potential for burning, low water solubility, and generally higher cost. Slow-release fertilizers are more appropriate to use during warmer months, when fertilizer burning can occur from fast-release fertilizers. There are several types of slow-release chemical fertilizers available, including isobutylidene diurea (IBDU), sulfur-coated urea (SCU), and plastic-coated fertilizers such as Osmocote.

Fast-release or soluble fertilizers are made up of ammonium nitrate or other ammonium or urea compounds. Water-soluble or liquid fertilizers can be used on greenhouse crops and herbaceous plantings when a quick shot of nitrogen is desired. Container plantings, for example, are typically given weekly watering with a soluble fertilizer.

It is important to read the ingredients and directions on a fertilizer bag or container before application. Rates of application depend on many variables, including type of fertilizer, crop, type of soil, weather, and time of year.

Chelated iron is used extensively for prevention and control of iron deficiency of azalea, rhododendron, and other acid-requiring plants. Also, various formulations of limestone products (and wood ashes) are used to raise soil pH for plants that need an alkaline soil. But the effectiveness of these products is strongly correlated to the degree of change needed to achieve the desired pH level. A public garden should, whenever possible, site plants into soils that approximate their pH and compositional needs.

Pruning

Trees and shrubs in public gardens can be displayed as individual specimens; grouped into groves, mass plantings, or hedges; or trained in specialty forms, such as pollards or espaliers. All woody plants will require ongoing pruning to achieve the intended results and to be vigorous plants with maximum aesthetic appeal.

Pruning and training trees from a young age can ensure structurally strong specimens that will be safer and require less corrective pruning as they mature. Training should take advantage of the tree's natural growth habit, whether that is with a strong, straight trunk (excurrent habit), a spreading, diffused form (decurrent habit), or a weeping habit.

Flowering trees and shrubs flower on two separate types of growth: new or current season's growth and older or previous season's growth. For example, common butterfly bush (*Buddleia davidii*) flowers on the current season's growth, while border forsythia (*Forsythia* × *intermedia*) blooms on the previous season's growth. Woody plants that bloom on the previous season's growth are generally pruned in midsummer to shape or train. More serious pruning to rejuvenate the plant

Figure 13-3: *Cornus officinalis* displaying typical excurrent growth habit.

Cornell Plantations

Figure 13-4: *Acer rubrum* 'Somerset' displaying typical decurrent growth habit.

Cornell Plantations

should be performed in late winter or early spring when the plant is dormant; doing so, however, will reduce that spring's flowering. Trees and shrubs that flower on the current season's growth are typically pruned before flowering when the plant is dormant. A modest amount of pruning can also be done in the growing season as well to maintain a specific shape or size.

Woody plants that are not grown primarily for their flowering, such as shade trees, conifers, and some broadleaf evergreens, are generally pruned in winter when dormant to reduce spread of disease or in midsummer after the spring flush of new growth has hardened off. As with flowering woody plants, this is a good time to shape trees and shrubs. Severe pruning should not be performed during the growing season, as plants may be damaged or made more susceptible to diseases.

Shrubs that are being grown primarily for their display of colorful stems, such as shrubby dogwoods and willows, should be ground-pruned (coppiced) every two to three years to maintain their colorful form. Cultivars that do not respond well to coppicing and are very slow to develop new stems should be thinned every year to keep new stems continually developing. Otherwise, stems will develop more mature bark layers that lack the attractive pigments.

Plant vigor will determine the type and severity of the pruning. Plants in good health have a better chance of recovering from severe pruning than ones in poor condition. However, proper pruning techniques can reenergize older trees and shrubs and improve plant health and aesthetics.

Arborists, who typically perform the majority of pruning in public gardens, may also be responsible for assessing the structural health of trees. A tree risk assessment program (TRAP) can be established so that every mature tree on the grounds is monitored and evaluated for potential for failure and so that records are maintained. Among the techniques that may be required are cabling of branches, removal of weak or broken branches, and removal of the entire tree.

Proper pruning tools are essential in maintaining handsome trees and shrubs that will produce vigorous growth, showy flowers, and fruit. The most important tools are handheld pruning shears, lopping shears, and a handsaw. There are several types of handheld pruners and lopping shears, but a bypass type is the most appropriate. This type of pruner works like a scissor and is effective because it will cleanly cut branches without crushing them. All pruning tools must be kept sharp, clean, and well oiled. Regular maintenance will ensure the effectiveness of these valuable tools. Failure to properly maintain tools may result in unnecessary damage to plants.

Figure 13-5: Winter is an ideal time to assess the integrity of trees. TRAP records can be kept in a paper file or in an electronic database, such as FileMaker.

Photo by Donna Levy, courtesy Cornell Plantations

Integrated Pest Management

Integrated pest management (IPM) is an approach to garden maintenance that has as its main goal the development of sustainable ways of managing pests to minimize environmental, health, and economic risks. The main types of pest management in a successful IPM program include biological, cultural, physical, or mechanical and chemical means, as well as proper plant selection.

The most important practice associated with IPM is monitoring or scouting of the landscape to observe the quantities and types of pests present. Thresholds need to be established for acceptable levels of a particular pest for any given plant species. Some pest populations can be monitored with pest traps such as pheromone traps and sticky cards. Once pest populations reach a certain threshold or level of concern, it may be necessary to take action.

Typically in IPM, proper plant health care and preventative measures are the first lines of defense. Mechanical measures

Figure 13-6: A successful IPM program is based on regular and thorough monitoring of pests.

Photo by Donna Levy, courtesy Cornell Plantations

such as pruning out localized infestations or infections can prevent pest outbreaks. Biological controls can be effective and include the use of beneficial insects and other organisms, including releasing parasitic wasps in a greenhouse or inoculating soil with beneficial nematodes. Finally, biological, minimum-risk, and reduced-risk pesticides are chosen as the least toxic control options.

The use of chemical pesticides is usually considered a last resort in an effective IPM program. If pesticides are needed to control pests, the safest, least harmful product to the environment should be considered first. Good examples of lower-toxicity pesticides are horticultural oils and soaps, which break down quickly in the environment with little residue.

REDUCED RISK PESTICIDES

Since 1993 the Environmental Protection Agency (EPA) has expedited the registration of conventional pesticides with characteristics such as very low toxicity to humans and nontarget organisms including fish and birds, low risk of groundwater contamination or runoff, low potential for pesticide resistance, demonstrated efficacy, and compatibility with IPM. Materials meeting these criteria are referred to by EPA as "reduced-risk." Minimum-risk pesticides are certain products that are exempted from EPA registration (and therefore have no EPA registration number). Biopesticides, or biological pesticides as defined by EPA, are certain types of pesticides derived from such natural materials as animals, plants, bacteria, and minerals (Cornell Cooperative Extension Pest Management Guidelines 2010.

Another facet of IPM that can also be very effective is the use of new, genetically superior plant cultivars. These plants are bred for pest resistance, drought tolerance, and improved aesthetic value. Many experts feel that the use of more robust plants in appropriate locations will significantly reduce pest problems and the use of pesticides. Their appropriateness in a public garden is predicated on the collections policy of that garden.

Equally important are the control of invasive weeds and the monitoring of landscape plants to reduce the risk of introducing invasive plants. Invasive plants continue to have a serious impact on our environment and economy and need to be evaluated closely. Many universities administer plant evaluation and breeding programs to determine if new cultivars display the potential for invasiveness. An increasing number of public gardens have signed on to the Voluntary Codes of Conduct for Botanic Gardens and Arboreta to eliminate all invasive or suspected-of-being invasive plants from their cultivated collections (Center for Plant Conservation 2002).

Record keeping and recording vital information as it relates to pesticide use and IPM procedures are very important and, in some cases, regulated by law. State environmental protection agencies require that certain records and information be maintained as part of a pest management program. States may also require that records be easily accessible in the event of an on-site inspection. If pesticides are being utilized, a certification or license is often required along with proper ongoing training. Pesticides include insecticides, miticides, fungicides, herbicides, rodenticides, and repellents. Those materials with an EPA registration number are regulated by law.

The types of records that are typically maintained by horticultural professionals include date pest was detected, host plant(s), growing degree day information, symptoms, action taken, date of action, and location of pest in the garden, as well as name, concentration, and amount of the pesticide or treatment method used. Follow-up efficacy notes are also important. These records create a history and timeline that can be referred back to when tracking and evaluating pest populations.

Roads, Pathways, and Infrastructure

Functional and safe roads and pathways are extremely important in a public garden. Not only do roadways and pathways provide access to gardens, greenhouses, buildings, and other vital facilities, but they are also visual elements that add to the aesthetics of the garden. Safe, level, and easy-to-navigate roads and pathways are an important component in the visitor's experience.

Road Maintenance

Maintenance of roadways depends on the composition of the surface. In most cases, the primary roads in a public garden are constructed of asphalt (blacktop). The integrity and life of asphalt depend on the quality of its preparation and application. Roadbeds should consist of up to 6 inches of some type of crushed stone that has been compacted before asphalt is applied. The thickness of the asphalt layer will usually dictate the life span of a road. At least several inches of blacktop is usually applied over a crushed gravel base. Secondary and tertiary roads are often less elaborate and can be made of loose gravel or dirt. These roads need regular maintenance and grading to reduce ruts and erosion.

Pathway surfaces can also vary. Pathways can be made of blacktop, concrete, paving stones, gravel, wood chips, or dirt. There are important advantages and disadvantages of each to consider.

- **Blacktop** (asphalt). More weather resistant than concrete and more stable than gravel, blacktop is flexible and has the ability to contract and expand without sustaining damage. Relative to their durability and life span, asphalt surfaces are fairly inexpensive and easy to repair. Disadvantages include limited durability in warmer climates and the regular maintenance needed to seal cracks and potholes over time.

- **Concrete.** Concrete is durable, moderately priced, and long-lasting. However, it is susceptible to cracking and breakage from freezing and thawing, especially in cold climates. Unlike asphalt, concrete is not easily repaired when cracks and breaks occur. Concrete walkways are also susceptible to damage from road salt and other chemicals in colder climates.

- **Pea gravel, bluestone dust, and other stone by-products.** The advantages of loose gravel products are that they are easy to apply and maintain, inexpensive, and aesthetically pleasing. However, these surfaces can easily move around, especially on slopes, and need to be stabilized regularly to avoid tripping hazards. A firm base of several inches of recycled concrete (RCA) applied as a base will help stabilize a top layer of ornamental gravel.

- **Pavers.** Paving blocks are popular in public settings and come in a wide variety of colors and sizes. Once a sand or RCA base has been established, pavers are installed like bricks and other loose stones. Pavers are durable and long-lasting and can range in price from moderate to expensive depending on the quality and thickness of the material.

- **Wood chips.** Wood chips are often a desirable pathway surface because they are easy to apply and are inexpensive or free and easily available. Finer grades of mulch are easier to walk on and compact better for a smoother surface. However, regular monitoring, maintenance, and replenishment are needed to repair washouts or gullies caused by erosion. Wood chips typically last just one year and thus need to be renewed annually. In times of severe drought, wetting down wood chip paths may be required to reduce risk of fire.

- **Dirt.** Maintaining dirt roads and pathways can be quite challenging. They require the most monitoring and maintenance of all surfaces. While there is no initial investment of money, regular grading and leveling to repair erosion will require time, equipment, and labor. Dirt roads can also become inaccessible during excessively wet weather and dusty during droughts. A dirt surface is generally appropriate only on secondary roads and pathways, especially in woodland areas and in less cultivated areas of the garden.

It is important to note that when roadways and pathways are created, they should have a slight crown in the center to allow for runoff so that puddles do not form. Even more important is that roadways and pathways that lead to buildings and garden features must be compliant with the Americans with Disabilities Act.

Snow and Ice Removal Options

In areas of the country that are subject to cold winters, there are special considerations and challenges to maintaining safe and accessible roads and pathways. The winter elements can cause serious safety concerns in public gardens that impact general visitation, special events, and maintenance of facilities. Some public gardens will close certain roadways during winter to reduce the need for snow removal and to provide special places for visitors to enjoy winter sports.

Here is a list of potential tools and techniques to address winter elements in a public garden:

- **Plowing.** Plowing is typically the fastest and most efficient way to remove significant quantities of snow in large or open areas. However, the purchase and maintenance of equipment can be costly, and staff members need to be properly trained in its safe use. Also, damage from plows to hardscape, turf, and other aesthetic features of the garden is often inevitable and requires repair.

- **Revolving brush on a truck.** A revolving brush can also be an effective tool to battle the elements. It tends to be less

Figure 13-7: Power equipment, kept in proper working order, is essential for gardens that receive heavy snows.

Smithsonian Institution, Smithsonian Gardens

damaging to asphalt and other hardscape features in the garden. However, brushes are generally used only on roads and pathways with light accumulations of snow.

- **Sanding.** Sanding can be used after larger accumulations of snow and ice have been cleared or when accumulation is minimal but the potential for a slippery surface still exists. Sand is an inexpensive way to create traction on roadways and pathways. One disadvantage of applying sand is the need for sand-spreading equipment for larger areas such as roads; this can be costly. Extra caution should also be taken near buildings, since sand can be quite damaging to rugs and flooring surfaces.

- **De-icers.** De-icers have largely replaced conventional road salt, also known as rock salt (sodium chloride), which can be quite damaging to equipment, vehicles, roads and other hardscape surfaces, and, more important, plants. De-icers are generally more expensive than sand or a mixture of sand and rock salt but are very effective and more ecofriendly. De-icers may contain calcium chloride, magnesium chloride, potassium chloride, or urea. All may cause some level of damage to plants, especially at high doses, but not as much as conventional road salt. Newer products such as calcium magnesium acetate (CMA) are more ecofriendly than most other de-icers and less likely to damage plants or pollute the environment.

Water Features

Water features in a public garden not only create a serene, calm atmosphere and aesthetic appeal but also have functional value. The ambience that a water feature provides is often underestimated. Water features can be man-made or naturally occurring. From a large lake to a small pond or pool, water offers a sense of tranquility. Water features can also provide functional value as irrigation water storage vessels and storm-water retention ponds. While there is an inherent risk factor and liability concern with water features, if they are properly planned, designed, and implemented, they can significantly enhance the visitor experience.

Maintaining Water Quality

Water quality is an important issue in maintaining water features. Good-quality water can be defined as:

- Water with no offensive odor or unnatural color.

- Water with no excessive turbidity, which relates to water clarity. The required water clarity is measured in terms of nephelometric turbidity units. These readings measure water transparency.

- Water with adequate circulation.

- A water surface with minimal filamentous or suspended algae and minimal debris and foam.

Another water quality issue that must be monitored on a regular basis is nutrient loading caused by aquatic animals, vegetation, fertilizer, stormwater, or waterfowl. Buildup of salinity, acidity, phosphate, nitrate, and sediment can also cause problems.

Algae and particulate matter can be problematic to the heath of water and to the health and viability of fish and beneficial organisms. Good filter and pumping systems, aeration, and circulation all help to reduce algae growth and particulate matter buildup. In smaller ponds, reducing sunlight to the surface of the water by proper use of aquatic plants will also help to reduce algae growth.

Water quality can be managed through best management practices (BMPs). These management approaches address watershed management and runoff issues that can help public gardens maintain healthy water features and reduce the risk of polluted water (Stevens 2003).

Water Features for Irrigation

The potential use of water features for irrigation in a public garden depends on the size of the water feature, how it is recharged, and if a local water authority or environmental agency will permit such activity. If permitted, specialized water pumps are designed to pump water from a body of water to an irrigation system. Using this water to irrigate can save money, but the water must be of sufficient quality to ensure no damage to plant collections.

Sustainable Landscape Practices

Sustainability is integrated into many aspects of public garden landscape practices, including IPM, plant health care, recycling, composting, organic gardening, energy efficiency, use of alternative fuels, water conservation, and much more. It is this collective effort that reduces the environmental impact of our resource use.

Selecting Appropriate Plants

One of the most important components of sustainability is the development and selection of plants with reduced resource needs. These are plants selected for their genetic superiority in pest resistance, drought tolerance, cold tolerance, and limited fertilizer needs. Many universities have plant evaluation and breeding programs to introduce superior plants. The results from these programs are featured at public gardens for the benefit of nurserymen, gardeners, retailers, and eventually home owners.

Many public gardens have also increased their use of plants native to their region. While native plants are not necessarily free of pests and cultural problems, they are more likely than non-natives to be adapted to the soil conditions and humidity and temperature extremes of the locality. Consequently, they often require less soil amending and fertilizer and fewer pesticides than non-native counterparts.

Recycling

Now more than ever, public gardens need to use recycled materials and to recycle their own waste products. Materials

Table 13-3: Basic Water Clarity Measurements

Trophic State (Nutrient Enrichment)	Secchi Disk Transparency Range (meters)
Eutrophic (very enriched)	0–3.0
Mesotrophic (moderately enriched)	3.0–5.5
Oligotrophic (nutrient poor)	> 5.5

that can be recycled include paper, cardboard, cans, plastic, and glass. Well-designed, easy-to-identify receptacles placed in strategic locations in eating areas or buildings can encourage staff, volunteers, and the public to help with recycling efforts.

Recycled materials should also be used whenever possible in the garden. For example, children's gardens are required by law to be accessible, and for liability reasons the floor surfaces should be soft and able to take impact to reduce injury when a child falls. The types of recycled products commonly used for this purpose are engineered wood fiber, loose rubberized mulch, poured-in-place rubber, and rubber tiles. The rubber products are made from recycled tires and come in a wide range of colors and sizes. Recycled rubber also can be fabricated into bridges, railings, and stairs.

Wise Water Management

Water reclamation is another important way to recycle in a public garden. Rainwater can be collected from buildings or greenhouse complexes and stored for future irrigation use. Barrels and other collection devices can be connected to gutters and leaders to collect rainwater. At Mount Auburn Cemetery in Cambridge, Massachusetts, 12,000 gallons of rainwater were collected in 2009 from the greenhouse complex for reuse (Barnett 2010).

In 1981, the Denver Water District coined the term *xeriscaping* to describe an approach to water-wise gardening. Though more appropriate in areas prone to drought than in humid temperate regions such as the Northeast, xeriscaping principles can be adopted in public gardens throughout North America.

THE SEVEN PRINCIPLES OF XERISCAPING

Thoughtful planning and design to use water most efficiently

Efficient irrigation systems, properly designed and maintained

Use of mulch to reduce water loss from soil surface

Soil preparation and modification to maximize soil water retention

Limited areas of turf

Water-efficient plant material, including use of less water-consumptive turf types

Appropriate levels of maintenance (Iannotti 2010)

Mowing Habits

Changing and improving mowing habits in public gardens can greatly improve the health of the landscape while minimally impacting aesthetics. Many gardens are reducing mowing areas or mowing less often simply as a response to reduced labor resources or the need to economize operations. Mowing less visible or less frequently used areas monthly or even once or twice a year can significantly reduce maintenance. Raising mowing heights will also reduce maintenance. Use of mulching mowers instead of bagging grass clippings adds nutrients back to the turf and reduces the need for chemical fertilizers. Areas left to revert into grassy meadows can create habitat for and encourage insects, birds, and other beneficials. Leaving turf longer under mature trees is especially helpful during times of drought.

A variation on this practice is to transform traditional turf areas into native lawns. The appropriate seed mix will vary by region, but the concept is to sow native grasses and other thin-bladed species onto a well-prepared seedbed. As with any newly seeded plot, this will need to be lightly watered daily until seedlings emerge. But once the bed becomes established, the need for mowing, fertilizing, and irrigating should be much less than that for traditional turf.

Finally, bear in mind that few people visit public gardens to admire the quality of the turf. They care about the quality of the collections, the beauty of the landscape design, and the diversity of education programs. So as long as the turf is green and regularly mowed in visible or often-used areas, visitors are typically quite tolerant of less-than-perfect lawns.

Composting

Proper composting requires a mix of raw materials, a large enough area, regular turning, and water and oxygen. Many types of microorganisms are needed to break down the different organic components that make up a compost pile. At the beginning of the composting process (0–40°C), mesophilic bacteria predominate. As the compost heats up above 40°C, thermophilic bacteria take over. Finally, at the highest temperatures, bacteria of the genus *Thermus* have been isolated, but little additional decomposition takes place. Frequent turning of the compost pile aerates it and prevents it from heating up to this range.

In compost, fungi are important because they break down tough debris, enabling bacteria to continue the decomposition process once most of the cellulose has been exhausted. Fungi spread and grow vigorously by producing many cells and filaments and can attack organic residues that are too dry, acidic, or low in nitrogen for bacterial decomposition (Trautmann and Olynciw 1996).

Table 13-4: Soil Amendments

Organic	Inorganic
Compost (humus)	Gravel
Manure	Vermiculite or perlite
Sphagnum peat moss	Sand
Wood chips	Limestone
Leaf mold	Gypsum
Biochar	
Wood ash	

Finished compost can be used in a number of ways, including as potting soil, as top dressing for turf, for soil amendment, and to brew compost tea. Brewing compost tea is a very complex procedure that requires specific knowledge of soils and composting. Compost tea brewers can be purchased assembled or can be custom-built depending on the resources available. Essentially, a properly brewed tea can be sprayed on or drenched into the soil or sprayed on the foliage of plants to improve soil biology and enhance plant vigor. This practice is still relatively new, and research continues in this area.

Biochar

Another new technology intended to make landscapes more sustainable is biochar. Biochar is a type of charcoal that is primarily used to capture and store atmospheric carbon. Biochar is of increasing interest because of concerns about climate change caused by emissions of carbon dioxide (CO_2) and other greenhouse gases. Biochar draws carbon from the atmosphere and is being evaluated as a tool in reducing the impact of farming. It can improve water quality, increase soil fertility, and reduce pressure on old-growth forests.

Fuel-Efficient Machinery

Fuel-efficient equipment and the consequent lowering of emissions is another major component of sustainable landscape practices. Many companies are now manufacturing cars, trucks, utility carts, chain saws, trimmers, and blowers that are more fuel efficient and less polluting. New technologies are yielding electric vehicles that are easier to operate and maintain and have sufficient power to meet the garden's needs.

Public Garden Security

While budgets play a major role in the type and size of security programs, the safety and security of staff, volunteers, and visitors are high priorities for all public gardens. Providing adequate security for the garden will ensure that its valuable features and resources are protected. With increased concern about liability and threats to public safety, maintaining the safety and security of public facilities requires considerable planning and resources. Theft, vandalism, and even more serious crimes can all be potential issues when managing a public garden. The factors that will affect safety and security include the location and size of the facility, number of staff, number of visitors, number and type of events, type and significance of buildings, garden features, plant collections, and, of course, budget.

In most cases, security staff members are unarmed but in close contact with local police. Security staff members should be easily identifiable, with uniforms and well-marked security vehicles. Their function is to deter negative behavior, assist visitors with directions and other needs, monitor the garden, and respond to incidents as needed.

There are two primary staffing options: in-house security or outsourced security. Larger gardens tend to choose in-house security because that option offers more control and oversight of scheduling and supervision and is sometime more cost-effective. However, with the rising cost of payroll taxes and benefits, many public gardens choose to contract with a private firm for security staffing, a practice that can be particularly beneficial to smaller public gardens with only modest security needs. Gardens that choose the outsourcing approach usually do so to eliminate the time and responsibility required to train and supervise in-house staff and to allow garden administrators to focus on more mission-related activities and the overall operation of the facility.

Security Equipment

In addition to a competent, well-trained security staff, monitoring and technology-enhanced security features can be effective tools to reduce risk and ensure safety in a public garden. Security cameras, motion sensors, and remote-area phones can all be incorporated into a security system. Security staff as well as operations and horticultural staff should possess reliable two-way radios for efficient communication.

Typically, cameras and other monitoring devices are located in and around buildings and potentially troublesome areas of the grounds. These systems not only allow security staff to monitor larger areas but also act as deterrents to potential criminal activity.

Remote-area phones, often used by universities, can also provide a unique form of security. Strategically placed phone stations allow a person in distress to report a crime or emergency while on the grounds of a public facility. These systems can be powered by electricity or by solar panels. Remote-area phones can also include features such as speakers as part of an emergency broadcast system. In many facilities, public address announcements are linked to cell phones, email, and voice mail to alert employees to emergencies or important events.

Other Security Measures

In addition to high-tech efforts, simple procedures that are made part of everyday operations can help to reduce theft and vandalism in a public garden. Appropriately lighting areas can both deter criminal activity and lead to a greater sense of security among visitors. Limiting points of access by vehicles and individuals on foot with physical barriers such as fences, locked gates to roads, or locked doors to buildings can also reduce the risk of crime. It is important for every staff member to pay attention and report a crime as soon as it occurs so it can be addressed quickly. For example, if vandalism has occurred, reporting it to authorities and then immediately repairing any damage conveys the message that the garden is serious about maintaining a clean, professional infrastructure.

Event Security

Many public gardens offer special events that can present a variety of challenges, including monitoring vehicular and pedestrian traffic and parking. Often gardens will hire additional security staff to work special events and/or work with local police forces to manage a large event. It is important that all phases of the security program are in place prior to a special event, including good communication among security staff, garden staff, and the local authorities such as police and fire departments. This will allow for the deployment of appropriate staffing levels as well as positioning and monitoring of specific areas or activities.

Emergency Management Plan

One very important component of a security plan for a public garden, regardless of size or type, is an emergency management plan (EMP). An emergency management plan provides vital information on disaster planning and emergency preparedness and includes emergency contact information, an evacuation plan for buildings and the facility as a whole, and other standard practices and procedures. The purpose of the EMP is to establish policies, procedures, and an organizational structure for response to an emergency situation. Many plans incorporate operating procedures from the Incident Command System (ICS) for handling emergencies resulting from fires, floods, storms, earthquakes, hazardous materials, and other potential disasters. The goal is to coordinate efforts between garden staff, security staff, and local police, fire, and EMT services so they can respond quickly to an emergency. ICS training information can be obtained through the Emergency Management Institute, coordinated by the Federal Emergency Management Agency (Emergency Management Institute 2010).

It is important to note that the role of the security staff in public gardens has changed over the years. Security staff members are no longer present simply to deter unwanted behavior or respond to criminal activity or emergencies. In many public gardens, security staff members are the first to greet and interact with visitors, providing helpful information and assisting visitors with special needs. Security staff members are ambassadors for the garden and foster camaraderie with other internal staff as well as appreciation and cooperation among visitors to the garden (Shakespear 2003).

Summary

The quality of grounds management practices can significantly impact how the public perceives a particular public garden. The focus of the grounds management program should be on the plant collections, but all components of the living and built landscape contribute to overall impressions. Successful grounds management programs are based on appropriate staffing and equipment, well-developed schedules, proper landscape designs, and coordination of activities. Sustainable practices are increasingly important in grounds management and include recycling, composting, wise use of water, and reduced frequency of mowing. A well-designed security program will protect collections, facilities, and people. Security officers can interact with visitors and serve as first responders when problems develop.

Annotated Resources

Grounds Maintenance (http://www.grounds-mag.com). An exceptionally informative website with detailed articles and information on irrigation, equipment, turf, and general grounds maintenance practices.

Trautmann, N., and E. Olynciw. 1996. *Compost microorganisms*. http://compost.css.cornell.edu/microorg.html. Basic biological information on the composting process.

Trowbridge, P., and N. Bassuk. 2004. *Trees in the urban landscape: Site assessment, design, and installation*. Hoboken, N.J.: John Wiley and Sons. Despite the title, provides detailed instructions on all aspects of site assessment.

United States Access Board Website (www.access-board.gov/). Guidelines for historic sites and modern construction on how to provide full accessibility and to be in compliance with the Americans with Disabilities Act.

PART IV

Programmatic Functions

CHAPTER 14

Public Gardens and Their Communities: The Value of Outreach

SUSAN LACERTE

Introduction

Some define outreach as programs and activities that occur outside the garden gates, while others consider it programs or activities—whether on-site or off—that bring a garden to the attention of those who may not know about the facility and its offerings.

Outreach initiatives are usually driven by the acknowledgment that barriers prevent people from knowing about an institution. These barriers may be physical (such as the existence of a river or a highway), political (a garden may have the name of one city yet be situated in or near another), practical (there may be transportation and accessibility issues), or self-imposed (as by having an admission fee). Other barriers are social: when existing programs underserve groups of people, such as those under or over certain ages; when the organization is unfamiliar with the customs or habits of people from other cultures; or when some groups are excluded because of lack of financial means or by some sort of physical, mental, or learning condition. More often than not, outreach initiatives are launched simply because people do not know that an organization exists.

Promoting knowledge of plants is part of the mission of most public gardens, and outreach can be a powerful tool in helping an organization realize its mission. Outreach is a two-way street that allows an exchange of information: garden

> ### KEY TERMS
>
> **Community gardens:** gardens designed, created, and maintained by a group of people for the benefit of the community at large.
>
> **Demographics:** statistical classification of people by age, sex, income, and other factors used for market research purposes.
>
> **Horticultural therapy:** any of a number of methods involving plants used for the purpose of promoting healing.
>
> **Psychographics:** market research classifying people according to attitudes, fears, values, and other psychological factors.
>
> **Special-needs audiences:** groups of people with a common disadvantage as the result of emotional, mental, physical, or other factor or combination of factors.
>
> **Visitor survey:** a poll to determine visitors' usage of, attitudes toward, and knowledge of various facilities, services, and programs.

professionals and volunteers share knowledge and promote a greater understanding of plants while providing a forum for community members to share knowledge and needs.

While school, adult education, and volunteer programs and various exhibit initiatives also serve outreach functions, these are all covered in other chapters of this book.

What Are Some of the Ways to Conduct Outreach?

The most widely utilized techniques for reaching out to the community involve mounting public programs, showcasing the performing arts, facilitating community gardening, and offering horticultural therapy and wellness programs. Gardens also use motor vehicles, speakers' bureaus, and competitions to further their outreach. Finally, many gardens go straight to the community with information or combine temporary exhibits with programming. The various techniques are often used together, and opportunities for creativity abound.

Utilizing Holidays and Cultural Events

Reaching new audiences is a key to remaining relevant in a community and realizing the education mission that is core to most public gardens. It's natural to utilize holidays, especially those involving planting, harvesting, and food, as a way to conduct outreach. In most cultures, holidays bring people together to celebrate a shared tradition or history. Increasingly, as a way to promote understanding, gardens are utilizing cultural, national, and religious holidays, anniversaries, and events as forums to introduce members of different backgrounds to each other and create a new, shared experience.

Working with Cultural Communities

North America has long been a melting pot, its population comprising both natives and immigrants from all over the world. When working with cultural communities, partnerships are key, as is the inclusion of members from different cultural communities on the board and staff and in the volunteer corps. It is generally most effective to work through a leader or

Figure 14-1: Public gardens are wonderful places where people from different cultures may gather together to celebrate shared traditions and create new ones. Here the Lion Dance, symbolic of prosperity and good luck, is performed at the Queens Botanical Garden.

Queens Botanical Garden

elder. Different social etiquettes and customs exist within different cultures, and there are differences in needs and desires between first- and second-generation immigrants. People in some cultures defer to elders, in others to men. All dates for events need to be checked to ensure that they offend no sensitivities and to determine whether they are "lucky dates" if that concept is relevant. A general rule of thumb is to avoid scheduling events on holy days and to remember that history plays a role in getting people from different groups to work together. Different cultures also have different senses of time and uses of color. Everyone wants to be respected; some groups

---

THE BENEFITS AND CHALLENGES OF USING TRANSLATION

Including translation on program brochures and in exhibits lets people from other cultures know that your organization is serious about connecting with them. However, utilizing translation can set up false expectations that these languages will be available in other aspects of the garden.

Translation should be used selectively—with greetings, headings, or key information—or more extensively if the budget allows and doing so enhances the program or initiative. Some cultural or social service groups, colleges, hospitals, banks, and governmental agencies offer free or low-cost translation services.

Some computer programs and printers treat foreign characters as graphics, not as text, but the characters may be available from the websites of various cultural groups. The written forms of different languages take up more or less space, and printing needs to be planned accordingly. Board members and volunteers from relevant groups may be invited to proofread materials and to look for, save, and translate articles from the ethnic press. Because reporters are often bilingual, it may not be necessary to translate press releases.

CASE STUDY: QUEENS BOTANICAL GARDEN

Observing that participation in programs did not reflect the observed demographics of its visitors, the Queens Botanical Garden (QBG) took a targeted approach to getting to know its neighbors. The Garden engaged "cultural specialists" to help create cultural advisory committees to answer questions such as these: What are the ten plants and holidays that are most important to the target culture? Who are the community leaders? What are the most important mechanisms of communication?

As a result, QBG added plants in the garden: tree peonies for the Chinese, rose of Sharon for the Koreans, bougainvillea for Latin Americans. To preserve the knowledge gained, results were printed in *Harvesting Our History: A Botanical and Cultural Guide to Queens' Chinese, Korean and Latin American Communities.* An annual Gardening Day program, which incorporated regular gardening topics in addition to a special feature, was developed. Cultural specialists identified presenters, translators, and interpreters and provided introductions to community leaders and reporters.

The first year's focus on the tree peony resulted in an audience in which 56 percent of all participants were of Asian heritage; the flower-arranging focus brought a 35 percent participation rate from the Hispanic/Latino community; and the community-focused program on orchids produced a 76 percent Korean participation rate. In each year, program materials were translated and printed in each respective language.

After recruiting the founder of a multilingual advertising agency for its board, QBG, with a consultant, conducted a visitor survey in four languages. QBG discovered that an astounding 75 percent of visitors spoke a language other than English at home, underscoring the importance of the cultural vision and the challenges and opportunities in designing programs and exhibits for a culturally diverse audience.

Staff continued to develop outreach initiatives that have included tours of the ethnic markets in Queens, writings on the lore and plants in the *botánicas*, an "ambassador" program of multiethnic volunteers, and frequent coponsoring of events such as the Moon Festival, the Lunar New Year, Diwali, the Burmese Water Festival, the Day of the Dead, Latkes and Lights, and more. The Garden regularly involves people from different cultural communities in planning efforts and celebrations and invited Native Americans to conduct a sage-burning ritual to honor the ground before the start of a construction project. Members of the Korean community started a friends group for the Garden, which is also host for a large group of tai chi practitioners. QBG's activities have led to a diversification of support as people from these cultural communities experience the Garden's sincerity firsthand, adopt trees and benches, become members, help with public programs, serve as advocates to elected officials, and help build a stronger garden and community.

Figure 14-2: The beauty of public gardens makes them perfect venues for outdoor performances. Concerts, theater, and strolling interpreters help attract new audiences and please existing patrons. Here Time for Three performs in the Rose Arbor at Longwood Gardens in Kennett Square, Pennsylvania.

Longwood Garden/L. Albee

are fearful about exploitation and being used as a token, so approach developing a relationship with authenticity and care.

The Queens Botanical Garden (QBG) embraces working with the many cultures that call Queens, New York, home. As one of the most popular destinations for new immigrants in America and a place where more than 130 languages are spoken, Queens—and thus the QBG—is a great laboratory for showcasing techniques for working successfully with cultural communities.

Using Performing Arts as a Mechanism to Develop New Audiences

In the past two decades there has been a sea change in attitudes about the role of the performing arts in public gardens. Not long ago, public gardens were viewed as sanctuaries for plants and the people who were serious about studying them, and even the thought of hosting performances in the garden brought looks of disdain.

Now many gardens embrace performances in the garden as excellent mechanisms to attract new audiences and please existing ones. Longwood Gardens in Pennsylvania includes the performing arts in its mission and has a long history of putting on events, from major orchestras accompanied by sensational fountain and fireworks displays to strolling costumed artists interacting with visitors.

Many gardens, especially those that have smaller budgets or are located in culturally diverse areas, use a grassroots approach that relies on making connections with local performers who provide programs at little or no cost in exchange for the opportunity to share their art. The garden must make its expectations clear to the performers to ensure a successful collaboration, and questions such as what compensation the performers will receive, how they can promote themselves, and what music they will perform must be answered. Using this approach couples the built-in audience of another organization with the garden's interesting facility.

Bringing in artists can attract people who might not otherwise visit a garden. In turn, gardens are excellent sites that may help the artists meet grant-related outreach requirements.

State and local arts organizations are often helpful in making connections with local artists or arts presenters. The National Endowment for the Arts' website includes information on these groups. Other arts presenters may be part of booking or routing consortiums that work together to keep down the costs of presenting national and international artists by creating tours that allow artists to amortize costs and offer lower performance fees. Working with concert promoters or local performing arts centers helps gardens reach new audiences and make garden dollars stretch. Working with established ticket vendors can help ease the marketing pressure that goes along with offering high-profile events; however, such businesses usually can't offer the same level of customer service as public garden staff. Putting on performances with high-profile artists takes a good deal of staff, logistical, and marketing coordination. Including garden admission in the price of the ticket and doing things to encourage visitors to arrive early helps concertgoers know why they must return and visit the garden.

Using Outreach Vehicles

Many gardens utilize outreach vehicles—which serve as traveling billboards—to take their programs into the community. Take every opportunity to put the name of the organization in front of the eyes of potential future visitors. Whether it is a recreational vehicle with indoor exhibits, such as the American Museum of Natural History's Moveable Museum, a smaller vehicle that can fit four plastic tubs, such as Minnesota Landscape Arboretum's Plantmobile, or Queens Botanical Garden's Gro-Cart, which gets hitched to a small truck, make sure the organization's name, logo, and an interesting graphic or a catchy phrase are stenciled on or affixed with a magnetic sign.

Scheduling is of paramount importance so that double bookings do not occur and adequate travel and parking time are built in. Depending on the size of the vehicle, special licensing and driving skills may be necessary. Utilize vehicles as energy efficiently as possible, allowing the public to see that the organization practices what it preaches. Designate a

Figure 14-3: Vehicles are traveling billboards! Use every opportunity to put the name of the public garden in front of the eyes of future visitors.

Minnesota Landscape Arboretum

The Missouri Botanical Garden (MOBOT), which has research scientists working around the world, took outreach to a new level locally by looking to serve neighboring southwest Illinois. With the Mississippi creating a physical and psychological barrier between the two states, the Shaw's Garden East Initiative was developed to bridge this barrier and to increase awareness of the Garden among the 25 percent of the metropolitan area's population who live in Illinois. The goal of the initiative was to promote regionalism and to increase the number of visitors, members, and education program participants from Illinois. MOBOT used the name of the Garden's beloved founder, Henry Shaw, to soften the focus on the state division. A key business leader was identified and asked to chair the initiative and find like-minded committee members. The twenty-four-member committee included college presidents and business and community leaders; a full-time staff member served as coordinator. Interviews of members and regular meetings allowed staff to identify potential partnerships and to introduce community leaders to the programs and work of the Garden. A market analysis indicated that the focus should be on three cities within a fifteen-to-forty-five-minute drive to avoid stretching resources too thin. Initially, programs that worked well on the Missouri side of the river were offered on the Illinois side, including teacher professional development, community gardening, and horticultural therapy programs at a nursing home. Staff also took on speaking opportunities and joined parks and other committees. Eventually the Signature Garden concept was developed, whereby MOBOT would approve, or "brand," physical gardens in Illinois as approved MOBOT sites. This approval depended on each site meeting design, horticulture, maintenance, and public access criteria. The first Signature Garden was located at Lewis and Clark College; it was followed by gardens at two other colleges, each of which stands on it own financially and is reviewed annually. MOBOT provided grant funding for the Initiative and sponsors provided funds for specific programs. Three beautiful gardens on college campuses remain the lasting legacy of this innovative outreach program.

single staff person to ensure that vehicles are properly maintained and inspections kept up to date. Have a travel log to keep track of the use of the vehicle and help allocate costs appropriately.

Speakers' Bureaus, Collaborations, and More

If members of the public reach out to staff, find a way to reach back: such inquiries indicate community need. Whether the garden has an officially named speakers' bureau or not, most gardens accommodate requests for presenters. Staff members at the Cheyenne Botanic Gardens view appearances at luncheons with women's groups, civic associations, and service clubs as the most cost-effective and efficient method of outreach for this small garden. Similarly, since the tiny, interesting plants at the Betty Ford Alpine Gardens, in Vail, Colorado, are visible only between snowmelt and snowfall, outreach takes on great importance during the cold months. Connections with the noted Cooperative Extension Service's master gardener program help stretch resources at this alpine garden and at many others around the nation.

Filling requests for speakers can sometimes seem like filling a bottomless pit. While there will always be a need to provide some programs free, keep the long-term financial sustainability of the organization in mind. Establish an appropriate fee schedule, one that recognizes the time involved in preparation and travel, and have appropriate teaching materials available. At the Arizona-Sonora Desert Museum, which includes a zoo and an earth science center, volunteers run the free speakers' bureau, while the staff handle requests for presentations involving live animals.

Reaching Out to Special-Needs Audiences

A number of gardens have reached out to the community with wellness programs. The Minnesota Landscape Arboretum, part of the University of Minnesota, has done a spectacular job of connecting with existing groups to offer programs to those with special needs through work with a domestic abuse shelter, an eating disorders clinic, a prison and center for chemical dependency, and Parkinson's and Alzheimer's centers.

A reassuring aspect for gardens working with health-related organizations is that typically such programs operate on a fee-for-service basis, relieving the fund-raising pressure on the gardens and helping to ensure the long-term financial sustainability of the programs.

Outreach Through a Focus on Plants and Gardens

While many gardens focus on programs that deal with plants and related topics, others focus directly on plants and gardens in the community and the people who take care of them. Several examples give plenty of food for thought.

CASE STUDY: THE ENID A. HAUPT GLASS GARDEN

Nancy Chambers, Director of the Glass Garden

One in five Americans lives with some kind of sensory, physical, psychological, or cognitive disability. This is the largest minority group in the United States and a vast, often untapped, audience for public garden outreach. Serving the needs of the disabled requires the expertise and training of professional horticultural therapists.

The Enid A. Haupt Glass Garden is a small garden in the middle of New York City that opened in 1959 as part of a large teaching hospital and university complex. What makes this garden unique is that its seven professional staff members are all horticultural therapists. This enables the Glass Garden to offer programs to patients young and old and on any unit of the hospital, and to reach out to special-needs populations throughout the community.

One example of outreach is the Garden's work with P.S. 811, a New York City high school for severely disabled children. Many of the students have no language ability and most need full physical care for dressing, bathing, and eating. The school offers science classes as part of its regular curriculum, but staff approached the Garden to provide a more hands-on, direct learning experience for teaching about photosynthesis, seeds,

habitats, and herbs. The school originally contracted for a series of five classes; the program was so successful it added an additional seventy-five classes.

The Glass Garden has also developed a vocational training program for individuals with moderate psychological or cognitive limitations. Various clinical and administrative departments pay the Glass Garden for staff to maintain plants throughout the hospital. This maintenance also provides the opportunity for training individuals for competitive jobs in the plantscape industry—a huge and vibrant business in New York City. The training program is recognized by the State Department of Vocational Rehabilitation, which pays the Glass Garden a fee for training and subsequent job placement of students.

Offering horticultural therapy outreach programs can benefit public gardens by building bridges to new constituencies and community organizations; opening doors to new funding and cost-sharing sources; engaging families and caregivers as well as those with special needs; leading staff to new and innovative thinking; and offering opportunities for media coverage, tie-ins, and special events.

Figure 14-4: Horticultural therapy training programs make public gardens important participants in the health of local communities. Here a trainee at the Glass Garden of the Rusk Institute in New York City learns plant care skills that may open the door to employment in the plantscape industry.

Glass Garden, Rusk Institute, NYU Medical Center

Phipps Conservatory and Botanical Garden in Pittsburgh, Pennsylvania, has woven together various strands of what public gardens are all about into an outreach program with both depth and breadth. Project Green Heart takes what's been done through its award-winning conservatory, said by some to be the greenest conservatory in the world, out to the community of home and nursery owners. The concept is simple: create demand for plants that need fewer resources—water, nutrients, pest control—and less maintenance. The website annually features a list of Top 10 Sustainable Plants, along with pictures of the plants and information on the nurseries where these plants may be purchased. The Top 10 are planted in the garden and introduced to home owners and landscapers through a series of programs. When home owners see the success of their neighbors' gardens, they contact the Garden and change their gardening habits.

Recognizing that person-to-person contact is often the most effective method of communication, the Morton Arboretum created a Tree Advocate Program to link the expertise at the Arboretum with the needs of municipal leaders and home owners in one of the fastest-growing counties in Illinois. Activities included meeting with home owners' associations and sharing information on best species and practices, creating cooperative tree-buying and -planting projects, reviewing specifications for tree planting as part of construction projects, helping with information on tree pests, and advocating for tree conservation legislation.

Recognizing the large gap in understanding and appreciation between native peoples and more recent inhabitants of Quebec, the Montreal Botanical Garden (MBG) inaugurated its First Nations Garden project on the 300th anniversary of the signing of the first peace agreement between New France and the thirty-nine First Nations of North America. MBG presented the idea for the project to the Assembly of the First Nations of Quebec and Labrador. With the consent of the assembly's elders, MBG sent questionnaires to aboriginal people, and interviews followed. Native people helped identify plants for the garden and contributed to decisions about the garden's layout and ideas for interpretive and educational themes. Once planting was complete, events and tours by native performers and guides, publications, and posters helped introduce visitors to gardening and the uses of plants by native peoples. MBG has continued its work

CASE STUDY: COMMUNITY GARDENS AND PUBLIC GARDENS AS NATURAL ALLIES

Ellen Kirby

Community gardens are created and maintained by groups of people for the benefit of the community at large. Unlike an institutional garden, the community garden is designed and maintained by the public. Recently, there has been a dramatic upsurge in the number of these gardens.

Community gardeners turn rubbish-filled lots into havens for people and plants. Community gardens provide social contact and foster community development, meet the needs of people for fresh, locally grown food, and are havens for wildlife, native plants, and composting education.

There are a multitude of types of community gardens, with many including a mixture of types and functions:

Gardens for children and youth

Gardens to grow food, including market gardens and food bank gardens

Gardens for neighborhood beautification

Gardens organized by specific ethnic/language groups

Gardens for meditation, rest, enjoyment

Gardens for the arts and music

Gardens for therapeutic horticulture

Gardens to demonstrate sustainable practices

Public gardens can become major allies with community gardens by:

• Providing horticultural resources: plants, education, and tools

• Sponsoring a community garden (sometimes on-site)

• Providing arenas for networking through organized groups, meetings, and conferences

• Developing courses such as tree pruning and composting education

• Launching demonstration gardens for gardening with wildlife, native plants, and sensory plants

• Producing newsletters and tip sheets for community gardens

• Designating staff and volunteers to assist with special plantings and offer workshops

• Collaborating with other agencies on grant applications

Although many community gardens fail within a few years due to a lack of resources, their chance for success is greatly enhanced by collaboration with public gardens. For the public garden, the benefits of expanding horticulture into the public arena are huge. The community garden is often the first introduction to plants for many people. A connection between the public garden and the community garden can provide for mutual identification and support.

Figure 14-5: Two students from the Chicago Botanic Garden's Green Youth Farm Program in North Lawndale, on Chicago's West Side, hold a photo of a site before it was transformed into a successful youth-operated urban agriculture garden.

Chicago Botanic Garden

with native peoples in pilot programs to teach science and traditional knowledge, using themes of traditional medicine. MBG has involved Inuit schools in a project on climate change and the impact on the tundra, with a goal of mentoring young people and encouraging greater participation in higher education. All projects are community based and participatory.

Outreach Through Community Gardening

Within the mission and purpose of most public gardens there are goals relating to the extension of the resources of the garden into the public arena. The community garden provides an exciting opportunity to get outside the garden gates to achieve these goals.

The Pennsylvania Horticultural Society (PHS), which also puts on the famed Philadelphia Flower Show and has helped support Philadelphia's 500 community gardens, has adapted to a changing funding climate by also working with a local prison to provide inmates with marketable skills and to grow produce that is distributed to people with little access to nutritious food. The Horticultural Society of New York also has an impressive record of working with prison populations and creating reading gardens and programs with libraries.

Figure 14-6: The Chicago Botanic Garden operates the Cook County Boot Camp Gardening Program with the local sheriff's office. Inmates are trained to plant, maintain, and harvest organic vegetables, which supply their mess hall and local community food pantries. The project is part of Windy City Harvest, the Garden's workforce training and urban agriculture production program.

Chicago Botanic Garden

The Chicago Botanic Garden has been engaged in community gardening for decades and developed programs to meet changing societal needs. It has utilized government funding to help with beautification initiatives with a decidedly horticultural emphasis as well as initiatives that focus on workforce and "green jobs" development and the creation of sustainable communities through local food production. This dynamic garden keeps its development department busy applying for grants and working with federal funding agencies including the U.S. Department of Agriculture, the U.S. Environmental Protection Agency, the Institute of Museum and Library Services, and the Bureau of Land Management, as well as state and local government agencies, foundations, corporations, and individuals, to match their programming with community needs and funding opportunities.

Issues-Based Initiatives and the Power of Collaborations

In the past few decades there has been a flowering in the growth of nonprofits to address specific issues, including waste reduction, accessibility to nutritious and affordable food, water conservation, community development, and environmental activism. Just as partnering with community gardening initiatives provides opportunities for public gardens to work in the community, so collaborating with nonprofit and government entities provides an opportunity to get outside the garden gates and combine with other resources in a more effective way.

Waste Reduction

The public gardens in New York City—Brooklyn Botanic Garden, New York Botanical Garden, Queens Botanical Garden, and Staten Island Botanical Garden—were all given a boost in their outreach efforts by the creation in the mid-1990s of a citywide composting program by the city's Department of Sanitation. This initiative addressed the need of the city to reduce the amount of garbage in the waste stream with the strength of institutions known for being able to reach people. All of these gardens have now developed much stronger outreach programs, which focus on composting, waste reduction, tree care, and environmentally friendly gardening. The New York City Compost Project shows the power of working on a large, collaborative scale.

Food

For more than twenty years Urban Harvest and its predecessor organization in Houston, Texas, have been focused on dealing with hunger issues by teaching people to grow nutritious foods close to home. This holistic organization saw many

Figure 14-7: Teaching people early about the value of plants and growing food locally is a goal of Urban Harvest, a nonprofit that connects people with plants in a different way. Here children and an instructor observe a pond in an outdoor classroom.

Bob Randall, Ph.D.

connected needs and became an agent of community development by sponsoring programs to foster youth education and empowerment and farmers' markets within parks and public spaces. Although not a public garden, it provides many of the same services: adult education classes and training for community gardeners, including training in essential nonhorticultural skills such as leadership development, volunteer management, and fund-raising. Urban farming programs attract the attention of foundations, corporations, government, and the media, and this can help a public garden realize outreach goals.

Water

The mission of the Water Conservation Garden (WCG) in San Diego is "promoting water conservation in the southern California landscape." The Garden was started by water agencies in response to a regional drought, and water agencies are still major financial supporters. Rather than just using changes in water rules and rates to lessen water consumption, water agencies charged this garden with using education. Garden staff asked, listened, and found that the number one question was, "How do I get rid of my lawn?" and the second was, "What do I do next?" In response, they created demonstration gardens and programs such as Toss the Turf and H2O 911. WCG personnel take every possible speaking opportunity and disseminate information in water authority communications. The garden had a 50 percent increase in visitation in one year

and, through a visitor survey, discovered that 50 percent of visitors had made a change in their home landscape after visiting the Garden.

Community Development

Chicago's Garfield Park Conservatory Alliance was created with various nongovernmental organizations, including Friends of the Parks and the Chicago Park District. When initiatives to revitalize Chicago's West Side were getting under way, the alliance was the obvious partner to work with the Local Initiative Support Coalition, a national nonprofit dedicated to helping residents with community development. The restoration of the Garfield Park Conservatory became the focal point. Chicago was an early leader in the wave of green development that was starting to sweep the nation; in the city various incentives were being offered to land and housing developers to use more recycled materials and environmentally sensitive water management methods. This helped a "green consciousness" gain ground. The alliance became part of this larger initiative, hosting and managing a community demonstration garden that served as a model for engagement, resulting in the involvement of more people and the creation of other community gardens, which helped transform the area. The various partners created other training programs for business and workforce development, along with teen councils. After an evaluation, those components that worked well were continued, and those that did not were eliminated. The restoration of the Garfield Park

Figure 14-8: The entry point of any public garden is often the best place to gain information from visitors. Here, people going to the Water Conservation Garden in San Diego, California, learn about water-saving plants, practices, and landscaping.

Helix Water District

Figure 14-9: The Fulton Garden is one of the community gardens facilitated by the Garfield Park Conservatory Alliance. Here gardeners admire the results of their work, sharing gardening tips and fellowship.

Garfield Park Conservatory Alliance

THE GREENEST BLOCK IN BROOKLYN COMPETITION

In a borough once better known for its bagels than its begonias and with a goal of encouraging residents to improve the appearance of New York City, the Brooklyn Botanic Garden (BBG) inaugurated the Greenest Block in Brooklyn contest in 1994. The Garden uses a variety of tools and techniques to encourage participation, including offering window box kits at a reduced price, donating tools and materials to participants, holding neighborhood street clinics to demonstrate good planting and gardening techniques, holding a press conference on the winning residential block, posting photos of the winners on the BBG website, presenting cash prizes at an awards events, giving signs for winners to post outdoors, and printing postcards of winning gardens. Judges are selected from local horticultural and community agencies. The contest is supported by the Borough of Brooklyn, a local community foundation, and BBG, and the names and logos of all three are presented together. The competition has been the subject of radio and television reports, in which sponsoring officials and gardeners are interviewed. The print articles are shared with funders and others, helping build community pride and connection with BBG. In addition to seeing many more beautiful, well-kept gardens in Brooklyn, BBG has seen an increase in membership from areas where participation is highest, and the contest has grown to include storefront, commercial, and community garden entries.

Figure 14-10: Brooklyn Botanic Garden's Greenest Block in Brooklyn contest spurred residents of Vanderveer Place in Flatbush, Brooklyn, to get out and garden. Different categories—from best window box to best storefront garden—allow for wide participation, many prizes, a more beautiful borough, and increased participation with the BBG.

Photo courtesy of GreenBridge/BBG

Conservatory shows the role a public garden can play in meeting societal and community needs.

Contests and Awards

School science fairs, plant society shows, and agricultural fairs are models for utilizing contests and competitions as outreach tools. Contests invite people of different socioeconomic, cultural, and geographic backgrounds to strive for excellence. If done sensitively and fairly, competitions can be one of the most effective ways of informing a wide audience about the services of the public garden.

The Arizona Department of Water Resources partnered with the Tucson Botanical Gardens to sponsor the Annual Xeriscape Contest, which recognizes people who incorporate native and low-water plants and practices into their landscapes. The California Friendly Landscape Contest was started by a water district to give awards for water-wise gardening.

Planning an Outreach Program

Some public gardens have separate units dedicated to outreach, while others may include outreach efforts in education, public programs, marketing, or membership departments. There is a fine line between outreach, which is considered programmatic, and marketing, which is considered "administrative and general," according to accounting and tax rules.

Wherever it is placed within the organization, outreach helps a garden build a stronger constituency and works best when it is carefully planned. Planning for outreach employs the same principles and practices as planning for any program: articulate goals, identify key participants and potential partners—including funding and marketing partners—then involve all in the creation of the project, carry out the project, and evaluate.

Articulate Goals

What is the problem to be solved? What is the target community to be reached? Understanding both questions will help with the articulation of goals. Flesh out the questions by exploring the issues. Is there a difference between the people who visit the garden and those who sign up for programs? Do people from the communities right outside the garden gates visit? Has the demographic composition of the neighborhood changed? Is there a governmental initiative to help with realization of the goal? Is the garden drawing people from the entire community or only from one neighborhood? Look for commonalities.

Develop Partnerships

To develop partnerships, the first step is to find other organizations that serve people in the target community. In building successful partnerships, it is imperative to involve members of the target group to be sure the needs of all are being met. Partnerships help bring the strongest elements of each organization to the initiative at hand: gardens have the real estate, plant collections, and educational skill to offer, while other partners have greater access to the target communities and to the media and social service organizations that support the target community.

Establish Baseline Information

Understanding who is *not* visiting the garden or using its services is often of central importance. To be able to judge success, establish baseline data by collecting information that will facilitate comparison later. For example, if the goal is to diversify the garden's audience, conduct a sampling of the cultural composition at the beginning. If the goal is to build membership, document how many members the garden currently has. If attracting people from a different part of town is the intention, ask visitors at the beginning of a project for zip codes, then take a poll again at the end. Keeping key information each year will provide a basis for analysis. Related information—trends in donations, membership, gift store sales, and parking receipts—are ancillary measures of the garden's impact in attracting new audiences. Simple spreadsheets help organize information and reveal patterns.

Admissions Point: Barrier and Opportunity

Charging admission is both a barrier to entry and a great opportunity to learn more about visitors. Some public gardens are prohibited from charging admission; others have multiple entrances, so collecting admissions is impractical or financially unfeasible. However, points of entry present the very best places to gather information and to learn who visits and why. Such knowledge makes it easier to chart a path for the use of staff and marketing resources, and helps in developing strategies to transform visitors into participants and donors.

When a garden charges admission or moves from free admission to charging a fee, there is an even greater need for conducting outreach. Through programs and other services, focus the public on the value your garden provides, helping get people through the gate and giving them reasons to return time after time.

Visitor Surveys

Visitor surveys provide information on visitor demographics and psychographics. Demographic information gives a profile: age, sex, ethnic and cultural background, household composition, where a visitor lives, education and income level, and languages spoken. Psychographic information concerns psychological variables, such as the motivation for visiting, and accompanying lifestyle choices. Visitor surveys can confirm that the garden's strategies for reaching its target audiences are effective or that they need to be changed. Surveys help direct outreach and marketing dollars to where they are most effective (e.g., sending a mailing to a locale where there are already many participants will likely yield even more participants). The ability to express a need and report on results are especially important when cultivating and reporting to funders and elected and community leaders.

An entrance survey is often a poll to obtain the basic visitor profile and information on how visitors know about the institution. An exit survey is designed to understand visitors' experiences and levels of satisfaction with the gardens, programs, and amenities (food service, restrooms, parking). Visitor surveys also help identify the garden's competitors, visitor media preferences (print, electronic, radio, television), when the visit was planned, and the visitor's means of transportation. Some

questionnaires include open-ended questions. For those gardens without gate counting capacity, a visitor count may be accomplished as part of the same effort.

It's especially helpful to work with experienced audience research consultants. Colleagues can provide suggestions, as can professional associations and market or audience research firms. Consultants who may later get a contract are often very willing to help guide the understanding and articulation of needs, which is an essential part of a fund-raising proposal. Local professors of business, tourism, and marketing are often looking for projects for students and may be willing to help in designing and carrying out a survey. Increasingly, gardens are also using post-event email surveys to capture feedback and suggestions; such strategies could be utilized with general visitors as well.

Some consultants will conduct the entire project, from drafting the questionnaire to finding and training people to collect the data to tabulating the results and writing the report. Some consultants will do parts, serving as a guide in helping draft the questionnaire and tabulate, map, and understand the

TIPS FOR A SUCCESSFUL VISITOR SURVEY

- Decide what you want to know. If you're not certain, start with these basic questions:

    Who are the visitors? (age, gender, income, education)

    What is the composition of the visiting party?

    Where do visitors live?

    Why do people choose to visit?

    How often people visit?

    Are the visitors also members of the organization?

    How satisfied were the visitors with the experience?

    How did the visitors hear about the garden?

- Always collect zip code information, which is quick to obtain and easily mapped.

- Keep the survey to two sides of one page for best results.

- Design questions to avoid ambiguity.

- Include a time period. Check-off boxes help. For example: "In the past year, have you visited 1–2 times? 3–6 times? more than 6 times?"

- Test the survey before finalizing it.

- Get a robust sample. With more questions, you'll need more completed questionnaires.

- If you need the survey to have statistical significance, ask an expert to help determine how many completed questionnaires are needed. One expert says to strive for fifty responses per cell minimum when doing cross-tabular analysis.

- If information that gives a basic idea will do, get what feels to be a robust and unbiased sample, which will likely provide directional information.

- Understand that the season and weather play a big role; collect data for *all* days.

- Recruit and train volunteers to help administer the survey.

- Have extra clipboards and writing utensils on hand.

- Come up with a plan to get a representative sample and avoid bias. For example, instruct surveyors to intercept every nth person (e.g., fifth).

- Ask the decision-making adult in a group to complete the survey.

- Often a simple thank-you is the only incentive people need to participate; sometimes gifts (a pencil, for instance) are offered.

- Take cultural sensitivities into account.

- Remind people that the survey is anonymous; make this clear near income questions.

results, while the garden takes the lead in administering the survey with staff and volunteers. Another economical way to obtain information is to ask another group—a chamber of commerce, another cultural institution, a tourism organization—to include a few questions about the garden in its survey. In-person surveys generally give the most comprehensive, unbiased results, but other methods, including conducting surveys by mail, telephone, email, or online, are worth considering for specific projects such as a membership study or reaching potential visitors through a market study.

Funding Outreach

Funding outreach initiatives requires just as much creativity as funding other programs. Foundations have a similar agenda: to bring change or support those who are not participating in various parts of the community. This provides a great opportunity to make the case that the garden is relevant within the community. Corporations often will provide sponsorship dollars in communities in which they do business, but unless the project can become a regional or national model, it's often much easier to approach local businesses than to try to penetrate corporate bureaucracy. Elected officials look for opportunities for visibility and usually have some discretionary money to distribute. Federal, state, and provincial governments often have programs to try to solve a variety of issues and offer funding to those who can help realize larger social goals. It's important to understand the need funders have to be able to show that their investment provides meaningful results.

Outreach is about the community and provides plenty of opportunity for an organization to partner with others who want to be seen doing good things. Every program or initiative has a beginning and an end. Be willing to let go of some initiatives and move on to others. Don't just rely on donations. Design programs that meet a social need and can support themselves through fees. This is the path to true sustainability.

Assessing Success

When evaluating results, remember that much of the feedback is anecdotal, coming in casual conversations that cannot be quantified. Unlike in business, where results are measured in numbers of items sold and in profit, public garden results and benefits are often intangible and relate to improved quality of life. Still, hard data command respect, so try to get them. Celebrate successes by sharing stories and putting them in print. An attractive printed piece or story on the garden's website will make the initiative live beyond the event or program and extend outreach even further.

The benefits of outreach show up in many different ways. Outreach can help build a stronger base both in the community (by bringing change and by engendering goodwill and respect for the knowledge of the organization) and within the institution (by validating work and bringing media attention and financial support). Outreach benefits all by creating a stronger and more informed constituency.

Summary

In this chapter, the reasons for conducting outreach were examined, the primary one being the need to overcome some sort of barrier that exists in reaching people. Various techniques for engaging in outreach were articulated, and numerous examples of ways to achieve success and avoid pitfalls were given. Finally, directions for getting started with outreach and details on important building blocks were enumerated. Outreach will help deepen and strengthen the role of a public garden within the community, ensuring its relevance and sustainability in an ever changing world.

Annotated Resources

American Association of Museums (aam-us.org) has many resources, including a Museum Marketplace page for finding visitor survey consultants and a Committee on Audience Research and Evaluation.

American Community Gardening Association (communitygarden.org).

American Horticultural Therapy Association (ahta.org).

American Public Gardens Association (publicgardens.org) is also known by its previous name, American Association of Botanical Gardens and Arboreta. *The Public Garden,* its journal, is an excellent source for information on gardens, programs, services, and outreach activities.

Association of Performing Arts Presenters (artspresenters.org) has a listing of state arts agencies on its website.

ESRI Press. 2009. *Source book of county demographics.* Redlands, Calif.: ESRI Press. Regularly updated information book.

Kirby, E., and E. Peters. 2008. *Community gardening.* Brooklyn Botanic Garden All-Region Guides, Handbook #190. Brooklyn: Brooklyn Botanic Garden.

Regional arts organizations and foundations, including:
   The Southern Arts Federation (southarts.org)
   Arts Midwest (artsmidwest.org)
   Western Arts Alliance (westarts.org)
   New England Foundation for the Arts (nefa.org)
   Mid Atlantic Arts Foundation (midatlanticarts.org)

Relf, D., ed. 1992. *Role of horticulture in human well-being and social development.* Portland, Ore.: Timber Press. A comprehensive collection of papers related to human issues in horticulture.

Rothert, G. 1994. *Enabling garden.* Dallas, Tex.: Taylor Publishing. Describes how to garden with disabilities.

Simson, S., and M. Straus, eds. 1998. *Horticulture as therapy: Principles and practice.* Binghamton, N.Y.: Haworth Press. A complete textbook on horticultural therapy including history and program implementation.

USDA (United States Department of Agriculture) Cooperative Extension System (csrees.usda.gov/Extension, ahs.org/master_gardeners). The extension system is a nationwide educational network in the United States. Each state and territory has an office at its land grant university as well as a network of local offices. The Master Gardener Program, conducted throughout the United States and Canada, trains avid gardeners to become leaders in sharing information within the community.

CHAPTER 15

Formal Education for Students, Teachers, and Youth at Public Gardens

PATSY BENVENISTE AND JENNIFER SCHWARZ-BALLARD

Introduction

It could be argued that the question of whether gardens should be places of education was answered unequivocally in the Book of Genesis: "No eating from the Tree of Knowledge!"

Despite the heavy sanction that Adam and Eve suffered for their disobedience, gardens have continued to be cultivated throughout history for pleasure, for beauty, for health, and as a crucial means by which humans gain and share a better understanding of the natural world and their place in it.

It was toward the end of the sixteenth century in Europe that botanical gardens emerged as centers for formalized student education. Michel Conan, a noted American landscape scholar

KEY TERMS

Civic engagement: taking personal responsibility for the quality of life in a community, through both political and nonpolitical processes.

Ecoliteracy: the knowledge, ability, and motivation to think critically and holistically about ecosystems and the way humans interact with them.

Environmental education: organized efforts to teach about the relevance, structure, and function of the natural world and how human beings can manage behaviors to help sustain the integrity of ecosystems.

Experiential learning: the process of making meaning from direct experience; learning by doing.

Formal education: education provided through an organized, instructed educational experience with guided activities and specific learning goals.

Inquiry-based learning: a way of exploring the natural or material world that leads to the asking of questions, exploration and discovery about any subject.

Moral development: the process through which children develop responsible attitudes and behaviors toward other living things through example, direct teaching, and social interaction.

Plant-based learning: education that uses the natural world, especially plant biology, as the foundation for integrated learning in and across disciplines.

Project-based learning: education that organizes learning around projects or problems that require active learner engagement and problem solving.

Standards alignment: correspondence in content and depth between a given education program and formal subject requirements per National Science Education or state academic standards.

Student-directed learning: learner-designed and -driven activity.

Sustainability education: education that teaches how life choices and behaviors can help preserve the earth's resources, biodiversity, and ecosystems for future generations.

and garden historian, describes the rise of the botanical garden as "a quintessentially modern phenomenon . . . a felicitous by-product of the . . . scientific revolution . . . a process which also saw the creation of the academy and scientific society." Conan notes that in their linkage to established academic institutions, those gardens spurred the development of the modern scientific consciousness, in which the scientist "felt disposed to share his knowledge with disciples and students, to measure his work against that of colleagues, and to forge links with *molti amici in molti luoghi* (many friends in many places)" (Conan 2005).

Four hundred years later, contemporary public gardens enjoy the benefits of the scientific revolution and the core teaching strategies that their antecedents helped to establish as common practice: direct student observation, description, demonstration, inquiry, and experimentation—that is, experiential learning.

While education is usually cited as a major institutional mission of public gardens in both developed and developing countries worldwide, the education of children, youth, and teachers through pedagogically sound, developmentally appropriate, and professionally instructed programs is extremely variable from garden to garden. The resources and expertise required to support strong education programs for this population are significant and can be daunting to smaller institutions.

It is the purpose of this chapter to examine the compelling argument for strong pre-K–12 education by public gardens, despite the challenge of cost; to present widely endorsed criteria for establishing and maintaining good educational programs; and to share examples of some educational best practices in public garden education for this audience. In this chapter, the term *formal education* does not denote instruction that takes place in the school classroom over weeks or months, but rather garden-sponsored lessons and activities that convene children and teachers in a structured way under the guidance of a subject-qualified teacher; have defined educational goals with associated curricula and materials; and are capable of evaluation and replication.

Rationale

As for all other museums with a public agenda, formal education programs are the primary means by which a public garden

- Signals its philosophy, values, and future direction

- Communicates in depth with the larger knowledge community

- Effects change

The traditional, cognitive-outcome model of education that emphasizes mastery of facts and data is only one aspect of the way in which public gardens serve their mission, the needs

of their audience, and the general good. Because they are so well suited to do so and because it is essential for our collective future, educationally ambitious public gardens also pay special attention to programs that help develop moral sensibility, ecoliteracy, and civic engagement in children and youth.

Moral Development

Moral development refers to the process through which an individual acquires sensibilities, concepts, attitudes, and behaviors that recognize the welfare, rights and fair treatment of persons (Nucci 1997)—in other words, the rules by which mature individuals interact ethically with each other, the community, and their environment. One of the critical components of moral development is empathy. Formal education at public gardens provides a structured format for helping children develop empathy via meaningful and memorable encounters with unfamiliar and fascinating life. Through their experience of the plants and habitats, their guided activity, and the actions of people around them, they are exposed to an ethos of caring and a demonstrated respect and responsibility for other living things. Through the lens of the garden, they can observe how rules guide actions, that actions can have both positive and negative impacts on individuals and communities, and that there is a universal standard of good that guides actions (Piaget 1965; Kohlberg and Turiel 1971).

Ecoliteracy

Among natural collection institutions, public gardens are best equipped to help their audiences become ecoliterate. This responsibility is paramount in the education of children, students, and teachers. Fritjof Capra, a scientist, author, and founder of the Center for Ecoliteracy in Berkeley, California, said:

> The first step in this endeavor [to build and nurture sustainable communities] is to understand the principles of organization that ecosystems have developed to sustain the web of life. This understanding is what we call ecological literacy. Teaching this ecological knowledge . . . will be the most important role of education in the next century.

Formal programs delivered by knowledgeable staff offer the necessary structure through which a child's experiences of nature can give rise to deep reflection and connection-making, which in turn give meaning to what was before an unexamined pile of facts or physical phenomena. Telling a student that the common red worm, an introduced species in North America, eats huge amounts of leaf litter on which forest ecosystems depend for seed growth, and thereby helps destroy

Figure 15-1: A Chicago Botanic Garden Science First student samples aquatic biota with her class for further investigation.
Photo by Robin Carlson, courtesy of the Chicago Botanic Garden

the biodiversity of the forest floor, is communicating facts. By contrast, in education for ecoliteracy, students may be asked to think about analogous processes in other ecosystems, and then to think about the relative benefits or harm that such activity causes to wider networks of living organisms.

In the best of circumstances, gardens will have the physical resources to illustrate the dynamics of the natural world and the intellectual capital to teach about those resources and model attitudes and practices. Teaching and nurturing ecoliteracy through formal programs at the garden and through educational outreach and training of teachers is a fundamental responsibility of public gardens.

Civic Engagement

Climate change, environmental degradation, and species loss are now common topics in the news media and the focus of national and international economic and policy decisions. Because environmental impacts are not yet obvious in most regions in the United States and have not significantly compromised quality of life, they are perceived as secondary to more immediate concerns. Consequently, even educated individuals are not necessarily inspired or motivated to change their actions or participate in political decisions at a higher level (Schwarz, Havens, and Vitt 2008).

Public gardens can engage youth in activities that illustrate in concrete ways how the environment is affected by human actions. Formal education programs offer a forum for communicating the importance of our actions, their impact on the environment, and the ways in which individual actions can make a difference. Through organized investigation into water quality, ecosystem interactions, plant responses to climate change, invasive species, and biodiversity, gardens can clearly demonstrate that the planet's environment is indeed changing in visible and identifiable ways. By participating in these programs, particularly those with a service-learning component, youth are empowered to participate personally and publicly in creating a sustainable society.

Claude Stephens, Education Director, Bernheim Arboretum and Research Forest

What makes Bernheim Arboretum and Research Forest especially valuable to students are its passionate environmental educators and beautiful natural settings. At Bernheim, a 15,000-acre arboretum and natural area in central Kentucky, students have opportunities to:

- Experience healthy native ecosystems, often for the first time
- Interact with people deeply committed to the human-nature connection
- Learn something important and memorable.

Roof to Stream: Water Education with Flow

This Bernheim program explores connections between the built environment and stream ecology. As students step off of the bus, they are introduced to their water adventure and engaged in a discussion about how people impact water resources. The Bernheim teacher pours a bucket of water at their feet (sometimes on them) to see where a hypothetical drop of oil leaking from their bus might go. The flow is followed to the Visitor Center past bioswales and a sloped parking pad that uses myco-remediation techniques to deal with polluted runoff. The group passes underground cisterns, where water collected from the roof is stored for flushing toilets. After a restroom break, the students continue following the flow of wastewater by exploring Bernheim's biological peat filtration system, where the dark water is cleaned before being put to use as nursery irrigation. The group breaks into smaller teams, each led by a paid or volunteer educator, to better explore dry sinks, experimental vegetated roof planting beds, native landscaping, erosion controls, and the host of design strategies that help the Arboretum conserve precious water.

From the built environment, the groups travel to Wilson Creek, where a restoration effort has returned a 400-foot section of stream back to a meandering creek with riffles and pools. Like most streams in the central region of Kentucky, it was channelized through historical agricultural practices. The students learn about biodiversity, try to net fish, measure dissolved oxygen, and investigate the floodplains and detached wetlands.

Play is indispensable to the students' experience. The Arboretum's staff and volunteers help students (and teachers and class chaperones) have fun in and with the water—listening to ripples, encouraging mud play, and stacking rocks. The children imagine sticks as boats and watch where the stream takes them. Some students report that they have never been allowed to touch a stream before. Imagine that. As Rachel Carson said, "When introducing a child to the excitement of the natural world, it's not half so important to know as to feel."

Figure 15-2: School field trip students in the Roof to Stream program explore the Arboretum's creek restoration project.

Bernheim Arboretum and Research Forest

Scope and Character of Formal Education in Public Gardens

There are more than 700 public gardens in the United States, but only a fraction of these places make the necessary investment in planning, funding, staffing, and garden-wide coordination necessary to achieve truly good formal education programs.

Formal education encompasses the entire range of structured programs that take place at public gardens, including summer camp, Scouting, and family programs; school-related programs such as field trips and student internship programs; and teacher training and development. By focusing on and investigating different aspects of a garden, such as its landscapes, plant species, or ecosystem characteristics, formal education programs deepen the learner's experiences in a way that free-choice, informal interactions—as rewarding as they may be—can never achieve.

The opportunity to engage a child in a carefully crafted and well-taught education program is important. Edith Cobb, an influential writer who deeply researched the imagination of childhood, believed that there is a special period—"the middle age of childhood, approximately from five or six to eleven or twelve—between the strivings of animal infancy and the storms of adolescence—when the natural world is experienced in some highly evocative way, producing in the child a sense of profound continuity with natural processes and presenting overt evidence of a biological basis of intuition" (Cobb 1959). The opportunity for public gardens to capture and feed that appetite is one that should be seized and fully exploited, since the implications for the future are so great. The vast majority of adults who describe themselves as environmentally aware can trace their interest to meaningful, positive childhood experiences in nature that were supported by an adult (Chawla 1986). Formal education programs at public gardens thus help to address key challenges facing society.

School Student Education Models

Over the past twenty years especially, education initiatives in public garden settings have increased significantly for children from the pre-K years through grade 12. Older American gardens such as the New York Botanical Garden, the Brooklyn Botanic Garden, and the Missouri Botanical Garden have helped establish a standard of quality that is widely cited. The Brooklyn Botanic Garden, through its physical campus and environmental education expertise, collaborates with the New York public school system in running the Brooklyn Academy of Science and the Environment for more than 400 students

in grades 9–12. The Huntington Botanical Gardens, in San Marino, California, boasts an expansive new student teaching facility that includes a large wet lab, fascinating plant tech exhibits, and an exhibit garden designed to appeal to the elementary school–age child.

The Morris Arboretum of the University of Pennsylvania runs a Children's Education Program for K–12 that is endorsed by the Commonwealth of Pennsylvania through its educational improvement tax credit as a way of promoting education that goes beyond the normal offerings of a K–12 public school curriculum and program.

University gardens, such as the University of California Botanical Garden at Berkeley and Cornell Plantations, can access a deep well of academic expertise and create very sophisticated pedagogical resources. Berkeley's Math in the Garden, developed in collaboration with the Lawrence Hall of Science, is a nationally used curriculum, as is Botany on My Plate.

Out-of-School Programs

Out-of-school programs refer to education offerings for children and teens who come to the garden (or to whom the garden comes) outside of school hours. The conduit for these students may be Scouting programs, park district or private summer camps, or even entire family groups seeking a structured educational experience. Organized, fee-based summer camps hosted by and at public gardens are another major element in this category. Increasingly, out-of-school student cohorts are being created by the public garden itself in order to provide educational, mentoring, and work experiences for underserved youth. This is the case with the Chicago Botanic Garden's Science First, College First, and Green Youth Farm programs, which all occur during the summer—both at the Garden and at off-site locations—and for which participants are directly recruited, with the cooperation of the schools, by the Garden's education staff.

Another interesting audience for out-of-school programming provided by some public gardens is home-schooled children. While public gardens may be unwitting hosts to home-schooled children who are brought by their parents, the Desert Botanical Garden in Phoenix actively serves this audience through an extensive menu of garden-based K–8 programs, Learning Labs for Homeschoolers.

Teacher Education Models

In addition to an extensive student education commitment, the Missouri Botanical Garden (MOBOT) has a standing arrangement with the St. Louis school district to provide teacher training classes via dedicated Garden classrooms, teaching

Figure 15-3: Summer camp students catching pollinators in the Chicago Botanic Garden's 15-acre native prairie.

Photo by Robin Carlson, courtesy of the Chicago Botanic Garden

laboratories and greenhouses. Thousands of St. Louis–area teachers have gone through MOBOT's teacher professional development programs over the past two decades.

The Chicago Botanic Garden, like many other larger public gardens, invests extensive financial resources and staff effort into teacher professional development programs. Every year, the Garden conducts two weeklong Teacher Garden Camps in partnership with other environmental and plant education organizations, runs an annual school gardening conference for regional educators, and holds many other multiple-day workshops for teachers who are seeking to enhance their classroom practice and gain educational endorsements.

Figure 15-4: The Chicago Botanic Garden's woodlands curator, Jim Steffen, explaining forest biodiversity to a class of teachers.

Photo by Robin Carlson, courtesy of the Chicago Botanic Garden

Inspiration from Abroad

In looking for examples of best practices and effective programming, a student of public garden education should not fail to look overseas. Botanic Gardens Conservation International (BGCI), headquartered in Surrey, England, maintains a substantial website with links to garden education programs around the world, as well as a library of resources and curriculum materials. In 1994, BGCI published *Environmental Education in Botanic Gardens: Guidelines for Developing Individual Strategies*, which still stands as an in-depth, remarkably undated set of instructions for implementing a whole-garden approach to plant and conservation education.

Desirable Characteristics of Formal Education Programs

Positive short- and long-term impacts of museum experiences are directly related to the quality of the program and the opportunity of the participant to make personal connections, have novel experiences, and fulfill a personal agenda. Formal programming allows the garden to mediate visitors' experiences so that these conditions are met appropriately. Structured programs serve participants by creating a contextual framework for content, focusing their attention on compelling and exemplary aspects of the garden, and providing an instructor who can modify programming in response to participants' interests and needs. Indeed, some of the most effective pedagogies are grounded in the rich experiential learning found in nonschool settings. The physical and intellectual resources at public gardens offer a unique platform for education in which children, youth, and professional educators can have a direct and multisensory experience of the subject. Organized programming also provides opportunities for individuals to interact with garden staff and others in ways that reinforce the experience and the lesson.

While the garden's resources, the individual program goal, and the intended audience will influence the characteristics of any single program, it is generally true that successful public garden education programs will reflect or include many of the following features:

- **Place-based.** Education programs that rely directly on the features and/or novelty of a particular location or landscape to motivate interest in a concept or activity will enhance understanding and appreciation of garden resources.

- **Project-based.** A hands-on interactive approach interests and engages both children and adults through investigation, problem solving, experimentation, and fieldwork.

- **Developmentally appropriate.** Meeting the developmental needs of program participants may require a range of activities and difficulty levels, particularly in mixed-age or multigenerational programs.

- **Accessible.** Successful programs align the content, schedule, and location with the needs of the intended audience.

- **Internally collaborative.** Resources from other departments at a garden enrich educational programming by incorporating their botanical and horticultural expertise.

- **Sensitive to formal schooling requirements.** Both parents and teachers look for educational programs that will help their children in school. Incorporating regional learning standards when appropriate can make programs more appealing.

- **Evaluated.** Initial and ongoing program evaluation will ensure that programs are meeting both educational goals and participant expectations.

These aspects of specific programming are developed in the context of the larger garden mission, resources, and broad educational goals.

Where to Start: Structure and Operations

A garden's mission, resources, broad educational goals, audience, and location drive the structure and operations of the education department. Before developing individual programs, a focused needs assessment in collaboration with other garden departments can be helpful. The results can then inform the organizational and operational structure of the education department and its suite of programs.

Goals Assessment

Taking a close look at the garden's larger mission and translating that into educational goals is critical to establishing a consistent overall message and developing appropriate educational programs. For example, educational programs developed around a conservation mission will look very different from those developed around a therapeutic or aesthetic mission. This is not to say that a single garden cannot support multiple programmatic foci; rather, these foci should be clearly identified

Sally Isaacson, Director of Education, Santa Barbara Botanic Garden

Public gardens that display native regional flora, and especially those that include natural areas of indigenous vegetation, have a special opportunity—even mandate—to teach about local ecology in focused ways.

Whether in a child or adult, the desire to conserve native species and their natural habitats must proceed from curiosity. Interactive and hands-on programs that focus on interesting local species, their unique adaptations for survival, and plant/animal interactions are especially compelling for children.

The Santa Barbara Botanic Garden (SBBG) focuses on California native plants, and over the last decade its family and children's education programs have been characterized by an increasing emphasis on local ecology. Garden educators believe that it is of primary importance to teach children about species that they are likely to encounter in their local area.

The Santa Barbara Botanic Garden has developed on-site laboratory and tour programs to teach school children about the ecology of California's oak woodlands, riparian woodlands, and chaparral. While outdoors, children have close encounters with plants, observe pollination in action, and catch stream invertebrates for later study in the lab. Indoors, kids use microscopes as they dissect flowers, examine butterflies and other insects, study seed dispersal mechanisms, and much more.

One of SBBG's most successful and recognized ecology-based programs is Fam Camp: Adventures in Nature from Garden to Forest. Since 2002, the Santa Barbara Botanic Garden and the Los Padres National Forest have cosponsored this educational camping program that brings less privileged families with school-age children for twenty-four-hour, carefully structured campouts in the national forest.

Instructors and organizers are experienced educators from the Botanic Garden and the National Forest. Pre-trip orientation slide shows are given during after-school programs at local public schools. Grant funds pay for busing, food, instructional materials, and staffing. The National Forest provides tents, sleeping bags, foam pads, and cooking equipment.

During each program, families learn to erect and take down tents, cook in the outdoors, and take care of their campsite. Nature hikes, stream explorations, short campfire talks, and displays on geology, fauna, flora, and Native American history of the area are included. Local volunteer groups provide astronomy demonstrations, and National Forest staff and volunteers give presentations complete with firefighting equipment and horses.

Families, including many recent immigrants and first-generation Americans, go home with heightened curiosity and a deeper appreciation for their natural surroundings and for local plants and animals. Having learned that camping is a fun, educational, and inexpensive family activity, many of the program participants return later to explore the area with their friends.

Figure 15-5: Adults and children in the Santa Barbara Botanic Garden's Fam Camp program explore riparian woodlands and stream in Los Padres National Forest.

Photo by Sally Isaacson

and understood before educational programming is developed. An interesting exercise is to identify the top three educational goals, define how they relate to the overall mission, and then describe how the garden's resources can be used to achieve those goals.

Physical Context and Resources

One of the unique advantages of programming at a public garden is the ability to immerse participants in nature. To do this effectively, it is necessary to inventory the garden's physical resources. Types of landscaping, native habitats, water features, seasonal changes, permanent and changing exhibits, library collections, and available programming space are some variables to consider. Internal communication with other garden departments is necessary to identify restrictions or requirements for using either natural areas or programming locations. It is also useful to have regular communication with horticulturists and curators about rich environments that can be used for education programs and those that may be sensitive to disturbance. Restoration activities, for example, may limit access to some areas.

Audience

Effective public garden educators know their community, including its geography and demography; people's values, beliefs, and knowledge levels; and relevant social and economic factors. In addition to personal knowledge, such information can be gleaned from member databases, if they exist, and from records of past program participants. School systems, local government, houses of worship, and agencies that serve the local community are major stores of information about, and access to, formal program participants. Once the target audience is defined, an appropriate program structure can be developed. Often gardens have multiple audiences, each of which will require a different strategic approach. Programming for school groups will need to be marketed to teachers and aligned with learning standards and school schedules. Teacher professional development programs must offer appealing content that can be translated to the school classroom and offer appropriate continuing education and graduate credit. Family programs might take into account parent work schedules, intergenerational dynamics, and topics of special interest.

Internal Collaborations

While each garden may divide up functions differently, executing educational programming requires the coordination of multiple areas in a garden, both logistical and substantive.

Coordinating with security, maintenance, visitor operations, and volunteer services among others is necessary to ensure that programs are staffed, participants are safe, and the setup is appropriate. A respectful, friendly dialogue with other staff, consideration for other departments' needs and limitations, and appreciative gestures for those who have helped out facilitate the successful implementation of educational programming.

In addition, there is much to be gained by leveraging the knowledge and expertise of a garden's researchers and horticulturists in the development of education programming. Particularly for gardens that have strategic research initiatives, incorporating new expert information and findings into public education programs provides additional depth and meaning. Given the mission to communicate new and existing knowledge about plants and the environment, gardens should strive to share such knowledge—homegrown or from the broader domain—in very accessible and comprehensible ways.

Community Partnerships

Becoming familiar with the programs and resources available at nearby museums, park districts, and cultural organizations allows the garden educator to identify gaps in existing garden education programs and to spot potential program collaborators. Programming can then be targeted first to audiences whose needs are not currently being met. Often there are other local or regional museums, science centers, nature centers, and formal education institutions that have education goals complementary to those of the public garden. Combining resources with these kinds of organizations can enrich environmental educational programming, provide a way for collaborators to expand program choices, and make deeper connections with the community.

As an example, the Chicago Botanic Garden and the Field Museum in Chicago partner on an annual youth science symposium attended by more than 200 high school students from twenty different schools. The Chicago Botanic Garden coordinates the speakers and school participation, while the Field Museum provides staff and space so the symposium can be held in a central location. Such partnerships are not limited to other environmentally focused organizations. Combining different content areas such as music, art, or history with environmental science can enliven activities and expand audience appeal. The Fairchild Challenge, developed by the Fairchild Tropical Botanic Garden in Coral Gables, Florida, and implemented in a number of public garden sites nationally (and internationally), invites high school students to communicate about the environment using music, poetry, fashion, and photography, among other media.

There are many other successful, replicable program models that can provide expert guidance for new gardens. The Earth Partnership for Schools curriculum and teacher professional development program, developed by the University of Wisconsin-Madison Arboretum, offers a well-tested program, originally funded by the National Science Foundation, that enables public gardens to offer in-depth training for K–12 teachers who want to implement habitat restoration projects with their students. In Ithaca, New York, Cornell Plantations has partnered with six local museums and the county library in the Discovery Trail Partnership, which involves structured exploration of all eight sites by all pre-K through fifth-grade students in the Ithaca City School District. Last but not least, the Midwest Public Garden Collaborative won the American Public Gardens Association's 1998 award for program excellence for Partners for Growing Science, a K–8 plant science curriculum that was co-developed by educators at the Holden Arboretum, the Minnesota Landscape Arboretum, the Missouri Botanical Garden, the Morton Arboretum, and the Chicago Botanic Garden.

Thinking Like a Business

Creating a business plan can improve a program's chance for success by concretely identifying cost of inputs versus expected participation rates and other positive benefits to the garden. These benefits may be quantified in dollars, good public relations, donor satisfaction, valuable contacts, and leveraging effect on other garden operations. In some cases, it may mean all of these things; in other cases, conducting a business plan will reveal that the return is not likely to be commensurate with the investment.

While the overall goal of education programs may not be revenue generation, programs can cover their costs and in some cases even contribute revenue to the garden. Good garden educators identify *all* program expenses, including materials, staffing, overhead, promotion, and transportation, and then determine how much it will cost to run one session of the program. Depending on revenue goals, this calculation helps determine registration fees, the number of registrants needed to cover costs, or the grant funds that need to be raised.

Like any other public service, successful education programs require good product development, marketing, delivery, and customer support, all of which must be carried out in a fiscally responsible way. Audience needs, garden goals, and available resources should guide program development. Particularly for fee-based programs, acceptance, registration, and cancellation processes and policies should be clearly defined up front

Figure 15-6: Brownies help plant garden beds as part of an after-school badge program.

Photo by Robin Carlson, courtesy of the Chicago Botanic Garden

to avoid participant confusion. Marketing should be targeted to potential participants and delivered via the media that most effectively reach them, whether print, electronic, or both.

There are two basic components to successful program delivery: participant expectations and instructional/program quality. It is important to be clear about what individuals should expect as program participants, such as whether the program will take place outside, whether participants will receive take-away materials, the size of the classes, and the developmental level at which participants will be taught.

Well-run public gardens understand that participants in education programs are important customers and that they bring an array of needs to their garden visit. Effective educators do not simply address the program's curriculum. They will pay close attention to all aspects of a garden visit and strive to make the participant's experience—whether the visitor is a two-year-old or a senior teacher—satisfying on many fronts. Customers come back, either through their own agency or through schools and teachers and parents, because they have had an enjoyable time in an educational, aesthetic, recreational, and even culinary way.

Department and Program Development

High-quality, well-trained staff people are the hallmark of successful programs in any educational setting. Public gardens are no exception.

Start with Staff

The majority of public gardens in North America were established to house and display horticultural collections. Research and education typically arrived later, if at all. As a result, most public gardens still have a small formal education staff—perhaps two or three full-time educators plus contracted instructors supplemented by the efforts of volunteers. This model is the prevailing reality where the garden's educational mission is not perceived by itself or by the community as paramount, or where the dollars to support more ambitious programming are simply not available.

Large gardens that have sizable endowments or enjoy generous annual giving by foundations and corporations have the opportunity to build staff capacity. Education staff specialization can range from early childhood to the challenges of working with teens to understanding the content and standards alignment requirements that classroom educators need so they can translate plant-based curricula into the schoolroom. Senior public garden education staff members do not always come from a horticultural, botanical, or environmental science background. Program development and management expertise in public garden settings can be found in staff with graduate-level training in curriculum and instruction, evaluation, the humanities, and even health-related fields such as occupational therapy.

Most typically, however, garden education staff will be drawn from the ranks of public horticulture program graduates, former classroom science teachers, and informal environmental educators. The skills, training, and character of these individuals will directly shape the quality and future prospects of a public garden education program, so it is crucial to find the best-qualified individuals possible. It is preferable to have one highly qualified and motivated educator rather than three mediocre staff members. That one individual is much more likely to be creative and resourceful in developing new funding streams that can help the garden grow its capacity.

Professional Development for Education Staff

Professional staff development is the not-so-secret ingredient that helps keep educators motivated and supports ongoing program innovation and vitality. The American Public Gardens Association and its conferences and interest groups comprise a major professional resource for public garden educators, and the National Science Teachers Association, the North American Association for Environmental Education, the Botanical Society of America, the American Association for the Advancement of Science, the American Association of Museums, and numerous other national professional organizations offer curricula, information sharing, and opportunities for peer and cause-related communication that can greatly enrich an educator's experience and knowledge.

Locally, professional development is often available through state agency programs, such as state departments of natural resources, community-of-practice networks, county-supported programs, and grant-supported university training courses that are typically geared for classroom science teachers but for which garden educators may qualify. The lack of dedicated travel and professional development dollars should not pose an absolute impediment. Creative networking, free or low-cost Web-based programs, and informal educational gatherings at the garden site can help address educators' needs for communication with peers, information sharing between disciplines, and development of best practices.

Funding Formal Education

Public gardens, like other living collection, science, and cultural organizations, depend on earned revenue from admission and program fees, memberships, government grants, and contributions from individuals, foundations, and corporations. Some combination of these, plus interest generated from endowments, is what keeps public gardens running day to day.

Formal education programs are, happily, one of the favored funding targets for both private sector donors and government agencies. Many private foundations direct all or part of their philanthropic dollars to support programs that serve student education and help train teachers. Minority and economically disadvantaged students are a particular focus for corporate and foundation giving, as they are for many federal agency grants.

For those gardens that have well-staffed development and sponsorship departments, there is good opportunity to make a match between programs and funders. In the United States, the Institute of Museum and Library Services is the major federal funding agency for public gardens. The National Science Foundation, through its Informal Science Education program, funds the development and dissemination of environmental science and STEM (science technology, engineering, and mathematics) programs delivered in informal settings such as public gardens. Agencies including the U.S. National Aeronautics and Space Administration are also supporting garden-sponsored programming in citizen science. The United States departments of Education, Health and Human Services, Labor, and Agriculture are also possible funding sources.

The inclusion of the No Child Left Inside (NCLI) Act as a part of the 2010 reauthorization of the Elementary and Secondary Education Act is an important development for public gardens. As noted by the NCLI Coalition, "The bill authorizes funding for states to provide high-quality, environmental instruction. Funds would support outdoor learning activities both at school and in non-formal environmental education centers, teacher professional development, and the creation of state environmental literacy plans."

Finally, the most direct and reliable way to help offset the cost of formal education programs in public gardens is to offer programs that people desire and for which they are willing to pay. Developing competitive, fee-based programs that generate a steady stream of revenue is the foundation for most public gardens. In certain cases, gardens can earn consulting fees for training and services through contracts with other organizations and school districts.

Ongoing Operations

Once an education department is up and running, with qualified staff and a menu of solid programs, maintenance and ongoing improvement become the main concerns. A good operating plan must take into account continuity and growth, collaboration, and improvement.

Program Continuity and Growth

A garden's education programs define the personality of the garden for participants and can help drive the support of key political and opinion leaders in ways that benefit the entire garden. Paying close attention to education programming pays off in significant ways. Whenever possible, programs should be closely linked to the garden's expertise in collections, natural habitats, and plant science research. The feedback loops thus created can help bootstrap small programs and allow all programs, big or small, to evolve appropriately as audiences and topics of interest change and new scientific discoveries are made.

Even with the best systems in place, staff transitions occur that can potentially disrupt successful programs. Several program management procedures can smooth transitions when staff members depart. At the beginning of each program, the responsible staff person should contribute to an operations manual that includes all the details of program operations: budgets, recruitment, materials, locations, internal and external collaborators, and any other information relevant to the program operation. Because programs develop and change over time, it is advisable to update the operations manual annually, or as needed. As more efficient and effective ways of coordinating programs are identified, those should be added. Maintaining operations manuals ensures that, whether because of a temporary gap in supervision or the learning curve of a new employee, any staff member will have the information needed to effectively manage the program.

While an operations manual is helpful, nothing substitutes for hands-on training and experience, so cross-training staff also ensures that programs continue smoothly despite staffing hiccups. Opportunities to discuss program operations, attend relevant volunteer trainings, and shadow each other periodically help staff develop a working knowledge of all the education programs.

Evaluation and Program Improvement

Evaluation, which is discussed in detail in Chapter 18, is a requirement for successful ongoing program operations. The likelihood is that even with careful planning, there will be aspects of program operations or content requiring modification. Ongoing assessment is essential to the long-term success of education programming: it helps ensure that participants are enjoying the program and that content remains relevant to the audience. For program performance aspects that are not self-evident, short satisfaction surveys completed by participants can be helpful.

POSSIBLE SATISFACTION SURVEY QUESTIONS

Questions to Ask about Program Attendance

Are program registration numbers acceptable?

Is the intended audience participating?

Is the marketing strategy reaching the intended audience?

Are participants satisfied?

Do participants feel that they can now teach this material themselves?

Are participants returning for additional programs?

Questions to Ask about Curriculum, Content, and Topic

Are participants engaged?

Are instructional/educational goals met?

Are activities received as intended?

Does the program effectively utilize garden resources?

Does the program relate to the garden's mission?

Questions to Ask about Instruction Quality

Are participants engaged?

Is the instructor knowledgeable?

Is the instruction hands-on?

Is the teaching style appropriate for the subject matter and audience?

Caroline Lewis, Former Director of Education, Fairchild Tropical Botanic Garden

The growing role of gardens in public education challenges educators to become more ambitious and creative in their public outreach. The wording of institutional missions may vary, but common agendas include developing lifelong learners who appreciate the beauty and value of nature. Programs such as the Fairchild Challenge can help public gardens cultivate large, diverse, untapped audiences and promote botanical and environmental awareness, scholarship and stewardship.

The Fairchild Challenge is a free, annual, voluntary, standards-based, interdisciplinary program that targets teenagers and, by extension, their teachers, parents, friends, and communities. Its mission is to foster interest in the environment by encouraging young people to appreciate the beauty and value of nature, develop critical thinking skills, understand the need for biodiversity and conservation, tap community resources, become actively engaged citizens, and recognize that individuals do indeed make a difference.

The overall goal is for students and schools to accrue points through entries in Challenge options staggered throughout the school year, each with stated requirements, points, and deadlines. The menu of contest options is diverse: writing opinion and research papers; performing songs, poetry, and skits; creating school gardens, artwork, videos, and newsletters; conducting intergenerational ethnobotany interviews; capturing school energy, water, and tree canopy data; designing solar devices; and formulating green cuisine menus, to name a few. The interdisciplinary quality of Challenge options allows teens to connect with nature physically, emotionally, creatively, and intellectually.

Promoting the program through schools maximizes youth involvement and weaves attention to nature into the daily lives of young people, regardless of age, race, religion, socioeconomic status, and ability. The schools involved are diverse—large and small, public and independent, Title I and magnet schools, schools that serve special-needs children, and community/after-school centers for at-risk students. Very fluidly, the Challenge is able to include, embrace, and promote a range of other nature-friendly initiatives, supporting the work of like-minded organizations. The Challenge partners with colleges/universities, parks, nature centers, government agencies, community groups, and private businesses to support and promote the students, teachers, and schools involved in the Fairchild Challenge. The school district, funders, partners, and sponsors embrace the program for its appeal to diverse learners, hands-on approach to connecting youth with nature, positive impact on school climate, and celebratory design.

The Fairchild Challenge is proving to be a scalable and replicable program that infuses entire school systems with meaningful, appealing environmental education opportunities. The Fairchild Challenge is currently being delivered in Florida, Illinois, California, Utah, Pennsylvania, and Costa Rica. Educators from forty-six sites have now been trained to replicate the Fairchild Challenge in cities around the country and internationally. The scope and potential of the program to link teachers and students around environmental issues is profound. The program model is also one that can inspire and help shape secondary school educational strategies in schools around the country.

Figure 15-7: High school students at the Fairchild Tropical Botanic Garden preparing for the Fairchild Challenge Poetry Slam competition.

Fairchild Tropical Botanic Garden

Positioning Public Gardens to Teach Ecoliteracy

In his foreword to *Ecological Literacy: Educating Our Children for a Sustainable World* (2005), David Orr, one of the nation's leading environmental educators, makes the following important points:

- The ecological crisis is in every way a crisis of education.

- All education is environmental education . . . by what is included or excluded, we teach the young that they are a part of, or apart from, the natural world.

- The goal is not just mastery of subject matter but making connections between head, hand, heart, and cultivation of the capacity to discern systems.

If all education is environmental education, public gardens enjoy an incalculable advantage over traditional school classrooms. Their programs, well conceived and executed, can model a kind of educational experience that, true to its root meaning, "leads out" the student to a fuller command of his or her potential. By having good educators employ the best pedagogical methods in the context of a rich and rewarding physical environment, the public garden trumps all other education venues that are normally available to the school-age child.

Summary

The programs discussed in this chapter reflect a considerable range of curricular goals and approaches, but all share a belief in the primacy of experience, the power of place, and the indispensability of careful preparation and good teaching. The three case studies included here report on programs that are grounded in the educator's belief that such experiences can make a lasting difference by connecting students to a story about nature that becomes a story about themselves. These programs, and no less the other programs mentioned in this chapter, signal the philosophy and values of their gardens, communicate with a larger knowledge community, and seek to effect change in profound ways.

We will continue to depend on educated citizens to carry the debate about what our communities, our states, and our nation require for a sustainable society. That sustainability is both measured in the health of plant and animal species and ecosystems and of the human communities that depend on those systems. Formal pre-K–12 education in public gardens is a powerful engine for science literacy, conservation awareness and advocacy, and personal human growth. The engine has barely turned over, however, and we can look forward to a future of transformative lessons from the garden.

Figure 15-8: Chicago Botanic Garden summer camp "green thumbs" getting instructions on how to pot.

Photo by Robin Carlson, courtesy of the Chicago Botanic Garden

Annotated Resources

Research, Best Practice, and Program Development Guides

Center for Ecoliteracy (www.ecoliteracy.org/strategies/place-based-learning). Web-based guides to place-based and project-based learning.

Lewis, S. P. 2005. *Uses of active plant-based learning in K–12 educational settings*. A white paper prepared for the Partnership for Plant-Based Learning. www.ahs.org/youth_gardening/plant_based_education.htm.

No Child Left Inside (NCLI) Consortium (www.cbf.org/Page.aspx?pid=687).

North American Association for Environmental Education (NAAEE) (www.naaee.org/programs-and-initiatives/guidelines-for-excellence).

School Garden Wizard (www.schoolgardenwizard.org). Website created by the United States Botanic Garden and Chicago Botanic Garden.

Schwarz-Ballard, J. *Summer science: Reaching urban youth through environmental science*. Chicago: Chicago Botanic Garden. www.chicagobotanic.org/ctl/publications.

Sobel, D. 2005. *Place-based education: Connecting classrooms and communities*. Great Barrington, Mass.: Orion Society. www.orionmagazine.org/cart/index.php?crn=207&rn=517&action=show_detail.

White, H. 2008. *Connecting today's kids with nature: A policy action plan*. Reston, Va.: National Wildlife Federation. www.nwf.org/News-and-Magazines/Media-Center/Reports/Archive/2008/Connecting-Todays-Kids-With-Nature.aspx.

Willison, J. *1994. Environmental education in botanic gardens: Guidelines for developing individual strategies*. Richmond, U.K.: Botanic Gardens Conservation International. www.bgci.org/files/Worldwide/Education/EE_guidelines/ee_guidelines_english.pdf.

Curricula

Activities Integrating Math and Science (www.aimsedu.org).

Garden Mosaics (www.gardenmosaics.cornell.edu).

Great Explorations in Math and Science (www.lhsgems.org).

Growing in the Garden. Iowa State University 4-H Youth Development (www.extension.iastate.edu/growinginthegarden). Multidisciplinary curriculum with garden applications.

CHAPTER 16

Continuing, Professional, and Higher Education

LARRY DeBUHR

Introduction

Because of their plant collections, libraries, professional staff, and research facilities, public gardens have become centers for adult continuing, professional, and higher education. In some cases, public gardens have become the academic leaders in horticultural, botanical, and related education in their communities. In other cases, public gardens provide thousands of hours of leisure-time learning for adults who are curious about plants, gardening, and the natural world. There are many approaches, many audiences, and many opportunities for public gardens to educate adults in their communities and at the same time to serve the broader horticulture profession. This chapter explores those audiences, the types of programs offered at public gardens, how to develop new programs, and how to ensure the quality of these programs.

KEY TERMS

Continuing adult education: activities, classes, and programs offered to adult audiences for personal enrichment and the pursuit of personal knowledge.

Leisure time learning: a term often applicable to adults who enroll in educational programs during their leisure time for the satisfaction of learning, essentially making a choice about how to spend leisure or recreational time. The term is often applied to museum learning.

Lifelong learning: voluntary learning beyond formal schooling that occurs throughout the life of an individual for personal growth and development.

Professional education: educational activities that help prepare an individual for a career or provide an individual already trained in a profession with new information, skills, and knowledge that helps the person to advance his or her career.

Traditional formal academic education: educational programs established with the goal of leading to a degree or diploma and having a set of curriculum requirements that need to be completed before the degree or diploma is awarded.

Certificate programs: structured instruction certifying that participants have developed specialized knowledge in a particular area of study.

Internships: student educational programs that provide practical, hands-on experience working side by side with professional mentors for various lengths of time. Some internships are paid and other are unpaid.

Continuing education unit (CEU): a measure used to provide evidence that professional education has been met. One CEU is usually awarded after ten hours of participation in a recognized program with a qualified instructor.

International Association for Continuing Education and Training (IACET): an organization that has established standards for issuing CEUs.

Accrediting Council for Continuing Education and Training (ACCET): an organization that accredits continuing education and training programs to ensure that they meet minimum professional standards.

Audiences

Public gardens offer a wide variety of educational programs to numerous audiences. There is no single approach or model applicable at all public gardens. Each garden determines what it can do best and how continuing, professional, and higher education fits into its operations and programs. If there is one hard-and-fast rule, however, it is this: to be successful, know the audience and serve it accordingly. Understand the community the garden is in. Understand the mission and the strengths of the public garden and how they can be used to select programs that best serve appropriate audiences.

If the public garden is in an urban area, the audience includes apartment dwellers and home owners with small lots and limited space. In a suburban area, audiences will have large lots and much larger gardens. The garden's education staff needs to consider what programs might best serve these two groups. For example, arboreta in suburban settings that have large natural areas might want to plan programs for amateur naturalists, bird-watchers, and wildflower enthusiasts.

Adults Seeking New Knowledge and Enrichment

The largest audience for continuing education at public gardens is adults seeking new knowledge and enrichment as part of their leisure-time activities. They are often home owners looking for ways to maintain lawns and landscape their homes. Some may be apartment dwellers looking to learn how to grow plants in containers on the patio. Others might be fruit and vegetable growers looking for ways to grow crops organically, get bigger yields, or grow plants they have not grown before. Bird-watchers, photographers, and artists are all leisure-time learners whose interests can be advanced with classes at public gardens. Remember the curious naturalists who want to learn about plants, animals, and the natural world, and provide programs that serve them as well as home gardeners.

Leisure-time learners include both working adults looking for short courses in the evening or on the weekend and retired adults whose lives are enriched and whose curiosity is fed by continuing education classes. These individuals often enjoy the social interaction that comes with leisure-time learning. They expect quality instruction, and often like to challenge or question the instructor. Because of their interest and curiosity, they can be very satisfying students to teach. They will let the instructor know when they are happy or not pleased with the class. Many will develop allegiances to favorite teachers, and if they have good experiences, those same loyalties will be shown to the public garden through donations and increased memberships. The first exposure to the Missouri Botanical Garden for one of its largest private donors came from an adult continuing education class.

Adults Seeking Careers or Career Changes

Adults exploring new careers form another audience served by public gardens. Some of these individuals are unsure if they will enjoy jobs in horticulture, garden design, or related professions, so they take continuing education courses to explore the field. Others wish to start new careers and are looking at programs offered by public gardens that prepare them for jobs in the horticulture industry. The School of Professional Horticulture at the New York Botanical Garden provides an excellent model of state-licensed and accredited career training.

Adults Requiring Professional Credentials or New Professional Knowledge

A significant audience for public garden adult education programs is professionals in the horticulture, landscaping, landscape architecture, and related botanical and green industry fields. Many professions require continued education to maintain credentials. Research advances in many fields result in new knowledge, techniques, and information that professionals need in order to stay up to date in their current jobs. Public gardens provide valuable service to these audiences, including their own staff, through a wide range of approaches. For example, the Chicago Botanic Garden offers a Healthcare Garden Design Certificate program that helps educate health-care facility planners, architects, and landscape designers working with hospitals and other health facilities to install health and wellness gardens. The Missouri Botanical Garden sponsors a botanical symposium each year for botanical researchers.

Undergraduate and Graduate Students

Certain public gardens have a history of and reputation for botanical or horticultural research or excellence in certain public garden program areas. They have highly qualified staff and are able to serve both undergraduate and graduate students. In these models, partnerships are developed between the public gardens and colleges and universities. Examples of programs serving this audience are included later in this chapter and include public gardens such as Rancho Santa Ana Botanic Garden, the New York Botanical Garden, Missouri Botanical Garden, Chicago Botanic Garden, and others.

Adult Continuing Education and Lifelong Learning

The easiest and most financially profitable program for a public garden to operate is the adult continuing education program that serves individuals interested in leisure-time, recreational, lifelong learning.

In 1907, the University of Wisconsin–Madison became the first academic institution in the United States to offer a continuing education program (Gooch 1995). Since then many colleges, particularly community colleges, have become proficient in offering adult continuing education in a wide range of academic disciplines that serve an important community function. But colleges are not the only organizations offering adult continuing education. Museums, parks, municipal recreation departments, and educational nonprofits are other avenues open to adults looking for recreational leisure-time learning.

It is clear that public gardens have a great deal of competition in this arena. But public gardens have also been very successful competitors. Collectively, public gardens have hundreds of thousands of members and millions of visitors annually, all of whom are potential students for their programs. Because they are beautiful places in which to learn, public gardens have an advantage over other types of organizations. More important, public gardens can easily provide classes supporting existing avocations and interests of millions of adults, such as gardening, bird-watching, painting, photography, and natural history in general.

Lifelong Learning

The term *lifelong learning* emerged during the past few decades and has been applied in numerous ways to any educational activity for adult audiences beyond the formal education track. The idea of adults continuing to learn beyond formal schooling is certainly not new, and professional continuing education has been operating in organized ways for many decades. Philosophically, the idea of lifelong learning is that adults will continue to pursue knowledge on a voluntary basis throughout their lives. The learner is self-motivated. The rewards are intrinsic personal growth and development rather than a degree, diploma, or career. There is also a clear element of social interaction that often accompanies lifelong learning. The classes, lectures, field trips, and other activities provided by public gardens that serve the leisure-time learner fall well within the label of lifelong learning.

Traditional Academic Programs

Traditional academic programs are distinguished from lifelong learning in a number of ways. Traditional academic programs are established with the goal of providing formal education leading to a degree or diploma. Traditional academic programs have curriculum requirements that must be completed before the degree or diploma is awarded, and these programs are designed to prepare the learner for careers. The motivation of the learner is the attainment of the degree or diploma.

Opportunities for Public Gardens

Public gardens operate adult continuing education programs for a number of reasons. First, adult continuing education serves the interests of members and the constituents of the garden. Second, adult continuing education helps advance the mission of the public garden. Many public gardens have education as an important component of their missions. Finally, adult continuing education programs generate significant earned revenue. Many public gardens offer some level of adult continuing education, and larger gardens have implemented very extensive, diverse, and active programs.

The New York Botanical Garden's program offers classes for professionals, hobbyists, and leisure-time learners ranging from botanical art and garden writing to botany, horticultural therapy, and landscape design. The Missouri Botanical Garden's programs cover an equally wide range of courses, including horticulture, cooking, crafts and floral design, garden walks and

Figure 16-1: An adult wreath-making class.

Table 16-1: School of the Chicago Botanic Garden: Programs and Number of Registrations

	1996	1997	1998	1999	2000	2001	2002
Programs	154	158	167	274	366	380	383
Registrations	2,467	2,660	3,178	4,338	6,710	6,191	8,365

visits, landscaping, and nature study. The School of the Botanic Garden at the Chicago Botanic Garden offers continuing education and professional classes in five departments: Garden Design, Horticulture, Ecology and Nature Studies, Botanical Arts and Humanities, and Plant and People Interactions. Table 16-1 documents the Chicago program's rapid growth in its first seven years (Jones 2002).

But it isn't just the public gardens with large budgets that offer adult continuing education. Public gardens that operate on smaller budgets and smaller staff have been able to offer incredibly rich adult programming. For example, the Fort Worth Botanic Garden has joined with Texas Christian University's Extended Education to offer adult classes. The Marie Selby Botanical Garden teaches classes in art, photography, horticulture, green building, and health. Nor do public gardens need a long history before they offer adult programming, as the Frederick Meijer Gardens and Sculpture Park has demonstrated.

However, there is a relationship between the size of a public garden's budget and the existence of adult education programs at the garden. A survey of the websites of 154 gardens and arboreta based on the size of their budgets (large gardens had budgets of over $2 million; medium gardens had budgets of between $1 million and $2 million; small gardens had budgets of less than $1 million) shows that that 69 percent of large public gardens have adult education programs, as do 51 percent of medium gardens, but only 41 percent of small gardens do.

Professional Education

Learning doesn't stop when a person completes a high school diploma, a college degree, or gets a first job. New information is always being discovered. Unique ornamental plants are being developed. Research is revealing different and better horticultural techniques, including more sustainable practices. Professionals, not only those working at public gardens but also those in many related fields, have an obligation to keep up to date with these developments.

Public gardens contribute significantly to the professional education needs and interests of a large community of practicing individuals in fields such as landscape design and architecture, horticulture, the nursery industry, botanical research, visitor services, and others. The American Public Gardens Association sponsors professional development workshops for public garden professionals.

The types of programs that fall under the category of professional continuing education are as varied as the audiences they serve. Some of those approaches are described in more detail below. To this list can be added symposia, workshops, conferences, informal visits to colleagues at other sites, and even papers published in journals.

Certification Programs

Certificate programs allow participants to develop specialized knowledge in a particular area of study. They are not equivalent to a college degree, but they do provide participants with proof that they have completed some unit of study, such as a first-aid certificate, a certificate to apply pesticides, or a safety certificate to use certain equipment. The format of certificate programs is variable and can include a series of required courses taken at different times or a structured curriculum delivered in a set sequence of activities and lessons.

At public gardens, certificate programs are often developed for leisure-time learners as well as professional learners who want to develop a deeper understanding of a certain topic without having any goal other than enrichment. The Morton Arboretum, for example, offers a successful naturalist certificate program that serves a leisure-time audience. The awarding of the certificate is an incentive to keep the leisure-time learner engaged over an extended period of time.

Certificate programs specifically designed for professional audiences have more rigorous requirements than programs for leisure-time audiences, and they set higher expectations for participants. Public gardens of various sizes offer certificate programs in areas such as horticulture, landscape design and

Table 16-2: Examples of Certificate Programs at Nine Public Gardens

Arnold Arboretum

Landscape Design

Landscape Design History

Landscape Preservation

Chicago Botanic Garden

Ornamental Plant Materials

Professional Gardening Levels 1 and 2

Midwest Gardening

Garden Design

Healthcare Garden Design

Botanical Arts

The Morton Arboretum

Home Landscape Gardening

Nature Photography

Botanical Arts and Illustration

Ornithology

Naturalist

North Carolina Botanical Garden

Native Plant Studies

Botanic Illustrations

Phipps Conservatory and Botanical Gardens

Native Plants

Botanic Art and Illustration

Sustainable Horticulture

Landscape and Garden Design

Floral Design

Brooklyn Botanic Garden

Horticulture

Floral Design

Denver Botanic Gardens

Rocky Mountain Gardening

Botanical Art and Illustration

The New York Botanical Garden

Horticulture: Plant Production

Horticulture: Landscape Management

Horticulture: Ornamental Plant ID

Horticulture: Floral Garden Design

Gardening

Botany

Botanical Arts

Natural Science Illustration

Horticultural Therapy

Floral Design

Landscape Design

Environmental Gardening

The State Botanical Garden of Georgia

Native Plants

---

maintenance, horticultural therapy, botanical arts, nature, and botany (see Table 16-2).

Student Internships

Many horticulture degree programs at colleges and universities require students to work in an internship program. The purpose of these internships is to provide students and future public garden employees with practical, hands-on experience working side by side with professional mentors. Public gardens are exceptionally good locations for student internships. In addition to interns from degree programs, some public gardens offer internships for young adults regardless of their connection to an institution of higher education.

The benefits to a public garden of sponsoring internships are numerous. Most important, internships help train the next generation of public garden professionals who will contribute to the field and be better employees. In fact, internships are a good way to identify potential future staff members. It is not uncommon for institutions to hire interns when positions become available. Finally, all public gardens can use the extra help that interns provide.

Figure 16-2: Student intern helping with pollination studies at the Shaw Nature Reserve.

There are many variations of internships offered at public gardens. Some are for the summer; others are for six or twelve months. Some gardens use internships as a way to supplement staff. In most cases interns are paid for the work they perform, but some internships are unpaid.

If the internships are to be meaningful for the students and productive for the garden, professional staff must serve as mentors, providing supervision, guidance, and a genuine educational experience. Longwood Gardens operates an exceptional internship program that helps to train three different audiences: high school students, college students, and international students interested in gardening.

Employee Swaps between Gardens

In some case, employees at different public gardens will exchange jobs for a period of time. Cox and Edwards (1994) describe the value of such a job exchange, including seeing how other gardens operate, looking at new approaches and techniques, and examining new ideas in a different setting. Working in the same job for an extended time sometimes becomes routine. An exchange can help to professionally refresh an employee by temporarily experiencing a new work environment and new professional colleagues.

CEU Classes

Many professional associations (Association of Professional Landscape Designers, International Society of Arboriculture, American Horticultural Therapy Association, and Golf Course

The internship program at the Morris Arboretum of the University of Pennsylvania has operated for more than thirty years and trained well over 200 leaders who have gone on to careers in the horticulture industry, public gardens, government, research, education, and extension services.

Eight yearlong internship positions are available in arboriculture, education, horticulture, plant protection, urban forestry, flora of Pennsylvania, plant propagation, and the rose and flower garden. Each requires a different set of qualifications and experience. This is not a survey program, where interns sample multiple disciplines for short periods of time. It is an intensive experience that provides a combination of practical application as well as the development of management skills in a single area.

Each intern is enrolled in two graduate arboretum management courses offered through the Department of Landscape Architecture and Regional Planning at the University of Pennsylvania. The curriculum includes instruction on the living collections, which introduce interns to the Arboretum's woody plants and help interns develop skills in plant identification, use, and culture. The courses require interns to complete an independent study project that helps them advance their own career interests, to prepare a written report, and to make an oral presentation to Arboretum staff.

In addition, the interns are engaged in a series of informal educational activities. Seminars and practical sessions on a variety of topics held throughout the year enable the interns to interact with Arboretum staff and professionals from other institutions. Field trips to public gardens, museums, and natural areas give the interns opportunities to see how other organizations operate. The interns also staff the Arboretum's Plant Clinic, a walk-in/phone-in service that provides the public with information on plant pests and diseases as well as plant identifications.

The Morris Arboretum's internship program places successful applicants in positions that are as close to professional work experience as possible for a one-year training program. Interns receive an hourly wage for forty hours per week, are eligible for health, vision, and dental benefits through the University of Pennsylvania, receive paid vacation time, sick days, and paid holidays, and are eligible for tuition benefits at the University of Pennsylvania, Chestnut Hill College, and Temple University's Ambler Campus.

Superintendents Association of America, to name a few) either require or recommend that members continue their professional education after their formal education is completed. The measure often used to provide evidence that this requirement has been met is the continuing education unit, or CEU. One CEU is usually awarded after ten hours of participation in a recognized program with a qualified instructor. The International Association for Continuing Education and Training has established standards for CEUs. Many public gardens offer continuing education programs designed to satisfy some of these requirements.

Teacher Professional Development

Increasingly, public gardens are offering professional training for teachers. Successful teacher professional development programs at public gardens are those that conform to the recommendations of the National Science Standards and align with state and local curriculum guidelines. For example, the University of California Botanical Garden at Berkeley has a summer learning institute that provides botanical and/or horticultural curriculum training that teachers can use to satisfy state curriculum and their own professional requirements.

Higher Education

Over the past twenty-five years a notable trend in colleges and universities has significantly altered the nature of horticultural and botanical training. Numerous universities have moved into research and education programs focusing on cellular and molecular biology and biomedical research. Horticulture and botany departments have been either discontinued or subsumed into other academic units, where they continue to shrink in size and importance.

Although there remain some notable departments of botany and horticulture, such as those at Cornell University, Iowa State University, Purdue University, Michigan State University, and Pennsylvania State University, public gardens have recognized the need and increased their leadership in botany and horticulture through their research and educational efforts. Today, some of the world's most important centers of botanical research and horticulture are public gardens such as the Missouri Botanical Garden, the New York Botanical Garden, the Royal Botanic Garden at Kew, and the Kirstenbosch National Botanic Garden in South Africa.

But even though public gardens have assumed many of the research and educational roles of colleges, they cannot offer college credit. They are not accredited to issue degrees and cannot independently offer graduate programs. Partnerships between academic institutions and public gardens are, therefore, essential.

Partnerships

Many colleges and universities, such as the University of Pennsylvania (Morris Arboretum), the University of California, Berkeley, the University of North Carolina at Chapel Hill, and

Harvard University (Arnold Arboretum), own and operate public gardens. The American Public Gardens Association member list includes more than eighty public gardens owned and operated by colleges and universities. These are natural partnerships.

Public gardens not owned or operated by universities have developed diverse partnerships with colleges and universities. Some are as simple as the public garden and university sharing facilities. In others, public garden staff members teach at the college or university. It is common to find public gardens offering courses that qualify for college credit should students wish to pay the additional fees.

Public gardens have much to offer to college and university partners. First and foremost, public gardens employ highly qualified professional staff trained in horticulture, botany, soil science, genetics, cell biology, and other specializations. In some cases these professionals complement existing staff at higher education partners, and in other cases they represent the primary knowledge base for the partnership. For example, Northwestern University, in Evanston, Illinois, had not had a botanist on its faculty for more than twenty-six years prior to the development of a partnership with the Chicago Botanic Garden.

Public gardens have physical facilities, such as research labs, office space, garden space for growing plants for research, and greenhouses for maintaining research collections. Many of the great public gardens have exceptional botanical libraries, living collections of plants for research and study, and herbarium collections or other collections of specimens important to higher education. Finally, the great botanical centers of education and research that exist at public gardens have earned international reputations that help to attract scholars and students from around the world.

Figure 16-3: A modern, well-equipped teaching classroom at the Huntington Botanical Gardens.

Besides their professional staffs, faculty, research space, libraries, and classrooms, colleges and universities have accreditation that allow them to issue credit for course work and to confer degrees. No public garden currently possesses this accreditation. Colleges and universities also have already in place an infrastructure of administrative offices, such as admissions, enrollment, records, financial aid, and student services, that are needed for higher education programs.

Undergraduate Programs

Historically, public gardens have been informal learning sites for botany and horticulture students enrolled at colleges and universities. The strongest connections are those public gardens owned and operated by colleges and universities such as the Arnold Arboretum at Harvard University, which has a long history of supporting students' botanical studies.

More recently, the University of Maryland campus was transformed into a public garden. As a result of that transformation, Professor Marla McIntosh, director of the University of Maryland Arboretum and Botanical Garden, commented on the value of the garden in a March 5, 2009, press release; "Urban forestry students can learn the technical skills needed for the contemporary green workforce; environmental science students can assess the ecological value of trees to the urban ecosystem; and public policy students can examine the effect of trees on quality of life."

Rancho Santa Ana Botanic Garden and Pomona College have a long history of collaboration. Pomona College undergraduate biology students may take graduate courses at Rancho Santa Ana Botanic Garden and use the Garden to carry out research projects. The combined herbarium of Pomona College and Rancho Santa Ana is located at the Garden.

Graduate Programs

In the United States, the first higher education partnership with a university was established when Henry Shaw, the founder of the Missouri Botanical Garden, established the School of Botany at Washington University in St. Louis. Although the school no longer exists, the partnership continues in the form of a graduate program and joint academic appointments.

In 1927, Susanna Bixby Bryant started the Rancho Santa Ana Botanic Garden, which soon became home to the Botany Department of Claremont Graduate University, with graduate classes and laboratories, faculty and student offices, and all research facilities used by students located at the Garden.

The graduate program at the New York Botanical Garden has students in partnership with six universities: the City University of New York, Columbia University, Cornell University, New York University, Yale University, and Fordham University. Other public gardens have developed higher education programs with a single university. One of the best-known is the Longwood Graduate Program in partnership with the University of Delaware. The Longwood program, established in 1967 (Skelly and Hetzel 2005), offers a master's degree in public horticulture administration. The program allows students to select elective courses, research, or special projects that prepare them for their own specific career interests.

Cornell Plantations, in conjunction with the Department of Horticulture, has developed a four-semester graduate fellowship program in public garden leadership that results in a master's of professional studies (M.P.S.). An internship is required between the first and second years. Each fellow identifies a topic for graduate study and completes an action project before graduating.

The Chicago Botanic Garden initiated a joint graduate program at the master's level in plant science and conservation with Northwestern University in 2006 that expanded in 2008 to include a Ph.D. The Fairchild Tropical Botanic Garden has graduate programs in partnership with Florida International University and the University of Miami.

Accredited Programs

The School of Professional Horticulture at the New York Botanical Garden is the only independently accredited postsecondary

Figure 16-4: The catalog of the School of Professional Horticulture at the New York Botanical Garden.

CASE STUDY: SCHOOL OF PROFESSIONAL HORTICULTURE AT THE NEW YORK BOTANICAL GARDEN

The School of Professional Horticulture was started in 1919 as a vocational training program for returning war veterans. It became a professional gardener training program in 1932 and today claims a mission "to educate motivated individuals to become horticulturists of the highest caliber who will take on leadership positions in both the public and private sectors."

Potential students must be at least eighteen years of age, have a high school diploma or an equivalency, and must have completed 1,800 hours of previous experience. Two years of postsecondary education is strongly encouraged.

The curriculum takes twenty-six months to complete. Students take a minimum of 685 hours of required course work in botany, horticulture, communications, and landscape design and may also enroll for up to 60 hours of additional elective course work for personal enrichment. Students participate in plant identification walks and must pass a daylong plant

identification exam with a score of 70 percent or better. Formal instruction also includes required field trips to other institutions and attendance at professional lectures offered outside of regular class times.

The curriculum requires extensive hands-on practical experience. Students must complete nearly 1,000 hours of practical work rotations in eleven different areas of the Garden, including arboriculture, display gardens, Bronx Green-Up, family garden, conservatory, turf and grounds, rose culture, integrated pest management, greenhouse production, plant records and mapping, and alpine and native plant culture. First-year students work in teams to design, install, and maintain a student garden measuring 6 feet by 80 feet. In the spring and summer of the second year, students must complete an approved six-month internship at a business or botanical institution.

education program at a public garden in North America. It is a private school licensed by the New York State Education Department and accredited by the Accrediting Council for Continuing Education and Training (ACCET). As a condition of state licensing and ACCET accreditation, the school must meet and maintain minimum standards of quality in all areas of its operation. The school is also certified by the U.S. Department of Education to administer Title IV funds to qualified students. The school is not accredited to award college degrees. Accreditation and licensing also give the school a level of credibility that is helpful in recruiting students and placing students in jobs after they complete the program.

Developing New Programs

Although all public gardens will implement some programs that will not be successful, more programs succeed than fail. It doesn't matter if a public garden is planning a new course or an entire new department—careful research and planning will increase the likelihood of success and help save time and money.

Research the Possibilities

The first step in developing new programs is to devote some time and money to gathering information that can be used to make an informed decision about the strategic direction for new programs.

Mission and Strength of the Public Garden

In many cases, the mission of a public garden and an analysis of its strengths, weakness, and fundamental nature will help determine the direction for new programs. A public garden that specializes in ornamental plants and formal displays, such as Longwood Gardens, would offer a different set of programs than a garden that specializes predominantly in native plants, such as the Santa Barbara Botanic Garden. Similarly, a public garden with formal gardens would offer different programs than an arboretum with an extensive collection of woody plants. Any public garden with a large natural area, such as a prairie or forest, would be better able to offer nature classes than a public garden in an urban setting. When developing new programs, consider the mission of the garden, its environmental features, its location, the community, the collections, and the strengths and weaknesses of the staff.

Market Analysis

To prepare a market analysis, it is important to gather as much information as possible. What programs are other institutions in the region, such as nature centers, parks, or other public gardens, conducting? How much are they charging? Are nearby institutions of higher education offering large continuing education programs? How large is the nursery, landscaping, or green industry in the region? How many members do the local Audubon Society and the local garden clubs have? Also critical is researching relevant local occupational trends and industries to determine which ones are changing, growing, or shrinking.

A useful resource is the Cooperative Extension System, a nationwide, noncredit educational network. Each U.S. state and territory has a state office and a network of local or regional offices staffed by experts who provide useful, practical, and research-based information.

Consult with Others

Meet with representatives from some of the potential constituents and find out their interests and needs. Meet with the garden's membership officer and ask about member comments that might give some ideas for program direction. Talk directly to members. Attend professional meetings of the garden, nursery, landscape, or related industries. Visit with members of local nature clubs. Perhaps develop a short survey that can be sent to representatives of constituent groups, including students, whose feedback would be valuable. Anderson (2004) describes the New York Botanical Garden's student-centered approach, which uses student evaluations and enrollment patterns to help determine new programs.

Deciding on the Scope of the Program

Once information has been collected, the data can be used to help determine the scope of the program. Assemble a planning group of knowledgeable individuals from the garden staff and the community to provide direction for the program. Invite participants from landscaping, gardening, and the nursery industries to participate on an advisory group. A great many potential mistakes can be avoided with thoughtful input from a well-assembled advisory group.

Determine the Audience

The first decision is to determine the audience. Is the audience going to be adult leisure-time learners seeking new knowledge and enrichment, adults looking for new careers, professionals wanting professional development, or college students? This decision will inform additional planning and ensure that the development of the new program will be better focused. Jones (2002) describes the planning and creation of the School of the

Botanic Garden at the Chicago Botanic Garden and includes an analysis of the audiences served by the School.

Determine the Content Scope

At an early point in the process of developing new programs, the content scope of the classes needs to be determined. This is when the mission and strengths of the public garden should be considered.

In some content areas, such as art and photography, the types of courses that public gardens offer do not vary depending on the location or mission of the institution. Classes in introductory painting and digital photography will be pretty much the same regardless of the mission or location of a public garden. But in horticulture, gardening, and design, the mission and location of the garden will determine the content scope of the programs. For example, the Marie Selby Botanical Gardens, in Sarasota, Florida, offers horticulture classes emphasizing the growing of orchids and bromeliads, while the Desert Botanical Garden, in Phoenix, Arizona, offers classes on growing cacti and succulents.

Determine the Format for the Courses

A number of formats can be used when developing adult continuing education programs, depending on the size of the intended audience, the amount of material included in the course, and the purpose of the program. Each of these formats can be used with leisure-time adult continuing education audiences as well as professional audiences. Table 16-3 summarizes the characteristics of various continuing education program formats.

A diversity of instructional techniques is important. The least interesting classes are those where the instructor lectures and the students take notes or look at PowerPoint presentations. Classes that engage students in hands-on activities, such as transplanting plants, pruning, grafting, or a hundred other gardening and horticultural techniques, are much more interesting and popular with adult continuing education students. Students also respond well to classes in which they receive printed study material or have access to online material.

Regardless of which format or instructional techniques are used, credit may be available through a college or university. If credit is to be offered, college partners need to be consulted to work out the details. It will have to be determined if the course content is adequate for college credit and if the instructors teaching the course are qualified. Courses that qualify for credit usually require an additional fee.

Table 16-3: Characteristics of Various Continuing Education Formats

Format	Class Size	Number of Class Sessions	Content	Instructors/ Speakers	Instructional Techniques
Short course	Classroom size (20–40)	Single class session	One specific topic	Usually one instructor	Lecture, discussion, demonstration, hands-on activities
Single-speaker lecture	Large audience	Usually one hour-long lecture	One main topic	Single speaker	Lecture, possible slides or PowerPoint
Multiple-session courses	Classroom size (20–40)	Five to ten class periods	Multiple topics around one broad theme	One or several instructors	Lecture, discussion, demonstration, hands-on activities, field trips
Symposium	Large audience	One or two days of presentations	Multiple topics based on a broad theme	Multiple speakers	Lecture, with slides or PowerPoint
Certificate program	Classroom size (20–40)	A series of individual courses over various time periods	Many topics	Multiple instructors for numerous courses	Lecture, discussion, demonstration, hands-on activities, field trips

Determine a Business Plan and Budget

Before a new program can be implemented, it is important to develop a business plan, which should be informed by the size of the audience and by the earlier market analysis.

Table 16-4 illustrates the 2008 budgets of three adult continuing education programs, one a large and diverse program, one a small off-site program, and one a single event. The revenue was determined based on the total number of registrations expected and the cost of each class. As seen in Table 16-4, some of the expenses are fixed costs (expenses that will be incurred regardless of the number of people who register for the program) and include marketing and promotion, printing, postage, telephones, and instructor salaries and travel expenses. Variable costs are expenses associated with each participant and include the cost of instructional materials and supplies, lunches, and credit card services.

In the three examples, two of the programs were able to cover their costs with revenue, but one program was not. If the expenses to operate a program are high and the expected revenue is small or does not cover costs, a decision might be made not to offer that program. Alternatively, classes that generate a high profit can be used to subsidize classes that do not pay for themselves.

The content of the program may be so closely aligned to the mission of the institution that a public garden decides to offers a program whether or not the revenue meets expenses. In these cases, the expenses of the program are partly subsidized by the general operating budget or by more successful programs, or the public garden seeks a grant to help cover the expenses. The Chicago Botanic Garden's horticultural therapy program has been traditionally funded through earned revenue as well as grants from health-care organizations.

In the case of the three programs in Table 16-4, the large program and single event have continued. The small program, after losing money for several years, was discontinued.

Table 16-4: Actual Budgets from Three Continuing Education Programs (Rounded to the Nearest $100)

	Large Program	Small Program	Single Event
Description	100 short courses	19 off-site courses	One-day symposium
Revenue	$161,300	$14,800	$16,300
Fixed Expenses			
Instructor pay	$46,000	$3,300	$2,500
Marketing	$58,000	$10,300	$3,000
Postage	$16,200	$5,500	$1,700
Copy expenses	$2,100	$400	
Telephone	$3,300		
Room rental		$5,000	
Instructor travel	$4,000	$300	$2,000
Variable Expenses			
Instructional supplies	$12,300	$2,100	
Other supplies	$1,100		$300
Lunch			$4,400
Credit card services	$3,900	$300	$400
Total Expenses	$147,800	$27,000	$14,300
Net of Revenue	$13,500	($12,400)	$2,000

- Develop databases that tag different audiences, such as the adult continuing education leisure-time learner or the professional looking for CEU courses.

- Determine marketing approaches. Should postcards or emails be used to announce dates of upcoming programs or events? Will a catalog be printed or published online? Will special brochures be used for special audiences or events?

- Determine the registration processes. Will registration be online, phone-in, or mail-in, or will all three methods be used? Will registration software be developed in-house, or will commercial software be used?

- Develop institutional policies. Will members and employees be given discounts? What will the cancellation and refund policies be?

- Coordinate the mechanism used to collect revenue with the business office. Will credit card payments be allowed, as they are at most gardens? Credit card companies assess a fee (2–3 percent) on credit card purchases, and this should be included in the program budget.

- Identify class instructors. Most public gardens use garden staff as instructors. Some pay staff extra to teach classes in the evenings and on the weekends. Others require teaching as a part of the staff member's job responsibilities. Larger gardens almost always hire some outside instructors who are professionals in the nursery or gardening industries or teachers at colleges and universities. Network with local and regional professional organizations to maintain a list of potential instructors.

- Inventory the available facilities for program use. Develop programs to fit with the availability of classrooms and meeting spaces. For classes held outdoors, always have backup space available in case of bad weather. Is appropriate equipment, supplies, or materials available for the programs? Be sure the facilities have appropriate audiovisual equipment.

- Determine what materials and supplies are needed and budget for them. Be sure that supplies are purchased and available when the class is offered. Decide if an additional materials fee will be added to the cost of certain classes when the cost for supplies exceeds a minimum basic level.

Evaluate to Ensure Quality Programs

Ensuring a quality program requires constant attention to details and evaluation. Students enrolled in the program are one of the most important sources of information about quality. All continuing education programs should have evaluation processes in place at two levels.

First is an ongoing evaluation of each individual course, class, symposium, or program to access the quality of instruction and organization of the program. The purpose of this evaluation is not to judge an instructor but to identify problems that exist and need to be fixed, to determine what is working well and what isn't, and to allow students to provide feedback that can help improve the course. Whether they are called evaluations or feedback, students should be asked to complete written forms at the end of the class before they leave. When students are asked to take evaluation forms home and return them later, the return rate is low.

Second, public gardens should regularly solicit feedback from students about other administrative aspects of the program, including the course catalog, ease of registration processes, quality of facilities, and effectiveness of communication, among others. Ask the participants if they have any suggestions for changes or if there are problems that need to be solved.

Remember that in continuing adult education programs, the students are customers who need to be served in the same way that a retail company serves its customers.

Don't let issues and problems go unaddressed. Find out where the problems are, address the issues, and let the students know what was done to solve the problems. Students talk to each other, and problems that are not fixed will continue to be topics of discussion. Remember that students develop a sense of loyalty to a public garden and will return many times to take new courses if they are pleased with the program.

Summary

Adult continuing education programs at public gardens are diverse. They vary in the audiences they serve, the kinds of program formats that are used, the size of the programs, the number and types of partnerships that are developed, and the various management processes used. Public gardens conduct unique continuing education programs that are a reflection of their own missions and strengths.

The key to successful continuing education programs is comprehensive planning, exceptional customer service, continuous evaluation, and quality instruction and facilities. Successful programs solicit feedback from students and use the feedback to improve program content, implementation, and management.

Annotated Resources

Anderson, N. 2004. A marketing driven continuing education program: Formula for success. *The Public Garden* 19(1): 36–39. A good account of the ways to market a continuing education program at a large public garden.

Cox, M., and I. Edwards. 1994. Changing places. *Roots* 1(9), bgci.org/education/article/0462/. A short personal description of the effect of a job change on the careers of two public garden professionals.

Gooch, J. 1995. *Transplanting extension: A new look at the Wisconsin idea.* Madison: University of Wisconsin Extension Printing Services. A history of the beginning of continuing adult education as started at the University of Wisconsin in 1907.

Jones, L. 2002. To serve broadly: The mission of the School of the Chicago Botanic Garden. *The Public Garden* 17(3): 28–30. A look at the planning and development of the School of the Chicago Botanic Garden.

McFarlan, J. 2005. The Morris Arboretum internship program: Training public garden managers for 26 years. *The Public Garden* 20(3): 32–34. An outline of the Morris Arboretum internship program.

Skelly, S. M., and C. Hetzel. 2005. The role of academic institutions in developing future leaders. *The Public Garden* 20(3): 14–17. A description of the Longwood Graduate Program with some comments on the benefits of university and public garden partnerships.

Sutherland, P., and J. Crowther. 2008. *Lifelong learning concepts and context.* New York: Routledge. A comprehensive description of lifelong learning.

CHAPTER 17

Interpreting Gardens to Visitors

KITTY CONNOLLY

Introduction

Informal education programs invite visitors to learn about a garden's mission, collections, and displays on their own. As such, informal education is fundamentally distinct from formal education programs that are not self-directed. Interpretive media such as signage and exhibits bring a garden's educational messages directly to visitors. They provide frontline contact with audiences even when no staff or volunteers are present and visitors are completely on their own. Effective informal education intrigues and empowers visitors to appreciate and understand public gardens.

Informal education programs, especially those elements that are self-guided and permanent in the gardens, can be of low cost relative to the impact they can provide. Every person who comes to the garden has a chance of encountering them, while even the most ambitious of public or school programs is unlikely to impact as large an audience. Although projects such as permanent exhibits can run into the millions of dollars, a brochure for a self-guided tour can be produced for a modest sum.

Strong and lasting connections can be forged through informal education. Each year, millions of people choose to go to public gardens because they are drawn to plants and green spaces. This is an invaluable opportunity. At some level, these people are prepared to receive the messages that public gardens deliver: that gardens are valuable, intriguing, and delightful places. Informal educators can exploit that opportunity when they create programs and exhibits.

KEY TERMS

Exhibition: a three-dimensional environment of objects, text, and graphics that communicates a message or theme; sometimes called a show.

Exhibit: one component of an exhibition; consisting of exhibit elements such as labels, graphics, specimens, authentic objects, or re-created props.

Informal education: the lifelong process whereby every individual acquires attitudes, values, skills, and knowledge from daily experience and the educative influences and resources in his or her environment, including family and neighbors, work and play, the marketplace, libraries, and mass media.

Informal educators: professionals who interpret resources, including gardens, collections, and specific plants, for audiences.

Interpretation: a mission-based communication process that forges emotional and intellectual connections between the interests of the audience and meanings inherent in resources.

Interpretive media: means, methods, devices, or instruments by which the interpretive message is presented to the public.

Interpretive objectives: desired measurable outputs, outcomes, and impacts of interpretive services.

Interpretive theme: a succinct, central message about a topic of interest that a communicator wants to get across to an audience.

Target audience: a defined segment of visitors toward which a program is aimed.

What Is Informal Education?

Informal education is self-directed, voluntary learning that people undertake in their leisure time. It is often called free-choice learning. The learner chooses to engage in the process and is learning for the edification, rather than for specific outcomes. Informal education, broadly defined, can include reading, watching TV, discussing current events, and learning to cook. Informal learning is ongoing and does not have a predictable outcome. In this chapter, discussion is limited to those forms of informal education that public gardens deliver.

In contrast, formal education is directed and evaluated by others and is driven by a purpose such as gaining knowledge, skills, or certification (see Chapter 15). A professional teacher assigns and assesses students' work throughout a structured course. Much of formal education is compulsory, like school. Informal education also has learning objectives but is voluntary and generally not assessed. The teacher may be a part-time instructor or a volunteer. Classes, workshops, and even field trips are typical informal education offerings at public gardens.

Informal Education Reveals Meaning

Informal education affects an impressive range of attitudes and practices (Committee on Learning Science in Informal Environments 2009) and can have a profound impact over a person's lifetime. Gardens are repositories of complex information and serve as authorities on a wide range of subjects, but many visitors arrive unprepared to deal with advanced information about plants. In fact, many people come to the garden simply to relax or for recreation. Informal education creates a bridge between the resources of the garden and the starting point of visitors through interpreting the garden. It aims to reveal the meaning of those resources so that visitors can cultivate their own interests, knowledge, and skills.

In society at large, plants tend to be overlooked. Wandersee and Schussler (1999) have termed this failure to notice plants in one's own environment "plant blindness" and see it as the result of an optical and cultural bias against an interest in plants. Plants' static nature and seeming sameness make them fade into the background, visually and intellectually, so people often undervalue plants in ecological, social, and aesthetic terms and consider them inferior to animals. However, in public gardens, plants are the subject, not the setting for something else. Informal education in public gardens can combat plant blindness by revealing the relevance of plants and generating excitement about the plant world.

LEARNING OUTCOMES IN INFORMAL SETTINGS

Informal education helps visitors to develop their:

- Awareness of the subject and its importance
- Interest in the subject matter
- Motivation to learn more and to act on what one learns
- Identity as a person who knows, cares, and learns about the subject
- Social competencies, as a person comfortable and confident in his/her relationship with the subject
- Practices related to the subject
- Incremental knowledge of the subject
- Habits of mind that allow for further learning and practice

(Committee on Learning Science in Informal Environments 2009)

Why People Come to Public Gardens

To successfully serve visitors, informal educators need to understand what motivates people to come to public gardens. Like the amazing diversity of the gardens themselves, audiences are also diverse, but they do have some similarities. People's reasons for visiting a museum fall into roughly five categories, and any single visit can incorporate several motivations (Packer and Ballantyne 2002; Falk 2006).

- **Learning and discovery.** Some visitors are "explorers," seeking to learn new things and open to learning about many subjects and places. Their satisfaction is based on a sense of discovery or rediscovery.

- **Social interaction.** Some visitors are "facilitators" who attend primarily for the benefit of others, especially children. They see a public garden as a place for spending time with family and friends and meeting the needs of their companions. Asked about their visit, facilitators will reflect on how the experience was for others in their group.

- **Passive enjoyment.** Others are "experience seekers," consumers of places and events who often act on recommendations of what is important to do, what are the "must-sees." They come to have a good time, to be entertained, and to enjoy themselves. If they had fun, the visit was a success.

- **Restoration.** Those who are "spiritual pilgrims" visit in order to relax and recharge their minds and bodies. If they feel refreshed, the visit was a good one.

- **Self-fulfillment.** Professionals and hobbyists look to reconfirm or expand their knowledge, which is a necessary condition for a successful visit.

Learning in Informal Settings

Learning in public gardens happens within a social and physical context and is predicated on the preparation and motivation of the learner. If visitors are unprepared and unmotivated, little may be gained during their visit to a garden. At the same time, informal learning is not limited to the acquisition of facts and concepts, as is often the case in formal education. This section will focus on the process of learning.

Learning Is Personal

While informal educators present their teaching agenda, visitors bring their own learning agenda. Visitors' prior experience, interests, and the various motivations cited above determine which of many possible outcomes may occur. These learning agendas are tied to visitors' previous exposure to a topic or experience and to their motivation for that day's visit.

Learning in informal settings is also a process of personal choice on multiple levels. Not only is the choice made to visit the garden, but every visit is personalized. All individuals and groups choose the order and elements of their garden experience as well as the degree to which they will attend to those elements. The expression of choice is one of the main attractors in informal education. People like to control their leisure experiences.

Learning Is Contextual

Learning happens in social groups, through interaction with other visitors, volunteers, or garden staff. Although some visitors prefer a solitary garden experience, the majority either come explicitly to interact with others or welcome interactions afforded by the setting. They learn though conversation about what they see, do, and read.

Visitors also learn in a place. The garden is a manifestly physical, immersive environment. Visitors are surrounded by living and preserved collections, landscapes, and works of art that influence what they experience and the order in which they experience it. This is, of course, a basic tenet of landscape design and not a concept new to public gardens. Yet its impact on education can be easily overlooked. One objective in designing a new garden could be to maximize its educational potential. One of the objectives of informal educators is to develop that potential in a garden.

Learning Takes Time

Learning happens over the course of a visit to a public garden but also over the course of a lifetime. It is a product of engagement with informal education elements, and then a reflection on those observations, determining how they fit in with other information and experiences. The cumulative nature of this process makes it difficult to measure the immediate effects of a garden visit. Comments like this one from a study of visitors (Packer 2006) to informal education institutions demonstrate the role of time in learning: "The next time you see something,

Figure 17-1: Some people come to gardens so their family members can be exposed to nature at a young age.

Photo by Lisa Blackburn. Courtesy of The Huntington Library, Art Collections, and Botanical Gardens

Figure 17-2: Gardens can be a place for solitude. This man is relaxing at Vaux le Vicomte outside Paris.

Kitty Connolly

you'll have a better understanding of it—you can try to get something else out of it then." Informal learning is ongoing and does not have a predictable outcome.

Characteristics of Effective Interpretation

All informal education efforts that effectively deliver interpretation to audiences share some characteristics. Regardless of the program's topic or budget, these qualities are critical to keep in mind during project development.

Relevance to Audience

Interpretation at public gardens is more successful when it is interesting. This sounds like an obvious point, but many times program development begins with the directive "visitors *should* know this," rather than the approach "visitors *will want to* know this." Experts should choose the topic, but the approach to the topic should be developed with the goal of effective communication in mind.

Because people learn in different ways, making interpretation accessible to many types of learners also makes it more relevant to visitors. Some people learn best through manipulating objects, others through working in groups, still others

through finding patterns in nature. Planning for a variety of ways to engage with content will encourage people with different learning styles.

Varied Approaches to the Topic

Storytelling is one effective interpretive medium. People remember stories; they want to hear the end. The trick with storytelling in gardens is that the stories have to be short. Visitors spend, on average, about thirty seconds at any educational exhibit and linger only a few minutes in any one garden area. In addition, because it is difficult to control the path a visitor will take through a garden, a story often needs to be composed of brief, nonlinear segments. For example, what plants need to live and grow is a topic that can be broken down into discrete segments, encountered in any order, yet still add up to a whole.

Another approach is incorporating nonliving elements into interpretation. Many public gardens are not stand-alone entities: they are also historical sites, divisions of a college or university, holders of art and library collections, or repositories for herbaria. Gardens with disparate collections can find themselves with a disjointed public image: one audience may view the place as a garden, while others may see it as the setting for library, artistic or historical objects. Wide-ranging collections

The Desert Botanical Garden in Phoenix, Arizona, has an exceptional, long-standing exhibit. It is a creosote bush growing a few feet from the path with a nearby sign reading: "What does the desert smell like when it rains?" The exhibit also has a water tap that visitors can operate, and a small stand holding a basin with a sprig of creosote in it. The sign invites visitors to run a little water into the basin, releasing the plant's aromatic oils.

In many ways, it is the perfect interactive botanical exhibit: the operation is simple, the objectives are clear, and the exhibit meets many of the goals one could have for informal education. It is engaging, authentic, and multisensory, draws attention to the collections, is straightforward to use, and is physically and cognitively accessible to a wide range of visitors. Moreover, it is easy to maintain and has a foolproof reset. Once the exhibit's affective approach has captured the visitors' attention, the text panel and illustrations explain why creosote smells as it does and how the plant is adapted to scarce desert rains.

Moreover, the exhibit uses real plants to arouse visitors' interests. Those who are unfamiliar with the desert will be intrigued to learn that deserts have a particular smell during rain. It builds upon those interests to explain why the plant does what it does and what that means in the desert ecosystem. In other words, the exhibit interprets the mission of the garden: it brings to life the wonders of the desert.

can also create internal conflicts over interpretive priorities. Yet these gardens also have rich opportunities. When these gardens create exhibitions that integrate their collections and relate both living and nonliving collections in a thematic whole, they can reinforce their unity internally while making the subject approachable for the wider public.

Themes and Relation to Mission

Informal education supports the mission of the garden. Visitors should leave a public garden knowing something about the organization and the role it plays in supporting a shared cultural and natural heritage. Few gardens are so focused as to have only one interpretive theme, and many have a complex mission. Each program should highlight only one or two interrelated themes.

For example, the Missouri Botanical Garden's mission of "enriching life" allows for a focus on the medicinal and ritualistic value of plants, the ecological functions that plants perform in the environment, and the role of landscape design in creating beauty, as well as other themes. Each of these themes is played out in different aspects of garden interpretation.

Targeted to Particular Audiences

Interpretation needs to be created with an audience in mind. The adult nonspecialist is one such audience and constitutes the largest segment of garden visitors. Families with children between the ages of two and seven are another audience, and so on. There are many choices to be made when defining a target audience, and the staff that develops informal education programs must make those choices. While carefully designed programs can work across demographics, even those should be designed with one audience in mind. Very young children in particular require an interpretative approach that is fundamentally different from what works for older audiences. It is better to work very well for one audience than poorly for all audiences.

Developing Informal Education

The process of developing informal education projects varies from garden to garden, depending on staffing levels, budget, and the garden's relationship with visitors, but some general guidelines are useful.

Define the Big Idea

The big idea is a concept popularized by the influential book *Exhibit Labels: An Interpretive Approach* (Serrell 1996). The big idea is a clear, one-sentence statement of what an exhibition is about and why people should care. Big ideas are equally useful in program development. The big idea provides strong guidance for the development team. Without a strong big idea, every topic could potentially fit into the exhibition. With the big idea, the team has focus and limits. "Everything is important" may be true, but that approach will leave most visitors dismayed by overwhelming detail or baffled by the inclusion of seemingly random information that doesn't add up to a meaningful whole. The big idea helps to narrow down the topic and so to reach visitors with limited interest and capacity to understand the topic and those who are not subject matter experts.

From its initial conception through every aspect of operations, the Eden Project's mission of sustainability is evident, but it is through the consistent and comprehensive use of interpretive media that the program becomes meaningful to visitors. Constructed in the bowl of a spent quarry in Cornwall, southwest England, its origin is a story of reclamation and regeneration. Eden heavily promotes this aspect of its history through interpretive signs that prominently feature "before" photos of the site so visitors can marvel at the change. The local sources and amount of materials used to perform this transformation from waste site to cultural destination are readily shared. Resources used in current operations are equally transparent: all of the irrigation water is from rain captured on-site, its electricity is from wind turbines, and even the food in the café is locally sourced when possible.

From special graphics on the vending machines that highlight tropical forest conservation to the waterless urinals in the men's rooms, each aspect of visitor services makes sustainability an unmistakable priority. This theme might be most evident in the café. The dining patio is surrounded by a vegetable garden where mature produce is displayed next to the plants on which they grew. The connection between the land and fresh food is unmistakable. The core interpretive message of human dependence on plants is explicit throughout the site. In fact, the education building is called the Core and holds botanical exhibitions as well as classrooms. Outdoor gardens display a wide assortment of plants that people need for various uses, from fruits to fiber. The biome domes' interpretive signs and vignettes highlight human uses of plants. While these informal education elements emphasize how useful plants are to people today, they simultaneously emphasize how important it is to keep the plants around for the long term.

Figure 17-3: The vegetable garden surrounding the café patio at the Eden Project drives home the importance of eating locally sourced food.

Photo by Karina White. Courtesy of The Huntington Library, Art Collections, and Botanical Gardens

Identify the Target Audience

Determine the demographics of the target audience and its familiarity with the subject matter. The number of visitors is also important to assess. Attendance level has a determining influence on the methods of informal education that are practicable for a garden. Gardens that receive millions of visitors a year, such as the gardens of the Smithsonian Institution, cannot sustain the types of interpretation that are possible at less visited sites.

Define the Visitor Experience

For each program element, such as each exhibit within an exhibition, written objectives that the key people on the team agree on are very important. An objective is a statement of a specific, measurable, and observable result desired from an educational or interpretive activity or experience. If the objectives aren't explicit and commonly held, it is unlikely they will be achieved. Visitor experience objectives should include three major areas, and each program element may have multiple objectives:

- **Behavioral.** What will visitors do? What will they see, read, smell, touch, hear, taste, or say?

- **Cognitive.** What will visitors think? Will they remember something, realize something new, or make connections?

- **Affective.** What will visitors feel? Will they feel reassured, intrigued, delighted, enlightened, concerned, or surprised?

For behavioral objectives, ambitious interpreters plan beyond the visit when constructing objectives. What will visitors do *after* they leave the garden? For example, will they become actively involved in conservation issues? Will they start their own garden? Will they learn more about plants and gardening? These long-term goals are the primary reason informal education exists. Public garden educators may never be there to observe these behaviors, but they are an ultimate goal.

CASE STUDY: "PLANTS ARE UP TO SOMETHING"

"Plants Are Up to Something" is a permanent exhibition at the Huntington Botanical Gardens. The big idea for the exhibition was to have visitors use the scientific skills of observation, comparison, measurement, and analysis to understand the amazing things that plants do. Evaluation has shown the exhibition to be effective in teaching science skills and botanical content to its target audience of children and also to adults. These were the key exhibit development criteria:

1. Exhibits will be about precise concepts or phenomena that can be observed.

   • What specific concept or phenomenon is being communicated?

   • Why is this particular concept or phenomenon important to communicate?

   a. What are three different examples of this concept or phenomenon?

   b. What will visitors do?

   c. What are the experiential objectives of this exhibit?

   d. What are the learning objectives of this exhibit?

   e. What are the affective objectives of this exhibit?

2. Exhibits will feature dynamic, observable processes of plants whenever possible.

   a. Is most of the information presented concrete instead of abstract?

   b. Could this exhibit concept be better communicated in a book, program, or game?

   c. Does this particular plant process occur at perceptible temporal or spatial scales? If not, how will it be displayed?

3. Exhibits will use living plants whenever possible.

   a. What plants will best demonstrate the exhibit topic?

   b. Are these plants available?

   c. What maintenance requirements do these plants have?

Figure 17-4: This exhibit, "Leaves Are Full of Holes," is about photosynthesis and gives visitors multiple exposures to stomata: a living plant along with a hand lens, macro photographs of stomata, and a magnified view of a fresh leaf shared on a monitor.

Photo by Kitty Connolly. Courtesy of The Huntington Library, Art Collections, and Botanical Gardens

Consider the Budget and Scope of Project

Budget, of course, is critical in any program. Planning must include not only program development but also long-term needs. Will the program use supplies? How often will materials need to be replaced or updated? Do staffing costs need to be included in the program budget?

Maintenance is a major budget consideration when developing informal education programs. Since these are self-guided experiences, they may not get daily attention from staff. Informal education elements need to be designed so that they function and look good with the maintenance they are granted on however irregular a basis. Material choices should balance initial costs with replacement costs and the need for ongoing care.

The scope of the program and the budget influence each other. It's prudent to plan for different scenarios. One budget should anticipate full funding that allows for all the desired elements to be as elaborately fabricated as one could wish. This is the "blue sky" budget. Another, more realistic budget should reflect funding one could reasonably expect: not so many elaborate elements, or fewer elements overall. This is the budget most work from most of the time. A third, barebones budget should anticipate what could be done to meet the project's goals if no funding comes through. Could any on-hand materials and supplies be used? This is the fallback budget.

Identify Appropriate Staff

Project by project, staff needs change. Exhibitions and other self-guided projects need both content and interpretation specialists. As far as is practicable, defining the roles of project staff is critical for progress. On any team, one person has to be the acknowledged decision maker, even if the team reports to higher-ups. In any size organization, a core team of three seems to function best. A small group allows for frequent interaction without complex scheduling concerns and keeps each person accountable. If the organization is large, consider adding a copy editor, graphic designer, facilities coordinator, marketing specialist, and development officer. People with journalism backgrounds make excellent staff on exhibition projects.

Dedicated staff time is crucial for high-quality projects. Although educational and curatorial staff usually have too many demands on their time, it is better to not produce a project than to produce one that is underthought, underplanned, and underrealized. That's a disappointment for all concerned: audience, staff, administration, and funders.

Hire Consultants

Consultants serve two major functions: supplementing on-staff expertise and supplying dedicated labor. No garden staff, no matter the size, has all the experience, skills, and facilities needed for every project. Sometimes outside help is essential, especially when the garden is embarking on a new type of interpretation with which it has little experience. Consultants can help with conceptualization, interpretive planning, research, writing, design, media, marketing, evaluation, and fabrication. Consultants usually work for the garden on a work-for-hire basis, which means the garden owns the work product.

Invite Advisors

Distinct from consultants are project advisors. Although they are often paid a fee for their services, advisors do not work for the garden in the same way. Advisors for a large exhibition may be reimbursed for travel costs and receive an honorarium if the budget allows. A board of local teachers may give advice and receive only tea and cookies in return. Each supplies expertise that the garden should consider but is under no obligation to follow. Choose advisors from fields directly related to the project. Advisors can comment on specific content, interpretive approach, audience approach, appropriate media, and sustainable practices, among other issues. Choice of an advisor should be based on two critical qualities: how much this person can contribute to the project and how pleasant this person is to work with.

Role of Prototyping

Prototyping is critical in the development of labels and interactive elements. Prototyping can be accomplished quickly with valuable results if mock-ups of interpretive materials are created and then set out for visitors to see. Cardboard setups with hand-printed labels will work for mocking up exhibits. If the institution is uncomfortable with putting out an unfinished or unpolished prototype, add a note that the garden is developing

Figure 17-5: Even rudimentary prototypes can help developers determine whether interactive elements are effective. This is the prototype for an exhibit about the water-holding capacity of sphagnum moss.

Photo by Karina White. Courtesy of The Huntington Library, Art Collections, and Botanical Gardens

new interpretation and would like visitor input in improving it. For the most part, people love to share their opinions and are flattered to be asked.

Role of Evaluation

Whenever possible, all project elements should be evaluated with the target audience. (See Chapter 18 for a complete discussion of evaluation.) An exhibition is a failure if no one comes, but attendance is only one measure of success and not a very sophisticated one at that. If objectives were established during project development, measuring their achievement is possible. Observe visitors to see if they did what was hoped for. Interview visitors to ask what they did, what they thought it meant, and how it made them feel. Ask them to suggest improvements. It's likely that visitors will provide valuable direction for improvement.

Range of Interpretive Media

Informal education at a garden starts with the first interpretive message a visitor perceives, either on-site, online, or in print. The garden's messages continue to be conveyed throughout a site visit through a wide variety of media.

Interpretive Plant Labels

Nearly all gardens label their plants with identifying information: scientific name, family name, common name, distribution, and accession number. This information is vital to curation of

CASE STUDY: KWAZULU-NATAL NATIONAL BOTANICAL GARDEN, SOUTH AFRICA NATIONAL BIODIVERSITY INSTITUTE

Frustrated with the limited information found on traditional plant labels and inspired by work at the Alice Springs Desert Park, Australia, staff members of the KwaZulu-Natal National Botanical Garden developed a method to maximize the educational potential of plant labels (Roff 2002). They designed labels that contain both vital curatorial information and interpretation that is meaningful to visitors.

Each label includes standard plant data: scientific name, scientific family name, common names (in various languages), and distribution. In addition, labels include the common name of the family and a one-sentence fact about the plant highlighting its common name. One key to this type of label is the brevity of the text. The fewer the words on a label, the more likely it is that visitors will read it.

For example:

Herbal tea made from the leaves of wild mint is used to treat coughs and colds.

Mint Family (Lamiaceae)
Mentha longifolia
Ufuthane Lomhlange
Kruisement

The short stories on these labels reinforce themed interpretation, such as human uses of plants. This systematic and disciplined augmentation of plant labels can spread the interpretive theme of a public garden throughout its grounds without requiring expensive and intrusive signage.

Figure 17-6: This label both identifies the common wild fig and describes its ecological function.

Photo by John Roff. Courtesy of Hilton College

the collection, and visitors appreciate plant labels. But there are more interesting stories to tell about a plant than its name. Interpretative labels can convey these stories, adding meaning and creating excitement.

Interpretive Signs

Signs in the garden are probably the most common form of informal education and reach most visitors. Signs can be used to identify a garden area and introduce the topic or theme of that area or display. They can be used to draw attention to a plant or view or to highlight an ephemeral event. Signage is a powerful interpretive tool, and signs, especially if they are kept scarce, attract attention. Too many signs lead to fatigue and neglect. Visitors believe that a garden would not invest the time and materials unless a sign had something important to say.

To make each sign concise, meaningful, and attractive, attention needs to be paid to the following requirements:

- Care must be taken in the writing of the signs to avoid unintended and double meanings, especially when visitors do not share identical cultural backgrounds. Colloquialisms and humor can easily be misunderstood.

- Definitions and pronunciations of unfamiliar but key words must be included.

- There must be a payoff to reading the sign, an answer to "so what?"

- The design of the sign should ensure legibility while supporting the message.

- Text and illustrations should reinforce and complement each other.

- Placement of the sign should draw attention to the subject rather than block the view to the subject. Shadows and glare should be taken into account during placement as well.

Brochures

No single piece of interpretation reaches more visitors and reaches further beyond the garden than a brochure. Brochures are often keepsakes from visits and generate interest from potential tourists. Primarily used for marketing and orientation, typical brochures include the garden's mission and history, collections highlights, a map of the grounds, hours of operations, admission costs, and rules.

Specialized brochures can serve as guides for particular audience segments. Family and children's guides can support age-specific interpretation. Brochures in different languages are useful at gardens that serve linguistically diverse communities. Special events, exhibitions, or specific collections can also benefit from specialized brochures.

Audience interests can also drive brochure production. At the University of Copenhagen Botanical Garden and Museum, two bilingual brochures are offered, both generated by visitor interest: one a guide to poisonous plants and the other to plants of the Bible.

Exhibitions

Among the oldest traditions in public gardens is the presentation of plants for educational purpose and pleasure. Exhibitions generally have one of three goals:

- Aesthetic exhibitions present the most beautiful aspects of their subject and are largely nontextual.

- Evocative exhibitions provoke an emotional response in visitors, frequently through engaging visitors' senses in an immersive environment.

- Didactic exhibitions instruct, educate, and impart information, normally through the use of text.

Whatever the goal, exhibitions should provoke some response from visitors: pleasure, wonder, entertainment, enlightenment, empowerment. Exhibitions can be a powerfully effective form of informal education.

Exhibitions, or shows, come in the form of flat graphics and text panels with no objects, assemblages of plants and objects, interactive indoor or outdoor exhibits, interpreted landscapes, or self-guided trails. Individual exhibits constitute an exhibition and are themselves composed of exhibit elements such as objects, text panels, and graphics.

Object-Based Exhibitions

Whether they are in changing displays or permanent collections, things drive object-based exhibitions. Content arises from the physical characteristics of those objects or the objects' ecological, historical, or cultural context. For example, rather than developing an exhibition about pollination syndromes and using orchids as an example, an object-based exhibition begins with the decision to develop a show about the topic of orchids. The next decision is what to say about orchids. What is the theme? The exhibition could be about structure, function, or physical appearance. It could be about orchid

conservation. The difference might seem subtle, but it has a determining effect on object selection. Whatever the theme, the exhibition will revolve around the orchids that are the focus of the show.

Object-based exhibitions can center on just one object or involve a range of things. Most public gardens showcase living plants, although library and art collections, historical objects, and even commercial products may be exhibition subjects.

Concept-Based Exhibitions

Exhibitions based on themes, issues, or stories are concept-based. These exhibitions are often meant to be experienced in a particular order. Sample topics include photosynthesis

Figure 17-7: "Darwin's Garden" re-created the naturalist's study down to his notes on the desk and the view out his window in order to evoke the important role plants played in the development of his theories.

Photo by Mick Hales. Courtesy of The New York Botanical Garden

("Sugar from the Sun" at Garfield Park Conservatory), the role of botanical studies in the development of Darwin's ideas ("Darwin's Garden: An Evolutionary Adventure" at the New York Botanical Garden), and plant evolution ("Evolution House" at the Royal Botanical Gardens, Kew). In concept-based exhibitions, first the subject matter is selected and developed, and then plants and objects are assembled along with text and interactive elements that clarify or build on the ideas.

Permanent and Temporary Exhibitions

Exhibitions can be permanent with no scheduled ending, or temporary, generally lasting three months to more than a year but having a predetermined ending date. Permanent exhibitions, by definition, should have lasting relevance, so core, rather than topical, messages go into these exhibitions. They should be rich enough to reveal new experiences to repeat visitors, since they may be seen again and again. Incorporating some changing exhibit elements within permanent exhibitions is one way to keep them fresh. Permanent exhibitions must also hold up physically over time. They should be designed to be sustainable, with a view to required maintenance of the living and nonliving components.

Temporary exhibitions can attract new audiences and visitors with innovative displays featuring seasonal changes, current issues, and the depth of the collections. A February visit to see orchids in a warm conservatory is a welcome excursion for many North Americans. A re-created historical garden can mark the 200th anniversary of Carl Linnaeus' birth. Changing displays of outdoor artwork continue the enduring association of landscape design and sculpture, while gardens with libraries or herbaria can highlight their collections with curated exhibitions. Renting traveling exhibitions can allow gardens to enhance their schedule with ready-made shows complete from press releases to display cases.

Blockbusters, a subset of temporary, traveling exhibitions, draw huge crowds and often generate significant revenue and publicity. But there are some potential drawbacks to blockbusters. In addition to requiring substantial staff time to coordinate, a string of blockbusters can create the impression that the garden is worth visiting only when large exhibitions are showing. Exhibitions, including blockbusters, that are closely tied to the collections and practices of the institution reinforce the value of the place, rather than converting it into a fillable space little different from any other recreational setting. The unique nature of the public garden may be lost in the drive to increase revenue and attendance if attention to mission is not carefully considered.

Electronic Media

New media open up new connections with visitors and non-visitors alike. The fast-changing nature of technology makes a detailed discussion of various modes futile, but some decisions underlying the use of technology are timeless.

Quality electronic interpretation requires a significant investment in time and funds to ensure that the media serve the garden's interpretive goals rather than become the goal. If the use of technology is intended to position the garden in the forefront of electronic media rather than to convey the institution's mission or themes, perhaps it doesn't belong in the education department. The goal of all educational technology, like the goal of all educational programs, should be to bring visitors closer to the garden's mission, themes, and collections.

An exciting direction opened up by new media is the possibility of creating participatory interpretation. The very idea of inviting visitors to contribute their ideas and materials to gardens is a risky one that goes against centuries of curatorial practice, yet it is undeniably here. Like all informal education, it needs to be undertaken thoughtfully and with respect. If visitors are asked to, for example, share their memories of gardening as a child, what will be done with those contributions? Will they be relegated to a corner of the visitor center, or will a space in the garden be designed to re-create those remembered gardens? While physical reenactment is an extreme example, visitor contributions should be solicited only if there is a purpose for them, if they will be used and shared in a meaningful way. It is a complex undertaking but could generate a new relevance for all public gardens.

Mobile Guides

As technology becomes more pervasive and sophisticated, mobile guides will perform some of the functions that brochures and websites currently serve. But they are not limited to that alone. The most successful electronic interpretation provides what is not available on-site, such as behind-the-scenes tours or the curator's perspective on the garden. Specialized tours, information in multiple languages, and themed interpretation are some of the programs that can be created for mobile guides. If electronic guides come with voice narration, they must be written for that purpose and not just be audio recordings of print media, which may sound stilted when read aloud.

Stationary Interactives

Electronic kiosks are commonly used for orientation and as guides to collections or gardens. Generally, these guides are not comprehensive but show highlights and draw from a database of living collections, although with a specialized interface that is visitor friendly. As mobile technology becomes more sophisticated, it may replace stationary modes of interpretation since mobile guides can be consulted exactly where and when needed and require less of an investment in physical equipment.

Web Materials

For reaching people outside of the garden, the Web is unmatched. Once a site is established, investment in posting materials is relatively low, and the depth of material can be amazing. The Web is currently the best way to fulfill the expectations of hobbyists and specialists for specific information about a topic. But like most electronic media, websites need to be updated regularly to remain fresh and interesting, which requires staff time and resources.

Drop-in Programs

Many gardens offer opportunistic programs for visitors. These programs are not always announced in advance: they can be part of a special event like a festival, or they can follow a regular schedule. Drop-in programs are usually designed to be of short duration and can be performance-based, like a book reading; productive, like a craft activity; or demonstrative, like a rose pruning demonstration. Investment in the programs can be very slight, especially if no materials are consumed, or they can be quite extensive, such as a bonsai workshop offered

Figure 17-8: Discovery carts can be elaborate, like this modified electric cart at the Morris Arboretum of the University of Pennsylvania. It has the distinct advantage of being easy to move.

Photo by Kitty Connolly. Courtesy of The Huntington Library, Art Collections, and Botanical Gardens

Figure 17-9: A volunteer at this rolling cart interprets orchids inside the U.S. Botanic Garden Conservatory. Smaller discovery carts are easier to manipulate through narrow paths and inside buildings.

Photo by Kitty Connolly. Courtesy of The Huntington Library, Art Collections, and Botanical Gardens

in conjunction with a Japanese garden festival. Investment depends on the availability of funding and the amount of staff time devoted to the program. All drop-in programs should be clearly linked to the mission and themes of the garden.

Discovery Carts

Discovery carts are small, manned interpretive stations that can be moved about the garden as needed. These carts usually hold interactive exhibits or displays that support the interpretive theme of the garden as a whole or of specific areas within the garden. Similarly, activities on the carts can serve a specific audience or be designed to cut across wide audience segments.

Carts can be as simple as a wheeled utility cart or as elaborate as a converted electric cart. They should be designed so that the interpretation can be changed to keep up with seasonal changes or to serve for special events. Discovery carts are excellent venues for trying out different interpretive approaches, as they generally attract visitors who are eager to interact with staff and volunteers.

Summary

Informal education is a process that visitors to public gardens undertake by choice. Educators create a more effective range of programs when they keep in mind why people come to gardens and how they learn when they are there. A focused approach to developing informal education will pay off in communicating the garden's mission and themes, bringing meaning to the experience of visiting a garden, accommodating all learners, and creating lifelong connections between visitors and public gardens.

Annotated Resources

American Association of Museums (AAM) (www.aam-us.org). The umbrella organization for all object-based museums, including those with living collections. It is the authority on standards and best practices, a central source for information and networking, and the leading advocate on museum issues.

Association of Science-Technology Centers (ASTC) (www.astc .org). An international organization that aims to promote public understanding of science through professional development and publications.

Center for the Advancement of Informal Science Education (CAISE) (caise.insci.org). Serves to advance informal science education through documenting and promoting its impact, encouraging improved practice, and alerting practitioners to relevant funding opportunities.

ExhibitFiles.org (www.exhibitfiles.org). An international, online community of museum professionals who share case studies and reviews of exhibitions.

Falk, J. H., and L. D. Dierking. 2000. *Learning from museums: Visitor experiences and the making of meaning*. Walnut Creek, Calif.: Altamira Press. Supplies an in-depth examination of informal education in museums.

Hein, G. E., and M. Alexander. 1998. *Museums: Places of learning*. Washington, D.C.: American Association of Museums/AAM Education Committee. An excellent, concise summary of learning theory and practice in informal education.

Honig, M. 2000. *Making your garden come alive! Environmental interpretation in botanical gardens*. Southern African Botanical Diversity Network Report No. 9. Pretoria: SABONET. http://www.bgci.org/ education/making_your_garden_come_a/. An accessible guide full of practical guidance for real-world projects.

InformalScience.org (www.informalscience.org). Has a searchable database of research and evaluation studies that is a valuable resource for those wishing to learn from other projects.

McLean, K. 1993. *Planning for people in museum exhibitions*. Washington, D.C.: Association of Science-Technology Centers. Provides wide-ranging guidance for developing interpretive experiences.

National Association of Interpretation (NAI) (www.interpnet .com). Its mission is inspiring leadership and excellence in heritage interpretation through national and international meetings, training and certification, and helpful online resources.

Serrell, B. 1996. *Exhibit labels: An interpretive approach*. Walnut Creek, Calif.: Altamira Press. An invaluable reference for project development and writing for the public.

Serrell, B. 2006. *Judging exhibitions: Assessing excellence in exhibitions from a visitor-centered perspective*. Walnut Creek, Calif.: Left Coast Press. This framework for individually assessing exhibitions and then sharing it with a group not only creates a collective understanding of criteria for exhibition development but also helps to internalize standards for excellence.

Smithsonian Accessibility Program. 1996. *Smithsonian guidelines for accessible exhibition design*. Washington, D.C.: Smithsonian Institution Press. A complete reference for creating accessible labels and print materials. http://www .si.edu/opa/accessibility/exdesign/start.htm

Wandersee, J. H. and E. E. Schussler. 1999. Preventing plant blindness. *American Biology Teacher* 61(2): 82, 84, 86. Reports on the preference that young people have for animals over plants, and describes reasons for this "plant blindness."

CHAPTER 18

Evaluation of Garden Programming and Planning

JULIE WARSOWE

Introduction

Education is a cornerstone of the public garden's mission. Yet simply offering educational programs is not sufficient; these programs must be demonstrably successful. Programs that don't work well waste money, time, and effort; even worse, they fail a garden's commitment to its mission. As public gardens become more visitor centered and service oriented, their approach to educational programs is changing. No longer can public gardens create programs in a vacuum, confidently determining the needs of participants without ever consulting them. Instead, public gardens and their funders need to know whether projects and programs are achieving intended goals and impacts—and if not, whether they should be continued or how they could be improved. Evaluation studies provide this information.

What Is Evaluation?

For public gardens, evaluation is the systematic collection and assessment of information, gathered for a specific audience to provide practical, focused feedback about a project or program (Trochim 2006; Hein 1998). Evaluation studies can occur and are valuable at all phases of the life span of a project or program.

Who Uses Evaluation Data?

Education program planners use evaluation data to determine whether intended program goals and learning objectives were met, as well as to understand participants' demographics,

needs, motivations, prior knowledge, interest, and satisfaction. Other garden staff also use education program evaluation: it helps marketing staff target efforts to increase attendance and participation, guides exhibit and graphic designers to make practical improvements during exhibition development, tells current funders and administrators if their money was well spent, and influences prospective funders' decisions as to whether they should offer new funds.

Why Evaluate?

Evaluation may demand a judgment, but merit or value can and should be determined in a rigorous, scientific manner without "relying on intuition, opinion, or trained sensibility" (Weiss 1998). Informal feedback can be valuable, but anecdotal evidence and gut feelings are not the same as an evaluation and cannot take its place in providing recommendations based on meaningful, empirical data. For others to have confidence that the review is legitimate, and be likely to follow recommendations for change or believe judgments of merit, evaluation in public gardens must be rigorous and systematic. Thus for a review to be considered an evaluation it must:

1. Be formally and intentionally planned and implemented

2. Collect data using sound, established methods

3. Contain an analysis, recommendations, and conclusions that are used to examine, improve, or develop an internal program

In contrast with academic research, evaluation studies do not tend to look for cause-and-effect relationships or attempt longitudinal investigations. Nor are evaluation results typically generalizable beyond the specific situation, or published for a wide audience. In a public garden, evaluation is intended to yield helpful observations for immediate internal use or for an external funder. It is a management tool.

A Brief History of Museum Program Evaluation

In the 1970s, taking a cue from the government's evaluation of social programs, both museum funding agencies and museums began to encourage evaluations as a justification for new or continued financial support. The Museum and Library Services Act of 1996 combined two older federal agencies into a new agency called the Institute of Museum and Library Services (IMLS), dedicated to promoting and supporting museums and libraries. The act requires the creation of procedures for reviewing and evaluating all funded projects.

Large funding bodies such as IMLS and the National Science Foundation (NSF), in first encouraging and eventually requiring evaluation of their funded projects, went a long way toward embedding evaluation in museum planning, especially in the exhibit development process. Other funding agencies, including private sponsors, began to follow suit: "Many museums entered the arena of visitor studies only because they were forced to carry out visitor studies as a requirement of their funding sources, but enter it they did" (Hein 1998). According to Weil, "Donors and grant-makers are decreasingly willing to accept simply as a matter of faith that recipient museums have achieved their educational or other intended outcomes. More and more, they are asking for some proof of performance" (2003).

Barriers to Conducting Evaluation

There are a number of barriers, whether real or perceived, that can make it difficult to embrace an evaluation study. Misconceptions and lack of understanding should be addressed when looking to undertake an evaluation. Common barriers include:

- Confusion of evaluation with academic research and thus a misconception that it is too difficult, expensive, or time-consuming

- Lack of confidence in the ability to carry out an evaluation internally

- Fear that evaluation is an assessment of staff performance

- Belief that evaluation is not necessary: faith that staff already know what's best, concern that staff will lose control over program decisions, confidence that anecdotal evidence is sufficient, a view that the program is too new to warrant evaluation

- Concern that money spent on evaluation drains resources away from actual programs

- Lack of trust in the accuracy of the data or its analysis

- Doubt that the evaluation will have any real impact

- Concern that the garden cannot afford evaluation

Look Within

Often the first step in an evaluation project is tackling these negative attitudes within the organization. Developing an institutional understanding of and support for evaluation, and transforming attitudes within the organizational culture to be more supportive of the evaluation process, are not easy tasks. Yet ignoring these barriers will not make them disappear. From the start, serious attention to concerns and misperceptions about evaluation, an awareness of the emotional sensitivity around evaluation, and a responsive, open attitude will go a long way in challenging negative attitudes that can derail an evaluation.

Who Does It?

Internal Evaluations

Internal evaluation, also called in-house evaluation, is planned, conducted, analyzed, and used primarily by staff from the organization of the program being evaluated. An individual or a team, the people who plan and run the program to be evaluated, or staff from another area of the garden can conduct an internal evaluation study.

External Evaluations

An external evaluation is conducted by outsiders—typically a consulting firm or academic researcher. The external evaluator will plan, carry out, and report on the evaluation with input, but limited assistance, from public garden staff. The garden is responsible for utilizing the evaluation recommendations. Generally a staff liaison works closely with the external evaluator.

Hiring an external evaluator does not magically absolve the garden of responsibility. Working with an external evaluator takes time and planning. Public garden staff members must help the evaluator learn about the organization, the program, and its participants. The external evaluator cannot create the program's goals, objectives, and desired outcomes or impacts to be evaluated. Once the evaluation is complete, utilization of the results and implementation of the recommendations will fall to garden staff. Whether the evaluation is conducted internally or externally, there are advantages and disadvantages to consider (see Table 18-1).

In a hybrid evaluation, responsibilities are shared by public garden staff and an outside consulting firm or university. For example, a consultant could create a survey that is administered by garden staff, or an outside firm could transcribe and analyze interviews conducted by in-house staff.

What to Look for in an External Evaluator

An RFP (request for proposal) or RFQ (request for qualifications) will help evaluators understand the program to be evaluated. Lists of evaluators can be found through InformalScience .org, the American Evaluation Association, or the Committee on Audience Research of the American Association of Museums. Public garden staff should look for an external evaluator who is already familiar with conducting evaluations in public gardens or parks and who understands the type of program to be evaluated and the unique challenges of a living collection.

If the evaluation budget is small, travel fees can be avoided by using local consultants. Likewise, professors in statistics, social sciences, education, or museum studies may see the garden's program evaluation as a real-world service and learning opportunity for their undergraduate or graduate students, at no or minimal cost to the garden.

Table 18-1: Advantages and Disadvantages to Internal and External Evaluators

Pros	Cons
Internal Evaluator	
Greater familiarity with institution, mission, history	Difficulty seeing the institution with fresh eyes
Greater knowledge of program being evaluated	Staff without formal training in evaluation could compromise evaluation rigor
Is present to remind others of results and supervise utilization	Day-to-day operations may get in the way of conducting evaluation or carrying out recommendations
Rapport, credibility, and trust already established with other staff, enabling open communication	Attempt at objectivity could be more difficult; participants might exaggerate positive feedback rather than offend someone they know
If program schedule changes, evaluation timing can shift	Time spent developing or running the program could cut into time for its evaluation
External Evaluator	
Gives greater sense of objectivity	Takes longer to become familiar with institution, program, organizational culture
Greater knowledge of evaluation techniques and more experience	Staff must still work closely with external evaluators; it takes time and energy to supervise consultants
Has knowledge of how other similar programs work	More expensive
Makes dedicated time for project	May be juggling projects from other organizations that take priority

(Fitzpatrick, Sanders, and Worthen 2004; Posavac and Carey 2007; Diamond 1999)

Timing Is Everything

Front-end, formative, and summative evaluations are timed to occur at the beginning, middle, and end of a project, respectively, although in practice the distinctions may blur, especially for programs without a true end. When evaluation is embedded in program planning, it can become a cyclical process with no exact end or beginning. Still, these three terms are commonly used and helpful in determining when and what kind of evaluation is needed (see Table 18-2).

Front-End Evaluation

Evaluation that is conducted before a program exists, in order to test the waters, gather information, assess needs, and justify development, is called front-end evaluation. Front-end evaluation gathers information from stakeholders and intended participants in the beginning stages of program development. A front-end evaluation might study level of interest in overall themes and specific topics by the program's intended audiences, their prior knowledge, or their misconceptions about the topic. Front-end evaluation might investigate whether a community needs the new program, whether other organizations in the community offer similar programs, what issues might shape the program, or what resources might be needed.

Formative Evaluation

Evaluation that is conducted as a program is being developed is called formative evaluation. Formative evaluations attempt to identify what is and is not working so that the program can be improved or revised while still under development. Formative evaluation takes the pulse of a program in process so that errors, pitfalls, and areas of confusion can be discovered before the program is fully implemented.

Formative evaluation can be an iterative process, that is, evaluation results may suggest an improvement, and once that improvement is made, further evaluation can test if the change has had the desired effect. This cycle of evaluation, change, and reevaluation can result in much stronger programs, but the number of iterations will depend on time and budget.

Table 18-2: **Where Does Evaluation Fit?**

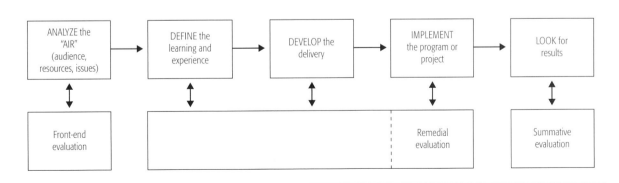

(Parsons 2009)

To save money, develop internal skills, and gather data that staff would find credible, the Atlanta Botanical Garden conducted a hybrid evaluation study of current visitors. The hybrid process created buy-in for evaluation and helped the Garden become more aware of visitor needs and interests.

The evaluation was a mix of front-end and remedial types. Some questions gathered front-end information for the development of an interpretive plan of a new area of the Garden. Other questions were geared toward remedial evaluation by gathering information that led to suggestions for improvements to completed projects (new interpretive signs and a newly opened visitor center). Issues explored included:

- Visitor awareness of the Garden's mission and activities, and their perceived value

- Motivations, expectations, and preferences in visiting

- Interest in, knowledge of, and expectations of content in new gardens

- Perception of the Garden's role as an environmental leader

- Use of existing information delivery systems

External consultants defined the interview questionnaire, determined the appropriate sample size, trained staff to administer the survey, analyzed the data, prepared a summary report, and presented findings and recommendations. Internally, staff managed the interviewers' recruitment and scheduling, and conducted interviews.

Summative Evaluation

Evaluation that takes place once a program or project has been completed and launched is termed summative. Generally, summative evaluation does not suggest changes that can be made to improve the project; when it does, it is sometimes called remedial evaluation. Evaluation that tests whether a program is being implemented as intended is sometimes called implementation evaluation. Summative evaluation measures how people changed as a result of the program or project: Do they feel, say, or do anything differently as a direct result? Were the intended goals achieved? Summative evaluations are conducted primarily for funders and administrators, though educators may also use the results for future programs.

What Can Be Learned from Evaluation?

Evaluation can measure five basic data types (see Table 18-3). The questions an evaluation study will attempt to answer should fall into one or more of these types. Wells and Butler (2004) organized these data types into an evaluation hierarchy, a pyramid that illustrates the increasing difficulty and complexity of measurement. That is, measuring descriptive data (A) is simpler than studying long-term effects (E).

All of these data types can be valuable, and generally a program evaluation plan will investigate a combination. It is crucial that the data collected do not "generate answers to the questions no one is asking . . . Such divergence could defeat

Table 18-3: Evaluation Data Types

Data Type	Examples
A. Descriptive data: products, numbers, demographics	How many people came to the program? What neighborhoods did they come from?
B. Psychographic data: participants' motivations, interests, curiosity, prior knowledge, expectations	Are participants interested in the program topic? What do participants already know about the topic before participating in the program?
C. Satisfaction data: participants' perception of success	Did the participants have fun? Did they think it was a worthwhile experience?
D. Short-term outcomes: short-term learning; immediate change in participants' knowledge or attitude	What do visitors do, think, and feel during or shortly after the experience?
E. Long-term impacts and benefits: long-term learning; change in participants' knowledge, skill, attitude, behavior, status, life condition; societal benefits	What do visitors retain from the experience? What do they do differently as a result of the experience?

(Wells and Butler 2004; Institute of Museum and Library Services 2009a and 2009b)

the idea of action or decision-oriented research" (Loomis 1987). Evaluations that do not answer key questions or suggest useful improvements will wind up sitting on the shelf.

What Can't Be Measured

Some impacts realistically cannot be measured, or can be measured only by highly skilled evaluators using complex evaluation tools. Overarching societal benefits and truly long-term impacts are extremely difficult to measure in a setting as complex as a public garden's informal learning environment. Because participants are influenced by many complex factors that reach far beyond a public garden educational program, establishing causal relationships between a garden's educational programs and long-term learning or changes in attitude and behavior is notoriously difficult. These large changes are also rarely tackled effectively at an individual public garden or with short-term projects. Evaluation cannot measure outcomes that are beyond the scope of the program or tied to systems out of its control, such as test scores from a school system (Korn 2004). A public garden should be cautious of an evaluator who promises to measure these impacts.

Education programs should still strive to cause positive, long-term behavior changes in program participants; such changes are just very difficult to measure. Public garden educators' higher goals can and should include, for example, environmental awareness and stewardship, mental and physical health improvements, economic stability, and community solidarity, but measuring these impacts is extremely difficult. When developing an evaluation plan, whether internal or external, it is important to be realistic about the evaluation scope and the evaluator's skill.

Data Collection

Once it is determined when evaluation is needed in program development, who will conduct it, and the types of data to be gathered, next choose the data collection methods. The two overarching methodologies are qualitative and quantitative. Many evaluation studies use a mixed-methods strategy that combines both qualitative and quantitative methods to take advantage of the strength of each and diminish their weaknesses. Neither methodology is easier than the other. Both require additional study if they are to be developed and implemented effectively. Likewise, sampling (the process of selecting participants) is complex and requires separate study.

Quantitative Methods

Quantitative data are essentially numeric. Quantitative tools yield counts, measures, percentages—that is, responses that fall into predetermined categories. Because this information can be analyzed statistically, the results are generally considered more reliable. Reliability is a measure of the method's consistency; when a method is reliable, it should measure the same thing the same way every time (Diamond 1999). Once a measurement instrument has been created, quantitative data are often simpler

---

AN ENTIRELY DIFFERENT VIEW

Some have argued that evaluations examining outcomes and impacts (D and E in Table 18-3) are built on a model of teaching and learning that is rooted in traditional, formal school settings and as such cannot entirely address an informal learning environment such as a public garden. According to Hein (1995), this way of evaluating is valid but didactic: "These questions, typical of the kind that evaluators are often asked to address, make sense within a model of learning and teaching that is based on the teacher's perspective, where the theory of education stipulates that the teacher decides what is to be learned and the task of education is to organize the material and present it in such a way that it is transmitted to the student." Hein continues, "The more likely we are to construct something that is open, ambiguous and able to be manipulated in a variety of ways by the learner . . . the less likely we are to be able to predict precisely what has been learned."

NSF also struggles to define appropriate learning outcomes in informal science learning environments such as public gardens. Through its Informal Science Education division, NSF funded a study by the National Research Council (NRC), which notes that traditional academic achievement outcomes are of limited value because they:

1. Do not encompass the range of capabilities that informal settings can promote
2. Violate critical assumptions about these settings, such as their focus on leisure-based or voluntary experiences and non-standardized curriculum
3. Are not designed for the breadth of participants, many of whom are not K–12 students (National Research Council 2009)

NRC is addressing these concerns by proposing an entirely new "'strands of science learning' framework . . . The strands are distinct from, but overlap with, the science-specific knowledge, skills, attitudes, and dispositions that are ideally developed in schools." For example, in strand one, the participant experiences "excitement, interest, and motivation to learn about phenomena in the natural and physical world." The report emphasizes that educational programs must still be designed with specific learning objectives in mind, but that these objectives should be based on informal, not formal, learning theory, and a constructivist approach. It remains to be seen whether this new model will become popular in public gardens.

to gather, resulting in larger data sets that are more generalizable and easier to analyze. Because quantitative methods are basically about numbers, they may lack rich emotion or depth.

Qualitative Methods

Qualitative data are essentially narrative. Qualitative tools use conversation and open-ended questions. Qualitative methods usually yield data that are rich and contextual. Such methods may reveal overall trends, but they also allow for unanticipated data, exceptions, and complex responses. As Wells and Butler (2004) note, qualitative methods allow an evaluator to go beyond what visitors do and say to something deeper. They allow the evaluator to pay better "attention to processes such as creativity, concept formation, and the acquisition of attitudes, beliefs, and values" (Munley 1987). A qualitative approach also allows the evaluator to "understand the program from the inside, rather than standing aloof on the outside . . . In a real sense, the qualitative evaluator is viewed as the measurement instrument" (Posavac and Carey 2007).

While quantitative methods are considered more reliable, qualitative methods are often considered to be more valid. As Wells and Butler (2004) note, "Qualitative measurement better captures the real or true meaning of a phenomenon." Validity in research is a measure of how accurate and appropriate the tool and the results are. It can be *internal*, referring to accuracy within the environment and participants being studied. Or it can be *external*, referring either to how outside experts in the subject would rate the accuracy of the instrument or to "the degree to which the conclusions in your study would hold for other persons in other places and at other times" (Trochim 2006).

Because qualitative tools are more likely to yield unanticipated responses, they are useful in a front-end exploration phase. When the major issues or ideas are not yet clear, they can be generated through the evaluation process. Qualitative data are more time-consuming and difficult to gather, so the sample sizes are usually smaller and the results are less generalizable and more difficult to analyze. For example, it usually takes the same amount of time, or more, to collect data using a qualitative method as it does to describe or transcribe it: for every hour of interview time, an evaluator generally will spend an hour transcribing and coding the audio recording, while every hour of a video recording can take up to sixteen hours to thoroughly transcribe.

Same Idea, Different Story

Qualitative and quantitative methods can be used to gather the same data type. For example, satisfaction data can be gathered with a Likert-scale survey (quantitative; i.e., "rate on a scale of . . .") or through open-ended interviews (qualitative), though the results may be different. Likewise, qualitative data can be coded quantitatively. While journals may be used qualitatively to better understand an individual's experience, if the journals are analyzed based on the frequency of predetermined expressions (perhaps the number of times a botanical term is mentioned), the analysis can be considered quantitative.

Built-in Methods

Data collection tools may be part of the program being evaluated, or additional tools can be created. Especially in an internal evaluation, built-in methods present an efficient, cost-effective way to collect data, and they increase the likelihood that the data will actually be collected, analyzed, and summarized. Built-in methods can be qualitative, quantitative, or both. They are sometimes called traces, from a comparison to the way archeologists observe traces of what people leave behind. Examples include:

- Gate counts, admissions records
- Membership records
- Archival data
- Participant journals and portfolios
- Minutes, agendas, notes
- Log books
- Comment cards
- Vandalism reports, maintenance records

Special Considerations

Consent

Evaluation is like an experiment using human subjects. For both legal and ethical reasons, evaluators must protect the rights of those being evaluated. Most projects in public gardens pose no risks to privacy, physical health, or emotional health, but participants should still be informed about the evaluation project and how it could affect them (Diamond 1999). This is especially important if the evaluation involves children. Sometimes informed consent is as simple as a sign at the entrance to the area under observation explaining the project, the evaluation method, and how a visitor can opt out of the study. Other times, written consent forms may be needed for participants or their guardians to read and sign. Confidentiality must be maintained whenever personal information is used; if confidentiality is not possible, that must be clearly communicated. Err on the side of caution.

Compensation is common if the evaluation is time-consuming or somehow onerous (the compensation need not be large; a free souvenir or admission pass is often more than adequate).

Bias

Personal values, interpersonal relationships, financial relationships, and organizational relationships can all lead to a biased interpretation of data (Fitzpatrick, Sanders, and Worthen 2004) and reduced credibility. Today the debate is less about objectivity and subjectivity than it is about minimizing bias. A certain amount of bias in both qualitative and quantitative approaches is inevitable.

Quantitative evaluation is often perceived as less biased than qualitative evaluation, but the way questions are framed, the choice of sampling and variables, and the assumptions the evaluator makes about the participants will manifest themselves even in a survey or in the interpretation of numeric data. Getting to know the audience and pretesting quantitative instruments can help counterbalance bias.

In qualitative approaches the evaluator has more of a presence—and in some cases may be a participant—in the program or project being evaluated. This immersion would seem to make objectivity more difficult. Yet because this approach is so immersive, qualitative evaluators regularly employ strategies to avoid bias, such as working with a partner and comparing findings.

For both qualitative and quantitative approaches, it is important to look at what happens rather than look for particular behaviors (Fitzpatrick, Sanders, and Worthen 2004). "All we can directly discern about people is what they do and say; we cannot similarly note what they think or feel" unless they explicitly express it (Hein 1995). For example, an evaluator can't assume that a visitor has read a plant tag just because she is observed looking at it. To ensure the greatest likelihood of credibility in both qualitative and quantitative approaches, follow standards of good program evaluation, choose a mixed-method evaluation, and be aware of the sources of bias, both internal and external.

Creating an Evaluation Plan

Planning for an evaluation begins with gaining commitment for the evaluation from key stakeholders. This means getting a budget approved, assembling a team, and outlining a plan. An evaluation plan defines the evaluation study. A written evaluation plan should contain:

Scope and framework
    a. Program description: What will be evaluated? What is the scope of the evaluation?

    b. Situation: What is the context for the program? Why is evaluation needed?

c. Resources: Who will collect the data? What is the budget? Who are the stakeholders?

Focus

a. Questions: What kinds of data need to be gathered? What are the burning questions?

Design

a. Methods: Is the evaluation front-end, formative, summative, or a combination? Which data collection techniques best answer the questions? Who is the subject of the evaluation?

Work plan

a. Timing: When will the evaluation occur?

b. Special considerations: For example, is consent needed (i.e., for interviewing minors)?

Utilization

a. Analysis and reporting: How will the data be analyzed, and by whom? How will findings be communicated, when, and to whom? How will the evaluation results be used?

The term *logic model* describes a type of evaluation plan used mostly with new programs; it embeds evaluation in the program plan rather than tacking it on as a separate process. A logic model defines both the new program (context, needed resources, activities, and strategies) and its evaluation (intended results, outcomes, impacts, and indicators) (Klemmer 2004; Kellogg Foundation 2004; Institute of Museum and Library Science 2009).

Some grant proposals require an evaluation plan. So even before a program is funded, staff often must determine whether the evaluation will be internal or external, create a plan, and identify the evaluator.

CASE STUDY: THE HUNTINGTON BOTANICAL GARDENS

"Plants Are Up to Something" is the NSF-funded permanent exhibition in the Huntington Library, Art Collections, and Botanical Gardens' new conservatory. As required by NSF, the Huntington conducted front-end, formative, and summative evaluation using a combination of in-house staff and external consultants.

Front-end evaluation was used to develop the exhibition's key themes and discover the baseline knowledge of participants. The majority of time went to formative evaluation, where in addition to working directly with intended participants, the Huntington assembled an expert advisory panel. In multiple iterations of formative testing, hundreds of interviews were conducted to develop the interpretive plan, test concepts, and refine interactive, inquiry-based activities. Formative evaluation revealed which

activities needed modification, but also which should be cut: many seemed ideal in principle but in practice sent the wrong message, or were not engaging and easy to use. To examine overall effectiveness and ways to improve the exhibition in remedial and summative stages, data were collected using interviews (of people who visited the conservatory as well as those who didn't), tracking and timing studies, and observations.

The exhibition's success is clearly linked to the evaluation effort, resulting in a new, positive attitude throughout the institution toward engaging visitors and conducting evaluation. This is an example of a complete and well-funded evaluation. While most program evaluation is on a smaller scale, the Huntington is a valuable model.

WHAT IS OUTCOMES-BASED EVALUATION (OBE)?

There are many evaluation models, each taking a different approach to the range of questions and the manner in which they are addressed. Outcomes-based evaluation is one model. It is based on the clear definition of intended results. Outcomes-based evaluation is popular in public gardens and museums, primarily because it is the model funders often require. "It is a method of planning that begins with the end in mind—literally—by asking what overall impacts you want to achieve, what outcomes lead to those impacts, what they look like, and how they can be measured" (Klemmer 2004).

According to the Institute of Museum and Library Services (2009), "Outcome evaluation helps you know (and show) that your program creates the intended results. The organized process of developing an outcome-based program and a logic model

helps institutions articulate and establish clear program benefits (outcomes), identify ways to measure those program benefits (indicators), clarify the specific individuals or groups for which the program's benefits are intended (target audience), and design program services to reach that audience and achieve the desired results."

Outcomes-based evaluation is part of a "backward research design" approach, where the target audience and intended outcomes and impacts are considered before a program is conceived. Outcomes-based evaluation is useful because it requires stakeholders to clearly articulate the program and its objectives, builds a shared understanding for the work to be performed, and connects actions to results.

Summary

Program evaluation is not an end in and of itself. It is one part of the larger planning process and, once embedded in that process, results in stronger programs. Public garden educators and administrators need not be professional evaluators, but systematic evaluation is necessary to develop good educational programs. While this chapter delivers a grounding in evaluation's basic rationale and process, further study in specific data collection methods will be necessary to carry out an evaluation.

Educators gather feedback every day—when they ask children about their favorite parts of a school field trip as they get back on the bus, or read the comment card left by a disgruntled visitor. They may even make programmatic changes based on these responses. Yet a thoughtfully planned evaluation at the beginning, middle, or end of a project ensures that programs are based not on anecdotal evidence, assumptions, and good intentions but on real evidence systematically gathered from stakeholders and participants. Only when program developers "treat evaluation as an integral part of the total planning and teaching process, adopting the attitude that improvement is an ongoing need" (Bennett 1989) can public gardens fulfill their educational mission.

Annotated Resources

Evaluation Techniques

General, Practical

Bond, S. L., S. E. Boyd, and K. A. Rapp. 1997. *Taking stock: A practical guide to evaluating your own programs*. Chapel Hill, N.C.: Horizon Research. Retrieved September 20, 2009, from www.horizon-research.com/reports/1997/stock.pdf. Great overview that assumes no prior knowledge of evaluation theory or techniques, but lacks the detail to serve as a stand-alone manual.

Diamond, J. 1999. *Practical evaluation guide: Tools for museums and other informal educational settings*. Walnut Creek, Calif.: AltaMira Press. Covers evaluation in museums and informal education settings. The focus is on how-to techniques without much theory.

Posavac, E. J., and R. G. Carey. 2007. *Program evaluation: Methods and case studies*, 7th ed. Upper Saddle River, N.J.: Pearson Prentice Hall. Introductory text for evaluation students. Covers the basics with real-world (though not garden-world) case studies. Not a stand-alone manual, but addresses how to justify, plan, and encourage utilization of evaluation.

Robson, C. 2000. *Small-scale evaluation*. London: Sage Publications. Great internal evaluation resource. End-of-chapter tasks enable the reader to create, perform, analyze, and report on a real evaluation by the book's conclusion.

Focus Groups

Morgan, D. L. 1997. *Focus groups as qualitative research*, 2nd ed. Thousand Oaks, Calif.: Sage Publications. Short enough to read in one sitting but with all the information necessary to design, conduct, and analyze a focus group. Geared more toward the academic researcher, but public garden staff will find more in common with academic research than market research.

Surveys

Salant, P., and D. Dillman. 1994. *How to conduct your own survey*. New York: John Wiley and Sons. Clear, step-by-step approach. Doesn't include online or email surveys and the analysis section is dated, but the information on developing questions, managing, coding, and reporting data is solid.

Interviews

Weiss, R. 1994. *Learning from strangers: The art and method of qualitative interview studies*. New York: Free Press. Conversational book that covers all the bases: choosing and recruiting respondents, creating an interview guide, length and format, ethics and confidentiality, interviewer bias, data coding, and analysis.

Observation

Lofland, J., and L. H. Lofland. 1995. *Analyzing social settings: A guide to qualitative observation and analysis*, 3rd ed. Belmont, Calif.: Wadsworth Publishing. Great book for learning about naturalistic research and participant observation. Information on carrying out participant observation and how to log, analyze, and report data.

Mahoney, C. 1997. Common qualitative methods. In *User-friendly handbook for mixed method evaluations*, ed. J. Frechtling and L. Sharp. Washington, D.C.: National Science Foundation, Division of Research, Evaluation and Communication. Retrieved September 20, 2009, from www.nsf.gov/pubs/1997/nsf97153/chap_3.htm. Nice summary of the pros and cons of observation as a formal method of data collection and what information can be gathered through observation. Does not give as much information on creating your own observation form. Link to the full document: www.nsf.gov/pubs/1997/nsf97153/start.htm.

Web Resources

Association of Science and Technology Centers (ASTC) (www.astc.org). Public gardens have a lot in common with science centers. See the Visitor Studies section of the Resources tab.

Committee on Audience Research and Evaluation (CARE) (www.care-aam.org). A committee of the American Association of Museums, CARE posts a biannual list of evaluators and PDFs of conference presentations.

Informal Science (www.informalscience.org). Evaluation section features a database of evaluation projects and evaluators, numerous links to other sites offering how-to guides, and other online evaluation resources.

Innovation Network (www.innonet.org). Lots of free resources and tools are available to those who register. The Logic Model Builder and Evaluation Plan Builder allows for the creation of customized plans.

My Environmental Education Evaluation Resource Assistant (www.meera.snre.umich.edu). Online tutorial intended for environmental education programs but works for public garden programs.

Shaping Outcomes (www.shapingoutcomes.org). On-line tutorial in outcomes-based evaluation.

Research Methods Knowledge Base (www.socialresearchmethods .net/kb). Essentially an online undergraduate course in social research methods, with clear definitions of terms and concepts.

Visitor Studies Association (www.visitorstudies.org). VSA members include researchers, educators, exhibit designers, and administrators from organizations that serve visitors.

CHAPTER 19

Public Relations and Marketing Communications

LEEANN LAVIN AND ELIZABETH RANDOLPH

Introduction

All public gardens have stories to be told, inspiring and informing diverse audiences with tales from the world of plants. For the garden's audiences, these stories come in many forms, from brochures and press releases to blogs and YouTube videos, but they all share an essential function: they communicate the garden's value to the public because the public is essential to the garden. Whether garden staff refers to this work as public relations or communications or puts it under the umbrella of marketing, the goal is the same: to nurture interest in and support for the garden among members of key audiences. These audiences are made up primarily of current and potential

---

KEY TERMS

Brand: the impression a garden makes on the public. Includes the garden's products by which it is known (e.g., educational programming) and the words, images, and emotions that communicate the garden's personality. Two key attributes of a brand are that it differentiates the institution from its competitors and that it reinforces the institution's relevance to the public.

Core messages: key phrases, terms, and definitions that reflect an institution's unique qualities that are used repeatedly throughout communication resources.

Logo: an easily recognized symbol of the garden or organization.

Marketing: the business of creating, communicating, delivering, and exchanging ideas, information, and experiences that have relevance and value for garden audiences and potential audiences (American Marketing Association 2010).

Marketing portfolio: a collection of resources that communicate what the garden does and why it is important to the public.

Market segmentation: the process of subdividing a market into distinct subsets of customers that behave in the same way or have similar needs (American Marketing Association 2010).

Media relations: ongoing interactions with mass-communication media, including websites, blogs, television, radio, newspapers, magazines, and journals.

Social media: media designed to be disseminated through social interaction, using highly accessible and scalable publishing techniques.

SWOT analysis: an examination of internal strengths and weaknesses and external opportunities and threats; often done within the marketing planning process.

Tagline: the verbal or written portion of a message that summarizes the main idea in a few memorable words (American Marketing Association 2010).

Target audience: the primary group of people to whom a marketing communication is directed. Target audiences can be people of a certain age group or gender, or they can be identified according to particular interests, such as home gardening. Discovering the appropriate target audiences to market a product or service is one of the most important results of market research.

Value proposition: what is promised by an institution's marketing efforts and fulfilled by its delivery and customer service processes (American Marketing Association 2010).

visitors, members, volunteers, and donors, as well as community leaders and officials and the internal audiences of staff and board. Some gardens need to attract visitors from across the state or country to generate revenue through admissions and public programs. All gardens, particularly those with free admission, need to build political, corporate, institutional, and social support to sustain their operations. But the goal remains the same: to identify means of support and to cultivate that support from the public they serve.

Media relations, member communications, visitor communications, internal communications, special events, tourism, community relations and events, publications, advertising, and online media are all part of marketing. This chapter focuses on the basics of marketing communications for a garden: how to create a mission-related garden brand, what a marketing portfolio is and how to evaluate it, why market research and formal marketing plans are important, and how to use media relations and social networking as marketing communications platforms. Because marketing staff or volunteers often have several communications responsibilities, this chapter also addresses planning for crisis communications.

Using the Mission to Market the Garden

Chapter 4 emphasizes that a mission statement defines why an organization exists, what its primary activities are, and whom it serves. Effective marketing looks at the mission statement from the public perspective, not just the viewpoints of staff and board, and asks: "What does the garden do that interests me? Why is the garden important to me?"

Examining the mission from the point of view of the garden's current and potential audiences is critical to creating a strong identity or brand, interchangeable terms for the impression a garden or any institution makes on the public. The brand differentiates an organization in the minds of the public. The brand reflects the garden's personality, evoking thoughts, images, and emotions that inspire actions of support. Those actions include visiting the garden, attending a class, becoming a member, making a donation, and recommending the garden to others. A sustainable brand evolves to accommodate change both inside and outside the garden while staying true to its mission.

Specific answers to the following questions can help marketing staff clarify the value and relevance of the garden to its audiences and potential audiences:

- Whom does the garden serve—amateur and professional horticulturists, tourists (general, educational), city residents, college students and professors, elementary school students, multigenerational family groups, scientists?

- What are the functional benefits the garden offers to these audiences (e.g., a beautiful conservatory to enjoy in winter, green space to roam)?

- What are the emotional benefits the garden offers (relaxation from stress, spiritual uplift)?

- Which programs, collections, and events at the garden attract significant numbers of people to visit or to support the garden?

- Why is the garden important to the people it currently serves? Is this a neighborhood institution? Does it offer green space in an area where there is no other? Is it a community meeting space? Does it offer much needed educational programs?

Core Messages Articulate the Garden's Mission

Reflecting the unique qualities of the garden's mission, core messages are key phrases, terms, and definitions that are used repeatedly throughout communication resources to reflect those issues most relevant to the mission of the individual garden. In general, those messages convey the benefits provided by the programs and services offered by the garden. The core message is often further refined to a catchy tagline.

Fairchild Tropical Botanic Garden's mission is "to save tropical plant diversity by exploring, explaining and conserving the world of tropical plants; fundamental to this task is inspiring a greater knowledge and love for plants and gardening so that all can enjoy the beauty and bounty of the tropical world." To ensure that the central message of the garden's mission is heard by its many current and potential audiences, the garden's easily remembered tagline, "Exploring, Explaining and Conserving the World of Tropical Plants," is used throughout its internal and external communications, including the website, phone greetings, news releases, signage, talking points, brochures, and advertising.

Phipps Conservatory and Botanical Gardens identifies itself as the "Green Heart of Pittsburgh." Its mission, "to inspire and educate visitors with the beauty and importance of plants; to advance sustainability and worldwide biodiversity through action and research; and to celebrate its historic glasshouse," is reflected repeatedly throughout its communication pieces.

Marketing Portfolio

Intentionally or not, all gardens have a marketing portfolio—a collection of resources that communicate to the public what the garden does and why it is important. These materials present the look and language of the garden, making an impression even when people can't experience the garden in person. Marketing materials that reach outside, such as the website, advertising, and brochures, should relate to communications materials inside the garden that may not fall under the umbrella of marketing, such as signage and gift shop merchandise.

Consistency is a key element in an effective portfolio. Every garden should establish basic guidelines for graphic design and language, including a writer's reference guide for style and usage, to keep materials consistent. The garden logo, an easily recognized symbol, is the graphic element most often used to represent the garden. The guidelines should address its color, size, placement, and use with or without a tagline. Palettes of signature colors and fonts can make the graphic design process easier and the end results more consistent. The guidelines should be known and available to everyone who has a part in creating marketing materials, from interns to contract designers.

The resources in a garden's marketing portfolio need to be routinely evaluated to determine their effectiveness. Included in that evaluation should be format, content, graphic style, verbal style, and even methods of dissemination and the intended audience for each application. Strong portfolios usually contain material geared to different audience segments based on both demographic information and lifestyle or behavior indicators.

A garden may have the most appealing communications materials possible, but if they aren't effectively disseminated, they can't help the garden. Dissemination options are many and depend on target audiences, their demographics, and their lifestyles. If, for example, the garden is trying to reach out to younger audiences, dissemination through social media sources such as Facebook and Twitter may be most appropriate. But such an approach may be completely lost on an older, ethnic audience, for whom articles in a native-language community newsletter may be much more effective. Likewise, advertisements for a family-oriented event have a better chance of reaching families if disseminated through local parenting news outlets. Don't dismiss such approaches simply because they are low-tech; that may be just what is called for with certain specialty audiences.

Reaching target audiences with repeated messages through various media is often necessary to achieve the intended goal. Options include brochures or other print product placements, paid or free advertising placements (print, broadcast, Web), electronic tools (email and website), and social networking. Each approach should be regularly evaluated based on

preestablished measurement criteria to gauge their effectiveness. Those that are deemed to be ineffective should be dropped.

Gardens are visually arresting places, so imagery becomes essential to a garden's marketing portfolio. If possible, gardens should work with professional photographers or professionally trained staff members who know how to shoot exactly what's needed and save it in the various technical formats required by different communications outlets. Many media outlets, commercial businesses, and tourist bureaus turn to public gardens when they want beautiful, seasonal images. An easy-to-use library of current images can provide many free promotional opportunities.

Planning for Successful Marketing

Just like landscape design, a plant collections policy, or a capital campaign, marketing is much more effective if it has written goals and strategies developed, approved, and implemented by the pertinent players. The planning process involves defining goals, conducting market research (which often dictate the goals), identifying target audiences, developing strategies and tactics, charting timelines and budgets, and evaluating effectiveness.

Goals

The goals of the marketing plan should be developed to support the mission of the garden. The institution's strategic plan and budget often outline marketing goals that support the garden's specific needs. Goals should consider all stakeholder groups including past, present, and future visitors, members, and donors, as well as the local and business communities, media, suppliers, volunteers, staff, and board members.

Goals should be measurable and quantifiable and may include both financial and nonfinancial measurement options. For example, a marketing goal may be to increase annual visitation by 10 percent, or to improve media relations as reflected in a 25 percent increase in local media coverage. Goals may also reflect the increases in the number of job applicants applying for positions, increases in attendance at a workshop, and/or increases in conversion rates of visitors to members.

Market Trend Research

Public gardens should regularly gather information about issues important to the public, consumer attitudes in the community and society in general, communication trends, and visitor impressions and expectations. This research can help provide firsthand data to supplement anecdotal data and balance out staff attitudes and impressions. While this data only provides a snapshot of public opinion, it is useful in helping to identify the important issues to specific target audiences that would be interested in the garden. Through market research, the Minnesota Landscape Arboretum was informed that physical fitness was a growing trend in the Twin Cities region (and nationally). Based on this information, the Arboretum staff developed health and fitness themes in targeting recreational planners and community fitness groups to promote the Arboretum's 12.5 miles of garden paths and hiking trails, ski-touring and snowshoe trails, and a 3-mile drive open to walkers, bikers, and runners year-round.

Audience Research

Knowing both the garden's existing and potential audiences is an important part of planning for successful marketing. This knowledge helps focus marketing efforts where they will have the most impact. Chapter 14 provides information on collecting visitor demographics such as age, gender, ethnicity, education level, household income, and profession, as well as geographic factors such as where they live and psychographic factors that focus on lifestyle, attitudes, values, and motivation.

SWOT Analysis

A SWOT (strengths, weaknesses, opportunities and threats) analysis done in-house can also help a public garden improve its marketing outreach. What does the garden do well? What are its strongest resources—community connections, history of the garden, plant collections, educational and outreach programs, board members with media connections, volunteers with website design experience? The garden should face its weaknesses: What does it lack? What mistakes has it made and why? Next, it should look for potential marketing opportunities and threats. Can the garden take a leadership role on local community issues? Can it capitalize on conservation and

other issue-based trends? How can it use social media to market the garden? What pressures could cause problems for the garden—a sluggish economy, the neighboring state park, a new highway that will change traffic and development near the garden? Bradley (2002) identifies five types of environments that gardens should monitor for both positive and negative challenges: competitive, political, economic, technological, and cultural. Using this type of analysis can help identify key areas in which marketing efforts play a role.

Marketing Plans

At the Morton Arboretum, the marketing team develops a comprehensive strategic marketing plan for the calendar year that correlates directly with the Arboretum's overall strategic plan and budget. Its marketing plan includes a succinct list of goals and objectives with projected statistics for earned income, attendance, and fund-raising. Marketing team members work alongside different departments to craft tailored marketing plans that target audiences for education, membership, facility rental, restaurant, gift shop, and group tours. They also develop separate marketing plans for new initiatives such as expanding digital outreach or major exhibitions.

The Minnesota Landscape Arboretum's management sets specific, measurable marketing goals each year, including numbers for visitorship, membership revenue, fund-raising revenue from special events, visits to selected Web pages, and e-news subscribers. The process of creating an annual written strategic marketing group plan includes a creative session in which the team members pool ideas and strategies, which are recorded on paper or on a screen. This process generates healthy discussions about what projects are in the works, what new strategies staff members would like to test, what successful strategies should be refreshed, and how collaboration among staff can be increased.

With input from the Arboretum's visitor services, education and programming, and operations and grounds departments, the marketing team collaboratively develops a strategic plan that clearly identifies not only visitor and marketing goals but also marketing services for each business segment (membership, facility rental, adults' and children's education programs, gift store, restaurant, exhibition, and events) to help reach revenue and visitation goals. These tactical plans focus on who is responsible for each phase as implementation partners. This plan also serves the purpose of identifying needs for potential community or promotional partners.

The Desert Botanical Garden has a big-picture marketing plan that groups its audiences as newer members (members for less than two years), long-term members (members for more than

amazon.com

SDHdZV6kVR

Returns Are Easy!
Visit http://www.amazon.com/returns to return any item - including gifts - in unopened or original condition within 30 days for a full refund (other restrictions apply). Please have your order ID ready.

Your order of September 18, 2011 (Order ID 002-0916962-8811448)

Qty.	Item	Item Price	Total
1	**Public Garden Management** Hardcover (** P-2-A61D645 **) X00080LGUL amzn1.wdsku.v1.131278413963425878 (**Sold by Warehouse Deals, Inc**)	$56.99	$56.99

This shipment completes your order.

Have feedback on how we packaged your order? Tell us at www.amazon.com/packaging.

Subtotal	$56.99
Order Total	$56.99
Paid via credit/debit	$56.99
Balance due	$0.00

2/DHdZV6kVR/-1 of 1-//1M/second/7163028/0919-15:00/0919-06:05/tdoe

1A3

two years), locals, and tourists. For day-to-day operations, the garden organizes its yearly marketing plan by season. Within each season there are five components: paid advertising, direct mail to garden members, brochure distributions to local tourist-related businesses, media relations promoting the season and related events, and online media, including the website, e-newsletter, and social media. They rely on their regional tourist bureaus to reach audiences outside the Phoenix metropolitan area.

Fairchild Tropical Botanic Garden incorporates all aspects of marketing into integrated plans, ranging from three months to eighteen months in scope. Special events such as the International Mango Festival and International Chocolate Festival are critical components of its plans because they appeal to audiences that are not attracted by mission-specific messages.

The marketing staff collaborate with other departments to create attractive reasons for people to come to Fairchild, experience the world of tropical plants, and ultimately make Fairchild part of their lives. Ten to 20 percent of their visitors become members.

When the Tyler Arboretum decided to develop and implement its first formal marketing plan for a seasonal exhibition, the results were illuminating. The exhibition of tree houses designed and built by local artisans launched the Arboretum into a new stratum. Admission revenue increased by over 600 percent, and gift shop revenue increased by 230 percent. The success of the exhibition was due in equal parts to the appeal of the individual exhibits, the quality of the visitor programs, and the marketing plan. The thoughtful process of establishing marketing goals, identifying target audiences, and crafting marketing strategies dramatically improved the efficiency and efficacy of Tyler's outreach.

Organize the Details

Working documents that give detailed instructions about how to execute marketing strategies make it much easier to get things done. They also provide critical information if there are sudden staff changes and serve as a useful reference for future planning. Spreadsheets or other flexible formats allow detailed information on schedules, responsibilities, and costs to be organized and reorganized according to different criteria.

Scheduling information should incorporate all deadlines appropriate to the time frame and project: newsletters, website updates, editorial media, advertising media, designers, printers, staff review. Responsibility information should identify who does what, from continuing education interns writing press releases on upcoming classes to contracted graphic designers working on the new direct-mail membership campaign. Detailed information on costs should make it easy to break out expenses according to marketing objectives. It should also provide a baseline for future budgets.

Evaluating Marketing Effectiveness

Conolly (2010) asserts that an important step in the marketing process is the evaluation and measurement of return on marketing investments. Every garden should assess the effectiveness and efficiency of the marketing strategies used. The outcomes can have important implications. For the marketing professional, it provides an opportunity to demonstrate the impacts that marketing programs have on the ability to grow net revenues and meet mission-related goals. For senior management and directors, it provides a valuable tool for understanding the impacts associated with marketing spending.

When original marketing goals are made measurable and quantifiable, their effectiveness can be assessed. Evaluation should include financial and nonfinancial measurements and may be simple or complex. It may reflect short-term or long-term effects. The key is to look for ways to link the causal marketing strategy to the ensuing result.

A standard tool is a summary report at the completion of a marketing program, which gives a comprehensive overview of the program and documents the effectiveness of tools used. Many gardens survey visitors after events, through either short on-site surveys or standardized emails sent to addresses captured when individuals register for a class or purchase tickets to an event. A summary report also provides staff with a starting point that is more beneficial than just attendance statistics or a list of media coverage or advertising placements in planning for future programs.

Where to Find Help

For many gardens, marketing is folded into other responsibilities, including membership, volunteer management, interpretation, visitor programs, or even the directorship. Finding the time, resources, and expertise to develop a marketing plan can be challenging. Professional assistance from outside organizations and consultants that are willing to help on a pro bono or reduced-fee basis can make the planning process easier.

The Scott Arboretum of Swarthmore College found help through the American Association of Museum's Museum Assessment Program (MAP). The Arboretum completed a public dimension assessment in 2009 that took marketing off the Arboretum's back burner and helped move it forward. The MAP consultants guided them through designing and conducting simple audience research on the local community and Arboretum members. A marketing professor at a state university assisted with more sophisticated surveys and analyses. As a result, the Arboretum identified steps staff can take in the near future, such as creating a sign for the nearby train station and staffing the

---

COMMUNITY RESOURCES

- Associations for communications and marketing professionals
- Chambers of commerce
- Colleges and universities with business, marketing, and tourism programs
- Local, county, and state tourism bureaus
- Peer institutions
- Regional cultural alliances
- RSVP (part of the Corporation for National and Community Service)

Arboretum office on weekends when visitation is highest. The MAP study also highlighted important strategies to consider, such as including paid advertising in public programming plans.

Many excellent community resources are available to public gardens that want to develop marketing plans and conduct audience research. These same resources may offer networking opportunities and collaborative marketing ventures.

Media Relations

Cultivating strong relationships with the media is a powerful marketing strategy. The process of defining garden audiences for marketing plans will in turn help target an appropriate mix of websites, television, radio, newspapers, magazines, and other media outlets.

An up-to-date media database that can be easily sorted according to target audience, distribution range, and information needs is very important. Media outlets should be periodically surveyed to find out if they even want materials, and if so, the appropriate contact, lead time, and preferred format for communications and images. While most communications are electronic, gardens should still keep up-to-date records of postal addresses for mailing tangible materials.

Hospitality is an easy and effective way to cultivate media relationships. Events that bring media on-site give them an opportunity to personally engage with staff and the garden. At Longwood Gardens, media previews of new exhibitions, garden openings, and other events welcome journalists with light refreshments, customized tours, and diverse opportunities for photos, video footage, and interviews. Longwood staff members accommodate special requests from the media with "I'm so glad you asked" willingness that ultimately helps Longwood generate consistently strong media coverage.

Staff and volunteers are excellent sources of interesting stories and personable subjects for media interviews. Firsthand stories told by the people who actually tend the vegetable garden, install the holiday light display, or conduct the plant research resonate with an authenticity that a public relations administrator can't duplicate. Practical tips and guidance on how to be an effective spokesperson are important for staff members who aren't accustomed to it. The garden's primary media liaison may benefit from formal training with an outside consultant and can then serve as the teacher for other staff. At the Chicago Botanic Garden, media training for staff contributed to the success of a 3½-minute segment on its Japanese Garden that aired on a national news network and on the network's website (Markgraf 2002).

Media tracking services range from free Google alerts to pay-for-service companies that provide reports and copies of print, broadcast, and online news coverage that result from the garden's media outreach efforts.

Being prepared to seize a news-generating moment on short notice is an important part of media relations. When the Brooklyn Botanic Garden's (BBG) titan arum, Baby, began exhibiting signs that it was getting ready to bloom and perfume the air with its notorious scent, the garden quickly pulled a team together to mark what would be a major plant event: the first titan arum to bloom in New York City in more than sixty-seven years. This spontaneous phenomenon gave the garden an opportunity to position BBG as an exciting, fun place to learn about plants.

A task force was established with representatives from horticulture, security, maintenance, education, the gift shop, visitor services, and communications. The titan arum was moved to a display area in the Bonsai Museum so that visitors could easily view the large plant. A video camera was set up so that online audiences could watch Baby's progress 24/7. Security was briefed, and extra guards were called in for the anticipated increase in visitors.

Visitor services and education quickly produced informative signage about the plant and its family. Education arranged for its Garden Apprentice Program students to staff the education plant carts near key areas of the visitor queue. The first blog at BBG was produced to provide readers with behind-the-scenes insights into Baby's bloom—and the anticipated stinky smell.

Communications conveyed to the media that BBG had exciting, once-in-a-generation news that was very visual—a big plant growing inches a day. A media advisory was written and disseminated to all relevant media, and calls to key journalists alerted them that Baby's bloom—and the accompanying odor—was imminent. The upsurge in media coverage was evident by Friday: the phones were ringing off the hook. Key spokespeople, including the president, director of horticulture, and director of plant propagation, provided telephone and on-site interviews to a steady stream of journalists. By Saturday and Sunday there was major news coverage in national and international news organizations in addition to Brooklyn media.

The Garden's visitation was enormous, especially when compared to a normal hot August weekend. Many visitors came to the Garden for the first time. BBG continued to enjoy a large visitor audience and sustained media coverage throughout the following week.

FORMATTING MEDIA COMMUNICATIONS

Technology keeps changing the methods for communicating with the media, but the content still follows traditional formats, with a digital twist.

- **Calendar listing:** brief listing of ongoing programs, seasonal displays, and special events

- **News release:** more detailed information that expands on displays, events, and unusual stories, such as the flowering of a rare plant or the opening of a new garden

- **Media advisor:** brief notice of an interesting event that is occurring with short notice or as a quick reminder of the beautiful scenery at the garden during a display

- **Photographs and videos:** a picture is worth a thousand words, especially for journalists without time to shoot it themselves

- **Fact sheet:** short, interesting facts and figures about the garden, such as the establishment year, history, governing authority, acreage, collections, or volunteer statistics

- **Website media room:** a comprehensive online source for press releases, images, and other media materials

Digital Marketing and Social Networking

Websites are now standard in garden marketing portfolios and often serve as the pivot point for garden communications. A website requires frequent maintenance to be an effective marketing tool. If a garden's website is maintained by an outside firm, the garden should make sure staff or volunteers are trained to update time-sensitive information rather than having to wait for someone else to do it. A garden risks losing audiences and credibility if its website isn't current.

E-newsletters are augmenting or replacing paper versions at many gardens. Gardens use e-newsletters to deliver short, timely messages and reminders about upcoming activities and events. The subject line is critical to prompting people to open the e-newsletter. When the Gardens of Spring Creek started an e-newsletter, class attendance and event participation increased by almost 20 percent. When the Botanical Garden of the Ozarks distributes its e-newsletter, online ticket purchases and membership renewals spike and content from the newsletter appears in local newspapers (King and Provaznik 2009).

Online social media are still a relatively new marketing forum for public gardens, but gardens are rapidly embracing

John Sallot, Desert Botanical Garden Marketing Manager

A recent week at the Desert Botanical Garden (DBG) was a turning point in our participation in social media. On Wednesday night of that week, the Garden hosted Yelp in Bloom, a special event to recognize 900 active Yelp.com online reviewers. For many it was their first time visiting the Garden since grade school days, and for quite a few it was their first time ever.

At the event, we were able to promote our mission to this group, as well as our robust spring season of exhibits, activities, and events, including Spiked! Thursdays at DBG, a cocktail hour that moves to a new location in the Garden each week and features bands, DJs, and food. It was a terrific opportunity to communicate with this audience.

The next evening at Spiked!, I received a text on my phone from the person who monitors social media on our behalf telling us that a Yelp in Bloom attendee was at Spiked!, unhappy, and tweeting (posting a comment to Twitter) about it. The garden's website had stated that there would be a vegetarian option—and there wasn't. I quickly found the event coordinator, and we soon discovered that the caterer had left out that option without informing the Garden. We communicated back to the guest, who was still at Spiked!, indicating that we needed some time to fully investigate, and that we would get back to him the following day. We also asked if we could take the conversation offline—the guest had 1,500 followers on Twitter and we did not want this to get out of hand. He agreed.

The next morning, our event coordinator communicated directly with the guest via email, offered our apologies, an explanation, and tickets to a future Spiked! or a complete refund. The guest was happy with our response and let his followers know on Twitter.

The experience was a great opportunity for us to see social media in action. If we had not been monitoring the social media sites, we never would have been able to respond to a complaint that was as valid as one we might have received in person, by letter, via email, or on the phone. And this complaint came with an audience of 1,500 followers. While the person was at our event, somewhere in our vicinity, we never saw or spoke to him. This all occurred through the Internet.

We would never suggest that it is necessary to monitor social media sites 24/7, but when you are hosting an event or activity that might have people involved in social media, you should make sure that someone is monitoring. It's not necessary to respond immediately, but definitely do so within the next twenty-four hours.

---

online networking because the public expects it, and it works. Gardens should do a thorough analysis of social media under consideration and consult with social media specialists and peer institutions. They should also make sure that new components and concepts created for social media can be used for other purposes if that forum should become obsolete.

Crisis Communications

All public gardens should have a crisis communications plan to help them make the best decisions when faced with catastrophes such as hurricanes, tornadoes, fires, or accidents. Even capital projects bring with them the potential for a crisis.

Sabina Howell Carr, director of marketing, Atlanta Botanical Garden, offers five basic tips for gardens in a crisis situation:

- Stay calm.

- Hire professional crisis counselors.

- Stick to your message and refer inquiries to the appropriate parties.

- Don't assume anything; make sure staff know the correct protocols for handling media.

- Be transparent in communicating with the public, stakeholders, and the media.

The Morton Arboretum assigns specific crisis communications responsibilities to key staff.

- Crisis response message creation is handled by the vice president of marketing, the public relations manager, the security supervisor, and possibly the director of visitor programs. If necessary, it would also include the president and CEO.

- The spokesperson is the public relations manager or president and CEO, as appropriate.

- Serving as media liaison (responding to and coordinating responses to media inquiries) are the public relations manager and public relations coordinator.

- Emergency personnel liaison duties, involving interacting with emergency personnel, fall to the security supervisor.

- The operations/program liaison, who manages operational and program scheduling and interruptions, is the director of visitor programs.

- The human resources liaison, who manages potential staff support responses such as provision of counseling, is the director of human resources.

Sabina Howell Carr, Director of Marketing, Atlanta Botanical Garden

On the morning of December 19, 2008, the Atlanta Botanical Garden was expecting several reporters to film and photograph the latest construction phase of a new attraction. The Canopy Walk, designed to soar 40 feet above a woodland garden, was a major part of a multimillion-dollar expansion.

Then tragedy struck. As construction workers began to pour concrete onto the walkway, the structure collapsed. Mary Pat Matheson, the Garden's executive director, and her communications team, Sabina Carr and Danny Flanders, were among the first on the scene. Emergency crews soon confirmed that one construction worker was dead and seventeen injured.

Carr and her team immediately began to assess the situation. "It was all about staying calm," said Carr. "We had to start planning for the next minute, the next ten minutes, and the next hour." The Garden's leaders coordinated duties and the flow of information among the various stakeholders. Matheson gave a short statement to the press in time for noon newscasts.

The Garden's executive team decided to engage Edelman Public Relations, a communications firm well known for its crisis management practice. "Our team is not specifically trained in crisis communications," Carr said. "We always knew we would call in a firm if something serious happened."

Edelman's experts counseled them to refer media questions about injuries to emergency responders and let the construction company answer inquiries about the accident. That strategy allowed the Garden to focus on crafting messages that not only would give the public information but also protect the garden's reputation. "We decided to be the voice of reason and sympathy," said Flanders. "We reiterated that the Garden is a place of healing, not tragedy."

Garden executives learned an invaluable lesson about crisis management: never assume anything, because everyone reacts differently. Carr and Flanders made sure that staff who answered phones were specifically instructed to log media inquiries in detail: reporter's name, news organization, deadlines. The instinct of some staffers was to tell reporters that no information was available and simply hang up—a well-intentioned but potentially damaging response.

As the day progressed, Garden leaders realized news coverage would extend far beyond Atlanta. The communications team decided to be proactive and emailed Garden leaders across the country, explaining what had happened.

Within twenty-four hours, the team also began to think about the long-term impact of the accident. How much of its marketing plan would change? How would it reposition and communicate the new attractions? How would the Garden express its sympathy to the workers' families?

The Garden forged strong partnerships with other players, including the lead construction company, and announced a memorial fund. The communications team also began planning how to communicate the rebuilding of the walk, deciding to be open and transparent with stakeholders and the media.

Summary

Marketing communicates a public garden's potential value to individual lives. Some institutions refer to this work as public relations or communications, while others call it marketing or promotion, but the goal is the same: to nurture community engagement and support. Looking at the garden's mission from the public's perspective is critical to creating a sustainable brand and developing core messages for the garden.

The garden's marketing portfolio communicates what the garden does and why it is important to the public. It presents the look and language of the garden, making an impression even when people can't experience the garden in person. Marketing materials need to be consistent, accurate and appealing to be effective. Format, content, distribution, graphic style, and verbal style should be routinely evaluated.

Formal marketing plans greatly contribute to a public garden's success. Analyzing the garden, its environments, and its audiences provides information needed to develop realistic and specific goals and strategies. Organized schedules and budgets make it easier to keep track of deadlines, objectives, costs, and responsibilities. Media relations and social networking are powerful and economical marketing strategies for all public gardens. Evaluation of marketing projects provides information useful for the next year or initiative.

Developing a crisis communications plan before an emergency occurs allows public gardens to calmly identify and assess their responsibilities, procedures, and policies when faced with a crisis.

Annotated Resources

American Marketing Association (www.marketingpower.com). A useful source of information about marketing terms, trends, and current issues.

Andreasen, A., and P. Kotler. 1995. *Strategic marketing for nonprofit organizations.* Upper Saddle River, N.J.: Prentice Hall. A practical examination of marketing in nonprofit organizations that encompasses the entire marketing process, including strategic evaluations, positioning, and market targeting.

Colbert, F., S. Bilodeau, J. Brunet, J. Nantel, and J. D. Rich. 2007. *Marketing culture and the arts*, 3rd ed. Montreal: Presses HEC. Takes traditional marketing concepts and applies them to the special cases of culture and the arts.

Convince and Convert (www.convinceandconvert.com/jason-baer). Social media strategy consultant Jay Baer, founder of Convince & Convert, provides social media consulting and training to leading companies and public relations firms and writes the Convince and Convert blog.

Durham, S. 2010. *Brandraising: How nonprofits raise visibility and money through smart communications.* San Francisco: Jossey-Bass.

Getting Attention (www.gettingattention.org). The focus of this e-newsletter is assisting nonprofits to develop marketing tools and strategies that will enable them to thrive.

Holland, D. K. 2006. *Branding for nonprofits: Developing identity with integrity.* New York: Allworth Press. A useful guide to the processes, tools, and thinking needed to brand or to rebrand, with case studies of nonprofits that have successfully created branding opportunities.

International Association of Business Communicators (www.iabc.com). Provides a professional network of more than 15,500 business communication professionals in more than 80 countries.

Kotler, N., and P. Kotler. 2008. *Museum marketing and strategy: Designing missions, building audiences, generating revenue and resources.* San Francisco: Jossey-Bass. Classic resource on museum marketing and strategy. It provides a proven framework for examining marketing and strategic goals in relation to a museum's mission, resources, opportunities, and challenges.

Pew Research Center (http://people-press.org). A nonpartisan "fact tank" that provides information on the issues, attitudes, and trends shaping America and the world. Current survey results are made available free of charge on its website.

CHAPTER 20

Collections Management

DAVID C. MICHENER

Introduction

Like other museums, public gardens are focused on collections and the management of those collections. While gardens can include a range of collections including works of art, herbarium specimens, and books, it is the living collections that are the vibrant heart of every public garden. Beyond their beauty and scientific value, these collections are valued because they inspire diverse audiences to enjoy, reflect, engage, and learn.

As living collections grow in size and scope, so too do the volume and detail of information related to them. It is the responsibility of those entrusted with the management of those collections to collect, track, evaluate, and distill that information so that it is useful to garden staff and a wide range of visitors. This work often leads to the creation of paper and digital lists, maps, Web pages, and special reports tailored to the user's needs. These needs may range from a visitor's questions about specific plants to a researcher's need for collection documentation. When those tasks also include the planning and evaluation of the collection's relevancy and quality, collections management is called curation.

The collections curator is responsible for overall management of the collections. This includes making decisions (often in consultation with horticulturists, researchers, educators, or landscape designers) about which plants will be added to the accessioned collections, when particular specimens need to be deaccessioned, how plant records will be managed, and what nomenclatural sources will be used. The plant recorder responds to decisions made by the curator, recording all new accessions and deaccessions and, in some cases, determining the correct nomenclature for accessioned taxa. They are often also responsible for establishing the GIS coordinates for each accession in the collections, although in larger gardens this may fall to a separate GIS manager.

There is no one best or correct method to manage living collections; instead, there are current best practices. Each institution's approach to collections management is based on its mission and situation, especially the collections' purposes and scope. This chapter examines major issues involved in the management of plant collections and the information about those collections. Hohn (2008) presents a valuable consideration of botanical garden collections management policies and practices; *The Darwin Technical Manual* (Leadlay and Greene 1998) is especially useful for conservation-focused gardens. Readers unfamiliar with the museum context out of which many protocols originated should explore this chapter's annotated resources as well as the resources available from the American Association of Museums, the American Public Gardens Association, and Botanic Gardens Conservation International.

What Are Living Collections?

In order to manage collections, they have to be defined. In the broadest sense, living collections are all the plants and landscapes that have records. Depending on the type of collection, those records may be specific to individual plants or related to specific landscapes. Having appropriate documentation of the plants and their management is a distinguishing element of all public gardens, whether they are botanical gardens, arboreta, historical landscapes, research collections, or natural areas. The plants may be in traditional collections, as is the case of the camellia collection at Descanso Gardens; in naturalistic gardens, similar to those at the Garden in the Woods (Lowe 1995); or natural areas such as the Crosby Arboretum.

Accession: an individual or group of identical-parentage plants (single taxon) from one source at the same time; assigned a code or number for tracking purposes.

Acquisition: a plant or propagule that has been brought to the garden to be accessioned and cataloged.

Aesthetics: a sense of design and style; frequently used to imply harmonious integration of grace and beauty.

Catalog: a list of accessions with additional information, traditionally done on paper but now almost entirely supplanted by computerized databases. It can also refer to creating such files and adding the information in paper or digital form.

Collection: a set of plants assembled for a purpose. An accession can belong to multiple collections at the same time.

Conservation: for plant conservation, refers to actions that preserve a population and ultimately a species. For historic specimens and key features of a garden, refers to actions that stabilize an individual object or historic element for the indefinite future.

Curation: the activities that involve the planning and management of collections in a professional and ethical manner.

Database: the information in digital tables that are an institution's records; quite distinct from the software that interacts with the data, such as Access or BG-BASE.

Design: the physical layout of living and nonliving objects in a garden or landscape. A garden's design history is partially recorded in and often deduced from the collection records and maps.

Display: the arrangement of plants in an area. Displays can be temporary (discarded when done), rotating (potted and reused after storage/reinvigoration), or planted/permanent.

Ethics: the set of values guiding decisions. As related to this chapter, usually centered on acquisition and disposal issues where the cash value or legal restrictions create the potential for conflict of interest among staff with responsibilities to acquire and dispose.

Gap: a conceptual break in a collection, as a missing set of years in a historic cultivar collection, or missing species where the collection is taxonomic.

Invasive: a term applied to introduced plants that escape and thrive outside their original geographic range.

Inventory: a physical or digital list of plants and/or accessions present in an area on a date; also, the action of making such lists. Additional information about specific accessions as condition and size is often recorded at this time.

Label: a sign that identifies a plant for the public. Additional information may be present, but without a plant name, it is an interpretive sign. Small tags with inventory numbers and related information are specialized labels.

Map: a plan showing selected characteristics, such as accession for an inventory or site features for field confirmation; now usually an output from geospatial databases.

Natural area: an area managed as an ecological system, usually implying presettlement vegetation in North America. Natural areas may be intact fragments of once-widespread vegetation types, reclaimed or restored disturbed sites, or combinations that include monitored individuals and/or populations.

Nomenclature: the internationally honored rules and systems of creating technical names so they are consistent across time and cultures.

Ownership: a legal status authorizing control. In living collections the plant records document ownership of the plants by purchase, gift, or other means.

Plant records: suite of collection policies, databases, maps, and related files that document the institution's living collections.

Policy: written guidelines setting out objectives and procedures to meet those objectives. Collection policy and invasive plant policy are two common examples.

Provenance: the original source; used both as a specific location (wild population vs. nursery grown) and a concept (as wild-collected vs. cultivated stock).

Taxon (pl., *taxa*): a group of plants that form a named unit, including all their components. Genus and species are familiar taxonomic ranks.

In addition, seed, pollen, and/or plant tissue cultures such as the endangered species maintained at the University of Hawaii's Harold L. Lyon Arboretum are all part of the living collections. Each collection type has fundamentally similar information and management needs. In this chapter, the traditional collection is presented so that the others can be seen as variants.

Collections Are Objects Gathered for a Purpose

This functional definition is deeply embedded in museum and library culture, and living collections are no exception. In this case, plants are the objects that are recorded, monitored, and evaluated. One plant is not always one object. A clone

Figure 20-1: The peony collection at the University of Michigan was opened in 1927 to hold nearly 400 pairs of peony cultivars. The original comparative purpose has become historical cultivar conservation as part of the North American Plant Collections Consortium, with more than forty American, Canadian, and European breeders represented.

Matthaei Botanical Gardens and Nichols Arboretum

Collection Types

Although each public garden defines its collections according to its mission and traditions, there are broad categories of living collections across institutions, which can be generalized as thematic, taxonomic, conservation and reference, recurrent display, trial, and research. Any accession can belong to multiple collections as long as it meets each collection's criteria.

- **Thematic collections** demonstrate an ongoing concept based in human culture, geography (such as continental or biome/regional), or horticultural/ecological needs (perennials, wetland plants, epiphytes). Human culture is wide-ranging and can embrace historical periods and design styles such as Victorian gardens, cultural meaning (e.g., plants featured in Shakespeare's works), and other human constructs.

- **Taxonomic collections** organize the specimens into evolutionary groups of closest kin. Familiar examples are collections by plant family or genus (for example, palms).

- **Conservation and reference collections** hold a diverse set of (often endangered) plants in trust for future generations. These collections can be of either wild provenance or historical cultivars.

- **Recurrent displays** have a fleeting seasonality and/or purpose. Common examples are displays of orchids, bromeliads, nonhardy bulbs, and bonsai/*penjing*.

- **Trial collections** are for evaluating plants under observation. Familiar examples include the All-America Rose Selections trial gardens and the National Crabapple Evaluation program.

- **Research collections** are specialized inquiry and reference tools of potentially great value. Traditionally, these were assembled by researchers with no planning for their fate after the project's completion, but increasingly, all collections with adequate records are deemed research-worthy.

in a conservation collection can be many plants, but it still represents only one genetic individual (just as duplicate books do not add diversity to a library). By contrast, some mass plantings of ornamental materials may be treated as one object, even though each is genetically distinct. An additional subtlety is that unlike typical museum objects, living collections ultimately die. The record system has to keep pace with relevant information during the plant's life and close with physical death, including if it is cloned to continue living in another location.

Gathering, in terms of living collections, refers to how the plant was procured for the institution. Procurement includes exchange, propagation, purchase, plant collecting, and exploration. This information is important since plants from wild populations have conservation value, unlike nursery-grown plants of the same name. Likewise, cultivated plants from nurseries that introduced particular cultivars have more reference value than plants from the open trade. The purpose of a collection is the reason the specific collection is needed to serve the institution's mission. Examples of purpose include foci on aesthetics, cultural identity, ecological diversity, ornamental value, plant geography, historical period, and native species.

Accessions Are the Building Blocks

Permanent collections almost always consist of accessioned plants. Accessioning a plant is a critical threshold in collection management. Accessioning differentiates one plant from other past, current, or future individuals and sets the stage for unique records to be created and linked to the plant for years to come. The complexity of each accession's record, beyond

Figure 20-2: The significant conifer collection at the Dawes Arboretum allows the genera to be mixed. Here pines and spruces provide the framework specimens that highlight other genera.

Photo courtesy of the Dawes Arboretum

basic identity, source, and location, depends on the standards of the collection category. Accessioned plants are given a code, typically a number, so that the object on the grounds and the records stored in digital and paper files can be linked. An important step to stabilize this link is to affix a tag, often metal, to the plant with its name and accession code.

Commonly encountered nonaccessioned collections tend to be either temporary materials or naturalistic collections and natural areas where all individuals are not tracked. Examples of temporary collections are trial and seasonal displays where taxon-based information about identity, source, and condition is captured for review and performance evaluation. Here the function is ongoing, but the materials are fleeting—pragmatically, the meaningful records don't require

Figure 20-3: Naturalistic design of part of the New England Wild Flower Society creates a visual context as well as ecologically and horticulturally appropriate microsites for the regional flora conserved here.

© New England Wild Flower Society/Steven Ziglar

Figure 20-4: *Spigelia marilandica* is one of the regionally significant species conserved and displayed.

© New England Wild Flower Society/Steven Ziglar

Figure 20-5: Orchids are typically displayed when in flower; displays show only a small fraction of the entire collection. The orchid display at the U.S. Botanic Garden is integrated into a verdant staging with rocks and ferns, thus hiding the pots.

U.S. Botanic Garden

accessioning for long-term retrieval. In naturalistic and natural areas, a few specific individuals may be accessioned for data capture and to serve as markers for all others of that taxon in the area. Furthermore, plants in the nursery/propagation system may be unaccessioned if the institution assigns accession numbers only once plants have survived to establishment size. In this case, temporary labeling and records maintain the basic information until the plants are accessioned.

Collections, Areas, and Displays

Areas, collections, and displays are sometimes confused with each other, but they are distinct for management purposes.

Public gardens present the visitor with a visually rich landscape—a tapestry of named spaces, each with its own identity. In museums and gardens, areas are essential to organize space, to display materials for the mission's purposes, to choreograph the visitor experience, and to assign staff responsibilities. However, such spaces do not define the collections; the definition refers to the institution's purpose in gathering, not where specimens are currently planted. Consequently, areas are useful but not complete organizing concepts in collection management. For example, at the San Diego Botanical Garden, the Palm Canyon presents many magnificent palm specimens, but not all of the specimens in the institution's palm collection are in this location. This situation is the norm in most gardens due to soils, design intent, history, and other circumstances. In collections management, it is important to know the location of all the objects of a particular type and manage them as parts of a single collection.

Display quality is important in museum galleries and garden areas. Unlike most works of art, plants have such strong seasonal changes that many public audiences view them only when they are in flower. Thus, permanently planted collections change in display value through the year, but they can't be moved or easily modified. The collection is present whether it is in display mode or not.

Figure 20-6: Crabapple cultivars at the Seacrest Arboretum are arranged to promote comparative examination as well as provide a stunning floral display. The fruit display is equally engaging and informative.

Seacrest Arboretum, Ohio State University

Displays of long-lived portable units, such as bonsai or orchids in pots, are featured in public areas when they are in peak viewing condition. Often the display is staged in one area but individuals are rotated in and out to keep the entire display in peak condition. In these cases it is clear that the collection is larger than the current display or area.

Yet another distinction is the temporary display. Typical examples are forced extravaganzas of annuals, bulbs, or poinsettias. These materials are ephemeral, and since they aren't retained, they are often excluded from accessioning. In all the above examples, the display and the collection are different entities.

Foundations of Successful Collections

Why are some gardens so well-known for their living collections regardless of collection type, institutional size, or geographic location? Excellent collections are exemplars for simultaneously upholding three components: quality, depth, and aesthetics. Standards are set for these three criteria, and the collections developed and managed to attain them.

Dosmann (2006) articulates the critical role of intrinsic quality standards, not size or numbers, for building living collections.

- **Quality** addresses the fit with the purpose of the specific collection. This may include source documentation, such as wild genotypes or acquisition of cultivars from the originator or a known reference set. Identification by recognized experts and the clarity and completeness of relevant records are also important.

- **Depth** is the degree of completeness for the collection's theme. If the theme is taxonomic (as a genus), depth is the percentage of what can be grown in the climate. If it is historical or cultural, depth is the percentage of the available pool of plants that potentially fit the specific theme. Depth also includes the competence of the material; for example, if the theme requires flowers, nonblooming specimens don't provide depth.

- **Aesthetics** embraces the horticultural care and condition of the individual plants as well as their arrangement in a visually pleasing manner that encourages visitor engagement.

CASE STUDY: CHICAGO BOTANIC GARDEN

The Chicago Botanic Garden has built internationally recognized living collections that carry out the institution's mission to promote the enjoyment, understanding, and conservation of plants and the natural world. Conceptually, living collections are one of four mission components; the other three are education, research/conservation, and public service. To build meaningful collections, the institution established a distinctive planning perspective to concurrently reinforce and increase collections, education, and research integration. This led to significant collection planning.

The Garden's collections development plan conceives of the living collections in two groups: specialized and general. There is a shared set of roles, expectations, and resource prioritization. Specific directives are established, and each collection has its own criteria for selecting taxa.

- **Specialized collections** are mission critical, destined to become nationally significant; the Garden is to be an authority in these collection types. These create collection depth, and there are now seventeen such collections.

- **General collections** are for beauty, fulfill a landscape need, and support classes. These create collection breadth.

  This approach focuses the institution's efforts on the materials with the highest significance and avoids "collection creep" of unplanned acquisitions simply because they were available, momentarily attractive, or offered.

  The collection criteria cover a range of program issues; the Garden prefers materials that meet as many criteria as possible.

The material must be useful to constituents from visitors to staff. Note that general collections are primarily driven by visitor need, whereas the specialized collections provide depth for research and education; within this envelope, more demanding criteria come into play.

- **Institutional support** includes building and land facilities, equipment capacity, financial resources, and the necessary curatorial staff resources to acquire, develop, study, and disseminate the findings associated with a plant group.

- **Value to the mission** has to span opportunities for research and add value in terms of conservation, natural areas management, or advancement and dissemination of knowledge related to the group.

- **Cultural appropriateness** is the fit of the plant with the soil and weather conditions of the Midwest.

- **Landscape value** is assessed from a holistic perspective and includes season-long aesthetic interest, varying landscape conditions, growth form, and commercial availability.

Several key lessons can be learned from the Chicago Botanical Garden's approach to collections development. The main ones are the value of coordinated planning from the Garden's inception; investing in staff training to work with, manage, share, and understand the collections; and thorough collection documentation. A critical element is the development and maintenance of a culture of individual and shared responsibility.

Attaining excellence requires standards and quantifiable goals. Following an intense study of leading gardens around the world, the Chicago Botanic Garden (CBG) staff (Gates 2006) identified twelve characteristics of exemplary living plant collections. Every leading institution has its set of characteristics, though few have codified them as clearly as CBG, where all these criteria are achieved, not just selected ones.

1. **Collections policy and development plans:** based on a unified vision with clear objectives

2. **High diversity:** breadth in taxa and the germplasm represented

3. **Depth of specialization:** including building collection networks with other institutions to end duplicated efforts

4. **Thorough record keeping:** excellent documentation for research and education, not just accession and maintenance records

5. **Care and maintenance:** thriving, nurtured collections

6. **Verification:** ongoing assessment to ensure material is accurately named and authenticated

7. **Original source materials:** provenance from a known wild population or the introducing nursery or other authenticated source

8. **Conservation value:** individual plants as well as plant communities are managed for the ecological benefits

9. **Expert staff:** knowledge acquired is proprietary and disseminated as such

10. **Public access:** user-friendly collections with broad sharing of knowledge from professional staff

11. **Local or international plant exploration:** for the acquisition of targeted taxa

12. **Relevance:** information, expertise, and collections to meet the needs of diverse audiences over time

Collections Policy

The purpose of a collections policy is to guide collection development and assessment so that the collections support the garden's mission and its programs. The policy usually establishes a management process that indicates who is involved in decision making and subsequent management. A collections policy often has these specific elements:

• Collections mission

• Collections scope, including invasives policy

• Acquisition and documentation standards

• Deaccession/disposal standards

• Access, intellectual rights, ethics

Every garden customizes these and additional elements to fit the institution's particular context and history. In addition, other types of reports and policies may be necessary for specific situations, such as how donor or memorialized trees and objects are handled, how reviews are conducted, or how artworks are integrated into gardens and landscapes.

Collections Mission

The living collection needs to have an articulated mission that states how it specifically supports the institution. This is typically where important collections are identified, standards of documentation are enumerated, and the expected audiences for whom the collections are managed are defined. These points all give direction to collection development. For example, the institutional mission may speak of conservation, and the collection mission identifies what is meant by that, such as plant conservation programs related to germplasm conservation, reintroduction work in this climate, plantings of species of regional conservation concern, or a combination of these elements.

Collections Scope and Invasives Policy

Once the collection mission sets the priorities, the collection scope helps resolve how deep the various collections should be and their need to draw on resources. In the Chicago Botanic Garden case study, this is directly addressed with the division into collection kind—specialty and general. Other gardens give all collections equal priority. The drawback of this approach is that it presumes all collections have equal rights to resources when they are tight, whereas in reality some collections are more critical than others. Regardless of the approach, the institution needs to identify the intended scope of each collection to answer the question, "What is enough and when are we done?"

As an example, if *Rosa* is a priority, this section states if the target is species, cultivars, or a mix. Given the vast number of taxa, the scope indicates what physical or conceptual features are desired, such as sections of a genus, diverse morphology, particular fruiting characteristics, particular breeders and their work, or sheer beauty and ease of culture for the region. Clearly, each collection can't be all things to all people.

Figure 20-7: Invasive buckthorns (*Rhamnus*), honeysuckles (*Lonicera*), and Norway maples (*Acer platanoides*) were added to the collections of the Nichols Arboretum early in the twentieth century. All have become invasive pests requiring eradication—here with a student crew.

Matthaei Botanical Gardens and Nichols Arboretum

Invasive species are an increasingly significant ecological problem, and gardens are historically leading sources of and dispersal institutions for invasive plants. This historical reality means gardens have to be vigilant both to keep new invasives out of their collections and to deal with those already present. This is a fundamentally a profound ethical issue since institutions must deliver public goods and services. Jefferson, Havens, and Ault (2004) present a current best-practices approach in considering potential invasives in gardens.

An invasive species policy should include the points in the Codes of Conduct of the St. Louis Declaration (see Chapter 22). For new plants (those of unknown invasiveness), the policy should indicate how the institution would monitor and evaluate new acquisitions.

Acquisition and Documentation Standards

It is important for the policy to state that plants have to be acquired legally, ethically, and in accordance with the institution's additional documentation standards. The policy should state who procures or accepts plants on the institution's behalf. The record system's capture of plant name, provenance, type of material acquired, and date of acquisition are a logical application of decisions listed here and are important in establishing legal ownership of the accessions in the collection.

Conservation and reference collections need detailed information on source and plant characteristics; the latter may only be evident after the plant has grown for some time, but the information needs to be captured. Certain thematic collections may require records of floral or foliage attributes and geographic origin. Historical cultivar collection may require post-planting information such as actual flower form, color markings, fragrance, and bloom period compared to others in the genus. The critical element is to reduce the documentation standards to the smallest number of elements so that they are recorded; long lists of interesting attributes may only dilute the work effort.

Deaccession and Disposal Standards

Other than for natural causes such as death and disease, removal requires a decision. The policy needs to dictate the criteria for such decisions. Accessions should be removed whenever the material fails to meet acquisition standards, fails to meet aesthetic requirements, or no longer meets the collection's objectives. Other possibilities include the availability of superior material or the current material proving to be an invasive and undesirable. Records should identify the specific reason the material failed. Deaccessioned materials are usually composted, but some may be traded, sold, or gifted. The policy should state what these conditions are and who makes the decisions. To avoid a conflict of interest, the recipient cannot be involved in the decision to remove a plant.

Ethics, Intellectual Rights, and Access

Gardens are physically open to the public, but that does not mean that all collections must be publicly accessible, all complete records must be available, or all requests for study materials must be met. The driving concern for this policy is meeting current ethical standards, beginning with acquisition. For conservation work, a foundation is the Convention on Biological Diversity (see Chapter 22). There are strong ethical issues (Galbraith 1998), especially where commercialization, such as new releases, plant products, and extractions (including DNA), is involved. Most U.S. gardens operate on the premise that materials are completely accessible in concept, with intellectual rights belonging to the organization. In order to protect the collections, access is often restricted based on plant rarity, difficulty of replacement, and intellectual issues. The policy should outline the institution's rationale for access restrictions.

Record Systems

The record system developed by collections management becomes the institution's working memory, a vital and evolving resource built by each generation and passed on to the next. This institutional memory is the basis for strategic decisions, and once transferred to the archives, it is a legacy that far outlives any project, staff member, or team.

Two issues are central to good management: first, defining what is required versus what is optional information for the system to track, and second, identifying what software system holds the information within the resources of the institution. It is critical that all required information be present and complete, and that the records for optional information be accessible. These core data give the collections its conceptual value. The software platform should be one that works for the institution and can meet evolving needs.

Required Information

Based on the acquisition standards, every plant has core information that should be completely tracked. Typically this includes:

Name, scientific and common
Plant family
Source type
Source
Type of material received

Number of materials received
Date received
Accession number
Accession condition with date
Accession location with date
Deaccession reason
Deaccession date

This information is effectively stored and managed in relational databases such as Microsoft Access or BG-BASE. The information splits into two categories: information that relates to the name and information that relates to the particular accession. This distinction is important because information that is known from one set should not overwrite the other. For example, from the name of a plant, it can immediately be known where the plant species is native, its habit, and, if a flowering plant, the color of the petals. However, if in verifying an individual accession the flower color is not in conformance, the record for that individual has to be maintained and the anomaly flagged. In this case, the floral color is actually two separate fields: correct-to-name color and actual color. Such distinctions are important and the reason why records quickly become complex and require thoughtful development.

Consistent records are essential for evaluating collections over time. For specialized collection types, additional information is needed beyond the list above. Each type will have logically derived information that must be field-confirmed. For all types, routine maintenance and vigor records are typically developed. These are sometimes called condition records. Here a consistent suite of plant attributes including height, width, and overall health are captured to provide baseline data for meaningful collection stewardship.

Relational Databases

Historically, card files were used to track institutional plant records. Some institutions then migrated to accounting software such as Microsoft Excel. These cost-effective, time-efficient systems work as long as there are fewer than 500 accessions and the number of fields tracked is limited. Once the information becomes more complex, it is more efficient to migrate the information to a relational database.

The efficiency of relational databases is that much information need be entered only once. The next record sharing the same logical link is automatically populated with the related data. Likewise, updates are made once and applied everywhere. For example, if the genus *Penstemon* is moved from Scrophulariaceae to Plantaginaceae, this change is made once in a relational database rather than for every *Penstemon* record. Relational databases also link effectively with photographs, maps, and other digitized information such as reports and Web-based inquiries. These functions are all beyond the capabilities of card files or simple spreadsheets.

BG-BASE is widely used by nearly 200 institutions in thirty-two countries. It is a turnkey system, with screens, fields, and reports already created. There are layers of information that can be turned off or customized, as the institution requires. Ongoing technical support and ongoing upgrades are available. Mapping modules are available via BG-Map (AutoCAD) and ArcGIS (ESRI). Not all gardens use BG-BASE for a variety of reasons, such as its relatively high initial cost (which may be prohibitive for smaller institutions) or software purchase and support decisions (which may apply to governmental units).

Access is a Microsoft product offered as part of a commercially powerful software suite. Gardens that use Access typically develop their own system and reports from scratch based on their own information technology staff and skills. These institutions tend to be IT-savvy and desire the freedom to manipulate and link data among applications, including Google Earth.

Inventories

Inventories are critical review and assessment tools that underlie all strategic planning; they allow gaps to be identified and quantified. Inventories allow garden staff to determine if the accession is still present and in the same condition as last recorded. Inventories keep the records and the ground reality in compliance with each other. Routine inventories are typically done on a periodic cycle—every three, five, or seven years, depending on the type of materials under consideration. Pragmatically, inventories are usually structured primarily either by area (e.g., Mediterranean garden, aquatic garden) or by taxonomic level (e.g., all Sapindaceae or all *Quercus*). An advantage to working by area is the clear sense of completion as areas are reviewed. An advantage to working by taxon is any nomenclatural problems that surface can be dealt with at one time, which can be a great time saver. The migration to GIS-based information systems changes the software, reports, and skills used in inventorying, but not the inventory's roles and importance. However it is structured, there should be no unaccounted-for accessions (such as missing in reality or missing in the records) when inventories are complete.

Voucher herbarium specimens are a special tool to document accession identity, presence, and phenology for reference and research collections. Voucher specimens allow other experts to assess the accuracy of inventory identifications at any time of year, or even decades after the accession has died, since they are physical samples. Herbarium specimens are valuable when both the inventory accession numbers are recorded

INVENTORIES BY AREA

Inventories can be initially daunting: every accession has to be found. Approaching inventories by area has the advantage of breaking up the task into a series of feasible units while visually tracking the completion status. Marking maps, either hand-drawn or output from BG-Map or GIS software, greatly facilitates the work. Key steps include:

- Define the space to be inventoried, usually existing management zones. If so large as to be confusing, spaces can be subdivided, such as along path and bed edges.

- Generate the list of the accessions that should be present (usually a database report). Values should include the name and accession number for each accession. Organize the list either alphabetically or numerically for ease of use. Go to the site and find the plants with their accession tags. Check off the list for each accession found. If the accession tag number is not on the list, this becomes a mislocation problem to resolve with the complete records. Either the tag was moved or the plant was moved, and the records were not updated. Determine which and correct the records. These problems are usually resolved in a batch at the end of each area so as not to interrupt the concentration in fieldwork.

- Locate all plants that lack accession tags or can't be clearly linked to the records. Identify them to the extent possible.

- From the list of what should be present or what was in the last inventory, attempt to relink the current plant with its records, provided the plant size and planting data are reasonably congruent. If more than one accession of the same name is present, but according to the records they are from different sources, assign a new accession number with the source as "mixed" and indicate which old number(s) may be involved. The old numbers should be noted as inactive, with pointers to the new, mixed-source accession. In this case the inventory process updates the records so that future record views can detect that the collection quality has been degraded.

- If plants still remain unaccounted for, the staff for the area needs to be interviewed for the site history. Such plants are an indication of either a lapse in following protocols to properly update records or unauthorized additions by staff or public.

and the key features for identification are preserved. Elsik (1989) and Michener (1989) present standard protocols. New DNA-based protocols will likely emerge over time.

Plant Names in the Records

Plants in gardens should be property identified. In order to communicate with the broad range of visitors, gardens use a mixture of common and scientific plant names. Since the purpose of names is to enable precise and consistent communication, it may seem intuitive that common names are ideal. The reality is that common names may vary by geographic or cultural region. Furthermore, every plant has a botanical name, but only some have common names. Thus, common names are useful in relatively restricted contexts. For clarity and precision in identifying a plant, scientific names have no rival. Over the past 250 years, Western-trained scientists have devised systems of classifying and naming plants. Currently there are several international nomenclatural conventions, called codes, that guide the correct naming of wild and cultivated plants. Moore (2006) provides an overview of the issues.

Collection/Inventory Maps

Maps are visual presentations of records information and spatial information. Because maps have only three elements—points, lines, and shapes—the information to be displayed has to be distilled; it is this simplicity that makes maps clear communication tools. Add-ons such as color, pop-ups (when the maps are live on the Web), and animated graphics embellish the map's fundamental simplicity.

Maps are critical tools for living collections management once basic inventory needs have been met. Mapping should not be undertaken in lieu of an inventory process; it should either be concurrent with the inventory or follow it. Once a digital mapping program is successfully established, it quickly becomes useful to internal and external users beyond the original audience (Burke and Morgan 2009).

The key roles maps fulfill for collection managers are:

- **Clarity of accession location.** A point or shape on a scaled map is unambiguous in ways unattainable by words.

- **Ease of comprehension.** Maps present information spatially; text and tables are linear sets of information.

- **Maps can show change over time.** Text and tables have no such ability; instead, related charts have to be constructed.

- **Maps raise deeper questions** and inspire another way to think about the area or situation, such as patterns of where plants thrive or fail.

- **Maps connect to new audiences and allow the institution to meet new needs.** This raises the utility of the collections and institution and builds new relationships.

- **Maps are visually attractive.** People enjoy looking at and thinking about information that is presented in a beautiful manner.

NOMENCLATURE FOR NONSPECIALISTS

Collection managers and curators have to decide how up to date they wish to keep the names in their plant records and, implicitly, all outputs from those records, such as plant labels and queries from Web pages. Plant nomenclature can be quite nuanced, but a simple pragmatic approach is recommended for institutions that are not actively engaged in taxonomic research: just follow seasoned experts.

1. Plant families are basic units that are becoming better understood with molecular data. The family definitions at the Angiosperm Phylogeny Website are widely used as current best knowledge.

2. Use names from national agencies, such as the USDA's Plants Database and Germplasm Resources Information Network (GRIN).

3. Use the plant lists of the major research gardens, including publicly shared lists such as that of North American Plant Collections Consortium (NAPCC) and those used among BG-BASE members. Leading gardens, such as the Chicago Botanic Garden, New York Botanical Garden, Missouri Botanical Garden, Montreal Botanical Garden, Royal Botanical Gardens, and Royal Botanic Gardens, Kew, make a point of having up-to-date names. Visit Web-based resources such as Tropicos and eFloras.

4. For uncommon species and cultivars, explore the authoritative lists and links found through the websites of the Royal Horticultural Society and the International Cultivar Registration Authorities.

5. Avoid names from trade sources that can't also be found in the above sources. If the name can't be found, leave it as not further identified at the next rank up and note the received name as dubious.

Table 20-1: Integrating the plant records system into a geoinformatics environment is almost always incremental. The staff at the UC Davis Arboretum has worked with numerous institutions to develop this overview of the progression. To meet the demands for higher-level outcomes such as reports requires investment in the underlying resources and staffing needs.

	"Lite"	"Regular"	"Extra Strength"	"Double-Double Espresso"
Plant Records	Index Cards Notebooks	Excel Filemaker (flat-file) Access (flat-file)	Relational DB Tools: Access BG-Base Filemaker, etc.	High-end DB Tools: SQL – Oracle, etc.
Facility Base Map	Aerial Photograph – Usually donated	Aerial Photograph – Usually purchased	Digital basemap or CAD base map of facility (often already available from cities or campus)	Surveyed base maps of facility; extreme accuracy; may be already available
Data Capture Tools	Walking Around- Sharpie, Pens, Pencils Paper	"Head's Up Digitizing" – Draw 'on-screen' on transparent digital layer on office computer	Ruggedized PDAs (Trimble, etc) and GPS equipment for capture of points – lat /long, accurate to 6-12"; med-level workstation	"Total Station"- digital capture of surveyed points of plants and features; absolutely accurate; mid- to high-end workstation typically used
GIS – Analysis	Limited- Requires access to experienced staff	ArcView	ArcGIS or *open-source GIS*	ArcGIS or *open-source GIS*
"Reports" – Information Products	List, Binders Copy Machines Cannot publish on web	ArcView Reports - plant collection and facility inventories; web ready	Sophisticated GIS reports for daily management of workflow; web ready	Sophisticated GIS reports for daily management of work-flow; web ready
Usefulness for Facility Planning and Exhibit Development	Reports will be useful as baseline information for landscape architects and planners; costs for 'next step' will be borne by CAD drawings for each project	Relatively accurate data set will be useful for landscape architects and planners; may be able to easily import into their in-house CAD systems	Very accurate GIS data set can go straight to landscape architects and planners for facility and exhibit planning and development	Extremely accurate GIS data set can go straight to architects and engineers for facility and exhibit building; i.e., this is *surveyed* data

Chart courtesy of M. Burke, UC Davis Arboretum

CASE STUDY: UC DAVIS ARBORETUM

In 1982, the UC Davis Arboretum was responsible for approximately 100 acres; 60 were under cultivation. The last inventory was from the mid-1960s, and years of severe staffing cuts meant the paper records, maps, and their notes were difficult to link, but at least the plants had tags. The best solution to determine what was where was the slowest one: work through the collection and map every plant one by one. Advantages to this approach were that every plant would be accounted for, every accession-tagged plant would be recovered, and users, including docents, students, and researchers, would be able to find the plants without much staff assistance.

The first "cartoon" maps (1982–1989) were made with paper, pen, and vellum. This was inexpensive and easy and helped drive data collection. However, these maps were soon out of date and difficult to update. The next move was to digital maps (1988) in a now extinct software. A campus team of faculty in landscape design, geography-cartography, and horticulture was recruited, a teaching improvement grant acquired, and the first digital maps of a small area created. Advantages were that experience was gained for choosing a better approach to digital mapping given the available human resources, win-win relationships were established with new partners, and one complex garden area finally had adequate maps and records. Since 2003, all the collaborating audiences wanted the maps in ArcGIS so that the Arboretum's maps and information would link with other projects across the university and its teaching labs. This was a chance to upgrade to survey-quality outputs, even though the software is complex. Out of this effort came the Institute of Museum and Library Services–funded grant with several zoos and gardens to develop a standard GIS data model for use by any garden. This has given rise to the Alliance for Public Garden GIS.

Bringing Records to the Web

The move to Web-accessible records is a fundamental step in assisting external users and potential collaborators. Such an institutional shift allows virtual visitors to find useful information even if they never visit the physical garden; many gardens have extensive inventories available online. One internal benefit to the institution is that the accuracy level of the records becomes obvious to any user. For example, at the University of Michigan's Matthaei Botanical Gardens and Nichols Arboretum, moving all the tribute tree and bench information online has increased staff awareness of the program, shared responsibilities, and resolved tribute histories.

Online exchanges as part of networking enable participating garden staff to see the holdings at other gardens. Examples include the shared inventories of BG-BASE institutions and NAPCC participants. In the end, such networking may help to rationalize and reprioritize collections in institutions across North America and lead to a more comprehensive approach to multi-institutional collections management.

Celebrating Collection Diversity

The rich diversity of living collection types, their history, and their missions make collection management both challenging and rewarding. Understanding collections as physical manifestations of ideas becomes a core base for management. Those ideas (the stated purposes for which the collection is gathered or the natural areas managed) help to guide the relevant record types and management approaches. In other words, given the diverse array of collection types, one manages for outcomes: useful information related to the collection's purpose.

This chapter has dealt with generalized collections management issues and processes. However, within North American public gardens are recurrent issues related to collections management. Few are found at all gardens, but among the issues meriting consideration are general and deep collecting; historical gardens and heritage plants; managing collections for aesthetics; natural areas and collections management; and native plants, natural areas, and the perspectives of indigenous nations.

General and Deep Collecting

Collections can range from general to deep. Neither general nor deep collections are inherently preferable. Where an institution aims to position itself on the spectrum of general to deep collecting depends on its mission and audience needs.

With their broad but shallow range of diversity, general collections can encompass many themes, and relatively small changes to the collections can give a sense of a new direction. For collections management, key issues are identifying and articulating what drives the choice of materials and whether or not to respect past choices over time.

By contrast, deep collections are quite narrowly defined and aim for completeness. Depending on the size of the target, deep collections can be small but of very high quality. Gardens may develop multiple collections of varied but significant depth rather than one general collection.

Deep collections are a means to achieve distinction through specialization, but to become a known reference requires an institutional commitment to develop that collection as a fundamental tool for advancing its mission. Examples of deep collections include the orchids and other epiphytes at Marie Selby Botanical Gardens and the succulents at the Huntington Botanical Gardens.

Historical Collections and Heritage Plants

Since public gardens are intended to last for centuries, over time historical collections accrue at every garden, whether intentionally or not. Many North American gardens were established over the last century and parts of their collections are reaching the end of the typical life span of framework plants, resulting in a potential loss of design and content history. The natural turnover of living collections brings several collection-planning issues to the fore. Assuming collections will be maintained at their given size and resource allocation, should collections remain focused on their historical roots? Should collections be refocused to include the best of the past and present? Or should the historical elements be discarded and the collection begun anew? The answers to these questions may lie in the garden's mission or the needs of its audiences; Barnett (1996) provides several examples.

Historical integrity requires quality documentation, not just retention of old accessions. Additional documentation may include verification of period authenticity, contextual documentation of local sources and companies, and reasons why the particular plants are viewed as meritorious by standards of another era. It can be particularly valuable to have documents that tie local plant materials to local history and local human-interest stories. The websites of the National Park Service and the National Trust for Historic Preservation provide additional resources.

The fact that heritage cultivars are going extinct at a high rate is a driving issue for agencies and gardens concerned

Figure 20-8: The distinctive and venerable landscape of the Mount Auburn Cemetery balances the slowly changing needs of an active cemetery, a historical landscape, and a diverse plant collection while preserving the integrity of each component.

Mount Auburn Cemetery

with heritage seed, garden, and crop plants as well as historical design. Institutions that constantly address historic garden preservation and cultivar issues include Filioi, Historic Hudson Valley, Monticello, Mount Auburn Cemetery, Planting Fields Arboretum, and Winterthur.

Collections Managed for Aesthetics

Every garden strives to be beautiful (see Folsom 2000 and Meinig 1976 for discussions of the meaning of aesthetics in this context). Some institutions demand the collections be displayed as an aesthetic unit. This overriding aesthetic needs to be stated, documented, and mapped so that future staff can maintain or restore it with confidence. Written and image-based documentation has to be very clear in order to break through the conceptual frames of reference different specialists will bring in subsequent years.

Aesthetic criteria include vistas and enclosure, serenity, and congruence (how all the elements hold together to create a unique sense of place). Serenity itself is often an umbrella term for nondistraction and ranges from the details of colorful fruit and bloom through various psychological issues that involve carefully controlling perceptions of sound and motion. Periodic aesthetic reviews are typically conducted by individuals with design training rather than collections managers. As with all other collections, the plants do need records, and especially those related to their roles and positions that

contribute to the intended aesthetic. Gardens known for exemplary aesthetic experiences include the Bloedel Reserve, Chanticleer, Ganna Walska Lotusland, Longwood Gardens, and Naumkeag.

Natural Areas and Collections Management

If collections are objects assembled for a purpose, can the definition be expanded to management of a set of immovable objects or complex landscapes? Clearly the answer is yes, and a number of gardens manage natural and restored areas as well as more traditional collections (Parsons 1995). Indeed, these three sets—natural areas, naturalized collections, and traditional collections—have intense but similar records and information needs. Information about which plants are where and their condition, management, and care vary only by the scale of the base units, which are masses or populations in natural areas rather than the individual accessions of traditional collections. Likewise, natural areas and naturalized collections need collection policy statements about their roles, what they are to contain, and records documentation standards. For the purposes of collections management, the necessary basic information includes:

- statement of objectives for which these areas are managed

- physical delimitation of the properties being managed in this way

Figure 20-9: The Fountain Garden at Lotusland is managed as an aesthetic unit. Lotusland is well-known for its integration of collection depth and defining sense of design.

Bill Dewey

- Periodic inventories of the property so that the plant record system is accurate for species presence and abundance

- Protocols and management plans tailored to the vegetation and natural systems

- Dated records/maps as to the management practices used in subareas for ascertaining their impacts (intended or otherwise) and their efficacy

Once uncommon, gardens known for natural-area collections (ranging from the traditional to those of extensive research caliber) are expanding. Rather than being sited in just one town, some have reached out and developed regional networks. Well-established examples include Bernheim Arboretum and Research Forest, Cornell Plantations, Missouri Botanical Garden/Shaw Arboretum, Matthaei Botanical Gardens and Nichols Arboretum, and New England Wildflower Society/Garden in the Woods.

Figure 20-10: The Coker Arboretum has collections in a traditional campus context.

P. S. White

Figure 20-11: The Coastal Plain Garden at the North Carolina Botanical Garden is a naturalistic display and collection of plants of the ecoregion.

P. S. White

CASE STUDY: NORTH CAROLINA BOTANICAL GARDEN

The North Carolina Botanical Garden is based on a spectrum of properties that includes two arboreta, native plant display gardens, restored areas, and natural/research areas that are home to populations of threatened species. This suite of collection types and landscapes is perceived and managed as a coherent set. The unifying themes of conservation biology, ecology, and regional natural and cultural heritage are expressed differently depending on the site history and plants. Placing planted gardens, naturalized gardens, and natural areas in the context of their own natural systems highlights such ecosystem services as pollinators, rainwater retention, and decomposition/recycling.

For understanding natural area management, not only were university faculty and staff critical, but assistance from the state heritage program and the expertise of colleagues at the Nature Conservancy have been welcome. Key plan elements include:

- Invasive species
- Fire management protocols
- Trail hazards
- Monitoring plans and protocols
- Visitor access protocols
- Deer control protocols

Natural areas as collections allow visitors to see remnants of the regional ecosystems that are being studied, protected, and reinterpreted in the naturalistic gardens. Likewise, the suite of landscape scales, properties, and collections allows pollinators, fruit dispersers, related wildlife, and the fascination they provide visitors to come right into the core of town life.

All the plant species present in the natural and restored areas are considered integral parts of the living collections and natural systems of the North Carolina Botanical Garden. The following baseline information allows staff to detect changes in species presence related to disturbances such as past, current, and future management practices and passage of time.

- **Complete plant species checklist.** All species are listed and recorded by area. An individual may be accessioned for mapping/reference as a proxy for the population.
- **Unique individuals.** These include largest trees, reference specimens, and plants of note. These may be accessioned for individual record tracking. For extremely rare plants, permanent plots are established and every stem mapped. This allows individual tracking as with an accession.
- **Soils, geologic, and topographic maps.** These can be found or made.

- **Thorough documentation of site history.** This includes deeds from the colonial period to university stewardship as well as studies/awareness of sites that may represent First Nations use prior to European contact.
- **Bibliographies.** These may be of any kind; they capture student work, especially student theses and projects.

All of these are maintained with the expectation of long-term periodic updates. The baseline information for sites has also been bound as reference materials and deposited in the libraries of the Garden and the university.

Figure 20-12: The natural areas are considered an integral part of the North Carolina Botanical Garden's collections, with the vegetation units, not individual accessions, as basic elements.

P. S. White

Native Plants, Natural Areas, and First Nations

As North American gardens develop native plant collections and manage naturalistic landscapes and significant natural areas, the perspectives of First Nations elders whose cultures are indigenous to the sites and plant communities would be expected to be included.

Most Native Americans have retained knowledge of places and plants from which they were displaced. Yet native voices, perspectives, and participation in living collection development and landscape management are uncommon.

Existing ethnobotanical collections and interpreted trails created without tribal collaboration need serious review, even if the tribe is completely displaced from the region. Leadership in this complex domain of living collection development and interpretation in consultation with First Nations is found in relatively few institutions. Foremost is the Montreal Botanical Garden, which embarked upon a multiyear collaboration with several diverse indigenous peoples (Cuerrier and Paré 2006). In the United States, the Arizona-Sonora Desert Museum and the Denver Botanic Gardens have meaningfully engaged Native American perspectives related to the living collections and their development.

Summary

Living collections are the heart of every garden. Fundamentally, meaningful living collections are plants gathered and managed for a lasting societal purpose. Types of living collections range from culturally based themes to conservation-based collections that serve research and stewardship objectives.

A clearly written collections policy is the fundamental management tool. It keeps the collections' guiding purpose consistent over time. Key elements include collections mission; invasives; acquisition, documentation, and disposal standards; and ethics, intellectual rights, and access. The policy allows periodic reviews to refocus the collections—individual units as well as the assembled whole—to best fit the intended purpose with the required level of records accuracy, thematic depth, and aesthetic qualities.

Accessions are the fundamental unit for most living collections. The record system has to track the accessions over time and maintain critical information about the source, location, and ongoing condition. Myriad other fields will be needed for each type of collection. Relational databases are essential to maintain the plant records beyond a very basic level. From the database it is easy to develop reports that promote sound collections management. The basic one is the inventory. Inventories are devices to keep the records and the grounds linked while allowing intense accession and collections review and updating. Unless an institution is an active authority on a group of plants, the nomenclature is often best handled in a conservative manner, since the purpose of names is to help people find the plants and information they want.

Maps are perhaps the most useful interface between the collections records and most visitors, including staff. The revolution in mapping software and related informatics is one of the most dynamic aspects of contemporary plant records management. Real-time institution-wide information from the records, linked to maps and photographs, is becoming available on the Web and thus downloadable to handheld devices. The underlying information has to be accurate, complete, and relevant. Meeting this need highlights the shift of plant records to institutional information management.

The great breadth of living collections is part of our cultural heritage. No one institution has the entire range of collection types or is ever likely to. This diversity among institutions and their collections is a societal strength—especially as collections are joined in working and formal networks such as the North American Plant Collections Consortium. But each institution has to maintain the highest standard collections possible, and leading that charge is a key role of collection management.

Annotated Resources

Armstrong, G. D. 2003. Collections profile: University of Wisconsin Arboretum. *The Public Garden* 18(4): 42–44. Thumbnail sketch of the range of collections at the UW Arboretum, from taxonomic collections to the classic restored biological communities envisioned by Leopold, Longnecker, and Fassett in the 1930s.

Barnett, D. P. 1996. Historic landscape preservation: Obstacle to change? *The Public Garden* 11(2): 21–23, 39. A comparison of how four historic institutions approach living collection issues of preservation, restoration, rehabilitation, and reconstruction.

Burke, M. T., and B. J. Morgan. 2009. Digital mapping: Beyond living collection curation. *The Public Garden* 24(3): 9–10. A call to take maps beyond their origin in collection management.

Carter, D., and A. K. Walker, eds. 1999. *Care and conservation of natural history collections*. Oxford: Butterworth-Heinemann. A contemporary review of the natural history museum protocol, the tradition in which living collection management practices is rooted.

Collins, D. 2008. Collaboration on a large scale: The NAPCC multi-institutional *Quercus* collection. *The Public Garden* 23(1): 27–30. Showing benefits of a specific collection, in which fifteen institutions collaborate to house 168 taxa (more than 2,300 accessions) and target the priority of unrepresented taxa as a team. See Otis (2001) for another perspective.

Cuerrier, A., and S. Paré. 2006. The First Nations Garden: Where cultural diversity meets biodiversity. *The Public Garden* 21(4): 22–25. The inclusion of First Nations perspectives in living collection development.

Dosmann, M. S. 2006. Research in the garden: Averting the collection crisis. *Botanical Review* 72: 207–34. A thoughtful articulation of the important roles of living collections based on shared information, collaboration, and new research agendas, as well as the critical issue of intrinsic value of the collections based on their quality, not size.

Elsik, S. 1989. From each a voucher: Collecting in the living collections. *Arnoldia* 49(1): 21–27. A case study of how to voucher the accessions with teams of trained volunteers.

Folsom, J. P. 2000. The terms of beauty. *The Public Garden* 15(2): 3–6. What is meant by beauty in gardens and its components?

Galbraith, D. A. 1998. Biodiversity ethics: A challenge to botanical gardens for the next millennium. *The Public Garden* 13(3): 16–19. A call to consider the ethical challenge in addressing the use of living collections as genetic resources.

Gardner, J. B., and E. Merritt. 2004. *The AAM guide to collections planning*. AAM Professional Education Series. Washington, D.C.: American Association of Museums. A lucid guide to writing a collection plan.

Gates, G. 2006. Characteristics of an exemplary plant collection. *The Public Garden* 21(1): 28–31. Synopsis from a study of leading gardens as to what features contribute to superior living collections and their management.

Hohn, T. C. 2008. *Curatorial practices for botanical gardens*. Lanham, N.Y.: AltaMira Press. The extensive bibliography reviews the literature to the publication date.

Jefferson, L., K. Havens, and J. Ault. 2004. Implementing invasive screening procedures: The Chicago Botanic Garden model. *Weed Technology* 18: 1434–40. Discussion of the logic-and-actions model for assessing potential weediness of unfamiliar plants.

Kister, S. 2008. Sustaining a living legacy: Longwood's tree management program. *The Public Garden* 23(3–4): 32–34. Tree management, assessment, and monitoring as a special case of collection management.

Leadlay, E., and J. Greene, eds. 1998. *The Darwin technical manual for botanic gardens*. London: Botanic Gardens Conservation International. Chapter 4 outlines conservation collection types and reviews acquisition, labeling, identification, evaluation, and deaccessioning objectives.

Lowe, C. 1995. Managing the woodland garden. *The Public Garden* 10(3): 11–13. An experienced perspective on woodland gardens as collections.

Meinig, D. W. 1976. The beholding eye: Ten versions of the same scene. *Landscape Architecture* 66: 47–56. Ten perspectives of one landscape; a classic reference on learning to recognize and shift conceptual frames of reference.

Michener, D. 1989. To each a name: Verifying the living collections. *Arnoldia* 49(1): 36–41. A case study of the process of verifying vouchers using staff and experts around the world.

Moore, G. 2006. Current state of botanical nomenclature. *The Public Garden* 21(3): 34–37. An overview of the issues in plant nomenclature relevant to collection management.

Otis, D. 2001. Maples in North America: Developing a network of NAPCC *Acer* collections. *The Public Garden* 16(1): 22–27. A perspective on building multi-institution living collections, outlining the steps to make a focused consortium work.

Parsons, B. 1995. The role of woodlands at the Holden Arboretum. *The Public Garden* 10(3): 21–23. An overview of the division of the arboretum into different categories of lands management.

Reibel, D. B. 1997. *Registration methods for the small museum*. 3rd ed. American Association for State and Local History Book Series. Walnut Creek, Calif.: AltaMira Press. This is especially useful for small institutions that are intending to include the grounds, gardens, or landscapes.

Ripley, N. 2006. Re-exploring the known: The mystique of native plants. *The Public Garden* 21(4): 26–28. The native habitat approach to displaying alpines at the Betty Ford Alpine Garden.

Roggenkamp, K., and S. Woodbury. 2009. Native plant gardens at the Shaw Nature Reserve. *The Public Garden* 24(4):

12–14. Development of native plant gardens focused on educating gardeners in the use of local natives.

Simmons, J. 2006. *Things great and small: Collections management policies*. Washington, D.C.: American Association of Museums. A clear presentation of the range of management policies and their purposes, all with real-world examples.

Stansfield, G., J. Mathias, and G. Reid, eds. 1994. *Manual of natural history curatorship*. London: HMSO. Another perspective on natural history collection management, the tradition in which living collection management is rooted.

Tan, B. 2001. Mesoamerican cloud forest at Strybing Arboretum. *The Public Garden* 16(1): 36, 38–40, 42–43. An overview of a distinctive ecogeographic collection, its intended roles, and how it was developed.

CHAPTER 21

Research at Public Gardens

KAYRI HAVENS

Introduction

Research has always played an important role in the development of public gardens. In fact, many early gardens were developed specifically as collections to support research activities, including plant taxonomic research and studies of the medicinal or economic uses of plants. Throughout most of their post-Renaissance history, public gardens have primarily served as horticultural collections of plants from around the world. These unusual, exotic collections have intrigued and delighted visitors. In the past few decades, with the recognition of an impending extinction crisis, the mission of many public gardens has evolved from developing a horticultural collection to playing an active role in plant conservation, including conservation-related research.

Conservation actions can take many forms, from strictly educational efforts to seed-banking activities, natural area management and restoration, and related basic and applied research. This chapter focuses on basic and applied research, while the next chapter focuses on other conservation activities. The need for botanical research has never been greater. Botanical expertise is fundamental to addressing climate change, invasive species problems, renewable-energy issues, ecosystem restoration, and the conservation and sustainable use of biodiversity. These critical needs coincide with a continuing loss or reduction of botany programs at many universities (Eshbaugh and Wilson 1969; Affolter 2003; Sundberg 2004). Plant collecting is also currently declining in the United States (Prather et al. 2004), as is collections-based research at natural history organizations (Dosmann 2006).

Many land management agencies are severely understaffed in botanical experts. For instance, on average one botanist for the Bureau of Land Management is responsible for the management of nearly 4 million acres, and the situation is similar at other federal agencies (Roberson 2002). Botanic Gardens Conservation International (U.S.) and Chicago Botanic Garden recently conducted a survey of several plant science communities in the United States (academia, government, nonprofit organizations, and consulting firms) to assess if there is sufficient capacity (primarily in terms of staff numbers and expertise) to meet the country's botanical research and management needs. The survey indicated that there is a critical need to increase botanical capacity, particularly in government sectors, where 91 percent of respondents indicated that their agency does not have enough staff to address its current botanical questions. This trend is likely to continue because 45 percent of current botanists in federal agencies who responded plan to retire within the next decade and 60 percent expect to retire in the next fifteen years, according to unpublished data collected by Havens, Kramer, and Zorn-Arnold.

Botanical gardens are ideally situated to help fill the void in botanical research, plant conservation, and education. All botanical gardens maintain documented collections of living plants, and many also maintain herbaria and seed collections. The multiple roles of gardens in botanical capacity building are increasingly recognized by governments and international agencies. Many gardens are developing new techniques for seed banking, plant propagation, plant reintroduction, and habitat management and restoration. Botanical garden networks like Botanic Gardens Conservation International and the Center for Plant Conservation help coordinate activities between gardens (Wyse Jackson and Sutherland 2000).

The botanical research activities carried out by gardens are highly variable, ranging from traditional systematics to conservation research, from horticultural studies to the emerging field of human/plant interactions. Many of those disciplines are discussed later in this chapter.

Abiotic: nonliving (chemical and physical) factors in the environment.

Autecology: the study of the interactions of an individual organism or a single species with its environment.

Bioclimatic envelope modeling: determining where climatic and environmental conditions are suitable for a species using current and recent historical records of its distribution. This envelope can be used to predict where species could live under future climate scenarios.

Biotic: living factors in the environment.

Ecotype: a genetically distinct population or race within a species, due to adaptation to local environmental conditions.

Ethnobotany: the study of the relationships that exist between people and plants.

Ex situ conservation: conservation of an organism outside its native habitat (such as at a botanical garden or zoo).

Floristics: the study of the distribution and relationships of plant species over geographic areas.

Georeferencing: an approach to defining the location of something, such as an individual plant or plant population in space, typically establishing a location on a map or in a coordinate system. Global positioning system (GPS) technology is most frequently used today.

Herbarium: a collection of preserved plant specimens. Specimens are typically pressed, dried, mounted on a sheet of paper, and labeled with collection location and other information. Specimens may also be kept in alcohol or another preservative, depending on the material to be preserved. Herbarium specimens are often called *vouchers* because they provide permanent documentation of a study.

Inbreeding depression: a reduction of offspring fitness or yield when genetically related individuals are crossed or when plants self-pollinate.

In situ conservation: conservation of an organism in its native habitat.

Mycorrhizae: fungi that form an association with plant roots. In this symbiotic relationship, the fungus helps the plant absorb water and minerals and the plant provides sugars to the fungus.

Outbreeding depression: a reduction of offspring fitness or yield when genetically dissimilar individuals, such as plants from widely separated populations, are crossed.

Phenology: the study of the timing of natural events, such as first leaf break, first flower opening, peak flowering, and so on. Phenology also applies to the timing of migration of animal species, etc.

Phylogeny: the evolutionary history or pattern of descent of a group of organisms.

Population viability analysis (PVA): a modeling approach to determine the likelihood of a population's persistence or extinction over a given period of time. PVAs can take into account multiple threats or management actions and identify key recovery actions for a species.

Propagule: any plant part used to produce a new plant, such as seeds, spores, cuttings, bulbs, tubers, and other vegetative reproductive structures.

Restoration ecology: the study of how a damaged or degraded ecosystem may be recovered through human intervention. Restoration activities may include removal of invasive species, reestablishment of natural processes such as fire and hydrology, and reintroduction of native species.

Systematics: the study of the diversification of living organisms, both past and present, and the relationships among living things through time.

Taxonomy: the science of describing, identifying, classifying, and naming organisms.

How to Establish a Research Program

Research programs can exist at several funding levels and sizes. Planning is the key to a successful research program. Whether developing a new research program or reenvisioning the priorities of an existing research program, a research strategic plan is an extremely beneficial starting point. A good strategic plan allows a public garden to determine appropriate research niche(s) and partners that will maximize the likelihood of developing a sustainable research program. Research strategic planning mirrors the process for institutional strategic planning. This process is further described in *The Darwin Technical Manual for Botanic Gardens* (Leadlay and Greene 1998).

Funding and Infrastructure Considerations

Research program size and expenses at a public garden are extremely variable. Some gardens may employ just one full- or part-time person in research; others have dozens or even hundreds of scientific staff. Similarly, expenses may be modest to very significant (several million dollars per year). Some gardens build their own research facilities on-site; others may partner with universities or other institutions for access to laboratories.

While grant funding is available for scientific activities, it is probably not reasonable to expect a research program to be entirely self-supporting. In a benchmarking study of twenty public gardens, the most common funding scenario was an approximately 50-50 split between institutional support and

- **Determine the mission.** Ask what types of research are valued, where the garden can make a significant contribution, how the collections can best be utilized in support of research, and what types of research the garden should *not* carry out. A benchmarking study of other botanical institutions in a particular region or in the country can be useful in determining the focus.

- **Define the goals and objectives.** Goals and objectives should translate the mission into achievable pieces.

- **Assess resource needs.** Determine what resources (human, financial, and capital, including laboratories and equipment) are needed to achieve the goals. Develop a plan for acquiring those resources.

- **Define the timeline.** Most strategic plans have a medium- to long-term view (three to ten years). Shorter operating plans

are also useful to undertake annually as part of the budgeting process.

- **Incorporate a SWOT analysis.** This type of analysis allows the garden to build on its strengths, address its weaknesses, capitalize on opportunities, and avoid threats.

- **Involve as many people as possible.** Strategic plans should represent as many voices as possible. Including not only research staff but staff from education, development, communications, and horticulture broadens perspectives and helps achieve institutional buy-in. Outside research review committees can also provide beneficial feedback.

- **Determine measures of success.** A good plan is SMART (specific, measurable, achievable, relevant, and time-bound). Determine what should be achieved, when to do it, and how to measure success.

grant support (Havens, unpublished data). Aligning some research with government agency priorities can increase funding options. Federal agencies are often interested in applied research related to restoration, invasive species control, adaptation to climate change, fire ecology, and native plant materials development. Partnerships with universities, other public gardens in the region, and other collections-based institutions can make limited funding stretch further. For instance, it may not be necessary to invest in a library, herbarium, seed storage facility, or molecular genetics laboratory if those resources can be accessed through partnerships.

Gardens can also stretch limited funding by attracting outside researchers to use their collections. Gardens can often bring in visiting scientists relatively economically by providing collaborative opportunities, small research grants, space (office, lab, or greenhouse), and access to plant collections (Dosmann 2006). Several gardens, including the Missouri Botanical Garden, Chicago Botanic Garden, and Fairchild Tropical Botanic Garden, have active research associate programs where visiting scientists are given garden membership benefits as well. Primack and Miller-Rushing (2009) highlight ways they have used the collections (living, herbarium, and photographic) at the Arnold Arboretum for their work on plants and climate change. Another way to build capacity is to strengthen collaborations between gardens and land management agencies. The Georgia Plant Conservation Alliance provides a nice example of a network that facilitates cooperation between gardens and agencies to conduct research.

Lastly, many gardens have used citizen scientists very successfully to extend the reach of their research programs. Volunteer rare-plant monitoring programs, such as the Plant

Conservation Volunteer Corps, coordinated by the New England Wild Flower Society, and Plants of Concern, coordinated by the Chicago Botanic Garden, provide valuable data for plant population management. Other successful citizen science projects include a national plant phenology monitoring program called Project BudBurst (Figure 21-1; www.budburst.org) and invasive plant monitoring. In addition to gathering data sets larger than any scientist could on his or her own, citizen science projects have the added benefit of increasing scientific literacy of the participants by engaging them in the scientific process. The Cornell Lab of Ornithology has numerous online resources about developing or participating in citizen science projects (http://www.birds.cornell.edu/citscitoolkit).

Figure 21-1: High school students collecting data on plant phenology for Project BudBurst at the Chicago Botanic Garden.

Courtesy Chicago Botanic Garden; photo by Robin Carlson

Systematics, Floristics, and Herbarium-Associated Research

Plant taxonomy, systematics, and floristics have long been a traditional role, and remain a continuing focus, for many botanical gardens. The Missouri Botanical Garden, New York Botanical Garden, and Royal Botanic Gardens, Kew, are well known around the world for their work in this area. Other gardens also make significant contributions, often specializing in a particular plant group or groups, such as the work of the Fairchild Tropical Botanic Garden on palms and cycads, or in the production of local floras exemplified by the New England Wildflower Society and the State Botanical Garden of Georgia. In today's world, where biodiversity is rapidly disappearing, there is an increased urgency to describe and name species before they become extinct. The initial target of the Global Strategy for Plant Conservation (GSPC) is the development of a working list of the world's flora.

Knowing what plants grow in a region and their relative abundance is the first step in prioritizing species for conservation action via the red-listing process of the World Conservation Union (IUCN) in most countries or the global rank determination carried out by NatureServe in North America, and ultimately legal protection of species. The IUCN Red List of Threatened Species has increasingly been adopted as the gold standard for information on the conservation status of species, but unfortunately, the listing process for plants has been progressing relatively slowly compared to that for vertebrates and other animals. As of 2009, less than 4 percent of vascular plants had been assessed using the IUCN Red List categories and criteria, and only two groups of plants (conifers and cycads) had been comprehensively assessed (Schatz 2009). Scientists from the Missouri Botanical Garden and the Royal Botanic Gardens, Kew, are particularly active in conservation assessments.

CASE STUDY: BOTANICAL GARDENS AND THE IUCN RED LIST

George Schatz, Missouri Botanical Garden

Botanical gardens and their associated herbaria must play a critical role in rapidly increasing the representation of plants on the IUCN Red List to better inform conservation planning. Herbarium specimens constitute the foundation upon which all of our knowledge of the diversity and distribution of plant species ultimately lies. Indeed, many plant species are known only in the herbarium, in extreme cases perhaps only from their type specimen, which forms the basis for their original description. Moreover, herbarium specimens represent primary occurrence data that document the geographic range of plant species, in the form of either extent of occurrence or area of occupancy, both of which are important factors in IUCN Red List assessments. In combination with knowledge on threats and their potential impact on population sizes, plant species can be readily assessed for their risk of extinction according to a series of threshold values for geographic range size (Figure 21-2).

The Missouri Botanical Garden has been collaborating with IUCN to assess the conservation status of plants endemic to three global hot spots: the Caucasus region, the Eastern Arc Mountains and coastal forests of Kenya and Tanzania, and Madagascar. All three projects rely on the synthesis and georeferencing of herbarium specimens to paint a picture of the geographic range and history of the target species using basic GIS tools. However, mechanically comparing the values of geographic range size against the Red List criteria thresholds is insufficient to arrive at a valid assessment in the absence of an intimate understanding of on-the-ground threats. Thus, the success of each project has been dependent upon the formation of a network of local botanists with expertise in both the species themselves and threats to their habitats. These essential networks of local experts assist in validating the assessments, formulating regional plant conservation strategies, and ultimately making recommendations to both governmental and nongovernmental organizations to mitigate the loss of plant diversity.

Figure 21-2: *Campanula raddeana* Trautv., a bellflower from the Caucasus region, which is a center of diversity for *Campanula*. It was assessed as endangered (EN) by the IUCN Red Listing procedure.

Photo by George E. Schatz

The advent of Web-accessible herbarium records and the creation of red lists have facilitated the designation of important plant areas (IPAs), which are high-priority regions for land acquisition and protection. IPAs are sites of exceptional botanical richness that often contain threatened species or habitats. They support the implementation of Target 5 of the Global Strategy for Plant Conservation, which aims for "protection of 50% of the world's most important areas for plant diversity assured by 2010." Much of the work to date on designating IPAs has been carried out in Europe by Plantlife International, which is currently training other countries in the methodology for carrying out the IPA process.

More recently, herbarium specimens have been used as sources of DNA for systematics work, including the study of species now globally extinct or extinct in the wild. Researchers remove a small leaf or leaf portion from the herbarium sheet and extract its DNA. To facilitate this type of work in the future, many herbaria are maintaining DNA vouchers that are linked to a herbarium sheet. DNA vouchers typically consist of a leaf or two from the same individual as the herbarium voucher that are then dried in silica gel and frozen. This practice allows for better preservation of the DNA and keeps the herbarium specimen intact.

Another growing role for herbaria is in research on global change. We know that bloom times of many species are changing as the climate changes. Herbarium sheets serve as a permanent record of the phenological phase of an individual plant on a given date. These can be compared with contemporary bloom dates. For some longer-lived species, vouchers of a garden's living collection can be associated with the living plant from which they were collected (Figure 21-3) and bloom dates of the same individual compared over time (Primack and Miller-Rushing 2009). Bioclimatic envelope modeling is increasingly being used to predict shifts in the geographic ranges of plants under climate change. These models depend on data about the current and historical ranges of species often derived from herbarium records (Donaldson 2009).

Conservation-Focused Research
Autecology

Autecological studies, those that focus on a particular species, are crucial to developing conservation plans. Understanding how a particular species interacts with its environment, both abiotic and biotic, is necessary both for management *in situ* and for designing reintroduction plans. Many plant species have obligate relationships with other organisms, including pollinators, seed dispersal agents, mycorrhizal fungi, host plants, and nurse plants. Because it wastes resources to manage or reintroduce a species where it is doomed to fail, studying these mutualisms, as well as requirements for particular soil types, moisture, aspect, exposure, and disturbance regime, are important areas of investigation.

Many public gardens within the Center for Plant Conservation network have conducted experimental rare plant reintroductions, which remain a fruitful area of research. Numerous variables can be tested in a reintroduction, including but not limited to propagule type (seeds or transplants), source populations, number and relatedness of founders, habitat characteristics, site preparation, post-planting care, and timing of planting (Guerrant 1996; Guerrant and Kaye 2007). For instance, Berry Botanic Garden researchers have studied the effects of seed age and *ex situ* storage, propagule type (seed vs. bulb), and removal of ground cover on the reintroduction success of the western lily (*Lilium occidentale*). North Carolina Botanical Garden scientists have investigated the effects of site preparation on survivorship of the riverine species harperella (*Ptilimnium nodosum*) (Figure 21-4); testing methods of anchoring transplants, using coir matting, cobble, and other techniques, in swift-flowing streams has been the focus of their work. Researchers at the Morton Arboretum and Chicago Botanic Garden have been studying effects of seed source on the reintroduction success of Pitcher's thistle (*Cirsium pitcheri*) in Illinois. They have also been using population viability analyses (PVAs) on natural and reintroduced populations of the species to measure success.

Figure 21-3: Abe Miller-Rushing (left) and Richard Primack (right) compare bloom dates of a *Rhododendron* herbarium specimen collected in 1938 and a living specimen.

Photo by Anica Miller-Rushing

Figure 21-4: Harperella (*Ptilimnium nodosum*), a rare riverine species, planted in coir matting to keep it from washing away, in a reintroduction carried out by the North Carolina Botanical Garden.

Photo by Johnny Randall

Community Ecology

Community ecology studies often focus on the roles of interspecific interactions (e.g., plant/animal or plant/fungus relationships) in the structure and resilience of communities. Environmental change, due to numerous anthropogenic threats, can affect ecological communities and ecosystem function. While some threats, such as land development, lend themselves to policy solutions, others (e.g., climate change, invasive species, habitat fragmentation) can benefit substantially from research conducted in tandem with policy and legislative approaches. For instance, understanding how species fare in novel climates is an area of research that public gardens are ideally suited to undertake (Primack and Miller-Rushing 2009). Gardens already grow thousands of species outside of their native ranges and could work collaboratively to improve bioclimatic envelope modeling efforts that aim to predict where species are likely to survive in the future.

Invasive species are recognized as the second-greatest threat to biodiversity after habitat loss. The majority of invasive plant species has been, and continues to be, deliberately introduced through horticulture and agriculture. Determining the potential invasive risk of these species and cultivars prior to introduction is a fruitful area of research (Jefferson, Havens, and Ault 2004). Other current areas of study are modeling the invasive risk of cultivars relative to their parent species and breeding sterility into invasive but otherwise desirable ornamental plants (Li et al. 2004; Anderson, Gomez, and Galatowitsch 2006; Anderson, Galatowitsch, and Gomez 2006). Other invasive species research

has focused on management techniques, including biocontrol methods, to eradicate or minimize the impact of problem species. Cornell University has a large research program on biocontrol agents (e.g., Blossey, Skinner, and Taylor 2001).

Restoration Ecology

Restoration ecology, the science of assisting the recovery of degraded or destroyed natural communities, is another area of active research. Understanding patterns of ecotypic variation and local adaptation of species used in restoration projects will help determine the most appropriate sources of plants or seeds for a restoration site. Similarly, understanding patterns of genetic variation spatially (within and between populations) and temporally will assist the development of seed collection strategies that capture high amounts of genetic variation. The combination of quantitative and molecular genetic approaches will generally provide better information to guide restoration practices than either approach alone (Kramer and Havens 2009).

Habitat restoration starts from the ground up and is often focused on the successful establishment of native plant communities. Restoration researchers and practitioners alike recognize the importance of choosing the right source material to ensure the success of plant restoration efforts (see McKay et al. 2005 for discussion). In many cases, the default method of approximating this is to match climatic conditions between the source site and the restoration site, ensuring that plants placed in a restoration site will be adapted to and able to tolerate expected climatic fluctuations.

Plants and climate are, however, only two pieces of the ecological restoration puzzle. Numerous other biological components are necessary for successful ecological functioning, including plant-animal interactions such as pollination, seed dispersal, and predator-prey relationships. These interactions are capable of altering what the most appropriate source material for a given restoration site may be and should be taken into consideration. For example, Chicago Botanic Garden scientists Andrea Kramer, Jeremie Fant, and Becky Tonietto studied differences between populations of several traits for three species of beardtongue (*Penstemon*). They found that significant differences, including the shape and size of flowers, from different populations of the same species of beardtongue (*Penstemon deustus*) appear to be more connected to local biological interactions than to abiotic factors. To investigate whether plant/pollinator interactions may be driving observed differences in flowers, they surveyed the pollinator communities on different mountain ranges throughout the region. When combined, floral morphology and pollinator community data present a picture of adaptation to different pollinator communities, with significant

Figure 21-5: Floral morphological variation between populations of *Penstemon deustus*. Row A: flowers from a population in the Desatoya Mountains (elevation 2,025 m; 6,643 ft.) visited solely by small bees (< 6 mm). Row B: flowers from a population in the Pinenut Mountains (elevation 1,861 m; 6,105 ft.) visited by a suite of small to medium-size bee (5–10 mm). Row C: flowers from a population in the Schell Creek Range (elevation 2,649 m; 8,691 ft.) visited primarily by medium to large bees (> 8 mm).

Courtesy Chicago Botanic Garden; photos by Rebecca Tonietto and drawings by Jeremie Fant

implications for restoration in the region (Figure 21-5). Plants on a mountain range in the western portion of the region produced small short flowers and were visited nearly exclusively by small bees that entered each flower they visited. Nearly 500 km (1,640 ft.) to the east, populations of the same plant species produced large flowers visited primarily by bumblebees hovering outside the flower. With these results, it is clear that moving seeds from the western source site to a restoration site in the east may result in a mismatch between flower and pollinator shape and size, which could lead to the failure of a restoration if flowers are not successfully pollinated and therefore do not produce seeds for the next generation.

Seed Biology

Seed banking is a fundamental activity of many public gardens. Seeds of most flowering plant species are orthodox, able to withstand the drying and freezing necessary for long-term storage. Properly dried and frozen (at −20°C), orthodox seeds can retain viability for decades to hundreds of years, and cryopreservation (in liquid nitrogen) shows promise for increasing seed storage life by one or more orders of magnitude (Li and Pritchard 2009). Research into storage conditions, desiccation practices, and the effects of seed aging for both orthodox seeds and recalcitrant seeds (those that cannot tolerate drying and freezing) has improved seed longevity and continues to do so (Smith et al. 2003; Walters 2004; Pritchard 2004; Li and Pritchard 2009). Periodic viability testing requires knowledge about species-specific germination protocols, another common area of research for public gardens. Carol and Jerry Baskin (2004) have outlined a series of experiments to determine dormancy-breaking and germination requirements, providing an effective template for seed germination research. Their guidelines can be used to obtain the most information from the least amount of seed, making the most of the small sample sizes typical of rare plant research. The Berry Botanic Garden, a very small garden with a staff of approximately five people, was well-known for its work on seed storage and germination, demonstrating that high-quality research can be done at gardens of all sizes.

Population Biology and Genetics

Understanding ecological and genetic dynamics in wild populations is also critical for conservation efforts. Many scientists at public gardens are conducting research on demography and genetics of native plant populations, including the impact of factors such as habitat fragmentation, on population viability. For instance, small or fragmented populations with low genetic diversity can suffer inbreeding depression or even reproductive failure (Wagenius 2006). Demographic studies can highlight specific stages of the life cycle, such as seedling establishment or flowering, that may be limiting population growth. Management targeted at helping a species through these vulnerable transitions can increase population size. Similarly, demographic studies of invasive species can help managers target life cycle stages where control or removal may be particularly effective. Studies of a species' reproductive biology can also inform management. For example, a study of the demographic consequences of increasing fruit set via hand pollination in a threatened orchid, *Platanthera leucophaea* (Figure 21-7), led to recommendations about optimal pollination levels for population persistence and the production of seed for restoration efforts (Vitt 2001).

Edward O. Guerrant Jr., formerly of the Berry Botanic Garden

Berry Botanic Garden scientists conduct a wide range of research projects involving seed germination, all of which revolve around two basic questions: what is the best way to germinate a particular species, and how well does it survive long-term storage?

Given extremely small individual sample sizes, we generally use only five to ten seeds each in a battery of up to six tests involving two variables: cold stratification (0, 8, or 16 weeks, at 5°C in a refrigerator) and temperature regime (constant 20°C or fluctuating 10°C/20°C). We omit some treatments if we have prior knowledge (e.g., cold stratification required), and may use other techniques such as physically scarifying hard-seeded species (e.g., many members of the legume family, *Fabaceae*). Even though the results provide low statistical power to distinguish among treatments or trials taking place in different years (Guerrant and Fielder 2004), the results do provide useful information. Even in the absence of knowledge about a species, valuable information can be gained from what is known about related species or genera. Baskin and Baskin (1998, 2004) provide a valuable overview of the relationships among phylogeny, embryo types, and dormancy types, and their correlations with germination requirements.

Beyond standard housekeeping tests and retests of seed bank accessions, to determine germination protocols and later survivorship over time, we also conduct related research on both common and rare species. One ongoing project is a small component of a much larger effort by the U.S. government to develop genetically appropriate native plants for use in restoring public lands after fires and other large-scale land disturbances. We began by conducting the full battery of six treatments described above on much larger samples (200 seeds each) of up to three populations each of nineteen common species native to the Intermountain West (Figure 21-6). Using the most successful protocol for each population, we have retested them after 1, 2 and 4 years of storage, either in cool (15°C), dry (22% RH) conditions or as frozen samples that had been equilibrated to the cool, dry conditions. In order to see if there are any ecological differences in germination requirements among populations within species, we tested some samples from widely separated sites and, indeed, found significant differences. These studies will help match seed sources to restoration sites, improving restoration outcomes.

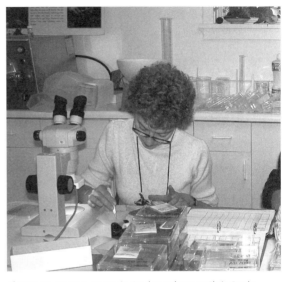

Figure 21-6: Berry Botanic Garden volunteer Chris Sarda carefully setting out five replicate germination boxes of forty seeds each to test their germination after two years in storage.

Photo by Edward O. Guerrant Jr.

Soil Science

Soil not only is a reservoir of water and mineral nutrients but also contains a diversity of plant, microbial, and animal life that affect the physical and chemical properties of the soil. These biotic and abiotic factors influence the aboveground plant community and provide ecosystem services including carbon storage and improved water quality. Today, scientists have a limited understanding of the diversity and function of organisms within the soil environment and how they might be altered by anthropogenic factors such as climate change and nitrogen pollution. Relatively few public gardens are currently studying soil science and soil ecology despite its importance both to plants and to terrestrial ecosystems in general. Some exceptions to that rule include the Holden Arboretum, Morton Arboretum, Chicago Botanic Garden, and Kings Park and Botanic Garden. For example, scientists at the Holden Arboretum are looking at whether population-level differences in aboveground growth of trees are a function of differences in root system carbon demands. They have found that fine root system production and life span vary between populations of loblolly pine and may be associated with variation in aboveground yield. Scientists at both the Morton Arboretum and the Chicago Botanic Garden are looking at carbon and nitrogen dynamics in soils, including urban soils and soils under restored plant communities. At Kings Park and Botanic Garden in Perth, Australia, considerable progress is being made in understanding the association between orchids

Figure 21-7: Chicago Botanic Garden intern Jennifer Taylor hand-pollinating an eastern prairie white-fringed orchid (*Platanthera leucophaea*).

Courtesy Chicago Botanic Garden, photo by Pati Vitt

and mycorrhizal fungi. Scientists there are using a variety of methods including soil assays, root assays, and "baiting" for fungus in soils to determine the diversity and functional significance of fungi colonizing orchid roots (Swarts and Dixon 2009).

Human/Plant Interactions

Several gardens, notably the Missouri Botanical Garden and the New York Botanical Garden, have research programs focusing on ethnobotany, the study of past and present relationships between people and plants, and are furthering that work by conserving useful plant species and traditional knowledge for the benefit of future generations. Ethnobotanists typically work with indigenous peoples to understand and promote the sustainable use of plant resources. They may also work with pharmaceutical and agricultural companies to study the chemicals in plants that show promise for the development of new drugs, crops, or other products.

For useful plants, it is important to harvest at levels that minimize harm to the population. Any plant used by humans must be harvested in some way, which can alter the population

CASE STUDY: SNOW LOTUS THREATENED BY OVERHARVEST

Jan Salick and Wayne Law, Missouri Botanical Garden

Our ethnobotanical research focuses on two culturally important and valuable snow lotus species under different harvesting pressures (Figure 21-8). Snow lotuses (*Saussurea* spp.) are threatened species native to the highest reaches of the eastern Himalayan mountains (4,000 m; 13,123 ft. and higher) and are important medicinal plants in traditional Tibetan medicine. We work with two sister species of snow lotus (*S. laniceps* and *S. medusa*) and analyze the consequences of human harvest on plant morphology and population growth rates, in the end leading to models of sustainable harvest.

The evolutionary consequences of harvesting can be very rapid: traits can change over a few generations. As collectors preferentially select larger plants, which have alleged greater potency and monetary value, they exert strong selective pressure. By analyzing herbarium specimens from early collecting expeditions as well as present day specimens, we detected a significant negative trend in plant height over 100 years for *S. laniceps*. Additionally, this size difference is observed in present-day heavily harvested populations, which are 9 cm (0.3 ft.) smaller than lightly harvested populations. Findings of this sort are particularly important because plants that are smaller have lower seed yield (Law and Salick 2005).

Finally, we constructed models of population growth incorporating the information collected above, as well as yearly variation found in populations of snow lotus. Current levels of harvest are not sustainable for *S. laniceps*, nor for *S. medusa* if pollen limitation is incorporated. Additionally, impacts of climate change

are severe in the Himalayan alpine habitats of snow lotus and will undoubtedly further change their population dynamics. If the harvest of these species were limited to traditional practices of Tibetan doctors, and rampant commercial harvest were banned, snow lotus populations would be stable. These results stress the need for active conservation measures and the engagement of local citizens in conservation decision making. People/plant interactions are still little appreciated, and understanding human impact is critical in developing successful management practices.

Figure 21-8: Snow lotus (*Saussurea laniceps*) growing on a steep alpine cliff in Yunnan, China.

Photo by Wayne Law

genetics and demographics of the target species. Sustainable harvest involves the extraction of a natural resource at a level where the exploitation can continue indefinitely. Whenever possible, levels of sustainable harvest for exploited species should be determined empirically (Peters 1994), and an excellent example is provided by the Missouri Botanical Garden's work with snow lotus harvest.

Environmental Horticultural Research, Plant Breeding, and Evaluation

Environmental horticulture is the practice of improving the quality, sustainability, and aesthetics of the human-created landscapes and gardens in which we work and play. Environmentally sound horticultural practices—using drought-tolerant plants to lessen water use, using pest- and disease-resistant plants to lessen chemical use, using plants that provide shelter and food for our native fauna—not only improve the health of urban landscapes but also ultimately lessen the impact of human activities on adjacent natural habitats.

Several public gardens have well-established horticultural research programs. Many gardens have resident expertise in plant propagation, using both traditional techniques and tissue culture. Many species are difficult to germinate, let alone grow to maturity, and public garden horticulturists are often the first to develop protocols to do both. For instance, scientists at several gardens have investigated the role of plant-derived smoke in breaking dormancy of species from fire-prone environments, including the fynbos of South Africa (Brown 1993), the *Banksia* woodlands of southwestern Australia (Rokich and Dixon 2007), and the tallgrass prairie in the United States (Jefferson et al. 2008). Tissue culture propagation has both horticultural and conservation applications. For *ex situ* conservation activities, many species fail to produce adequate numbers of seeds for seed banking or produce recalcitrant seeds that do not withstand drying and freezing. For these species, tissue culture offers options for propagation and medium-term storage. The Harold L. Lyon Arboretum in Hawaii has an active tissue culture program working with numerous critically endangered Hawaiian endemic species. Tissue culture protocols are also being developed for the non-seed-bearing bryophytes and pteridophytes (Pence 2004).

Many gardens are actively developing new ornamental crops, including the University of British Columbia Botanical Garden in Canada, Kings Park and Botanic Garden in Australia, and the Chicago Botanic Garden in the United States. The Chicago Botanic Garden's breeding program focuses on developing new cultivars of herbaceous perennials well adapted to Midwestern and equivalent landscapes, primarily from traditional breeding of genera native to the United States. Plants are selected to be highly ornamental but also environmentally friendly by being noninvasive, cold hardy, and resistant to drought, heat, and pests, thereby lessening inputs of water and chemicals. Breeding programs may require a significant amount of in-ground nursery space and are best done in cooperation with several institutions willing to evaluate potential releases. It is important to know how the new plant performs in a variety of climates before taking it to market.

In a world quickly becoming more interconnected due to global trade, comprehensive testing of new plants in multiple climate zones is important because these plants are widely available via the Internet regardless of their origin. In addition, the market is being flooded with new plants, and sifting through all the garden options to select hardy, geographically appropriate plants can be a daunting task. Public gardens can use their plant evaluation results to educate the horticultural industry and home gardeners about the best plants for their region, that is, those that are beautiful and hardy but not weedy or disease-prone. The largest plant evaluation program in the United States is found at the Chicago Botanic Garden; it focuses on perennials, vines, and shrubs for home and commercial landscapes and, more recently, on plants for use on green roofs (Figure 21-9).

Figure 21-9: Richard Hawke evaluating taxa in the genus *Tradescantia* at Chicago Botanic Garden for garden use in the upper Midwest.

Courtesy Chicago Botanic Garden, photo by Robin Carlson

Richard Hawke, Chicago Botanic Garden

The Chicago Botanic Garden's Plant Evaluation Program utilizes comparative trials to evaluate species and cultivars of selected genera in side-by-side plots for easy comparison. Plants are evaluated in-ground for a set term—four years for perennials and six years for shrubs and vines—with data collected regularly on ornamental traits, adaptability to edaphic and environmental conditions of the test site, invasiveness, susceptibility to diseases and pests, and winter hardiness. The test site is monitored for light and wind exposure, soil type, and pH. Water is provided as needed, and mulch consisting of shredded leaves and wood chips helps with water conservation and weed suppression. Plants are not fertilized, winter-mulched, or chemically treated for insect or disease problems. The Garden has always taken a sustainable approach to plant evaluation by keeping maintenance practices to a minimum, allowing plants to thrive or fail under natural conditions, thus compiling a list of recommended plants grown using sustainable gardening practices.

Plants are regularly monitored using thirty characterization criteria to track their performance throughout the evaluation term. Data are collected on, among other things, ornamental traits such as bloom period, flower color and size, habit assessment, height and width, weedy or invasive potential, fall color effectiveness, and winter character; landscape performance and adaptability, including health and cultural or environmental issues related to soil, drainage, or climate; disease and pest problems; and winter survivability, such as degree of crown damage or woody dieback.

Reporting the results of a trial is an essential component of a plant evaluation program. *Plant Evaluation Notes*, the Garden's principal vehicle for reporting results, is broadly distributed in both print and electronic formats to researchers, horticulture professionals, and the gardening public, reaching hundreds of thousands of readers with each issue. Results are routinely cited in gardening and trade publications such as *Horticulture, The American Gardener, American Nurseryman, NMPro, Perennial Plants*, and *Gartenpraxis*. Recommendations are also distributed at such Garden programs as the annual plant sale, Plant Information Service, and Best Plants of Illinois website.

Summary

The need for increased capacity in plant research has never been greater. Many of today's most pressing environmental issues, including climate change, invasive species, and habitat loss and fragmentation, as well as the development and impact of biofuels, require botanical knowledge. Yet we are experiencing a continuing loss in botanical capacity with each passing year from the elimination of botany programs at universities and the retirement of botanists in land management agencies. And each day more plant species are lost to us forever.

Public gardens are already making significant contributions to plant science and are ideally positioned to do more to fill this critical research niche. Much of the fundamental work in biodiversity conservation is being done by public gardens, including classifying plant species, determining relationships among plant families, and understanding plant use around the world. Other garden scientists are making important discoveries about the management of anthropogenic threats to plants. This improves our understanding of the biology of plants and their communities so that we can conserve and restore them more successfully and efficiently.

Public garden research also reaches beyond basic plant science and conservation applications. Horticultural research addresses plant propagation problems, breeds new ornamental plants, and evaluates plants for different climates and uses, thereby improving the palette of plants available for home gardeners and green industry professionals. The common theme in garden research is the desire to improve human welfare and increase the understanding of plants in a world where plant-based solutions to environmental problems are critically needed.

Annotated Resources

Convention on Biological Diversity. 2002. *The global strategy for plant conservation*. Montreal: Secretariat of the Convention on Biological Diversity. Document approved and adopted at the sixth Conference of the Parties to the Convention on Biological Diversity (CBD). The decision represents the first time plant conservation received detailed scrutiny by the governments of the 183 countries that are parties to the CBD and the first time targets were set to guide plant conservation action on a global scale.

Crane, P. R., S. D. Hopper, P. H. Raven, and D. W. Stevenson. 2009. Plant science research in botanic gardens. *Trends in Plant Science* 14: 575–77. An introduction to a special issue of *Trends in Plant Science* titled "Plant science research in botanic gardens." Articles in this special issue focus on a number of timely issues, including orchid science and conservation (Swarts and Dixon), conservation genetics (Kramer and Havens), conservation and global change research (Donaldson), *ex situ* plant conservation (Li and Pritchard), plant diversity information management (Lughadha and Miller), biodiversity informatics (Paton), plant red-listing (Schatz), *in situ* conservation in the tropics (Chen, Cannon, and Hu), tree conservation (Oldfield), and the Global Strategy for Plant Conservation (Wyse Jackson and Kennedy).

Dosmann, M. S. 2006. Research in the garden: Averting the collections crisis. *The Botanical Review* 72: 207–34. An extensive review of the importance of collections-based research and how to increase the use of living plant collections.

Leadlay, E., and J. Greene. 1998. *The Darwin technical manual for botanic gardens.* London: Botanic Gardens Conservation International. This manual does not explicitly address research, but contains a wealth of information on public garden planning and management.

Primack, R. B., and A. J. Miller-Rushing. 2009. The role of botanical gardens in climate change research. *New Phytologist* 182: 303–13. A very nice review of how public gardens have contributed to climate change research and how they can continue to contribute in the future.

Wyse Jackson, P. S., and L. A. Sutherland. 2000. *International agenda for botanic gardens in conservation.* London: Botanic Gardens Conservation International. A framework for how public gardens can develop programs and policies in support of global plant conservation regardless of garden size, history, or collections.

CHAPTER 22

Conservation Practices at Public Gardens

SARAH REICHARD

Introduction

The Earth is changing rapidly. Human populations continue to grow, with the United Nations estimating up to 11 billion people on this planet by 2050, if fertility and death rates remain at current levels. We currently add 74 million people per year, and by 2050 it may be as high as 169 million per year. Each of those people will consume resources at varying levels, but all will need shelter, food, and other basic resources. Just as we have seen wild lands decrease in the last century as agriculture

and housing expanded, we will continue to see loss of suitable habitat for plants and animals.

When a species is proposed for listing under the U.S. Endangered Species Act, agencies publish a notice in the U.S. Federal Register that includes why scientists think the species is in trouble. A study of those listings found that in the United States, habitat loss, fragmentation, and degradation are the largest contributors to imperilment of plants (Wilcove et al. 1999), with introduced invasive species, overcollection from

KEY TERMS

Artificial selection: selection by humans for certain traits. This can be intentional, for breeding purposes. When species are grown for a long time in cultivation, however, surviving plants may undergo unintentional selection for the growing conditions. The survivors among nursery-grown plants may be genetically disadvantaged in wild populations.

Congeners/conspecifics: species in the same genus are known as congeners; individuals or populations in the same species may be called conspecifics.

Ecosystem services: the benefits of nature to human beings. Examples include forests and soils slowing water runoff and preventing erosion, pollination of crop species, and providing sequestration of carbon produced by internal combustion engines.

Ex situ conservation: conservation of an organism outside its native habitat (such as at a botanical garden or zoo).

Imperiled species: species that are likely to go extinct without intervention.

In situ conservation: conservation of an organism in its native habitat.

Maternal lines: plants descended from a single individual. When seeds are collected, they are recorded and stored separately by maternal lines.

Orthodox seeds: seeds that survive drying and freezing and may be stored for extended periods of time under those conditions without dying. Many temperate species are orthodox.

Plant respiration: plants' release of energy from stored sources produced by photosynthesis for metabolic processes. Slowing down respiration in orthodox seeds allows them to survive longer.

Recalcitrant seeds: seeds that do not survive drying and freezing. Most tropical and some temperate species such as oaks have recalcitrant seeds.

the wild, and disease also taking their toll. It is expected that these results may extend to the global level.

Climate change will also result in the degradation of habitat. Increasing carbon dioxide, methane, nitrous oxide, and other greenhouse gases are having a number of effects, including increasing average temperatures in most parts of the world and changing precipitation patterns (IPCC 2007). The changes will affect all organisms on Earth, but plants may be among the hardest hit because of their limited dispersal ability. Among the plants, montane species may have the most difficulty: as temperatures rise, montane species have been able to increase their altitudinal distribution—a study of 171 forest species in Europe found an average elevation increase of about 95 feet per decade (Lenoir et al. 2008). At some point they will run out of mountain and be at the top. For some alpine species, that time is now. Because alpine species generally do not have effective long-distance dispersal, they will go extinct unless they can adapt their physiological tolerances to warmer temperature.

Globally, the numbers are staggering. By 2050, we could lose, or be very close to losing, 100,000 of the 300,000 plant species we know about (Raven 1999). By the end of the century we could lose another 100,000. The estimate of 300,000 plant species on Earth includes 50,000 we have not yet discovered and described. We will not even know what we have lost in those cases: a cure for a form of cancer, a species that could be hybridized with a known crop species to increase disease resistance, or species that perform valuable ecosystem services for us. Plants nourish us, keep soil in place, hold carbon to reduce global warming, and delight us with their beauty.

There is another disturbing global trend, and that is the shrinking of traditional botanical expertise in universities. Public gardens have botanical and horticultural expertise and facilities and are therefore in an excellent position to address critical needs in conservation. Some gardens, especially those affiliated with universities, may be able to train graduate students who want to work for governmental and nonprofit agencies doing applied work. They may be able to use lands they manage to do restoration work, or use facilities to grow plants for reintroduction into the wild. Gardens with laboratories can perform critical types of applied research. They may be able to provide public classes, lectures, and displays that will stimulate support for plant conservation work. Collectively they also have 150 million visitors per year, providing an excellent educational opportunity (Wyse Jackson and Sutherland 2000). The point is that there is something that every garden, of every size, can contribute to increasing the security of plants on Earth.

Approaches to Plant Conservation
In Situ Conservation

In situ means "on site" and refers to conservation work done where the species occurs naturally. This is always preferable because it preserves the genetic diversity of the species in its ecological context.

Natural Areas

Many public gardens manage natural areas in addition to their display gardens. Overall, U.S. and Canadian public gardens manage 62,539 acres (25,328 hectares) of natural areas (Garcia-Dominguez and Kennedy 2003). Some are quite large: the Bernheim Arboretum and Research Forest in Kentucky has 14,000 acres (5,670 hectares). Large natural areas can be used for land management research techniques, for restoration, or for planting rare species when appropriate. Smaller natural areas may be mostly or entirely "edge" and subject to edge effects of increased light and disturbance that makes the habitat less suitable (Galbraith 2003). Assume that about 100 m (328 ft.) into the habitat from the actual transition is edge. Even the Delaware Center for Horticulture's single acre, the smallest reported by Garcia-Dominguez and Kennedy, can be useful for *in situ* conservation as an education site where people can learn about native species. Managing a natural area, however, is different from managing a garden and requires diverse knowledge and skill sets among garden personnel.

When possible, it is important for gardens to be involved with *in situ* work. Agencies that monitor rare plants, such as the U.S. Fish and Wildlife Service (USFWS) and state natural heritage programs in the United States, should be contacted before beginning a project. If the garden does not own the land, landowners should also be contacted to determine their priorities. All conservation work should be done as part of an organized plan for the recovery of the species. The USFWS leads planning for species formally listed as endangered, but some unlisted species may also have plans. Biologists from several agencies and gardens with knowledge of the species may be asked to participate in developing the plan, which will discuss the steps needed for the species to be considered secure, as well as gaps in knowledge and priorities for research. It should also be noted that some species, such as those with specific soil requirements, are naturally rare and not necessarily imperiled and perhaps should not be the highest priority. Working with relevant agencies will help determine the priority species.

Assisting Agencies with In Situ Conservation

Even if a public garden has no natural areas in its land holdings, it can assist with *in situ* conservation. Federal, state, and

Trained volunteers who assist in data collection can be useful in extending the reach of garden personnel, as well as in providing a useful outreach tool about plant conservation. The volunteers, working in groups with garden staff or as individuals, are assigned populations of rare species to locate and document or instructed to look for specific invasive species. The documentation is returned to the garden and information given to the land managers and state tracking agencies so species and populations are better managed.

Since 2001, the Rare Care Program at the University of Washington Botanic Gardens has trained volunteers to independently monitor the status of rare plant populations. All volunteers must have at least two years of post-high-school biological training, sign a confidentiality statement to protect the site location, and go through a one-day training session with Rare Care. Additional training in plant identification and navigation is also offered. Rare Care works with agencies to determine which populations should be monitored, and the volunteer completes a lengthy data form, which is then shared with the landowner and the state database. Between 2001 and 2009, nearly 500 populations were monitored in more than 200 species. In addition, while relocating known populations, 25 new populations were discovered.

The goal of the Invasive Plant Atlas of New England (IPANE) is to develop a comprehensive Web-based database of the invasive species in the region. The database can then be used for analyses, education, and early detection of new species. Professional botanists collect some of the data, but much is collected by volunteers trained by the New England Wildflower Society's Garden in the Woods. Trainings are offered around the region each year, and volunteers collect and enter their findings into the database.

Figure 22-1: A Rare Care volunteer takes field notes as he monitors a rare plant in Washington.

Photo by Katie Messick

The Fairchild Tropical Botanic Garden near Miami, Florida, invites residents of the area, especially children, to explore their own neighborhoods in the Fairchild Challenge program If You Plant It, Will They Come? As participants discover one of three specified native plant species, they observe them to see what insects or animals visit the plant. The observations are posted on a map the Garden maintains. The goal is to create pockets and corridors of habitats for native organisms, as well as to engage children and adults about landscape plant selection and its effects.

local public agencies and nonprofit organizations often have an insufficient number of botanists on staff to monitor and maintain natural populations. Gardens can encourage staff to collaborate with agencies to assist with management of the populations and extend the reach of the garden. The agencies often need help locating populations, verifying identification, observing pollinators, looking for obvious threats, and providing assistance with restoration activities such as controlled burns and planting associated native species. Gardens may also be able to use their expertise and facilities to grow rare plant species for population introductions and augmentations.

Ex Situ Conservation

Live Collections

Conservation that occurs away from the site of the wild population is called *ex situ* ("off site") conservation. *Ex situ* conservation may be done alone or integrated with *in situ* work. Plants

are collected from the wild populations, either as cuttings or seeds, and the source well documented (today precise GPS data are usually taken, along with detailed collection descriptions). One form of *ex situ* conservation is to grow plants within a garden setting, whether as part of a display or in a dedicated conservation area. There can be a powerful educational message if the plants are grown as part of a display. Just as visitors to a zoo may become more supportive of tiger conservation if they watch the animals on display, a visitor to a public garden may be engaged by observing a rare plant. An obvious disadvantage, however, prevents this from being a truly effective conservation tool: many individual plants are needed to represent even a fraction of the genetic diversity in the wild. With small herbaceous plants it may be possible to fit many into a relatively small space, but trying to conserve the genetic diversity of trees in a public garden setting is virtually impossible. Herbaceous species, however, are also not well suited to

FRANKLINIA AND WOLLEMIA: OUT OF THE WILD AND INTO THE GARDEN

John Bartram, a farmer and early American plant explorer, along with his son, William, saw an unusual small tree growing along the Altamaha River in Georgia. It had large white camellia-like flowers that bloomed late in the summer. He described it and named it *Franklinia alatamaha* after John Bartram's friend Benjamin Franklin. William later collected seeds from the plants and sent them to England, noting at one point that they had only observed the one population. For reasons unknown, that population no longer exists and no others have been found—no wild plants have been known since the early 1800s. If not for the Bartrams' intervention, this species would be extinct. Between 1998 and 2000, Bartram's Garden (still in existence near Philadelphia and open to the public) surveyed to determine how many plants may be found worldwide; they estimate about 2,000 plants, in several countries. Because these are the offspring of the relatively small sample of seeds that William took, a new population established in the wild might have lower evolutionary potential to adapt to changing conditions. At least their presence in gardens allows this beautiful species to continue to be known and enjoyed.

A more recent example is the discovery of *Wollemia nobilis* (Wollemi pine) in Australia in 1994. Previously known from fossils from the Jurassic, making them contemporaries of dinosaurs, about 100 trees were found growing in a deep canyon in eastern Australia. The population is carefully guarded, but propagated materials are available to public gardens and commercially

through a thoughtfully organized plan that returns some of the proceeds from each sale (beginning in 2005) to conservation of the species. If only *Franklinia* had been subject to such foresight and protection in the 1700s!

Figure 22-2: *Franklinia* is extinct in the wild but survives in the collections of many public gardens.

Photo by Michael Dosmann

---

this sort of *ex situ* conservation. They are likely to be relatively short-lived and will need to be continually repropagated. Doing that by cuttings or some other asexual propagation methods may be considered genetically stable, but collection of seeds from those plants would need to be considered as "garden origin," or not genetically representative of the wild population. The seeds may be the result of artificial selection or hybridization from related species grown in the garden. Plants grown in gardens for reintroduction in the wild should be carefully monitored for the transmission of weeds, insects, and pathogens before planting.

All rare plants grown in the garden should have security, especially smaller plants. Many gardens have stories of rare alpine plants smuggled out in a purse, or rampant and disfiguring cuttings taken from shrubs and trees. Some gardens prefer not to label rare plants, although that defeats the purpose of engaging the thoughtful visitor. It is also a good idea to have additional plants outside the display area in case of theft. If a rare plant is in decline, cuttings should also be taken from it, if possible, for reestablishment in the garden.

It is doubtful that the plants grown in gardens will be suitable for reintroduction in the wild, unless the growing conditions in the garden are identical to those for the wild population. Just as natural selection results in the individuals most suited to the immediate environment surviving and reproducing and less fit individuals dying, artificial selection results in plants best suited to the conditions of the garden. If this must be done, the garden needs to maintain impeccable records about the lineage of each individual, to ensure that more than the progeny of one or just a few mother plants are reintroduced, which would result in an overintroduction of one genetic type. Another problem is hybridization with congeners or even garden-origin conspecifics in the population, which can lead to individuals unfit for reintroduction. If there is an intention to use living plants for introduction into the wild, gene flow with close relatives must be eliminated.

Seed Banks

A more feasible way to preserve genetic diversity of rare plants away from the site of a rare population is through seed banking.

Seeds are durable living organisms, consisting of the embryonic plant, a starchy nutrient source (endosperm), and a hard seed coat that protects the embryo and endosperm. These sturdy packages, if treated correctly, can survive for decades. Careful collection, followed by careful storage, can be a viable tool in plant conservation. This includes the collection of rare species, as well as the collection of more common native seed for later use in restoration. It should be noted that not all seeds are suitable for storage. So-called orthodox seeds are those that store well and include many temperate species. Recalcitrant seeds cannot be stored for long periods of time, and complicated tissue culture or cryopreservation, beyond the scope of most public gardens, are needed for these plants. These include oaks and many tropical species (Guerrant, Havens, and Maunder 2004).

The first step is to carefully collect the seeds to maximize genetic diversity. It is important to take a small sample from each population, because it is irresponsible to collect all the seeds from a population unless the population is destined for destruction. This must be done carefully, to ensure that most seed remains in each population to regenerate it, that no maternal line is completely removed, and that the genetic diversity of the entire population is represented in the sample. Determining how much seed is acceptable to take from a population is a bit tricky. Excellent detailed guidelines are given in Appendix 3 of Guerrant, Havens, and Maunder (2004). In general, it is important to take a small amount of seeds from a number of individuals, storing the seeds from each individual plant separately (collecting along maternal lines); this can be critical in planning the use of the seeds later. Collect from throughout each population and store temporarily in containers that allow air exchange such as paper bags. After collection, the seeds should be carefully cleaned of pods, chaff, and other materials. They should be counted, and each maternal line should be entered as a separate accession into a records book or file and given a tracking number. Collecting from multiple populations usually increases the genetic diversity represented in the seed bank.

Many things, including species, age of seed, and storage conditions, determine the life span of a seed. Seed respiration must be reduced for longevity. This is achieved by cool temperatures and, even more important, low humidity. However, extremes of either cold or dryness can also kill the seeds. As soon as possible, the collected seed should be placed in cold storage. Drying the seeds to about 15–20 percent relative humidity first is ideal. Large gardens may build a secure seed vault with humidity controls, but dessicant gels and dehumidifiers can be used if data loggers or other devices that record

Figure 22-3: A volunteer cleans, checks, and counts seeds prior to packaging them for long-term storage. Each accession includes the seeds from only one plant, and records are carefully tracked.

Photo by Jennifer Youngman

relative humidity are used. Once the seeds are sufficiently dry, they should be sealed into containers (many types, such as metal envelopes and jars, are available) and frozen at -20 to $-25°C$. Much more information can be found in Pritchard (2004) and Guerrant, Havens, and Maunder (2004). Properly handled and stored, seeds should be able to live for 30–100 years or even more. Some moss and fern spores can also be stored under similar conditions (Pence 2004). Recently, there has been research demonstrating that cryopreservation, or the freezing of seeds in ultra-low-temperature liquid nitrogen, is ultimately the best way to preserve even orthodox seeds. Because of the high cost of doing this, however, it is likely that few public gardens will use these methods. The same is also true of tissue culture, which preserves and propagates species through asexual methods using small bits of plant tissue on a nutrient and hormone gel. Conventional seed storage still provides excellent results for conservation for most species.

Gardens interested in collecting seeds of rare native species but not yet ready to dedicate space for climate-controlled facilities can partner with other gardens. Many that are members of the Center for Plant Conservation (see Annotated Resources) might be good partners. The National Center for Genetic Resources Preservation in Fort Collins, Colorado, and the Millennium Seed Bank may be able to accept seeds if contacted in advance.

Ideally, at the time of collection, a small random sample across maternal lines would be germinated to determine the viability of the seeds. Other viability tests can also be used. At intervals of perhaps about five years, seeds should be withdrawn from storage and their viability retested to determine if re-collection from that population should be attempted. Because little is know about propagation of most rare plant species and public gardens usually have considerable expertise, experimentally germinating the seeds at the time of collection may provide useful information for future reintroductions.

While not focusing on rare species, efforts such as Seeds of Success (SOS) work to bank seeds of common native species for eventual restoration projects (Byrne and Olwell 2008). It uses teams across the country to collect seeds that are sent to England for the Millennium Seed Bank, which is doing similar collecting in other countries. Some seeds are also sent to the U.S. Department of Agriculture's National Plant Germplasm System.

Ex situ conservation is intended to preserve genetic diversity, but there is a loss of genetic diversity at every step in the process. For instance, when collecting seed, only some of the seeds are taken from the population, representing a fraction of the genetic diversity in the population. Of those seeds, some are not viable, and still more are lost in propagation, nursery production, and transplanting. While a valuable tool, it should never be considered a preferred alterative to *in situ* conservation, but as an integrated component of a larger conservation plan.

Engaging the Garden in Conservation

A conservation garden is one that integrates conservation into every aspect of its operations, as the North Carolina Botanical Garden and the Eden Project have done. Displays in gardens can also promote conservation activities that are not directly related to plant conservation but can affect it. For instance, water conservation is also an important concern. Freshwater is limited, and much of it is wasted and polluted when it sheets off impervious surfaces. Public gardens can display rainwater capture through cisterns or rain barrels and use rain gardens or bioswales (Dunnett and Clayden 2007) to demonstrate the cleansing of water before it rejoins natural water sources. Gardens can also display plants demonstrating how attractive xeriscaping gardens can be (Eberhardt 2008). These educational efforts help conservation overall.

When new buildings are developed, the materials should be as sustainable as possible and from local sources. Energy efficiency should be a primary consideration. In some places, solar or geothermal energy sources may be initially more expensive but pay for themselves over time. The Leadership in Energy and Environmental Design (LEED) program of the Green Building Council provides a number of ideas for buildings.

Even garden operations can become part of the conservation garden. Trams for tours and carts for horticulture staff use should be energy efficient. In food service, efforts can be made to include local and organic foods, shade-grown coffee (which protects bird habitat), and reusable and compostable dishes and cutlery. Nearly every operation should contribute to the success of the conservation program. Staff, boards, and members all play a role in determining the appropriate level of conservation engagement for the garden.

Determining Appropriate Integration of Conservation

Display and Pleasure Gardens

Gardens whose primary mission is to display plants may still find ways to communicate the importance of plant conservation. Those with good security might include some rare species and interpretation about them in the collection. An ecogeographic display about the region's native species could include messages about causes of local species endangerment. A display about eastern U.S. plants could include interpretation about the impacts of overharvesting American ginseng (*Panax quinquefolius*). Interpreting composting, water conservation, or green building techniques can also increase visitor engagement about conservation. While the mission of these gardens may not be focused on education, informal messages enhance the visitor experience and further general knowledge about conservation issues.

CASE STUDY: BETTY FORD ALPINE GARDEN

At 8,200 feet in elevation, the Betty Ford Alpine Garden is the highest in the world, with the goal of displaying and conserving the world's alpine plant species. The garden was established in 1985 by the Vail Alpine Garden Foundation and in 1988 was named after the wife of the thirty-eighth U.S. president, Gerald Ford. Although small, it has more than 3,000 alpine species in the collection. The trustees and staff serve conservation of such species in several ways. They integrate the Global Strategy for Plant Conservation into every aspect of their planning and program development (see the Annotated Resources for more information about this strategy). They partner with federal and state conservation agencies on projects, including using volunteers to monitor native rare alpine species. Recognizing that a trail through a subalpine wetland was impacting it, the Garden built a boardwalk that routes visitors through less sensitive areas and keeps them off the ground, allowing the wetland to recover. Its collections policy incorporates clear statements about the importance of having wild-collected material in the collection for conservation, but also about how responsible wild-collection should be done. Finally, the Garden works with larger organizations such as Botanic Gardens Conservation International and Conservation International on plant conservation issues.

Advocacy Gardens

A relatively new concept in public gardens, advocacy gardens are issue-oriented, with a mission to change how humans relate to the Earth (Hoversten and Jones 2002). These gardens integrate that message across all of their activities. There may be an integration of information about plants, soils, climate, human healing, and art. A good example is the Eden Project, in Cornwall, England. According to its website, the project "exists to explore our dependence on the natural world, rebuilding connections of understanding that have faded from many people's lives. Much of the Eden Project site tells the story of how plants support our social, economic, and environmental well-being" (www.edenproject.com). The Eden Project, in addition to its displays and interpretations about plants and the Earth, also has

---

CASE STUDY: THE LADY BIRD JOHNSON WILDFLOWER CENTER

The Lady Bird Johnson Wildflower Center (LBJWC) is located in Austin, Texas. Austin gets only about 32 inches of rain a year, much of it in heavy downpours (compare to Boston, with 42 inches, and New York City, with 60 inches). It sits at the northeast end of the Edwards Aquifer, one of the largest aquifers in the world, serving 2 million people, including the cities of Austin and San Antonio, as well as agriculture. Water conservation is important in the region. The LBJWC collects water off the roofs of its buildings and stores up to 300,000 gallons of rainwater per year in cisterns to use for irrigation. The water collection pipes are visible to the public and a 21,000 gallon cistern is at the entrance to the garden, making interpretation about rain harvest and water conservation clear. Altogether, their rainwater harvest can potentially capture 376,000 gallons per year. The water is then pumped out of the cisterns to assist in irrigating the collection. The LBJWC is a good example of a garden that integrates conservation into most of its activities and interprets that for visitors. Gardens can also interpret water conservation through permeable paving, rainwater gardens, and green roofs.

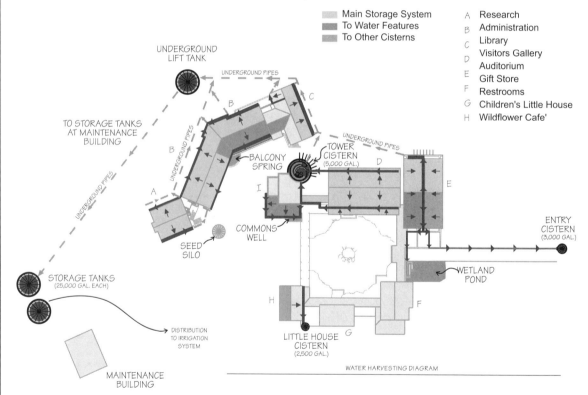

Figure 22-4: Rainwater captured from roofs at the Lady Bird Johnson Wildflower Center in Austin, Texas, is channeled into several cisterns and tanks so that it can be used for irrigation.

Map courtesy of Lady Bird Johnson Wildflower Center

environmental art and carries its conservation message all the way to extensive recycling in its food service and a policy of purchasing more recycled products than products it recycles or disposes of in other ways. The Arizona-Sonora Desert Museum is an example of an advocacy garden that focuses on interpreting the Sonoran Desert ecosystem and its plants, animals, geology, and art. It promotes understanding and conservation of the unique system. A garden does not have to completely become an advocacy garden, however. It is possible to have some displays that promote advocacy and others that do not.

Research and Teaching Gardens

Research and teaching gardens are often large and complex. Many universities, especially land grant universities in the United States, also include public gardens that do important conservation research work and educate students about conservation activities. The North Carolina Botanical Garden has a strong conservation mission and calls itself a conservation garden (White 1996). It focuses on regionally native plants, and conservation is central to every aspect of the garden, including

CASE STUDY: MISSOURI BOTANICAL GARDEN

The Missouri Botanical Garden (MOBOT) was founded in 1859 by Henry Shaw. It has a wonderful series of display gardens, but its real strength is unseen by most visitors. MOBOT employs dozens of Ph.D. scientists, many of whom actually work in other countries on basic and applied research. Much of that work is in plant classification, but many also work on conservation issues. MOBOT is the host institution for the Center for Plant Conservation and works with that organization on conservation of native Missourian plants. Scientists also study plants in Asia, Latin America, and Africa and hold training programs in seven countries. Working with local universities, they have about thirty graduate students training in research, about half from outside the United States. Some of the Garden's most valuable contributions are the many databases that are available through its website. Need a checklist of the plants of Peru or Madagascar? It's there. Need to know the chromosome numbers of a rare species? Chances are that information will be in the Index to Plant Chromosome Numbers. MOBOT's dedication to conservation goes beyond research, however. It is one of a number of gardens that are integrating conservation into everything they do. In 1998 it was one of the first to demand that its new buildings be sustainable, built with recycled materials, sustainably harvested lumber, increased energy efficiency, fewer impermeable surfaces, and more. It is hard to imagine a public garden more dedicated to international plant conservation or one that is more of an inspiration to gardens everywhere.

buildings, collection policies, education and interpretation, and planning. In addition to the main garden adjacent to the university and an arboretum on campus, it maintains several public and nonpublic natural areas throughout the state in which it promotes rare and native plant restoration.

Nonprofit and municipal gardens also have extensive programs. For instance, the Missouri Botanical Garden is one of the oldest in the United States, with an international reputation for excellence in teaching and research. Its staff may have university affiliations, but they are employees of the Garden. Similarly, the Chicago Botanic Garden, since its opening in 1972, has quickly developed a stellar program.

Organizations and Plans to Help Conservation Integration

There are organizations and international strategies and conventions addressing plant conservation, including some specific to public gardens. These suggest a number of conservation activities, some of which are important to all gardens and others that may be more important to those emphasizing conservation.

Botanic Gardens Conservation International

Gardens with substantial conservation goals may choose to join networks of similar public gardens, including Botanic Gardens Conservation International (BGCI), which provides technical support and information for every level of garden around the world. With hundreds of member institutions in 118 countries, BGCI is perhaps the largest international group working on plant conservation. Members include gardens from all levels of conservation interest, and the work of other member gardens often inspires ideas for new projects at home. Headquartered in England, BGCI has offices in the United States, Singapore, and China and resources available in numerous languages. BGCI also provides links to other networks, such as the African Botanic Gardens Network.

Center for Plant Conservation

In the United States, the Center for Plant Conservation (CPC) links a number of gardens that have made a substantial commitment to conservation. Interested gardens must apply and go through a screening process to become part of the network. The CPC takes a regional approach, with gardens from Massachusetts to Hawaii taking leadership on plant conservation in their areas. Each garden is responsible for certain key species in its area, which CPC refers to as the National Collection of Endangered Plants. Gardens must report annually about the *in situ* and *ex situ* work done on these species. While they may also work on species not included in the National Collection, this approach ensures that there is an institution working explicitly on the rarest species in the country. The CPC is headquartered at the Missouri Botanical Garden in St. Louis. All CPC affiliated gardens work closely with appropriate agencies in their regions.

Convention on International Trade in Endangered Species

The International Union for the Conservation of Nature (IUCN) maintains and updates the Convention on International Trade in Endangered Species (CITES). This is an international agreement between countries to prevent trade from creating a loss of biological diversity. CITES was signed in 1975 by eighty countries, including the United States, and now covers more than 30,000 plants and animals on its regularly updated Red List. It does not replace national law, but gives a framework for each nation to develop its own. In general, permits are needed for the legitimate movement of listed species. For more information, see www.cites.org.

Convention on Biological Diversity

The Convention on Biological Diversity (CBD) became effective in 1993. Its goals are the conservation and sustainable use of biodiversity and the equitable sharing of resources. The financial gain from any plants imported after the effective date for each country (when it signed), as well as their offspring and DNA, must be shared with the country from which they were collected. Because botanical gardens are sometimes used by commercial horticulturists and even pharmaceutical companies for source material, plant exploration must be done in a way that ensures that source countries are compensated. The United States has not ratified the CBD, but most countries have, and public gardens everywhere should adhere to its standards (available at www.cbd.int).

Global Strategy for Plant Conservation

The Global Strategy for Plant Conservation (GSPC) was developed to manage plants under the CBD and was agreed to by 180 countries in 2002. Public gardens were instrumental in its development and in its implementation (Oldfield 2007). It has sixteen targets and an ambitious time frame for completion (see www.cbd.int/gspc). It calls for a working list of known plant species and an assessment of their conservation status. Public gardens with significant holdings and knowledge of particular plant taxa or regional floras could assist with this effort. In addition, there are region-specific plans, such as the North American Botanic Garden Strategy for Plant Conservation, in consultation with a number of U.S., Canadian, and Mexican groups.

International Agenda for Botanic Gardens in Plant Conservation

This agenda was developed in 2000 to provide a framework for public gardens to address the CBD (see www.bgci.org/ourwork/international_agenda). While the GSPC later spurred gardens in some regions to develop specific plans after its development in 2002, the agenda was the first effort to try to address CBD issues through gardens. Its structure is different from that of the GSPC, but it covers the same issues. Registering a public garden on the BGCI website in support of the agenda is one way that gardens can show support for the GSPC and assist international efforts.

Gran Canaria Declaration on Climate Change and Plant Conservation II

This 2006 declaration is an update of an earlier effort and looks beyond the 2010 deadline for the GSPC. It affirms that public gardens have a critical role to play in conserving plants under climate change through *ex situ* conservation and education. It recommends specific research topics and policy priorities (see www.bgci.org/ourwork/gcdccpc).

Leadership on Invasive Plant Issues

This chapter has focused on the conservation of rare species, but one conservation area in which nearly all gardens can actively participate is preventing the display and promotion of regionally invasive species. Except for a few gardens that focus

Figure 22-5: Kudzu (*Pueraria montana* var. *lobata*), a vine native to Asia, covers native forest trees in eastern Tennessee. Originally introduced for ornamental use, it has also been planted for erosion control.

Photo by Sarah Reichard

exclusively on native species, most public gardens include non-native plants, the majority of which are regionally appropriate from both cultural and conservation standpoints. A few, however, can become problem species. These non-native invasive plants may compete with native species in wildlands for resources such as water, light, and soil nutrients (Mack et al. 2000). They may also affect ecosystem properties, including soil nutrient cycling and hydrological processes, and the changes may be difficult to reverse (Vitousek and Walker 1989; Sala, Smith, and Devitt 1996; Mack et al. 2000; Dougherty and Reichard 2004). Conservative estimates are that invasive species cost the United States several billion dollars annually in control costs and damages (Pimental, Zuniga, and Morrison 2005). Unfortunately, many of these wildland invaders are used for horticulture, and many are common in gardens (Reichard 1997).

The Missouri Botanical Garden hosted a workshop in 2001 that was attended by nearly 100 professionals from public gardens, nurseries, landscape architects, and government agencies that grow and promote non-native plants. Amateur gardeners were also included. Each group developed its own code of conduct or best management practices around invasive species issues. In addition, all participants agreed to guiding principles that were foundational to their codes. By agreement, the participants titled the product of the workshop the St. Louis Declaration. All the guiding principles, codes of conduct, and proceedings from this workshop and a later one at the Chicago Botanic Garden can be found on the website of the Center for Plant Conservation (see Annotated Resources).

Implementing the Codes and Developing a Conservation Policy

The American Public Gardens Association and many individual gardens have endorsed the St. Louis Declaration, but the challenge is in the implementation. The first code calls for an

The University of Washington Botanic Gardens wanted a conservation policy that extended beyond the brief mentions of conservation in its collection policy. The policy begins with a statement of the importance of conservation values to the institution and its mission. Using the documents discussed in the section "Organizations and Plans to Help Conservation Integration" and the St. Louis Declaration, objectives were developed affirming the understanding and documentation of diversity, conserving diversity, promoting public education, awareness, research, and display about plant diversity, and building capacity for conservation diversity. Under the objectives, goals were laid out that would help the institution achieve its objectives. Using the objectives and goals, staff then began developing strategic work plans.

institution-wide assessment. For many gardens, the definition of *institution* might be a simple matter, but university and college gardens might want to consider the entire organization as the institution. Because the codes are wide-ranging in scope, implementation should involve staff from a number of relevant areas of the garden, including curation, education, and conservation (Havens 2002).

Implementation may also take place as part of developing a larger conservation plan. Regardless of the size or mission of the garden, it is useful for all institutions to develop a conservation policy. Most have a collections policy that guides development of the collections, but few have extended this to include conservation. A conservation policy can be included in a collections policy, but it is often worthwhile to have an independent one that covers issues other than the accessioning and deaccessioning of collection plants. The extended policy might also include water and energy conservation, use of compostable utensils in food service, and other concerns.

Measuring the Success of Conservation Programs

Many public gardens, like many other types of nonprofit organizations, have difficulty knowing when their efforts are successful. It may be useful to do a self-assessment a few years after developing a conservation policy. Using the goals set out in the policy, staff and volunteers within each unit should attempt to grade themselves on achieving the goals. In addition, units within the garden should independently grade each other. Finally, members of support organizations and outside partners (such as federal agencies working with the garden on

species recovery or other local nonprofit organizations) should be invited to do the exercise as well. While their efforts may be less well informed, the results may show where communication about successful activities is limited.

Comparisons of the results of the assessment from the different groups will likely give a good picture of where the conservation goals are being met and where efforts are less satisfactory. The information can be used to develop new goals, or better plans to achieve existing goals.

Summary

Developing a successful conservation program has many rewards. Most public gardens have a mission to foster awareness of the importance of plants to humans and other animals on Earth. Because of their shared values, staff members are generally committed to this vision and find implementing increased conservation deeply satisfying. Leading by example, as well as by explicit education, provides positive steps toward mitigating the effects of climate change and habitat loss. Gardens that actually become engaged in active plant conservation may make the difference between a species surviving on Earth or becoming extinct. Every garden should take steps appropriate to its mission and style to promote conservation.

Annotated Resources

Botanical Gardens Conservation International website (www.bgci.org). Links to several important publications and to networks of gardens doing conservation work throughout the world.

Center for Plant Conservation (www.centerforplantconservation.org). Offers valuable information about plant conservation in the United States, invasive species, and the St. Louis Declaration. Provides links to public gardens doing conservation in the United States and other plant conservation professionals. CPC maintains the National Collection of Endangered Plants, tracking several hundred rare U.S. species.

Leadership in Energy and Environmental Design Web page (www.usgbc.org/DisplayPage.aspx?CategoryID=19). Gives information about green building. The Sustainable Sites Initiative, an effort to extend green building strategies to the landscape, is managed by the same group at www.sustainablesites.org.

Byrne, M., and P. Olwell. 2008. Seeds of success: The national native seed collection program in the United States. *The Public Garden*. 23 (3): 24–25. Describes a seed collection program in the United States.

Eberhardt, M. 2007. The water conservation garden: A good idea that has become a necessity. *The Public Garden* 22 (1): 30–31. Describes xeriscaping and how to make it interesting in a public garden.

Guerrant, E. O., K. Havens, and M. Maunder. 2004. Ex situ *plant conservation: Supporting species survival in the wild*. Washington, D.C.: Island Press. The definitive book on *ex situ* conservation, with both theoretical and applied information.

Havens, K., P. Vitt, M. Maunder, E. O. Guerrant, and K. Dixon. 2006. *Ex situ* plant conservation and beyond. *BioScience* 56: 525–31. This paper provides an excellent overview of *ex situ* plant conservation.

IPCC. 2007. Climate change 2007: Synthesis report. Contribution of working groups I, II and III to the fourth assessment report of the Intergovernmental Panel on Climate Change, ed. R. K. Pachauri and A. Reisinger. Geneva, Switzerland: IPCC. Definitive document on climate change.

National Center for Germplasm Resources Preservation (http://www.ars.usda.gov/Main/docs.htm?docid=17923). Contains good details about seed collection and storage.

Oldfield, S. 2007. Working together in plant conservation. *The Public Garden* 22 (2): 8–9. Article about Botanic Gardens Conservation International.

PART V

Long-Term Initiatives

CHAPTER 23

A Strategic Approach to Leadership and Management

KATHLEEN SOCOLOFSKY AND MARY BURKE

Introduction

No one is born an effective leader, and few people instinctively know how to become a good manager. However, much like plant propagation and exhibit design, there are key skills that can be learned. The fields of management and leadership have been the focus of intense research and practice in the business community for many decades. Leaders of innovative public gardens, continually challenged to do more with less, benefit from the best of this work: they continually study new advances and then test approaches that promise to leverage limited public garden staffing and funding into extremely well-organized collaborative efforts.

Public garden leaders and managers use leadership and management skills to carefully consider and then align all resources available to them—people, budgets, partnerships inside and outside the organization, energy, attention, and enthusiasm—to accomplish clear goals that can make a difference in their local community and, in some cases, the entire world. Best of all, a public garden that promotes management and leadership skills across all departments and at every level of staffing can transform itself into a lively, energetic, and passionate workplace, where the impact of the staff's daily work is felt far beyond the garden borders.

This chapter examines the special tools and concepts that great leaders and great managers have used to transform their

KEY TERMS

Leadership: the art of establishing, sharing, and ensuring the realization of a vision for an organization, while balancing and coordinating the diverse interests of the organization's stakeholders.

Management: organization and coordination of the work of an organization; the art of getting things done through others.

Strategic planning: a process of imagining a desired future or vision for an organization and developing the goals, objectives, resources, and action steps to reach that vision.

SWOT analysis: a tool designed to help develop organizational strategy by looking at the organization's strengths, weaknesses, opportunities, and threats.

Stakeholder: person, group, or organization that has a stake in the organization.

Vision: a description of a desired future for an organization that will have a significant positive impact on the community and/or larger world and that serves to motivate its stakeholders.

Consultative decision making: a style of decision making in which the leader or manager asks for advice and opinions from subordinates, partners, or experts before making a decision. Responsibility for the final decision remains with the leader or manager.

gardens into thriving centers of horticulture, science, and education, and reviews some important approaches that help answer the fundamental questions facing all public gardens: what should be done, in what order; who should do it; and how can it be accomplished most effectively and efficiently, with the fewest resources (people, money, equipment, time, etc.).

The Difference Between Leadership and Management

> Management is doing things right; leadership is doing the right things.
>
> —*Peter Drucker*

Managing a complex institution such as a public garden, which has the infrastructure headaches of a small city, the educational goals of a college, the collection and curatorial issues of a museum, the health and safety issues of an amusement park, and the management concerns of a farm, requires extremely tight integration of leadership and management skills. This integration is so multifaceted that in real life it is difficult to tease apart leadership and management, and most public garden leaders have deep skills in both areas. However, it is helpful to consider how leadership and management differ conceptually. When projects or plans begin to go awry, this broad understanding allows a leader to quickly determine what part of the system has failed and swiftly begin repairs by mobilizing people with exactly the right skill set.

Leadership

Leaders are attuned to the future. Leaders are responsible for setting the overall direction of a public garden, a department within the garden, or even a volunteer team. Closely attuned to the world outside the garden walls, the best leaders listen carefully to the voices of visitors and supporters, stay sharply aware of shifts taking place in science and society, imagine new roles the garden might take in addressing or solving these issues, and, most important, remain keenly aware of both new opportunities and real dangers ahead that might either energize or crush the institution. Leaders must bring together a whole community and ensure that any new vision that emerges is built on the true strengths and history of the garden, is fully believable and attainable, and has the potential to make a significant impact by addressing critical issues in science and society. Finally, once an overall vision is firmly in place for the garden, leaders must inspire people and align them into high-performance partnerships and teams that have clear goals and

objectives. Leaders must constantly watch the far horizon and, with their eyes on the future, ensure that the most strategically important work is accomplished to advance major initiatives, while simultaneously adapting both short- and long-range plans in response to changing realities.

Leadership, then, is about developing both a vision and strategies to achieve that vision, and aligning people into partnerships, teams, and coalitions to execute the vision. Great leaders inspire change; they build consensus around big ideas and transform visions into attainable goals, clear objectives, and focused plans. In short, leaders decide what should be done and which major steps must be taken, in what order, to achieve those goals.

Management

Managers are focused on the now. Practical, direct, and achievement-oriented, great managers are responsible for executing the major projects that help public gardens have tremendous impact either locally or globally. Responsible for the day-to-day work of the public garden, managers oversee teams of people, monitor budgets and timelines, solve real-world problems, and have the talent to shift resources to the people and projects that can advance the garden's mission most rapidly. Managers provide clear objectives, timetables, and detailed processes, and then delegate authority and responsibility to individuals and teams. Unlike leaders, who are responsible for driving change and adapting to external forces, managers are expected to help a public garden perform in an orderly and predictable way, by setting up systems that help staff meet budgets and achieve critical targets. A manager works with the leader to understand what must be done, then organizes the people (who) and the processes (how) to ensure that major initiatives are completed on time and on budget. Management skills, then, help a leader execute all the plans and tasks needed to reach long-term goals and fulfill the vision and mission of the public garden.

Tools for Strategic Leadership: From a Shared Vision to a Plan

Leaders inspire and drive change with one simple tool: a focus on the gap between a possible, realistic, and wonderful future for a particular public garden and the hard, cold reality of where that same garden is right now. That gap, that tension between current reality and a more inspiring yet attainable future, is what energizes people to achieve great things. If the community was part of imagining and designing this new vision, people are primed and excited about working hard to help make it happen. There is nothing more powerful than consensus around a truly inspiring shared vision or mission. Beginning in the late 1990s, the Queens Botanical Garden in Flushing, New York, undertook a community-oriented master planning process. As the staff participated in this somewhat messy, open, but deeply engaging conversation with its community, an exciting vision for the Garden emerged, as well as a newly energized team of staff and supporters to carry it out. The master plan, adopted in 2001, developed around the universal theme of water, created a framework for physical development that prioritized environmental stewardship and cultural expression. In the years that followed, a great deal of activity—new grants, education programs, and building projects—started to align with these big goals. Today, the Queens Botanical Garden is widely regarded within the network of public gardens as a national leader in sustainability.

Public gardens that succeed best—those with the greatest positive impact in their local community or nationally or worldwide—are those that are most clear and exacting about what they are doing and why. Their leaders continually align and adjust resources to help staff and volunteers reach explicit goals. From the smallest of everyday decisions, such as how to set priorities for a person or a team, to the most high-profile public planning exercises, these public garden leaders make decisions and take actions that propel their gardens forward with focused efforts that can result in profound impacts in just a few years.

Built as a repository of horticultural excellence by Henry W. Phipps in 1893 at the height of Pittsburgh's industrial prowess, Phipps Conservatory and Botanical Gardens has evolved into a distinguished ecochampion among North America's approximately 700 public gardens. When Phipps began planning a three-phrase, multiyear expansion before the turn of the millennium, green building principles and practices had not yet reached broad public awareness. Like many other gardens, Phipps was focused on updating the visitor experience and support facilities in the more than 100-year-old institution. Inspiration to create one of the world's most energy-efficient and sustainable conservatories came from within. Once the leadership at Phipps learned about green buildings, the organization decided to complete its project in the most ecofriendly way possible. As the design progressed, Phipps' staff continually asked "what if" and challenged the designers, questioning everything and looking at each challenge as an opportunity to do things in a new way. While it was not the intent when the design started, Phipps found that by the time the project was completed, they had transformed a Victorian glass house into one of the world's greenest gardens. This pacesetting model for advanced green building practices,

sustainable development, and environmental awareness resulted in fourteen prestigious awards and its selection by President Barack Obama as the site for the 2009 Pittsburgh G-20 summit welcome reception and dinner for world leaders.

Catapulting a garden forward in this way depends entirely upon full access to the rich resources of a fully engaged community of leaders, managers, staff, funders, partners, and supporters, all united by a shared vision. The following are guidelines for public gardens seeking to build and cultivate an engaged community.

Develop a Clear Vision

Successful public gardens depend on the active participation and engagement of an entire community, both within and outside the garden. A clear vision, if built upon the garden's strengths and history, will guide its work and inspire people to commit to the work ahead; internally, it can encourage greater organizational effectiveness and impact at every level of the organization. These shared visions succeed best if they are authentic, inspiring, and built with the help of many stakeholders.

Involve Stakeholders

A wide range of stakeholders, garden staff, volunteers, and board members as well as potential external donors or partners should be part of the conversation and consensus building from the start. A vision crafted in isolation by a leader or a board of directors is a high-risk venture: it may be read with interest but never adopted. Every strong vision for the future is grounded in careful listening. The actual experience is often profound as other voices and viewpoints enlarge and expand the understanding of possibilities and alternative futures. New ideas about what is truly important emerge from what is heard. Those invited to share their ideas become enthusiastic about what is possible and begin to imagine a better future—and often come up with suggestions about how they personally can be a part of moving the institution in these new directions.

Make It Authentic

One of the primary tasks of a public garden leader is to help find the special niche for the garden: to help the organization discover what it can be best at in the world. When that niche is discovered, a great deal of energy and enthusiasm is suddenly released, and new people, new resources, and new closely linked projects, programs, and partners seem to emerge on every side. Many gardeners understand intuitively that the magic of a beautiful landscape or public space is that it somehow captures what Alexander Pope called "the genius of the place."

The best public gardens build off this genius to develop unique visions that would not have been likely to arise elsewhere. These authentic visions emerge from the history of the place, the constraints facing the garden, the special circumstances of the region, and the strengths of the leaders, board, and key staff. The living collections of the Arnold Arboretum of Harvard University are an inspiring example: with more than 15,000 plants, the Arboretum's collections are distinguished as one of the most thoroughly documented collections of temperate woody plants in the world. Building on a rich legacy of plant explorers and scientists on staff who specialized in the floras of China, Japan, Korea, and North America, the Arnold Arboretum fills a special niche in North American public gardens by focusing on its roles as a model of excellence in curatorial and collection practice as well as an international model of the use of living plant collections for scientific research.

CASE STUDY: MISSOURI BOTANICAL GARDEN'S CREATION OF AN INSPIRING VISION

In 2007, the Missouri Botanical Garden—guided by its board of trustees and AEA Consulting, New York—engaged in an eight-month planning process that involved diverse garden stakeholders as well as an intensive scan of critical issues and hard realities in the outside world. During this process, the Garden's leadership consulted with more than eighty people—board members, peer institutions in St. Louis and around the world, opinion leaders in St. Louis, funders, volunteers, staff members, and others—and had intensive discussions with staff. The planning team reviewed recent organizational successes and disappointments, articulated the garden's vision and core values, assessed the Garden's strengths and weaknesses, and identified the most important obstacles to the future vitality of the institution. They confronted the grave problems facing the globe in the face of habitat destruction, loss of biodiversity, and cultural pressures for consumption. Key stakeholders worked closely with the Garden leaders to consider where the Garden could make the most impact addressing these issues.

Locally, the visitor sites at the Missouri Botanical Garden provide opportunities for visitors to connect with plants and their environment in ways that inspire, inform, and enlighten. Nationally, the Garden has long been a leader in using Web-based technologies to support conservation and plant science. Internationally, the quality and scope of the Garden's globally important contributions to plant science and conservation distinguish it from all but a few other institutions in the world. The planning team at the Missouri Botanical Garden quickly understood that the Garden was uniquely suited to provide both national and international leadership in creating new models for a sustainable future.

The fragile balance of life on the Earth, with some species at risk of vanishing forever, may depend in large part on the efforts made by public gardens over the next few decades. With core strengths in mind—scientific leadership, extensive partnerships worldwide, a history of technological excellence, and a history of being a global force in plant conservation—the Missouri Botanical Garden realized that it was well positioned to launch compelling new national and international initiatives that would foster sustainability and the conservation of natural resources. Enhanced cooperation with the major botanical institutions of the world and other key partners is essential to achieving this goal—and the Missouri Botanical Garden already had the key global partnerships in place to build upon. To protect plants and ecosystems and thus enhance life for people and all living things, the Garden elevated sustainability as a core principle in all its work—its programs of research and conservation, horticulture, and education and ongoing operations—and, in its new strategic plan, committed to making the relevance of sustainability evident to all its visitors, both at its physical facilities and on the Web.

To sustain a healthy environment for people and other living organisms in St. Louis and around the world will require an extraordinary effort that must extend into the indefinite future. With this plan, the garden commits itself, together with its partners, to the following achievements by 2014:

- Creation of the Checklist of Plants of the World, a global database on all plant species, providing basic information in a highly accessible way to users around the world

- Production of Web pages on all 350,000 of the world's plant species as part of the Encyclopedia of Life

- Publication of *The Flora of North America, Flora of China, Flora Mesoamericana, Manual de Plantas de Costa Rica, Flora of Missouri, Catalog of the Plants of Madagascar*, and *Moss Flora of China* (collectively covering, with other garden scientific publications, 40 percent of the world's flora)

- Development of practical ways to support critical international conservation goals in key regions

- Building an international cadre of well-trained, committed biologists and conservationists who are engaged in plant research, conservation, and sustainability activities with these regions

- Becoming a global leader in educating the public about conservation and sustainability, recognized at home and abroad for the imaginative and effective ways research is linked to displays and exhibits, interpretation and education programs, media messages, and operations

For more details, see the Missouri Botanical Garden 2008–2014 Strategic Plan.

Make It Inspiring

An inspiring vision should be clearly grounded in the strengths and potential of the garden, but it should also be deeply meaningful and profound enough to require a real leap—of faith, of commitment, of focus—to succeed. Big goals inspire people to change, to stretch, and to set aside the turf battles and conservatism that often derails change in organizations. The San Diego Zoo and Wild Animal Park is an example of a public institution that created a bold vision and transformed itself from a traditional zoo to a powerhouse of global wildlife preservation. For decades, zoo staff members have worked with scientists and field biologists worldwide to save wildlife species from extinction. The groundbreaking work on plant collections at the zoo has helped people understand how critical appropriate plants and habitat are for the successful reproduction of captive animal populations.

Create a Work Plan

A vision is most powerful when it is tied to an executable plan. Strategic planning is the process by which public gardens develop the path to the future and align their desired vision and goals with appropriate resources, strategies, and actions. A successful strategic planning effort involves a wide range of stakeholders and effectively aligns all of the work of the garden, from the smallest tasks to the largest initiatives. Choosing an appropriate timeline for a strategic plan is an important first step: young gardens may need ten to fifteen years to launch major initiatives, build support groups, and stabilize funding, while more mature gardens, with large staffs, established endowments, political support, and thriving collections and programs, may wish to create a sense of urgency by focusing the staff and community's attention on a three-to-five-year period.

It is important to realize that not every strategic plan is undertaken to redesign the vision and mission of a public garden. However, in all successful strategic plans, leaders must make a concerted effort to scan the world beyond the garden gates. They must ask what the most significant concerns of science and society today are, and how the garden can contribute. After structured discussions with staff, garden members, influential community members, and the public are completed and an analysis of external realities is finished, the leadership develops a focused plan: a set of long-term goals linked to clear objectives, projects, and tasks with assigned deadlines. Excellent tools have been developed that can assist leaders as they embark on the preparation of a strategic plan; however, one of the best ways to start is to examine examples of public

gardens of different sizes and reflecting different purposes. Two widely used strategic planning approaches are a SWOT analysis and a self-assessment.

SWOT Analysis: Strengths, Weaknesses, Opportunities, Threats

An effective ways to quickly gather the critical information for decision making is a SWOT analysis, a strategic planning method that evaluates the strengths, weaknesses, opportunities, and threats of any project or institution. Widely used by businesses, public garden leaders can also use a SWOT analysis to engage stakeholders in discussions about the development of a strategic plan that is grounded in the current best understanding of the institution, builds on the garden's historical and current strengths, and safeguards the garden against threats and weaknesses.

Self-Assessment and Long-Range Planning

Developing an inspiring vision, building consensus around a long-range plan, and transforming a public garden can remain an elusive goal. For this reason, many public gardens depend upon outside specialists in long-range and master planning. Good consultants can bring a special viewpoint to the table: because the consultants are outsiders, people may speak more freely with them, sharing concerns that are difficult to bring up with colleagues. In addition, consultants sometimes see natural connections or synergies that staff and supporters miss.

However, some public gardens undertake this planning work independently, using tools and approaches developed by experts and supported by books, workshops, and training institutes. For example, the "five most important questions" and the step-by-step approach detailed in the Drucker Foundation Self-Assessment Tool can guide any public garden through an inexpensive but transformative six-to-twelve-month exercise that results in a long-range plan, a budget and a timeline, and an engaged community of participants.

Continually Review and Adapt the Plan

Public gardens strive to develop strategic and long-range plans that are living documents: highly focused and flexible plans that can be adapted as necessary to reflect changing circumstances. Once strategic results are identified, staff members work with the garden leadership to develop the short-range operational plans that clarify the tasks, activities, and resources that will help achieve these goals. Next the projects and tasks are delegated to individuals or teams for implementation. The following practices can help ensure that a strategic plan stays

CASE STUDY: THE DRUCKER SELF-ASSESSMENT PROCESS AT THE UC DAVIS ARBORETUM

In 2001–2002, Kathleen Socolofsky, the director of the UC Davis Arboretum, guided by strategic consultant Gary Stern of Stern International, led the sixty-five-year-old public garden through a long-range planning exercise, the Drucker Foundation Self-Assessment Process, that helped develop both an exciting new shared vision and the critical clear, practical work plans that were needed to turn the new vision into reality.

The community was invited to participate with the leadership team through a series of highly structured events and outreach tools: public meetings, focus groups, interviews, and email questionnaires. The community's passion for the Arboretum took the staff by surprise: more than 4,000 people responded, including over 400 faculty, more than 1,800 students, and legions of university staff, plus Arboretum members, volunteers, and donors. Campus and community leaders all joined the conversation about the potential and possibilities for a new role for the Arboretum on campus and in the community.

Through this process, the wider community helped determine key goals for the Arboretum's long-term plan by identifying critical gaps—important areas where much improvement was needed. For example, there had long been some internal tension among the UC Davis Arboretum staff and members about educational signage: some felt that signs and plant labels detracted from the purity of a beautiful garden experience, while others felt that educational signage was critical at a university botanical garden. However, the voice of the customer was unanimous: across all groups, respondents felt that educational signs and plant labels would greatly enhance the visitor experience.

The ten-year plan that resulted was extremely focused and clearly limited the number of overarching goals: four programmatic goals (the "what do we deliver") and two resource goals, one about money and the other about people (the "how do we deliver") were permitted. Constraining the number of goals helped the UC Davis staff and partners move into intensely targeted discussions about how to deliver quickly on these goals and establish institutional priorities to address the goals. Working from the ten-year plan, priorities for key projects were quickly set and a detailed three-year plan resulted. Following the Drucker Process, the leadership team then identified the critical

next steps within this three-year plan, and a detailed work plan for the current year, the one-year plan, was suddenly in place.

With close to unanimous buy-in across staff, membership, university leadership, and the community, people throughout the organization were anxious to get working on these exciting new ventures. Socolofsky set up new cross-disciplinary teams around the goals and required staff from all operational areas to work together on some of the most important goals. For example, the renovation of the Arboretum's Redwood Grove cut across all six goals and pulled together horticulturists with donors, Davis service clubs with students living in the dorms, education specialists with landscape architects. By carefully aligning work and projects, momentum built, and people had the wonderful experience of delivering on multiple goals simultaneously: new collections were built, curation practices improved, funding increased from both earned income and direct donations, exciting new educational programs were launched, and new partnerships with donors and the community were established.

The Drucker Process also provided new, tightly structured management tools: the plan is regularly reviewed and adapted through a series of staff meetings and quarterly meetings that track progress. These meetings allow the director and team leaders a chance to evaluate progress and adapt as they encounter new opportunities and reshape priorities based on internal and external changes. Problems are quickly identified and solved, and resources devoted to projects bogged down by unforeseen complications are shifted to new high-priority projects that have great potential for moving forward on major goals.

Best of all, the Drucker Self-Assessment Process brought together an engaged community of staff, students, faculty, volunteers, donors, community members, and campus leaders who are all working together to create a new kind of university public garden, where the excellence of UC Davis—in science, the arts, the humanities, and horticulture—is shared with the public through the new places, programs, and partnerships at the Arboretum. Without question, this process led to a transformation of how the university, city, and region view the garden and how the staff and close partners understood new possibilities for this campus garden.

on track and relevant, and that the garden is positioned to raise the funds it needs to execute its plan.

Adopt a Dynamic Review Process

Consistent and regular monitoring of progress toward shared short-term goals is a critical step toward aligning strategic plans throughout a public garden. Strategic plans are best reviewed frequently at staff meetings or team meetings when comments about what is working and what is not help leaders and

managers revise and improve the plan. Clarifying what is working and why helps staff find new ways to apply successful strategies in one area to other projects and initiatives.

Adjust Priorities

Plans and priorities naturally shift as time goes on. Inevitably, new opportunities emerge and a few projects unexpectedly get mired down by complex issues. Discussing and shifting project plans and tasks ensure that key results will be achieved quickly. Although time is one of an organization's greatest resources, there is often very little discussion about how to use this resource effectively. Focusing work time on the most strategic tasks, instead of automatically defaulting to the most urgent tasks, can help a public garden advance rapidly on major initiatives. A regular process for quickly adjusting staff priorities ensures that the projects with the most strategic impact get the time, attention, and resources they need.

Public gardens that let the power of the inspiring vision pull them forward are the gardens that are most successful at fulfilling the promise of their long-range plans, even in the face of major upheavals. For example, strategic plans crafted in a thriving economic environment and then executed during an economic downtown may succeed only if the original plan is reconsidered. When staff, supporters, donors, and outside partners have all been part of developing the plan, the community will still want to see the plan succeed, even if the timeline or the full scope of particular projects must be adjusted to fit new realities. Facing hardships together while trying to move major initiatives forward can inspire the whole community to think creatively about how to accomplish shared goals.

Tools for Strategic Management: From a Plan to Reality

People are the greatest resource of any public garden. The energy of a great staff, motivated by deeply meaningful shared goals, attracts other great people and encourages participation throughout the entire community. Big plans become new realities only when public garden staff, volunteers, and key partners work together to align resources and make things happen in the face of competing demands on time and attention.

A self-reliant team or staff with a clear sense of strategic purpose that is free to adapt the plan (within clear boundaries) can be a huge asset in transforming a plan from idea into reality. Managers at public gardens have two special responsibilities critical for successfully executing any plan: deciding who the best people are to undertake the specific projects identified in the plan and deciding how they will be trained, organized, and managed to work most effectively.

Build High-Performance Teams

The traditional approach to managing staff is often tightly bound to ineffective management conventions: rigid job descriptions, a yearly evaluation, and a nod to occasional professional training. Decades of research and practice from the most successful businesses and nonprofits demonstrate that the best managers are able to deliver rapid results and encourage excellence by creating high-performance, flexible, project-based teams: small, fleeting, rapidly emerging and disappearing mini-organizations that place each person in the right place, at the right time, with the right partners, to get work done. Successful managers encourage a high level of engagement from the people who work with them by creating teams where people can work to their strengths, ensuring that individuals and teams know what is expected of them, and, when problems or unexpected events occur, readjusting team membership or adapting the plan to keep advancement toward major goals on track.

Great managers are attuned to the strengths of the people who work for them: what each person can do easily with a high degree of excellence and success. Rather than attempting to train away or shore up weakness of individual employees, effective managers create teams that partner people with others who have complementary strengths, and then encourage people to do what they do best. For example, some people enjoy planning and thrive in intensive collaborative meetings; others find satisfaction working alone, arranging and tracking detailed information; while still others struggle through meetings or detailed reports but excel once a project enters the real world and requires an action-oriented leader who can trouble-shoot unexpected problems.

New practical strategies and tools, based on 1.7 million interviews and decades of research, have been developed by the Gallup Organization for managers interested in developing a strengths-based workplace. Focusing on strengths can be one of the most creative and rewarding ways to improve performance in the workplace. The intensively tested recommendations of the Gallup Organization can guide public garden managers who are interested in experimenting with these effective and innovative approaches to management.

Encourage Strategic Thinking and Communication

No plan survives intact after contact with the enemy—those unexpected events that blow up work plans. Rapid progress toward shared goals depends on staff at every level exercising strategic decision making when confronted with the daily challenge of deciding exactly what to do next. Frequent discussions about which key tasks are likely to have the most important strategic results help a team get in the habit of focusing its efforts there. Similarly, other rapid assessment tools—such as training public garden staff to quickly assess the importance versus the urgency of the multiple tasks on their work list—can improve on-the-fly decision making and keep work focused on projects that consistently deliver the greatest impact for the whole institution. Communicating the mission to outsiders and potential new supporters is another key task for all members of the public garden community. Garden leaders should encourage staff and close partners to seek opportunities to communicate the garden's mission: in grant applications and newspaper articles, with donors, at internal staff meetings, at presentations, in training sessions for volunteers, and in casual conversations.

Have a Clear Team Process

As public gardens experiment with new team-based organizational structures, power and decision making gradually shift to the person closest to the action, but only when that person has completed critical leadership and management training. For distributed decision making to be successful, careful preparation is required, which should incorporate the following elements.

Create a Climate of Innovation Through Experimentation and Evaluation

Solving problems requires experimentation and thinking in new directions. Staff members who are growing into leadership positions must therefore be encouraged to experiment. But because testing is inherently risky and not all experiments meet with success, experiments should be permitted only in areas where a failure will not cause grave problems for the institution. Public gardens that wish to build a culture of innovation encourage staff to question assumptions, generate ideas, propose ways to test the best ideas, and then reflect on what was learned and where to start next. Evaluating failures and successes and then adjusting the strategic plan in light of the new understanding can help a public garden to accomplish long-range goals, but only if unexpected failures are seen as an opportunity to examine what went wrong, why, and how.

Adopt a Sound Process for Consultative Decision Making

A structured approach can help ensure that distributed decision making is successful. Generally, in a team framework, most decisions need a consultative approach in which the small team to whom decision making is delegated is required to consult with key people as advisors. Consultative decision making is often more effective than consensus, which is an all-or-nothing method that has frustrated many hardworking people who have tried to work in teams.

One of the most successful approaches is for the leader or manager who is delegating the assignment to work with the team leader and team members to clarify the key issues and goals and to set the parameters for the decision making. For example, a team might be asked to develop a program to improve the visitor experience at a public garden. The director or manager might first work with the team to clarify the primary issue—that visitors are confused about where to go when they arrive at the garden. From there, the group might work together to develop goals and parameters for decision making that might include the following: (1) provide an experience that gives visitors the confidence to know where to go and what to do when they arrive; (2) set the stage for a great experience that reflects and introduces them to the mission; (3) ensure that they feel welcomed and will be eager to return; (4) provide for accessibility; and (5) exceed their expectations. It is also important to develop a list of budgetary and timeline constraints that will affect decision making. Constraints of time, money, and other key factors often drive tremendous creativity and innovation when people put their minds together to find workable solutions. Time and again, constraints have helped public garden teams make the big leaps of insight that give rise to unexpected win-win solutions and new ways of partners working together to meet shared goals.

Once the team understands the goals and parameters for decision making and has consulted with appropriate resource people, they are ready to generate a series of options. After brainstorming and discussion concludes and only the best options remain on the table, an information gathering phase begins, and team members research the alternatives and organize their findings so the pros and cons of each option can be evaluated, along with potential risk and reward. Finally, a recommendation is made to the leader or manager to whom the leader has delegated the decision-making authority.

Naturally, not all work at a public garden takes place within a team framework. Some critical decisions (e.g., how to handle an emergency or major budget crisis) require an immediate and clear decision by the leader with responsibility in that area. Minor decisions made by trusted and experienced leaders do not require the entire decision-making process. However, when issues are complex and need integrative solutions, returning to a more formal decision-making process can be very helpful because it clarifies the issues, sets the goals and parameters, identifies consultative partners, and examines the pros and cons of proposed options.

Summary

Leaders of innovative public gardens have been quick to see the benefits of carefully aligning and leveraging the garden's resources into high performance organizations that can have tremendous impact. Leaders who are focused on achieving excellence study the field of leadership and management, select approaches that are backed by sound research and extensive testing and refinement, and then experiment with these new ideas within their organizations. The good news is that even the smallest of public gardens can participate: concentrated time, rather than significant new funding, is the most critical ingredient for successful leadership and management.

As leadership and management skills are honed and understanding of complex systems deepens, the public garden leader will find that key projects speed to completion, staff and volunteers quickly adapt and respond to changing realities, donors want to increase their commitment, and money is saved by aligning networks of people who begin to self-organize to accomplish the mission of the garden. Best of all, as everyone is invited to share the passion, the public garden workplace can become a dynamic and creative place that has a profound impact in the real world as well as on the people who are transformed by working together on something bigger and grander than could have been accomplished alone.

Annotated Resources

American Association of Museums, Center for the Future of Museums (www.futureofmuseums.org/about). AAM's Center for the Future of Museums (CFM) helps museums explore the cultural, political, and economic challenges facing society and devise strategies to shape a better tomorrow.

Buckingham, M., and C. Coffman. 1999. *First, break all the rules: What the world's greatest managers do differently*. New York: Simon and Schuster. Learn how the best managers do things differently to create successful organizations.

Buckingham, M., and D. O. Clifton. 2001. *Now, discover your strengths*. New York: Free Press. The best managers play to their employees' strengths. This book teaches you how to identify key talents, suggests ways these talents can be developed into strengths, and gives managers new tools to help manage employees in strength-based teams.

Cary, D., and K. Socolofsky. 2003. Long-range planning for real results: Start with self-assessment and audience research. *The Public Garden* 18 (4): 10–13. A summary of the planning work completed at the UC Davis Arboretum and its impact on the garden and the campus community.

Crutchfield, L., and H. M. Grant. 2007. *Forces for good: The six practices of high-impact nonprofits*. San Francisco: Jossey-Bass. Through extensive surveys and interviews, the authors identify six practices shared by high-performance nonprofit organizations.

Drucker, P. 2001. *The essential Drucker: The best of sixty years of Peter Drucker's essential writings on management*. New York: Harper Business. This classic text includes a wonderful selection of the best of Peter Drucker's writing during his long and illustrious career.

Drucker, P., and G. Stern. 1998. *The Drucker Foundation self-assessment tool set* (includes the revised Process Guide and Participant Workbook). Drucker Foundation Series. San Francisco: Jossey-Bass. A set of books that can help any organization, with or without an expert consultant, lead a self-assessment process that results in a strategic or long range plan for their organization. The Process Guide is for the small team that will lead the entire process; the Participant Workbook will be used by all stakeholders who participate in the public planning process.

Kotter, J. P. 1996. *Leading change*. Cambridge: Harvard Business School Press. This book is a practical and realistic assessment of what it really takes to transform an organization. This book is informed by much experience and a deep understanding of what works and what fails. If you are attempting to change an institution, this sober book will save you many missteps and position your organization for success.

Mind Tools. 2009. *SWOT analysis: Discover new opportunities. Manage and eliminate threats*. www.mindtools.com/pages/article/newTMC_05.htm, September 21. This article introduces key questions as a helpful framework for quickly leading a project team or organization through a SWOT analysis.

CHAPTER 24

Associations and Partnerships

CLAIRE SAWYERS

Introduction

Public gardens can, in many arenas and parts of their operations, more efficiently and effectively fulfill their missions by working synergistically with other organizations or in partnership with other entities. In this chapter examples of partnerships will be described, successes will be profiled, and the pros and cons of forming such relationships will be identified.

Less binding than formal partnerships are programs offered by a number of professional organizations or associations related to living collections and museums. These organizations and programs will also be explored.

Nationally Based Professional Associations
American Association of Museums

Founded in 1906, the American Association of Museums (AAM) is a not-for-profit, membership-supported organization dedicated to furthering excellence within the museum community and identifying best practices by gathering and sharing knowledge nationwide and for all types of museums. Through advocacy, professional education, an accreditation program, and offerings of resources to help achieve professional standards and performance, AAM staff members help museum staffs, board members, and volunteers to better meet their missions and serve the public. With more than 15,000 individual, 3,000 institutional, and 300 corporate members, AAM represents a broad base of the museum profession.

Examples of AAM's standing committees with relevance to public gardens include the Committee on Audience Research

and Evaluation, Committee on Education, Committee on Museum Professional Training, Public Relations and Marketing Committee, and Development and Membership Committee.

The organization's flagship publication, *Museum*, published bimonthly and a key resource for museum professionals, is accessible on the AAM website. The organization publishes books and offers an extensive collection of reference materials through its bookstore, including *National Standards and Best Practices for US Museums*, published by AAM in 2008. Of its many educational programs, the largest is its annual meeting, drawing over 6,000 participants. Two AAM programs of particular value to public gardens include the Accreditation Program and the Museum Assessment Program.

AAM Accreditation Program

AAM established the accreditation process in response to President Lyndon B. Johnson's 1967 request to the U.S. Federal Council on the Arts and Humanities to study the status of American museums and recommend ways to strengthen them.

Within months of the 1970 release of *Museum Accreditation: A Report to the Profession*, applications from museums were accepted into the newly formed accreditation process. In 1971 the first sixteen museums received accreditation.

The accreditation process continues to be refined to better serve the profession and strengthen standards and best practices, measuring different aspects such as ethics and transparency, community involvement, diversity, and use of technology. Today more than 750 museums have accredited status in the AAM program, of which only 2 percent are public gardens.

Unlike other professional fields, no licensing or regulatory body oversees the use of such words as *museum* or *public garden*. Anyone can hang a shingle and proclaim his or her backyard an arboretum. The accreditation process is one way to provide substantiation of professional standards to the broad array of institutions that describe themselves as public gardens.

When AAM staff members canvass museum professionals to learn how the accreditation program has served their institutions, a variety of factors are cited: recognition on a national level; a clearer sense of purpose and validation of fulfilling the mission; strengthened fund-raising and marketing abilities; enhanced credibility with other agencies, potential partners, potential employees, and donors; a better-informed and engaged staff and board; and strengthened policies and procedures, which is perhaps the most important result, given the impetus to establish the program. Accreditation is a means by which AAM has been able to advance the field and a self-regulating process from which all museums can benefit.

Museum Assessment Program

The Institute of Museum and Library Services, a federal agency, formed a cooperative agreement with AAM to administer the Museum Assessment Program (MAP). MAP uses a confidential process of self-exploration and consultative peer review to help museums, including public gardens, see how they stack up against best practices, receive suggestions for improvements, and get help in addressing priorities and resource allocation.

Created in 1981, the program has provided more than 5,000 assessments to over 3,500 institutions. More than 1,250 peer reviewers contribute more than 28,000 volunteer hours to the program annually. The yearlong effort involves a self-study process and a visiting peer review, followed by implementation of suggestions in the review team's report. The four types of assessment available include Institutional Assessment, Collections Management Assessment, Public Dimension Assessment, and Governance Assessment.

American Public Gardens Association

Founded in 1940 as the American Association of Botanical Gardens and Arboreta, the American Public Gardens Association (APGA) is committed to increasing professionalism in the public garden field through knowledge sharing, professional development, and research, and to supporting and promoting the work of public gardens so that they may better serve their visitors and fulfill their missions

The Public Garden, APGA's primary publication, devotes each issue to a particular topic important to the public garden profession. APGA organizes periodic professional development symposia and webinars and an annual meeting attended by as many as 700 professionals.

The organization regularly conducts surveys of public gardens, including a salary survey of public garden professionals and a benchmarking survey of operations based on size of operating budgets. The APGA Resource Center serves as a professional lending library of public gardens materials and programs. Its 500 institutional members represent sites throughout North America and six other countries.

APGA PROFESSIONAL AND GARDEN SECTIONS

The APGA Professional and Garden Sections represent the interests and activities of the membership.

College and University Gardens Section

Conservatory and Support Facilities Section

Design and Planning Section

Education Section

Grounds Management Section

Historic Landscapes Section

Information Technology Section

People-Plant Interaction Section

Plant Collections Section

Plant Conservation Section

Plant Nomenclature and Registration Section

Small Gardens Section

Volunteer Management Section

Warm Climate Conifer Curatorial Group

North American Plant Collections Consortium

Sponsored by APGA in cooperation with the U.S. Department of Agriculture's Agricultural Research Service, the North American Plant Collections Consortium (NAPCC) is a network of public gardens in a coordinated, nationwide approach to preserve plant germplasm and to promote high standards of plant collection management. Participating institutions agree to hold and develop a living plant collection meeting specified standards and to make long-term commitments to curate and preserve the collection. These serve as reference collections for plant identification and cultivar registration. The benefits of holding NAPCC collections, according to participating institutions, are strengthened collections, increased potential for collaboration with other institutions, and the opportunity for enhanced grant-funded projects.

PlantCollections

A program/partnership known as PlantCollections is a joint collaboration between three primary partners: APGA, the Chicago Botanic Garden, and the University of Kansas. Fifteen public gardens nationwide have committed to participate in the project. The program's aim is to develop a database system for Web-based querying that will allow plant records systems in different formats to be accessed and integrated into a comprehensive inventory as a first step in developing a nationwide effort to preserve plant germplasm.

The Garden Conservancy

The Garden Conservancy exemplifies the use of partnerships for the common goal of garden preservation. Founded in 1989 by distinguished horticulturist Frank Cabot, the organization is devoted to saving and preserving America's exceptional gardens for the education and enjoyment of the public. It does so through broad financial support from a national membership base. The conservancy provides technical support and leadership to private gardens to help them transition to public entities, assisting with legal strategies, management structure, and establishment of sound financial and organizational operations. More than ninety significant gardens in the United States have benefited from some form of short-term or long-term partnership with the Garden Conservancy, which has developed tools such as the handbook *Taking a Garden Public* to outline issues and strategies involved in preserving and sustaining a garden through time.

The conservancy also helps grow public awareness of gardens and raises program funding through its annual Open Days program, a nationwide initiative in which more than 300 private gardens in twenty-three states are visited by over 70,000 participants.

Center for Plant Conservation

The Center for Plant Conservation (CPC), founded in 1984, is devoted to preventing the extinction of America's imperiled native plants and consists of a network of public gardens and institutions committed to conservation work. Thirty-six institutions participate in the National Collection of Endangered Plants, which totals more than 700 plant taxa. Each collection serves as a safeguard against extinction and provides material for restoration work and scientific study.

In addition to coordinating and managing the network of gardens and the National Collection of Endangered Plants, the organization gains support through a membership base. Through its quarterly, *Plant Conservation*, and through the symposia and other educational activities it sponsors, CPC broadens public awareness of the need for enhanced strategies and tactics for plant preservation.

International Associations
Botanic Gardens Conservation International

Established in 1987 to work toward saving the world's imperiled flora, Botanic Gardens Conservation International (BGCI) is the world's only global network dedicated to plant conservation in public gardens. The mission is "to mobilize botanic gardens and engage partners in securing plant diversity for the well-being of people and the planet." Today the organization includes more than 700 members, mostly botanic gardens, in 118 countries. Member publications include the semiannual *BGjournal* and *Roots*, which covers topics such as education for sustainability, teacher training, interpretation, and research. BGCI works to empower its member institutions by enhancing their knowledge of ways to reverse the threat of plant extinction through publications, exhibitions, international gatherings, training courses, and direct conservation programs. The head office is located at the Royal Botanic Gardens, Kew, in London, with regional offices in Kenya, the United States, Singapore, and China. The U.S. BGCI office is housed at the Chicago Botanic Garden and works with more than eighty partner gardens and organizations committed to conservation.

The International Agenda for Botanic Gardens in Conservation, published in 2000 and produced by BGCI, has been signed by 472 botanic gardens from eighty-three countries confirming their commitment to plant conservation.

Forming Partnerships

Public gardens enter into formal partnerships for a variety of reasons: to share governance, to support and broaden the impact of their mission, to enhance the reach of educational programming, to raise revenue, or for operation of visitor services not directly related to the mission of the garden.

For Governance

Many public gardens have a partnership of shared governance with government agencies, universities, or other organizations such as the Garden Conservancy. Descriptions of these forms of governance were addressed in Chapter 1.

The Water Conservation Garden at Cuyamaca College

The creation of the Water Conservation Garden was the result of shared concerns and a multiagency partnership. After an extended drought, the Helix and Otay Water Districts in California recognized the importance of educating the public about outdoor water conservation techniques. The districts joined with a third partner, Cuyamaca College, which agreed to provide the land for the Water Conservation Garden. The Water Conservation Garden Authority (WCGA) incorporated in 1992 with the task of funding, developing, and maintaining the Garden, which opened as a public garden in 1999. The Garden's governing board includes representatives from each of the sponsoring public agencies and additional sponsoring groups. The Sweetwater Authority joined the WCGA in 2007, and in the same year the Garden joined the Environmental Protection Agency's WaterSense partners program.

For Shared and Enhanced Mission

Partnerships with other organizations can help a public garden fulfill its mission when staff and budget are limited. By banding together, like-minded organizations can reach a broader audience. In some instances, organizations with different kinds of expertise working together are better able to achieve a common goal.

Lady Bird Johnson Wildflower Center Affiliate Program

Located in Austin, Texas, the Lady Bird Johnson Wildflower Center's aim is to inspire people to conserve native plant habitat, restore native plant communities, and integrate native plants into landscapes of North America. To accomplish that goal on a national scale, it has developed a program of affiliates, which has defined criteria and benefits for both the Wildflower Center and the affiliates. Benefits to the Wildflower Center include broader outreach to complement the Wildflower Center's mission and vision, geographic extension of the Wildflower Center's constituency, and encouragement of regional efforts to conserve wildflowers and native plants. Affiliate benefits include official association with the Lady Bird Johnson Wildflower Center; collaboration with the center on programs, activities, and funding proposals; and access to publications and communication channels developed by the Wildflower Center. Currently the program has twenty-seven affiliates in three countries and more than a dozen states in the United States.

Nebraska Statewide Arboretum

The Nebraska Statewide Arboretum (NSA) is a unique statewide network of sites linked in a partnership to promote the knowledge and appreciation of plants and excellence in landscapes in the state. Organizations and institutions in Nebraska can become a part of the network through two affiliate programs: one is for stewardship sites, including historic sites, parks, campuses, schoolyards, and landscapes of cultural significance, while the second is for public gardens and arboreta. Some of the benefits for affiliates include statewide exposure through NSA publications and website; utilization of the NSA logo, plant labels, signs, and publications; participation in a research consortium; technical support from the NSA staff; access to financial support through NSA grant programs; and the ability to receive tax-deductible contributions through NSA's tax-exempt status. Currently twenty-five sites participate as arboreta affiliates, eleven as historic landmark sites, and fifty as landscape steward sites.

For Enhanced Educational Programming

Partnerships based on a specific educational objective or program may lead to a broader audience, shared expertise in curriculum development, and the ability to grant degrees through an accredited program.

Perennial Plant and Woody Plant Conferences

In 1983, a group of public organizations in the Philadelphia region joined forces to plan and sponsor an annual day-long conference devoted to perennial plants. The original group included the Scott Arboretum of Swarthmore College, Longwood Gardens, the Pennsylvania Horticultural Society, and the Hardy Plant Society/Mid-Atlantic Group and was later joined by Chanticleer. A committee of staff representatives from each organization manages conference planning and evaluation and sets policies. Conference staging responsibilities are divided among the cosponsors: the Scott Arboretum hosts the event, Chanticleer assumes publicity responsibilities, Longwood Gardens handles registration, the Pennsylvania Horticultural Society handles speaker arrangements, and the Hardy Plant Society assembles conference packets and a segment of the program. Many years the conference has drawn 600 attendees. Proceeds are divided among the co-sponsors once expenses are paid. Following the success of this collaboration, a similarly constructed annual conference was added devoted to woody plants.

The Longwood Graduate Program
Longwood Gardens partnered with the University of Delaware in 1967 to form the Longwood Graduate Program, one of the earliest graduate-level degree programs to prepare students for a leadership career in public horticulture. In addition to coursework at the University of Delaware, the program, which offers fellowships to students, includes activities and work experiences during two summers at Longwood Gardens. Graduates receive a master of science degree in public horticulture. Longwood Gardens not only helps shape the leadership for the public garden field through this program but also benefits from the research and special garden projects conducted by the fellows.

Plants for a Livable Delaware
Plants for a Livable Delaware is a campaign designed to educate homeowners about problems with invasive plants and to suggest suitable alternatives for landscapes. The program is a collaboration between Delaware Cooperative Extension, the Delaware Center for Horticulture (a public garden based in Wilmington, Delaware), the Delaware Nature Society, the Delaware Department of Agriculture, and the Delaware Nature and Landscape Association. A grant from the Delaware Estuary and the National Urban and Community Forestry Advisory Council Program provided funding.

For Collections Preservation
In addition to the plant preservation and conservation organizations such as CPC and BGCI, gardens have formed effective partnerships on regional and international levels to more effectively accomplish goals related to plant conservation.

Georgia Plant Conservation Alliance
The Georgia Plant Conservation Alliance is a network of public gardens coupled with governmental and environmental agencies working together to preserve Georgia's endangered flora. Its stated mission is "to study and preserve Georgia's flora through multidisciplinary research, education, and advocacy." Established in 1995, the alliance works to protect natural habitats and biodiversity and educate the public. The strategy involves a team of botanical garden staff, land managers, state and federal botanists, and university-based scientists working together.

Research findings by members of the Alliance are disseminated through school programs that encourage direct engagement in native plant conservation. Another benefit of the partnership as expressed by Jim Affolter, its chair, has been to "cut through some red tape and bureaucratic inertia in the process."

For Collection, Crop, and Cultivar Development
Partnerships of various kinds have been effective means to enhance the collections at gardens, including the North American Plant Collections Consortium and partnerships with plant societies. The American Conifer Society, American Hosta Society, and Holly Society of America are examples of plant societies that have developed partnerships on various levels that have resulted in stronger plant collections at the public gardens and a broader audience and plant collection resources for the plant societies. Chicagoland Grows is an example of a partnership between public gardens, growers, and wholesale nurseries that develops, evaluates, and introduces worthy landscape plants.

Holly Society of America
The Holly Society of America has a program of official holly arboreta or experimental test centers. The garden or site pays annual dues, complies with society guidelines for maintaining records and labels, and submits an annual report on the status and conditions of the hollies based on an annual inventory. To become an official holly arboretum, organizations must submit an application that is reviewed and approved by the society's trustees.

For Enhanced Marketing
In several regions of the United States, public gardens have developed partnerships to market themselves and the region collectively.

Greater Philadelphia Gardens
In 1989, a group of Philadelphia region gardens led by the Morris Arboretum received funding from the Pew Charitable Trust to work together as a consortium to better market the member gardens to encourage visitorship and to market the Philadelphia region nationally as a garden-rich area to visit. After a number of years of joint efforts, outside funding was no longer available; the partnership continued with eligibility requirements, expected commitments, and annual membership fees. The collaborative continues to focus on publicity and marketing efforts through a joint website and coordinated events planning and marketing. The nearly thirty participating gardens in three states are all within an hour's drive of Philadelphia.

For Financial Support

Partnerships are commonplace now between not-for-profit museums and for-profit enterprises. With a grant or financial gift, programs may be funded that support an objective of the garden and fulfill the corporation's philanthropic aims in the community. Examples include a cosmetic company underwriting the costs to "make over" the Brooklyn Botanic Garden's rose garden beds with new soil, and an Italian foods manufacturing company supporting a Garden Chefs series at the Chicago Botanic Garden. Among other examples are the many public gardens that are able to offer discounts offered by local businesses as incentives for joining their membership programs.

While both the garden and the corporation benefit, the public trust and ethical integrity of the public garden need to be safeguarded. Looking at ethical guidelines and best-practice standards outlined by the American Association of Museums on the subject of corporate sponsorship may be one way to avoid issues.

International Partnerships

To further their research, plant conservation/preservation, and educational programs, public gardens have formed partnerships with gardens in other countries.

The State Botanical Garden of Georgia

The State Botanical Garden of Georgia has developed partnerships with sister gardens in Latin America to further its programs related to conservation, environmental education, and new crops development. In the province of Córdoba, Argentina, the Garden has partnered with the Jardín Botánico Dr. Miguel J. Culaciati, which has led to several staff exchanges and collaborations on medicinal plant conservation and environmental education projects. In addition, the Garden's research staff is working in partnership with a university in Costa Rica to develop a new botanical garden on the campus of the University of Georgia's San Luis Research Station in the Monteverde cloud forest region. This also involves a collaboration with ProNativas, a local nonprofit in Monteverde, to select, propagate, and evaluate native Costa Rican species with economic potential as ornamental plants.

Summary

Public gardens are museums with living collections. Many of the best practices for collection management and curation, education and interpretation, audience development, fund-raising, volunteer management, and other operations are similar to those of other museums. Professional organizations addressing museum practices and standards may be valuable resources to gardens and their staffs. A number of professional organizations related specifically to gardens and plant collection development serve as valuable resources for public garden professionals. These associations can help public gardens to develop and achieve their institutional missions, expand their programs, and promote their institutions. Examples of effective partnerships described in this chapter are designed to serve as models that can be adapted to the needs of many public gardens.

Annotated Resources

The American Association of Museums. 2008. *National standards and best practices for U.S. museums*. Ed. E. Merrit. Washington, D.C.: John Strand.

Andorka, C., L. Brockway, and W. Noble. 2001. *Taking a garden public*. 2 vols. Garden Conservancy Preservation Handbook Series. Cold Spring, N.Y.: Garden Conservancy.

Professional associations and related organizations

American Association for Museum Volunteers (www.aamv.org)
American Association of Museums (www.aam-us.org)
American Public Gardens Association (www.publicgardens.org
American Society for Horticultural Science (www.ashs.org)
Association of College and University Museums and Galleries (www.acumg.org)
Association of Zoological Horticulture, Inc. (www.azh.org)
Botanic Garden Conservation International (www.bgci.org)
Center for Plant Conservation (www.centerforplantconservation .org)
Council on Botanical and Horticultural Libraries (www.cbhl.net)
Garden Conservancy (www.gardenconservancy.org)
Institute of Museum and Library Services (IMLS) (www.imls.gov)
International Council of Museums (ICOM) (www.icom .museum)
International Plant Propagator's Society (www.ipps.org)
Museum Store Association (www.museumdistrict.com)
National Trust for Historic Preservation (www.preservationnation .org)
Nebraska Statewide Arboretum (www.arboretum.unl.edu)
New England Museum Association (NEMA) (www.nemanet.org)
North American Association for Environmental Education (www.naaee.org)
Lady Bird Johnson Wildflower Center (www.wildflower.org)
Travel Industry Association of America (www.ustravel.org)
Visitors Studies Association (www.visitorstudies.org)
Western Museums Association (WMA) (westmuse.wordpress .com)

CHAPTER 25

Facility Expansion

BRIAN HOLLEY

Introduction

While public gardens focus much attention on the development and refinement of their collections and programs, most eventually reach a point where further development is limited by inadequate facilities. Facility expansion can take on many forms and functions, but there are a few key elements that define a successful public garden expansion:

It meets the needs of the garden and its audiences.
It is built and operates in a sustainable manner.
It is built within budget.

KEY TERMS

AIA: American Institute of Architects.

APGA: American Public Gardens Association.

Civil engineer: develops plans for site development, including roads, drainage, and grading.

Concept phase: the first phase of design. It organizes elements of the facilities program into logical relationships and provides scale for elements such as parking and ticketing.

Construction administration: the services that the architect or landscape architect provides to oversee the project during construction.

Construction document (CD) phase: phase for the preparation of detailed drawings of the project, which will be used to construct it.

Construction manager (CM): develops bid documents, oversees bidding process and performance of subcontractors.

Cost consultant: develops detailed estimates of the cost of the project.

Design development (DD) phase: phase in which the building materials and general look of the finishes are determined.

Electrical engineer: develops plans for electrical service. May also design audiovisual systems, lighting controls, computer systems, and phone systems.

FF&E: furniture, fixtures, and equipment.

General contractor (GC): contracts to undertake the entire project. May have staff that perform some or all of the construction.

GMP: guaranteed maximum price.

HVAC: heating, ventilating, and air-conditioning.

LEED: Leadership in Energy and Environmental Design.

Mechanical engineer: develops plans for plumbing and HVAC (heating, ventilating, and air-conditioning).

OACs: owner/architect/contractor meetings.

Owner's representative: acts on behalf of the owner during project design and construction.

Partnering: a system of dispute avoidance and resolution that emphasizes the shared responsibility of the team to resolve issues.

Schematic design phase: includes the style of the facility and the arrangement and size of rooms.

Structural engineer: develops plans for structures and structural components of the project.

Subcontractor: contractor who performs work under contract with the general contractor or construction manager.

Value engineering (VE): the process of examining all aspects of the project to ensure that it is being designed to be built in a cost-efficient manner. This often involves eliminating nonessential components of the project.

Figure 25-1: An aerial view of the new Brazilian Garden at the Naples Botanical Garden.
Photo provided by Aero Photo

For most institutions, their expanded facilities have included experiences that are directed at broadening the traditional public garden audience by engaging families through children's gardens, discovery rooms with hands-on activities such as the Montreal Botanical Garden's Insectarium, and immersive conservatory experiences.

Education

When expansion involves the creation of additional spaces for educational activities, it is very important to consider how those spaces can be used for alternative activities. A sloped-floor auditorium works well for lectures but can't be used for flower shows or as a venue for special-event rentals such as wedding receptions. Placing classrooms where they have views of the gardens can make them very attractive for corporate retreats and other rental opportunities, as will high-quality audiovisual (A/V), wireless Internet access, and videoconferencing. Incorporating sinks and long counters into classrooms makes them more versatile, allowing for programs such as flower arranging and plant propagation as well as for setting up for a garden club buffet lunch. A garden that hosts many floral design events may wish to include floor sinks in or near classrooms.

When designing educational spaces, it is important to enlist the assistance of an A/V specialist, who can assist in determining the size and location of screens, speakers, projectors, cameras, and controls. These specialists may come from a design/build firm, as independent contractors, or through the mechanical engineering firm.

Libraries

Libraries are going through a tremendous transformation, with ever-greater amounts of information available electronically.

It is completed on time.

It is functional.

It is aesthetically pleasing.

This chapter will provide an overview of the expansion process and key strategies to ensure success.

Why Expand Facilities?

There are myriad reasons for undertaking an expansion. Overcrowded offices, insufficient propagation space, lack of facilities for new programs, and inadequate classroom space are common motivators for considering a facility expansion. In other cases, the desire to generate earned income, create a better visitor experience, or make the organization more efficient drives the decision to pursue an expansion.

Very often the decision to address needs in one area leads to a consideration of the needs of the whole organization and a much more integrated expansion program. For example, adding attractions such as children's gardens and conservatories also requires providing high-quality visitor amenities such as food service and retail offerings as well as expanded parking, restrooms, ticketing, offices, support areas, and classrooms.

The Visitor Experience

Public gardens compete for people's time, interest, cases money. Using a program of facility expansio compelling plant-based visitor experience can have impact on a garden's ability to meet its mission. Th in the recent transformations of the Phipps Cons Botanical Garden, New York Botanical Garden, Atla Garden, Cleveland Botanical Garden, and Morton In many instances, these institutions have seen a do bling of their attendance and a dramatic change in awareness and perception. In some cases, institutio able to dramatically expand education, communi and conservation initiatives because of the increa revenue and change in perceived community impor

Expanded facilities can dramatically enhanc collections and the ability to communicate inforn the collections. The Atlanta Botanical Garden's Hi House is a good example. The sophisticated enviro trols have allowed the Garden to develop a collect from the Cloud Forest of the Andes Mountains and that unique collection as part of the visitor experie

---

CASE STUDY: FACILITY EXPANSION AT THE MORTON ARBORET

Gerard T. Donnelly, Ph.D., President and CEO, Morton Arboretum

The Morton Arboretum is a large public garden dedicated to the planting and conservation of trees located in the western suburbs of Chicago (www.mortonarb.org). The Arboretum created a comprehensive master plan for its 1,700-acre site in 1997, its seventy-fifth anniversary year. This plan included land use zones, improvements to plant collections, enhanced circulation for people and vehicles, parking, buildings, and hydrology. It provided capacity for audience growth to as many as 750,000 visitors per year (compared to 287,000 in 1997) once the entire plan was implemented.

The master plan provided the basis for additional plans for plant collections, interpretation, storm water management, and utilities. A more detailed site plan was developed in 1999 for the Arboretum's central area, including its main entrance, visitor center, gardens, and other staff and visitor facilities.

The first phase of development of the master plan was launched in 2002, with a $45 million capital initiative that included multiple projects designed to attract and serve a broader public audience. A new entrance, gatehouse array, and arrival roads were constructed, together with a 500-car porous pavement parking lot designed as a model to inspire other environmental parking innovations. The existing visitor center was replaced with a larger (36,000 sq. ft.), attractive, and energy-efficient facility.

A 4.5-acre children's garden was created, along with a 1-acre maze garden and enhanced horticultural landscapes throughout

the central area of the Arboretum. The second in a visitor stations was built along the road circuit to enco of plant collections, trails, and natural areas. A centra redeveloped for improved water quality, aesthetics, ronmental value. Expanded plant production and oth facilities were also included. The development was ph three and a half years, utilizing a temporary visitor cer and food service facilities.

The capital development initiative was coupled with marketing and public programming designed to tran public face of the Morton Arboretum and the audienc It certainly has achieved that goal. Attendance and m expanded rapidly upon completion and opening of the ities in 2004 and 2005 and has continued. Attendanc grew to 830,000, and membership to 34,000 househ only the first phase of master plan development.

The children's garden in particular has had a ma on audience growth, and the visitor profile now inclu more children and young families. This new audience is also more culturally diverse than in the past. Awar grown substantially, and the Arboretum has become tion for people well beyond the Chicago metropolitan

Earned revenue has grown substantially, more thai since the opening of the new facilities to a total of lion. Operating costs have also grown during this time requiring careful budget planning.

Library expansions seem to fall into four categories: enhancing research capabilities, enhancing public access to information, creating space for community programs, and enhancing the environment for rare book and archive storage. While these are all compelling reasons to expand, the institution must also consider how the digitization of books and ubiquity of electronic information may call for a reduction rather than expansion of space devoted to a library.

One specialized aspect to be considered during library expansion is the temporary storage of rare books and archival materials. Several information resources as well as consultants can help plan this process: the Regional Alliance for Preservation, the American Association of Museums, the Institute of Museum and Library Services, and CoOl (Conservation Online) are a few of the many great resources (See Appendix E).

Horticulture, Conservation, Research, and Collections

Most public gardens have as part of their mission the display of diverse horticultural collections and/or research programs that relate to plant biodiversity, conservation, or basic biology. A garden's ability to fulfill its mission can be limited by the quality or size of available facilities.

Prior to expanding the physical plant to support collections expansion, it is advisable to apply for a grant through the Institute of Museum and Library Services to undertake a collections assessment under the Museum Assessment Program. Public garden professionals with extensive experience conduct the assessments, which can be directed to living or nonliving collections and result in reports that are very useful for developing plans that both protect collections and help direct their growth.

These studies will provide a clear picture of how to prioritize facilities to best support collections development. This level of information is really critical when seeking the governing body's approval to proceed with the design process.

The most commonly needed facility to support research programs is propagation space, which can take many forms, from nurseries to greenhouses to low-tech hoop houses. Growth chambers, used primarily for controlled experiments, consume enormous amounts of energy and produce a great deal of waste heat, so it is critical that the HVAC system is designed to aggressively vent or cool the area. Sophisticated refrigeration units may also be needed for long-term seed storage or storage of plant tissue samples.

When building greenhouses for propagation or collections, there are many considerations, including the primary purpose,

initial cost, useful life of the structure, operating costs, ease of operations, and the climate.

If the purpose of the greenhouse is to produce seasonal bedding plants, it may be worth talking with local growers to see if there is an opportunity to have them custom-grow the crops rather than tie up large amounts of capital, operating funds, and staff time in on-site facilities.

It is very common to hire a design/build firm when developing working greenhouses. These firms will take the program for the greenhouse and design and build the space to meet precise criteria. This process can be very straightforward if the greenhouse is for general use; it may be more complex if collections involve plants that require specialized conditions, such as cloud forest plants, or if there needs to be very precise control of temperature, humidity, light, and air movement. It is very important that careful consideration be given to how the space may be used in the future as well as in the short term. A system that provides greater flexibility may be more expensive initially but a good investment in the long run.

The garden's location plays a significant role in the choice of materials as well as the heating and cooling systems for a greenhouse. Typically, the further north a garden, the more important it is to use glazing materials that have greater insulating value and to possibly invest in insulating blankets that can be pulled at night to trap the heat. Greenhouses in northern locations also benefit from auxiliary lighting to extend day length during the winter. Areas with drier climates can be cooled very efficiently by evaporative transpiration systems.

Before the Master Plan

A well-researched master plan is critical to a comprehensive facility expansion program. Public gardens generally hire a landscape architecture or architecture firm that specializes in the master planning of public gardens to lead the process.

Before planning begins it is useful to have a clear consensus between all constituents about the future direction for the institution. Otherwise, the master plan can become a staff and/or board wish list of pet projects, and the garden ends up with a plan that isn't feasible to implement. Some gardens have gone through multiple master plans costing hundreds of thousands of dollars without ever building anything.

To develop that clear consensus, it is often helpful to engage the services of a facilitator to undertake some preliminary planning and to help with the selection of the master-planning firm. Another approach is to engage the services of an owner's representative at the beginning of the process. This is especially useful for independent gardens with prior experience with facility expansion. The role of the owner's representative is to protect the owners, guide them through the process, and help them to make good decisions. The representative should be very experienced in all aspects of project development, from developing master plans to managing the general contractor or construction manager. While such services can be expensive, they can more than make up for the cost by saving the garden from making serious mistakes. Most large universities and governmental units have facilities departments with extensive project management experience, so owner's representatives are not needed.

Using a different master-planning strategy, administrators at the Naples Botanical Garden brought together a team of four talented landscape architects who specialize in tropical gardens and a very creative architect with a strong background in sustainable design. They worked together in a series of design workshops over a period of several months to create the master plan; then each landscape architect was charged with designing a particular garden within the master plan, and the architect designed the buildings.

Master Plan Committee

The garden's master plan committee should be a relatively small group (six to ten participants), including members of the staff whose programs will be most affected by the facility expansion, board members with particular areas of expertise that support the project, representatives from the architectural firm, and, if the garden is part of a parent organization such as a university or municipality, a representative from that entity. Both the CEO and board chair should be part of the committee. In choosing between the various constituencies, it may be necessary to prioritize needs to keep the size of the group within scale.

Important skills for committee members include experience in construction management, financial management, legal knowledge, fund-raising, retail, food service, and marketing. The committee should meet frequently, either biweekly or monthly, during the planning process, and report to the garden's governing body at key points in the plan's development.

Recently gardens have begun to create teams with the owner's representative rather than the architect at the center of the design team. Architects will always include mechanical and structural engineers in their contract, but most other consultants

Figure 25-2: The Naples Botanical Garden master plan design team gathers to review concept drawings. From left to right: Brian Holley and landscape architects Ellin Goetz, Raymond Jungles, Made Wijawa, and Robert Truskowski.

will contract directly with the owner and be coordinated by the owner's representative. This structure makes every participant an equal part of the team and allows the owners to place resources where they feel they are most important and to source the best talent. This section will go through the process of developing a design team for a complex project with limited internal resources.

At one time, developing a national or international team was very expensive because of the travel costs. Today, many firms have videoconferencing capability, point sites where the design team members can post drawings, and programs that allow for the design team to meet online and manipulate drawings. As a result of these technologies, it is more financially feasible to go outside the local region in search of talent.

Staff Input

A garden embarking upon developing a master plan needs to engage all staff for both ideas and feedback early in the process. This can be done in a variety of ways, but one of the most effective is developing interdisciplinary teams to study various aspects of the garden and make recommendations for future development. Using a staff team that includes people from different departments, including facilities, horticulture, education, finance, and volunteer management, brings a diversity of perspectives to planning. The resulting staff reports can form the basis for informing the master plan committee and the design team.

Developing the Master Plan

The development of the facilities master plan is an iterative process taking many steps. Each should be checked for viability and buy-in as the plan develops. Chapter 6 provides in-depth descriptions of the steps in the master-planning process.

Once the concept phase of the master plan is complete, the master plan committee will need to determine how much the project will cost, what funds are available, likely operating costs for the facility, expected operating income from the facility, and details about the contract.

How Much Will the Project Cost?

A cost estimate can be remarkably accurate in predicting the cost of the project even in the early design phase. A construction manager or a professional cost estimator (cost consultant) can be brought onto the team or contracted to provide this service. With complex projects, it can be valuable to have a cost consultant and the construction manager both creating estimates to ensure that the owner is getting competitive pricing.

Detailed cost estimates at this phase are useful in identifying what each part of the project is likely to cost. This in turn often leads to the first session of value engineering—modifying the project to keep it within the budget.

It is important to recognize that facilities expansion is complex and expensive. According to Herb Schaal, one of the leading designers of children's gardens, intensively developed children's gardens cost about $2 million per acre. The budget for a conservatory with an immersion experience is about $1,000 per square foot, according to Linda Rhodes, cofounder of RhodesDahl, a project management firm.

How Much Money Can Be Raised?

If the implementation of the plan will require a fund-raising campaign, this is also the time to test the level of support that the garden's donor base is likely to commit to the project and whether key audiences view the project as vital. This is called a capital campaign feasibility study, which can be conducted by a fund-raising counsel who will interview donors to the garden and key audiences members.

Several years ago, the Cleveland Botanical Garden undertook a capital campaign feasibility study based on its initial master plan and discovered that its donors would not support the full intent of the plan, indicating instead that $6 million to $8 million was a feasible campaign target. Furthermore, the donors wanted a much more exciting plan. The planners went back to the drawing board, selected a new team led by a nationally significant architect, developed a more engaging visitor experience, and ultimately were able to raise $50 million.

How Much Will It Cost to Operate?

Another key study is an estimate of future operating costs, including additional staff, utilities, insurance, and maintenance. A rough initial estimate often can be done in-house by simply taking the cost per square foot of existing facilities and multiplying that by the square footage of the expansion. It is also very useful to get operating costs from organizations with facilities similar to those under consideration. Finally, the American Public Gardens Association produces salary studies which are enormously useful for estimating personnel costs.

How Much Operating Income Can Be Expected?

If the garden is developing facilities that will need admissions-based support, it is important to undertake market research to estimate the number of visitors that the new facilities are likely to attract as well as the suggested admission price. The market research may also help to identify visitor amenities not previously

Figure 25-3: Aerial view of the recently completed Smith Children's Garden at the Naples Botanical Garden in Florida.
Photo provided by Aero Photo

considered as well as the seasonal distribution of visitors and the percentage of visitors who are members.

There are many market research firms, but, not surprisingly, traditional information-gathering methods such as focus groups are quickly being replaced by massive online surveys that are much more accurate at predicting the market's response to a visitor experience.

Once projected attendance figures are established, they can be converted into projections of monthly, daily, and even hourly attendance. These are very useful for deciding on the size of ticketing, food service, and restroom facilities, as well as for developing a staffing plan for visitor services.

Other forms of income are retail, parking, special events, facility rentals, and food service. Retail and food service measure their income in several ways: most common are gross sales, sales per square foot, and sales per visitor (also called per capita). In 2008 the median sale per visitor for gardens with budgets in excess of $2.5 million was $2.04 (Directors of Large Gardens 2007).

It is very common for gardens to contract for food service, retail, and even facility rentals. While the financial returns may be smaller, there is also less risk and lower start-up costs. But the drawback with contracting these services is the loss of some control over how the garden presents itself through retail and food service, especially on sustainability and other environmental issues.

Many gardens are now undertaking very large special events such as flower shows, concert series, or sculpture installations. These can require extensive utility infrastructure, enormous amounts of staff time, and appropriate staging areas. Gardens considering staging events or large art shows should contact other gardens and similar venues to discuss the economic

Figure 25-4: The completed Brazilian Garden at the Naples Botanical Garden.

Photo by Vanessa Rogers, VanessaRogers.com

viability of special events. Again, undertaking market research would be a very good investment before making such as decision.

Contract Considerations

Once the team has been organized, they will need to address the development of requests for proposals (RFPs) and the letting of contracts. The RFP will describe the scope of the project, outcomes, deliverables, and special features such as LEED certification; give an overview of the garden; and identify what is expected to be included in the proposal and the submission date. A well-done RFP allows the team to readily compare each of the bidders and establish a short list of firms to be interviewed.

It is critically important to have experienced legal counsel review all contracts. Most design and construction contracts are based on templates developed by the American Institute of Architects (AIA), and it is best to use an attorney who has a good working knowledge of these contracts and can construct amendments that are favorable to the garden.

It is impossible to overstate the importance of paying due diligence to contracts in facility expansion. One garden found itself in a very difficult situation when it signed, without any legal review, a contract with a board member who was also an architect. The architect designed buildings that the garden couldn't afford and then wanted to charge the garden a new fee to design another, less expensive expansion. This conflict of interest created a rift in the board, upset the largest donor,

and exposed the garden to potential litigation. Fortunately, the garden hired legal counsel, corrected the situation, and went on to create a successful expansion.

A garden should let major contracts only after a careful selection process. A competitive process ensures that there is no conflict of interest with staff or board members and that the pricing is competitive.

Depending on the type and scale of the expansion, the master plan committee may be adapted into an implementation committee that may also include any of the following additional participants: cost consultant, retail consultant, food service consultant, graphic designer, LEED consultant, interpretive planner, information technology consultant, exhibit designer, or audiovisual designer. More and more projects are adding the general contractor to the project early on to help with cost estimating, value engineering, and constructability of the project. Again, this committee could become unwieldy, so only include individuals with the types of expertise that are required.

Traditionally, all consultants are included in the architect's contract and fees, but for unusual projects, that structure doesn't always work very well. For example, the architect's agreement for services with an exhibit designer may provide considerably less time and consequently less commitment than the owner would prefer. Also, if the exhibit designer reports through the architect, the architecture rather than the exhibit may take precedence.

Budgets

There are few worse feelings than finding that the project is over budget or can't be finished because key elements were not included in the project budget. There are five key elements in developing the project budget: pre-opening costs, soft costs, hard costs, hard cost contingency, and contractor's contingency.

Pre-opening Costs

Pre-opening costs are often about 20 percent of the total budget but can vary greatly with the size and structure of the institution and the scope of the project. These are the fund-raising costs of the capital campaign, marketing costs, those for specialty staff required for the project, such as an in-house construction manager or an interpretive specialist, and the costs associated with hiring staff such as a facility rental coordinator, who needs to begin selling rentals well before the new facility opens. These funds would also cover lost income if the garden is closed during construction.

Soft Costs

Typically 20 percent of the total project costs, soft costs include design fees and reimbursable expenses, legal fees, permits, travel, plan printing, and other costs associated with design and permitting. Complex projects and renovations often have significantly higher soft cost budgets. Soft cost contingency (also called design contingency) is included in the budget and is typically about 10 percent of the soft cost budget. As the design is completed, the balance is moved into the hard cost contingency.

Hard Costs

Hard costs represent about 60 percent of the project costs and include all activities related to the general contractor/construction manager (CM) and its subcontractors. Hard costs also need to cover any direct-to-owner contracts for construction services. For example, the garden may want to have the landscape contractor be supervised by its staff or owner's representative.

Key to staying within budget is careful oversight of the construction budget for allowances. When details aren't complete or there are components such as plants that are going to be purchased by the owner, the contractor will put in an allowance for them. Often the allowances are much lower than the elements will cost.

The hard costs also need to include funds for furniture, fixtures, and equipment (FF&E) to pay for new equipment that needs to be purchased but is not included in any existing contract. This includes freestanding furniture, phone systems, ticketing software and hardware, and cleaning equipment. FF&E also covers whatever equipment needs to be procured to operate the new facilities, which in public gardens may include trucks, track loaders, lifts, and specialized trailers.

Hard Cost Contingency

Typically about 10 percent of the hard cost budget will be designated as construction contingency. It is not wise to let the size of this contingency be known to the construction team because the contingency needs to be guarded. It is really critical to preserve the contingency as intact as possible to deal with the unforeseen, most of which seems to occur late in the project. If the project is completed under budget, the garden will have a happy board and, potentially, the beginning of a maintenance fund.

Contractor's Contingency

This contingency, roughly 3 percent of the budget, is used in two ways: to deal with unexpected problems that are not directly attributable to a particular subcontractor or designer and to fund lunches, T-shirts, and celebrations for the crew at key points during the construction, which help to build a positive attitude toward the project and the garden. The contractor's contingency may also be used as an incentive to reduce change orders and cost overruns and reward staying on schedule. The contractor's contract can include language that divides the balance of the contingency with the contractor 50-50 at the end of the project or other incentives for adhering to the project schedule.

Design Phases

Once the master plan is complete, the individual elements such as buildings, gardens, and parking lots need to be designed. The process has a series of steps during which the level of detail increases until plans for a buildable product are produced.

Architects generally have a clear design process that includes the following phases: concept, schematic, design development, construction drawings, and finally construction administration. Normally the architect's fees are tied to each of these phases: schematic design, 10 percent; design development, 20 percent; construction documents, 40 percent; bidding, 5 percent; construction administration, 25 percent. It is very common for design firms to underestimate the amount of time that will be required for construction administration.

The design process for landscape architects is often not as clearly delineated and the product is not as predictable for each phase, especially for smaller design companies with little experience in public gardens or government projects. It is not uncommon to have a design go from schematic to construction documents in one step—often an overwhelming step for the owner's team.

Very few landscape architects actually design the systems for their water features, relying instead on the water feature manufacturer and contractor to produce the design. This can be a challenge when the contract is put out to competitive bidding and the low bidder looks to cut corners to make a profit. At the Naples Botanical Garden, the contractor initially designed a system for a lily pond that used chlorinated water, like in a swimming pool—death to water lilies! Fortunately, this was changed before it was installed.

It is very important to contact references for all designers to ascertain how well they follow schedules, the quality of their work, the opportunity for owner input, and the ability to design to a budget.

Concept Phase

Generally, the concept phase for gardens and facilities occurs in the master-planning process. During this phase any prior information gathering is reflected in the general footprint of the buildings, facilities, and layout of the site. It is also critical to set a goal for the level of sustainability that needs to be incorporated into the project. Higher levels of LEED certification, especially Gold and Platinum, drive a significant amount of the design, from landscape to building orientation.

Schematic Design

Schematic design is when the form of the building begins to take shape. Architectural style, relationship to roads and paths, location of elements such as dumpsters and loading docks, sizes and relationships of interior spaces, and the primary type of construction are all considered and identified. It should also take into account major code issues such as setbacks (the distance a building needs to be from the street or an adjacent property) and fire access.

What the Garden Should Receive

Garden administrators should receive plan drawings showing interior layouts, cross sections, and sketches of what the exterior will look like (also called exterior elevations). A preliminary budget is usually included as well. It is not uncommon for architects and landscape architects to develop a study model at this point.

The Garden's Responsibility

The schematics phase is when the major decisions need to be made. If the drawings show a building location or major feature that needs to change, it should be determined at this stage. If the schematic design is approved and there is a subsequent desire to change major elements, additional design fees will be incurred and the project will be slowed down. This is an important time to get the designers to present the plan to the board for approval and to take the plans to other stakeholders such as staff, members, and donors for their feedback. This is also the time to do a second cost estimate.

Design Development

During design development, the project really takes shape as the details of the materials and the structural and mechanical systems (heating, ventilation, cooling, plumbing, and electrical) are developed. Design development drawings can be submitted to the local building department for initial review.

What the Garden Should Receive

Detailed drawings of floor plans, cross sections through each significant part of the building, and elevations of the exteriors should be received.

The Garden's Responsibility

If ever there was a good use of the phrase "the devil is in the details," design development review is it! It is really important to take an extended period of time to scrutinize the drawings with the architect and with the appropriate staff room by room and element by element. Things to look for are lighting controls, windows, door swings, heating and cooling duct locations, thermostat locations, telephone and computer jacks, outlets, hose bibs, exterior colors, and materials and interior finishes. The maintenance staff may want to weigh in on the mechanical systems, such as water heaters, pumps, and HVAC. It is also important at this point to check that the services are in place for equipment that is not in the contract, such as refrigerators.

This is a critical time to do a cost estimate and conduct value engineering to confirm any changes that need to be made before beginning the next phase.

Construction Drawings

Construction drawings (CDs) are the working drawings that are used to bid and build the project.

What the Garden Should Receive

Public gardens will often receive a few sets of construction documents based on the development of the final details. For complex projects, garden administrators may receive 50 percent, 75 percent, 90 percent, and 100 percent CDs. These phases allow for additional cost estimates that may affect decisions about finishes and trim levels.

The Garden's Responsibility

Final colors and finishes are usually decided during this phase. It is also important to review the plans for details such as breaker panel locations, restroom and kitchen fittings, and specifications for lighting and plumbing fixtures. It is very important to keep hard copies and electronic copies of the plans in a safe location.

Bidding

At this point the primary responsibility transfers from the implementation committee to the construction team. The construction manager (CM) will develop a list of qualified contactors to undertake the various components of the project. They will then circulate the bid packages and set a time for all bids to be submitted. Normally the CM will have one or more meetings where the prospective bidders can ask questions.

In some cases the lowest qualified bidder must be selected, but in many situations the garden can opt to interview two or three of the bidders and choose the firm that is preferred. This is particularly important for selecting the general and/or landscape contractor, but the maintenance staff may also want to interview the HVAC contactor.

Construction

It is important to recognize that once construction begins it is the CM who controls access to the site, not the owner. The CM sets the access requirements for safety equipment, footwear, and restricted areas. The garden will need to determine

Figure 25-5: An aerial view of the Naples Botanical Garden after three months of construction.

Photo provided by Aero Photo

which staff members need regular access to the site and must provide them with hard hats and any other safety gear that might be required. When garden administrators are bringing guests such as donors to the site, the visit must have been approved by the site superintendent and the guest must have signed a waiver of liability provided by the CM. Typically CMs prefer that visits take place in the late afternoon or on weekends, when the construction workers are off the site; the visitors are safer at these times and won't disrupt the work.

Project Committee

Once design has been completed, the master plan committee's role is complete. The governing body should have approved the project budget and the construction contract, thus allowing staff to go forward with overseeing the project. During construction, however, the garden's governing body needs to be able to track the project schedule and budget as well as any potential litigation or major changes in the project. For this purpose a project committee may be formed that includes the treasurer, board chair, CEO, CFO, and individuals from the board with legal or construction experience if possible. This group should meet on a regular basis (monthly if possible) and review the project's status and report to the board.

The project committee should also be called upon if there are any major issues that will impact the project or the garden. For example, at the Naples Botanical Garden, the geotechnical consultant did extensive testing for underground conditions because a layer of cap rock (very hard limestone) occurs erratically in the area. However, the pattern of testing missed a large area of cap rock that wound its way between test bores. The cap rock needed to be blasted, creating significant concerns about the budget, potential litigation, and neighborhood relationships. Once the team became aware of the situation, it notified the project committee and regularly updated them. Ultimately, the area of cap rock was less than an acre, the blasting cost was covered by the contingency, and there was no significant impact on the project or the garden.

Owner, Architect, and Contractor Meetings

Normally the owner, architect, and contractor get together every week or two. These owner/architect/contractor meetings (OACs) provide an opportunity for inspection of the work in progress, discussion of issues, and updates on the project schedule.

As great as a particular team might be, issues will come up that must be resolved before they head to court. The best way to avoid major issues is to begin a program of partnering before construction begins. The essence of partnering is to avoid absolutes on the part of all parties, and to calmly and deliberately come up with a solution to disputes. It can be a very effective tool for saving the owner and the team a great deal of money in legal fees.

Managing the Site During Construction

It is not unusual for it to seem to take forever before a building starts to come up out of the ground and the site ceases to be a big mud pile. The underground work is often very extensive and may require a long line of cement trucks. Three things to keep in mind about heavy equipment on the site: trucks leaving the site covered with mud can make a real mess of nearby streets, and the CM needs to have a street cleaner on duty; mud turns to dust that can be a nuisance to existing facilities and neighbors; and the on-site construction roads can create heavily compacted soils and terrible drainage that should be corrected before planting begins.

If there are neighbors nearby, the garden should take the time to explain what it is doing, what the neighbors can expect during construction, and whom they should contact if they have a question or concern. Sending regular updates to a community association can make the neighbors feel that they are part of the process and can preempt conflicts.

To Close or Not to Close

Construction can profoundly impact a garden's operations even if it is separate from the existing facilities. Safety is always the biggest concern, but costs, inconvenience, eroded visitor experience, and logistics such as where to have the construction workers park can all influence the decision of whether to close the garden. If the garden stays open during construction, it can employ one or more of the following strategies: reduce admission for the duration of the work, offer free events such as classes or workshops, or develop special exhibits that serve as visitor draws.

If the garden does opt to close, it should have a very clear message to both its constituents and the media as to why the decision was made (for example, "We are closed during construction so we can develop a more exciting and diverse garden next year"). If it has to move to a temporary off-site location, it must inform GPS programs. In either case, tourism websites and offices should be notified of the change. If phone numbers must be changed, the new numbers should be prominent on the garden's website and in all publicity.

Whether the garden closes or stays open, it must plan for how the construction will affect the care of the collections, the

Figure 25-6: A typical scene during the site work phase of construction at the Naples Botanical Garden. Soil dredged from the lake excavation is being spread to dry. The mulch pile is shredded melaleuca, an invasive species that covered the site. The Garden insisted that all organic materials be shredded and stay on-site for mulch and soil amendment. In the lower left are some loose boulders that were in the excavated material.

© Donna E. Meneley

ability to conduct educational programs, and how staff carry out their work.

Summary

At some point, almost every garden expands its facilities. The process can redefine the garden and invigorate the staff and board, or it can be demoralizing and result in the departure of the chief executive. The key to success is to provide adequate lead time for all aspects of planning and for the development of a solid team of professionals. The garden should have a clear understanding of how the proposed expansion furthers its mission and relates to an overall physical master plan. Both the affordability of the project and its potential income-generating capacity must also be determined. The members of the project team should be familiar with every aspect of the process, from concept design through the completion of construction.

Annotated Resources

American Institute of Architects (www.aia.org/contractdocs/index.htm). AIA contract documents.

Associated General Contractors of America (www.agc.org/cs/industry_topics). Industry topics.

Construction Jargon (www.constructionjargon.com/Dictionary-A.html). Dictionary of construction terms.

Constructionplace.com Incorporated. (www.constructionplace.com/glossary.asp) Glossary of construction terms.

Missouri Botanical Garden (www.mobot.org) and the New York Botanical Garden (www.nybg.org) provide excellent overviews of the diverse functions of a contemporary garden library. The Council on Botanical and Horticultural Libraries (www.CBHL.net) is another resource.

CHAPTER 26

The Shape of Gardens to Come

PAUL B. REDMAN

Introduction

As we look to the future of public gardens, we must look to the past to remind us of our origins. Public gardens have evolved from their early inception as gathering places for people to learn about and enjoy plants, to centers of study and celebration of biodiversity and human culture. As they continue to develop, the primary objective for public gardens today is to maintain relevance in a rapidly changing, connected, global community.

Time-Tested, Enduring Features of Early Gardens
Pleasure

The most widely recognized and well-known examples of pleasure gardens originated as part of the grand estates in Europe and England. The term *pleasure garden* originated in England and referred to what would now be known as an estate garden. Although often opened to the public for special events and celebrations, most pleasure gardens were private

---

KEY TERMS

Pleasure garden: a private estate garden that traditionally would have been used both for strolling and for special events, such as concerts. In the past, many were quite opulent, reflecting the owners' wealth and power.

Physic garden: a garden whose collections were used to train students in apothecary medicine (pharmaceuticals). Each of the plants in such a garden would have had putative medicinally active properties.

Large garden: based on the categorization by the American Public Gardens Association, public gardens whose annual operating budget is above $2.5 million.

Capital project: new construction, or an expansion, renovation, or replacement project for an existing facility or infrastructure that helps maintain or improve existing conditions.

LEED certification: an internationally recognized green building certification system developed by the U.S. Green Building Council. It provides third-party verification that a building or community was designed and built using strategies aimed at improving performance across the metrics that most affect sustainability in terms of energy savings, water efficiency, CO_2 emissions reduction, improved indoor environmental quality, and stewardship of resources.

Demographics: the characteristics of a human population as used in government, marketing, or opinion research.

Second Life: a free 3-D virtual world where users can socialize, connect, and create, using voice and text chat.

New Urbanism: an urban design movement that promotes walkable neighborhoods containing a range of housing and job types. It arose in the United States in the early 1980s and continues to reform many aspects of real estate development and urban planning.

and were often a statement of status and wealth. An example of the most famous of all pleasure gardens is the Château de Versailles, whose formal gardens were designed by the famous landscape designer André Le Nôtre and completed in May 1664. The gardens of Versailles were the site of one of Louis XIV's great celebrations, Plaisirs de l'Isle enchantée, which lasted for three days and included a parade, performances, music, and fireworks.

Fruits of Exploration

Early European and North American gardens reflected the academic and cultural developments of the eighteenth, nineteenth, and early twentieth centuries. The early glass houses or conservatories served as places to cultivate and display exotic and unusual plants that were brought back from exploration trips. The primary purposes of such trips were to advance science and colonial development. Plants of agricultural, horticultural, economic, or medicinal value were of interest. This practice continued well into the mid-twentieth century, at which time plant conservation and preservation took on a more important role with the onset of the environmental movement.

Curiosity About the Unusual

The status of early public gardens was often based upon their ownership of rare, curious, and interesting plants. One objective of these gardens was to have at least one plant or group of plants that could be studied or seen only at that garden. The colonial garden at Peradeniya in Sri Lanka had what was described as a spectacular Nicaraguan aroid (*Draconticum gigas*) with a lurid purple hooded spathe that gave off strong and offensive odors. The Trinidad Botanic Garden had a cannonball tree (*Couroupita guianensis*) in 1890 whose trunk appeared as though it had been pummeled with cannonballs.

The most famous and popular plants in the early 1800s were orchids, which were viewed as curiosities because of their diverse forms and erotic flowers. In 1819 the Glasgow Botanic Garden was the first public garden to successfully flower what was then considered a novelty, *Cattleya labiata*. Orchids became such a rage and status symbol for public gardens that Kew Gardens built a special conservatory to display orchids from India and Australia.

A great Victorian-era curiosity was *Victoria amazonica*, the Victoria water lily. Competition among public gardens developed to see which garden could be the first to successfully flower a Victoria water lily. Queen Victoria visited Kew Gardens three times in a matter of weeks to see the large and unusual water platters. Because of royal curiosity, public

Figure 26-1: *Victoria* 'Longwood Hybrid'. Longwood Gardens' water lily display features the first hybrid of the famous *Victoria amazonica*, named after and enjoyed by Queen Victoria.

© Longwood Gardens

excitement developed. Kew credited the popularity and success of the Victoria water lily for the garden's resurrection and high public perception after a low point in its history. By 1852, Kew had dedicated an entire house to water lilies, and other public gardens shortly followed suit.

Advancement of Science and Agriculture

The Orto Botanico Padua (established 1545), recognized as one of the oldest gardens in the Western world, still reflects its original layout. It was established by the medical faculty of the University of Padua to support scientific research and education programs. Padua was the beginning of the physic or apothecary's gardens that supported the healing arts of the time. These gardens cultivated and displayed plants of medicinal interest and use. Physic gardens were established throughout Europe and eventually expanded their role to include nonmedicinal plants. One of the more famous of the European apothecary gardens is the Chelsea Physic Garden, which was established in 1673 to serve as a training site for doctors and pharmacists of the time and to improve knowledge of the natural world.

Public gardens of the colonial period served an important role as agricultural plant research stations to advance economic development. These gardens helped the establishment of young, emerging colonies by providing seeds or plants when crops failed. They also helped to build awareness of the need for alternatives to mass single-crop production or monoculture. Sugar cane was introduced to West India by a British colonial botanical garden in 1796. Public gardens also supported the advancement of forestry practices through the production and distribution of saplings for silk, fruit, and logwood. British and Dutch colonial gardens supported the establishment of cinchona tree plantations throughout Asia, particularly in Ceylon, and India; the bark of the cinchona tree provided the only known cure for malaria.

Multidimensional Experience

The rapid industrialization and population growth of cities around the world in the nineteenth century led to the demand for green space and places for leisure. It was during this time that the role of public gardens as places of leisure became more important. This was not without conflict among curatorial professionals, who felt pressure to turn their attention from scientific botany and horticulture to creating pleasure parks for recreation and relaxation. As the colonial governor of Mauritius noted, the botanical garden was chiefly a place for public amusement, and it was a necessity to maintain the grounds for pleasure.

The Trinidad Botanical Garden stuffed and displayed animals and snakes that were caught in the gardens. The Sydney Botanic Garden established a museum in 1900 with more than 700 exhibits. The Hong Kong Botanical Garden constructed a bandstand in 1866. Colonial garden administrators observed that the number of patrons increased when entertainment such as bands was provided. Kew Gardens established the first museum of economic botany in the world on its grounds in 1847. The years 1857 and 1863 included the addition of new buildings to display items such as seed vessels, fibers, papers, oils, extracts, and other preparations from plants.

Public gardens were among the first institutions to display living, exotic animals. Aviaries were common design elements in many early public gardens. The Jardin des Plantes in Paris had a collection of exotic birds and animals. Kew Gardens at one point had flamingos, pelicans, and penguins. The Singapore Botanical Garden had a collection of large animals that included orangutans, leopards, tigers, and even crocodiles—until one of the crocodiles devoured an employee.

Figure 26-2: The Philadelphia Orchestra performing in Longwood Gardens' Open Air Theatre on May 18, 1941, with Eugene Ormandy conducting.

© Longwood Gardens

Conservatories became a common architectural feature of public gardens in the nineteenth century, establishing new places for city residents to gather. Early exhibits in these gardens under glass were formal displays of plants in a Linnaean order by family. In the early twentieth century, the landscape architect Jens Jensen changed the conservatory experience by dismantling the Linnaean display experience. Jensen created a series of naturalistic displays at the Garfield Park Conservatory in Chicago, Illinois, to immerse visitors in what appeared and felt like a real jungle or forest setting.

Issues Public Gardens Face Today

In many ways, the issues that public gardens face today are similar to those faced by early gardens. Contemporary curatorial and noncuratorial professionals still debate the importance and relevance of programming outside of the realm of science, but those same professionals recognize the importance of curatorial, educational, and horticultural staff working together to give the visitor the most positive, holistic, and educational experience possible. The missions of earlier public gardens emphasized information gathering and sharing to advance science as well as to develop a better understanding of the world. Building upon this tradition, public gardens now emphasize scientific gathering of information for the active preservation and conservation of the global garden.

Two great issues for all public gardens in the twenty-first century are relevance and resources. The status of public gardens today is based not only upon the number of their living and nonliving collections but also upon community relevance as evidenced through direct measures such as gate admissions and public or private financial support.

Audience expectations are influenced by the rapidly changing world of the twenty-first century. With the advancement of technology, access to information has never been faster and easier. People can experience remote jungles, gardens, and botanical libraries through a virtual world that substitutes for the real thing to younger generations.

Cultural institutions, such as public gardens, art museums, zoos, and science centers, no longer have clearly defined boundaries determined by core purpose and location. With the removal of distance through technology and overlapping, similar programs, which some refer to as mission creep, the lines between institutions have become vague. For example, many zoos now include the term *botanical garden* in their names and present horticultural programs. Art museums include floral design classes among their programs and feature outdoor gardens designed by famous landscape architects. In a similar vein, public gardens include more artwork and animals within their collections and programming. Of course, everyone is competing to promote unique, earth-friendly, green programs to connect to the environmental consciousness of the twenty-first-century consumer.

Public gardens of the early twenty-first century describe their purpose as display, education, or research. Commonly used phrases in the mission statements of contemporary public gardens include "connecting plants and people," "place for inspiration," "learn how to grow," "enhance the environment," "discover and share knowledge," "celebrate the lives of individuals," "serve all people," "teach children," "reach out," "promote the understanding of conservation," and "enjoyment." Such phrases and terms reflect the diverse community needs that public gardens are trying to fulfill in order to remain relevant.

Competition

Competition today is daunting and goes well beyond having the greatest number of taxa in a collection or having a certain rare orchid flower first. In the twenty-first century, public gardens are competing for the attention, leisure time, and discretionary dollars of consumers and for public and private dollars to fund operations and capital endeavors.

What is the competition public gardens face? The answer is simple: it is everything. No matter where they are located, public gardens compete with the World Wide Web, fast-food outlets, zoos, art museums, children's science centers, amusement parks, movie theaters, the United Way, auto dealers, and other public gardens.

An important factor in this competition is that the manner in which visitors receive information and purchase goods influences the manner in which those individuals determine whether or not they will attend or support a public garden. Public gardens must present themselves in a way that will motivate potential visitors to direct their attention to the garden above and beyond all of the other pressures and marketing influences they face. The key to survival in the twenty-first-century marketplace is to create a one-of-a-kind opportunity and instill in potential visitors a sense of urgency to experience that opportunity before it disappears.

The popular perception that public gardens are pretty places to visit immediately skews their potential audience and prevents them from being recognized not only as unique institutions to visit but also as central to economic and community development.

A 2008 study by the Greater Philadelphia Cultural Alliance found that performing arts organizations spend $5.75 per visitor on marketing as compared to cultural institutions (including public gardens), which spend $1.58 per visitor, and service organizations, which spend $15.81 per visitor.

Public gardens continue to lag behind other industries because gardens have not made marketing and public relations an institutional priority. What is the solution? Public gardens must have well-funded, sophisticated, multifaceted marketing and public relations programs to actively compete in an information-rich world.

Audience Profile Changes

The population of the United States tripled from 76 million in 1900 to 281 million in 2000. As a result, the United States is becoming a denser and more urban nation, with an estimated 80 people per square mile. Its population is also becoming older. The most significant growth of population in the late twentieth century occurred in the sector of individuals sixty-five and older. It is also becoming a more diverse nation. Both whites and blacks now represent a smaller share of the population in the United States. Asian and Pacific Islander populations tripled and Hispanic populations doubled during the last two decades of the twentieth century, with Hispanics now accounting for more than 12 percent of the population. For the first time in

Figure 26-3: Huaxia Edison Dance Troupe performance in Longwood Gardens' Exhibition Hall, 2005.

© Longwood Gardens

the history of the U.S. census, four states (Texas, California, New Mexico, and Colorado) and the District of Columbia had populations that were 48 percent or more minority. Household demographics have also changed, as married couple households declined from 78 percent to 52 percent.

The United States is one of the most populous countries in the world; however, its share of the global population has decreased every decade since 1950. By the end of the twentieth century the developed countries of Germany, the United Kingdom, and Italy were no longer among the most populous. Less-developed and emerging countries such as Pakistan, Nigeria, and Bangladesh are growing rapidly and becoming among the most populous countries in the world, with rising middle classes. China alone comprises 20 percent of the world's population.

In terms of the public garden demographic, the typical visitor today is female, white, and between the ages of thirty-five and sixty-five. Clearly, public gardens have before them an audience that is changing—and that change is influencing how programs are developed and delivered. Because of the lack of diversity among the professional staff who make programmatic decisions, public gardens are challenged to establish programs and displays that connect with diverse constituencies.

The rapid increase of the global population has also placed the environment at the forefront of programming. Audiences in the United States now expect and demand that most businesses, and especially public gardens, have composting, recycling, and other ecofriendly practices.

Financial Vulnerability

Economic volatility is one of the greatest challenges facing public gardens in the twenty-first century, which began with an unprecedented economic boom only to be followed by one of the most severe economic busts since the Great Depression. In the boom years, public gardens were experiencing growth and planning for the future, as evidenced by capital campaign drives totaling almost $1 billion. After the recession, many public gardens were making significant budget reductions, streamlining operations, and realigning capital campaign goals.

Because they lack reliable, sustainable funds and are subject to increasing and uncontrollable costs such as health care and utilities, public gardens in the twenty-first century are financially vulnerable. Government support for arts and culture organizations in the United States has decreased as a percentage of GDP. Most institutions have very little, if any, endowment, and very few communities in North America have adopted measures to support cultural organizations through dedicated tax funding.

Prior to the 2008 recession, as stock prices soared and corporate community philanthropy budgets increased, cultural institutions relied upon corporate donations. One of the most comprehensive and telling regional economic studies of cultural institutions was conducted by the Greater Philadelphia Cultural Alliance. During the ten-year period of the study, revenue grew 52 percent and expenses increased 49 percent among arts and culture organizations. Contributions represented the greatest component of the income mix. The fastest-growing expense for organizations was utility costs. The results of the study are revealing because they demonstrate the narrow margins in which cultural institutions such as public gardens operate and survive.

Climate Change

Because of its programmatic and economic implications, one of the critical strategic pressures facing public gardens is climate change. The increasing world population, along with the production of more goods and services to support the demands of the emerging middle classes in developing countries, is leading to a loss of forests and habitats and increased pollution. Climate change is defining a new, time-sensitive role for public gardens that is beyond a passing fad.

The unifying core and foundation of all public gardens are their plant collections, manifested in inspirational displays. Gardens' fundamental mission of education, display, and research emanates from plants. In the face of impending climate change, public gardens must establish protocols for protection of the species they currently house and begin to develop strategies for incorporating new plant material that is suitable for a warmer climate.

Climate change is also impacting the manner in which public gardens plan for the care and development of their facilities and infrastructure. This is a complicated issue because public gardens are caught in the crosshairs of the past and present. Because most gardens were established between 1890 and 1990, their infrastructure is aging and not environmentally sensitive. Ideally, all new facilities in public gardens should be less reliant upon nonrenewable energy and should be LEED (Leadership in Environmental and Energy Design) certified, but the greater capital cost of renewable energy and LEED-certified buildings is prohibitive for many institutions.

Technology

Public gardens lag behind other institutions in their use of technology to advance mission and vision. Furthermore, public gardens are not in the forefront of innovation to help develop new technology. This is a fundamental issue because

Figure 26-4: Longwood Gardens established a progressive composting program that incorporates all carbon-based organic waste, including food. Dining utensils, water bottles, and drinking cups are compostable and incorporated into the compost program. Longwood Gardens produces more than 2,200 cubic yards of organic compost on average each year to support its horticultural operations and land management program.

© Longwood Gardens

technology has become a key factor in maintaining relevance in a rapidly changing world.

A 2009 survey of large public gardens in the United States was revealing. When asked to provide "specific examples of technology that your garden is utilizing to support programs," respondents answered "not enough" or "woefully lacking." Technologies that public gardens currently utilize include:

- Web-based tools for ticket and membership sales

- Web-based tools for tour and education registrations

- Mobile phone tours (e.g., Guide by Cell)

- Social networking websites and tools

- MP3 podcasts

- iPhone applications

- Personal audio wands

- Database management software for plant collections

- Digital image libraries

- Global positioning systems for site mapping

- Video signage

- Chalkboards

- Point-of-sale systems

- Email

People now expect to receive information quickly and in sound bites and want full control over when they receive that information. Public garden guests use technology to determine if and when they visit. They also use technology to define their own unique experience at a public garden. The presence of mobile phone guides, podcasts, and iPhone applications in public gardens as interpretative tools demonstrates the change that technology has already made in the visitor's experience of a public garden.

Unlike other cultural institutions that are fixed by buildings in which they exist, public gardens are defined by geography that many still believe requires a personal, on-site immersive experience that engages all of the senses. However, technology influences the conceptual and physical boundaries of proximity and distance. It is also reshaping how public gardens define a visitor. The collections, programs, and resources of universities, art museums, libraries, and public gardens around the world can be accessed via the World Wide Web through digital libraries, collection databases, and virtual tours.

Figure 26-5: Peirce's Park at Longwood Gardens. The original arboretum, known as Peirce's Arboretum, purchased by Pierre S. du Pont in 1906.

© Longwood Gardens

Technology has defined a new segment, virtual public garden visitors, who are measured by click-throughs and whose visits last seconds or minutes instead of hours. Other professions are realizing the benefits of technology. Universities integrated online learning management systems years ago. One in four university students takes at least one online course, and the demand is growing. Universities as well as for-profit corporations are using videoconferencing technologies as an accepted daily practice for meetings and the delivery of programs. A trend among universities, social service organizations, and art museums is to establish a presence in the virtual three-dimensional world of Second Life, accessible on the Internet. These institutions are discovering that class enrollments, fundraising, and on-site paid admissions are increasing because of Second Life.

Longwood Gardens has taken aggressive steps to utilize technology to fulfill its mission and to attract the public garden visitors of the twenty-first century. Longwood has implemented an online learning management system (Desire2Learn) that will provide hybrid and synchronic delivery of its education programs to anyone in the world. It is also using technology to enhance the delivery of customer service. A new point-of-sale software system allows Longwood to track customer loyalty and provide immediate concierge-level service by phone or on-site.

Public gardens are faced with a dilemma when it comes to incorporating new, advanced technologies into their operations. Does technology place less value on the core product of public gardens—a live, genuine experience? As with marketing, public gardens will lag behind other institutions until technology is embraced and appropriately invested.

The Public Garden of the Future

The aforementioned issues should be viewed as opportunities to define the future. It is an exciting time to lead or be involved in a public garden, probably the most exciting time since the early nineteenth century, when botanical gardens influenced the cultural and economic development of the world. The twenty-first century has brought to public gardens an opportunity to create a greater understanding of connectedness in a world that should be seen as a garden. Public gardens have an opportunity to lead the way in determining how we care for this global garden and feed people. The twenty-first century could very well become known as the century of the public garden.

They Did It Right the First Time

Public gardens must look to the past in order to establish the path for the future. While there were and still are many types of gardens, their fundamental qualities have not changed and remain relevant to guide the development of public gardens in the twenty-first century, including their role in promoting pleasure, exploration, curiosity about the unusual, learning and advancement of science and agriculture, conservation, and multidimensional experiences.

Public gardens of the twenty-first century have discovered, just as the gardens of the nineteenth century did, that colorful, fanciful, seasonal horticultural displays and entertainment that are in keeping with the garden's mission have a positive impact on visitation. Public gardens that were once the best-kept

Figure 26-6: Longwood Gardens' use of technology to connect guests with its gardens and plant collections.

© Longwood Gardens

Figure 26-7: *Disa uniflora* (Pride of Table Mountain), considered one of the most beautiful native wildflowers of South Africa. Collected and introduced by Dr. Russell Seibert, Longwood Gardens Director, 1967.

© Longwood Gardens

secrets in communities, had limited visitation, and served as isolated havens for academics have busted the doors wide open, not only for survival but also to engage broader audiences in their missions.

The public garden of the present and the future is no longer one specific type of garden; rather, it combines all of the qualities that previously defined individual gardens into a more holistic, multidimensional presentation of plants.

The World Is Flat: Collaboration and Partnerships Required

New York Times columnist Thomas Friedman in his book *The World Is Flat* (2005) takes as his primary premise that technology has leveled or flattened the global economic playing field. The primary challenge for public gardens in a flattened world is that the profession is not technologically advanced, nor is it actively participating in the innovation of new technology to support its advancement. This technological deficiency must be financially and creatively addressed in order for public gardens to simply be on the same plane in the new world order of flatness.

The flattened world of the early twenty-first century has made outreach, partnerships, and collaborations easier than ever before in history. A 2009 survey of large public gardens provides the framework to understand the status of partnerships. Seventy percent of the responding gardens were involved in local and regional collaborations, but only 48 percent had national partnerships and even fewer, 37 percent, had global partnerships. The same survey asked respondents to describe

collaborations or partnerships that were under consideration for the future. Interestingly, only 42 percent were considering national collaborations and 33 percent were considering global partnerships. The collaborative nature of public gardens and public garden professionals is evident in their strong local and regional partnerships, but as the survey demonstrates, public gardens are not playing on as large a field as they could in the twenty-first century.

Email and the World Wide Web have made it possible for any nonprofit to identify potential new partners and to reach out to them to establish new collaborations. Such collaborations offer many benefits:

- Decreased expenses through expense sharing or elimination of redundancies

- Increased revenue through joint programming and marketing

- Broadened base of support

- Introductions to new audiences

- Innovative new programs

- Advancing the outreach of mission-based programs

- Enhanced perception as value to society.

Partnerships require creativity, work, and the commitment of resources but are necessary for the survival of the twenty-first-century public garden. Technology has made it possible for us to identify those things that are common among all public

Figure 26-8: Longwood Gardens partnered with the Chinese Floral Arts Foundation of Taiwan to present a successful flower show in 2006.

© Longwood Gardens

gardens. Through global partnerships, public gardens can unite to combine their resources to advance the stewardship of the global garden.

Institutional Flexibility and Adaptability for Survival

The management skills that a gardener instinctually uses to have a productive garden are relevant to the administration of a public garden in the twenty-first century. Any gardener knows that the key to a successful garden is to have a plan. The plan sets forth a vision and establishes the parameters within which decisions are to be made in order to reach the vision. Gardeners understand that the plan requires nurturing, evaluation, and flexibility, because more often than not things don't happen as planned; even so, the vision remains intact. The principles of planning, flexibility, and adaptability are essential for public gardens of the future to succeed.

Public gardens currently achieve flexibility and adaptability by:

- Conducting regular surveys of visitors and benchmarking surveys to understand industry and cultural trends (increasingly, these are conducted electronically so that large numbers of participants can be recorded and results can be analyzed in a number of modes)

- Developing innovative exhibitions that can be adapted based on audience feedback

- Broadening their bases of income, consistent with the institution's mission

- Identifying and assessing the competition, and striving to engage the competition in collaboration and partnerships

- Avoiding bureaucratic organizational structure

- Fostering a culture of experimentation by taking risks

- Engaging younger employees, students, and interns to gain fresh perspectives

- Receiving constructive criticism

- Encouraging staff involvement in the community to ensure relevance

- Using more technology

- Continually assessing their strategic plans

Public gardens that are inflexible and not prepared for change are operationally weak and vulnerable to failure. Two primary operational areas of public gardens that are prone to vulnerability are finances and programs.

As with other cultural institutions, the financial model of public gardens is often not strong. They may be dependent upon one primary source of income, such as an endowment or government subsidy. In addition, the operating margin is frequently too narrow, and simply breaking even is considered an

Figure 26-9: Longwood Gardens established the Wine and Jazz Festival in 2007 in fulfillment of its strategic plan to present quick, limited-time festivals and events to broaden its audience base.

© Longwood Gardens

accepted business practice. Public gardens in the twenty-first century need financial flexibility with a diversified revenue stream to survive the inevitable fluctuations of the economy.

Public gardens of the future also require an innovative, entrepreneurial approach to the development and delivery of programs. This requires diligence, awareness of consumer trends, a commitment to risk, and flexibility in order to be successful.

Leading and Effecting Social Change

Cultural organizations such as public gardens serve an important role in their communities to effect positive social change. Plants are the medium by which public gardens create greater cultural understanding and effect social change. Plants are one of the great equalizers in life. Besides air and water, plants are a common thread that connects all living things. We need them for the air we breathe, the food we eat, and the medicines that heal us; they are also the inspiration for the creation of beautiful works of art. Planet Earth depends on plants for its very survival.

Public gardens, no matter the type, serve to connect people and plants. Because of global warming and other environmental threats, public gardens have been given a historic opportunity to lead and effect change through the development and demonstration of innovative stewardship practices. People are concerned and want real solutions.

A benchmarking study commissioned by Longwood Gardens revealed that sustainability is an emerging business practice in the public garden sector. Activities at public gardens have a heavier emphasis on understanding and communicating sustainable concepts than on improving them. Very few globally adopted best practices exist, nor is there a clear articulation of what constitutes a best practice for public gardens. The focus to date has been on ad hoc environmental programs.

The American Society of Landscape Architects, the U.S. Botanic Garden, and the Lady Bird Johnson Wildflower Center worked in partnership to create voluntary national guidelines and performance benchmarks for sustainable land design, construction, and maintenance practices. Phipps Conservatory and Botanical Garden is leading the way with a multiphased project to go green in the construction of new facilities and the renovation of its historic 1893 conservatory.

Summary

The American Public Gardens Association anecdotally notes that the majority of all those who make phone inquiries to the association ask, "How do I start a public garden?" This interest in starting new gardens is supported by the fact that 75 percent of the association's members are small and emerging gardens. It is these gardens that have the greatest opportunity to blaze new trails for public gardens, which must be driven by missions firmly rooted in education, display, research, and conservation, while at the same time being more mindful that the garden experience must be accessible to a diverse world.

Figure 26-10: Longwood Gardens is working to define and promote a greater understanding of what may be called the American meadow garden, composed of native plants and designed to nurture a native ecosystem.

© Longwood Gardens

Without losing sight of their origins as centers of science, research, pleasure, curiosity, learning, and advancement of agriculture, public gardens must meet their current challenges of remaining relevant and finding the resources to support their efforts. In so doing, gardens must become more flexible and collaborative in their operations and programming. They must also upgrade their technological tools and marketing efforts to compete for the attention of new audiences and to become leaders in promoting the preservation of the environment

The public garden of the future should be a center of and resource for economic development to sustain and advance a connected, global community that encompasses a shared philosophy that the world is a garden and that all public gardens are connected in a noble cause to effect change. Public gardens are living sanctuaries of inspirational beauty and the models to which individuals will look for healthier, more responsible living and for ways to promote the sustainability of the planet.

Factors in the Development and Management of Canadian Public Gardens

MELANIE SIFTON AND DAVID GALBRAITH

Introduction

Canadian public gardens differ from their U.S. counterparts in their origins, governance, operations, and funding models. Relatively few are derived from large private estates or are associated with federal or provincial governments, but many are university or college units, with the balance divided among municipal parks and botanical societies. Local botanical or horticultural societies have had a significant role in starting most of the newer public gardens in the country.

Earliest Canadian Public Gardens

The first botanical garden in Canada was developed in 1861 by George Lawson, founder of the Botanical Society of Canada, at Queen's College in Kingston, Ontario (now Queen's University), to train physicians in the use of medicinal plants and as a teaching tool for botany. The original Queen's Botanical Garden endured only until the end of the decade, as interest faded when Lawson left Kingston for Dalhousie University in Halifax, Nova Scotia, in 1863. Interestingly, the site of this first garden is now identified by Queen's University as its arboretum. It is not clear whether Lawson's move to Nova Scotia influenced the development of the formal Victorian

Halifax Public Gardens, started in 1867, but he was most certainly involved in horticultural science in this area around the time of its early establishment. Halifax Public Gardens now stands out as one of the oldest continually operating public garden in Canada, and one of the few good remaining examples of a historic Victorian-style garden in North America.

Historic Federal Public Gardens

Although Canada lacks an official national botanical garden or arboretum, two federally managed public gardens were established as agricultural research centers quite early in the country's history. The first official Canadian arboretum was formally established in 1889 as Ottawa's Dominion Arboretum and Ornamental Gardens. The Dominion's collection is now run as part of the Central Experimental Farm of Agriculture and Agri-Food Canada and features more than 3,000 specimens of trees, shrubs, and ornamental plants originally planted to test for cold-hardiness. The Morden Arboretum in Alberta was similarly established in 1915 by the federal Department of Agriculture as a research center focusing on crop and tree research applicable to plains farmers. Although its main focus is agricultural research, Morden continues to trial roses and other display horticultural crops and maintains cultivated garden areas and walking trails through its plantations.

Provincial Botanical Gardens

The drive for U.S. tourism and goodwill has been a notable influence in the development of some of the oldest Canadian public gardens, particularly those run through provincial government funding. Examples include the Niagara Parks Commission public gardens and natural areas, spanning 4,250 acres along the Canadian side of the Niagara River, and the 2,339-acre International Peace Garden, located on the border of Manitoba and North Dakota.

Niagara Parks Botanical Gardens

Dating back to 1885, when the North American national parks movement was first under way, the Niagara Parks Commission was originally devised to protect and enhance the areas close to Niagara Falls. While the Niagara Parks Commission is a provincial entity, it is self-funded through its own revenue-generating activities, which mostly revolve around tourism. In 1936, the Commission set up an elite gardener training school modeled after the Royal Botanic Gardens, Kew, training program. Now called the Niagara Parks Commission School of Horticulture, the grounds of the school have expanded through the work of the students and staff into a botanical garden, arboretum, and butterfly conservatory. For many decades, the school has also had a significant impact on the public garden field through its many graduates who have become influential in public horticulture throughout Canada and internationally.

International Peace Garden

The International Peace Garden (IPG) has its origins firmly rooted in cross-border tourism and filial affection between the two countries sharing the world's longest unprotected border. Opened in 1932, IPG sits on the border between Canada and the United States near Boissevain, Manitoba, and Dunseith, North Dakota, and is, in fact, in two countries. The garden was the beneficiary of Depression-era work programs on both sides of the border, including the U.S. Civilian Conservation Corps and dominion government programs through the Department of Public Works of Manitoba. Popular highlights include sunken parterre gardens, a floral clock, an interpretive center, and a conservatory, as well as memorial sites dedicated to various causes focusing on peace and conflict resolution. Native prairie plants and cold-hardy, prairie-tolerant plants make up the bulk of IPG's woody plant collections, but natural areas also include aspen parkland forest and more than 100 acres of simulated native prairie. Primary operational funding for IPG is uniquely split between the province of Manitoba and the state of North Dakota.

Royal Botanical Gardens

One of Ontario's largest cultural attractions is the Royal Botanical Gardens (RBG), which is both a 200-acre botanical garden and a very large urban natural area of approximately 2,000 acres. RBG originated from efforts in the 1920s to beautify the northwest entrance to the city of Hamilton with formal gardens. Initially part of the city parks board, the first gardens opened to the public in 1932. In 1941 the Province of Ontario established it as a not-for-profit agency. It now operates as a self-governing charitable organization with support from the Province of Ontario, City of Hamilton, and Regional Municipality of Halton. Its development as an educational and research institution dates from 1947. Living collections include more than 14,200 accessions in five major garden areas, including one of the world's most diverse lilac collections. Other resources include a significant botanical library and archives and an herbarium of 80,000 specimens. Research programs include plant taxonomy, wetland ecology, and conservation policy. The natural areas are recognized as home to the highest spontaneous plant diversity area in Canada (approximately 24 percent of the flora of Canada) and include some of the most important remaining Great Lakes coastal wetlands.

University and College Gardens with Research or Training Focus

Research-oriented public gardens associated with a university or college make up approximately half of Canada's public gardens.

Setting the standard for all Canadian university gardens is the University of British Columbia Botanical Garden and Centre (UBCBGC) for Plant Research, the oldest continuously operating university garden in the country. Started in 1916 by John Davidson, the first provincial botanist, the UBC Botanical Garden was originally established for research in plants native to British Columbia and is now one of the most well-established botanical institutions in the country. Its mission has since expanded to include conservation, research, and education on temperate plants from around the world. The UBCBG holds around 12,000 accessions, with notable Asian, alpine, physic, winter, food, and native plant display collections, and maintains facilities and plants for scientific research including *ex situ* conservation, phylogenetics, plant biology, and biotechnology. It also conducts scientific breeding programs for its Plant Introduction Scheme, which works with the British

Columbia nursery industry to bring forth dependable and appealing landscape plants.

Other important university gardens that engage in botanical research and display include, in order of establishment, McGill University's Morgan Arboretum, in Montreal (est. 1945); the University of Alberta's Devonian Botanical Garden, near Edmonton (est. 1959); the University of Guelph's Arboretum, in Ontario (est. 1970); Memorial University of Newfoundland's Botanical Garden, in St. John's (est. 1971); the Roger-Van den Hende Botanical Garden at Université Laval, in Hochelaga, Québec (est. 1978); the Laurentian University Arboretum, in Sudbury, Ontario (est. 1982); and the Harriet Irving Botanical Garden at Acadia University, in Wolfville, Nova Scotia (est. 2002). Each of these gardens also hosts herbaria and various other plant research facilities or works in conjunction with university departments that do.

Some Canadian colleges run public gardens as training facilities for students in horticulture and landscape trades. Since the Cuddy Gardens estate in Strathroy, Ontario, was donated to Fanshawe College in 2007, the gardens have been run by the college's Horticultural Technician Program as a hands-on teaching facility. The Olds College Botanic Garden (Alberta) likewise acts as a living classroom and applied research site for its horticulture programs, as do the Jardin Daniel A. Séguin of the Institut de Technologie Agroalimentaire in Saint-Hyacinthe, Québec, the Humber Arboretum of Humber College (Ontario), and the gardens at the Nova Scotia Agricultural College.

Municipal Gardens

Another significant category of Canadian public gardens consists of institutions operated by municipalities. Many municipal public gardens stem from a long-standing cultural fascination with display horticulture as a means of improving landscapes in and around cities, and the public's expectation that municipalities, charities, or businesses will allocate resources toward the creation or support of such displays (Martin 2001). While it can be said that no two Canadian municipal gardens are alike, it should be noted that municipal gardens rarely operate solely with municipal funding or governance. Sometimes closely aligned with parks and recreation departments, municipal gardens often feature unique governance structures and hybrid funding models that split management and funding with educational institutions, horticulture societies, or foundations.

Municipal Gardens and Educational Institutions

The Jardin botanique de Montréal is the largest public garden in Canada in terms of budget, collections, visitor attendance,

and programs. The garden has its origins in the Botanical Institute of the Université de Montréal, founded in 1920 by Brother Marie-Victorin, and a subsequent plan to become a municipal garden, realized in 1931. Today the Institut de recherche en biologie végétale (Botanical Research Institute) is officially a joint undertaking between the City of Montréal and the Université de Montréal and is on-site at the garden. With 100 staff members involved in research, the Jardin botanique de Montréal is both a city garden and a university garden, and one of the most successful and highly regarded public gardens in the world. Significant collections include Japanese, Chinese, alpine, native, rose, and tropical plants displayed in ten exhibition greenhouses. The Jardin botanique de Montréal also houses a herbarium, a children's garden, a horticultural training school, and the Montréal Biodiversity Center, a center of excellence in conservation and digitization of biological collections. As part of the Muséums Nature Montréal, it is associated with the city's Insectarium, Biodôme, and Planetarium. The Jardin botanique de Montréal is also noted for its highly successful cultural programming and educational interpretation.

Another example of a municipal garden hybrid that pairs city resources with formal education, the Humber Arboretum is located at Humber College and acts as an outdoor classroom and training facility for landscape, horticulture, arboriculture, and education and sustainability programs. Established in 1977, the Humber Arboretum is a partnership between the City of Toronto, the Toronto and Region Conservation Authority, and Humber College. Although unique in its management structure, it is representative of how many municipal public gardens leverage complex partnerships with other conservation, education and charitable organizations. It features a mix of ornamental display gardens and managed natural areas among Humber River valley lands and woodland trails.

Municipal Gardens and Plant-Related Nonprofit Organizations

Horticultural societies may also be closely connected to the management, governance, or financial support of municipal public gardens and have been known to take over operation and development of existing municipal public gardens. One example is the 4-acre Toronto Botanical Garden, which was recently annexed from the city of Toronto's Edwards Gardens and is now operated as a gardening education center by a conglomerate of horticultural societies, master gardeners associations, and volunteers. Another example of a municipal public garden now run in partnership with a volunteer-based charity is the Riverwood Conservancy in Mississauga, Ontario.

In some cases, municipal gardens officially split operational duties between the city and a nonprofit association. Deftly demonstrating this balance, the horticultural and curatorial operations of the VanDusen Botanical Garden are managed by the Vancouver Board of Parks and Recreation, while the Vancouver Botanical Garden Association provides other aspects, such as educational programs. Located on a site that was converted from a golf course in the 1970s, VanDusen is known for its stunning landscapes and plant collections featuring more than 7,000 taxa arranged primarily by geographic origin; the collections include a rare Elizabethan hedge maze, rhododendrons, azaleas, magnolias, and cherry trees. As exemplified by the design of its new Visitor Centre as a living building, VanDusen also dedicates significant effort to plant conservation, environmental stewardship, and landscape sustainability.

Municipal Conservatories

Many of the larger Canadian municipalities also own and operate glass houses and conservatories as part of their parks or community services departments. Muttart Conservatory features tropical, temperate, and arid horticulture displays in glass pyramids run by the city of Edmonton, Alberta. Toronto operates six public glass houses at Allan Gardens, a park that dates back to the 1850s and features a historic palm house built in 1910. The City of Vancouver's Parks Department operates the Bloedel Conservatory in Queen Elizabeth Park, which features tropical plant and bird collections.

Estate Gardens

Only a handful of Canada's public gardens originated as estates. One notable example is Jardins de Métis/Reford Gardens in remote Grand-Métis, Québec, which traces its origins to the tenacity of Elsie Reford and her railroad baron heritage. Jardins de Métis/Reford Gardens is noteworthy for its annual contemporary landscape installation, art festival, native plants, education programs, and splendid historic gardens where Elsie trialed plants from all over the world, proving that many could be successfully grown in a harsh northern location through crafty use of microclimates and soil amendment. The emblematic plant of the gardens is the finicky *Meconopsis betonicifolia* (Himalayan blue poppy), which Elsie famously naturalized throughout Reford's woodland gardens. The province of Québec opened the gardens to the public from 1962 to 1995, but thereafter sold it to a charitable organization, Les Amis des Jardins de Métis.

Other examples include the Columbia Valley Botanical Garden in British Columbia, which owes its existence to the donation of land by Randolf Bruce, a former lieutenant governor of British Columbia. More historic farm site than estate, George Pegg Botanic Garden in west-central Alberta is located on the site of the former homestead of the celebrated botanist and taxonomist after whom the garden is named.

Significant Influences on the Development of Canadian Public Gardens

Canada is an enormous country that has a relatively small and geographically widespread population. If institutional membership in a professional organization, such as the American Public Gardens Association or Botanic Gardens Conservation International, is an indicator of public garden status, then there are perhaps fifteen to twenty Canadian public gardens. Based on a comparison of the ratios of public gardens to overall population, Canada has one-quarter of the number of gardens that might be expected on the basis of the country's population relative to that of the United States.

The paucity of public gardens in Canada is due in part to the absence of an accepted model for public gardens generated by any level of government. Canada also has no tradition of wealthy estates converting to public gardens. Most Canadian public gardens are hybrids combining differing governance models and initial private intentions. Searching for funding is the hallmark of Canadian public gardens, with governance and operations often changing in response to whatever funding appears to be most sustainable.

Conservation and Natural Areas

Despite the relatively small number of public gardens per capita, according to the current listing of participants on the BGCI website Canada has twenty-three institutions that use the International Agenda for Botanic Gardens in Conservation (compared to twenty-eight for all of the United States), which puts it first behind the United States and points to the tendency of Canadian horticultural institutions to include plant conservation within their mandates. The inclusion of natural areas as part of a public garden's holdings is another distinguishing feature of Canadian public gardens. Based on a 2003 survey, almost 75 percent of Canadian gardens own or manage natural areas, whereas in the United States only about 25 percent do so. Because several of Canada's major public gardens also manage natural areas for public use, the line between parks and botanical gardens is often blurred, particularly in regard to organizational identity and public perception. While problematic, this situation also promotes a wider appreciation for plants in a variety of contexts and presents a broader range of educational opportunities than are presented by designed gardens alone.

Foundations and Philanthropy

In contrast to the focus on endowment and foundation funding in U.S. public gardens, Canadian gardens receive much less support from these sources, a fact that may be related to cultural attitudes toward philanthropy, political attitudes toward public amenities, and even Canadian tax law.

Inherent in Canadian society is a general expectation that the government is primarily responsible for the stewardship of activities relating to arts, culture, science, education, and the environment. Taxes, in part, support these functions, which are some of the most vital activities undertaken by Canadian public gardens. The result is that gardens, as with most Canadian cultural, environmental and educational institutions, generally rely heavily on government funding, either directly or indirectly through grants.

Though gifts to charitable organizations are eligible for tax receipts, which should encourage donations, the fact that most Canadian public gardens either receive significant government support or are governed by a governmental unit is both a complication and a deterrence. Many Canadian governmental units are not allowed to accept certain types of charitable donations, and because of their affiliation with governmental units, gardens are sometimes unable to accept gifts as well. Many public gardens have been able to work around these regulations by establishing a separate foundation or other registered nonprofit organization to steward tax-deductible donations for the garden or for special projects. A good example is the VanDusen Botanical Gardens Association, which jointly funds and operates VanDusen Botanical Gardens with the City of Vancouver.

Although Canadians are less inclined to charitable giving than their American counterparts, individual donations and bequests can help to fill funding gaps. Roughly the same percentage of taxpayers donate to charities in Canada and the United States, but Americans tend to donate two and a half times as much money as Canadians (LeRoy, Veldhuis, and Clemens 2002).

According to Susan Raymond's comparison of philanthropic trends in Canada and the United States, tax policy appears to be an important determination of giving in Canada (Raymond 2001). The Canadian taxation system supports public programs, but higher taxation rates also mean that individuals accumulate less personal wealth and consequently have less ability to personally direct their wealth toward philanthropic endeavors than Americans do. Canada's per capita personal disposable income (PDI) in 2001 was 70.4 percent of that of the United States (Sharpe 2002), and in 2005, Canada's tax revenue as a percentage of GDP averaged 8.2 percent more than the United States (Read 2007).

While personal wealth does not often accumulate to levels that match those in the United States, corporate wealth is not as limited. Although there is not much of a tax incentive for Canadian corporations and businesses to donate to charities (Rotstein 2008), Canadian public gardens frequently seek funding from corporate foundations and corporate social responsibility initiatives, which can provide significant monetary and in-kind support.

Governance

If a garden has a charitable foundation or nonprofit organization involved in its governance, then Canadian federal and provincial legal regulations require a board of directors for oversight of its activities. However, the fact that many Canadian public gardens are run through either public educational institutions or some other governmental unit has a profound effect on governance structure. Because of these relationships, independent boards of directors are less commonly involved in the primary governance of Canadian gardens. Since educational and government organizations running public gardens may not wish to give primary decision-making power to an outside board of directors, it is common for management boards to be appointed through the garden's parent organization(s) or for ultimate governance be handled through a board of trustees of a university or college.

Staffing

Because there are relatively few Canadian public gardens and because of the distances between them, most garden staff members come from outside of the public garden community, and movement of staff between institutions is rare. Individual institutions must continue to invest heavily in training staff in just what a public garden is and does.

Unions are an important part of Canadian society, and Canadian labor law is quite strong (e.g., constructive dismissal does not exist in U.S. labor law but is very important in Canada). About half of Canada's public gardens are university based, and many others are tied to municipal or provincial governments, which means that personnel policies are determined outside of the garden. Upper management is bound by the challenges of the academic or government environment in terms of productivity and advancement, a difficult set of circumstances that are hard to reconcile with managing a garden as a public amenity and a research center.

Table A-1: Canadian Public Gardens

Garden Name	Parent Organization	Governance
Alberta Crop Diversification Centre South	Agriculture and Agrifood Canada	Government, Federal
Annapolis Royal Historic Gardens	Annapolis Royal Historic Gardens Society	Not for Profit
Aurora Community Arboretum	Self	Not for Profit
Assiniboine Park	City of Winnipeg	Government, Municipal
Biodôme de Montréal	City of Montreal	Government, Municipal
Bloedel Conservatory	City of Vancouver Park Board	Government, Municipal
Calgary Zoo & Botanical Garden	Self	Not for Profit
Canadian Museum of Nature (no living collections)	Museums Canada	Government, Federal
Columbia Valley Botanical Gardens	Self	Not for Profit
Devonian Botanic Garden	University of Alberta	University Unit
Domaine Joly-De Lotbinière	Self	Not for Profit
Dominion Arboretum	Agriculture and Agrifood Canada	Government, Federal
Finnerty Gardens	University of Victoria	University Unit
George Pegg Botanic Garden	Self	Not for Profit
Halifax Public Gardens	Halifax Regional Municipality	Government, Municipal
Harriet Irving Botanical Gardens	Acadia University	University Unit
Humber Arboretum	Humber College, City of Toronto, TRCA	Government, Municipal; Conservation Authority; College Unit
Jardin botanique de Montréal	City of Montreal; Université de Montréal	Government, Municipal; University Unit
Jardin botanique du Nouveau-Brunswick	New Brunswick Botanical Garden Society	Not for Profit
Jardin botanique Roger-Van den Hende	Université Laval	University Unit
Le Parc Marie-Victorin	Municipality of Kingsey Falls	Government, Municipal
Lakehead University Arboretum	Lakehead Arboretum	University Unit
Les Jardins de Métis/Reford Gardens	Self	Not for Profit
Memorial University of Newfoundland Botanical Garden	Memorial University of Newfoundland	University Unit

City/Province	Website
Brooks, AB	www1.agric.gov.ab.ca/$department/deptdocs.nsf/all/opp4386
Annapolis Royal, NS	www.historicgardens.com/
Aurora, ON	www.auroraarboretum.ca
Winnipeg, MB	www.winnipeg.ca/cms/ape/conservatory/
Montreal, QC	www2.ville.montreal.qc.ca/biodome/
Vancouver, BC	http://vancouver.ca/PARKS/PARKS/bloedel/index.htm
Calgary, AB	www.calgaryzoo.org/
Ottawa, ON	www.nature.ca
Invermere, BC	www.conservancy.bc.ca/CVBG/
Edmonton, AB	www.ales.ualberta.ca/devonian/
Sainte-Croix, QC	http://domainejoly.com
Ottawa, ON	www.agr.gc.ca/sci/arboretum/
Victoria, BC	http://external.uvic.ca/gardens/index.php
Glenevis, AB	www.pegggarden.org/
Halifax, NS	http://halifaxpublicgardens.ca
Wolfville, NS	http://botanicalgardens.acadiau.ca/
Toronto, ON	www.humberarboretum.on.ca/
Montreal, QC	www2.ville.montreal.qc.ca/jardin/jardin.htm
Saint-Jacques, NB	http://jardinbotaniquenb.com
Quebec, QC	www.jardin.ulaval.ca/
Kingsey Falls, QC	www.parmarievictorin.com
Thunder Bay, ON	laurentian.ca/Laurentian/Home/Departments/Biology/About_Biology/arb.htm
Grand-Métis, QC	www.jardinsmetis.com/
St. John's, NL	www.mun.ca/botgarden/

Table A-1: Canadian Public Gardens (*continued*)

Garden Name	Parent Organization	Governance
Milner Gardens and Woodland	Vancouver Island University	University Unit
Morden Research Station Arboretum	Agriculture and Agrifood Canada	Government, Federal
Morgan Arboretum	McGill University	University Unit
Musée de la Nature et des Sciences	Self	Not for Profit
Musée du Château Ramezay	Self	Not for Profit
Muttart Conservatory	City of Edmonton	Government, Municipal
Niagara Parks Botanical Gardens and School of Horticulture	Niagara Parks Commission	Government, Provincial
Nikka Yuko Japanese Garden	Self	Not for Profit
Nova Scotia Agricultural College Gardens	Nova Scotia Agricultural College	College Unit
Olds College Botanic Garden	Olds College	College Unit
Oshawa Valley Botanical Gardens	City of Oshawa	Government, Municipal
PFRA Indian Head Tree Nursery	Agriculture and Agrifood Canada	Government, Federal
Riverwood Conservancy (formerly Mississauga Garden Council)	Self	Not for Profit
Royal Botanical Gardens	Self	Not for Profit (Provincial, Municipal partners)
Royal Roads University Botanical Garden	Royal Roads University	University Unit
Sherwood Fox Arboretum	University of Western Ontario	University Unit
Sunshine Coast Botanical Garden Society	Self	Not for Profit
The Arboretum	University of Guelph	University Unit
The Gardens of Fanshawe College	Fanshawe College	College Unit
Tofino Botanical Gardens	Self	Not for Profit
Toronto Botanical Garden	Self	Not for Profit
Toronto Zoo	City of Toronto	Government, Municipal
University of British Columbia Botanical Garden and Centre for Plant Research	University of British Columbia	University Unit
VanDusen Botanical Garden	City of Vancouver, Self	Joint Municipal Government/Not for Profit

City/Province	Website
Qualicum Beach, BC	www.viu.ca/milnergardens/
Morden, NB	dir.gardenweb.com/directory/mrc/
Ste.-Anne-de-Bellevue, QC	www.morganarboretum.org/
Sherbrooke, QC	www.naturesciences.qc.ca/
Montreal, QC	www.chateauramezay.qc.ca/index2.htm
Edmonton, AB	www.muttartconservatory.ca
Niagara Falls, ON	www.niagaraparks.com/garden-trail/botanical-gardens.html
Lethbridge, AB	www.nikkayuko.com/
Truro, NS	nsac.ca/envsci/gardengate/alumni.asp
Olds, AB	www.oldscollege.ca/botanicgarden/
Oshawa, ON	ovbgoshawa.ca/
Indian Head, SK	www4.agr.gc.ca/AAFC-AAC/display-afficher.do?id=1186517615847&lang=eng
Mississauga, ON	www.riverwoodconservancy.org
Hamilton, ON	www.rbg.ca
Victoria, BC	www.hatleypark.ca/
London, ON	www.uwo.ca/biology/arboretum/
Sechelt, BC	www.coastbotanicalgarden.org/
Guelph, ON	www.uoguelph.ca/arboretum/
London, ON	www.fanshawec.ca
Tofino, BC	www.tbgf.org/
Toronto, ON	www.torontobotanicalgarden.ca/
Toronto, ON	www.torontozoo.com/
Vancouver, BC	www.ubcbotanicalgarden.org/
Vancouver, BC	vancouver.ca/parks/parks/vandusen/website/index.htm

Since Canadian public gardens tend to be underfunded, many must turn to the cultivation of a volunteer workforce in order to help offset the need for staff. Some, such as the Toronto Botanical Garden, have even been created out of volunteer associations. Because of the strong presence of unions within many public garden staffing systems, there are often restrictions placed on the use of volunteers as a significant portion of a garden's workforce. This factor can be particularly challenging in municipal, university, and college gardens, which tend to have union-based work forces.

National Initiatives

In the 1940s, professionals in Canada were involved in the launch of the American Association of Botanical Gardens and Arboreta (now the American Public Gardens Association). In the early 1970s efforts to formalize links between Canadian horticultural institutions reached a point at which a National Botanical Gardens System for Canada was proposed. The Royal Botanical Gardens hosted a major conference to flesh out the proposal, which was forwarded to the government of Canada but not acted upon.

The Rio Earth Summit of 1992 and the subsequent Convention on Biological Diversity (CBD) in 1993 renewed efforts to bring botanical gardens into the forefront of conservation programs. In 1995 the Canadian Botanical Conservation Network (CBCN) was founded at the Royal Botanical Gardens in response to the absence of a serious role for botanical gardens in the Canadian Biodiversity Strategy, Canada's national response to the CBD. Canada is a party to the Convention on Biological Diversity, whereas the United States has not ratified this important treaty. As a result, the federal environment ministry in Canada has been supportive of efforts to organize the botanical gardens community, resulting in several action plans and national meetings in the 1990s and 2000s.

Since 1998, there has been a consistent effort by the volunteer Ottawa Botanical Garden Society to establish a botanical garden in the capital city of Ottawa, and to have this project designated as the national botanical garden. The idea of a national garden in Canada is not new. Efforts date back well over 100 years to the inception of the Dominion Arboretum and a botanical garden at the federal Central Experimental Farm but have yet to come to fruition. This is due in part to the fact that botanical gardens, rightly or wrongly, are strongly associated with ornamental horticulture and have not had a consistent champion within any government department.

Summary

While the Canadian public garden sector is still growing and in some senses struggling to formulate a national identity, new public gardens are being developed throughout the country and existing institutions continue to strengthen their programs and capacities. Factors that are likely to have profound effects on these gardens include the growing movement toward sustainability, rising interest in native plant conservation and research, and the maturation of the Canadian philanthropic sector. Also likely to occur is a more active and innovative response to Canadian multiculturalism and globalized tourism. Though it is difficult to generalize about Canadian public gardens as a whole because of the diversity of their origins, funding models, governance structures, and mandates, it is likely to be this very variety that will allow these organizations to be flexible enough to meet the changing needs and demographics of Canadian society.

The Importance of Plant Exploration Today

PAUL W. MEYER

Botanical gardens, from the earliest of times, have been repositories of plants collected in faraway lands. Plants for food or medicine, or other economically useful plants, were especially coveted, as were plants that offered special beauty or novelty in the garden. From the early physic gardens such as Pisa's (1544) to gardens such as the Royal Botanic Garden, Kew, that developed during the age of exploration in the sixteenth and seventeenth centuries, the growing, displaying, and studying of plants collected abroad was central to their mission.

This work was built upon and extended in the nineteenth century by emerging American institutions such as the Missouri Botanical Garden (1859) and the Arnold Arboretum (1872). During this era China and Japan were becoming more accessible to European and American plant explorers, and a steady stream of dried herbarium specimens, living plants, and seeds flowed into botanical institutions. Among the most notable and famous of the early plant collectors was Ernest Henry "Chinese" Wilson, an Englishman with affiliations with Kew and later the Arnold Arboretum. In addition to his energy and fearlessness, Wilson brought a scientific rigor to his work, carefully documenting his living collections with herbarium specimens, plant descriptions, and collection site data. He, along with leading peers of his day, set a new standard that plant explorers continue to emulate. His introductions and others from that era continue to have a major impact on American horticulture, and his dried specimens hold great value in herbaria collections throughout the world.

The work of plant explorers continues to be central to the collections, scientific research, and education programs of modern public gardens. Today's plant explorers often focus on a specific geographic area or a particular plant group. The objective may be documenting with herbarium specimens, photos, and written descriptions, or it may also involve collection of seeds or other living plant material. With the accelerating loss of natural habitat throughout the world, herbarium specimens, seeds and living plants of wild-collected, scientifically documented origin are an important and in some cases urgent component of plant conservation. Because intraspecific genetic variation can be significant, it is important that accessions of a species in collections represent many different parts of the natural range of that species. This variation could be manifested through different horticultural forms, or it might be a hidden trait, observed only in an individual plant's adaptability to various conditions such as heat, cold, drought, or salt spray.

Today, a plant collection expedition is usually the result of collaboration involving a number of scientists representing several institutions. It is rare for a garden staff member to be totally devoted only to exploration. Contemporary plant explorers tend to be curators, botanists, or horticulturists with a myriad of other responsibilities at their home institution. So it is important that the responsibilities of planning, executing, and following up an expedition are shared. Also, in the field, much work needs to be done, including collecting and pressing specimens, taking photos, recording collection observations and data, and collecting seeds. Ideally the seeds collected should represent a diversity of individual plants, which often makes the task of actually gathering the seeds time-consuming.

Although it is possible for a plant explorer to do solo expeditions, a team approach facilitates the work. As with any team, members bring diverse areas of expertise. An ideal team might include a taxonomist, a horticulturist, an older experienced collector, and a young athletic collector able to climb tall trees. The collaborative approach also brings critical benefits after the trip, when the living material is being grown on and evaluated. It gives observers a chance to see how a plant performs under a variety of conditions and multiple sites and serves as an insurance policy, helping to guard the young collection from loss as a result of insects, disease, or drought. This is especially important in this era of climate change. Plants that have grown well in one location in the past may not necessarily continue to do so in the future as conditions change. Similarly, urbanization creates dramatic microclimate changes that accentuate the need for varying plant adaptabilities.

The potential of introducing an invasive plant is a special concern today. Though the majority of plant introductions are well behaved and a positive addition to our landscapes, invasive plants that have the ability to overrun a habitat must be scrupulously avoided. Again, a collaborative approach among gardens gives multiple opportunities to grow and observe a plant under different circumstances and to exchange data before making a new introduction. It is also important not to introduce a plant until it can be evaluated for possible invasive potential.

An example of one successful plant exploration collaboration is the 1984 collection trip to South Korea to collect seeds of *Camellia japonica* from a very northern population offering the potential of greater winter hardiness. Organized by Barry Yinger, U.S. National Arboretum, the team included collectors from the Morris Arboretum of the University of Pennsylvania, Longwood Gardens, and the Holden Arboretum. Seed collections were made from isolated populations from a group of islands off the northwest coast of South Korea. Multiple accessions were made, and when possible, seeds from multiple individual plants in a given locale were included in an accession. Living collections were also vouchered with herbarium specimens that were later deposited at both North American and Korean institutions.

The camellia seeds germinated well, and within a few years seedlings were planted out for testing at institutions including the Morris Arboretum, the U.S. National Arboretum, Longwood Gardens, and the Holden Arboretum. As might be expected, the camellias were not cold-hardy enough for northeast Ohio winters, but many plants were successfully grown at the other institutions. Now, more that twenty-five years later, a number of clones are being introduced for their garden characteristics and superior winter hardiness (Aiello 2009).

The North American–China Plant Exploration Consortium (NACPEC) is another example of successful plant exploration collaboration. Founded in 1991, this group of seven gardens has worked with Chinese colleagues to sponsor nine expeditions to China between 1991 and 2008. The objective has been to explore the riches of China's north temperate flora in areas that have a climate similar to areas in the northeastern United States. In all, the database of NACPEC collections lists 1,348 accessions with more than 6,000 plants in nine institutions. Individual plants are attracting attention as possible cultivar introductions, but in addition to the horticultural quality of these plants, someday some "ugly duckling" might be found to contain genes for resistance to some still unknown virulent disease or insect, or may contain a compound effective in the fight against cancer. No doubt the value of these collections will continue to emerge for decades to come. One species of special interest is Chinese hemlock (*Tsuga chinensis*), which demonstrates resistance to the hemlock wooly adelgid (*Adeges tsugae*), currently plaguing the native Canada hemlock (*Tsuga canadensis*). Already Chinese hemlock is being used at the U.S. National Arboretum in breeding programs for which the hope is to combine the characteristics of native Canada hemlock with the insect resistance of Chinese hemlock. It is important to note that all collections were brought into the country in accordance with the regulatory restrictions of both China and the United States. All seeds, seedlings, and herbarium specimens were declared and subject to inspection both at the point of entry into the United States and in a more formal inspection at the Plant Introduction Center at Beltsville, Maryland.

Plant exploration does not necessarily require travel to faraway places. Riches of unusual, useful, and well-adapted plants might be found along local roadsides and in meadows and forests closer to home. But wherever a plant explorer collects, the principles of careful observation and documentation still apply. Whether collected nearby or abroad, wild-collected and documented plants hold the most value in a well-curated public garden collection.

APPENDIX C

Herbaria

BARBARA M. THIERS

For the past three centuries, scientists have documented the Earth's plant diversity by collecting portions of living plants and preserving them in collections called herbaria. The first herbaria were rooms in medieval monasteries where monks stored bundles of dried plants for the concoction of herbal medicines. The innovation of pressing plants and gluing them to paper is attributed to Luca Ghini (1500–1566), a professor at the University of Bologna. In Ghini's herbarium the sheets of specimens were compiled into bound volumes. Even though species with medicinal properties may well have been the focus in Ghini's herbarium, his innovation in storage method suggests that by his day the herbarium was viewed as a scholarly reference rather than an herbalist's workshop. Carl Linnaeus (1707–1778), who invented the current system for naming plants, abandoned the book format for herbarium specimens, choosing instead to store the sheets layered horizontally in cabinets. This change allowed Linnaeus to make more active use of specimens in classifying plants—loose specimens were easier to compare and to rearrange as he refined his classification system.

The basic technique for preparation and storage of specimens is remarkably unchanged since Linnaeus' time, although the materials and techniques we use today help ensure the longevity of the specimens. Herbaria are now routinely stored in specially designed fire- and waterproof steel cabinets, specimen preparation uses archival-quality paper and glue, and regular pest control procedures such as freezing prevent the introduction and spread of specimen-eating insects.

There are approximately 3,400 herbaria in the world today. Collectively they contain an estimated 350,000,000 specimens, documenting 400 years of the earth's vegetational history (Thiers 2010). This wealth of data has allowed scientists a deep understanding of plant biology, but the work started by Linnaeus to document the world's plant biodiversity is still far from complete. We still have names for less than 50 percent of the earth's plant species, even fewer in more poorly known groups such as bryophytes, algae, and fungi, which also are stored in herbaria.

Among the approximately 600 active herbaria in the United States, most are associated with universities (473 herbaria, or 82 percent). Governmental institutions house about 9 percent of the nation's herbaria (54), natural history museums house 5 percent (29), and 4 percent of herbaria are associated with public gardens (24 herbaria). Although relatively small in number, the herbaria associated with public gardens tend to be large in size. Of the approximately 79 million herbarium specimens in the United States, 22 percent, or 16 million, are held in herbaria associated with public gardens (Thiers 2010).

Herbaria in the United States are fairly consistent in management and use, regardless of the type of institution with which they are affiliated. In general, herbaria associated with large public gardens (for example, the New York Botanical Garden, Arnold Arboretum, and Missouri Botanical Garden) have an eclectic acquisition policy, accepting specimens across a wide taxonomic and geographic range, emphasizing the research interests of associated scientists more than the geographic location of the garden. Some herbaria in public gardens emphasize cultivated plants (e.g., the Arnold Arboretum), and all document to some extent the plants that have grown on their own grounds. Because understanding the evolutionary history of cultivated plants can be very complicated, herbarium collections of such plants, especially historical collections, may be critical to unraveling their ancestry and determining the course of future breeding programs.

Most of the major herbaria in the world have embarked on a digitization program for their specimens. Information from specimen labels (e.g., the name of the plant, where and by whom it was collected) is transcribed into a database, and sometimes digital images of the specimens are captured as well. Herbaria associated with public gardens have been leaders and innovators in sharing herbarium data online. The Missouri Botanical Garden, through its online TROPICOS system (Missouri Botanical Garden 2010), allows users to trace plant names to their original source of publication and often links to a scanned image of that publication. The New York Botanical Garden's Virtual Herbarium is an actively growing database of specimen label information and images and also provides online identification tools for selected plant groups or geographic regions (New York Botanical Garden 2010). The Chicago Botanic Garden and the Morton Arboretum are both part of an innovative program called V-Plants, which is a virtual herbarium of plants growing in the greater Chicago region, designed primarily as an educational tool and reference for citizen scientists (V-Plants Project 2010).

Most herbaria share their digitized specimen data online through their own websites, through a regional Web portal, or through the international Global Biodiversity Information Facility (GBIF). Currently the GBIF Data Portal, the world's largest aggregator of herbarium specimen records, serves more than 39 million records from herbaria around the world (Global Biodiversity Information Facility 2010). Making such data available online helps scientists to document plant biodiversity more efficiently and has also opened the herbarium doors to a wider range of scientific analyses. Comparing information about what plants grow where now and where they used to grow can provide the basis for a profile of the conditions favored by different species. Scientists then can extrapolate about how those plants might fare in response to future changes in climate.

Public Garden Archives

SHEILA CONNOR

> Since the beginning of human time, we have
> expressed ourselves through the gardens we have
> made. They live on as records of our private beliefs
> and public values, good and bad.
> —Mark Francis and Randolph T. Hester Jr.

Archives are essential. They provide the intellectual infrastructure that documents the history of a public garden's endeavors and are the repository of its permanently valuable records. The records held by an archive serve as confirmation of decisions made and actions taken; they capture the work, creativity, and thinking of both individuals and departments or units within the institution; and they give insight and evidence about the culture of the organization.

Archivists collect, describe, preserve, protect, process, and organize these unique records. They determine which records are of enduring value and champion their use. Access to these records can foster a greater understanding of a garden's traditions and a common sense of place and purpose. Archivists also provide reference assistance to researchers as they search for that elusive quote or fact and as they learn about the documentary legacy, resources, and practice of the institution.

All public gardens, including arboreta, botanical gardens, conservatories, historical landscapes, and natural, display, and entertainment gardens, as well as special collections, generate important organizational documents. A cursory survey of garden websites reveals detailed timelines, well-written histories, impressive mission statements, and excellent historical photographs, all based, presumably, on documents the garden holds. At the same time, staff members in the garden's programs and departments are all generating new records that document the garden's current activities. The management of these documents through the creation of an archive often presents a challenge for gardens. Establishing an archive is a commitment undertaken by the governing institution and requires the funding of knowledgeable staff, appropriate equipment, space, and supplies.

To be effective, archives need to be organized into units or groups that best reflect the institution and have a mission statement, goals, and a strategic plan. A collection development policy for the archives also needs to be established. While the management of archives of those gardens associated with an educational institution or other governing entity may be prescribed by the parent institution, most garden archives need to generate their own standards for the retention and disposal of records and protocols for the transfer of inactive records from the individual or department to the archives.

Records to be archived will arrive in various conditions and in all sizes, shapes, and formats: handwritten manuscripts; correspondence, both handwritten and typed; images, including prints, negatives, and slides; maps, plans, journals, diaries, films, and video and sound recordings (many of which may now include an electronic component, or arrive in only electronic form); poor-quality printed matter; and other three-dimensional objects. The archivist must have a general understanding of how to preserve these different papers, inks, textiles, and photographic materials and be familiar with the adhesives that may have been used on these objects. Records may also be copied onto other formats to protect the original and to make them more easily and widely accessible.

Once the material is on-site, it is assessed and processed. This procedure includes many steps, from the finger-numbing removal of rusted staples to the writing of a finding aid.

EXAMPLE OF MISSION STATEMENT, GOALS, AND STRATEGIC PLAN FOR ARCHIVES

Mission

To acquire, manage, preserve, and make accessible for reference and research materials that document the founding, development, organization, management, and achievements of the garden and its role in research, plant exploration, landscape management, education, conservation, and horticulture

Goal

To make available to staff, students, and scholars the records that provide a comprehensive documentary history of the institution

Strategic Plan

• To identify, acquire, and manage institutional records that have permanent administrative, historical, or scientific value

• To develop and implement a set of procedures and policies, supported by an institutional management program, that ensures the acquisition and management of appropriate records

• To arrange, describe, and curate these records through sound archival practices and to make them accessible through the creation of guides, often identified as finding aids and other cataloging and descriptive means

• To provide the appropriate environmental controls and proper materials to house the archives in order to ensure their permanent preservation and their availability for continued use

• To ensure ongoing physical access to, and information about, the archives and to assist researchers in the use of these resources

---

BASIC ELEMENTS OF A FINDING AID

Title

Descriptive Summary
  Repository

  Call No.

  Location

  Title

  Date(s)

  Creator

  Quantity

Abstract

Acquisition Information
  Provenance

Processing Information
  Processed

Terms of Access

Terms of Use

Biographical/Historical Note

Scope and Content

Arrangement

Container List

While the creation of an in-house processing manual is invaluable, a simple work plan for the steps in processing includes:

• **Appraisal:** determining the originator/creator, subject, and title of the collection and what type of material it includes

• **Current state of the collection:** provenance, original order, size, date of creation, and date range

• **Preservation:** any preservation steps that may need to be taken

• **Arrangement:** the proposed arrangement for the collection and series defined and the level of description determined, along with a general description of each series

Archival records can be damaged by a variety of environmental conditions, including temperature, relative humidity, and light. Infestations of fungus, mold, insects, and rodents can also adversely affect collections. Nor are archives exempt from abuse or disasters. Environmental conditions must be monitored and stabilized, and plans and policies need to be in place to prevent infestations and abuse. Having an emergency plan and supplies on hand will help mitigate disasters.

Finally, an overview of the collection and guidelines for its use should be available to visitors and posted on the garden's Web page, and an annual report should be produced.

Two excellent, readable references that are short, simple, and very practical are *Starting an Archives* by Elizabeth Yakel and *Organizing Archival Records* by David Carmicheal. The first is an introduction to establishing an archival program within an institution; the second provides guidance on how to process collections for archivists in small institutions. Also, *Keeping Archives* is the name of the third edition of a comprehensive guide to establishing, managing, and developing archives published by the Australian Society of Archivists.

The Library in a Public Garden

RITA M. HASSERT

If you have a garden and a library, you have everything you need.

—Cicero

The intersection of the garden and the library has been formally documented in Western history since the early gardens of the sixteenth century. The botanical gardens at Padua and Pisa in Italy followed what has been described as a classic arrangement of three key garden elements: the living collections of the gardens, the dried plant collections of the herbarium, and the book collections of the library (MacPhail 1989). These three elements all unite to document, preserve, record, share, and expand our knowledge and understanding of plants and gardens. While library collections might no longer be limited solely to books, this essential triad continues to flourish today.

Embedding the library within the garden continues to allow for the seamless access to plant knowledge and information within the garden community. The garden library has become a crucial stakeholder not only in the acquisition, preservation, management, and dissemination of plant information, resources, and knowledge, but also in the public garden's education and outreach efforts.

The library provides information, resources, and services to all the members of the public garden community. Directly supporting the research of the garden's staff and the garden's education programs, the library also often serves the informational needs of the garden's volunteers and members. The library's collections typically focus on selected subjects closely allied with the mission of the garden. Within these subjects,

the library's collections often range from the expert level to the recreational. Resources within these collections can include a recently published monograph on conifers, an 1893 nursery catalog, a children's book about trees, an audiotaped interview with a retired staff member, access to a database on garden literature, a book for the beginning gardener, early landscape plans, a journal on native plants, a taxonomist's field notebook, a born-digital collection of garden images, a pen-and-ink drawing of a white oak tree, a photograph of a recently introduced sugar maple cultivar, and early institutional documents. Selecting, acquiring, organizing, managing, and preserving these resources and making them accessible are goals of the public garden librarian.

With the librarian's knowledge and understanding of the garden's mission, programs, and collections, resources are selected and acquired from a variety of vendors and sources. Once the resources are acquired, they are cataloged and integrated into the library's online public access catalog (OPAC) and holdings. Increasingly, next-generation OPACs are adding enriched content, including reviews, cover images, summaries, cloud tags, comments, and additional search capabilities, creating a more user-centric focus. To manage resources, the OPAC has a module to maintain patron records and track circulation.

Efforts to digitize collections within the library may be pursued in-house or contracted to outside service providers. Digital asset management systems, whether stand-alone or consortial, provide electronic access to a multitude of digitized and born-digital resources within the garden library. Reference services and outreach efforts encourage and facilitate access to collections in all formats. The librarian navigates this array of resources by capitalizing on knowledge of the library's subject interests, collection strengths, and access to a wide range of information portals. In addition, the library embraces current technologies to enhance access to collections and communication with their constituents. Blogs, wikis, and other tools are used to create proactive services within the garden community.

The library, through its resources and programs, also seeks to educate, inspire, and enrich the external community. Tours, classes, displays, exhibits, programs, and activities within the library all enhance the garden's outreach efforts to its community. Members of the local community often value the garden library as a unique resource that makes available to them materials usually not found in their public and school libraries. Dovetailing with the garden's education program and outreach efforts, the library is one more way to attract community members to the garden.

A key professional community for organizations and individuals concerned with botanical and horticultural literature is the Council on Botanical and Horticultural Libraries (CBHL). Created in 1969, CBHL "is an international organization of individuals, organizations and institutions concerned with the development, maintenance and use of libraries of botanical and horticultural literature." CBHL fosters cooperation, collaboration, and community among its member institutions. Building on the success of CBHL, the European Botanical and Horticultural Libraries Group (EBHL) was founded in the early 1990s "to promote and facilitate co-operation and communication between those working in botanical and horticultural libraries, archives and related institutions in Europe." Through publications, meetings, and other activities, both CBHL and EBHL work to encourage resource sharing and collaboration among botanical and horticultural libraries and communities.

The sharing of resources among botanical and horticultural libraries encouraged by CBHL and EBHL greatly enhances community and staff access to information. Resource sharing through a variety of vehicles allows for libraries to ensure that their patrons and communities have access to a wealth of information. Traditional interlibrary loan avenues including local, regional, and international consortia allow for access to resources not held by the library. Increasingly, a host of digital resources and repositories are available through venues such as the Biodiversity Heritage Library. No longer constrained by the on-site library's collection, the library user is presented with a wide range of resources and tools. In this way, the library within a public garden becomes a library without walls—able to access a broad palette of resources and provide a high level of services. By sharing the richness of the library collections with others, a greater community is consequently impacted by the garden's mission.

The library is often involved in the development and implementation of emerging technologies to support teaching, learning and research within the garden. Library 2.0 technologies such as blogs, wikis, RSS feeds, instant messaging, and other social software tools allow for engaged and dynamic participation by the garden community. This focus on technology allows for the adoption of new and innovative ways of presenting and packaging information. All of these successes increase the potential impact and outreach efforts of the library and further the dissemination of the garden's knowledge capital.

The creation of those early gardens in Padua and Pisa heralded not only a new age in gardens and plants but also a new age for libraries. The library continues to flourish right alongside the living plant collections and the preserved plant specimens of the herbarium. Our knowledge of plants has been gathered, preserved, dispersed, studied, discounted, rediscovered, reviewed, and examined under the leadership and purview of the public garden library. Tools and resources change, but the spirit of the library continues to impact the garden and the community.

Horticultural Therapy and Public Gardens

KAREN L. KENNEDY

Horticultural therapy (HT) is "a professionally conducted client-centered treatment modality that utilizes horticulture activities to meet specific therapeutic or rehabilitative goals of its participants. The focus is to maximize social, cognitive, physical and/or psychological functioning and/or to enhance general health and wellness" (Haller and Kramer 2006). The distinguishing characteristics of horticultural therapy are the participant's goals and the relationship between the participant, the therapist, and plants. The desired outcomes of such programs are focused on individuals and the improvement in their health and wellness. While most individuals feel an improvement in their mental and/or physical health after working in the garden, it is the intentional outcomes facilitated by a horticultural therapist that distinguish a program as horticultural therapy.

History of Horticultural Therapy in Public Gardens

Public gardens have long been a source of plant knowledge and inspiration to visitors of all ages. People seek out gardens to provide restorative experiences and relief from the stresses of daily life. Horticultural therapy programs in public gardens developed as a result of increased awareness of these factors, an increased desire to connect with people in their communities, and the rise of public concern for the rights of people with disabilities. Particularly for publicly funded gardens, the acknowledgment that people with disabilities are among the constituencies the gardens are charged to serve further promoted the development of HT programs.

The earliest programs, in the mid-1950s, were the result of the work of such pioneers as Lewis Lipp and Maude (Mrs. Warren H.) Corning of the Holden Arboretum, near Cleveland, Ohio. Those early programs brought underprivileged older adults, children with disabilities, and adults in physical rehabilitation programs to the Arboretum for planting activities. In 1973 the National Council for Therapy and Rehabilitation Through Horticulture (now the American Horticultural Therapy Association) was founded and began formalizing the profession. At the same time, more programs formed with specially trained staff at public gardens around the country: the North Carolina Botanical Garden, Chicago Botanic Garden, Cleveland Botanical Garden, Enid A. Haupt Garden, and Denver Botanic Gardens. According to the authors of a horticultural therapy textbook, "These programs led gardens to reach out to groups not traditionally served and have elevated the profile of public gardens in their communities and cities" (Simson and Straus 1998).

HT Services in Public Gardens Today

Hands-on horticultural therapy programs and training programs for therapists and other allied health professionals at public gardens have helped to increase the gardens' relevance in their communities. Gardens have become valuable resources for the health and human service community through programs that emphasize the wellness benefits of integrating plant-rich environments into their organizations. Some public gardens, such as the Chicago Botanic Garden and Missouri Botanical Garden, also provide therapeutic and enabling garden design consultation services to these same organizations.

HT programs provide experiences with and knowledge about plants and gardening in hands-on programs that enrich the lives of those not traditionally served and who might not have the means or opportunity to access a garden. Horticultural therapists use a natural interest in plants and gardens to motivate program participants to work on vocational or health-related goals. HT staff specially design activity sessions to meet the goals of the participants. Missouri Botanical Garden's Room with a Bloom program focuses the goals of the monthly flower-arranging activity on the needs of residents in independent-living, assisted-living, or skilled-nursing homes.

Gardens, tools, and even the process of planting are adapted to fit the mental or physical capabilities of participants in all types of programs. The Minnesota Landscape Arboretum (MLA) states as its program goal "to maximize individual quality of life, develop the skills necessary for self determination, and promote community integration through the simple pleasures of the garden." Both on- and off-site program opportunities for individuals and groups are tailored to promote decision making, daily living skills, and independence. The MLA Sensory Garden and North Carolina Botanical Garden's Horticultural Therapy Demonstration Garden are among those that not only demonstrate garden adaptations to professionals and the public but also provide on-site HT programming space.

HT programs are successful with adults and children, including people with intellectual disabilities, physical impairments resulting from accidents or strokes, traumatic brain injuries, and mental illness. The Chicago Botanic Garden offers indoor, outdoor, and year-round contractual services to facilities in the community and adjusts the program to address therapeutic, vocational, or wellness issues. Included in the services are all of the program materials, session plans, and a therapist to conduct the programs.

Through HT programs, public gardens can serve people in diverse life situations. HT can help people dealing with cancer and chronic illness to develop improved coping skills; it can help others maintain wellness as they age, and it can aid in the rehabilitation of substance abusers and criminal offenders.

While HT programs in public gardens share many commonalities, program emphasis and services are as diverse as the people they serve. Programs vary from single life-enrichment sessions to multiple sessions on- or off-site. Others focus on ongoing relationships, integrating the HT service with occupational or recreational therapy departments of health as well as human service organizations. On-site programming is often offered in the garden's own enabling and/or sensory garden. The fees for service may be based on annual or semiannual contracts, or arranged on a program basis one or more times per year.

In terms of outreach to the entire community, many public gardens offer very popular HT programs in stress management, mental health, cardiovascular fitness, and overall wellness that demonstrate the role plants and gardens play in promoting human health and well-being

Community Partnerships

Partnering with community-based health and human service organizations enables public gardens to reach individuals who can benefit from HT services and at the same time expand their audience. Partnerships also open the door to new marketing and additional educational opportunities for both organizations.

Some public gardens with horticultural therapy programs also offer consultation services to health and human service organizations that want to integrate green spaces into their facilities and create gardens suitable for individuals with a range of behavioral, physical, and mental disabilities.

Enabling Gardens and Theme Gardens

Many public gardens have created enabling gardens that serve as living demonstrations of how gardens can be created to serve individuals with disabilities. A garden that is enabling has design features that allow people with disabilities to access and to work in the garden. Raised beds, hanging baskets on pulleys, vertical garden walls, and raised hose attachments are examples of modifications that accommodate physical disabilities. The Chicago Botanic Garden, for example, is well-known for its Buehler Enabling Garden, which incorporates appropriate plants and design elements to accommodate a wide variety of people with physical and intellectual abilities.

Public gardens use other types of theme gardens to engage visitors with special needs and facilitate interaction with the garden. The Elizabeth and Nona Evans Restorative Garden at the Cleveland Botanical Garden includes tranquil places to sit and get away from the hustle of the other public areas, a reflecting pool that highlights a magnolia tree, and a dramatic rock wall with native stones and plants, ending in a water feature designed for touching. The walkways are fully accessible, and the grass is a special species that will accommodate wheelchair traffic.

The Portland Memory Garden within the city of Portland's park system is an excellent example of another theme garden that was designed to accommodate some of the unique attributes of people with dementia yet is also delightful for all visitors. By incorporating a returning loop path system, visual scanning opportunities that encompass the whole enclosed garden, and many seating areas, visitors are motivated to wander through and explore the garden. It is planted to stimulate all the senses, create new memories, and evoke fond childhood memories as well.

Summary

The missions of many public gardens include providing educational opportunities as well as enjoyment and restorative experiences to their visitors and communities. It is natural to connect those dots and realize that this mission extends to promoting the overall health and well-being of its visitors. There is much compelling evidence that demonstrates the impact of plant-rich environments on behavioral, physical, and mental health. Horticultural therapy programs go a step further by expanding the garden's reach and ability to make a significant impact on the health and well-being of individuals in their community well beyond their gates.

References

Chapter 2: The History and Significance of Public Gardens

Diamond, J. 2005. *Collapse: How societies choose to fail or succeed.* New York: Viking Press.

Evans, S. T. 2007. Precious beauty: The aesthetic and economic value of Aztec gardens. In *Botanical progress, horticultural innovations, and cultural changes*, edited by M. Conan and W. J. Kress, 81–101. Washington, D.C.: Dumbarton Oaks Research Library and Collection and Spacemaker Press.

Fallen, A. C. 2007. *A public garden for the nation.* Washington, D.C.: Government Printing Office.

Gothein, M.-L. 1928. *A history of garden art.* Vol. 2. London: J. M. Dent.

Hunt, J. D. 2000. *Greater perfections: The practice of garden theory.* Penn Studies in Landscape Architecture. Philadelphia: University of Pennsylvania Press.

Kellert, S. R., and E. O. Wilson, eds. 1993. *The biophilia hypothesis.* Washington, D.C.: Island Press.

Lawler, A. 2009. Beyond the Yellow River: How China became China. *Science* 325: 930–38.

Tudge, C. 1998. *Neanderthals, bandits and farmers: How agriculture really began.* Darwinism Today series. New Haven: Yale University Press.

Turner, T. 2005. *Garden history: Philosophy and design 2000 B.C.–2000 A.D.* New York: Spon Press.

UNFPA. 2007. *State of world population 2007: Unleashing the potential of urban growth.* United Nations Population Fund.

Wilson, E. O. 1984. *Biophilia: The human bond with other species.* Cambridge: Harvard University Press.

Chapter 3: Critical Issues in Starting a Public Garden

Gagliardi, J. 2009. An analysis of the initial planning process of new public horticulture institutions. MS thesis. University of Delaware.

Lyons, R. E. 1999. Arboreta and gardens: Teaching laboratories in the undergraduate curriculum—Introduction. *HortTechnology* 9: 548.

Rakow, D. 2006a. Starting a botanical garden or arboretum at a college or public institution, part I. Special report. *The Public Garden* 21(1): 33–37.

———. 2006b. Starting a botanical garden or arboretum at a college or public institution, part II. Moving from planning to reality. Special report. *The Public Garden* 21(2): 32–35.

Stephens, M., A. Steil, M. Gray, A. Hird, S. Lepper, E. Moydell, J. Paul, C. Prestowitz, C. Sharber, T. Sturman, and R. E. Lyons. 2006. Endowment strategies for the University of Delaware Botanic Garden through case study analysis. *HortTechnology* 16: 570–78.

Chapter 4: The Process of Organizing a New Public Garden

Boardsource. www.boardsource.org.

Brooklyn Botanic Garden. Mission and vision statements. www.bbg.org/abo/mission.html.

Cheekwood. Mission statement. www.cheekwood.org/About/History_of_Cheekwood.aspx.

Coastal Maine Botanical Gardens. 2009. *History of the Gardens.* Booth Bay, Maine: Coastal Maine Botanical Gardens. www.mainegardens.org/about/history.

Cornell Plantations. Mission statement. www.cornellplantations.org/about/mission.

Franklin Park Conservatory. Mission statement. www.fpconservatory.org/about.htm.

Garvan Woodland Gardens. Mission statement. www.garvangardens.org.

Internal Revenue Service. 2010. *Tax information for charities and other nonprofits.* Internal Revenue Service. www.irs.gov/charities.

Minnesota Council for Nonprofits. Info central: Governance. www.mncn.org/info_govern.htm.

Missouri Botanical Garden. Mission statement. www.mobot
.org/mobot/research.
Powell Gardens. n.d. Historical archive. Powell Gardens.
Radtke, J. M. 1998. *Strategic communications for non-profit
organizations: Seven steps to creating a successful plan.*
New York: John Wiley and Sons.
San Diego Botanic Garden. Mission statement.
www.sdbgarden.org.

Chapter 8: Volunteer Recruitment and Management

Ellis, S. 1996. *From the top down: The executive role in volunteer program success.* Philadelphia: Energize.

Chapter 9: Budgeting and Financial Planning

Dropkin, M., and B. LaTouche. 1998. *The budget-building
book for nonprofits: A step-by-step guide for managers and
boards.* San Francisco: Jossey-Bass.
Drucker, P. F. 1990. *Managing the non-profit organization:
Practices and principles.* New York: Harper Collins.
Epstein, M. J. 2008. *Making sustainability work: Best practices
in managing and measuring corporate social, environmental, and economic impacts.* San Francisco: Berrett-Koehler.
Oster, S. M. 1995. *Strategic management for nonprofit
organizations: Theory and cases.* New York: Oxford
University Press.
Savitz, A. W., and K. Weber. 2006. *The triple bottom line:
How today's best-run companies are achieving economic,
social, and environmental success—and how you can too.*
San Francisco: Jossey-Bass.
Western States Arts Federation and the Washington State Arts
Commission. 2008. Perspectives on cultural tax districts.
Proceedings from a seminar, February 11 and 12 in Seattle,
Washington.

Chapter 10: Fund-raising and Membership Development

Greenfield, J. M. 1991. *Fund-raising: Evaluating and managing the fund development process.* New York: John Wiley
and Sons.
Fund Raising School. 2002. *Principles and techniques of fund
raising.* Indianapolis: Center on Philanthropy at Indiana
University.
Havens, J. J., M. A. O'Herlihy, and P. G. Schervish. 2006.
Charitable giving: How much, by whom, to what, and
how? In *The nonprofit sector: A research handbook,*
edited by W. W. Powell and R. Steinberg, 542–67. New
Haven: Yale University Press.

Levy, B., and R. L. Cherry, eds. 1996–2003. The AFP fundraising dictionary. www.afpnet.org.
Rich, P., and D. Hines. 2002. *Membership development: An
action plan for results.* Sudbury, Mass.: Jones and Bartlett
Publishers.
Seiler, T. L. 2003. Plan to succeed. In *Hank Rosso's achieving
excellence in fund raising,* edited by E. R. Tempel, 23–29.
San Francisco: Jossey-Bass.

Chapter 11: Earned Income Opportunities

Daley, R. 2008. *Report to the directors of large gardens:
Synopsis benchmarking study 2008.* St. Louis: EMD
Consulting Group.
Merritt, E. E. 2006. *2006 museum financial information.*
Washington, D.C.: American Association of Museums.
Museum Store Association. 2006. *2006 MSA retail industry
report: Financial, operations, and salary data.* Denver:
Museum Store Association.

Chapter 13: Grounds Management and Security

Barnett, D. 2010. *Sustainability initiatives at Mount Auburn
Cemetery.* Cambridge, Mass.: Mount Auburn Cemetery.
Bauerle, T. 2009. Cornell University Department of
Horticulture. Current projects on irrigation. http://hort
.cals.cornell.edu/cals/hort/research/bauerle/current_
projects.cfm.
Brede, D. 2000. *Turfgrass maintenance reduction handbook:
Sports, lawns, and golf.* Chelsea, Mich.: Ann Arbor Press.
Brundtland Commission Report.1983. *Our common future.*
Oxford: Oxford University Press.
Cave, J., ed. 2000. *The complete garden guide.*
Charlottesville, Va.: Time-Life Books.
Center for Plant Conservation. 2002. Voluntary code of conduct for botanic gardens and arboreta. www.centerforplant
conservation.org/invasives.
Center for Transportation Research and Transportation. 2006.
The roadway. In *Local roads maintenance workers' manual.* www.ctre.iastate.edu/pubs/maint_worker/chap3.pdf.
Cornell Cooperative Extension Pest Management Guidelines.
2010. http://ipmguidelines.org/turfgrass/
Cornell University Sustainability Website. www.cornell
.edu/sustainability.
Emergency Management Institute. 2010. http://training.fema.gov.
Grounds Maintenance. 2010. Irrigation systems.
http://grounds-mag.com/irrigation.
Gussack, E., and F. S. Rossi. 2001. *Turfgrass problems: Picture
clues and management options.* Ithaca, N.Y.: Natural
Resource, Agriculture, and Engineering Service.

Iannotti, M. 2010. Xeriscape gardening—planning for a water wise garden. http://gardening.about .com/od/gardendesign/a/Xeriscaping_2.htm.

Jefferson, T. 1987. Letter from Jefferson to Charles Willson Peale, poplar forest, August 20, 1811. In *Thomas Jefferson: The Garden and Farm Books*, edited by R. C. Baron, 199. Golden, Colo.: Fulcrum Publishing.

Lanfranchi, M. *Contract vs. in-house security: Working with the experts for specialized services.* www.alliedbarton. com/about/InTheNewsPdfs/ContractSecurityVsInHouse-WorkingwithExpertsforSpecializedServices.pdf.

Lerner, J. M. 2001. Maintenance chart. In *Anyone can landscape*, 67. Batavia, Ill.: Ball Publishing.

Miller, M. M. F. 2010. All together now: Making play safe and accessible. *Recreation Management*, March, 18–25.

Penn State Agronomy Guide. http://agguide.agronomy.psu .edu/cm/sec2/sec23.cfm.

Planting Fields Arboretum State Historic Park. 2006. *Planting Fields Arboretum State Historic Park emergency action plan*. Report.

Rakow, D., and R. Weir. 1996. *Pruning: An illustrated guide to pruning ornamental trees and shrubs*. 3rd ed. Ithaca, NY: Cornell University Cooperative Extension Service.

Rose, M. A., and E. Smith. *Fertilizing landscape plants*. Ohio State University Fact Sheet, Horticulture and Crop Science. http://ohioline.osu.edu/hyg-fact/1000/1002.html.

Shakespear, G. 2003. Public safety on public grounds. *The Public Garden* 18(1): 12–15.

Simeone, V. A. 2005. *Great flowering landscape shrubs*. Batavia, Ill.: Ball Publishing.

Smith, C. 2009. Go "no-mow" lawns for a better planet. *Cornell Plantations Magazine* 64(1): 14–19.

Smith and Hawken. 1996. *The book of outdoor gardening*. New York: Workman Publishing Company.

Soil Foodweb. www.soilfoodweb.com.

Stevens, D. 2003. Designing naturalistic decorative water features: Criteria for water safety, water quality, and management. *The Public Garden* 18(1): 30–33.

Trautmann, N., and E. Olynciw. 1996. *Compost microorganisms*. http://compost.css.cornell.edu/microorg.html.

United States Access Board. www.access-board.gov.

University of Georgia Cooperative Extension. http://pubs .caes.uga.edu/caespubs/pubs/PDF/C802.pdf.

Vermont Agency of Natural Resources. www.anr.state.vt.us/ env03/activities/Water%20Activity.pdf.

Walker, P. 2009. Composting at Mount Auburn's new and improved recycling yard. *E-ternally Green Newsletter* December.

Chapter 15: Formal Education for Students, Teachers, and Youth at Public Gardens

Anderson, D., M. Storksdieck, and M. Spock. 2007. Understanding the long-term impacts of museum experiences. In *In principle, in practice: Museums as learning institutions,* edited by J. H. Falk, L. D. Dierking, and S. Foutz, 197–215. Lanham, Md.: AltaMira Press.

Capra, F. 1999. Ecoliteracy: The challenge for education in the next century. Paper presented at the Liverpool Schumacher Lectures, March 20, 1999, in Liverpool, England.

Chawla, L. 1986. The ecology of environmental memory. *Children's Environments Quarterly* 3(4): 34–42.

Clayton, S., and G. Myers. 2009. *Conservation psychology: Understanding and promoting human care for nature.* Hoboken, N. J.: Wiley-Blackwell.

Cobb, E. 1959. The ecology of imagination in childhood. *Daedalus* 88(3): 538–48.

Cole, M. 1998. *Cultural psychology: A once and future discipline.* Cambridge: Harvard University Press, Belknap Press.

Conan, M. 2005. *Baroque garden cultures: Emulation, sublimation, subversion.* Cambridge: Harvard University Press.

Gilligan, C. 1982. *In a different voice: Psychological theory and women's development.* Cambridge: Harvard University Press.

Kohlberg, L., and E. Turiel. 1971. Moral development and moral education. In *Psychology and educational practice*, edited by G. Lesser. Glenview, Ill.: Scott Foresman.

Lorenzoni, I., and N. Pidgeon. 2006. Public views on climate change: European and USA perspectives. *Climactic Change* 77: 73–95.

Lowe, T., K. Brown, S. Dessai, M. de Franca Doria, K. Haynes, and K. Vincent. 2006. Does tomorrow ever come? Disaster narrative and public perceptions of climate change. *Public Understanding of Science* 15(4): 435–57.

Nucci, L. 1997. Moral development and character formation. In *Psychology and educational practice,* edited by H. J. Walberg and G. D. Haertel, 27–157. Richmond: McCutchan Publishing.

Orr, D. 2005. Foreword. In *Ecological literacy: Educating our children for a sustainable world,* edited by M. K. Stone and Z. Barlow, x–xi. San Francisco: Sierra Club Books.

Piaget, J. 1965. *The moral judgment of the child.* Translated by M. Gabain. New York: The Free Press.

Schwarz, J., K. Havens, and P. Vitt. 2008. Understanding climate change through citizen science. *Roots* 5(1): 18–22.

Wertsch, J. V. 1991. *Voices of the mind: A sociocultural approach to mediated action.* Cambridge: Harvard University Press.

Chapter 16: Continuing, Professional, and Higher Education

Anderson, N. 2004. A marketing driven continuing education program: Formula for success. *The Public Garden* 19(1): 36–39.

Cox, M., and I. Edwards. 1994. Changing places. *Roots* 1(9). www.bgci.org/education/article/0462.

Gooch, J. 1995. *Transplanting extension: A new look at the Wisconsin idea.* Madison: UW-Extension Printing Services.

Jones, L. 2002. To serve broadly: The mission of the School of the Chicago Botanic Garden. *The Public Garden* 17(3): 28–30.

McFarlan, J. 2005. The Morris Arboretum internship program: Training public garden managers for 26 years. *The Public Garden* 20(3): 32–34.

Skelly, S. M., and C. Hetzel. 2005. The role of academic institutions in developing future leaders. *The Public Garden* 20(3): 14–17.

Chapter 17: Interpreting Gardens to Visitors

Committee on Learning Science in Informal Environments, National Research Council. 2009. *Learning science in informal environments: People, places, and pursuits*, edited by P. Bell, B. Lewenstein, A. W. Shouse, and M. A. Feder. Washington, D.C.: National Academies Press.

Falk, J. H. 2006. An identity-centered approach to understanding museum learning. *Curator* 49: 151–66.

Packer, J. 2006. Learning for fun: The unique contribution of educational leisure experiences. *Curator* 49: 329–44.

Packer, J., and R. Ballantyne. 2002. Motivational factors and the visitor experience: A comparison of three sites. *Curator* 45: 183–98.

Roff, J. 2002. An interpretive revolution. *Roots* 24 (June 2002). www.bgci.org/resources/article/0308.

Serrell, B. 2006. *Judging exhibitions: Assessing excellence in exhibitions from a visitor-centered perspective.* Walnut Creek, Calif.: Left Coast Press.

Chapter 18: Evaluation of Garden Programming and Planning

Bennett, D.B. 1989. Four steps to evaluating environmental education learning experiences. *The Journal of Environmental Education* 20(2): 14–21

Borun, M. 2001. The exhibit as educator: Assessing the impact. *The Public Garden* 16(3): 10–12.

Butler, B. 2004. Evaluation. *The Public Garden* 19(2): 7.

Caffarella, R. S. 2002. *Planning programs for adult learners: A practical guide for educators.* San Francisco: Jossey-Bass.

Diamond, J. 1999. *Practical evaluation guide: Tools for museums and other informal educational settings.* Walnut Creek, Calif.: AltaMira Press.

Eberbach, C., and K. Crowley. 2004. Learning research in public gardens. *The Public Garden* 19(2): 14–16.

Fitzpatrick, J. L., J. R. Sanders, and B. R. Worthen. 2004. *Program evaluation: Alternative approaches and practical guidelines.* Boston: Pearson Education.

Friedman, A., ed. 2008. *Frameworks for evaluating impacts of informal science education projects.* http://caise.insci.org/uploads/docs/Eval_Framework.pdf.

Gibbons, E. 2001. *Sustaining our heritage: The IMLS achievement.* Washington, D.C.: Institute of Museum and Library Services. http://imls.gov/pdf/WholeBrochure.pdf.

Hein, G. E. 1995. Evaluating teaching and learning in museums. In *Museum, media, message*, edited by E. Hooper-Greenhill, 190–205. London: Routledge.

Hein, G. E. 1998. *Learning in the museum.* New York: Routledge.

Institute for Museum and Library Services. 2009a. *Webinar on reporting and evaluation for Museums for America grantees.* www.imls.gov/ppt/IMLS_Museums_for_America_Webinar.ppt.

Institute for Museum and Library Services. 2009b. *Outcomes based evaluation: Frequently asked questions.* www.imls.gov/applicants/faqs.shtm.

Institute for Museum and Library Services. 2010. *Museum and Library Services Act of 1996*: Public Law 104-208, Title II, 104th Congress. http://imls.gov/pdf/1996.pdf.

Kellogg Foundation. 2004. *Logic model development guide.* Battle Creek, Mich.: Kellogg Foundation.

Klemmer, C. D. 2004. An evaluation primer. *The Public Garden* 19(2): 8–10.

Korn, R. 2004. Nonprofits, foundations, and evaluators, or where's the Advil? *The Public Garden* 19(2): 17, 39–40.

Loomis, R. J. 1987. *Museum visitor evaluation.* Nashville: American Association for State and Local History.

Munley, M. E. 1987. Intentions and accomplishments: Principles of museum evaluation research. In *Past meets present: Essays about historic interpretation and public audiences,* edited by J. Blatti, 116–30. Washington, D.C.: Smithsonian Institution Press.

National Research Council. 2009. *Learning science in informal environments: People, places, and pursuits.* Washington, D.C.: National Academies Press.

Parsons, C. 2009. *Where does evaluation fit?* Table used with permission, personal correspondence, August 2009.

Posavac, E. J., and R. G. Carey. 2007. *Program evaluation: Methods and case studies.* Upper Saddle River, N.J.: Pearson Prentice Hall.

Roberts, L. C. 1997. *From knowledge to narrative: Educators and the changing museum.* Washington, D.C.: Smithsonian Institution Press.

Rudzinski, M., and L. Wilson. 2003. *Leveraging audience insight: Segmentation tools and applications for museums.* Conference presentation conducted at the 11th Annual Conference of the Visitors Studies Association, Columbus, Ohio.

Soren, B. J. 2007 Audience-based measures of success: Evaluating museum learning. In *The manual of museum learning*, edited by B. Lord, 221–51. Lanham, Md.: AltaMira Press.

Trochim, W. M. 2006. *The research methods knowledge base.* 2nd ed. Ithaca, N.Y.: Trochim. www.socialresearch methods.net/kb/evaluation.php.

Visitor Studies Association. 2004. *Who we are.* Retrieved August 7, 2004 from visitorstudies.org/whatweare.htm.

Wagner, K. 1996. Acceptance or excuses?: The institutionalization of evaluation. *Visitor Behavior* 11: 11–13. www.historicalvoices.org/pbuilder/pbfiles/Project38/Scheme325/VSA-a0a1j8-a_5730.pdf.

Weil, S. E. 1999. From being about something to being for somebody: The ongoing transformation of the American museum. *Daedelus* 128: 229–58.

Weil, S.E. 2003. Beyond big and awesome: Outcome-based evaluation. *Museum News* 82(6): 40–45, 52–53

Weiss, C. 1998. *Evaluation*, 2nd ed. Upper Saddle River, N.J.: Prentice Hall.

Wells, M., and B. Butler. 2004. A visitor-centered evaluation hierarchy. *The Public Garden* 19(2): 11–13.

Chapter 19: Public Relations and Marketing Communications

American Marketing Association. 2010. www.marketing power.com.

Bradley, N. 2002. Marketing for nonprofits: 101. *The Public Garden* 17(2): 8–9, 39.

Conolly, N. B. 2010. Return on marketing investment: An investigation into how public garden organizations successfully evaluate and measure marketing performance. MPS thesis, Cornell University.

King, S., and M. Provaznik. 2009. A conversation about two small gardens' adventures in digital marketing. *The Public Garden* 24(3): 19–20.

Markgraf, S. 2002. Public relations can help botanic gardens draw new audiences. *The Public Garden* 17(3): 8–10.

Chapter 20: Collections Management

Alliance for Public Garden GIS, groups.google.com/group/apgg?hl=en.

American Association of Museums. www.aam-us.org.

American Public Garden Association. www.publicgardens.org.

American Public Garden Association Resource Center. www.publicgardens.org/custom/ResourceLibrary.

Angiosperm Phylogeny Website. www.mobot.org/MOBOT/research/APweb/welcome.html.

Barnett, D. P. 1996. Historic landscape preservation: Obstacle to change? *The Public Garden* 11(2): 21–23, 39.

BG-BASE. www.bg-base.com.

Botanic Gardens Conservation International. www.bgci.org.

Burke, M. T., and B. J. Morgan. 2009. Digital mapping: Beyond living collection curation. *The Public Garden* 24(3): 9–10.

Center for Plant Conservation—Voluntary Codes. www.centerforplantconservation.org/invasives/gardensN.html.

Convention on Biological Diversity. http://www.cbd.int.

Cuerrier, A., and S. Paré. 2006. The First Nations Garden: Where cultural diversity meets biodiversity. *The Public Garden* 21(4): 22–25.

Dosmann, M. S. 2006. Research in the garden: Averting the collection crisis. *Botanical Review* 72: 207–34.

e-floras. www.efloras.org.

Elsik, S. 1989. From each a voucher: Collecting in the living collections. *Arnoldia* 49(1): 21–27.

Folsom, J. P. 2000. The terms of beauty. *The Public Garden* 15(2): 3–6.

Galbraith, D. A. 1998. Biodiversity ethics: A challenge to botanical gardens for the next millennium. *The Public Garden* 13(3): 16–19.

Gates, G. 2006. Characteristics of an exemplary plant collection. *The Public Garden* 21(1): 28–31.

GRIN: Germplasm Resources Information System. www.ars-grin.gov.

Hohn, T. C. 2008. *Curatorial practices for botanical gardens.* Lanham, Md.: AltaMira Press.

Institute of Museum and Library Services. www.imls.gov.

International Cultivar Registration Authorities. www.ishs.org/sci/icra.htm.

International Plant Names Index. www.ipni.org.

Jefferson, L., K. Havens, and J. Ault. 2004. Implementing invasive screening procedures: The Chicago Botanic Garden model. *Weed Technology* 18: 1434–40.

Leadlay, E., and J. Greene, eds. 1998. *The Darwin technical manual for botanic gardens*. London: Botanic Gardens Conservation International.

Lowe, C. 1995. Managing the woodland garden. *The Public Garden* 10(3): 11–13.

Meinig, D. W. 1976. The beholding eye: Ten versions of the same scene. *Landscape Architecture* 66: 47– 56.

Michener, D. 1989. To each a name: Verifying the living collections. *Arnoldia* 49(1): 36–41.

Moore, G. 2006. Current state of botanical nomenclature. *The Public Garden* 21(3): 34–37.

National Park Service. Historic Preservation Guidelines. www.nps.gov/history/hps/hli/landscape_guidelines/index.htm.

National Trust for Historic Preservation. www.preservationnation.org.

North American Plant Collection Consortium. www.publicgardens.org/web/2006/06/napcc_home.aspx.

Otis, D. 2001. Maples in North America: Developing a network of NAPCC *Acer* collections. *The Public Garden* 16(1): 22–27.

Parsons, B. 1995. The role of woodlands at the Holden Arboretum. *The Public Garden* 10(3): 21–23.

Royal Horticultural Society. Registrations page. www.rhs.org.uk/Plants/Plant-science/Plant-registration.

Chapter 21: Research at Public Gardens

Affolter, J. 2003. Botanical gardens and the survival of traditional botany. *The Public Garden* 18(4): 17–19, 22.

Anderson, N. O., S. M. Galatowitsch, and N. Gomez. 2006. Selection strategies to reduce invasive potential in introduced plants. *Euphytica* 148: 203–16.

Anderson, N. O., N. Gomez, and S. M. Galatowitsch. 2006. A non-invasive crop ideotype to reduce invasive potential. *Euphytica* 148: 185–202.

Baskin, C. C., and J. M. Baskin. 1998. *Seeds: Ecology, biogeography, and evolution of dormancy and germination*. New York: Academic Press.

———. 2004. Determining dormancy-breaking and germination requirements from the fewest seeds. In Ex situ *plant conservation: Supporting species survival in the wild,* edited by E. O. Guerrant Jr., K. Havens, and M. Maunder, 162–79. Washington, D.C.: Island Press.

Blossey, B., L. C. Skinner, and J. Taylor. 2001. Impact and management of purple loosestrife (*Lythrum salicaria*) in North America. *Biodiversity and Conservation* 10: 1787–807.

Brown, N. A. C. 1993. Promotion of germination of fynbos seeds by plant-derived smoke. *New Phytologist* 123: 575–83.

Convention on Biological Diversity. 2002. *The global strategy for plant conservation*. Montreal: Secretariat of the Convention on Biological Diversity.

Donaldson, J. S. 2009. Botanic gardens science for conservation and global change. *Trends in Plant Science* 14: 608–13.

Dosmann, M. S. 2006. Research in the garden: Averting the collections crisis. *The Botanical Review* 72: 207–34.

Eshbaugh, W. H., and T. K. Wilson. 1969. Departments of botany, passé? *Bioscience* 19: 1072–74.

Guerrant, E. O., Jr. 1996. Designing populations: Demographic, genetic, and horticultural dimensions. In *Restoring diversity: Strategies for reintroduction of endangered species*, edited by D. A. Falk, C. I. Millar, and M. Olwell, 171–207. Washington, D.C.: Island Press.

Guerrant, E. O., Jr., and P. L Fiedler. 2004. Accounting for sample decline during *ex situ* storage and reintroduction. In Ex Situ *plant conservation: Supporting species survival in the wild,* edited by E. O. Guerrant Jr., K. Havens, and M. Maunder, 365–85. Washington. D.C.: Island Press.

Guerrant, E. O., Jr., and T. N. Kaye. 2007. Reintroduction of rare and endangered plants: Common factors, questions, and approaches. *Australian Journal of Botany* 55: 362–70.

Jefferson, L., K. Havens, and J. Ault. 2004. Implementing invasive screening procedures: The Chicago Botanic Garden model. *Weed Technology* 18: 1434–40.

Jefferson, L., M. Pennacchio, K. Havens, B. Forsberg, D. Sollenberger, and J. Ault. 2008. *Ex situ* germination responses of midwestern USA prairie species to plant-derived smoke. *American Midland Naturalist* 159: 251–56.

Kramer, A. T., and K. Havens. 2009. Plant conservation genetics in a changing world. *Trends in Plant Science* 14: 599–607.

Law, W. and J. Salick. 2005. Human induced dwarfing of Himalayan Snow Lotus (*Saussurea laniceps (Asteraceae)*). *PNAS* 102: 10218–20.

Leadlay, E., and J. Greene, eds. 1998. *The Darwin technical manual for botanic gardens*. London: Botanic Gardens Conservation International.

Li, D.-Z., and H. W. Pritchard. 2009. The science and economics of *ex situ* plant conservation. *Trends in Plant Science* 14: 614–21.

Li, Y., Z. Cheng, W. A. Smith, D. R. Ellis, Y. Chen, X. Zheng, Y. Pei, K. Luo, D. Zhao, Q. Yao, H. Duan, and Q. Li. 2004. Invasive ornamental plants: Problems, challenges, and molecular tools to neutralize their invasiveness. *Critical Reviews in Plant Sciences* 23: 381–89.

McKay, J. K., C. E. Christian, S. Harrison, and K. J. Rice. 2005. How local is local? A review of practical and conceptual issues in the genetics of restoration. *Restoration Ecology* 13: 432–40.

Pence, V. C. 2004. *Ex situ* conservation methods for bryophytes and pteridophytes. In Ex situ *plant conservation: Supporting species survival in the wild,* edited by E. O. Guerrant Jr., K. Havens, and M. Maunder, 206–28. Washington, D.C.: Island Press.

Peters, C. M. 1994. *Sustainable harvest of non-timber plant resources in tropical moist forest: An ecological primer.* Washington, D.C.: Biodiversity Support Program.

Prather, L. A., O. Alvarez-Fuentes, M. H. Mayfield, and C. J. Ferguson. 2004. The decline of plant collecting in the United States: A threat to the infrastructure of biodiversity studies. *Systematic Botany* 29: 15–28.

Primack, R. B., and A. J. Miller-Rushing. 2009. The role of botanical gardens in climate change research. *New Phytologist* 182: 303–13.

Pritchard, H. W. 2004. Classification of seed storage types for *ex situ* conservation in relation to temperature and moisture. In Ex situ *plant conservation: Supporting species survival in the wild,* edited by E. O. Guerrant Jr., K. Havens, and M. Maunder, 139–61. Washington, D.C.: Island Press.

Roberson, E. B. 2002. *Barriers to native plant conservation in the United States: Funding, staffing, law.* Sacramento: Native Plant Conservation Campaign, California Native Plant Society, and Tucson: Center for Biological Diversity.

Rokich, D. P., and K. W. Dixon. 2007. Recent advances in restoration ecology, with a focus on the *Banksia* woodland and the smoke germination tool. *Australian Journal of Botany* 55: 375–89.

Schatz, G. E. 2009. Plants on the IUCN Red List: Setting priorities to inform conservation. *Trends in Plant Science* 14: 638–42.

Smith, R. D., J. B. Dickie, S. H. Linington, H. W. Pritchard, and R. J. Probert, eds. 2003. *Seed conservation: Turning science into practice.* London: Royal Botanic Gardens, Kew.

Sundberg, M. D. 2004. Where is botany going? *Plant Science Bulletin* 50: 2–6.

Swarts, N. D., and K. W. Dixon. 2009. Perspectives on orchid conservation in botanic gardens. *Trends in Plant Science* 14: 590–98.

Vitt, P. 2001. *Effects of hand pollination on reproduction and survival of the eastern prairie fringed orchid.* Unpublished report to U.S. Fish and Wildlife Service.

Wagenius, S. 2006. Scale dependence of reproductive failure in fragmented *Echinacea* populations. *Ecology* 87: 931–41.

Walters, C. 2004. Principles for preserving germplasm in gene banks. In Ex situ *plant conservation: Supporting species survival in the wild,* edited by E. O. Guerrant Jr., K. Havens, and M. Maunder, 113–38. Washington, D.C.: Island Press.

Wyse Jackson, P. S., and L. A. Sutherland. 2000. *International agenda for botanic gardens in conservation.* London: Botanic Gardens Conservation International.

Chapter 22: Conservation Practices in Public Gardens

Byrne, M., and P. Olwell. 2008. Seeds of success: The National Native Seed Collection Program in the United States. *The Public Garden* 23(3): 24–25.

Dougherty, D., and S. Reichard. 2004. Factors affecting the control of *Cytisus scoparius* and restoration of invaded sites. *Plant Protection Quarterly* 19: 137–42.

Dunnett, N., and A. Clayden. 2007. *Rain gardens: Managing water sustainably in the garden and designed landscapes.* Portland, Ore.: Timber Press.

Eberhardt, M. 2007. The water conservation garden: A good idea that has become a necessity. *The Public Garden* 22(1): 30–31.

Galbraith, D. A. 2003. Natural areas at public gardens: Creative tensions and conservation opportunities. *The Public Garden* 18(3): 10–13.

Garcia-Dominguez, E., and K. Kennedy. 2003. Benefits of working with natural areas. *The Public Garden* 18(3): 8–9, 44.

Guerrant, E. O., Jr., K. Havens, and M. Maunder, eds. 2004. Ex situ *plant conservation: Supporting species survival in the wild.* Washington, D.C.: Island Press.

Havens, K. 2002. Developing an invasive plant policy: The Chicago Botanic Garden's experience. *The Public Garden* 17(4): 16–17.

Havens, K., P. Vitt, M. Maunder, E. O. Guerrant Jr., and K. Dixon. 2006. *Ex situ* plant conservation and beyond. *BioScience* 56: 525–31.

Hoversten, M. E., and S. B. Jones. 2002. The advocacy garden: An emerging model. *The Public Garden* 17(4): 34–37.

IPCC. 2007. *Climate change 2007: Synthesis report.* Geneva, Switzerland: IPCC.

Lenoir, J., J. C. Gégout, P. A. Marquet, P. de Ruffray, and H. Brisse. 2008. A significant upward shift in plant species optimum elevation during the 20th century. *Science* 320: 1768–71.

Mack, R. N., D. Simberloff, W. M. Lonsdale, H. Evans, M. Clout, and F. A. Bazzaz. 2000. Biotic invasions: Causes, epidemiology, global consequences, and control. *Ecological Applications* 10: 689–710.

Oldfield, S. 2007. Working together in plant conservation. *The Public Garden* 22(2): 8–9.

Pence, V. 2004. *Ex situ* conservation methods for bryophytes and pteridophytes. In Ex situ *plant conservation: Supporting species survival in the wild,* edited by E. O. Guerrant Jr., K. Havens, and M. Maunder, 206–28. Washington, D.C.: Island Press.

Pimentel, D., R. Zuniga, and D. Morrison. 2005. Update on the environmental and economic costs associated with alien-invasive species in the United States. *Ecological Economics* 52: 273–88.

Pritchard, H. W. 2004. Classification of seed storage types for *ex situ* conservation in relation to temperature and moisture. In Ex situ *plant conservation: Supporting species survival in the wild,* edited by E. O. Guerrant Jr., K. Havens, and M. Maunder, 139–61. Washington, D.C.: Island Press.

Raven, P. H. 1999. Plants in peril: A call to action. *The Public Garden* 14(4): 28–31.

Reichard, S. 1997. Preventing the introduction of invasive plants. In *Assessment and management of plant invasions,* edited by J. Luken and J. Thieret, 215–27. New York: Springer-Verlag.

Sala, A., S. Smith, and D. Devitt. 1996. Water use by *Tamarix ramosissima* and associated phreatophytes in a Mojave Desert floodplain. *Ecological Applications* 6: 888–98.

Vitousek, P. M., and L. Walker. 1989. Biological invasion by *Myrica faya* in Hawai'i: Plant demography, nitrogen-fixation, ecosystem effects. *Ecological Monographs* 59: 247–65.

White, P. S. 1996. In search of the conservation garden. *The Public Garden* 11(2): 11–13, 40.

Chapter 23: A Strategic Approach to Leadership and Management

American Association of Museums. The Center for the Future of Museums. http://www.futureofmuseums.org/about.

Buckingham, M., and D. Clifton. 2001. *Now discover your strengths.* New York: Free Press.

Buckingham, M., and C. Coffman. 1999. *First break all the rules: What the world's greatest managers do differently.* New York: Simon and Schuster.

Cary, D., and K. Socolofsky. 2003. Long-range planning for real results: Start with self-assessment and audience research. *The Public Garden:* 18(4): 10–13.

Crutchfield, L., and H. McLeod Grant. 2007. *Forces for good: The six practices of high-impact nonprofits.* San Francisco: Jossey-Bass.

Drucker, P. 2001. *The essential Drucker: The best of sixty years of Peter Drucker's essential writings on management.* New York: Harper Business.

Drucker, P., and G. Stern. 1998. *The Drucker Foundation self-assessment tool set.* San Francisco: Jossey-Bass.

Kotter, J. 1996. *Leading change.* Boston: Harvard Business School Press.

Mind Tools. 2009. *SWOT analysis: Discover new opportunities. Manage and eliminate threats.* www.mindtools.com/pages/article/newTMC_05.htm.

Chapter 25: Facility Expansion

Brault, D., and R. Denis. 1995. Contracting for design and engineering services. *The Public Garden* 10(2): 28–29.

Directors of Large Gardens. 2007. *2007 Medium and small garden benchmarking study.* Wilmington, Del.: American Public Garden Association.

Dobbs, V. 2009. Paradise found: A new tropical garden, Naples Botanic Garden. *The Public Garden* 24(4): 28–29.

Holley, B. 2003. Cleveland Botanic Garden. *The Public Garden* 18(2): 8–11.

Rich, P. E. 1987. Planning for small public gardens. *The Public Garden* 2(2): 9–11.

———. 1999. Managing garden construction. Special report. *The Public Garden* 14(1): 37–38.

Chapter 26: The Shape of Gardens to Come

Anisko, T. 2006. *Plant exploration for Longwood Gardens.* Portland, Ore.: Timber Press.

Cunningham, A. S. 2000. *Crystal palaces: Garden conservatories of the United States.* Portland, Ore.: Timber Press.

Friedman, T. L. 2005. *The world is flat.* New York: Farrar, Straus and Giroux.

Greater Philadelphia Cultural Alliance. 2008. 2008 Portfolio. www.issuu.com/philaculture/docs/2008_portfolio_fullreport.

Hobby, F., and N. Stoops. 2002. *Demographic trends in the 20th century*. Census 2000 Special Reports. Washington, D. C.: U.S. Government Printing Office.

McCracken, D. P. 1997. *Gardens of empire: Botanical institutions of the Victorian British Empire*. London: Leicester University Press.

Minter, S. 2001. *The apothecaries' garden: A history of Chelsea Physic Garden*. Stroud, U.K.: Sutton Publishing.

Monem, N., ed. 2007 *Botanic gardens: A living history*. London: Black Dog Publishing.

Reinikka, M. A. 1995. *A history of the orchid*. Portland, Ore.: Timber Press.

Appendix A: Factors in the Development and Management of Canadian Public Gardens

Chan, A. P. 1972. A national botanical garden for Canada—a history of failures. In *Proceedings of the Symposium on a National Botanical Garden System for Canada*, edited by P. F. Rice, 22–27. Hamilton, Ont.: Royal Botanical Gardens.

Connor, J. T. H. 1986. To promote the cause of science: George Lawson and the Botanical Society of Canada, 1860–1863. *Scientia Canadensis: Canadian Journal of the History of Science, Technology, and Medicine* 10(1): 3–33.

DesMarais, A. 1972. Report from the Ministry of State for Science and Technology. In *Proceedings of the Symposium on a National Botanical Garden System for Canada*, edited by P. F. Rice, 55–58. Hamilton, Ont.: Royal Botanical Gardens.

Dewing, M. 2008. Federal government policy on arts and culture. PRB-0841e. December 11. http://www2.parl .gc.ca/Content/LOP/ResearchPublications/prb0841-e.htm.

English, J., and R. Bélanger, eds. 2000. Lawson, George. In *Dictionary of Canadian biography online*. www.biographi .ca/009004-119.01-e.php?&id_nbr=6222.

Francis, J., and J. Clemens. 1999. Fraser Forum: Charitable donations and tax incentives. The Fraser Institute. http:// oldfraser.lexi.net/publications/forum/1999/06/04_chari table_donations.html.

Klose, E., and D. Whitehouse. 2004. The Niagara Parks Commission School of Horticulture. In *Acta Horticulturae* (ISHS) 641: 145–46. http://www.actahort .org/books/641/641_19.htm.

Laking, L. 2006. *Love, sweat, and soil: A history of Royal Botanical Gardens from 1930 to 1981*. Hamilton, Ont.: Royal Botanical Gardens Auxiliary.

Lawson, G., and Nova Scotian Institute of Natural Science. 1883. *Notice of new and rare plants*. n.p. (Halifax, N.S.).

———. 1891. Notes for a flora of Nova Scotia. Part I. In *Proceedings and transactions of the Nova Scotian Institute of Science* 8(1): 84–110. http://dalspace.library.dal .ca/dspace/handle/10222/12374?show=full.

LeRoy, S., N. Veldhuis, and J. Clemens. 2002. The 2002 generosity index: Comparing charitable giving in Canada and the U.S. *The Fraser Forum*, December 2002, 13–18. http://www.fraserinstitute.org/commerce.web/product_ files/FraserForum_December2002.pdf

———. 2004. How giving are Canadians? The 2004 Generosity Index. *The Fraser Forum*, December 2004, 9–14. www.fraserinstitute.org/commerce.web/product_ files/FraserForum_December2004.pdf.

Martin, C. 2001. *Cultivating Canadian gardens: A history of gardening in Canada*. http://epe.lac-bac .gc.ca/100/200/301/nlc-bnc/cultivating_cdn_gardens- ef/2008/www.lac-bac.gc.ca/2/11/h11-2005-e.html.

Nova Scotian Institute of Science. 1895. *The proceedings and transactions of the Nova Scotian Institute of Science*, vol. 9. Halifax, N.S.: Nova Scotian Institute of Science.

Popadiouk, R. 2000. *Old trees in the Dominion Arboretum*. Ottawa Horticultural Society. www.ottawahort .org/yearbook2000-2.htm.

Raymond, S. 2001. North of the border: Canada-U.S. comparisons in philanthropy. www.onphilanthropy.com/site/ News2?page=NewsArticle&id=5920.

Read, C. 2007. A comparison of tax rates in the OECD. March 20. http://www.craigread.com/displayArticle. aspx?contentID=548&subgroupID=5.

Rotstein, G. 2008. Cross border philanthropy: The more we are different, the more we are the same. May 15. www.onphilanthropy. com/site/News2?page=NewsArticle&id=7489.

Sharpe, A. 2002. Raising Canadian living standards: A framework for analysis. *International Productivity Monitor* 5 (Fall): 25–40. http://ideas.repec.org/a/sls/ipmsls/ v5y20022.html

Speirs, R. 1999. Tax surprise: Most of us pay less than Americans. *Toronto Star*, November 6. www .canadiansocialresearch.net/taxes.htm.

Thomsen, C. 1996. A border vision: The International Peace Garden. *Manitoba History: The Journal of the Manitoba Historical Society* 31 (Spring). www.mhs.mb.ca/docs/ mb_history/31/peacegarden.shtml.

United North America. 2010. Similarities and differences between Canada and United States. www.united northamerica.org/simdiff.htm.

Vancouver Board of Parks and Recreation. 2003a. Bloedel
Floral Conservatory. http://vancouver.ca/PARKS/PARKS/
bloe del/index.htm.

———. 2003b. Queen Elizabeth Park—Bloedel Floral
Conservatory. http://van couver.ca/PARKS/PARKS/
queenelizabeth/index.htm.

Whysall, S. 2009. Fate of Bloedel Conservatory in the balance.
Vancouver Sun, November 19. http://communities
.canada.com/vancouversun/print.aspx?postid=566238.

Wolff, M., P. Rutten, A. Bayers III, and World Rank Research
Team. 1992. *Where we stand: Can America make it in the
global race for wealth, health, and happiness?* New York:
Bantam Books.

Appendix B: The Importance of Plant Exploration Today

Aiello, A. S. 2005. Evaluating *Cornus kousa* cold hardiness.
American Nurseryman 201: 32–39.

———. 2009. Seeking cold-hardy camellias. *Arnoldia* 67: 20–30.

Anisko, T. 2006. *Plant exploration for Longwood Gardens*.
Portland, Ore.: Timber Press.

Meyer, P. W. 1985. Botanical riches from afar. *Morris
Arboretum Newsletter* 14: 4–5.

———. 1994. Plant collecting expeditions: A modern perspective. *The Public Garden* 14(2): 3–7.

———. 1999. Plant collecting expeditions: A modern perspective. In *Plant exploration: Protocols for the present,
concerns for the future: Symposium proceedings, March
18–19, 1999, Chicago Botanic Garden, Glencoe, Illinois*,
edited by J. R. Ault. Glencoe, Ill.: Chicago Botanic Gardens.

Meyer, P. W., and S. Royer. 1993. The North American Plant
Collections Consortium. *The Public Garden* 13(3): 20–23.

Yinger, B. 1989a. Plant trek: In pursuit of a hardy camellia.
Flower and Garden 33:104–6.

———. 1989b. Plant trek: On site with hardy camellias,
Sochong Island, Korea. *Flower and Garden* 33: 62–66.

Appendix C: Herbaria

Global Biodiversity Information Facility. 2010. Data portal.
http://data.gbif.org/welcome.htm.

Missouri Botanical Garden. 2010. Tropicos.org. www.tropicos
.org.

Thiers, B. 2010. Index herbariorum: A global directory of public herbaria and associated staff. http://sciweb.nybg.org/
science2/IndexHerbariorum.asp. Continuously updated.

New York Botanical Garden. 2010. Virtual herbarium. http://
sciweb.nybg.org/science2/VirtualHerbarium.asp.

vPlants Project. 2001–2009. vPlants: A virtual herbarium of
the Chicago region. http://www.vplants.org.

Appendix E: The Library in a Public Garden

Biodiversity Heritage Library. www.biodiversitylibrary.org.

Council on Botanical and Horticultural Libraries, Inc. www
.cbhl.net.

European Botanical and Horticultural Libraries Group. www
.kew.org/ebhl/home.htm.

MacPhail, I. 1989. The garden and the book: Or how to run a
culture. *The Public Garden* 4(3): 12–13, 26–27.

Appendix F: Horticultural Therapy and Public Gardens

American Horticultural Therapy Association. www.ahta.org.

Haller, R. L., and C. L. Kramer. 2006. *Horticultural therapy
methods: Making connections in health care, human
service, and community programs*. Binghamton, N.Y.:
Haworth Press.

Simson, S. P., and M. C. Straus. 1998. *Horticulture as therapy:
Principles and practice*. Binghamton, N.Y.: Haworth Press.

Contributors

Patsy Benveniste

Patsy Benveniste, Vice President for Community Education Programs at the Chicago Botanic Garden, oversees the Garden's Center for Teaching and Learning, community gardening and outreach, the horticultural therapy services program, off-site youth leadership development programs, jobs training initiatives in sustainable urban agriculture models, and horticultural therapy programming and professional training. Benveniste forges strong, hands-on connections between the Garden's plant scientists and ecologists and formal, ongoing educational programs. Prior to joining the Garden, Benveniste was Director of Education at Lincoln Park Zoo, overseeing formal and informal education programs.

Mary Burke

Mary Burke, the Director of Collections and Planning at the UC Davis Arboretum, is a botanist with an interest in exploring how innovation, leadership, systems thinking, and technology can enhance experiential learning and enrich community life, as well as improve public garden management. She holds a master's degree in plant ecology.

Kitty Connolly

Kitty Connolly, the Associate Director of Education at the Huntington Library, Art Collections, and Botanical Gardens, directs programs ranging from teacher professional development to discovery carts. The major focus of her work is interpreting collections through exhibitions. She was one of the principal investigators for "Plants Are Up to Something," American Association of Museums 2007 winner of Excellence in Exhibitions, and co-curator and coordinator of exhibits at the Huntington and the Smithsonian Institution. She is a former APGA director-at-large. Connolly holds a bachelor's degree in environmental zoology and a master's degree in geography.

Sheila Connor

Sheila Connor has been the Horticultural Research Archivist at the Arnold Arboretum Horticultural Library since 1970. Connor served as principal investigator for grants awarded by the National Endowment for the Humanities, the Institute of Library and Museum Services, and Harvard's Library Digital Initiative. Most recently she has been involved with the digitization of the Arboretum's photographic archives. She has established the Arboretum's archival collection and authored a number of articles for *Arnoldia* and *The Public Garden*. Her book, *New England Natives: A Celebration of People and Trees* (Harvard University Press), is a cultural history that documents human conduct in a wooded land.

Richard H. Daley

Richard H. Daley is a founding partner of EMD Consulting Group, which provides strategic counsel on planning, revenue generation, and organizational issues to public gardens and other NGOs. He has worked with gardens large and small in the United States and abroad. Daley served as CEO of the Arizona-Sonora Desert Museum, Denver Botanic Gardens, and Massachusetts Horticultural Society, and held senior management positions at the Missouri Botanical Garden. He served on the boards of the American Public Gardens Association, Center for Plant Conservation, Botanical Gardens Conservation International-U.S., and Trust for Public Land. He is an accreditor for botanical institutions for the American Association of Museums.

Larry DeBuhr

Since 2008, Dr. Larry DeBuhr has been the Executive Director of the Rivers Institute at Hanover College. Previously at the Chicago Botanic Garden, DeBuhr was initially the Vice President of Education and Director of the Joseph Regenstein

Jr. School of the Botanic Garden and later Vice President of Academic Affairs. He led the development of a continuing education program that offered over 500 courses to more than 7,000 adults annually, numerous certificate programs, and partnerships with colleges and universities. Previously he was Director of Education at the Missouri Botanical Garden.

Gerard T. Donnelly

Dr. Gerard T. Donnelly is President and CEO of the Morton Arboretum, near Chicago. Previously, he was curator of the W. J. Beal Botanical Garden at Michigan State University and served on the faculty there and at Coe College. He has a Ph.D. in botany and plant pathology from Michigan State University. Donnelly has made leading contributions to the American Public Gardens Association, receiving its Service Award; Directors of Large Gardens; Center for Public Horticulture at the University of Delaware; development of the ArbNet network of arboreta; and a partnership with Botanic Gardens Conservation International promoting participation in the Global Trees Campaign.

Arlene Ferris

Arlene Ferris has been the Director of Volunteer Services at Fairchild Tropical Botanic Garden for twenty-four years. She serves on the Volunteerism Committee of the American Public Gardens Association and has presented programs on volunteering at the annual APGA conference and at Volunteer Interaction, a biennial conference for volunteer directors in public gardens.

Christine A. Flanagan

Dr. Christine A. Flanagan is Public Programs Manager at the U.S. Botanic Garden, where she has worked since 1996. Her division is responsible for exhibits, educational programs, partnerships, interpretation, and public relations. She is a frequent contributor to *The Public Garden* and serves on the board of the American Society of Plant Biologists Foundation. Recent awards include the American Public Gardens Association Professional Citation in 2008 and the Ecological Society of America's Eugene P. Odum Award for Excellence in Ecology Education in 2009. She holds a Ph.D. in ecology and evolutionary biology from the University of Arizona.

David Galbraith

Dr. David Galbraith, Head of Science at the Royal Botanical Gardens, is responsible for its research program, library, archives, and herbarium. He developed the Canadian Botanical

Conservation Network, promoting the role of botanical gardens in conservation and biodiversity programs, and is involved in endangered species recovery and habitat conservation projects: the Global Strategy for Plant Conservation, the North American Partnership for Plants, and the International Advisory Council of Botanic Gardens Conservation International. An Adjunct Professor in the Biology Department of McMaster University and a Conjoint Professor in the Environmental and Life Sciences Graduate Program of Trent University, he holds a Ph.D. from Queen's University at Kingston in wildlife biology.

Rita M. Hassert

A Librarian in the Sterling Morton Library of the Morton Arboretum since 1986, Rita M. Hassert received an M.S. in library and information science from the University of Illinois. As both a gardener and a researcher, she finds herself keenly interested in the intersection of gardens, people, information, community, plants, technology, and libraries. An active member of the Council on Botanical and Horticultural Libraries, she has served CBHL as a board member and president, meeting host, committee chair/member, and contributor to the CBHL Newsletter.

Kayri Havens

Dr. Kayri Havens is the Director of the Division of Plant Science and Conservation and Senior Scientist at the Chicago Botanic Garden. Previously she was the Conservation Biologist at the Missouri Botanical Garden. Her research interests include the effects of climate change on plant species, restoration genetics, the biology of plant rarity, and invasiveness. Havens serves on the boards of the Midwest Invasive Plant Network and Botanic Gardens Conservation International and on the IUCN Species Survival Commission's Plants Committee. She is coeditor of Ex Situ *Plant Conservation: Supporting Species Survival in the Wild.* Havens holds an M.A. in botany from Southern Illinois University and a Ph.D. in biology from Indiana University.

Maureen Heffernan

Maureen Heffernan, Executive Director of the Coastal Maine Botanical Gardens, has led the development of this 248-acre botanical garden, which opened in 2007. She was Education Coordinator at the American Horticultural Society, initiating the Youth Gardening Symposium. As Director of Public Programs at the Cleveland Botanical Garden, she helped develop the Hershey Children's Garden and Green Corps urban gardening program. She is the author of *Burpee Seed Starter; Hershey Children's Garden: A Place to Grow; Native*

Plants for Your Maine Garden; and *Fairy Houses of the Maine Coast*. She received the American Horticultural Society's Jane L. Taylor Award in 2004 and the American Public Gardens Association's Professional Citation in 2009.

Brian Holley

Brian Holley, Executive Director of the Naples Botanical Garden, has been involved in many projects over the course of his career. In Naples he is overseeing the development of a new garden from the ground up. Holley was the executive director of the Cleveland Botanical Garden, where he led the development and implementation of a long-term strategic plan that included expansion of the Garden's facilities and new program initiatives. Holley started his career at the Royal Botanical Gardens in Hamilton, Ontario, where he was involved in building a variety of structures and gardens. He has also consulted on developing garden and infrastructure projects across the country and abroad.

Karen L. Kennedy

Karen L. Kennedy, HTR, is an independent contractor for horticultural therapy and wellness programming to healthcare and social services organizations. For more than twenty years she managed the Horticultural Therapy and Wellness Program for the Holden Arboretum. She is on the faculty of the Horticultural Therapy Institute and is a contributor to textbooks in the field. She served on the board of the American Horticultural Therapy Association and is the recipient of the AHTA Rhea McCandliss Professional Service Award and the American Horticulture Society Horticultural Therapy Award. She holds a B.S. in horticultural therapy from Kansas State University.

Susan Lacerte

Susan Lacerte has loved plants for her entire life. Her earliest memories are of vegetable gardening with her father and enjoying the company of trees while on camping trips organized by her mother. She earned a B.A. in environmental horticulture from the University of Connecticut and a master's degree in public administration from New York University. Lacerte, who once headed adult education at the Brooklyn Botanic Garden and has served on the boards of the American Public Gardens Association, Metro Hort Group, and the Green Guerillas, has also led the transformation of the Queens Botanical Garden, serving as Executive Director since 1994. She teaches public garden management at the State University of New York at Farmingdale.

Leeann Lavin

Leeann Lavin is the former Director of Communications at the Brooklyn Botanic Garden, where she played a key role in driving attendance for special events. She previously worked at the New York Botanical Garden. Prior to her work in public gardens, Lavin was Director of Communications at Sony Electronics and worked at New York City public relations firms that specialized in technology. Lavin is an award-winning landscape designer and is currently principal of Duchess Designs, LLC.

Sharon A. Lee

Sharon Lee heads Sharon Lee & Associates, a firm specializing in marketing communications for public gardens, and is the creator and coordinator of Plant Lovers Discovery Tours, an educational tour program promoting public horticultural institutions in the Philadelphia region. Lee is the former Deputy Director of the American Public Gardens Association, where she managed the association's publications, outreach initiatives, and the Resource Center. She was the creator of *The Public Garden*, APGA's quarterly journal, and served as its editor for eighteen years. Lee holds an M.A. in English and an M.S. in television/radio/film.

Robert Lyons

As Program Director and Professor at the University of Delaware, Dr. Robert Lyons oversees the professional development of the students in the Longwood Graduate Program in Public Horticulture. Previously, Lyons held the J. C. Raulston Distinguished Professor Chair in Horticultural Science at North Carolina State University, where he was also the Director of the JC Raulston Arboretum. He was one of the founders and first director of the Hahn Horticulture Garden at Virginia Tech. Lyons is the Consulting Editor for the Public Horticulture section of *HortTechnology* and a Fellow in the American Society for Horticultural Science. He holds a Ph.D. in horticultural science from the University of Minnesota.

Lisa Macioce

Lisa Macioce has held the position of Chief Financial Officer of the Phipps Conservatory and Botanical Gardens since 2006. Macioce has more than seventeen years' experience in the nonprofit sector, including areas such as financial reporting, capital and operational budgeting, program profitability analyses, cost allocation, information technology, and operational process redesign. Macioce holds an M.B.A. from the University of Pittsburgh's Katz Graduate School of Business and a bachelor's degree in business administration from Robert Morris University in Pittsburgh. She is also a Certified Public Accountant.

Mary Pat Matheson

Mary Pat Matheson, Executive Director of the Atlanta Botanical Garden, is implementing a new master plan to create facilities that will enhance the visitor experience, education programs, accessibility, and model environmental sustainability. Her visionary outlook is leading the Garden in new directions and driving increased attendance through blockbusters such as "Niki in the Garden" and "Chihuly in the Garden." She is also the Director of the new Smithgall Woodland Garden. While Executive Director of the Red Butte Garden and Arboretum, Matheson oversaw the design and construction of eight display gardens, a children's garden, four miles of nature trails, an orangerie, and a visitor center. Matheson holds an executive master's degree in public administration from the University of Utah.

Paul W. Meyer

Paul Meyer, the F. Otto Haas Director of the Morris Arboretum of the University of Pennsylvania, has played a major role in restoration of its late Victorian gardens. He has taught urban horticulture at the University of Pennsylvania, contributes frequently to horticultural publications, and is a leader in the field of plant exploration and evaluation, having completed nine expeditions to China and Korea as well as expeditions to Armenia and the Republic of Georgia. He has been awarded the Pennsylvania Horticultural Society's Distinguished Achievement Medal, a Professional Citation from the American Association of Botanical Gardens and Arboreta, and the American Horticultural Society's Great American Gardeners Professional Award.

David C. Michener

Dr. David C. Michener, Associate Curator at the University of Michigan Matthaei Botanical Gardens and Nichols Arboretum, oversees collection development, renovation, and related information management, including the current move to Web-based geospatial access to the institution's records, for all four properties. He serves on the university's Museum Studies Program's steering committee and as a Faculty Associate in the Program in the Environment. Michener teaches in the Michigan Math and Science Scholars summer program. He has conducted more than a dozen on-site reviews of living collections for funding agencies. He holds a Ph.D. in botany from the Claremont Graduate School and Rancho Santa Ana Botanic Garden.

Nancy L. Peske

Nancy L. Peske, PHR, is Director of Human Resources at the Morton Arboretum, overseeing the administration of 330 employees and 950 volunteers. On staff since 1999, she holds a bachelor's degree from DePauw University and is certified as a Professional in Human Resources by the Society for Human Resource Management. Peske was named 2010 HR Professional of the Year by the Management Association of Illinois.

Richard V. Piacentini

Richard V. Piacentini is the Executive Director of Phipps Conservatory and Botanical Gardens. During his tenure he has led Phipps from public to private nonprofit management and the most ambitious capital expansion projects in its more-than-100-year history. He is responsible for the "green" transformation of Phipps, with a focus on green buildings and sustainable operations. Piacentini holds an M.S. in botany, an M.B.A., and a B.S. in pharmacy. He is a past president and treasurer of the APGA and recipient of its Professional Citation.

Donald A. Rakow

Dr. Donald A. Rakow is the Elizabeth Newman Wilds Director of Cornell Plantations and serves as an associate professor in the Cornell Department of Horticulture and the Director of the Cornell Graduate Program in Public Garden Leadership. His research interests include the history of botanical gardens in Europe and North America, the management of public gardens, and the interactions between plants and people. Actively involved in horticultural associations and education initiatives at many levels, Rakow was honored in 2009 for his service on the American Public Gardens Association board of directors and many of its committees with the APGA Service Award. Rakow holds a Ph.D. in horticulture from Cornell University.

Elizabeth Randolph

Elizabeth Randolph writes and farms in Pennsylvania. Through the stories she writes and the crops she grows, Randolph strives to sustain the natural world. As both staff member and freelancer, she has many years of experience with green institutions, including the American Association of Botanical Gardens and Arboreta, Chanticleer, Tyler Arboretum, Lancaster Farmland Trust, and USDA's Farm Service Agency, as well as eleven years in marketing at Longwood Gardens.

Paul B. Redman

Paul B. Redman is Director of Longwood Gardens, one of the world's premier horticultural display gardens, sponsor of important plant research and plant exploration trips, and a leader in educating new horticulturists. Redman oversees the 1,050-acre site and its 350 employees, 400-plus volunteers, and $50 million annual budget. Previously, Redman served as the Executive Director of the Franklin Park Conservatory and Botanical Garden. Redman serves on the boards of directors for the American Public Gardens Association and the Philadelphia Cultural Alliance. He is a member of the Advisory Board for the College of Agriculture and Natural Resources at the University of Delaware. Redman has been working and studying in public horticulture for more than eighteen years, receiving his B.S. and M.S. in horticulture from Oklahoma State University.

Sarah Reichard

Dr. Sarah Reichard, Professor at the University of Washington, founded and directs the conservation program at the University of Washington Botanic Gardens. Her research specialties include the biology of both rare and invasive plant species. She served for six years as an advisor to the federal government on invasive species issues and is author of *The Conscientious Gardener: Cultivating a Garden Ethic*, editor of *Invasive Species in the Pacific Northwest*, and author of numerous scientific and popular press articles. She received a B.S. in botany as well as an M.S. and Ph.D. in forest resources from the University of Washington.

Patricia Rich

Pat Rich, ACFRE, is a principal in EMD Consulting Group. She has consulted throughout the country and overseas on fundraising, planning, membership, and nonprofit management issues. She is one of eighty-five Advanced Certified Fundraising Executives in the country, the highest accreditation in the fund-raising profession. She is a frequent speaker at fund-raising conferences and meetings of nonprofit groups and teaches the fund-raising course at the University of Missouri–St. Louis. She has served on the National Board of the Association of Fundraising Professionals and is a member of the AFP National Research Council. Her book, *Membership Development: An Action Plan for Results*, is a leading source on membership programs.

Iain M. Robertson

Iain M. Robertson, ASLA, is an Associate Professor of Landscape Architecture at the University of Washington and an adjunct faculty member of the University of Washington Botanic Gardens. His academic interests center on design creativity and plants as a design medium, and he has developed novel ways for exploring and teaching about the distinctive design characteristics of plants. A registered landscape architect, he has consulted on a number of planning and design projects for botanical gardens, principally in the western United States. He is a contributor to *The Public Garden* and *Pacific Horticulture*. Robertson received his undergraduate degree in architecture from Edinburgh University and his M.L.A. from the University of Pennsylvania.

Claire Sawyers

Claire Sawyers, Director of the Scott Arboretum of Swarthmore College, oversees the development of a 300-acre campus-arboretum dubbed "the most beautiful campus in America" by *Garden Design* and ranked in the Top 10 Beautiful Campuses in *The Princeton Review*. Sawyers served as Commissioner for the American Association of Museums Accreditation program, co-chair for the Garden Conservancy screening committee, board member for Bartram's Garden, and on the Visiting Committee for Longwood Gardens. She is author of *The Authentic Garden: Five Principles for Cultivating a Sense of Place* and editor of three Brooklyn Botanic Garden handbooks. She holds master's degrees in horticulture from both Purdue University and the University of Delaware, where she was a Longwood Fellow.

Jennifer A. Schwarz-Ballard

As Director of the Center for Teaching and Learning at the Chicago Botanic Garden, Dr. Jennifer Schwarz-Ballard oversees the Garden's youth programs, teacher services, citizen science, and education research initiatives. She also supervises graduate students as Adjunct Faculty for the Northwestern University–Chicago Botanic Garden collaborative Plant Conservation Biology Program. As Lead Science Instructor for Project BudBurst, she supports public engagement in science and works for increased understanding of the impacts of climate change on the environment. She is author of the award-winning publication *Summer Science: Reaching Urban Youth Through Environmental Science*. Schwarz-Ballard holds a Ph.D. in the learning sciences from the School of Education and Social Policy at Northwestern University.

Melanie Sifton

Melanie Sifton, Director of the Humber Arboretum and Centre for Urban Ecology in Toronto, is passionate about urban public horticulture and dedicated to promoting landscape sustainability through public garden outreach and education. Sifton is a member of the Sustainable Sites Initiative team at the Lady

Bird Johnson Wildflower Center, forming guidelines and performance benchmarks for sustainable landscapes. A graduate of the Cornell Graduate Program in Public Garden Leadership, she focused on sustainable landscape design and operations in public gardens. Her background includes the Niagara Parks Commission School of Horticulture and Ontario Horticulture Technician Apprenticeship. Sifton holds an Honors B.A. from McGill University in English and art history.

Vincent A. Simeone

Vincent A. Simeone is Director of Planting Fields Arboretum State Historic Park, a position he has held for eighteen years. He teaches horticulture classes at the New York Botanical Garden and lectures nationwide for both professional and hobby gardeners. He has written numerous articles for Long Island–based publications as well as *Great Flowering Landscape Shrubs*, *Great Flowering Landscape Trees*, *Great Landscape Evergreens*, and *The Wonders of the Winter Landscape*. He received an A.A.S. degree in ornamental horticulture from SUNY Farmingdale and a B.S. in ornamental horticulture from the University of Georgia.

Kathleen Socolofsky

Kathleen Socolofsky, Assistant Vice Chancellor at the University of California, Davis and Arboretum Director at the UC Davis Arboretum, is cofounder of the California Center for Urban Horticulture, serves on the Visiting Committee of Longwood Gardens and as Vice Chair of the Center for Public Horticulture, and is a past board member of the American Public Gardens Association (APGA). Socolofsky is recipient of the APGA Professional Citation Award and served as Director of Education at the Desert Botanical Garden prior to her tenure at the UC Davis Arboretum. She holds a master's degree in educational leadership.

Barbara M. Thiers

Dr. Barbara M. Thiers is the Director of the William and Lynda Steere Herbarium at the New York Botanical Garden, which is the largest in the Western Hemisphere, with approximately 7.3 million specimens. She is also the editor of *Index Herbariorum*, the online guide to the world's approximately 3,300 public herbaria. She has been responsible for overseeing the development of the New York Botanical Garden's Virtual Herbarium, the online catalog of data and images from about 1.1 million specimens from the Herbarium. She received her Ph.D. in botany from the University of Massachusetts.

Eric Tschanz

Eric Tschanz, President and Executive Director of Powell Gardens, has implemented the first three phases of the Gardens' master plan, which included developing several theme gardens, a new visitor center, a meditation chapel, and the Heartland Harvest Garden. Previously, he served as the first Director of the San Antonio Botanical Garden, where he oversaw the completion of the first xeriscape garden in Texas, a refinement of its native plant display, and development and construction of the Halsell Conservatory. Throughout his career he has been involved with young, rapidly developing gardens. Tschanz holds a master's degree in public garden administration from the University of Delaware, where he was a Longwood Fellow.

Julie Warsowe

Julie Warsowe, Manager of Visitor Education at the Arnold Arboretum of Harvard University, has developed visitor testing and interpretive content for a comprehensive new wayfinding system, coordinated the first visitor study at the Arboretum in over ten years, and launched an interpretive master plan to develop interpretation and informal education in the landscape over the next five years. Before coming to the Arnold, Warsowe was first the Manager of Brooklyn GreenBridge and then Director of Adult Education at the Brooklyn Botanic Garden. Her master's thesis examined the evaluation of adult education programs in public gardens. She holds a master's degree from the Cornell Graduate Program in Public Garden Leadership.

Index

Burden Center, Louisiana State University AgCenter, Baton Rouge, Louisiana, 73–75
bureaucratic obstacles, founding strategies, 38
business manager, responsibilities of, 86
business plans, formal education program, 199

Callaway Gardens, Georgia, 10
Canada, 339–48
Cape Fear Botanical Garden, Fayetteville, North Carolina, 62
capital budget, 107–8
capital campaigns, fund-raising, 133
career changes, 206
Carnegie, Andrew, 6
case statement, fund-raising, 127
cash flow, budgeting and, 108
Center for Plant Conservation (CPC), 310
certification programs, 206, 208–11
Chanticleer, Wayne, Pennsylvania, 8, 27–28
Cheyenne Botanic Garden, Wyoming, 10, 99
Chicago Botanic Garden, Chicago, Illinois, 5, 130–31, 142, 149–50, 210, 258, 282
Chicago Horticultural Society, 11
chief executive officer (CEO), 86, 126, 144
chief financial officer (CFO), 86
chief operations officer (COO), 86
Chihuly Exhibitions, 138
circulation, site analysis, 69
city governments, public garden support, 12, 25. See also government organizations
civic engagement, 192
civic groups, donors, 126
Civil Rights Act of 1964, 91
climate, site analysis, 69
climate change
    conservation practices, 284–85
    future prospects, 332
Climatron conservatory, Missouri Botanic Garden, St. Louis, Missouri, 5, 6
Coastal Maine Botanical Gardens, Boothbay Harbor, Maine, 44, 58–61

collaborations
    community outreach techniques, 183–86
    formal education program, 198
collection management. See plant collections management
collective bargaining agreement, defined, 83
colleges, public garden support, 13–14
communications, management style, 305–6. See also public relations
communications director, responsibilities of, 86–87
community ecology, research programs, 277
community gardens, 179–83
community organizations, 65, 198–99
community outreach, 175–89
    defined, 175
    evaluation of, 188
    funding of, 188
    program planning, 186–88
    techniques for, 175–86
compensation
    budgeting, 111–12
    defined, 83
    personnel management, 90
competition, earned income, 144
composting, grounds management, 169–70
computer-aided design (CAD), detail drawings, 77
Conan, Michel, 190–91
concept identification, organizational management, 45–48
conceptual design, design process, 70–73
consent requirements, evaluation process, 239
conservation collections, 255
conservation-focused research, 276–80
conservation practices, 284–95
    evaluation of, 294
    ex situ practices, 286–87
    extinctions, 284–85
    garden integration, 289–92
    invasive species, 292–93
    St. Louis Declaration, 293–94
    seed banks, 287–89
    in situ practices, 285–86
conservatories
    described, 6–7

facilities, 156, 317
Conservatory of Flowers, Golden Gate Park San Francisco, California, 6
Conservatory Palm Dome, Buffalo and Erie County Botanical Gardens, Buffalo, New York, 72
Consolidated Omnibus Budget Reconciliation Act (COBRA), 91
constraints, site analysis, 68–69
construction documents, design process, 77
construction drawings, 77, 323–24
consultants
    defined, 66
    design process, 66–67
    design team, 77–78
    informal education, 226
contests, community outreach techniques, 186
continuing education, 205–18. See also education
    audiences for, 206
    graduate degrees, 211–14
    lifelong learning concept, 207–8
    professionalism, 206–11
    program development, 214–17
    program evaluation, 217
    volunteers, 101
contract documents, 66, 321
contracted services
    budgeting expense, 113
    earned income, 143
contractor, defined, 66
contribution revenue, budgeting, 110
core group factors, organizational management, 41–45
corporate donors, 125, 131
cost of goods sold, budgeting expense, 113
credentialing, 206, 208–11
Crystal Palace, London, England, 6
cultivation, fund-raising, 128
cultural events, community outreach techniques, 175–78
cultural tax districts, budgeting, 110–11
culture, public gardens, 22–29

data collection, evaluation process, 237–39
deaccessioning, of collections, 260–61
decision making, management style, 306
Denver Botanic Gardens, Colorado, 141

Huntington Botanical Gardens, San Marino, California, 225, 240
hydrology, 57, 69

ice removal, grounds management, 167
implementation, design process, 77
independent contractors, 91, 113
individual donors, 125
informal education, 219–31. *See also* education
    described, 220–22
    effective techniques in, 222–23
    importance of, 219
    interpretive media for, 226–30
    program development, 223–26
infrastructure. *See* facilities and infrastructure
in-kind gifts, fund-raising, 134
in situ conservation practices, 285–86
Institute of Museum and Library Services, 309
insurance expenses, budgeting, 112
integrated pest management, 158, 165–66
intellectual rights, 261
interactive media, informal education, 229–30
internal evaluations, 233–34
Internal Revenue Service (IRS), 50
international perspective
    collections, 349–50
    education programs, 196
    future prospects, 335–36
    partnerships, 313
    professional associations, 310
internships, 209–10
interpretation. *See* informal education
interpretive media, 226–30
invasive species, 259–60, 292–93
inventories, collections management, 262–63
inventory maps, collections management, 263–64
irrigation
    facilities and infrastructure, 147, 154, 168
    plant health care, 161–62
    staffing, 158
issue-based initiatives, community outreach techniques, 183–86
IUCN Red List, 275

JC Raulston Arboretum, North Carolina State University, Raleigh, 34
job description, elements of, 90
John Bartram Association, 9
John Hay National Wildlife Refuge, Lake Sunapee, New Hampshire, 8

Key West Tropical Forest and Botanical Garden, Key West, Florida, 85
Kwazulu-Natal National Botanical Garden, South Africa, 227

labels, 226–27
Lady Bird Johnson Wildflower Center, Austin, Texas, 290, 311
land acquisition
    biotic inventory, 57
    facilities and infrastructure, 145–46
    financing of, 55
    founding strategies, 38
    gifted land, 54–55
    hydrology, 57
    information resources and networking, 58
    leased land, 55
    microclimates, 57
    natural hazards, 58
    noise levels, 57
    permits, environmental and building, 58
    purchased land, 55
    size requirements, 55–56
    soils, 56
    topography, 56
    traffic factors, 57
    views, 57
    zoning laws, 57
landslide, land acquisition, 58
land use, site analysis, 69
language translation, 176
Lauritzen Gardens, Omaha, Nebraska, 47–48, 63
leadership and management style, 299–307
    communications, 305–6
    concepts in, 299–300
    flexibility, 303–5
    leadership, management contrasted, 300
    team approach, 305
    team process, 306

vision, 300–303
work plan, 303–4
Leadership in Energy and Environmental Design (LEED), 145, 321
leased land, land acquisition, 55
legal compliance, personnel management, 91
legal requirements, board structure and governance type, 50
library, 316–17, 355–56
lifelong learning concept, 207–8
long-term forecasting, budgeting oversight, 121–22
Longwood Gardens, Kennett Square, Pennsylvania, 8, 11, 334
Louisiana State University AgCenter, Burden Center, Baton Rouge, Louisiana, 73–75

maintenance facilities, 155
management, leadership contrasted, 300. *See also* leadership and management style; organizational management; personnel management; staff and staffing
maps, inventory maps, collections management, 263–64
marketing communications. *See* public relations
marketing coordinator, 84
marketing manager, 86–87
marketing portfolio, 244–45
market trend research, 246
master plan
    design process, 68, 73–75
    facilities and infrastructure, 145, 153–54
    facility expansion, 317–19
media relations, 248–49
membership director, responsibilities of, 87
membership programs, 129–31, 138–39
membership revenue, budgeting, 110
memorial program, fund-raising, 131–32
microclimates, 57, 69
mission statement
    defined, 41
    organizational management, 51–53
    public garden criteria, 4
    public relations, 244